Mexican American Civil Rights in Texas

LATINOS IN THE UNITED STATES SERIES

Mexican American Civil Rights in Texas

Edited by
Robert Brischetto and J. Richard Avena

Michigan State University Press • *East Lansing*

To all those who organized, picketed, marched and litigated to bring systemic change toward greater equality. And to those of the next generation of all ethnic origins who will carry el movimiento into the next fifty years.

Michigan State University Press
East Lansing, Michigan 48823-5245

This publication was made possible in part thanks to a grant by the Julian Samora Research Institute.

Library of Congress Cataloging-in-Publication Data
Names: Brischetto, Robert R., editor. | Avena, J. Richard, editor.
Title: Mexican American civil rights in Texas / edited by Robert Brischetto and J. Richard Avena.
Description: East Lansing : Michigan State University Press, [2021] |
Series: Latinos in the United States | Includes bibliographical references.
Identifiers: LCCN 2021001042 | ISBN 978-1-61186-404-5 (paperback) | ISBN 978-1-60917-679-2 (pdf) |
ISBN 978-1-62895-446-3 (epub) | ISBN 978-1-62896-440-0 (Kindle)
Subjects: LCSH: Mexican Americans—Civil rights—Texas. | Mexican Americans—Texas—Social conditions. | Race discrimination—Texas. | Social change—Texas. | Texas—Race relations.
Classification: LCC F395.M5 M476 2021 | DDC 323.1168/720764—dc23
LC record available at https://lccn.loc.gov/2021001042

Cover design by Charlie Sharp, Sharp Des!gns, East Lansing, Michigan
MAYO protest against Captain Allee of the Texas Rangers during the U.S. Commission on Civil Rights Hearings at Our Lady of the Lake University, San Antonio Express-News Photograph Collection E-0017-064-f34 / ZUMA Wire

Visit Michigan State University Press at *www.msupress.org*

Contents

RUBÉN MARTINEZ

Series Editor Foreword

The year 1968 was full of milestones, politically speaking. Revolutions and protests were occurring throughout the globe, including in the southwestern United States, the homeland of Mexican Americans, a population that was defining itself as Chicano and demanding its civil rights. In 1968, Chicanos were part of the U.S. armed forces fighting the Viet Nam Cong San, the guerrilla forces that fought alongside the North Vietnamese against South Vietnam and the United States. That was the deadliest year for U.S. forces as the Tet Offensive, a coordinated set of attacks on South Vietnam cities by North Vietnam forces, was launched in January, turning the tide in the war and leading to the ultimate withdrawal of American forces. It intensified the Vietnam antiwar movement here in America. It was also the year that Martin Luther King, Jr., and Robert Kennedy were assassinated, and fourteen people were killed and twenty-one wounded in a mass shooting in San Bernardino, California.

The year was a period of government hearings in the United States, mainly as a result of the passage of the Civil Rights Act of 1964, which established the Community Relations Service, expanded the Commission on Civil Rights, and wrote into statute the Equal Employment Opportunity Commission. It was also a period when the federal government took notice of Mexican Americans and their political grievances. The hearings that took place that year in San Antonio, Texas, may pale in comparison to the high-profile events that gripped the nation, but the hearings were milestones in terms of the presentation of grievances by community leaders. The events leading up to the hearings included a series of farmworker strikes in California, land grant struggles in New Mexico, protests against police brutality in Colorado, and student and leader walkouts at schools and commission hearings. Frustrations among Mexican American leaders increased during the decades following the end of World War II. Despite their honorable service in the American armed forces, the economic expansion of the 1950s, and promises by American presidents and federal government representatives, integration was not occurring as expected. Race relations were focused on Anglos and Negroes, to use the vernacular of the times, and Mexican Americans were both invisible to and unknown by most Anglo Americans outside of the Southwest, where they had been subordinated since the conclusion of the American Mexican War in 1848.

A major shift in the federal government's relations with Mexican American leaders occurred as a result of the walkouts that took place on March 28, 1966, at the Equal Employment Opportunity Commission's hearings in Albuquerque, New Mexico. Frustrated that the federal government's focus was on the black civil rights movement while neglecting the concerns of Mexican American communities, they made it clear that they expected their concerns to be addressed by the Johnson administration. President Lyndon Johnson, who had been planning a White House conference on civil rights focused on the "American Negro," responded by acknowledging that Mexican Americans suffered discrimination and should receive more attention from his administration. The White House Conference "To Fulfill These Rights," held on June 1–2, 1966, at the Sheraton-Park Hotel in Washington, DC, was attended by some 2,500 participants but by fewer than ten Mexican American leaders. A planning session was held on November 17–18, 1965, and months later President Johnson appointed a Council to the Conference of thirty members, none of whom were Mexican Americans or Chicanos. The 177-page report produced by the Council did not mention Mexican Americans, leading to increased frustrations among Mexican American leaders.

On June 9, 1967, President Johnson established the cabinet-level Inter-Agency Committee on Mexican American Affairs to ensure that federal programs were reaching and providing services to the communities of this population. On October 26-28, 1967, the Inter-Agency Committee held hearings in El Paso, Texas, that featured testimony by Mexican American leaders from throughout the nation, albeit mostly men. Fourteen months later, on December 9-14, 1968, the Commission on Civil Rights held hearings in San Antonio, where John Hannah, Chairman of the Commission and President of Michigan State University, made opening remarks about the purpose of the hearings. Testimony and exhibits were received from persons mostly from Texas, with a handful from New Mexico and California. This edited volume examines the importance and the impact of these hearings across the major life areas of Mexican Americans.

Despite erratic progress in the area of civil rights, the authors of the chapters highlight the little overall progress that has occurred in the life areas of Mexican Americans since the Congressional hearings were held in San Antonio in 1968. Persons who spoke at those hearings highlighted the scope and forms of oppression that characterized the lives of most Chicanos and their families. Unfortunately, civil rights advocates at the time were unaware that a group of political conservatives led by Barry Goldwater, a Republican, had latched on to libertarian ideologies rooted in the works of staunch, anticommunist Austrian economists. Although Democratic candidate John Kennedy became President of the United States in 1961, Goldwater and his conservative followers continued to organize, and by 1971, when Justice Powell crafted his infamous memorandum on free enterprise to send to the Director of the U.S. Chamber of Commerce, the roots of the neoliberal movement had already taken hold. The aim was to dismantle the so-called "welfare state," which they viewed as a threat to individual freedom, and replace it with a political philosophy of radical individualism, small government, and "free labor."

Of particular concern for the wealthy class was the transfer of personal income to the public coffers through taxation. The neoliberal torch was taken up by Ronald Reagan and passed from one generation of political leaders to another, such that in the 1990s Democratic President William Clinton was espousing neoliberal ideologies and supporting conservative policies. That political philosophy and its attendant policies have yielded enormous inequalities in society, especially in terms of income and wealth along racial lines. Most recently, the neoliberal torch was carried by Donald Trump, who used it to deregulate industries, reduce corporate taxes, weaken organized labor, and scorch American Democracy and its institutions. In his own business practices, he simply did not adhere to the thinking of the libertarian economist Milton Friedman, who argued that the singular pursuit of profits should abide by the rules of the game (regulations) without deception and fraud.

Where we go from here depends on the leadership and policies of President Joseph Biden and the influence of progressive forces seeking to transcend the regressive and unsustainable policies of neoliberalism. Already corporations have begun, since the Great Recession of 2007-2009, to rethink Friedman's emphasis on the singular pursuit of profits, to broaden the scope of their paradigm to include the environment and social and governance factors. Problems to be addressed not only for Latinos but for other marginalized groups as well include education, housing, employment, healthcare, criminal justice, voting rights, and immigrant rights, to name a few. This volume makes clear the challenges facing Mexican Americans and Latino communities as the nation attempts to move toward a more humane economic system that works for everyone.

DAVID MONTEJANO

Foreword

In order to understand the significance of the U.S. Commission on Civil Rights hearing in 1968 and the timeliness of this particular review, some historical context is necessary. During the first half of the twentieth century, Mexicans in the United States were generally seen as seasonal immigrants doing farm work or unskilled labor. Regardless of their historical roots in the Southwest, they were not considered citizenship material. Segregated Mexican communities were always subject to immigration sweeps, especially during economic downturns. During the Great Depression of the 1930s, more than half a million Mexican nationals and their Mexican American children were deported. World War II, however, signaled a sharp change in the status of the Mexican American people. The wartime service of an estimated half million soldiers of Mexican descent emboldened veteran-led organizations like the American GI Forum to claim first-class citizenship. Wartime service also made college enrollment and homeownership possible because of the GI Bill of Rights, and it earned preference for government employment at the postal service and the military bases.

Kelly Air Force Base, for example, played a central role in the rise of a stable Mexican American working class and middle class in San Antonio.

In the 1950s, the Mexican American community, no longer having to patch together a livelihood from migratory work, began to turn its attention to the obvious inequities of a segregated system—to matters like inferior schooling, housing, health, poverty, and restricted political participation. In the early 1960s, a restive middle class formed organizations like the Political Association of Spanish-Speaking Organizations (PASSO) in Texas and the Mexican American Political Association (MAPA) in California to address these issues. The Chicano movement that erupted a few years later, catalyzed by César Chávez and the farmworker strike in 1965, was a more militant expression of frustration and resolve by the working class of the Mexican American community. The youth, in particular, aggressively confronted the problems in schooling, in policing and in politics generally. The Mexican American community was asserting its presence in the country.

This was the milieu in which the U.S. Commission on Civil Rights convened its hearing on the education, employment, economic security, and administration of justice regarding Mexican Americans in December 1968. Farmworker strikes in California and Texas were ongoing and had been marked by police violence at the picket lines; dramatic high school walkouts protesting inferior conditions had taken place in Los Angeles and San Antonio; and college youth were organizing campus groups and national conferences in Denver and Santa Barbara, among other places. Outside the building where the hearings were being held, a young Mexican American Youth Organization (MAYO) was staging a protest against Texas Ranger brutality.

The hearing was a response to the emerging Chicano movement of the time. It represented an unprecedented recognition by the federal government of the Mexican American presence in the country. Until then, Mexican Americans had generally been a "forgotten people" in the American racial and ethnic tapestry as far as government policy was concerned. The occasional attention given Mexican Americans in government reports had generally dealt with agricultural labor or immigration. The hearing, on the other hand, proceeded on the premise that Mexican Americans were a permanent part of the American citizenry. The testimonies, of course, provided a vivid window into the life and work conditions of Mexican Americans at the time.

Now, on the eve of Mexican Americans becoming the largest racial/ ethnic group in Texas, the following collection of reports offers a comprehensive review of the progress that Mexican Americans have made since those historic hearings. Together, the reports regarding population growth, immigration, voting rights, education, housing, farm labor and employment, health, and criminal justice provide an encyclopedic assessment of the status of the Mexican American people at this time. The overall portrait is that of an ethnic community still dealing with poverty and discrimination. The volume also demonstrates the interrelated nature of discrimination—that voting rights, for example, impact education and housing policies. Each report concludes with a set of recommendations for future action, thus reminding us of the challenges that remain. As such, this collection is already an important document. It will serve as a benchmark for the next fifty years. The collection is also an important document in another respect. In spite of some somber undertones over the lack of progress, the volume itself, written by recognized experts in their respective fields, is a testament to the development of the Mexican American community. Unlike the situation fifty years ago, the volume makes clear that Mexican Americans now have a professional and academic voice, and that the advocacy organizations emerging from the Chicano movement of the late 1960s—Intercultural Development Research Association (IDRA), Mexican American Legal Defense and Education Fund (MALDEF), Southwest Voter Registration Education Project (SVREP), and Communities Organized for Public Service (COPS) to mention a few—have become well established. In the past fifty years, the Mexican American community has increased its intellectual and political capacity, an important point to keep in mind in the current era when our claim to American citizenship is being questioned. That capacity is being challenged. Whether the recommendations offered by the authors are realized over the next fifty years will obviously depend on the outcome of those challenges.

Preface

This book chronicles a critical era in the saga of an often-overlooked group of people concentrated in the southwestern part of the United States, who are aptly termed by *Los Angeles Times* columnist Rubén Salazar as "strangers in their own land."[1]

After the war with Mexico, the United States took almost half of Mexico by force. This included portions of what became Texas, New Mexico, Arizona, Colorado, Kansas, and Wyoming. With the signing of the Treaty of Guadalupe Hidalgo in 1848, both sides agreed that the land, civil rights, and language of the former Mexican citizens would be protected. Historians tell us that between 80,000 and 100,000 Mexicans became U.S. citizens overnight. In other words, they never crossed the border; the border crossed them.[2]

The Mexicans who lived in the newly annexed areas did have a choice of returning to Mexico, but most chose to stay, feeling secure that their rights would be protected as U.S. citizens. Many were descendants of people who had lived there for more than three hundred years. The differences from the Anglos inhabiting the same areas were in religion, language, color, and class. According to historian Neil Foley, "Anglo Texans had firmly established in their minds that Mexicans were more like Indians and Black Americans than Germans or French."[3] Another historian describes a new Anglo Texan's impression of the Mexicans as the "unfortunate race of Spaniard, Indian and African . . . so blended that the worst qualities of each predominate."[4] It was that attitude of racial superiority that formed the basis for a caste-like system with Anglos in control and Mexicans as the underclass.[5]

Fast forward a century later. The U.S. Commission on Civil Rights (USCCR) was established as a small, independent, federal agency in 1957 "to inform the development of national civil rights policy and enhance enforcement of federal civil rights laws." The agency studies "alleged deprivations of voting rights and alleged discrimination based on race, color, religion, sex, age disability or national origin, or the administration of justice."[6] With no enforcement power and with only the authority to compel sworn testimony, the commission makes policy recommendations to Congress and to the President.

A decade into its tenure, the agency decided to spend a sizable amount of its resources to document issues facing the Mexican American in the Southwest. The commission heard complaints from Mexican Americans a year earlier at a hearing in San Francisco, where Chicano youths staged a walkout. Among their complaints were concerns that no Mexican Americans had served on the commission and that the federal government did not understand them or their problems. Responding to their concerns, President Lyndon Johnson appointed Dr. Héctor García, founder of the American GI Forum, to the commission.

San Antonio was chosen as the site for a six-day hearing to be held in December 1968. The commission subpoenaed testimony from all sides of the issues. The commission heard from the Texas education commissioner, experts who cited research, and students who had protested school conditions with walkouts. It listened to farmworkers on strike in the lower Rio Grande Valley and the captain of the Texas Rangers, who was accused of trying to break the strike. It brought in administrators of human services as well as residents in the *colonias* along the border and urban barrios, elected officials, civil rights attorneys, and voters. For six days in December, testimony was given by more than seventy witnesses. Personal accounts and a number of studies on the conditions of Mexican Americans in the five southwestern states were presented by the Mexican American Studies Division of the commission.[7] Fr. Theodore Hesburgh, president of Notre Dame University and commission member, opened the hearing, saying the purpose was "to hold up a mirror to the community so it can see what the facts are."

The fiftieth anniversary of the 1968 meeting of the U.S. Commission on Civil Rights provided an opportunity to reflect on the progress in civil rights for Mexican Americans. It was a chance to pause and take stock of what had transpired as well as what lay ahead. A group of academicians, attorneys, and community activists came together in 2015 to discuss the idea of a report on the changes that had occurred since the landmark hearing. Potential authors began meeting monthly to discuss the issues addressed by the commission in 1968. A larger group began plans for a major conference in November 2018. More than 850 participants attended the two-day conference, "50 Years Later: Holding Up the Mirror," at Our Lady of the Lake University, the site of the original hearing.

The 1,304 pages of testimony transcript from the 1968 hearing and the many studies that arose from it provided a point of reference for charting progress. In the chapters that follow, twenty experts present research examining these changes in Texas ethnic relations. In addition to the civil rights problems examined in 1968, several important "new" civil rights issues were added that are crucial to the Mexican American community, not only in Texas but nationally: immigration, voting rights, housing, and health.

In the five decades since the USCCR 1968 hearing, it is clear that Mexican Americans have made much progress in Texas, yet many challenges remain. In this book we are concerned with how racism expresses itself in institutional patterns or social practices that create inequalities adversely affecting democracy and civil rights in Texas.

The authors who contributed to this work have devoted their lives to organizing and promoting *la raza*. Each chapter provides a unique perspective on the context in their particular field of expertise. The main questions they were asked to address in this "50 Years Later" report that accompanied the conference were: What has changed since 1968 and how will these changes affect the future of Latinos in Texas? What inequalities remain by race and ethnicity? What policy changes are needed to achieve greater equality going forward?

Charting Racial Inequalities

Despite the long history of persons of Hispanic origin in the United States, they were not counted in a consistent way in the national census until the late twentieth century. Latinos numbered 1.6 million in Texas in 1960. By 2018 they had increased seven times in number, to 11.4 million. This growth—from 16 to 40 percent of the state's population—had a major impact on the economy, the politics, and the culture of Texas in a way that will shape its future.

Demographer Rogelio Sáenz analyzes public-use microdata samples of Texas residents each decade from the 1960 to 2010 decennial censuses and the 2018 American Community Survey. By comparing racial/ethnic groups across almost six decades, he is able to discern trends in each group and the disparities in their socioeconomic characteristics. With his graphic analysis, he is able to show the disparities among racial groups and the inequalities that remain.

The premise of this book from its inception was that changes over the past fifty years can be measured. The socioeconomic indicators provided by Sáenz show progress for all groups in Texas. More importantly for the future, they show the gaps that remain among the racial groups and the extent to which they are changing over time.

Immigration Policy

The Immigration Act of 1965 represented a major shift in immigration policy. The act eliminated the nativist quotas established by Congress in 1921 and 1924, and thus prompted more immigration from previously restricted countries in eastern and southern Europe, Asia, and Africa. Immigration from Mexico, Central America, and South America continued to grow; by 1968 Mexicans represented the largest nationality group among immigrants.

The Texas-Mexico border was transformed over the past half century due to changes in the economies of the two countries, immigration policies, and security threats from cartels smuggling drugs into and guns out of the United States. The ebb and even greater flow of both legal and illegal migration from Mexico over the past five decades has resulted in increased restrictions and buildup of border enforcement. Texas and other border states became militarized zones dedicated to large-scale federal immigration enforcement. In the past twenty-five years, the federal government has detained and deported more individuals from Mexico and Central America than at any other time in our history.[8]

Since 2013 there has been a surge of Central Americans seeking refuge from gang violence and security threats in the Northern Triangle countries of Guatemala, Honduras, and El Salvador. The buildup of migrants along the border provided an opportunity for ultranationalists to test the political strength of anti-immigrant sentiment in this country.

Immigration attorney and law professor Lee Terán traces the history of immigration policies and practices. By tracking the changes in different indicators of immigration enforcement alongside changes in the laws and administrative practices, she is able to evaluate the impact of these changes on both immigrants and the receiving country.

Voting Rights

Latino voting potential had not been fully actualized at the time of the Civil Rights hearing of 1968. When the Voting Rights Act (VRA) of 1965 was amended in 1975, extending protection to language minorities and including all of Texas in section 5 "preclearance," the power of Latino voters was unleashed through a series of court cases and oversight of Texas voting jurisdictions by the Justice Department.

The 1975 and 1982 amendments to the Voting Rights Act provided the basis for hundreds of cases brought by the voting rights bar. Letters of objection were filed by the Department of Justice challenging at-large voting systems, as well as malapportionment, racial gerrymandering, and other devices that dilute minority voting strength. Voting rights organizations sued cities, school districts, and other political subdivisions, challenging at-large election systems with remarkable success.

Three chapters of this book address the changes that took place in support of Mexican American voting rights. Law professor José Roberto Juárez, with the assistance of Mexican American Legal Defense and Educational Fund attorney Ernest Herrera, gives a thorough review of the litigation on voting rights in Texas during the past half century. He shows that because of the efforts to enforce the VRA, Texas has undergone fundamental changes in election systems leading to improved representation of minorities on the state and local levels.

Political scientist Henry Flores, who served as an expert in a number of voting rights cases, shows that there is ample evidence to argue that the state of Texas has engaged in intentional discrimination in its effort to build barriers to Mexican American voting.

Quantitative analyst Kevin Morris and New York University law professor Myrna Pérez of the Brennan Center examine the impact of recent voter purges and other vote suppression tactics by the Texas Secretary of State and the Texas legislature.

Educational Equity

José A. Cárdenas, who testified as an education specialist in the commission hearing, became superintendent of San Antonio's Edgewood Independent School District (ISD) in 1968 when the district's parents were filing a lawsuit challenging the inequities in financing education based on local property values. Edgewood was the poorest district in Texas. Also testifying at the commission hearing was Aurelio Montemayor, a VISTA school counselor in the Del Rio ISD, where students had walked out in protest over a host of issues, ranging from segregation and punishment for speaking Spanish in the school systems to the quality of the curriculum and facilities.

Inspired by the school finance reform movement and funding from the Ford Foundation, Cárdenas founded Texans for Educational Excellence (TEE) to pursue equity in the funding of education. TEE was incorporated in 1974 under a different name, the Intercultural Development Research Association (IDRA), and Montemayor was one of the early staff engaged in reforming education. For Cárdenas, the battle on behalf of Edgewood parents was also his battle. He approached the Mexican American Legal Defense and Education Fund (MALDEF) attorney Albert Kauffman to devise a new approach to challenging inequalities in education funding based on the state's guarantee of equal funding for the same tax effort. Cárdenas put the IDRA research staff in support of the new litigation.

IDRA has been engaged in not only litigation research but also evaluation of Texas schools and equity in education since its inception. Its national director of policy David Hinojosa, president María "Cuca" Robledo Montecel, and senior education associate Montemayor examine the progress made toward educational equity in Texas.

Farmworkers of Texas

Farmworkers numbered almost three million in the United States at the time of the 1968 commission hearing and were the most underpaid and unprotected occupational class. In Starr County, Texas, 70 percent of the families earned less than $3,000 per year. Agribusiness was the county's second largest business, and most Mexican American residents there worked in the fields from March through October each year, with no minimum wage and stripped of the ability to effectively organize by the Taft-Hartley Law of 1947.[9]

César Chávez began organizing farmworkers in California in 1962 and four years later led a national boycott of California table grapes. Inspired and assisted by the organizers of the grape strike in California, the Texas farmworkers struck at La Casita Farms and three other growers of canta-loupe melons in Starr County on June 1, 1966.

The story of the Texas farmworkers' strike at La Casita Farms and their historic march to the Capitol in Austin to draw attention to their demands for a minimum wage and working conditions is told by Rebecca Flores with Juanita Valdez-Cox and James Harrington. For several decades they sup-ported farmworkers and their organizing efforts in the Rio Grande Valley, in the courts, and in the legislature.

Fair Housing

Four days after the assassination of Martin Luther King, Jr., and months before the USCCR hearing in San Antonio, President Johnson signed the Fair Housing Act of 1968 to protect disadvantaged groups from discrimina-tion in renting, buying, or securing financing for housing. In the fifty years since its enactment, hundreds of cases of discrimination in housing have been adjudicated. One measure of the success of the fair housing law is the extent to which disadvantaged groups have been able with some success to buy homes in neighborhoods of their choice. Research by the federal government itself has found serious discrimination in the housing market in the five decades since the law was enacted. According to Gary Orfield, an expert on desegregation research, these studies "demonstrate that the government failed to enforce both the notoriously weak 1968 fair housing law and the 1988 amendments."[10]

The question of affordability has always plagued those who advocate for neighborhood integration. In the early 2000s, the housing market had soared. Lenders pushed "subprime mortgages," extremely risky loans, to borrowers who would normally not have qualified. When interest rates on subprime loans rose in 2005 and 2006, millions of new homeowners were in trouble. The number of foreclosures rose by 79 percent in 2007. When the housing bubble burst in 2008, about half of all Latino families nationwide owned their own homes, a disproportionately large number of them with subprime loans.[11]

Two of the national experts on housing, Alejandro Becerra and Henry Cisneros, explore some of the unanswered questions on how Hispanics have fared in the fifty years since enactment of the Fair Housing Law. After serving as San Antonio mayor in the 1980s, Cisneros became the Secretary of Housing and Urban Development under President Bill Clinton, and Becerra has spent almost all of his professional life studying housing among Latinos.

Employment and Economic Security

Income inequality can be understood by analyzing occupational differences by race and ethnicity. The Equal Employment Opportunity Commission (EEOC) was established in 1965 precisely to examine charges of discrimination in employment. Ernest Gerlach, formerly with the U.S. Commission on Civil Rights and the Institute for Economic Development at the University of Texas at San Antonio, utilizes EEOC reports to determine the extent to which inequalities in occupational status have changed over the past half century in public and private sectors of the Texas economy. He found that while disparities persist overall in minority representation of higher job categories, there has been considerable progress made in some areas, such as San Antonio.

Economists Marie Mora and Alberto Dávila dig deeper to explain differences in economic security among racial and ethnic groups. They trace economic disparity indicators between native-born Mexican Americans and Anglos in Texas over the period from 1970 to 2016 and ask whether the ethnic group differences in earnings can be explained by education or other factors.

Public Health

In the 1968 commission hearing, San Antonio provided a case example of extreme economic deprivation affecting the health of Mexican Americans.

Living conditions on San Antonio's West Side had been broadcast nationally in a CBS Reports documentary film, "Hunger in America," in June of that year.[12] The film opened with a malnourished infant dying in San Antonio's Robert B. Green Hospital. San Antonio's near West Side—a neighborhood that from the early 1900s has remained about 98 percent Hispanic—was featured as one of four locations in America that typified the problem of hunger. The documentary estimated that more than 100,000 people in San Antonio were going to bed hungry every day. It sparked a firestorm of controversy over the extent of, causes of, and solutions to a problem that had long been ignored.[13]

While progress has been made during the past half century in providing food for the hungry through a food stamp program, health issues remain for Latinos in Texas. Juan Flores has spent most of his career in public health policy. He examines the health of the Latino population in Texas through the lens of *bienestar* (well-being), the concept of examining not only the health of Latinos, but their background and environment. He reviews the various social indicators that have an impact on the health of Latinos throughout Texas.

Criminal Justice System

Of major concern in the 1968 USCCR hearing in San Antonio was the unequal treatment of Mexican Americans in our country's system of justice. The commission had just completed an investigation into a range of violations revealed in its interviews in the southwestern states—from mistreatment by police to underrepresentation on juries to overrepresentation in jails and prisons and inadequate representation by counsel. Law professor and former state district judge Lupe Salinas updates the state of criminal justice in Texas by citing cases that illustrate many of the violations that continued after the 1968 hearing.

What the Commission on Civil Rights accomplished during its six days of testimony in 1968 was to give legitimacy to the many issues being raised by the Mexican American community. As a result of the hearing and reports published subsequent to the hearing, a people's struggles were brought into the light. For the first time, the U.S. government, through a comprehensive examination, was confirming discrimination against Mexican Americans.

While this book covers most of the issues affecting Mexican Americans raised in the 1968 commission hearing and some that have emerged since then, still others need to be explored. Not adequately examined here are the issues that especially impact women, such as reproductive rights. Also, one panel in the 2018 conference highlighted a group in the Mexican American community that previously had been hidden or ignored and deserves further attention. A crowded workshop was held on civil rights problems facing the LGBTQ (lesbian, gay, bisexual, transgender, questioning) community in Texas. The panel discussed the work of the LGBTQ community of San Antonio and South Texas. Community members were asking for the same recognition, dignity, and guarantee of civil and human rights as any other minority group that faces discrimination.

Another 2018 conference panel brought together some of the Chicano activists from five decades ago to "lay out a blueprint for what is needed to move into the next 50 years." Armando Rendon, author of the 1971 book *Chicano Manifesto*, launched an initiative as a sequel to the conference, MeXicanos 2070. The Think Collective was then formed to continue the conversation among the activists, scholars, artists, and professionals by reaching out to barrios and the universities throughout the country. They met again via a nationwide webinar on February 2, 2020, the anniversary of the signing of the Treaty of Guadalupe Hidalgo, and intend to continue working for change, so that in another fifty years a new generation may convene and carry the torch forward. This book is written with the same aspiration that by examining the past fifty years through an evidence-based lens, we might see what can be built upon to achieve a better future. If the price of freedom is eternal vigilance, our work should always be in progress.

We are grateful to the many who participated in the planning and execution of the 2018 conference and to the authors who contributed their expertise and time to prepare an analysis of what has changed in the half century since the 1968 commission hearing. That it was all accomplished without a grant speaks volumes of their dedication.

We are deeply indebted to attorneys José Garza, Al Kaufman, and George Korbel, who have dedicated their careers to civil rights for Mexican Americans, for comments and insights in the development of this book. We benefitted from the careful critiques and insights of journalist and political scientist Fernando Piñon and sociologist Chandler Davidson on some of the chapter drafts. Their writings that spanned more than fifty years on the rights of Mexican Americans also served us well in our attempt to get the historical facts right. Finally, we are truly grateful for the copy edits of Renee Haines and Christina Brischetto, both excellent wordsmiths, and David Duran for his masterful web page development promoting this book: MxAmTx.org

Notes

1. There are various names for these people: *Mexicanos*, Mexican Americans, Chicanos, Hispanics, Latinos, *raza*, and in Texas, Tejanos, Texas Mexicans, Mexican Texans—in this book we find them all acceptable.
2. Neil Foley, *Mexicans in the Making of America* (Cambridge, MA: Harvard University Press paperback edition, 2017), 31.
3. Foley, *Mexicans*, 26. In this book, "Anglos" are also referred to as "non-Hispanic whites" or just "whites." In the same manner, African Americans are referred to as "Blacks."
4. Arnoldo de León, *They Called Them Greasers: Anglo Attitudes Toward Mexicans in Texas, 1821–1900* (Austin: University of Texas Press), 7-9.
5. This caste-like relationship is described in a number of books on Texas history, including Zaragosa Vargas, *Crucible of Struggle: A History of Mexican Americans from Colonial Times to the Present Era* (New York: Oxford University Press, 2017), 114-120; Jesús F. de la Teja, Paula Marks, and Ron Tyler, *Texas: Crossroads of North America* (Belmont, CA: Wadsworth, 2004), Chapter 8; and Foley, *Mexicans in the Making of America*, 25-38.
6. U.S. Commission on Civil Rights (USCCR), "Mission," available online at usccr.gov.
7. U.S. Commission on Civil Rights (USCCR), *Hearing before the United States Commission on Civil Rights: San Antonio, TX, December 9-14, 1968* (Washington, DC: GPO, 1969). Also available at https://catalog.hathitrust.org/Record/001874430.
8. Lee J. Terán and Robert Brischetto, "We Have Criminalized Migrants and Terrorized Their Children," *San Antonio Express-News*, July 28, 2018, F1.
9. USCCR, *Hearing*, 396-397.
10. Gary Orfield and Susan E. Eaton, *Dismantling Desegregation: The Quiet Reversal of Brown v. Board of Education* (New York: The New Press, 1996), 299.
11. Kevin M. Kruse and Julian E. Zelizer, *Fault Lines: A History of the United States Since 1974* (New York: W. W. Norton & Company, 2019), 291.
12. CBS News, *Hunger in America*, written by Peter Davis and Martin Carr, featuring David Culhane,

Charles Kuralt, and A. J. Ploch, documentary film, first aired May 21, 1968, on *CBS Reports* (television program).

13. For a record of that controversy, see *Hunger in America: Documentary Sources from the Rafael Ruiz Collection,* Our Lady of the Lake University library archives, 2018.

ROBERT BRISCHETTO

Texas Mexicans in the Post-Civil Rights Era

On August 3, 2019, a white nationalist from Allen, Texas, posted an anti-immigrant manifesto online and then drove more than 500 miles to open fire in an El Paso Walmart with the intent to "kill as many Mexicans as possible," saying his attack was a "response to the Hispanic invasion of Texas."[1] Twenty-three innocent people lost their lives and two dozen more were injured in the largest domestic terrorist attack against Latinos in modern history.

The attack in El Paso was not an isolated incident. FBI Director Christopher Wray said the bureau made about one hundred domestic terrorism arrests in the nine months prior to the El Paso attack, the majority of which were "motivated by some version of what you might call white supremacist violence."[2]

The El Paso shooter was part of an online community of white nationalists that many consider to have been emboldened by anti-immigrant rhetoric from President Donald Trump. The shooter's hate-filled rant cites "the great replacement," a right-wing conspiracy theory that minority groups will overtake whites. It echoed the chants of "you will not replace us" from the 2017 Unite the Right rally in Charlottesville where neo-Nazis, Ku Klux Klan, and alt-right groups marched to protest against the perceived threat to the white race, erupting in violence and the death of a counter protester.

In spring of 2020, George Floyd, an African American, was killed when a white police officer handcuffed him and pinned him down by kneeling on his neck. The act sparked widespread outrage at the police violence regularly occurring against people of color, an issue brought to public attention by shockingly graphic videos posted to social media. The subsequent protests that erupted across the nation were in some respects reminiscent of the urban unrest of the late 1960s, when Watts, Newark, Detroit, and more than a hundred other cities were looted and burned. The 1967 riots led President Lyndon Johnson to appoint the Kerner Commission to determine "what happened, why did it happen [and] what can be done to prevent it from happening again?" After numerous studies and testimonials, its report in March 1968 concluded that "Our nation is moving toward two societies, one black, one white—separate and unequal."[3]

In December 1968 the U.S. Commission on Civil Rights (USCCR) conducted a hearing to examine the civil rights status of another minority group, Mexican Americans of the Southwest.[4] In this book, experts review our nation's progress with regard to Mexican Americans in Texas in the half century since then. As they examine the extent of racial polarization and inequality, we find that the United States has become fractured into multiple racial, ethnic, and economic groups, a reality that defines what has been labeled the post-civil rights era.

The Importance of Race and Ethnicity

It is perhaps shameful that for more than four centuries our nation has not been able to erase division by color. Racism and ethnocentrism are burned into our civic and cultural consciousness. Below the façade of constitutional guarantees of freedom and equality under the law, there remain class divisions that have guided our public behavior in the past and define our social relations today.

Latinos in both popular and social science literature are sometimes identified as a racial group, sometimes as an ethnic group, and sometimes as both. Current federal policy, including the U.S. Census, defines Hispanics as an ethnic group, not a race. That was not always so. From 1890 to 1930, the U.S. Census did not identify Latinos at all. In the 1930 Census, Mexicans were classified under a separate racial category and then ignored in 1940 and 1950. In 1960 they were counted separately only from samples of five Southwestern states and identified as "persons of Spanish surname." It was not until 1980 that all Latinos were singled out in the complete count of the census and allowed to self-identify in a separate question apart from race.

Regardless of the official federal definition, however, Pew Research Center polling finds that two out of three Latinos consider their racial and ethnic makeup to be inextricably intertwined.[5] This may be traced to the concept of "mestizaje" (mixing or blending), which some of the countries in Latin America used in the first half of the twentieth century to refer to their populations with indigenous ancestry as "mestizo" to avoid racial conflict and promote a unified national identity.[6] As many as a quarter (24 percent) of all U.S. Hispanics in a 2014 survey tied their identity to Afro-Latino origin.[7]

The ambiguity of racial identity disappears when one considers *race* not from a biological but from a sociopolitical perspective. Sociologist David Montejano explains how race is a social construct: "The bonds of culture, language, and common historical experience make the Mexican people of the Southwest a distinct ethnic population. But Mexicans . . . were also a 'race' whenever they were subjected to policies of discrimination or control."[8] In a similar vein, George Fredrickson sees race as "what happens when ethnicity is deemed essential or indelible and made hierarchical."[9] Or, as sociologist Robin DiAngelo put it, "Race is an evolving social idea that was created to legitimate racial inequality and protect white advantage."[10] Even the definition of who is included in the category of "white" changes, as Italian, Irish, and Polish immigrants learned earlier in the twentieth century, when they were not included.[11]

Racism and Ethnocentrism

It is important to note at the beginning of this volume that racism is a term that has different levels of meaning. As it is popularly used, racism refers to the attitudes or behavior of individuals toward members of another racial group. Similarly, ethnocentrism refers to the evaluation of other cultural groups based on the narrow lens of one's own culture. I use both terms here to identify structures of oppression. Institutions can be racist or ethnocentric in the way the rules that govern them treat and control racial or ethnic groups, independent of the intentions or actions of individuals.[12] Dominant group institutions that define intergroup relations are scrutinized in this volume. Racism is a "system of advantage based on race."[13]

Social scientists have written volumes examining racism and interracial conflict within the American caste system.[14] Their major concern has been more with Black-white relations.[15] However, with changes in the demographic landscape in the last three decades, the study of racism and race relations now requires a multicultural perspective. The binary paradigm must be modified to fit the new sociodemographic reality. We must examine all sides of the multifaceted cultural environment and update our theories to fit the changing racial makeup of the population. Latinos, African Americans, Native Americans, and Asian Americans—each group to a different degree—experiences racism and discrimination in the American caste system.

Political scientist Ashley Jardina acknowledges the changing racial/ethnic landscape in her "theory of dominant group identity," which proposes that white consciousness does not always emerge from learned prejudice and hostility toward minorities; it is often the product of attempts by whites to protect their privilege and power.[16] She compiled data from six national surveys during the period of 2010-2016 to create an unusually large, representative national sampling of whites. She found that a substantial number of whites—about 30 to 40 percent of them—score high on white solidarity, but the vast majority of these "reject assertions of white supremacy and racism."[17] Members of the historically dominant white majority fear they are on their way to becoming a political minority. From this perspective, their racism is not as much a matter of racial animus as it is a function of desire to sustain white dominance and control of social, economic, and political structures. Jardina argues that white attitudes are also driven by their concern that non-white immigrants threaten to undermine American culture and its economic and political institutions.

Recent national polls, however, indicate that anti-immigrant sentiment in the United States, far from being widespread, has actually waned in the past quarter century. The Pew Center in 2019 found that public views of the contributions of immigrants had done an about-face since 1994, when 63 percent of the general population felt that immigrants "*burdened* the country by taking jobs, housing and health care." The same proportion (62 percent) felt that "immigrants *strengthen* our country because of their hard work and talents" (emphasis added).[18]

What's changing is the degree to which attitudes toward immigrants have become polarized along partisan lines over the past three decades. While there was no significant difference by political party in the views toward immigrants in 1994, the same question asked in 2019 revealed that as many as 83 percent of Democrats said "immigrants *strengthen* our country," compared to only 38 percent of Republicans (emphasis added).[19] Attitude toward immigrants is increasingly associated with their affiliation.

Civil Rights of Texas Mexicans Before 1968

A thorough understanding of the emerging developments in the civil rights of Mexican Americans in Texas requires that we examine the making of public policies in light of what has taken place in the courts, the legislature, and the population over time. There are numerous excellent historical accounts of the Mexican American experience in the Southwest. This book traces the data on Latinos in Texas during the past half century and—because disparities among racial groups are so central to questions of civil rights—the focus is on those group differences. We present empirical research and not strictly an historical account; even so, one must acknowledge that to understand the present and plan for the future, history can be an important guide and a crucial starting point.

In 1848 when the war between the United States and Mexico ended, the territory that we know of today as the southwestern United States was taken in the Treaty of Guadalupe Hidalgo. Unless they formally declared their intent to remain Mexican citizens within a year of the signing, the Mexicans who lived there automatically became U.S. citizens. Property rights were to be respected.[20] Despite the treaty's promise, the experience of Mexicans was much like that of the Indian tribes who lost their lands because of broken treaties. As a state, Texas had jurisdiction over the land within its boundaries; "it claimed to be exempted from the Treaty of Guadalupe Hidalgo . . . and carried out its own deliberations concerning the status of the annexed Mexicans and their land grants."[21] Tejanos lost their land to Anglos through deceit and violence.[22] There ensued a systematic attempt of "racial replacement," bringing Anglos in to farm, mine, and build railroads on land that was once Mexico.[23]

Unsuccessful attempts were made in the drafting of the state's constitution to exclude Texas Mexicans (Tejanos) from the franchise, based mostly on their mixed racial background.[24] After Reconstruction brought freedom and the promise of full citizenship to slaves, gradual disfranchisement of both African Americans and Mexicans occurred in Texas through the enactment of Jim Crow laws. The Tejano vote had been decisive in many of the towns in South Texas. During the decade of Texas as a Republic, fifty-seven of the eighty-eight aldermen who served in San Antonio de Béjar had Spanish surnames. The ethnic ratio was reversed after only a decade of statehood, when almost five times as many Anglos as Tejanos served as aldermen.[25]

From the late nineteenth century to the mid-twentieth century, Anglo landowners and political party bosses controlled the votes of Tejano workers. In rural counties of South Texas, the votes of *peones* were regularly delivered by their *patrones*, the landowners and political bosses, not all of them Anglo. These political machines continued even into the post-World War II era, during which Lyndon Johnson owed them his razor-thin senatorial victory in 1948.[26]

The poll tax was added in 1902 as one of many impediments to voting for minorities.[27] A year later, Texas Democrats implemented the whites-only primary. In some counties, they excluded not just African Americans, but also Mexican Americans, who were seldom considered "white."[28] It was not until 1944—after twenty years of litigation and five decisions—that the U.S. Supreme Court finally found all-white primaries in violation of the Constitution, in *Smith v. Allwright*.[29] The poll tax was declared unconstitutional in federal elections in 1964, and in 1966 in state elections in Texas.[30]

The transformation of the South Texas economy from ranching to farming began in the first decade of the twentieth century. Railroads connected Brownsville with the Missouri-Pacific system in 1904 and San Antonio in 1909, laying the infrastructure for an agricultural revolution in Texas. With refrigerator cars to transport perishable crops from the farm to the merchants, there was an influx of Anglos from the North and Midwest in search of land to farm. Workers were drawn from Mexico. Land values skyrocketed and cow pastures were converted into plowed fields. Ranchers became farmers, and real estate and irrigation companies moved in to slice ranches into farm tracts.[31] The "Magic Valley" along the border quadrupled in population from 1900 to 1930 and the "Winter Garden" area of South Texas increased threefold. By 1920, with the exception of a few counties along the border, Texas Mexicans had been reduced to landless wage laborers.[32]

While far less common than the violent racism experienced by African Americans in the post-Reconstruction South, lynching and other forms of discrimination against Texas Mexicans are well documented.[33] The Porvenir massacre of fifteen Tejano residents in 1918 by Texas Rangers is just one incident of many in which executions were carried out without regard to due process.[34] The "Mexico Tejanos" formed *sociedades mutualistas* (mutual aid societies) for security, legal aid, and protection against discrimination.[35] It was in response to lynching in Texas in 1911 that the Primer Congreso Mexicanista (First Mexican Congress), a statewide meeting in Laredo, was called. The event drew three to four hundred and, in addition to lynching, addressed concerns of discrimination in education, the economy, and the loss of Spanish and Mexican culture.[36] Out of the Congreso was formed La Gran Liga Mexicanista (the Great Mexican League) and its women's affiliate, the Liga Femenil Mexicanista (League of Mexican Females). Numerous other Mexican and Mexican American organizations formed in the early twentieth century—both local and statewide—like the Alianza Hispano Americano (Hispanic American Alliance) in 1911, La Agrupación Protectiva Mexicana (Mexican Protective Group) in 1911-1915, the Order of the Sons of America (OSA) in 1921, and the League of United Latin American Citizens (LULAC) in 1929.[37] Cynthia Orozco traces the development of a "México Texano" identity among the middle class organizers of some of these associations during the period 1910-1930 to form the beginnings of a Mexican American civil rights movement.[38]

Texas Mexican workers organized to protect their rights to a fair wage and to fight employment discrimination.[39] In 1900 the Sociedad de Protección Mutua de Trabajadores Unidos (Society for the Mutual Protection of United Workers) was formed by factory workers.[40] It was during the Great Depression that the U.S. labor movement came of age, demanding fair wages and working conditions. Organizers like Emma Tenayuca, a self-described communist, mobilized pecan shellers on San Antonio's West Side in the 1930s. Perhaps because of its leftist organizers, the pecan shellers' strike was not backed by local chapters of LULAC; but multiethnic alliances were formed with labor unions—such as the American Federation of Labor (AFL)—that carried over into electoral politics for decades to come.[41] These alliances remained in the post-World War II era in which labor renewed its militancy in coalition with Black and Latino community organizers in the fight for civil rights.[42]

The fight for civil rights did not stop at demands for fair wages. Segregation in schools was another battle. Records from the early 1900s show that as few as one in five Mexican American students in Texas attended any school at all.[43] The first "Mexican School" was established in Seguin in 1902, and by 1930 nine out of ten schools in South Texas separated Mexican American children from Anglo children.[44] While whites and Blacks were separated by law, the first recorded challenge to de facto segregation of Mexican Americans in Texas schools was filed against the Del Rio School Board in 1929, when the board ordered an election to expand school facilities, including the "Mexican School." The state district court issued an injunction against separate facilities for Mexican Americans on the grounds that they were not being afforded equal protection of the law. But the Texas Court of Civil Appeals in *Independent School District v. Salvatierra* (1930)—while it agreed with the lower court that "school authorities have no power to arbitrarily segregate Mexican children . . . solely because they are Mexican"—voided the injunction, effectively legalizing segregation of Mexican students through the third grade. Separating the children by language ability was deemed within the "pedagogical wisdom" of educators.[45] Segregation of Mexican Americans remained the practice in Texas schools.

Attorney Gustavo (Gus) Garcia, with support from LULAC, challenged separation of Mexican Americans in Bastrop Independent School District (ISD) and three other districts (*Delgado v. Bastrop ISD,* Civil No. 388, W.D. Tex., June 15, 1948) as depriving children of "Mexican or other Latin American descent" of equal protection of the laws, in violation of the Fourteenth Amendment of the Constitution. Like previous state judges, however, the judge allowed segregation for "language handicap," as long as it was not done in an arbitrary and discriminatory way.[46] Of course, many Texas schools remained segregated via a variety of strategies, such as testing and tracking to place Mexican American children in special education classes.[47]

In his history of Anglo-Mexican relations in Texas, Montejano attributes the wearing down of the segregationist order to two main crises—World War II and the 1960s civil rights movement.[48] Coming home from fighting a racist enemy side-by-side with white comrades, Texas Mexican servicemen could no longer tolerate the barriers that segregated them in housing, schools, and the workplace. They organized to fight for equal rights in employment, education, and voting. In San Antonio after the war, there were the Loyal American Democrats (LAD), the West Side Voters League, the Alamo Democrats, and the School Improvement League.[49]

When Mexican American candidates were successful in local elections in urban areas, it was usually by mobilizing a coalition with Blacks and liberal whites. In 1948 attorney Gus Garcia was elected to the board of the San Antonio Independent School District.[50] Henry B. Gonzalez, Jr., also a coalition candidate, was elected in 1953 to the San Antonio City Council, in 1956 to the state senate, and in 1961 to become the first Mexican American from Texas to serve in Congress. Activist attorney Albert Peña, Jr., was behind much of the mobilization of San Antonio's Mexican American vote in the 1956 election, when he won a seat on the Bexar County Commissioner's Court.[51] With LULAC support, Raymond Telles was elected El Paso's mayor in 1957, becoming the first Mexican American mayor of a major city in the twentieth century.[52]

The first Mexican American civil rights case to reach the U.S. Supreme Court was in 1954, regarding the exclusion of Mexican Americans from juries in a murder case. Peter Hernandez had been indicted and convicted of murder by an all-Anglo jury in Jackson County, Texas, a county in which Mexican Americans for more than twenty-five years had been completely excluded from grand jury service. The appeals court had previously ruled that since Mexican people "are not a separate race but white people of Spanish descent," there was no discrimination based on race under the equal protection clause of the Fourteenth Amendment. On appeal to the U.S. Supreme Court, attorneys Gus Garcia, Carlos Cadena, and John Herrera challenged that premise and argued that Mexican Americans, while they were white, were not treated as white and thus constituted a distinct class that deserved protection against discrimination. The high court ruled in *Hernandez v. State of Texas* that excluding Mexican Americans was a violation of the equal protection clause of the Fourteenth Amendment.[53] Two weeks after the decision was handed down, a case of segregation of African American children gained national attention. In *Brown v. Board of Education,* the Supreme Court declared de jure segregation of children in public schools unconstitutional in violation of the Fourteenth Amendment and acknowledged that there might be "other groups which need the same protection."[54]

In 1955 Rosa Parks refused to give up her seat on a bus in Montgomery, Alabama, and Reverend Martin Luther King, Jr., led a bus boycott that set off a national movement against segregation. For more than a decade, nonviolent civil disobedience transformed the Jim Crow South. The struggle of African Americans for racial inclusion, culminating in important civil rights legislation, would democratize this country through desegregation and enfranchisement.

With the Civil Rights Act of 1957, the first civil rights law since Reconstruction, Congress created the U.S. Commission on Civil Rights. The commission was given the charge of making recommendations to the President and Congress on changes in policy or new legislation. While it was defined as a temporary agency, it has been reauthorized several times, most recently in 1994, as an "independent, bipartisan, fact-finding federal agency."[55]

From more than a decade of relentless organizing, marching, and protesting came key pieces of legislation that helped change the course of race relations in America: the Civil Rights Act of 1964, desegregating public facilities and codifying fair employment; the Voting Rights Act of 1965, putting the power of Justice Department into reviewing electoral system changes; and the Fair Housing Act of 1968, forbidding discrimination in housing. The civil rights movement would have the effect of democratizing the nation and the unintended consequence of polarizing the population by race, according to Harvard political scientists Steven Levitsky and Daniel Ziblatt, "posing the greatest challenge to the established forms of mutual toleration and forbearance since Reconstruction."[56]

The divisions were also drawn along ethnic lines. In February 1961 several Mexican American labor leaders from Viva Kennedy clubs in Texas decided to build on their success in the 1960 presidential election by forming a state organization, the Mexican American Political Association (MAPA). In May they brought together Latino political, labor and civil rights activists from throughout the state under a new name, the Political Association of Spanish-Speaking Organizations (PASSO, aka PASO), with Commissioner Albert Peña, Jr., as their standard bearer.[57] It was PASSO that demonstrated how the power of the Texas Mexican majority, once mobilized, could challenge Anglo rule. PASSO members organized a local slate—called Los Cinco Candidatos—to run for city council in Crystal City, a South Texas town of ten thousand some eighty miles west of San Antonio in 1963. Using labor organizers in a door-to-door poll tax recruitment campaign, they took complete control of city offices.[58] While some saw this as a pyrrhic victory lasting only two years, the takeover was an expression of grassroots democracy that was to serve as an inspiration to a generation of Chicano leaders that was to follow in Texas.

Another key labor organizer emerged in California who drew the attention of the entire nation. César Chávez began organizing farmworkers in Delano, forming a union under the banner of the National Farm Workers

Association in 1962. In 1965 the NFWA joined Filipino farmworkers in a strike, followed by a national boycott of grapes. California organizers Eugene Nelson, Antonio Orendain, and Gil Padilla went to Texas in support of a strike against La Casita Farms in the melon fields of the Rio Grande Valley (the Valley) in 1966.

The Valley strike became a *cause célèbre* when a coalition of labor activists joined the striking farmworkers in a 468-mile march from the Rio Grande City, winding through the Valley to Austin to urge Governor John Connally and the legislature to support a $1.25 minimum hourly wage and protection for farmworkers.

Texas had a number of laws to stifle union activity, including statutes forbidding mass picketing, prohibitions on secondary boycotts, and a "right to work" law to discourage the formation of unions. The Texas Rangers, who had a well-earned reputation for using lethal force, were there to break the farmworker strike, as were local law enforcement officers hired by the growers as private guards. The Texas Rangers arrested the main organizer, Eugene Nelson, on the first day of the strike.

Many Texas churches viewed the farmworker strike as more than a labor dispute, seeing it as a moral issue. By the second month of the strike, a march to the state capitol had been organized to garner public support statewide. Strikers and their sympathizers wound their way through the Valley to Austin, gathering farmworkers, other labor unions, churches, students, and even a Catholic bishop as they marched in the hot Texas sun, arriving at the capitol on Labor Day 1966.

A new generation of Chicano activists emerged in the southwestern states during the mid-1960s. Much like the Black civil rights movement, they embraced their own cultural identity in what came to be known as the Chicano Movement.[59] Unlike the older politicos of PASSO, MAPA, LULAC, and the American GI Forum, the Chicano activists were more confrontational in their approach to organizing and developed their own forms of protest around a multitude of issues.

In 1967 and 1968 three statewide Raza Unida conferences were organized by members of the newly formed Mexican American Youth Organization (MAYO).[60] By 1969 MAYO chapters had sprung up throughout Texas, and were credited with organizing as many as thirty-nine school walkouts among high school students.[61]

1968 as a Pivotal Year

The year 1968 will be remembered as a turning point in the quest for minority civil rights, as well as a year of turmoil and tragedies in this country. The country was divided on involvement in the Viet Nam War, which had reached a turning point with the Tet Offensive by Viet Cong forces. Latinos were dying on the front lines at a rate that far exceeded their proportion of the population. During the previous summer, riots and civil disorders were reported in 150 cities.[62] In 1968 King's dream went beyond winning civil and voting rights. In March of that year, he joined with more than fifty organizations representing American Indians, Mexican Americans, and civil rights organizations to launch the Poor People's Campaign with plans to gather in the U.S. Capitol to propose "a radical redistribution of economic power."[63] King was not able to complete his campaign for economic justice. His life was cut short by an assassin's bullet on April 4.

Two months after King's assassination, presidential candidate Senator Robert Kennedy was assassinated. Kennedy had earlier joined with César Chávez and Dolores Huerta in support of César's twenty-five-day hunger strike to draw attention to the plight of farmworkers who were protesting wages and working conditions in California. Kennedy had investigated the issues of race, class, and culture—with a specific focus on Mexican Americans—in the Senate Subcommittee on Migratory Labor.

The year 1968 was also when civil rights attorneys formed the Mexican American Legal Defense and Education Fund (MALDEF) in San Antonio to support their demands for equal rights under the law with a grant from the Ford Foundation. MALDEF was instrumental in building a civil rights bar to challenge discriminatory election systems, to fight in the courts for equity in funding education, to bring bilingual education to the classrooms, to protect the rights of immigrants, and to ensure fair employment opportunities for minorities and women.

In 1968, students walked out in protest about the conditions of education in districts with low property values and poor funding. Parents of the protesting students in San Antonio's Edgewood ISD filed suit in federal court that same year to challenge the system of funding education as discriminatory by wealth and ethnicity *(Rodríguez v. San Antonio ISD)*.

As 1968 drew to a close, the U.S. Commission on Civil Rights held a week-long fact-finding hearing at Our Lady of the Lake College in San Antonio on civil rights challenges faced by Mexican Americans. A team of civil rights lawyers, social scientists, and expert consultants had been working in the southwestern states for more than a year, gathering testimony on discrimination and violations of civil rights among Mexican Americans.[64]

As the hearing began, there was ample evidence of the need for attention to the conditions and rights of Mexican Americans. Hundreds filled the college auditorium. Farmworkers came from the Lower Rio Grande Valley to testify about the conditions they faced and the efforts of the Texas Rangers to break up their strike. Outside, there were demonstrations by students who had participated in school walkouts demanding changes in the education system. Because of the protests and the new civil rights acts of the mid-1960s, legal infrastructure was established that allowed institutions previously closed to minorities to open up. It seemed that America could now become the democracy and the meritocracy that it had promised.

Texas Mexican Civil Rights Since 1968

What progress has been made on the issues of importance to Latino civil rights in the past half century since the Civil Rights Commission initiated its investigation? How do we measure that progress? Have civil rights movements propelled us beyond our history of racism at both national and state levels?

To answer these questions, we asked twenty experts in their respective fields to study the changes that have taken place in the civil rights and conditions of Latinos in Texas over the past fifty years. Their research focuses on the issues raised in the 1968 USCCR hearing in San Antonio, along with the addition of immigration, voting rights, and public health.

CHARTING RACIAL INEQUALITIES

To begin the task of assessing the progress and inequalities among racial and ethnic groups, demographer Rogelio Sáenz analyzed Texas census data each decade from 1960 to 2018, comparing Latinos, Blacks, and Anglos on a variety of demographic, social, and economic indicators. His results are presented in graphic form in the following chapter, depicting trends for each racial/ethnic group. His charts provide evidence of changes in each of the groups and show the racial inequalities that persist. Some of his more remarkable findings include:

- **Population Growth.** Latinos have driven population growth in Texas, increasing from 1.5 million to 11.4 million since 1960. The expectation is that by 2022 Latinos will outnumber Anglos. And, three decades later, the number of Latinos is projected to double in Texas. These trends will impact the political and economic landscape of Texas in the next half century.
- **Immigration.** A large portion of Latino growth can be attributed to immigration, most from Mexico, but more recently, Central America. The percentage of foreign born among Latinos in Texas more than doubled over the half century, from 13 percent to 28 percent. Even so, 85 percent of Latinos in Texas in 2018 were of Mexican origin, down from 97 percent in 1960.
- **Education.** There was progress for all groups in high school completion during the past half century, but the gap between Anglos and Latinos has remained in higher education. The percentage of Latinos completing college increased from 3 percent to 15 percent over that period; by contrast, 39 percent Anglos had completed at least a bachelor's degree. Enrollment of very young Latinos in preschool programs increased from one in five in 1980 to two in five in 2018, still below the percentage of Anglo children enrolled, which was half.

- **Employment.** There was over the half century relatively high employment of both Latino and Anglo men of working age (25-64). Among women, participation rates increased even more. One in three Latinas (age 25-64) were working in 1970 and almost two-thirds by 2018. Clearly, gains by Latinas in education have facilitated their entry into the workforce.
- **Family Income.** While income levels improved for all groups, the dollar gap grew between Anglo families and Black or Latino families. And, while poverty has declined for all groups, especially minorities, in 2018 Latinos and Blacks were twice as likely to be poor as were Anglos, and the poverty rate was three times as great for children of color as for white children.

Overall, while progress was made on some socioeconomic indicators, substantial inequalities remained between whites, on the one hand, and Latinos and African Americans, on the other.

The fact that Latinos are a younger population is important to consider when projections are made for the future of Texas. Already, more than half of the students enrolled in K-12 are Latino and in the very near future more than half of the workforce will be Latino. This stresses the importance of improving the quality of their education and prospects for employment.

THE ISSUE OF IMMIGRATION REFORM

The Immigration and Nationality Act of 1965 removed a nativist quota system, ultimately leading to an increase in immigration from Latin America, Asia, Africa and the Middle East. By 2018, the proportion foreign born in the United States had tripled from 4.7 percent in 1970 to 14 percent, the same level that triggered the quota restrictions of 1924. Ethnic diversity began to increase in the 1970s at a time when economic growth slowed, especially for those who were on the bottom of the wealth distribution. The economic downturn after the Great Recession in 2007 brought greater inequality, less job security, longer working hours, and fewer opportunities for upward mobility. As a result, there is a growing social resentment among members of the white working class and greater polarization by race and class.[65]

Concerns about "the browning of America" and the dilution of U.S. citizenship entered the national political dialogue.

When our country's first African American president was elected in 2008, white replacement was seen as a partisan threat.[66] Political scientists have presented evidence that the racial divide in American politics increased during President Barack Obama's two terms in office.[67] The Tea Party—a populist movement on the political right with outspoken members who publicly espoused nativist views—emerged in 2009. This may have been, in part, a reaction to the fact that Obama was an African American with a foreign name; but it was also a response to the ascending numbers of immigrants and asylum seekers at the border. With the increases in immigration came renewed attempts to restrict immigration. Immigration became a hot-button issue that galvanized some Anglos to work within the political system to influence public policy and others, disillusioned with the political elite, to join the white populist movement known as the "alt-right."

Democrats and Republicans have been gridlocked on comprehensive immigration reform for more than two decades. The Trump administration took advantage of the inaction and issued a series of executive orders that imposed draconian measures on immigrants, sparking outrage and deepening an ethnic and partisan divide. Just during the first year of Trump's presidency, the administration:

- Expanded the removal dragnet to criminally prosecute and deport all adults who entered the country illegally. Trump's policy of "zero tolerance" toward unauthorized migrants created a huge challenge to the enforcement of human rights governing asylum.[68]
- Canceled the Deferred Action for Childhood Arrivals program (DACA)— initiated in 2012 by President Obama to provide temporary status to those who entered without documents as children. This put about 800,000 at risk of deportation.[69]
- Separated migrant children from the parents who were under prosecution, hoping that such cruelty would discourage others from seeking

asylum. The separation was declared by the courts to be a violation of the Constitution, but only after as many as three thousand children had been separated, some permanently, after their parents were removed from the United States.

- Stopped grants of temporary protective status (TPS) to Haitian and Central American nationals, putting more than a million migrants at risk of deportation. This action would test a 1990 law that allowed temporary status to victims of oppression and natural disasters.[70]
- Declared a rule that those migrants receiving social services, Medicaid, food stamps, and housing vouchers would not qualify for a Green Card that would grant them permanent residency. The "Public Charge" rule could affect millions of Texans, more than 1.6 million with U.S. citizen children, who may go without much-needed health care, food, and housing for fear of losing their chance for gaining a Green Card.[71]
- Ordered migrants seeking asylum to remain in Mexico as they awaited their day in court. The backlog of all cases in the immigration courts reached one million. In the first nine months of 2019, as many as 55,000 refugees were returned to Mexico to wait at great peril in the streets of border towns where there is no protection from gangs and drug cartels.[72]

For Latinos in Texas the immigration issue has always been both cultural and deeply personal. Almost half of all Texas Latino households have members who are immigrants, some unauthorized.[73] Undocumented immigrants are already integrated into Latino families and the Texas workforce. Now they seek a legal place in the larger community and culture.

Immigrants have become one of the most rapidly growing segments of the American electorate, almost doubling in number over the past two decades. The Pew Research Center estimated that 23.2 million immigrants would be eligible to vote in the 2020 election, one-third of them Hispanics.[74] The National Partnership for New Americans (NPNA) had projected that as many as 860,000 new Americans would be naturalized by election day, 96,000 of them in Texas.[75] That was in February 2020, just prior to when all public-facing processes in the naturalization process were brought to a halt due to the pandemic. A proposal to continue interviews and naturalizations via video conferencing by League of Women Voters was rejected by the U.S. Citizenship and Immigration Services (USCIS). The Trump Administration saw the coronavirus as an opportunity to further restrict immigration. The the president issued sixty-three executive actions from March through August 2020 that did just that, including travel bans on thirty-one countries, ending asylum at the United States-Mexico border, and suspension of several categories of visas.[76] Those restrictions were added to a previous proposal made in November 2019 to almost double the citizenship application fee, from $640 to $1,170.

One issue of great concern is the potential for violating the civil liberties of peaceful protesters. In the years following 9/11, the George W. Bush Administration created Customs and Border Protection (CBP). Several federal agencies were merged under the Department of Homeland Security to create what is now the largest federal law enforcement agency. The CBP has a budget of more than $20 billion, with more than 45,000 armed personnel. As protests developed after the police murder of George Floyd in Minneapolis, the CBP deployed its agents and its crowd-control weapons to quell unrest in urban areas such as Portland, Oregon, and even small towns in parts of South Texas, such as Kingsville and Refugio County. CBP has coordinated with nearly a dozen Texas law enforcement departments in response to planned protests. Human and civil rights groups have raised concerns about violations of First Amendment rights of assembly and free speech in the deployments.[77]

Immigration law professor emeritus Lee Terán traces the trend toward greater militarization of the Texas-Mexico border in her chapter of this book.

THE ISSUE OF VOTING RIGHTS

Returning to his own hometown in Crystal City in 1969, José Angel Gutiérrez, one of the MAYO founders, began building an effort that would demonstrate the ability of the Chicano movement to transform local politics in rural Texas. It began with the issue of discrimination in selecting the homecoming queen in the local high school, and grievances brought to the school board grew from there. He and his wife, Luz, worked with parents and students to form Ciudadanos Unidos and built support for a school walkout and a political force that grew under the banner of "Raza Unida." Within a year, Ciudadanos Unidos controlled both the school board and the city council in Crystal City.[78] Raza Unida activists in the South Texas Winter Garden Area also won places in several other nonpartisan municipal and school board elections in Cotulla and Carrizo Springs.[79]

RAZA UNIDA PARTY

The first real test of Raza Unida on the local level came in the fall of 1970, when it fielded candidates in partisan elections in Dimmit, La Salle, Zavala, and Hidalgo counties. It took some write-in campaigns, election fraud challenges, and several court battles to get candidates on the ballots. Fifteen of the sixteen Raza Unida candidates in the four counties were defeated. The only victory was in La Salle County, for a county commissioner's race.[80] Two years later, in Zavala County, Ciudadanos Unidos came back, adding the county commission to its takeover of the school board and Crystal City council.[81]

In a statewide meeting in San Antonio in 1970, some MAYO members formalized a plan discussed a year earlier about making Raza Unida a third political party in Texas.[82] During the next few years, Raza Unida Party (RUP) chapters were very successful in local elections in rural towns in South Texas. They won places on city councils, school boards, and county commissions in more than a dozen places. The Crystal City model proved to be a success in Pearsall, Kingsville, San Juan, Carrizo Springs, Asherton, Marathon, Anthony, Eagle Pass, San Marcos, Kyle, and Lockhart, and school boards in Cotulla, Robstown, Beeville, Hebbronville, La Joya, and Edcouch-Elsa, to mention a few.[83]

Buoyed by these local successes, Raza Unida sought and achieved official recognition as a state political party in 1972. With almost no vetting, it fielded a young lawyer and local MAYO leader from Waco, Ramsey Muñiz, for governor, along with a slate of candidates for six statewide offices. Muñiz received 6.3 percent of the vote, 114,000 more votes than the margin of victory by Democrat Dolph Briscoe, who garnered the lowest winning percentage in the history of the state.[84] This was close enough to cause concern within the Democratic Party establishment, which controlled all statewide offices and both houses of the legislature.

The 1972 election marked the first time that Chicanos had captured the attention of both of the major parties in a presidential election as well. *Laredo Times* editor Fernando Piñon, researching testimony given before the U.S. Senate Watergate Committee hearings, found a secret memo from Attorney General John Mitchell urging the Republican Party's Committee to Reelect the President (CREEP) to encourage the RUP with undercover funding to run presidential candidates in California and Texas. While that did not materialize, President Richard Nixon's political director used the administration's power of the purse to override Governor Briscoe's veto of a grant to the Zavala County Health Corporation, a proposal submitted by RUP's Gutiérrez as County Judge.[85] Gutiérrez made sure that Raza Unida Party remained neutral in the presidential contest, something he said it was planning to do all along.[86]

Although the RUP did not grow statewide in 1974, it again drew almost 6 percent of the vote in the election for governor, more than enough to keep its third-party status on the next ballot. There was evidence that the RUP had been under surveillance by the Department of Public Safety since its inception.[87] Texas Attorney General John Hill launched an investigation of Raza Unida officeholders in Crystal City, and in 1975 several Raza Unida officeholders were indicted, but not convicted, on charges of corruption. Ultimately, the party was brought down by misdeeds of Muñiz, its standard bearer, for trafficking marijuana from Mexico and jumping bail.[88]

The Raza Unida Party ran its last campaign in 1978 with Mario Compeán, the first chairman of the party, as its candidate for governor. He received less than 1 percent of the vote. But Democrat John Hill lost to Republican Bill Clements also by less than 1 percent of the vote, for the first gubernatorial win by a Republican since Reconstruction. The RUP disbanded after less than a decade, but the organizers of MAYO and many of those young Chicanos it trained continued to be active in the political and civic life of their communities. While the Raza Unida Party was unable to mount a successful campaign for statewide offices, its local victories in rural South Texas demonstrated that the Chicano vote was a force to be reckoned with in Texas.

At the time that Raza Unida Party was forming among the MAYO leaders, there was a nonpartisan effort to build Chicano political power initiated by another of the MAYO founders, William C. ("Willie") Velásquez. Velásquez was a St. Mary's University graduate student in economics who, like many Chicano activists at the time, began his organizing in support of the farmworker movement. Southwest Council of La Raza (SCLR) in Phoenix had tried to launch a regional voter registration effort among Mexican Americans in the Southwest beginning in 1969, modeled after the effort started by five Black civil rights organizations in the South, the Voter Education Project (VEP) in Atlanta. SCLR applied for tax-exempt status for its Citizens Voter Research Education Project (CVREP) and was denied twice by the IRS in 1971 and 1972. Velásquez was brought on as a consultant to CVREP with the assignment to raise the appropriate funds and file again for nonprofit status. A year later, CVREP was denied tax-exempt status a third time. It was not until President Nixon's adviser John Dean testified before the Senate Watergate Special Committee and presented White House memos from 1970 and 1971 asking the IRS to take actions against "left-wing" and "activist" organizations that Velásquez learned of the real reason for the denials.[89]

After President Nixon's resignation, Velásquez began once again applying to the IRS in his own hometown of San Antonio. He formed the Southwest Voter Registration Education Project (SVREP) with new sponsors. SVREP was granted tax exempt status in 1974. The project, supported mostly by foundation funds, expanded its reach to over two hundred communities in Texas, New Mexico, Arizona, Colorado and California. The number of Latinos registered doubled, reaching five million by the time of Velásquez's death in 1988. By then, the project had added the Southwest Voter Research Institute, hired an attorney, and initiated eighty-eight successful voting rights lawsuits. The record of its impact can be seen in an increase of more than eighteen hundred Latino elected officials in just fifteen years.[90]

Southwest Voter's influence went beyond its region. Using SVREP as a model, the Midwest Voter Registration Education project was incorporated in 1982 in Chicago. As of 2020, at least a half dozen voter registration organizations have formed to register Latino voters and SVREP continues its work among Mexican Americans in the five southwestern states.[91]

The collective efforts of Chicano activists over the past half century resulted in electing Texas Mexicans to mayor of San Antonio, numerous positions in the Texas legislature and the U.S. Congress, as Housing and Urban Development secretary twice, and in 2020 as a candidate to the U.S. presidency.

DISCRIMINATORY ELECTION SYSTEMS

To make the Latino vote count required changing the very election systems that discriminated against minority voters. Because voting was polarized along racial lines in Texas, the victories for Latinos were less common in urban election districts where Mexican Americans did not comprise a majority. It took a challenge of multimember countywide legislative districts in *Graves v. Barnes* (1972), unanimously affirmed by the U.S. Supreme Court in *White v. Regester*, 412 U.S. 755 (1973), to finally change the type of voting system. Multimember countywide districts with at-large voting prevented both African Americans and Mexican Americans from electing candidates of their choice in Bexar and Dallas counties. Single-member legislative districts were mandated in both counties. The second round of *Graves v. Barnes* (1974) created single-member districts in eight other urban counties, resulting in electing the first minorities to the legislature in these counties.[92] With the 1975 extension of the Voting Rights Act to language minorities, shepherded by Houston Congresswoman Barbara Jordan, an African American, activists launched new court challenges to discriminatory voting systems.

Under Section 5 of the Voting Rights Act amendments of 1975, states with histories of voter discrimination were required to have voting changes "precleared" by the Justice Department or the DC federal court. An early illustration of the power of Section 5 can be found in San Antonio. The city had been ruled for decades by an oligarchy of Anglo business elites. The

Good Government League (GGL) controlled city politics during the modern charter period from the early 1950s to the early 1970s with a system of voting at-large by place on the city council. Their nominees for city council, handpicked by a GGL nominating committee, were elected with very few exceptions during this period. Latino voters' choices were almost always defeated by the Anglo voters.[93]

When San Antonio annexed sixty-six square miles of new territory in 1972, there was concern by voting rights advocates that the added voters, most of them Anglo, would dilute the strength of minority voters' choices in citywide at-large elections with numbered seats. When the Voting Rights Act was amended in 1975 to include language minorities and all of Texas under Section 5, MALDEF filed a lawsuit (*Martínez v. Becker*) and the Department of Justice issued an objection to the San Antonio annexations.[94] The city settled by adopting ten single-member council districts and holding a special city charter election to ratify the change in 1976.

The charter amendment passed and voting by district in the 1977 election produced the first city council in San Antonio modern history with a majority who were minority-group members.[95] The change in the election system was followed by challenges to at-large elections in many other communities in Texas and throughout the Southwest. The litigation was often followed by voter registration drives to enlist new Latino voters and mobilize the electorate around candidates of their choice. The result of this two-step strategy was a dramatic increase in the number of Latinos elected to office on the local level in Texas cities and school districts, as much as a fourfold increase since 1975.[96]

The electoral gains by Texas Mexicans could not have been accomplished without the skills of attorneys who made up an informal "voting rights bar." MALDEF and SVREP joined forces to file eighty-eight lawsuits over the next decade (1974–1984) in Texas counties, cities, and school districts.[97] In a well-coordinated effort, other civil rights groups—LULAC, Texas Rural Legal Aid, the ACLU and local Latino political activists joined them to challenge voting discrimination in its many forms.

Whether elections are fair and do not discriminate against minorities may also depend on how electoral districts are drawn. The drawing of state legislative, congressional, and state board of education districts is delegated to the state legislature. If the state legislature fails to reach an agreement on state legislative districts, the task falls to the state Legislative Redistricting Board (LRB) in Texas.

Each decade, upon release of the decennial census, it is customary for the majority party to draw up plans for those districts. Gerrymandering is the practice of drawing lines to favor one party or racial group over another. It is illegal when done to disadvantage minority voters, but partisan gerrymanders have often been tolerated by the courts. The problem in Texas is that since parties have historically been divided along racial lines, it is virtually impossible to distinguish a partisan from a racial gerrymander, and courts have sometimes excused blatant racial gerrymanders as just politics.

While both major political parties in Texas have sometimes engaged in racial gerrymandering, the most egregious abuse of the power to redistrict was led by the U.S. House Majority Leader, Tom DeLay, out of cycle in 2003. Republicans packed Latino and African American voters into a small number of congressional districts in major metropolitan centers of Houston and Dallas. Six districts were shifted from Democrat to Republican in the 2004 election, giving Texas Republicans a net gain of twelve seats in Congress.[98]

Not to be outdone, in 2011 Texas Republicans adopted redistricting plans for Texas House districts that were found to be drawn to intentionally discriminate against minority voters, in violation of § 2 of the Voting Rights Act and the Fourteenth Amendment to the U.S. Constitution, in *Perez v. Abbott*, 250 F. Supp. 3d 123, 219 (W.D. Tex. 2017).

Then in 2013 voting reforms were slowed to a crawl by a U.S. Supreme Court decision, *Shelby County v. Holder*, invalidating the formula in the Voting Rights Act (VRA) for determining which jurisdictions require federal oversight of voting changes.[99] Texas and all of its subdivisions were no longer required to have proposed election changes reviewed before they were implemented. *Shelby* immobilized the most important provision of the VRA, and Congress was left to decide whether to draft a new formula for preclearance coverage or to effectively abandon the enforcement of minority voting rights.

VOTER SUPPRESSION

Within twenty-four hours of the high court's decision in *Shelby*, according to a Judiciary Committee report, Texas Republicans moved to reinstitute a draconian voter identification law that was later found more than once by a federal court to be intentional racial discrimination. The Secretary of State initiated a massive purge of the voter registration rolls of a suspected 95,000 noncitizens, many of them found to be naturalized citizens.[100] Additional unnecessarily burdensome voter registration requirements were added by the Texas legislature in a desperate attempt to suppress voting, making it more difficult for minorities and low-income citizens to vote.

As Texas voters approached the 2020 election, new voters faced a series of obstacles that had the effect of suppressing minority votes;[101]

- Texas had passed one of the toughest voter ID laws in the country in 2011. The law was challenged in court and some of the requirements were changed, but the tough photo ID requirement remained. When the law was first challenged, as many as one in four Latinos in Texas were estimated to lack the proper identification.
- Registration does not happen automatically when Texans update their drivers' licenses; they must print and mail a voter registration form to their county registrar.
- Voter registration organizations must get permission to register voters from each of the 254 counties where they intend to register voters.
- Texas was one of only ten states that required voters to register at least thirty days in advance of the election.
- The Texas legislature in 2019 passed a law prohibiting temporary polling locations.
- When the coronavirus pandemic caused concern about exposure at crowded polling places, vote by mail was expanded to all voters in most states, but not in Texas. Texas was one of only five states that would not allow all voters to vote by mail.[102]

- Governor Greg Abbott ordered all counties to allow no more than one absentee ballot drop-off place per county, at odds with the plans of many local voting administrators to secure multiple locations for those concerned about late delivery by the postal service. Harris County, with the largest population and the largest number of minority voters, had planned to set up twelve drop-off locations, but was restricted to one.

In response to requests from local election administrators, Governor Abbott extended the early voting period by six days. Early voting in person then became the preferred method for Texans to cast their ballots, with 9.7 million voting early, more than the total vote cast in the 2016 election. Turnout was almost 70 percent of all registered voters, higher than it had been in at least three decades.[103]

There are several chapters in this book devoted to examining issues of voting rights in the Latino community:

- Law professor and voting rights attorney José Roberto Juarez, assisted by MALDEF attorney Ernest Herrera, reviews the cases and Justice Department objections to voting rights violations brought in Texas during the past half century.
- Voting rights expert Henry Flores identifies the factors that go into a voting rights law suit and the evidence needed to prove intentional discrimination.
- Legal experts from the Brennan Center for Justice at New York University School of Law, Kevin Morris and Myrna Perez, develop measures of voter suppression.

THE ISSUE OF EQUITY IN EDUCATION

By far the greatest attention in the 1968 USCCR hearing was on the education system. School walkouts by Chicano students had already begun in Texas, drawing attention to demands protesting inadequate curriculum and teaching, seeking removal of sanctions against speaking Spanish on campus and of corporal punishment, and seeking support for bilingual/

bicultural education. With the support of MAYO chapters, the protests spread throughout parts of Texas by the end of 1969.[104]

The *Rodríguez* case—filed in 1968 by San Antonio's Edgewood ISD parents in the poorest school district in the state—presented evidence that local property taxes determined to a large extent the amount of revenue available for education in a district. A three-judge panel ruled in favor of the Edgewood parents in 1971 (*Rodríguez v. San Antonio ISD*). On appeal, the U.S. Supreme Court in 1973 overturned the lower court's ruling and declared that education was not a fundamental right guaranteed by the Constitution (*San Antonio ISD v. Rodríguez, et al.*)

Not to be deterred, a decade later, with the help of MALDEF, parents sued again, this time under the state constitutional guarantee of a thorough and efficient educational funding system. In and out of court for the next couple of decades, MALDEF attorney Albert Kaufman worked to obtain no fewer than five rulings requiring more equal distribution of tax revenue among Texas school districts. The battle for equity in funding education shifted from the courtroom to the halls of the Texas legislature and is still being waged.[105]

After the immigration reforms of 1965 dropped quotas from Latin American countries, the need to provide an education appropriate to the cultural and linguistic background of the new English language learners became clear.[106] The legislature passed legislation in 1969 authorizing bilingual education up to grade six and the Bilingual Education and Training Act of 1973, requiring districts with at least twenty students of limited English speaking proficiency to offer bilingual education in grades K–3. Bilingual education soon became a national mandate for schools with English-language learners in the *Lau v. Nichols* decision (414 U.S. 563) of the U.S. Supreme Court.[107] Less than a decade later, the high court established an open-door policy for immigrant children, regardless of their legal status, in *Plyler v. Doe* (457 U.S. 202, 1982). And in 2001 Texas became the first state to authorize in-state tuition rates for college students who were undocumented. From 2009 to 2017, as the number of white undergraduate students in the United States dropped by 1.7 million, the number of Latino undergraduates increased by 1.1 million.[108]

Achieving educational equity in Texas has been the goal of the Intercultural Development Research Association since its founding almost five decades ago. Attorney David Hinojosa, who was in charge of IDRA's Equity Assistance Center, IDRA president emeritus María "Cuca" Robledo Montecel, and senior education associate Aurelio Montemayor, discuss the educational equity efforts in Texas in their chapter of this book.

THE ISSUE OF ECONOMIC INEQUALITY

FARMWORKERS

In the half century since the 1968 USCCR hearing, the agricultural economy that had once relied on cheap Mexican labor was again transformed, this time by the forces of mechanization and globalization of the marketplace. The number of farms in Texas decreased by one-third between 1950 and 1970, and the workforce in agriculture was decimated by more than half.[109] While one-third of the Texas Mexican population had been employed as farmworkers in 1930, that had been reduced to less than 4 percent by 1980.[110]

The 1966 Valley strike was a bold move against growers in Texas, but it was doomed from the start. A year after it began, the strike was stopped by a court order banning all picketing of La Casita Farms. However, seven years later the strikers were finally vindicated when five Texas statutes were struck down by the U.S. Supreme Court—laws forbidding mass picketing, secondary strike, unlawful assembly, obstructing the streets, and unlawful assembly in *Allee v Medrano*, 416 U.S. (1974).

Today Texas is the third most productive state in agriculture. Food is grown, harvested, and packed by more than 200,000 farmworkers, roughly half of them undocumented. Increasingly, immigrants are coming in on H-2A guest worker visas, bound to one employer who controls their housing and worksites. They are sometimes charged illicit recruitment fees, putting them into debt bondage. Trafficking is difficult to prosecute since it requires an intent to force a person to work. This is a form of modern-day slavery.[111]

While the Texas farmworkers have diminished in number and been largely replaced by immigrant workers, the influence of the 1966 strike went well beyond the Valley to a larger Chicano movement that ultimately brought a transformation of the politics-as-usual in South Texas and reforms in the schools. Just finishing their college education, many of the leaders of that movement received on-the-job training as organizers. "*Viva la Causa*," their rallying cry, became the call to action for student walkouts, for equal political representation, for marches seeking equal justice in the courts, and for the rights of immigrants. The Texas melon strike and national grape boycott provided a training ground for Chicano activists who went on to ignite other organizational efforts during the next decade.

The impact of the farmworker movement in Texas and the historic Valley strike is delineated in the chapter by Rebecca Flores with the assistance of Juanita Valdez-Cox and James Harrington. They were involved as a key organizers of farmworkers in the Rio Grande Valley at various times from the early 1970s to the present.

HOUSING

More than five decades since the Fair Housing Act of 1968, racially segregated neighborhoods have been too often accepted as a fact of urban life by governments at all levels and neighborhood segregation has persisted. These residential patterns are the basis for much of the school segregation that persists.

Much of the segregation today by race and national origin continues because of economic disparities among these groups. Local governments can promote neighborhood desegregation through zoning policies and housing vouchers to pave a path toward greater neighborhood integration. Given the history of continued neighborhood patterns of economic and racial segregation in the past half century, elimination of this structural inequity will not occur through free-market forces without the assistance of local governments and the backing of the courts at the federal and state levels.

It took a U.S. Supreme Court ruling in 2015 (*Texas Department of Housing and Community Affairs v. The Inclusive Communities Project*) to remind local governments that the Fair Housing Act prohibited not only intentional discrimination, but also policies that have a disparate impact on minorities by race, national origin, sex, or religion. Within weeks of the Court's decision, the Obama administration issued a rule that local jurisdictions examine their patterns of racial segregation in housing, set goals in reducing it, and report progress every three to five years. The Trump administration replaced the Obama rule with a new one, "Preserving Community and Neighborhood Choice," which the National Association of Realtors predicts will lead to further discrimination since it "weakens the federal government's commitment to the goals of the Fair Housing Act."[112]

The residential segregation of families by socioeconomic status has grown significantly.[113] While there were great strides made in fair housing legislation since the late 1960s, there has been a failure to adequately enforce these laws. There is clear quantitative evidence that Latino families have lived in income-segregated communities and have become more isolated.[114] Racial, ethnic, and class isolation have much to do with the political conflicts of today. When racial and ethnic groups are residentially and socially segregated, they will naturally sort themselves into different political camps with different and sometimes conflicting worldviews. We then have the conditions for racial polarization.

Studies of housing discrimination against Mexican Americans as well as their progress in home ownership are discussed by housing expert Alejandro Becerra and former housing secretary Henry Cisneros in their chapter.

JOBS

With the expansion of Texas's urban areas in the twentieth century, the job opportunities were to be found in San Antonio, Houston, Dallas, and Fort Worth. Lacking inherited wealth, many Mexican Texans sought to move up the economic ladder through education and employment. Nowhere is this more evident than in San Antonio's Kelly Field, an Air Force base that offered thousands of blue- and white-collar jobs to Mexican Americans from the 1940s until the base closed in 2001. But the majority of the working class have remained in low-income jobs in inadequate public housing in neighborhoods that were often flooded or lacked adequate street repairs.

It was in the parishes on San Antonio's West Side and near Kelly Air Force Base that Ernesto Cortes, a University of Texas at Austin economics graduate student, began organizing neighborhoods in his hometown in the early 1970s. He was trained in grassroots organizing by Fred Ross of the Industrial Areas Foundation (IAF) in Chicago and Los Angeles. Cortes formed the Communities Organized for Public Service (COPS) in 1973, working primarily with parish leaders. COPS began with small issues that concerned the families and children in these lower middle-class neighborhoods, such as placing moms as traffic guards and addressing street flooding and drainage, and then working up to larger concerns like workforce development, fair wages, and the expenditure of tax revenues. In just a few years, COPS had spread to other parishes in the south and west sides and in a decade almost a dozen IAF organizations were organized in Texas—in Houston, El Paso, Dallas, Fort Worth, the Rio Grande Valley.[115] The local IAF groups formed a network of community groups that would influence policymaking all the way to the state legislature.

There remain large gaps separating racial and ethnic groups by income and even greater chasms in wealth. Economists on the Board of Governors of the Federal Reserve System reported the national median income in 2019 of Anglo households to be $69,000, compared to $40,700 for Hispanics and $40,300 for Blacks. The racial disparities in wealth (gross assets minus liabilities) are much larger. The median net worth of white families (those in the middle of their ethnic group) was $188,200, five times that of Hispanic families ($36,200) and eight times as great as Black families ($24,100).[116]

The tight U.S. labor market in 2019—with unemployment at 3.5 percent—was finally beginning to benefit working-class communities of color when the global pandemic arrived in 2020, hitting especially hard low-income workers, women, and people of color, wiping out their gains in the most recent expansion. By August 2020, unemployment reached 8.4 percent overall, with 10.5 percent among Hispanics and 13 percent among Blacks.[117]

Civil rights analyst and urban studies expert Ernest Gerlach explores inequalities in employment in his chapter, comparing jobs held in Texas with racial/ethnic composition of the state's population and a special focus on San Antonio.

Economics professors Marie Mora and Alberto Davila probe deeper into the trends and correlates of inequalities in their chapter, tracing the economic outcomes for native-born Mexican Americans over the past five decades in comparison to Anglos in Texas.

THE ISSUE OF PUBLIC HEALTH

Census data show that Texas had the highest number and percentage of persons without health insurance in 2018. Five million people were uninsured and the majority of them were Hispanics. Just before the Affordable Care Act (ACA or Obamacare) went into effect in 2014, 22.1 percent of Texans were uninsured. Over the next three years, the percent uninsured dropped each year, reaching 17 percent.

The ACA was to provide subsidized coverage for people at above 130 percent of the poverty level and expand Medicaid to people below that income level, if a state approved the expansion. Texas was one of fourteen states that refused to expand Medicaid for low-income adults. If the Texas political leaders were to participate in Medicaid expansion, more than 1.4 million Texans would become eligible for coverage.[118] By not accepting the $8-10 billion a year in federal funds available under the ACA for Medicaid expansion, the state lost jobs and revenue and removed health care from where it is most needed. As many as seventeen rural hospitals have closed in Texas since 2010.[119] The most recent Census survey numbers (for 2019) indicate that uninsured Texans numbered 5.2 million or 18.4 percent of the total population, the highest in the nation.[120]

A Georgetown University study found that states failing to expand Medicaid to adults have also seen increases in their child uninsured rates. By 2018 as many as 835,000 Texas children were without health insurance. The state had the highest rate of uninsured children, at 11.2 percent—more than twice the national average.[121]

State policies on women's reproductive health have put low-income women at a disadvantage. A new study by the Texas Evaluation Project at the University of Texas at Austin shows that Texas women have tried to end their pregnancies on their own three times more often than women in other states. The research looks at self-administered abortions before and after a 2013 state law that forced nearly half of the state's abortion clinics to close. The law required clinics to meet the same strict standards as hospital-style surgical centers and required physicians who performed abortions to obtain admitting privileges at a nearby hospital. By the time the U.S. Supreme Court struck down the law in 2016, the number of Texas clinics performing abortions had been reduced from forty-one to twenty-four.[122]

There are some fairly easy fixes to the safety net that policymakers could make to immediately improve the plight of those of those without health care and jobs, according to Anne Dunkelberg of Every Texan. Texas elected officials could join the thirty-eight other states that have taken advantage of Medicaid expansion made available by the Affordable Care Act. Failing that, Congress and the president could easily remove the glitch in the ACA that locks out low-income Texans from sliding-scale subsidies under the act. One out of four Texas children are in households with non-citizens members, some of them undocumented. Because of the aggressive stance taken by the Trump administration against immigrants, hundreds of thousands of Texans eligible for benefits have dropped Medicaid coverage for their children under the Child Health Insurance Program (CHIP) or failed to apply for food stamps for fear of harming the immigration status of family members. That too is something that could easily change if policymakers and administrators of these programs were to be more proactive in their outreach efforts.[123]

Juan Flores, a Latino health policy analyst and advocate for more than four decades, reviews studies that measure ethnic group disparities in health and social determinants of health in Texas in his chapter.

THE ISSUE OF FAIRNESS IN THE CRIMINAL JUSTICE SYSTEM

There is probably no institution in which white dominance is more apparent than in the criminal justice system. In a totalitarian state, the use of violent force is essential to maintain control. Our democratic government has checks to unmitigated force built into our legal system by utilizing the courts, citizen juries, a set of laws, and a constitution to guide us. But what happens when the system becomes unequal and constitutional rights are sacrificed?

Some who remembered the racial protests and riots of the 1960s have drawn parallels to the protests that accompanied the Black Lives Matter

movement since 2015. While many of their grievances and targets for reform were the same, the protesters differed in important respects. Blacks
predominated in the protests of the 1960s; half of the participants in the
2020 protests were white.[124] In a *New York Times* Voters Poll in late June, one
in five Latinos (21 percent) and Blacks (22 percent) said they had participated in Black Lives Matter protests.[125]

The racist police violence central to the Black Lives Matter movement
was also identified as a problem for Latinos when the Civil Rights Commission met a half century ago. Both groups have experienced shared human
rights violations within our criminal justice system. In the last chapter
of this book, Lupe Salinas, a professor at the Thurgood Marshall School of
Law in Houston with more than fifty years of experience as a civil rights
attorney, prosecutor, and state district judge, illustrates the structural racism embedded in our legal system. Salinas recounts cases brought since
the 1968 hearing in which Latinos were victims of police brutality, skewed
jury representation, unreasonable bail, and inadequate counsel. He adds
instances of prosecutorial misconduct, some resulting in the wrongful
assessment of the death penalty, and raises the issue of whether it is time
to abolish the death penalty in Texas.

The Challenges Ahead

Many changes in the status of Mexican Americans have occurred in Texas
over the past fifty years, most for the better, though only after hard-fought
battles in the courts, the legislatures, the ballot box, and the streets. The
civil rights movement of the 1950s and 1960s brought the combined effort of
all of these forces to challenge discrimination in voting, education, housing,
employment, and the application of criminal justice. The institutions of
our democracy were changed and made more equitable by both African
Americans and Mexican Americans raising the same issues in their own
struggles for greater equity in an increasingly diverse democracy.

But many concerns brought to the surface by the Black and Latino civil
rights movements of the past half century remain unresolved, as evidenced

by the persistent deep divisions and inequalities in Texas and the rest of the nation. Basic human rights and needs have become racial issues because of how unequally the resources of power and wealth have been distributed in our society.

THE GLOBAL PANDEMIC: 2020 TO ?

As the 2020 decade began, the issue that eclipsed all others worldwide was COVID-19. By mid-February the first cases of the virus had been confirmed in the United States. The next month, as the virus spread unabated, it became clear that there was a "kind of pandemic caste system" emerging from the statistics.[126] Preliminary data released in early April showed that this coronavirus was killing people of color in New York City at twice the rate of white people.[127] National tallies by the Centers for Disease Control and Prevention (CDC) revealed that Latinos, who make up 18 percent of the U.S. population, made up 34 percent of the COVID-19 cases.[128] By the end of May, Blacks and Latinos were found to be three times as likely to have been infected compared to the whites in their counties and were twice as likely to die from the virus.[129]

Texas was the only state in which more than half of all those dying from the virus were Latino. An analysis of CDC data by demographer Rogelio Sáenz found that among people of working age (twenty-five to sixty-four years) in Texas, Latinos were dying at a rate four times the rate of non-Hispanic whites.[130] One of the greatest hotspots was in the Rio Grande Valley. Another was El Paso, with hospitals at full capacity and intensive-care patients being exported to San Antonio.[131] The four border counties reported forty-nine deaths from the coronavirus in early June and almost two thousand by the end of August.[132]

To understand these racial disparities, one must unpack the structural conditions that lead to greater infections and higher mortality. Most vulnerable to the disease were frontline workers—those in health care, cleaning services, food service, public transit, delivery, and warehouse—essential to keep the economy open and provide for basic necessities. In Texas at least six in ten of these essential workers are people of color and one in five are immigrants.[133] Most of these essential workers could not work from home.

An Associated Press analysis of data from the U.S. Bureau of the Census on eleven Texas cities with the largest population of frontline workers shows that 62 percent were women.[134] Latinos aged forty to fifty-nine years were infected at five times the rate of whites in that age group.

A month after shutdowns began, Latino adults were asked about how their households were affected by the coronavirus. Six in ten Latinos in the United States—and four in ten white adults—suffered a job or wage loss due to the pandemic.[135] Almost half (46 percent) of Latinos surveyed in Texas in early April reported that one or more persons in their household continued to go to work outside the house. Three in ten of the households had someone who lost their job and one in four Latino-owned businesses had shut down or lost revenue. Of those households with someone working or schooling online from home, one in three (32 percent) said they did not have enough computers, laptops, or tablets for everyone.[136] The Texas cities of Brownsville and Pharr had the lowest digital connectivity of all U.S. cities; nearly half of their households were without broadband access in 2018.[137]

Higher incidence of prior health conditions and lack of insurance among Latinos and Blacks also played a role in COVID's disproportionate effect. Almost four in ten (38 percent) of working-age Latinos in Texas are not insured, compared with 20 percent of Blacks and 15 percent of whites.[138]

COVID-19 brought to the public's attention huge inequalities that exist along racial and economic lines and revealed a safety net riddled with holes. We are the only industrialized nation that does not have universal coverage of health care. Unlike all other advanced economies, employers in the United States are not required to grant paid sick leave or time off. Four in ten working Texans are without access to paid sick leave, and as many as eight in ten service-sector workers—where many Latinos and women are concentrated—are not covered.

When the pandemic hit, people lost jobs along with health insurance. The public interest nonprofit think tank Every Texan (formerly Center for Public Policy Priorities) reported that in the first six months after the closures began, 3.5 million Texans filed for unemployment relief. Almost 700,000 uninsured adults lost their health insurance in only the first two months of the pandemic shutdowns. More than 600,000 joined the ranks of the 3.8 million Texans who rely on food stamps to feed their families. Before the pandemic, the state required SNAP (Supplemental Nutrition Assistance Program) recipients to work at least thirty hours a week if they are to keep their benefits.[139]

When the Congress acted in mid-March by passing the Families First Coronavirus Response Act (FFCRA) and the Coronavirus Aid, Relief and Economic Security (CARES) Act many immigrants and mixed-status families were excluded from the recovery financial stimulus, putting at risk millions of other Texans and seriously undermining the ability to weather this crisis.[140]

Yet the first pandemic relief package the Republican Congress passed included a $90 billion tax adjustment for 2020 almost exclusively benefitting those who earn more than $1 million per year.[141] As New York University marketing professor Scott Galloway put it: "As the pandemic tore through our economy, we poured hundreds of billions into the coffers of big and small corporations, where it quickly found its way not into the dinner table of those without work or sick from the virus, but into the bank accounts of the shareholder class."[142]

EXTREME RACIAL DISPARITIES IN WEALTH

Freedom and equality are two distinct and worthwhile goals. Changes in the laws brought through litigation and legislation took a giant step toward freedom in the civil rights era. The challenge that remains is to achieve greater economic equality, something that King had envisioned in his attempt to form a rainbow coalition in support of the Poor People's Campaign. Unfortunately, the evidence in the fifty years since then is that extreme inequalities in wealth have accelerated the differences among racial and ethnic groups.

Economists have alerted us to the trend toward greater concentration of wealth and corporate control of politics during the past few decades. Gabriel Zucman maintains a World Inequality Database at the University of California at Berkeley. His analysis shows we have returned to levels of wealth concentration not seen since the Roaring Twenties. The top 0.1 percent of the population has increased its share of the national wealth since 1980 from 5 percent to 20 percent of the total national wealth, more than the combined wealth of the bottom 80 percent of the population. One in five American households have either zero assets or more debt than assets; their numbers have increased by one-third since 1983.[143] The bottom one-fourth of households (31 million families) have a median net worth of $200.[144]

An analysis of the stock market gains during 2020 shows that it was the wealthiest 10 percent—those who were well vested in stocks—that were profiting in the trillions of dollars as the markets soared during the pandemic. The Nasdaq was up 42 percent for the year, but the Main Street economy was down 3 percent. The 651 billionaires in the United States together accumulated an additional trillion dollars, while 47 percent of Hispanics reported financial difficulties.

INCREASED RACIAL POLARIZATION AND VOTER ALIENATION

One indicator of minority empowerment is the extent to which people are participating in the electoral process. Historical data show that African American voter participation reached its apex during Reconstruction, when two out of every three ex-slaves voted.[145] As Jim Crow laws were imposed in the South, barriers to registration and voting effectively excluded Blacks from participation. The extent of Black voter participation in the South dropped from 61 percent in 1880 to 2 percent in 1912.[146] It took federal litigation based on the Fourteenth and Fifteenth Amendments and the Voting Rights Act of 1965 for Blacks to finally regain the right to vote.

But there is a limit to what the courts can do to bring about change; they usually follow rather than make public opinion. As one prominent legal scholar reminds us, "Constitutional rights are generally limited to negative constraints on government."[147] They remove barriers, but do not ordinarily lead the charge for change. Elected officials can set policies and pass laws in the public interest, but even now that "most barriers are gone," political scientist Bernard Fraga points out, a "large, growing turnout gap" remains between white and minority voters a half century since the Voting Rights Act.[148] According to the most reliable national estimates of voting from 2006 to 2016, the average "turnout gap" over the past decade between white and Black voters was 15 percentage points, and 29 points between white and Latino voters.[149] Why was the turnout gap for Latinos so large? Fraga suggests that one issue could be that Latino voters "do not perceive their vote to matter."[150]

Willie Velásquez may have had the answer to Mexican Americans' lagging electoral engagement four decades ago. In communities where Latinos were frustrated in their attempts to elect candidates of their choice to the city council or school board, his strategy was to file litigation challenging structural barriers, such as the at-large elections, and follow with voter registration drives. Local Latino organizers would identify their own preferred candidates and conduct get-out-the-vote drives in their communities. By removing the barriers to voting, Latinos would have a more effective voice in the election outcome. Velásquez adopted the slogan *Su Voto Es Su Voz* (*Your Vote Is Your Voice*), which guides organizing drives among Latinos even today. His approach emphasized voter engagement and self-determination.[151]

As 200,000 Latinos come of voting age every year in Texas, their potential impact on statewide elections increases. In the 2020 U.S. presidential election, voter participation was up dramatically among all voters, Latinos included, and differences in voters' choices among racial groups in Texas were stark. The results of exit polls in 2020 give us some insights into Latinos' voting patterns and views. The *New York Times* reported that 38 percent of all votes cast in Texas were by Black, Latino, or Asian voters, with each non-white group favoring Biden. The *New York Times* polls indicate Trump's win in Texas was aided by strong support from white voters, especially Anglo men (71% Trump, 27% Biden) and white evangelicals (86% Trump, 13% Biden), who made up one-third of all voters.[152]

Election-eve phone surveys of 2020 voters conducted by a consortium of Latino Decisions, Asian American Decisions, and the African American Research Collaborative showed the following results for these racial/ethnic groups in Texas:

• Whites: 64% Trump, 33% Biden.
• Latinos: 29% Trump, 67% Biden.
• Blacks: 10% Trump, 86% Biden.

The Collaborative found patterns of support in the races for U.S. House and U.S. Senate very similar to those for president: among Anglo voters, twice as much support for the Republican as the Democrat; among Latino voters, more than twice as much support for the Democrat as the Republican; among African American voters, almost nine times more support for the Democrat as the Republican.[153] Polls by both the New York Times and the Latino Decisions consortium show that Texas voters clearly were polarized along racial and ethnic lines in the 2020 election.[154]

Behind the racial polarization is the concern among whites that the increases in the minority population will eventually bring minorities into power as the new majority. Demographers predict Latinos will account for at least half of the growth in the Texas population between 2010 and 2050. New census survey estimates for 2019 demonstrate that people of color already outnumber Anglos in the state. On the local level in many parts of the state some major realignment of power is taking place among racial and ethnic groups. On the state and national levels, the domination of politics by Anglos could give way under both demographic and political pressure to a pluralistic democracy characterized by greater equality and less tribalism.

RESURGENCE OF WHITE SUPREMACY

While some political polarization is healthy and necessary to advance different views in a democracy, there is a point at which social segregation and partisan rivalries lead to perceived mutual threats. According to Levitsky and Ziblatt, such distrust may "encourage the rise of anti-system groups that reject democracy's rules altogether. When that happens, democracy is in trouble."[155] We saw this in the case of the El Paso massacre of twenty-three Mexicans in 2019. The Southern Poverty Law Center has been following the rise of white supremacy and attacks on immigrants for two decades, showing an increase from 784 extremist groups in 2014, when immigrants from the northern triangle countries in Latin America began arriving in greater numbers, to as many as 1,020 hate groups in 2018.[156]

An analysis by the Center for Strategic and International Studies (CSIS) of 893 terrorist plots and attacks in the United States between January 1994 and May 2020 found the same alarming trend. They focused on domestic terrorism versions and found twice as many right-wing (57 percent) as left-wing (25 percent). The right-wing attacks had increased in number during the previous six years. Over the past two decades, attacks from the right were the deadliest, resulting in 335 deaths—compared to twenty-two deaths from left-wing attacks and five deaths from ethnonationalist terrorists.[157] Clearly the data signaled a need for a coordinated effort among all levels of government to protect against domestic terrorism.

On January 6, 2021, there was a seditious and violent attack on the nation's Capitol by supporters of Donald Trump. Hundreds stormed the Capitol to protest the results of the presidential election, attempting to interrupt the U.S. Senate's certification of the electoral college results. As the FBI carried out their investigation into the perpetrators of violence, their findings revealed that white nationalists and other far-right extremists had been involved in the planned assault. *Washington Post* columnist Michael Gersen characterized the invasion as "united by a belief that the White, Christian America of its imagination is on the version of destruction, and that it must be preserved by any means necessary."[158]

Alejandro Mayorkas, the newly appointed Secretary of Homeland Security, reported that for several years prior to the attack on the Capitol the country had suffered an upsurge in domestic violence extremism and the threat continues. Acknowledging that "the majority of these attacks have targeted communities of color and other minority groups," he designated domestic violent extremism as a National Priority Area.[159] The partisan polarization that was once based on policy differences had revealed itself as a racial divide.

How do we all meet the challenge of reducing racial polarization and its extreme expression in racial violence? How do we protect equality of opportunity and respect for civil rights? This will require looking back and analyzing what has worked and what has not. Our data-informed examination of the past half century in Texas reveals some real progress on which to build in a number of areas. The civil rights reforms of the 1960s have laid the foundation for a just democracy. The development of Latinos in Texas after 1968 was a consolidation and acceleration of the gains made by the civil rights struggles of the previous decades. The organizing of farmworkers in the Rio Grande Valley, the ongoing battle for comprehensive immigration reform, the fight for voting rights, the battle for equal educational opportunity, the effort to obtain affordable homes and better jobs, the improvement of public health, and the struggle for equal treatment in the justice system—these were all part of the Latino civil rights movement in Texas. There are many who continue working tirelessly to keep the civil rights era alive, propelling us forward.

A closer look at the changes during the past half century since the Civil Rights Commission's hearing on Mexican Americans reveals that we have yet to deal with the extreme economic inequality along racial/ethnic lines. As Sáenz shows in the next chapter, the gaps between racial and ethnic groups remain large. Until we address these inequities, we will not bring racial and ethnic groups closer together, nor ensure a pluralistic democracy.

Notes

1. Tim Arango, Nicholas Bogel-Burroughs, and Katie Benner, "Minutes Before El Paso Killing, Hate-Filled Manifesto Appears Online," *The New York Times*, August 3, 2019, 1.

2. Greg Miller, "Rise of Far-right Violence Leads Some to Call for Realignment of Post-9/11 National Security Priorities," *The Washington Post*, August 5, 2019.

3. National Advisory Commission on Civil Disorders, *The Kerner Report* (New York: Bantam Books, 1968), 1.

4. U.S. Commission on Civil Rights, *Hearing before the United States Commission on Civil Rights: San Antonio, TX, December 9–14, 1968* (Washington, DC: GPO, 1969). Also available at https://catalog.hathitrust.org/Record/001874430.

5. Ana González Barrera and Mark Hugo Lopez, "Is Being Hispanic a Matter of Race, Ethnicity or Both?" *FactTank*, Pew Research Center, June 18, 2015, available at PewResearch.org.

6. Ana González-Barrera, "'Mestizo' and 'mulatto': Mixed-Race Identities Among U.S. Hispanics," *FactTank*, Pew Research Center, July 10, 2015, PewResearch.org.

7. From a Pew Research Center poll, September 11-October 8, 2014, cited by Gustavo Lopez and Ana González-Barrera, "Afro-Latino: A Deeply Rooted Identity Among U.S. Hispanics," *FactTank*, Pew Research Center, March 1, 2016, PewResearch.org.

8. David Montejano, *Anglos and Mexicans in the Making of Texas, 1836-1986* (Austin: University of Texas Press, 1987), 5.

9. George M. Fredrickson, "Understanding Racism," in George M. Fredrickson, *The Comparative Imagination: On the History of Racism, Nationalism and Social Movements* (Berkeley: University of California Press, 1997), 778-97.

10. Robin DiAngelo, *White Fragility: Why It's So Hard for Anglo People to Talk About Racism* (Boston: Beacon Press, 2018), 17.

11. DiAngelo, *White Fragility*, 18.

12. A similar definition is given by DiAngelo, *White Fragility*, 20.

13. David T. Wellman, *Portraits of White Racism* (Cambridge, UK: Cambridge University Press, 1977).

14. Swedish sociologist Gunnar Myrdal in his two-volume work *An American Dilemma* (New York: Harper & Brothers, 1944), perhaps the most comprehensive study of race in America, describes the American society as a "caste system." Myrdal's contemporaries using the same description: Hortense Powdermaker, *After Freedom: A Cultural Study in the Deep South* (Madison: University of Wisconsin Press, 1939); Allison Davis, Burleigh B. Gardner, and Mary R. Gardner, *Deep South: A Social Anthropological Study of Caste and Class* (Chicago: University of Chicago Press, 1941); and Oliver Cromwell Cox, *Caste, Class, and Race: A Study in Social Dynamics* (New York: Doubleday, 1948).

15. Ashley Jardina, *White Identity Politics* (Cambridge, UK: Cambridge University Press, 2019), 11.

16. In this regard, Jardina cites the works (among others) of Herbert Blumer, "Race, Prejudice as a Sense of Group Position," *The Pacific Sociological Review* 1(1), 3-7, and Lawrence D. Bobo, "Prejudice as Group Position: Micro-Foundations of a Sociological Approach to Racism and Race Relations," *Journal of Social Issues* 55(3), 445-72; Christopher S. Marker and Matt A. Barreto, *Change Theory They Can't Believe In: The Tea Party and Reactionary Politics in America* (Princeton, NJ: Princeton University Press, 2013).

17. Jardina, *White Identity Politics*, 8.

18. Bradley Jones, "Majority of Americans Continue to Say Immigrants Strengthen the U.S.," Pew Research Center, January 31, 2019, PewResearch.org.

19. Jones, "Majority of Americans."

20. Neil Foley, *Mexicans in the Making of America* (Cambridge, MA: Harvard University Press, 2014), 31.

21. Montejano, *Anglos and Mexicans*, 38.

22. Zaragoza Vargas, *Crucible of Struggle: A History of Mexican Americans from Colonial Times to the Present Era* (New York: Oxford University Press, 2017), 146.

23. Paul R. Spickard, *Almost All Aliens: Immigration, Race and Colonialism in American History and Identity* (New York: Routledge, 2007), 156-57, as cited by Foley, *Mexicans in the Making of America*, 32-33.

24. Montejano, *Anglos and Mexicans*, 38-39. Also see Zaragosa Vargas, *Crucible*, 102; Jesús F. de la Teja, Paula Marks, and Ron Tyler, *Texas: Crossroads of North America* (Belmont, CA: Wadsworth, 2004), 234-36.

25. August Santelban, *A Texas Pioneer: Early Staging and Overland Freighting Days on the Frontiers of Texas and Mexico* (New York: Neale Publishing, 1910), 314-21, as cited by Montejano, *Anglos and Mexicans*, 40.

26. Much has been published on Johnson's U.S. Senate race against Coke Stephenson in 1948. A detailed account can be found in Robert A. Caro, *The Years of Lyndon Johnson: Means of Ascent* (New York: Alfred A. Knopf, 1990), Chap. 15.

27. Montejano, *Anglos and Mexicans*, 260.

28. Darlene Clark Hine, *Black Victory: The Rise and Fall of the Anglo Primary in Texas* (Millwood, NY: KTO Press, 1979).

29. For a history and an empirical test of Texas voting rights litigation in Texas through the 1980s, see Robert Brischetto, David R. Richards, Chandler Davidson, and Bernard Grofman, "Texas," 233-70, in Chandler Davidson and Bernard Grofman, eds., *Quiet Revolution in the South: The Impact of the Voting Rights Act, 1965-1990* (Princeton, NJ: Princeton University Press, 1994).

30. The Twenty-Fourth Amendment was ratified in 1964, prohibiting the tax as a voting require-ment in federal elections. Based on the Voting Rights Act of 1965, the U.S. Attorney General brought suit against the state's poll tax in *United States v. State of Texas* (1966).

31. Montejano, *Anglos and Mexicans*, 103–10.

32. Montejano, *Anglos and Mexicans*, 109–14.

33. See Montejano, *Anglos and Mexicans*, 15–128; Vargas, *Crucible*, 146–50.

34. Vargas, *Crucible*, 187.

35. Arnoldo De León, *The Tejano Community, 1836–1900* (Albuquerque: University of New Mexico Press, 1982); Arnoldo De León, *They Called Them Greasers: Anglo Attitudes Toward Mexicans in Texas, 1821–1900* (Austin: University of Texas Press, 1983); Arnoldo De León, *Mexican Americans in Texas: A Brief History* (Arlington Heights, IL: Harlan Davidson, 1993); Richard A. García, *Rise of the Mexican American Middle Class, San Antonio, 1919–1941* (College Station: Texas A&M University Press, 1991).

36. Cynthia Orozco, *No Mexicans, Women, or Dogs Allowed: The Rise of the Mexican American Civil Rights Movement* (Austin: University of Texas Press, 2009), 70.

37. In San Antonio alone, there were twenty-five mutual aid societies between 1915 and 1930, with a combined total of more than ten thousand members. Orozco, *No Mexicans*, 68; Benjamin Márquez, *LULAC: The Evolution of a Mexican American Political Organization* (Austin: University of Texas Press, 1993).

38. Orozco, *No Mexicans*, 24–39.

39. For early labor exploitation and discrimination, see Montejano, *Anglos and Mexicans*, Chaps. 2 and 4.

40. Fernando Piñon, *Searching for America in the Streets of Laredo: The Mexican American Experience in the Anglo American Narrative* (Mexico: Centro de Estudios Sociales Antonio Gramsci A.C., 2015), 97.

41. Max Krochmal, *Blue Texas: The Making of a Multiracial Democratic Coalition in the Civil Rights Era* (Chapel Hill: University of North Carolina Press, 2016), 7, 21–28. For a detailed account of the pecan shellers strike, see Zaragoza Vargas, "Tejana Radical: Emma Tenayuca and the San Antonio Labor Movement During the Great Depression," *Pacific Historical Review*, 66 no. 4 (1997): 553–80. Also see Vargas, "The Mexican American Struggle for Labor Rights in the Era of the Great Depression," *Crucible*, 212–40.

42. For a discussion of labor's politics in the postwar period, see Kevin Boyle, *The UAW and the Heyday of American Liberalism, 1945–1968* (Ithaca, NY: Cornell University Press, 1995). Also see Nelson Lichtenstein, *State of the Union: A Century of American Labor* (Princeton, NJ: Princeton University Press, 2002).

43. James D. Crockroft, *Latinos in the Struggle for Equal Education* (Danbury: Franklin Watts/Grolier, 1995), 12–13, as cited by José Angel Gutiérrez, *Albert A. Peña Jr.: Dean of Chicano Politics* (East Lansing: Michigan State University Press, 2017), 34.

44. Montejano, *Anglos and Mexicans*, 160.

45. Jorge C. Rangel and Carlos M. Alcalá, "De Jure Segregation of Chicanos in Texas Schools," *Harvard Civil Rights-Civil Liberties Law Review* 7 (March 1972): 307–91.

46. Foley, *Mexicans in the Making of America*, 156–57.

47. V. Carl Allsup, "Delgado v. Bastrop ISD," *Handbook of Texas Online*, tshaonline.org.

48. Montejano, *Anglos and Mexicans*, 259–61.

49. Montejano, *Anglos and Mexicans*, 279.

50. Krochmal, *Blue Texas*, 133.

51. Gutiérrez, *Albert A. Peña Jr.*, 61–64.

52. Brischetto et al., "Texas," 242.

53. Arnoldo De Leon and Robert A. Calvert, "Civil Rights," in *Handbook of Texas Online*; Vargas, *Crucible*, 287.

54. *Hernandez v. Texas*, 347 U.S. 475 (1954), as cited in Foley, *Mexicans in the Making of America*, 158. Also see PBS Documentary, "A Class Apart," premiered February 3, 2009, American Experience, at PBS.org.

55. U.S. Commission on Civil Rights, "Mission," available at usccr.gov.

56. Steven Levitsky and Daniel Ziblatt, *How Democracies Die* (New York: Broadway Books, 2018), 144.

57. Krochmal, *Blue Texas*, 232.

58. Gutiérrez, *Albert A. Peña Jr.*, 124–32.

59. For a discussion of the philosophy behind the movement, see Armando B. Rendón, *Chicano Manifesto: The History and Aspirations of the Second Largest Minority in America* (New York: Macmillan, 1971). For a history of the role of feminists in the movement, see Maylei Blackwell, *Chicana Power: Contested Histories of Feminism in the Chicano Movement* (Austin: University of Texas Press, 2011).

60. MAYO emerged in 1967 in San Antonio from a series of informal discussions after college classes in the Fountain Room near St. Mary's University. Besides Gutiérrez, the founders were Mario Compeán, Juan Patlán, Nacho Perez, and Willie Velásquez. Ignacio M. García, *United We Win: The Rise and Fall of La Raza Unida Party* (Tucson: University of Arizona Press, 1989), 15–22.

61. José Angel Gutiérrez, *The Making of a Chicano Militant: Lessons from Cristal* (Madison: University of Wisconsin Press, 1998), 142.

62. National Advisory Commission on Civil Disorders, *Kerner Report*, 32.

63. Michael K. Honey, *Going Down Jericho Road: The Memphis Strike, Martin Luther King's Last Campaign* (New York: W. W Norton, 2007), 186.

64. Henry M. Ramírez, *A Chicano in the White House: The Nixon No One Knew* (CreateSpace Independent Publications, 2014), 96.

65. Levitsky and Ziblatt, *How Democracies Die*, 228.

66. Rob Willer, Matthew Feinberg, and Rachel Wetts, "Threats to Racial Status Promote Party Support Among White Americans," SSRN working paper, 2016. Also see Shanto Iyengar and Sean J. Westwood, "Fear and Loathing Across Party Lines: New Evidence on Group Polarization," *American Journal of Political Science* 59, no. 3 (2015): 690–707.

67. Donald R. Kinder and Allson Dale-Riddle, *The End of Race? Obama 2008* (New Haven, CT: Yale University Press, 2012); Cindy D. Kam and Donald R. Kinder, "Ethnocentrism as a Short-Term Force in the 2008 Presidential Election," *American Journal of Political Science* 56, no. 2 (2012): 326–40.

68. PBS Frontline. See also discussion of these by Terán, later in this book.

69. Ryan Nunn, Jimmy O'Donnell, and Jay Shambaugh, "A Dozen Facts About Immigration," Report of Brookings Institution, October 6, 2018, available online at Brookings.org.

70. Jens Manuel Krogstad and Ana Gonzalez-Barrera, "Key Facts About U.S. Immigration Policies And Proposed Changes," *Fact Tank* (May 17, 2019), Pew Research Center website.

71. Anne Dunkelberg, "Dangerous Federal 'Public Charge' Rule Threatens 1 in 4 Texas Children," news release of Center on Public Policy Priorities, August 12, 2019.

72. Known officially as Migrant Protection Protocols (MPP), the program was started in January 2019 in San Diego and expanded to Calexico, El Paso, Laredo, and Brownsville. Sylvia Foster-Frau, "'Remain in Mexico' Policy Is Explained," *San Antonio Express-News*, September 5, 2019.

73. Data accessed from Census Microdata Series: Steven Ruggles et al., "Integrated Public Use Microdata Series USA: Version 8.0 Database," Minnesota Population Center, 2018, https://usa .ipums.org.

74. Abby Budiman, Luis Noe-Bustamante, and Mark Hugo Lopez, "Naturalized Citizens Make Up Record One-in-Ten U.S. Eligible Voters in 2020," Pew Research Center, February 26, 2020, pewresearch.org.

75. Diego Iniguez-López, "Naturalization Now, Vote Tomorrow: New Americans Vote 2020," report for National Partnership for New Americans, February 2020, available at Partnership-ForNewAmericans.org.

76. Eileen Guo, "New U.S. Citizens Were One of the Fastest-Growing Voting Blocs. But Not This Year," *Our 2020 Election Forecast*, FiveThirtyEight, August 31, 2020, available at fivethirtyeight .com.

77. St. John Barned-Smith, "Small Towns Are Loaned Big Firepower," *San Antonio Express-News*, December 13, 2020, A-1.

78. García, *United We Win*, 54–60.

79. Gutiérrez, *The Making of a Chicano Militant*, 187–88.

80. These battles in court are discussed by García, *United We Win*, 61–71.

81. For a more complete discussion of Zavala County governance, see Gutiérrez, *The Making of a Chicano Militant*, 242–66. Also, see García, *United We Win*, 37–74.

82. David Montejano, *Quixote's Soldiers: A Local History of the Chicano Movement, 1966–1981* (Austin: University of Texas Press, 2010), 148.

83. García, *United We Win*, 165–68.

84. Texas State Historical Association, "Elections of Texas Governors, 1950–1972," *Texas Almanac* website.

85. Piñon, *Searching for America*, 231–36.

86. García, *United We Win*, 124–25.

87. Montejano, *Quixote's Soldiers*, 224.

88. García, *United We Win*, 197. Muñiz failed to appear in federal court in 1976 and was convicted of jumping bail and drug charges. In 1984, he was released from prison, only to be charged and convicted ten years later for a third drug offense, when he received a life sentence as a repeat offender. Montejano, *Quixote's Soldiers*, 224–26.

89. Juan A. Sepúlveda, Jr., *The Life and Times of Willie Velasquez: Su Voto es Su Voz* (Houston: Arte Publico Press, 2003), 124-30.

90. Sepúlveda, *The Life and Times of Willie Velasquez, 387.*

91. The five states are Texas, California, Colorado, New Mexico and Arizona. After Willie's death, the Southwest Voter Research Institute was named the William C. Velazquez Institute.

92. *Graves v. Barnes*, 343 F. Supp. 704 (W.D. Tex. 1972); *White v. Regester*, 412 U.S. 755 (1973), *Graves v. Barnes*, 378 F. Supp. 640 (W.D. Tex.), vacated and remanded, 422 U.S. 935 (1975), as noted in Brischetto et al., "Texas," 244–45.

93. Robert Brischetto, Charles L. Cotrell, and R. Michael Stevens, "Conflict and Change in the Political Culture of San Antonio in the 1970s," in David R. Johnson, John A. Booth, and Richard J. Harris, eds., *The Politics of San Antonio: Community, Progress, & Power* (Lincoln: University of Nebraska Press, 1983), 75–94.

94. *Martínez v. Becker*, No. SA-75-CA-315 (W.D. Tex. 1975).

95. Brischetto et al., "Conflict and Change," 88–89. See also Charles L. Cotrell and Arnold Fleischmann, "The Change from At-Large to District Representation and Political Participation

of Minority Groups in Fort Worth and San Antonio, Texas," Paper presented at the annual meeting of the American Political Science Association, Washington, DC, August 30-September 3, 1979.

96. For a discussion of this strategy, see Robert Brischetto, "Today's Politics Not Velásquez's," *San Antonio Express-News*, May 9, 2014.

97. Montejano, *Anglos and Mexicans*, 296.

98. Steve Bickerstaff, *Lines in the Sand: Congressional Redistricting in Texas and the Downfall of Tom DeLay* (Austin: University of Texas Press, 2007), 133-70.

99. 570 U.S. 2 (2013)

100. Robert Brischetto, "A Number on Voters," *San Antonio Express-News*, March 10, 2019, F1, F6.

101. Benjamin Wermund, "Texas Is at Center of Fights over Voting Rights," *San Antonio Express-News*, September 20, 2020.

102. For a discussion of President Trump's campaign to cast doubt on the validity of vote-by-mail, see Robert Brischetto, "Don't Let Rhetoric, Obstacles Deter Your Vote," *San Antonio Express-News*, October 14, 2020, A23.

103. Texas Tribune, "At Least 9.7 Million Texans—57% of Registered Voters—Voted Early," accessed November 28, 2020, at texastribune.org.

104. Gutiérrez, *The Making of a Chicano Militant*, 142.

105. See a more complete discussion of litigation and legislation in Texas in the chapter by Hinojosa, Robledo Montecel, and Montemayor, later in this book.

106. A federal court decision (*US v. Texas*, 321 F. Supp. 1043; S.D. Tex. 1971) required a bilingual program for children in the San Felipe Del Rio school district.

107. This was a suit brought on behalf of children in San Francisco's Chinatown who could not speak English.

108. Rogelio Sáenz and Dudley L. Poston, Jr., "Children of Color Already Make Up the Majority of Kids in Many U.S. States," *The Conversation*, January 9, 2020, available at theconversation.com.

109. Montejano, *Anglos and Mexicans*, 273-74.

110. U.S. Department of Commerce, Bureau of the Census, 1930 and 1980 Decennial Census.

111. Dana Ullman, "Forgotten in the Fields," *The Texas Observer*, July/August 2019, 22.

112. Editorial, *San Antonio Express-News*, July 31, 2020.

113. Douglas S. Massey and Nancy Denton, *American Apartheid: Segregation and the Making of the Underclass* (Cambridge, MA: Harvard University Press, 1993).

114. Kendra Bischoff and Sean F. Reardon, "Residential Segregation by Income, 1970-2009," Report prepared for Project US2010, October 16, 2013; John R. Logan and Brian J. Stults, "The Persistence of Segregation in the Metropolis: New Findings from the 2010 Census," Census brief prepared for Project US2010, March 24, 2011, available at www.s4.brown.edu/us2010.

115. For a detailed account of the IAF, see Mary Beth Rogers, *Cold Anger: A Story of Faith and Power Politics* (Denton: University of North Texas Press, 1990).

116. Board of Governors of the Federal Reserve System, "Changes in U.S. Family Finances from 2016 to 2019: Evidence from the Survey of Consumer Finances," *Federal Reserve Bulletin* 106, no. 5 (September 2020).

117. Rachel Siegel, "Wealth Gaps Between Black and White Families Persisted Even at the Height of Economic Expansion," *The Washington Post*, September 28, 2020.

118. Center for Public Policy Priorities, "Red Flag: More Texans Uninsured for a Second Year," *Every Texan* (blog), Every Texan (formerly Center for Public Policy Priorities), September 10, 2019, available at EveryTexan.org.

119. Paul Krugman, "State-Inflicted Medical Misery," *San Antonio Express-News*, June 28, 1919.

120. U.S. Census Bureau, Health Insurance Coverage in the United States: 2019, Table A-3, available at census.gov.

121. Joan Alker and Lauren Roygardner, "The Number of Uninsured Children Is on the Rise," Georgetown University Center for Children and Families, October 2019, available at ccf.georgetown.edu.

122. Andrea Zelinski, "Abortions Tried at Home Much Higher In Texas," *San Antonio Express-News*, January 13, 2020, A1.

123. Anne Dunkelberg, "Will Plans Close Dangerous Gaps in Access?," *San Antonio Express-News*, September 27, 2020, A34.

124. Amanda Barroso and Rachel Minkin, "Recent Protest Attendees Are More Racially And Ethnically Diverse, Younger Than Americans Overall," *FactTank*, The Pew Research Center, June 24, 2020, available at PewResearch.org.

125. Jennifer Medina, "Latinos Back Black Lives Matter Protests. They Want Change for Themselves," *The New York Times*, July 3, 2020.

126. Noam Scheiber, Nelson D. Schwartz, and Tiffany Hsu, "'White-Collar Quarantine' Over Virus Spotlights Class Divide," *The New York Times*, March 27, 2020.

127. Jeffrey C. Mays and Andy Newman, "Virus Is Twice as Deadly for Black and Latino People than Whites in N.Y.C," *The New York Times*, April 14, 2020.

128. Shawn Hubler et al., "Many Latinos Couldn't Stay Home. Now Virus Cases Are Soaring in the Community," *The New York Times*, June 26, 2020.

129. Richard A. Oppel Jr. et al., "The Fullest Look Yet at the Racial Inequity of Coronavirus," *The New York Times*, July 5, 2020.

130. Rogelio Saénz, "Latinos, Black People Bear Brunt of COVID," *San Antonio Express-News*, August 30, 2020, A33; Abba Kuchment, Holly K. Hacker and Dianne Solis, "The Color of COVID," December 20, 2020.

131. Rogelio Saénz, "For Latinos, the COVID-19 Trends Are Getting Worse—and the Worst May Be Yet to Come," *Poynter* blog, October 30, 2020, available at poynter.com.

132. Karen Brooks Harper, "Balancing Higher Health Risks With Spotty Internet, Reopening College in the Rio Grande Valley Is a Challenge," *The Texas Tribune*, September 15, 2020, TexasTribune.org.

133. Luis Figueroa, "Immigrants Keep Texas Going and Deserve Protection," *Every Texan* (blog), April 30, 2020, available at EveryTexan.org

134. Shannon Najmabadi, "Texas Front-Line Workers in the Pandemic Are Predominantly Women and People of Color, Analysis Finds," *The Texas Tribune*, May 1, 2020, available at TexasTribune.org.

135. Mark Hugo López, Lee Rainie, and Abby Budman, "Financial and Health Impacts of Covid-10 Vary Widely By Race And Ethnicity," *FactTank*, The Pew Center, May 5, 2020, PewCenter.org.

136. From a national survey of 1,200 Latino adults conducted April 7-12, 2020, by Latino Decisions, available at LatinoDecisions.com

137. National Digital Inclusion Alliance, "Worse Connected Cities in 2018," from American Community Survey, 2018, available at DigitalInclusion.org.

138. Kuchment et al., "The Color of COVID."

139. Luis Figueroa, "CPPP Stands with Texans Grappling with COVID-19," *Every Texan* (blog), March 13, 2020, available at EveryTexan.org.

140. Figueroa, "Immigrants Keep Texas Going."

141. Jeff Stein, "Tax Change in Coronavirus Package Overwhelmingly Benefits Millionaires, Congressional Body Finds," *The Washington Post*, April 14, 2020.

142. Galloway, *Post Corona*, 163.

143. Gabriel Zucman, *Annual Review of Economics* 11 (2019): 109-38, available at economics.annual reviews.org.

144. Federal Reserve, "Changers in U.S. Family Finances from 2013 to 2016: Evidence from the Survey of Consumer Finances." September 2017, available at federalreserve.gov.

145. Chandler Davidson, "The Voting Rights Act: A Brief History," in Bernard Grofman and Chandler Davidson, eds., *Controversies in Minority Voting* (Washington, DC: Brookings Institution, 1992), 7-51. The "turnout gap" as used in political science refers to the percentage point difference between the turnout rate (percent of eligible citizens who turn out to vote) of non-Hispanic whites and the turnout rate of a different racial or ethnic group.

146. Stephen Tuck, "The Reversal of Black Voting Rights After Reconstruction," in Desmond King et al., eds., *Democratization in America: A Comparative Historical Analysis* (Baltimore: Johns Hopkins University Press, 2009), 140.

147. Michael L. Klarman, *From Jim Crow to Civil Rights: The Supreme Court and the Struggle for Racial Equality*, (New York: Oxford University Press, 2004), 461.

148. Bernard L. Fraga, *The Turnout Gap: Race, Ethnicity and Political Inequality in a Diversifying America* (New York: Cambridge University Press, 2018), 211.

149. Fraga, *The Turnout Gap*, 109.

150. Fraga, *The Turnout Gap*, 207.

151. For discussion of SVREP strategy, see Sepúlveda, *The Life and Times of Willie Velasquez*, 187.

152. "Texas Exit Polls: How Different Groups Voted," available at https://www.nytimes.com. The *New York Times* relied on the National Election Pool of 4,768 voters by Edison Research, pooling surveys of voters outside polling places or early voting sites, or by phone to capture mail-in voters.

153. Latino Decisions, "2020 American Election Eve Poll," available at https://latinodecisions.com/polls-and-research/american-election-eve-poll-2020. Three samples were taken of Texas voters: 400 Latinos, 400 Blacks—each with a ±4.9% margin of error—and 300 whites with a ±5.6% margin of error.

154. The fact that Latino voters in Texas border counties did not skew to the Democrats as much as in the previous presidential election is a reflection of the diversity among Latinos in Texas by class, education, and region, nuances of differences that pollsters often fail to capture. For example, a majority (52 percent) of Mexican American voters in Zapata County, a small county along the Texas-Mexico border, went for Trump. This might also reflect the greater outreach effort among younger Mexican American Republican activists there. See Arelis R. Hernández and Brittney Martin, "Why Texas's Overwhelmingly Latino Rio Grande Valley Turned Toward Trump," *The Washington Post*, November 9, 2020; Sylvia Foster-Frau, "Crossover to Trump Along the Border," *San Antonio Express-News*, November 14, 2020; Paul Stekler, "Blue Wave Fizzles, Yet Progress Continues," *San Antonio Express-News*, November 19, 2020.

155. Levitsky and Ziblatt, *How Democracies Die*, 115-16.

156. Southern Poverty Law Center, "Rage Against Change," *Intelligence Report* (Spring 2019): 37.

157. Seth G. Jones and Nicholas Harrington, "The Escalating Terrorism Problem in the United States," Center for Strategic and International Studies Briefs, June 17, 2020, available at CSIS .org.

158. Michael Gerson, "Opinion: Trump's Rot Has Reached the GOP's Roots," *The Washington Post*, February 15, 2021.

159. Alejandro N. Mayorkas, "Alejandro Mayorkas: How My DHS Will Combat Domestic Extremism," *Washington Post*, February 25, 2021.

ROGELIO SÁENZ

The Latino Population of Texas: 1960–2018

When the U.S. Commission on Civil Rights (the Commission) held its hearing on the status of Mexican Americans in the southwestern United States in 1968, witnesses described a young, rapidly growing population mired in poverty—a description that would not change for the next fifty years.[1]

The first witness, Domingo Reyes, a thirty-eight-year-old Mexican American social science analyst in the Research Division of the U.S. Commission on Civil Rights, described his work on two Commission reports on the Mexican American population in the Southwest, specifically in Texas. The Texas-born analyst described the clustering of the youthful Mexican American population in seventeen southwestern counties of Texas, and their urban concentration in San Antonio, El Paso, and Houston.[2]

Reyes portrayed a population marked by low levels of educational attainment and income, of high levels of impoverishment, and disproportionately relegated to work toiling as laborers and in other low-wage jobs. Nearly all (95 percent) of the 167,000 migrant farm workers in Texas in 1968 were Mexican American. Even when Mexican Americans gained employment in the federal government, they were overwhelmingly concentrated in jobs at lower pay grades.

Then, Latinos had been subjugated to keep them from gaining political and economic power.[3] Even today, as Latinos stand to become the largest racial/ethnic group in Texas in a few years, there are significant barriers in place that keep Latinos near the bottom of the state's social stratification system.[4]

The History of Mexican Americans in Texas

Shortly after Mexico gained its independence from Spain in 1821, Mexico, fearing that the United States would appropriate its land, opened up its northern territory—what is now Texas—to settlement by foreigners, drawn largely from the United States.[5] The Mexican government gave land to Stephen F. Austin to bring in settlers to develop Mexico's northern region.

American settlers receiving land had to abide by three agreements: (1) they had to pledge allegiance to Mexico; (2) they had to observe the Christian religion; and (3) they had to learn Spanish. The settlers largely ignored these requirements, hoping the land would eventually become U.S. territory. In a relatively short period of time, non-Mexicans would outnumber Mexicans by a ratio of five to one in what were then the Mexican states of Coahuila and Tejas.[6] Several years after Mexico abolished slavery in 1829, settlers who were slaveholders inserted the slavery issue into calls for a rebellion. Section 9 of the "General Provisions of the Constitution of the Republic of Texas," written in 1836, stated: "All persons of color who were slaves for life previous to their emigration to Texas, and who are now held in bondage, shall remain in the like state of servitude."[7] Mexican President and General Antonio López de Santa Anna marched his troops to San Antonio to quell the Texas revolt and its declaration for independence from Mexico, arriving at the Alamo in San Antonio. On March 6, 1836, Santa Anna led the killing of defenders of the Alamo at what would be called the Battle of the Alamo. Of the approximately 250 settlers who died defending the Alamo against the Mexican army, about nine were natives of what was then Mexico.[8] The

Mexican army was also victorious three weeks later at Goliad, in a battle led by General José de Urrea.

Nearly a month after the victory at Goliad, Santa Anna lost the Battle of San Jacinto (just outside what is today Houston) to settler-soldiers led by General Sam Houston, which ended Mexico's effort to overturn Texas's declaration of independence from Mexico. The United States annexed Texas on December 29, 1845, making U.S. citizens of Mexicans living in Texas. Tensions were already high when more U.S. settlers claimed lands in disputed territory between the Nueces and the Rio Grande rivers, and Mexico was provoked into war against the United States. At the conclusion of the Mexican-American War, and the signing of the Treaty of Guadalupe Hidalgo in 1848, Mexico ceded approximately half of its land to the United States. However, many Mexicans opted to remain on their land that now belonged to the United States and become U.S. citizens.[9]

WHITES DOMINATE A NEW STATE OF TEXAS

Once Texas became a U.S. state, the floodgates were open to migration from other U.S. states. By 1850, non-Hispanic whites outnumbered Mexican Americans by a ratio of sixteen to one. Despite its still strong ties to Mexico, and the indigenous populations of the region, Texas became essentially a predominantly non-Hispanic white (herein referred to as simply "white" or "Anglo") state very quickly. In 1860, Anglos comprised 95 percent of the Texas population, while Latinos—almost exclusively Mexican Americans—constituted less than 5 percent of the state's population. Texas began to recruit more settlers from midwestern and southern U.S. states in the early twentieth century as South Texas underwent a transformation from a ranching to a farming society. As more whites flooded into Texas, the institution of the Texas Rangers was used to keep Anglo newcomers "safe" from Mexican Americans in Texas. The Texas Rangers terrorized, killed, and sought to dominate Mexicans in Texas, all in the name of "law and order."[10]

The Mexican Revolution, a decade-long civil war beginning around 1910, uprooted many Mexicans, and many migrated to Texas seeking refuge, as their compatriots fought to change from a dictatorship to a constitutional republic. Texas employers, especially agricultural growers, hungered for cheap Mexican labor. In fact, while U.S. immigration restrictions were placed on Southern and Eastern Europeans and Asians, Texas growers exerted pressure on the U.S. Congress to exclude Mexicans from such restrictions in the Immigration Acts of 1917, 1921, and 1924.[11] One concession, however, was that the U.S. Border Patrol was established as part of the Immigration Act of 1924.[12]

The Texas Latino population grew by 62 percent between 1900 and 1910, by 67 percent between 1910 and 1920, and by 54 percent between 1920 and 1930. Latinos accounted for one-fourth of the Texas population growth between 1910 and 1920 and for 22 percent of its growth between 1920 and 1930. As the Latino population grew in Texas, whites established "Mexican schools" to segregate Latino and white children.[13] Advocates for segregated schools employed racist reasoning, portraying persons of Mexican origin as dirty, unhygienic, and diseased. Some used pseudo-pedagogical reasons, such as the idea that Mexican immigrant children did not know English and thus would slow down the learning of white children.

"Mexican schools" would exist in Texas for decades. The oft-heard rationale from white growers, clumping all persons of Mexican origin regardless of nativity, was "Give them too much education, and you lose a good cotton picker." The League of United Latin American Citizens, formed in 1929, combining the League of American Citizens and the Orden Hijos de America, demanded an end to the existence of the state's Mexican schools.[14]

PERSONS OF MEXICAN ORIGIN DURING WORLD WAR II

The advent of the Great Depression of the 1930s would bring about a temporary halt to the large-scale immigration of Mexicans to Texas. Immigrants from Mexico and U.S. citizens of Mexican origin became convenient scapegoats for the Great Depression. The U.S. government established the Repatriation Program, designed to deport Mexicans, including U.S.-born children, from the United States to Mexico.[15]

The Texas Latino population dropped by 12 percent between 1930 and 1940. At the same time, the white population, in the throes of the Great Depression, increased by 7 percent.[16] The shunning of Mexican immigrants was short-lived, as World War II led to domestic labor shortages. To meet this need, the

United States and Mexico established the Bracero Program, which brought contract laborers to work in the United States for limited periods of time.

Texas became notorious for the racism of its growers and terrible exploitation of Mexican laborers.[17] Indeed, the Mexican government banned Texas from recruiting Bracero workers from 1943 until 1947. Nonetheless, growers ignored Mexico's ban, opting to hire Mexican immigrants as undocumented workers. The Bracero Program became so popular with U.S. employers that the program was extended eighteen years beyond the end of World War II. Still, Mexican immigrant workers were not altogether welcome, as evidenced by the enactment of Operation Wetback in 1954. This program, which included a slur in its title to demean immigrants crossing the Rio Grande from Mexico to Texas, led to the deportation of approximately 1.1 million Mexicans.[18]

MEXICAN AMERICANS DEMAND CHANGE

World War II proved to be a watershed period for Mexican Americans in an important way. Mexican Americans were major contributors on the battlefield, fought valiantly, and earned a disproportionate share of Medals of Honor, the highest honors bestowed on U.S. soldiers.[19] Mexican American young men had left neighborhoods, or barrios, throughout the Southwest to enlist during World War II, where they met their peers from around the country. They learned their status was different from that of other Americans. When they returned to their homes after the war, many expected to be treated differently and for positive change to take effect in their communities. After all, they had proved that they were patriotic Americans and had fought valiantly.

Mexican American veterans discovered that nothing had changed in their communities after the war. They continued to be regarded as second-class citizens, especially in South Texas communities, and relegated to low-wage jobs, blocked from educational opportunities, and effectively barred from upward mobility.[20] The breaking point for Mexican American military veterans occurred in 1949 in Three Rivers, Texas, where a local funeral home did not allow a wake for the returned body of soldier Felix Longoria, a local young man who lost his life in World War II, because "the whites would not like it." This event galvanized Mexican American veterans, and caused Dr. Héctor García, a veteran and Texas physician, who had just founded the American G.I. Forum, to persuade then-U.S. Senator Lyndon B. Johnson of Texas to have Longoria's body buried alongside other U.S. soldiers at Arlington Cemetery outside of Washington, DC.[21]

The 1960s represented yet another significant watershed for the Mexican American community. The younger generation called for radical change, which clearly showed the generational split between what sociologist Rodolfo Alvarez called the "Mexican American generation" (consisting largely of World War II veterans) and the "Chicano generation" (Mexican American youth who called for more immediate, wider reaching changes). The early roots of the Chicano Movement also could be found in Crystal City, Texas, where Mexican Americans for the first time unseated the Anglo mayor and every Anglo city council member in 1963.[22]

The Mexican American Youth Organization (MAYO) was founded in 1967 by five students at St. Mary's University in San Antonio: José Angel Gutiérrez, Mario Compean, Juan Patlán, Ignacio "Nacho" Pérez, and Willie Velásquez.[23] MAYO became instrumental in the development of La Raza Unida Party, which challenged the two-party system in Texas during the 1970s. The Chicano Movement pressed for improving the social, economic, and political conditions of Mexican Americans. Major issues of the day included calling for an end to persistent poverty, discrimination, the lack of political representation, police brutality, unequal funding of education, and substandard housing.

PRE-1968 MEXICAN AMERICAN DEMOGRAPHICS

Significant demographic changes took place in Texas from its establishment to 1960. Between 1870 and 1960, the Texas white population increased from nearly 537,000 to close to 6.9 million, while the Latino population rose from about 35,000 to more than 1.5 million.[24] During this ninety-year period, the percentage of the Texas population that was white rose slightly from 66 percent in 1870 to 72 percent in 1960, while the percentage that was Latino ascended from 4 percent in 1870 to 16 percent in 1960. This represented the seeds of the major demographic shift that would take place in Texas over the next half century.

Yet when it came to socioeconomic status, Latinos continued to be largely marginalized and ranked among the poorest people in the United States. The facts were clear on the low standing of Latino Texans in 1960 (derived from the 1960 Public Use Microdata Sample):[25]

- Fifty-eight percent of Latinos sixteen to twenty-four years of age were not high school graduates and were not currently enrolled in school (the "status" dropout rate).
- Thirteen percent of Latinos ages twenty-five and older were high school graduates; 2 percent were college graduates.
- Eighty-six percent of Latinos ages twenty-five to sixty-four (the age of the experienced labor force) were employed.
- The median family income of Latinos was $25,758 (in 2018 dollars).
- Sixty-two percent of all Latinos and 69 percent of Latino children were living in poverty.

As the 1968 U.S. Civil Rights Commission (the Commission) prepared to meet in San Antonio for its hearing, the city had just a few months earlier introduced San Antonio to the world as the host of the 1968 World Fair. That same year, the documentary *Hunger in America*, narrated by national CBS television journalist Charles Kuralt, featured San Antonio as one of four U.S. cities/regions with extreme poverty and hunger.[26] The documentary called attention to the devastating impoverishment and hunger in the city's predominantly Mexican American West Side. One scene showed an infant taking his last breaths before dying from malnourishment. Later that year, the Commission hearing would be held in the heart of the city's West Side at the campus of Our Lady of the Lake College.

Demographics and Socioeconomics After 1960

The demographic and socioeconomic characteristics of Latinos in Texas over seven time periods, presented in the analysis that follows, are based on public-use microdata samples from the decennial censuses of 1960 to 2000 and from the U.S. Census Bureau's 2010 and 2018 American Community Surveys. While the 1968 U.S. Civil Rights Commission hearing focused on Mexican Americans, the larger pan-ethnic group comprising all Latinos grew measurably over time, including more than the three major Latino subgroups: Mexican Americans, Puerto Rican Americans, and Cuban Americans. Although the Latino population of Texas is home to more subgroups, persons of Mexican heritage represented 85 percent of the state's Latino population in 2018.[27]

Thus, the focus is on Latinos. The analysis compares Latinos to whites and African Americans and examines differences between U.S.-born and foreign-born Latinos, as well as variations between Latino men and Latina women. The analysis also compares the demographic and socioeconomic characteristics of Latinos across eight large metropolitan counties. Finally, population projections assess what the future holds for Latinos and the Texas population.

Demographic Trends From 1968 to 2018

When the U.S. Civil Rights Commission on Civil Rights met in 1968, the Mexican American population was beginning to exert some demographic influence on the face of the Texas population. During the next fifty years, the Latino population would become the dominant driver of Texas population growth.

LATINO POPULATION GROWTH

The Texas population grew significantly between 1960 and 2018, tripling from 9.6 million in 1960 to 28.7 million in 2018. During this period, Texas ascended from the sixth most populous state in 1960 to the second largest state in 2000. Latinos accounted for slightly more than half (52 percent, or 9.8 million) of the state's population growth of 19.1 million people between 1960 and 2018, while whites constituted slightly more than one-fourth (26 percent, or 5.0 million) of that growth.[28]

Latinos have dominated population growth across the state's three

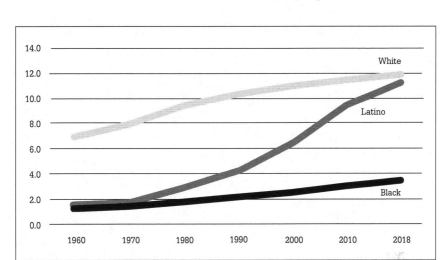

Figure 1. Texas Latino, White, and Black Population (millions), 1960–2018. *Source:* Integrated Public Use Microdata Series USA (Ruggles et al. 2019).

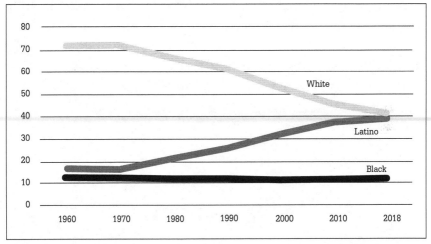

Figure 2. Percentage of Texas Population That Is Latino, White, and Black, 1960–2018. *Source:* Integrated Public Use Microdata Series USA (Ruggles et al. 2019).

major racial and ethnic groups. For example, the Latino population grew more than sevenfold, from approximately 1.5 million in 1960 to nearly 11.4 million in 2018 (Figure 1). During the same period, the state's African American population nearly tripled (from 1.2 to 3.4 million), while the Anglo population nearly doubled (from 6.9 to 11.9 million).[29]

Latinos have accounted for the largest share of Texas population growth in each decade since 1980. As such, the Latino population has increased its percentage share of the Texas population from 16 percent in 1960 to 40 percent in 2018 (Figure 2). By contrast, the white percentage of the state's total plunged from 72 percent in 1960 to approximately 41 percent in 2018. The African American population has consistently comprised about 12 percent of the Texas population.[30]

THE TEXAS CITIZEN VOTING-AGE POPULATION

The expanding Latino population has the potential to increase the political strength of Latinos. The demographic trends are reflected in the changing demography of the Texas citizen voting-age population (CVAP), individuals eighteen years of age and older who are U.S. citizens and, thus, eligible voters (Figure 3).

Although the Census Bureau did not collect information on citizenship status in 1960, the Latino share of the state's adult citizens more than doubled, from 12 percent in 1970 to 30 percent in 2018. The white share of the Texas CVAP slipped from slightly more than three-fourths in 1970 to just over half in 2018. African American and "other" (such as Asian American

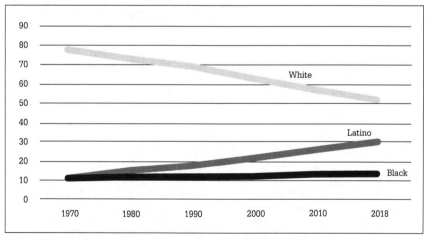

Figure 3. Percentage of Citizen Voting-Age Population (CVAP) by Race/Ethnic Group, 1970–2018. *Source:* Integrated Public Use Microdata Series USA (Ruggles et al. 2019).

and Native American) groups have seen their percentage share of the total CVAP increase slightly. It is only a matter of time until the Texas CVAP will become majority-minority, when whites comprise less than half of the state's eligible voters.[31]

LATINO DEMOGRAPHIC CHARACTERISTICS

The tremendous Latino population growth has been driven largely by its youthfulness, reflecting significant international migration and high levels of fertility. In 1960 the median age of the Latino population was an extremely young age of seventeen; it rose to twenty-eight years in 2018 (Figure 4). On the other hand, the white population is significantly older, with a median age of forty-two years in 2018, fourteen years older than the Latino median age. African Americans have been consistently older than Latinos and younger than whites.[32]

In particular, over the last half century the Latino population has been characterized by a relatively larger share of its population under the age of eighteen and a smaller portion being elderly. In 1960, one out of every two Latinos was a child younger than eighteen years of age, reflecting a high fertility rate; by 2018, one of every three Latinos was a child (Figure 5). By

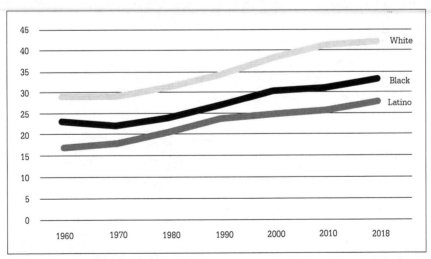

Figure 4. Median Age of Latinos, Whites, and Blacks, 1960–2018. *Source:* Integrated Public Use Microdata Series USA (Ruggles et al. 2019).

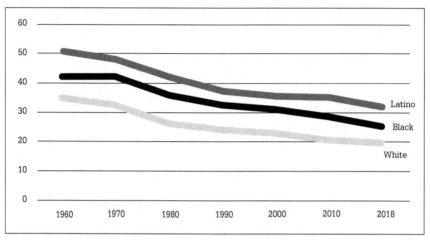

Figure 5. Percentage of Latino, White, and Black Population Who Are Children (younger than eighteen years of age), 1960–2018. *Source:* Integrated Public Use Microdata Series USA (Ruggles et al. 2019).

contrast, children comprised one of every five whites and one of every four African Americans in 2018.[33]

The large population of Latino children has the potential to increase the group's political strength. Latinos already accounted for 30 percent of the Texas citizen voting-age population (CVAP) in 2018. Latino children have represented the largest racial/ethnic group of children in Texas since 2002. In 2018, Latino children numbered nearly 3.7 million, or half of all children in the state. Each year, nearly 204,000 Latino children become eighteen years old, and since more than nine in ten of them (96 percent) are U.S. citizens, these are potential voters that will continue to make the Texas CVAP increasingly Latino in composition.

The elderly—persons sixty-five years of age and older—continue to comprise a small share (7 percent) of the Latino population (Figure 6). By contrast, the white population, as a whole, has become older over the last fifty years, with the percentage share of elderly rising from 9 percent in 1960 to 19 percent in 2018. The elderly among the African American population have increased only slightly, from 7 percent in 1960 to 10 percent in 2018.

One of the prominent features of the Latino population from 1968 to 2018 is its increasing diversity in national origin due to immigration from

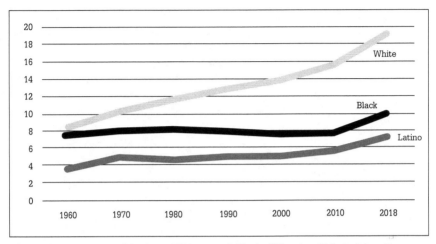

Figure 6. Percentage of Latinos, Whites, and Blacks Who Are Elderly (sixty-five years of age or older), 1960–2018. *Source:* Integrated Public Use Microdata Series USA (Ruggles et al. 2019).

different Latin American countries. Mexicans represented 70 percent of all U.S. Latinos in 1960 and 62 percent in 2018. In Texas, although the Latino population has become somewhat more varied on the basis of national origin, persons of Mexican origin have by far remained the predominant Latino group, accounting for 98 percent of the state's Latino population in 1960 and 85 percent in 2018 (Figure 7). The largest Latino subgroups, aside from the 9.7 million persons of Mexican origin in Texas in 2018, include Salvadorans (356,499), Puerto Ricans (213,809), Hondurans (176,931), and Guatemalans (107,723).[34]

This diversity is due to immigration. In 1960, fewer than one in seven Latinos in Texas were born outside of the United States or its outlying territories (Figure 7), though data for citizenship status were not available in the 1960 census, making it impossible to identify those who were born abroad to parents of whom at least one was a U.S. citizen and where the child was automatically a U.S. citizen at birth. Figure 7 also shows the percentage of Latinos who were technically immigrants (i.e., they were born outside of the United States and they were not U.S. citizens born abroad) from 1970 to 2018.

Slightly more than 13 percent of Latinos were foreign-born in 1970, with the percentage peaking at 32 percent in 2000. The percentage of Latinos

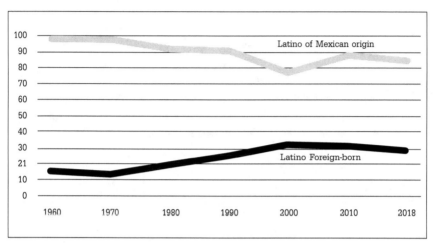

Figure 7. Percentage of Latinos of Mexican Origin and Texas Foreign-Born Latinos, 1960–2018. *Source:* Integrated Public Use Microdata Series USA (Ruggles et al. 2019).

who are foreign-born has declined slightly since 2000 as the volume of immigration from Latin America, especially from Mexico, has decreased significantly.[35] Nonetheless, the number of Texas Latinos who were foreign-born (mostly from Mexico) increased more than fourteen-fold, from 221,000 in 1960 to 3.2 million in 2018. The proportion of migrants who were from Mexico declined from 93 percent in 1960 to 78 percent in 2018.

The demographic trends associated with the growth of the Latino population in Texas over the last half century are dramatic. The demographic variations—in particular, the youthfulness of the Latino population and the aging of the white population—have been responsible for the much faster population growth of Latinos compared to whites over the last fifty years. A portion of this growth can be attributed to immigration from Mexico and Latin America.

The electorate will become increasingly Latino as today's Latino children turn eighteen years of age in the next couple of decades. We are likely to see even greater diversity of the Latino population in the near future, especially if migration from Mexico to Texas continues to be at the current low levels. What are the socioeconomic changes among Latinos since the U.S. Commission on Civil Rights hearing of 1968?

Socioeconomic Trends During the Last Half Century

From the events leading to the hearing on the socioeconomic status of Mexican Americans held in 1968 and at the hearing itself, it was abundantly clear that Mexican Americans lagged significantly behind whites and other groups throughout the Southwest and, in particular, in Texas. Much has changed in some respects since the hearing took place, and still, much has not changed in other respects.

LANGUAGE

Historically, language has always been an important dimension in the social stratification of Mexican Americans in Texas. Anglos commonly used the lack of English fluency to justify the placement of even English-fluent Mexican American students in Mexican schools throughout the period between the early and middle of the twentieth century in Texas. Lack of English fluency was also used to justify the low earnings of Latinos. The Census Bureau begin asking about language use in the 1980 decennial census.

The census questionnaire asked individuals who were at least five years of age two questions related to language: whether a language other than English was spoken at home, and, for these individuals, their level of fluency in English. Adults (age eighteen and older) can be divided into three categories: (1) English speakers (those speaking English at home); (2) bilingual (those speaking a language other than English at home and who speak English "well" or "very well"); and (3) non-English speakers (those speaking a language other than English at home and who speak English "not well" or "not at all").[36]

Across the last three decades, the majority of Latino adults born in the United States are bilingual speakers (i.e., they speak a language other than English at home and speak English "well" or "very well"), although the proportion who are bilingual has dropped from 79 percent in 1980 to 62 percent in 2018 (Table 1). By contrast, most foreign-born Latino adults have in earlier decades lacked English fluency (speak a language other than English at home and speak English "not well" or "not at all"), and for almost half this is the case in 2018.

Table 1. Percent of Texas Latinos Age Eighteen Years and Older by Nativity and Language Patterns, 1980–2018.

Nativity and language patterns	1980	1990	2000	2010	2018
Native-born:					
Bilingual	78.9	76.0	73.5	66.4	61.5
Speak English not well or not at all	11.9	8.4	5.9	4.0	3.4
Foreign-born:					
Bilingual	42.2	46.3	42.2	43.2	47.9
Speak English not well or not at all	55.6	49.3	51.7	53.6	47.8

Source: Integrated Public Use Microdata Series USA (Ruggles et al. 2019).

The question of whether English is spoken in the home gives a better insight into actual language usage as it relates to nativity. In 1980, only one in ten Latinos born in the United States spoke only English at home, as did only 2 percent of those who were foreign-born. By 2018, more than one in three native-born Latinos spoke English at home, with almost no change among foreign-born Latinos (Figure 8).

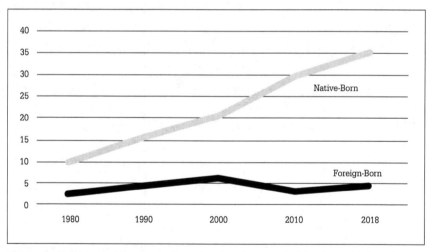

Figure 8. Percentage of Texas Latinos Age Eighteen and Older, by Nativity, Who Speak English at Home, 1980–2018.

PRESCHOOL ENROLLMENT

Latino children three and four years of age have consistently lagged behind their peers from other racial and ethnic groups in enrollment in preschool. This was true in Texas at the time of the Commission hearing in 1968 and it

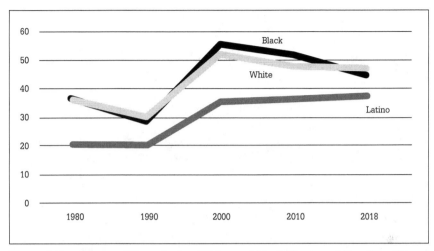

Figure 9. Percentage of Texas Latino, White, and Black Three- and Four-Year-Olds Enrolled in Preschool, 1980–2018. *Source:* Integrated Public Use Microdata Series USA (Ruggles et al. 2019).

is true today. While Latino children have made some progress in preschool enrollment since 1960, Anglo and African American children are still significantly more likely than Latino children to be attending preschool (Figure 9). In 2018, 47 percent of white children (ages three and four years) and 44.4 percent of African American children attended preschool programs, while only 38 percent of Latino children did so.

STATUS DROPOUT RATE

Education researchers use the term "status dropout rate" to gauge the school dropout level: essentially, the percentage of persons ages sixteen to twenty-four who are not high school graduates and who are not currently enrolled in school. Because the level of schooling is associated with nativity status, the status dropout rates of Latinos differ by native- and foreign-born status.[37]

While there has been a significant reduction in the status dropout rates of Latino youth across nativity groups, Latinos—including native-born Latinos—continue to have noticeably higher status dropout levels compared to their white and African American peers (Figure 10). This does not bode well for the socioeconomic sustainability of Latino youth as they mature in the coming decades.

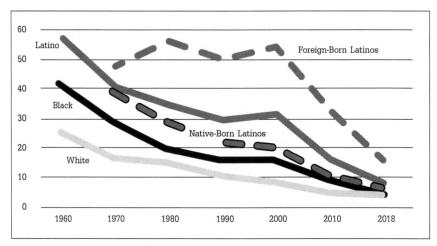

Figure 10. Status Dropout Rates of Latino, White, and Black Persons Sixteen to Twenty-Four Years of Age, 1960–2018. *Source:* Integrated Public Use Microdata Series USA (Ruggles et al. 2019).

HIGH SCHOOL DIPLOMAS AND BACHELOR'S DEGREES

Latinos twenty-five years of age and older also lag behind their white and African American peers with respect to the attainment of high school diplomas (Figure 11) and those with bachelor's degrees or more (Figure 12). Even native-born Latinos lag significantly behind whites and African

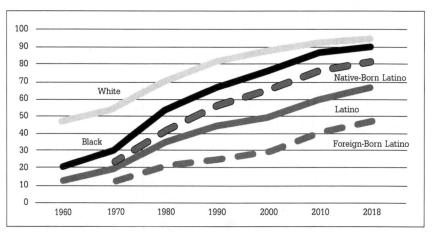

Figure 11. Percentage of Texas Latinos, Whites, and Blacks Age Twenty-Five and Older Who Are High School Graduates, 1960–2018. *Source:* Integrate Public Use Microdata Series USA (Ruggles et al. 2019).

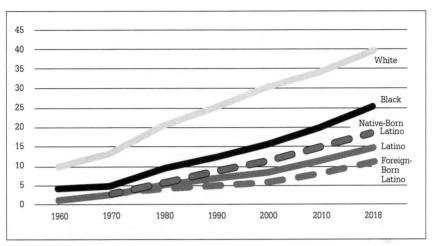

Figure 12. Percentage of Texas Latinos, Whites, and Blacks Age Twenty-Five and Older with Bachelor's Degree or Higher, 1960–2018. *Source:* Integrated Public Use Microdata Series USA (Ruggles et al. 2019).

Americans in the attainment of these educational credentials. Fewer than half of foreign-born Latinos have a high school diploma and only one in ten has a bachelor's degree. As with other educational indicators, the low levels of high school and college completion rates do not portend favorable socioeconomic outcomes for Latinos in the future.

EMPLOYMENT

There is often significant variation in unemployment patterns due to the state of the economy at any point in time, as well as the presence of discouraged workers who often exit the labor force and are not counted in the computation of unemployment rates. For these reasons, the focus is on the employment of the experienced labor force—persons twenty-five to sixty-four years of age. The level of employment continues to vary by sex.

For men twenty-five to sixty-four years of age, with the exception of foreign-born Latino men, the tendency has been decreasing levels of employment over time, until 2000 (Figure 13). While Latino men overall trailed whites somewhat in employment over time, the employment levels of the two groups drew even in 2010, with Latino men being more likely than white men to be employed by 2018. Nine in ten foreign-born

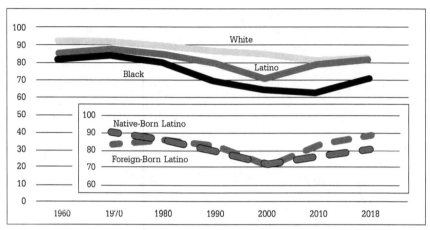

Figure 13. Percentage of Texas Latino, White, and Black Men Ages Twenty-Five to Sixty-Four Years Who Are Employed, 1960–2018. *Source:* Integrated Public Use Microdata Series USA (Ruggles et al. 2019).

Latino men were employed in 2018, compared to seven in ten African American men.

In contrast to men, there has been a significant increase in employment over time of women twenty-five to sixty-four years of age (Figure 14). Latina women have consistently had the lowest levels of employment, with African American women being the most likely to be working. What

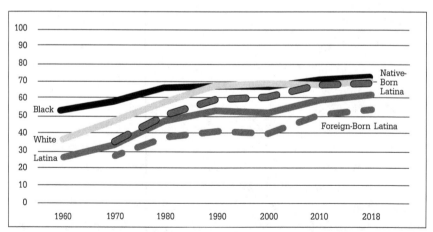

Figure 14. Percentage of Texas Latina, White, and Black Women Ages Twenty-Five to Sixty-Four Who Are Employed, 1960–2018. *Source:* Integrated Public Use Microdata Series USA (Ruggles et al. 2019).

is remarkable is that the employment levels of Latina women more than doubled from 1960 to 2018. Furthermore, in contrast to the case among men, native-born Latinas have higher employment rates than foreign-born Latinas, who are the least likely among all groups of women to be employed.

FAMILY INCOME

The median family income represents a measure associated with the returns that individuals and families receive for their human capital and related characteristics. Figure 15 presents median family incomes measured in 2018 dollars for Latinos, whites, and African Americans, as well as for native- and foreign-born Latinos over the seven time periods. A two-tier system is obvious from the demonstrably higher incomes enjoyed by Anglos, compared to Latino and African American families.

The median family income of non-Hispanic whites was $93,406 in 2018. The next highest median family income ($58,119) was that of native-born Latinos, approximately $35,000 below that of whites. Between 1970 and 2018, the median family income increased at about the same rate among African Americans (rising 53 percent), native-born Latinos (48 percent), and whites (45 percent) (Figure 15). Latino families overall had the smallest gain—a 39 percent increase—in their median family income between 1970 and 2018.

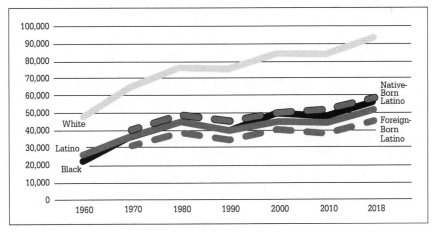

Figure 15. Median Family Income in 2018 Dollars of Latino, White, and Black Families, 1960–2018. *Source:* Integrated Public Use Microdata Series USA (Ruggles et al. 2019).

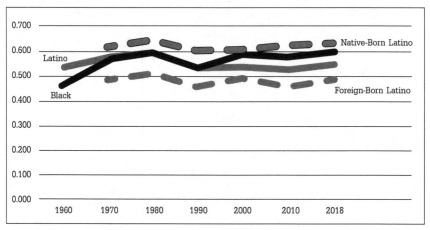

Figure 16. Median Family Income in 2018 Dollars of Latino and Black Families as a Percentage of the White Median Family Income, 1960–2018. *Source:* Integrated Public Use Microdata Series USA (Ruggles et al. 2019).

Latino families overall have the lowest median family income ($51,892) in 2018, with families headed by foreign-born Latinos having the lowest income level ($45,146).

While the incomes of all groups increased between 1960 (or 1970) and 2018, the gaps remained about the same in 2018. For example, Latino families earned 54 cents for every dollar that white families earned in 1960; by 2018, they earned 56 cents for every dollar earned by white families (Figure 16).

While the gap decreased more significantly for African American families between 1960 (45 cents for each dollar among whites) and 2018 (60 cents for each dollar), it reflects the extremely low median family income of African Americans in 1960 ($21,616 in 2018 dollars).

The African American-to-white median income gap remained fairly constant between 1970 (57 cents for each dollar) and 2018 (60 cents for each dollar) (Figure 16). Even the gap between families headed by native-born Latino and non-Hispanic white families did not change between 1970 (61 cents for each dollar) and 2018 (62 cents for each dollar). Families headed by foreign-born Latinos have the greatest disparity in median family income relative to white families, earning 48 cents for each dollar earned by white families in 2018.[38]

POVERTY

As is the case with racial variations in median family incomes, there is a racial/ethnic divide in poverty, with non-Hispanic whites having lower rates of poverty, and Latinos and African Americans having higher levels of impoverishment (Figure 17). Across all racial/ethnic groups, poverty rates were highest in 1960, especially for Latinos, with a 62 percent poverty level for all persons and a 69 percent poverty rate among children, and for African Americans (64 percent and 73 percent, respectively). The extremely high poverty rates plummeted significantly between 1960 and 1980. This is consistent with national trends, which demonstrated that programs associated with President Lyndon B. Johnson's War Against Poverty were effective in bringing down overall levels of impoverishment in the 1960s and 1970s.[39]

Despite the significant declines in poverty, large gaps remained along racial/ethnic lines. Latinos and African Americans had poverty rates that were 2.5 times and 2.4 times higher, respectively, than those of non-Hispanic whites in 2018 (Figure 17). Approximately one in five Latinos and African Americans lived in poverty in 2018, compared to less than one in twelve Anglos.

Poverty is even more pronounced among children, with 29 percent of Latino children and 28 percent of African American children living in

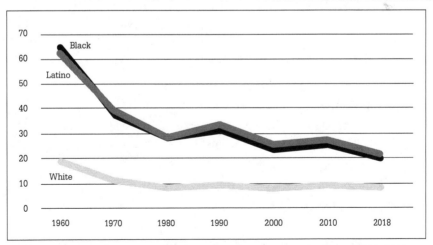

Figure 17. Percentage of Latino, White, and Black Persons in Poverty, 1960–2018. *Source:* Integrated Public Use Microdata Series USA (Ruggles et al. 2019).

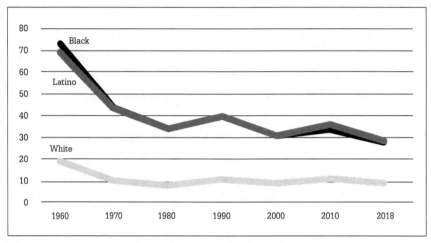

Figure 18. Percentage of Latino, White, and Black Children (younger than eighteen years) in Poverty, 1960–2018. *Source:* Integrated Public Use Microdata Series USA (Ruggles et al. 2019).

poverty in 2018. These children are slightly more than three times more likely to be poor than white children. (Figure 18).[40]

While Latinos lagged significantly behind on a wide variety of socio-economic characteristics in 1968, little change occurred over the following fifty years. Although Latinos experienced some improvements in their socioeconomic status, major gaps persist today between whites, on the one hand, and Latinos and African Americans, on the other.

GENDER VARIATIONS ON SOCIOECONOMIC CHANGES

Socioeconomic attainment has long been associated with gender, with males commonly having more favorable socioeconomic standing than females. Gender gaps within the Latino population are apparent by nativity status (U.S.-born versus foreign-born) from 1970 to 2018. (The Census Bureau did not ask about a person's place of birth in 1960.)

Latina women have achieved greater improvements in the area of education than men (Table 2). In 1970, Latina women were less likely than men to have completed their high school education and to earn a bachelor's degree. Their completion levels surpassed those of men in 2018, a trend observed among the native- and foreign-born population in Texas.

Table 2. Selected Socioeconomic Characteristics of Texas Latinos/Latinas, 1970–2018.

	Total		Native-born		Foreign-born	
	1970	2018	1970	2018	1970	2018
Percent of persons twenty-five and older high school graduates						
Male	22.3	65.6	24.6	80.9	15.1	46.2
Female	18.4	67.8	20.7	81.3	12.1	50.2
Percent of persons twenty-five and older with bachelor's degree or higher						
Male	4.3	13.4	3.8	16.3	5.8	9.8
Female	1.8	16.7	1.8	20.3	1.6	11.9
Percent of persons twenty-five to sixty-four working						
Male	87.6	83.7	88.6	79.5	83.5	89.1
Female	33.7	63.0	35.5	69.5	27.8	54.5
Median family income in 2018 dollars						
Male	$40,027	$59,157	$42,079	$68,498	$33,869	$51,892
Female	$17,447	$43,589	$16,763	$48,779	$18,474	$37,362
Percent of persons age eighteen and older in poverty						
Male	31.0	13.6	29.1	12.1	38.6	15.8
Females	35.5	20.4	33.9	17.7	40.6	24.4

Source: Integrated Public Use Microdata Series USA (Ruggles et al. 2019).

Among the experienced labor force (persons twenty-five to sixty-four years of age), women also made major gains compared to men. In 1970, roughly one-third of Latina women ages twenty-five to sixty-four were employed, but this level nearly doubled by 2018. Men in this age group for the most part experienced a reduction in employment activity, with an exception being foreign-born men. Nonetheless, even in 2018, women were significantly less likely than men to be employed. Foreign-born women were the least likely to be working in 2018.

The median family income (in 2018 dollars) of families headed by women more than doubled between 1970 and 2018, though the starting place was a very low income level in 1970. Overall, families headed by Latina women earned only 74 cents for every dollar attained by families headed by Latino men in 2018. Families headed by a foreign-born woman had the lowest median family income.

Latino men fared better than Latina women in the reduction of poverty, with men seeing their poverty rates cut in half between 1970 and 2018, while those of women declined at a slower pace. Overall, the poverty rate of Latina women was about 50 percent higher than that of Latino men in 2018, with foreign-born Latina women (nearly one in four) being the most likely to be poor in 2018.

Overall, while there have been improvements in the reduction of the socioeconomic gender gap among Latinos, this has taken place most evidently in women's gains in education and employment. Unfortunately, these improvements have not been able to erode gender gaps associated with income and poverty.

COUNTY VARIATIONS

The demographic and socioeconomic standings of Latinos vary greatly from county to county in Texas, as evident in Table 3 concerning selected demographic and socioeconomic characteristics for Latinos for 1960 and 2018 across eight selected counties: Bexar, Cameron, Dallas, El Paso, Harris, Hidalgo, Travis, and Webb.[41] Four of the counties are located on the Texas-Mexico border (Cameron, El Paso, Hidalgo, and Webb). Bexar County is located approximately 150 miles from the border, and the remaining three (Dallas, Harris, and Travis) are located in the interior of Texas.

All eight counties experienced major growth in their Latino populations, ranging from a quadrupling of Latinos in Cameron and Bexar counties to more than a twenty-five-fold growth in Dallas County. Bexar County had the largest Latino population in 1960, but fell to second place in 2018. Harris County, which had the fifth largest Latino population in 1960, became the county with the largest Latino population in 2018. Dallas County changed from the seventh largest county in Latino population in 1960 to the third largest in 2016.

Across the eight counties, the Latino population increased by 6.0 million people between 1960 and 2018. Harris County and Dallas County, located 240 miles apart, accounted for half of the Latino population growth occurring in the selected eight counties between 1960 and 2018, showing the expansion of the Latino population into the larger urban centers during this period.

The eight counties' Latino population is increasingly composed of persons born outside of the United States. Harris County and Dallas County

Table 3. Selected Demographic and Socioeconomic Characteristics for Latinos in Eight Selected Counties, 1960 and 2018.

	Bexar		Cameron		Dallas		El Paso	
	1960	2018	1960	2018	1960	2018	1960	2018
Latino population	281,200	1,201,757	100,480	380,719	41,960	1,068,351	149,800	697,539
Percent born outside United States*	13.1	17.9	20.3	25.6	11.0	42.7	27.1	29.2
Percent high school grads.†	14.1	75.8	10.5	64.7	22.6	55.1	18.5	73.8
Percent college grads.†	1.6	17.3	2.0	14.6	3.7	10.3	1.7	19.3
Percent men employed‡	86.2	80.9	84.6	79.4	86.8	90.8	87.2	80.8
Percent women employed‡	27.9	67.4	30.2	62.3	35.2	61.4	32.8	63.1
Median family income§	$29,382	$55,006	$18,315	$40,476	$39,608	$51,892	$34,560	$46,184
Percent adults in poverty	45.6	17.2	70.2	24.5	29.7	13.3	37.4	18.6

	Harris		Hidalgo		Travis		Webb	
	1960	2018	1960	2018	1960	2018	1960	2018
Latino population	84,980	2,035,010	132,960	800,000	19,500	423,043	54,060	263,267
Percent born outside United States*	14.6	40.1	21.4	29.9	10.1	30.2	23.0	25.2
Percent high school grads.†	20.3	62.3	8.4	62.9	14.8	70.9	16.3	64.9
Percent college grads.†	2.8	14.0	0.9	17.0	4.4	24.2	2.9	18.9
Percent men employed‡	91.9	88.5	87.4	79.5	85.6	87.0	84.3	80.8
Percent women employed‡	28.1	59.6	31.7	61.1	32.9	69.0	25.8	62.3
Median family income§	$38,054	$49,629	$17,301	$40,164	$27,699	$57,081	$20,753	$50,854
Percent adults in poverty	35.0	16.3	76.1	26.6	51.8	15.4	61.9	22.4

Source: Integrated Public Use Microdata Series USA (Ruggles et al. 2019).
* Not able to determine the citizenship status of individuals born outside of the United States.
† Based on persons age twenty-five and older.
‡ Based on persons twenty-five to sixty-four years of age.
§ In 2018 dollars.

experienced significant increases in the percentage of their Latino populations originating from outside of the country, demonstrating that a major
part of the Latino growth in these areas was associated with immigration.
While Dallas (43 percent) and Harris (40 percent) counties had the largest
percentages of persons born outside of the United States in 2018, Bexar
County (at 18 percent) was on the other end, with less than one-fifth of the
city's Latinos being foreign-born.

The eight counties also experienced significant gains across socioeconomic indicators. The largest increases in the percentage of high school
graduates between 1960 and 2018 occurred in the counties of Hidalgo (rising
from 8 percent to 63 percent), Cameron (from 11 percent to 65 percent),
and Bexar (from 14 percent to 76 percent). The counties reporting the most
favorable gains in the percentage of Latinos receiving four-year college
degrees were Hidalgo (from 1 percent to 17 percent), El Paso (from 2 percent
to 19 percent), and Bexar (from 2 percent to 17 percent).

The employment rate of men twenty-five to sixty-four years of age
declined between 1960 and 2018, with the exceptions being Dallas County
and Travis County, where work activity increased among Latino men. By
contrast, Latina women twenty-five to sixty-four years of age were much
more likely to be working in 2018 than in 1960, with the greatest gains
occurring in five counties where the percentage of women working doubled
during this period: Bexar, Webb, Harris, Travis, and Cameron.

Despite seeing their median incomes rise between 1960 and 2018, families in Hidalgo and Cameron counties had the lowest median incomes in
both years. By contrast, Latino families in Travis and Bexar counties had the
highest median family incomes in 2018.

Overall, the poverty rate of Latinos eighteen years old and older fell between 1960 and 2018. Yet despite seeing their poverty rates fall dramatically
from high levels in the range of 70 percent in 1960, Latino adults in Hidalgo
and Cameron, two border counties, continued to have the highest rates of
impoverishment—approximately one-fourth—in 2018. Latinos in Dallas
County had the lowest poverty rate in 2018, although it far exceeded the
county's white poverty rate.

Texas has witnessed large-scale growth in its Latino population, with Latinos increasingly choosing to live in Harris and Dallas counties over the last fifty years. While Latinos made significant strides in their socioeconomic status, part of the increase stems from very low educational and income levels in 1960, particularly in border counties such as Hidalgo and Cameron counties.

Projected Population Trends for the Next Thirty Years

Texas has experienced a major shift in its population since the Commission hearing in San Antonio in 1968, with a rapidly growing Latino population alongside a more slowly increasing Anglo population. The Texas population is projected to increase by 88 percent, from 25.1 million people in 2010 to 47.3 million in 2050.[42]

As has been the case over the last half century, the Latino population will be the principal driver of the projected population increases in Texas over the coming decades. The Latino population is expected to more than double, from 9.5 million in 2010 to 20.2 million in 2050 (Figure 19).[43] The

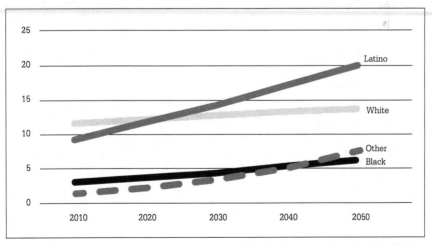

Figure 19. Projected Texas Population by Race/Ethnic Group (millions), 2010–2050. *Source:* Office of the State Demographer (2018).

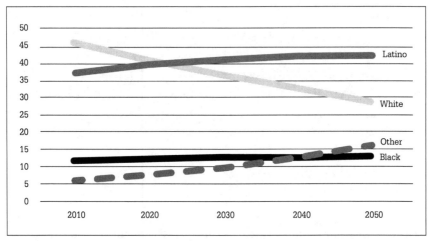

Figure 20. Percentage Distribution of Texas Projected Population by Race/Ethnic Group, 2010–2050. *Source:* Office of the State Demographer (2018).

non-Hispanic white population is projected to grow more slowly between 2010 and 2050, rising by 19 percent between 2010 and 2050. The population projections suggest that the Latino population will surpass the non-Hispanic white population by 2022. The African American population is expected to grow steadily over the coming decades, while the "other" population, primarily Asian Americans, is projected to more than double between 2010 and 2050. Overall, Latinos are projected to account for 48 percent of the Texas projected growth in population between 2010 and 2050.[44] Overall, the pace of growth of the Latino population has slowed since the 2008 due to a significant reduction in migration from Mexico and falling fertility rates.

Major shifts are projected to take place over the next three decades with respect to each race/ethnic group's percentage share of the state's projected population. The Latino population is expected to increase its share of the Texas population from 38 percent in 2010 to 43 percent in 2050 (Figure 20). By contrast, the non-Hispanic white population's representation of the state population is projected to fall from 45 percent in 2010 to 29 percent in 2050. The African American population is expected to increase slightly in its percentage share of the Texas population, but the other population, consisting largely of Asians, is projected to rise from 6 percent in 2010 to 16 percent in 2050.

Challenges Ahead

Demographically, the Latino population has blossomed, becoming the engine powering the Texas population growth. Latinos have been disproportionately responsible for Texas becoming the second largest state in the country and the state with the largest absolute growth. Texas was the primary winner in the reapportionment of U.S. House members following the 2010 census. The state was allotted four additional U.S. congressional seats because of rapid growth, stemming mostly from the expansion of the Latino population.

Socioeconomically, however, despite improvements in education, employment, and income over the last fifty years, Latinos continue to lag significantly behind whites and, in many instances, to not fare as well as African Americans. Indeed, even native-born Latinos have not closed the socioeconomic gaps.

The state of Texas since its beginnings has failed to recognize the importance of Latinos for the state's future. Texas has successfully fought in the courts to retain its unequal educational funding system, a system that has significantly shortchanged Latino and African American students. The unequal funding of education continues to be a reality a half century since the U.S. Commission on Civil Rights hearing in 1968. A Texas Supreme Court ruling in 2016 on the Texas system for funding public education described it as "byzantine," but good enough.[45] The Texas legislature refuses to acknowledge that the future of the state of Texas once again depends very heavily on Latino children being able to fulfill their educational, social, and economic potential as adults.

A Republican-dominated Texas legislature in recent decades redirected funding from public schools to less monitored charter schools, and paid more attention to loosening state gun ownership rules than to meaningful education reform. Policy changes are needed to improve the standing of Latinos in Texas, such as equal funding of education, access to health care, affordable housing, and support for DACA (Deferred Action for Childhood Arrivals) students.

Despite the growth of the Latino population, Latinos continue to lack the political power commensurate with their numbers in Texas. Some characteristics of the Latino population also limit the extent to which it can translate growing numbers into political influence. According to data from the 2018 American Community Survey, of the estimated nearly 11.4 million Latinos in Texas in 2018, only half were eligible to register to vote.[46] One in three Latinos cannot vote because they are younger than eighteen years of age, and about one in five cannot cast a ballot because they are adults who are not U.S. citizens.

By contrast, eight in ten of the 11.9 million non-Hispanic whites in Texas in 2018 were eligible to vote. In sheer numbers, the differences in the number of eligible voters is large: Anglo eligible voters numbered 9.4 million, compared to 5.6 million Latino eligible voters. To further widen that gap, Texas Republicans in public office have used effective ploys, such as enacting the strictest voter ID law in the country and gerrymandering voter districts, to intentionally dilute the influence of minority voters.

Recommendations

However, there is a ray of hope in another demographic factor. Latinos have outnumbered whites in numbers of children, dating back to 2002. In 2018, there were nearly 3.7 million Latino children younger than eighteen years of age in Texas, compared to 2.3 million white children.[47] Due to the youthfulness of the Latino population and the aging of the white population, these numbers favoring Latinos will only increase.

The approximately 3.7 million Latino children in Texas translate to nearly 204,000 Latino children turning eighteen every year, and 96 percent of these are U.S. citizens who will be eligible to vote. To unleash their future political power, parents must begin to engage their children politically at an early age. Parents and educators must teach them the importance of registering to vote, of actually voting, and engaging in the political debates that impact our future.

Civic and minority-rights organizations—including the American G.I. Forum, League of United Latin American Citizens (LULAC), National Association for the Advancement of Colored People (NAACP), and Southwest Voter Registration Education Project (SVREP), among others—along with Mexican American/Latina/o and African American Studies in high schools and universities should undertake massive efforts to educate students on the importance of registering and voting. As such, these organizations can play a role in developing critical thinkers and engaged citizens.

Latinos are on the eve of becoming the largest racial/ethnic group in the state. This is a very important period for which we have been waiting. We are either going to organize ourselves politically and press for a larger influence on the Texas legislature and local governments, or we are going to continue as a marginalized population with political interests that are easily ignored. The future is completely in our control, as no one is going to hand us political power. We have to start now. If we do not take advantage of this opportunity, the next half century will produce more of the same in demographic and socioeconomic indicators—some gains, but enduring gaps, in equity and opportunity.

Notes

1. U.S. Commission on Civil Rights, *Hearing before the United States Commission on Civil Rights: San Antonio, TX, December 9–14, 1968* (Washington, DC: GPO, 1969). Also available at https://catalog. hathitrust.org/Record/001874430; Domingo Nick Reyes. *Domingo Nick Reyes Papers, c. 1930–1985* (Austin, TX: The Nettie Lee Benson Latin American Collection, 1930–1985).
2. Rodolfo Acuña, *Occupied America: A History of Chicanos*, 8th Ed. (New York: Pearson Education, 2014); David Montejano, *Anglos and Mexicans in the Making of Texas, 1836–1986* (Austin: University of Texas Press, 1987).
3. Juan Flores and Rogelio Sáenz, "Fading American Dream for Texas Hispanics," *Beyond Chron* (June 25, 2015). http://beyondchron.org/fading-american-dream-for-texas-hispanics.
4. Rodolfo Alvarez, "The Psycho-Historical and Socioeconomic Development of the Chicano Community in the United States," *Social Science Quarterly* 53, no. 4 (1973): 920–42; Montejano, *Anglos and Mexicans*.
5. Alvarez, "The Psycho-Historical and Socioeconomic Development."
6. University of Texas, Austin, Jamail Center for Legal Research, Tarlton Law Library, "General Provisions, Constitution of the Republic of Texas (1836)."

7. Jesús F. de la Teja, "Tejanos and the Siege and Battle of the Alamo," Texas State Historical Association, https://tshaonline.org/handbook/online/articles/qst01.

8. Alvarez, "The Psycho-Historical and Socioeconomic Development."

9. F. Arturo Rosales, *Chicano! The History of the Mexican American Civil Rights Movement*, 2nd rev. ed. (Houston: Arte Publico Press, 1977); Monica Muñoz Martínez, *The Injustice Never Leaves You: Anti-Mexican Violence in Texas* (Cambridge, MA: Harvard University Press, 2018).

10. Rosales, *Chicano!*

11. Rogelio Sáenz and María Cristina Morales, *Latinos in the United States: Diversity and Change* (Cambridge, UK: Polity Press, 2015).

12. Jorge Bustamante, "The Wetback as 'Deviant': An Application of Labeling Theory," *American Journal of Sociology*, no. 4 (1972): 706-18.

13. Jennifer R. Najera, *The Borderlands of Race: Mexican Segregation in a South Texas Town* (Austin: University of Texas Press, 2015).

14. Benjamin Márquez, *LULAC: The Evolution of a Political Organization* (Austin: University of Texas Press, 1993).

15. Francisco E. Balderrama and Raymond Rodríguez, *Decade of Betrayal: Mexican American Repatriation in the 1930s* (Albuquerque: University of New Mexico Press, 2006).

16. Steven Ruggles, Sarah Flood, Ronald Goeken, Josiah Grover, Erin Meyer, José Pacas, and Matthew Sobek, "Integrated Public Use Microdata Series USA: Version 10.0" [Database], Minnesota Population Center, 2019, https://usa.ipums.org/usa.

17. Otey M. Scruggs, "Texas the Bracero Program, 1942-1947," *Pacific Historical Review* 32, no. 3 (1963): 251-64.

18. Kelly Lytle Hernández, "The Crimes and Consequences of Illegal Immigration: A Cross-Border Examination of Operation Wetback, 1943 to 1954," *Western Historical Quarterly* 37, no. 4 (2006): 421-44.

19. Maggie Rívas-Rodríguez, ed., *Mexican Americans and World War II* (Austin, TX, University of Texas Press, 2005); Rogelio Sáenz and Aurelia Lorena Murga, *Latino Issues: A Reference Handbook* (Santa Barbara, CA: ABC-CLIO, 2011).

20. Najera, *The Borderlands of Race*.

21. Patrick Carroll, *Felix Longoria's Wake: Bereavement, Racism, and the Rise of Mexican American Activism* (Austin, TX: University of Texas Press, 2003); *The Longoria Affair*, Directed by John J. Valadez, DVD, Independent Lens, http://www.thelongoriaaffair.com/Longoria_Affair_home.html.

22. José Angel Gutiérrez, *The Making of a Chicano Militant: Lessons from Cristal* (Madison: University of Wisconsin Press, 1998); John Staples Shockley, *Chicano Revolt in a Texas Town: Crystal City* (Notre Dame, IN: University of Notre Dame Press, 1974); Rosales, *Chicano!*

23. Gutiérrez, *The Making of a Chicano Militant*, 99.

24. Ruggles et al., "Integrated Public Use Microdata Series USA."

25. Ruggles et al., "Integrated Public Use Microdata Series USA."

26. David Martin Davies, "'Hunger in America': The 1968 Documentary that Exposed San Antonio Poverty," Texas Public Radio, June 8, 2018.

27. Ruggles et al., "Integrated Public Use Microdata Series USA."

28. Ruggles et al. "Integrated Public Use Microdata Series USA."

29. Ruggles et al., "Integrated Public Use Microdata Series USA."

30. Ruggles et al., "Integrated Public Use Microdata Series USA."

31. Ruggles et al., "Integrated Public Use Microdata Series USA."

32. Ruggles et al., "Integrated Public Use Microdata Series USA."

33. Ruggles et al., "Integrated Public Use Microdata Series USA."

34. Ruggles et al., "Integrated Public Use Microdata Series USA."

35. Rogelio Sáenz, "A Transformation in Mexican Migration to the United States," National Issue Brief #86, Casey Research, 2015; Ruggles "Microdata Series."

36. Ruggles et al., "Integrated Public use Microdata Series USA."

37. Rogelio Sáenz and Carlos Siordia, "The Inter-Cohort Reproduction of Mexican American Dropouts," *Race and Social Problems*, 4 no. 1 (2012): 68-81.

38. Ruggles et al., "Integrated Public Use Microdata Series USA."

39. Ron Haskins and Primus Wendell, "Welfare Reform and Poverty," Brookings Center on Children and Families, July 1, 2001; Dylan Matthews, "Poverty in the Fifty Years Since 'The Other America,' in Five Charts," *Washington Post*, July 11, 2012.

40. Ruggles et al., "Integrated Public Use Microdata Series USA."

41. Ruggles et al., "Integrated Public Use Microdata Series USA"; U.S. Census Bureau 2012-2016 American Community Survey Five-Year Sample; U.S. Census Bureau 2016 American Community Survey. Author's Note: Here we focus on eight counties where Latinos are concentrated and for which there are sufficient amounts of data for 1960 and 2016. Two methodological interventions are offered here. First, the 1960 Public Use Microdata Sample that we used in the analysis did not have data for Travis County, where Austin is located, but it did have information for the Austin metropolitan area, which is equivalent to Travis County. In this part of the analysis, we essentially treat the Austin metropolitan area as Travis County. Second, while the 1960 data are based on a 5 percent sample of the census of that year, the 2016 American Community Survey (ACS) data are based on a 1 percent sample for that year. In order to have more stable data for 2016, given that we are focusing on counties, we use the Census Bureau 2012-2016 ACS Five-Year Sample, which is a 5 percent sample.

42. Office of the Texas State Demographer, "2018: Population Projections for the State of Texas by Age, Sex and Race/Ethnicity for 2010-2050," Texas State Data Center 2018. We use population projections for the state of Texas generated by the Office of the State Demographer. The projection projections are constructed the total Texas population, as well as for five racial/ethnic groups (non-Hispanic white, non-Hispanic African American, Hispanic/Latino, non-Hispanic Asian, and non-Hispanic Other). For a methodology used to construct the population projections, the population projections are based on the scenario that assumes that the migration rates for 2010-2015 persist over the projection years up to 2050.

43. Office of the Texas State Demographer, "Population Projections."

44. Jill Cowan, "When Will Latinos Outnumber Non-Hispanic Whites in Texas? Experts Have a New Prediction," *Dallas Morning News,* June 21, 2018; Office of the Texas State Demographer, "Population Projections."

45. Kiah Collier, "Texas Supreme Court Rules School Funding System is Constitutional," *The Texas Tribune*, May 13, 2016.

46. Ruggles et al., "Integrated Public Use Microdata Series USA."

47. Ruggles et al., "Integrated Public Use Microdata Series USA."

LEE J. TERÁN

Civil Rights and Immigration: Fifty Years of Failed U.S. Immigration Laws

W hen the U.S. Commission on Civil Rights (the Commission) met in San Antonio, Texas, in 1968 to study the plight of Mexican Americans in the five southwestern states, the Commission focused its investigation on civil rights challenges, limiting consideration of immigration issues to the effect Mexican migrants had on job opportunities for border residents.[1]

In 1978, the Commission revisited the United States-Mexico border to investigate immigration and civil rights concerns of migrants and residents. In September 1980, the Commission released a report, "The Tarnished Golden Door: Civil Rights Issues in Immigration."[2] The report found that immigration law was discriminatory and that the "practices and procedures for the enforcement of those laws result[ed] in the denial of the rights of American citizens and aliens."[3]

Commission investigators would return again to the Southwest border after "federal immigration laws and their enforcement practices [had] undergone numerous, sweeping changes."[4] Fifteen years after publishing "The Tarnished Golden Door," the Arizona, California, New Mexico, and Texas

Advisory Committees to the U.S. Commission on Civil Rights conducted field research on the impact immigration enforcement had on the border. In March 1997, the Commission published yet another report, "Federal Immigration Law Enforcement in the Southwest: Civil Rights Impacts on Border Communities."[5] The report concluded that civil rights violations continued to plague the border after the advisory committees considered "information indicating that a pattern of abusive treatment by Border Patrol officials might exist."[6]

In April 2003, the Commission addressed border related violence and deaths in the report "Migrant Civil Rights Issues Along the Southwest Border."[7] The Commission expressed deep concern regarding a rise in migrant injuries and deaths along the border. In 2015, the Commission issued its report on immigration detention, "The State of Civil Rights at Immigration Detention Facilities."[8] The Commission found that immigration detention, especially of migrant children, was "shocking to the nation's conscience."[9]

In the weeks approaching the fiftieth anniversary of the 1968 Commission hearing in San Antonio, the word "shocking" was heard again in protests against the Trump administration's campaign in 2018 to clamp down on immigration. That campaign included separating children from their asylum-seeking parents as they crossed the border, locking them in caged areas in separate detention centers. Authorities kept watch, while lawsuits filed in courts across the United States sought to reunite the families.

The 1968 Commission hearing in San Antonio opened with testimony regarding the history of the Southwest. Jack B. Forbes testified that the southwestern United States, once part of Mexico, must be understood in terms of the region's past.[10] The experience of its residents, who are more native than immigrant, differs significantly from that of European migrants. What is today the U.S. Southwest withstood military conquest and an aggressive control of its conquered population.[11] Because the region "overlap[s] national boundaries,"[12] residents of the Southwest have maintained strong ties to Mexico.[13]

For more than 150 years after the 1848 Mexican War and the Treaty of Guadalupe, when Mexican land was ceded to the United States, cultural and economic ties did not diminish between the United States and Mexico.

Mexicans have crossed the United States-Mexico border, with and without authorization, in possibly the greatest migration between any two countries of the modern world.[14]

Unquestionably, Mexican migration has influenced U.S. immigration law and policy. As of 2018, Mexicans represent the largest national group within the population of legal residents admitted each year to the United States. Unauthorized Mexican migrants are the primary target of restrictive and punitive immigration legislation and a massive buildup of enforcement centered on the United States-Mexico border.

Early Patterns of Mexican Migration

Immigration to the United States increased to previously unseen levels during the mid-nineteenth century, and migrants arrived from areas new to most Anglo-Americans—from Asia, Southern and Eastern Europe, and Mexico. U.S. employers recruited Mexican migrants to meet demands in the Southwest, and it was Mexican labor that built the railroads, the ranching and agriculture empires, and mining and manufacturing industries throughout the Southwest.[15] In a first wave of migration in the early 1900s, Mexicans labored primarily in Texas, but also traveled to work in California, Arizona, and New Mexico.[16]

The need for Mexican labor in the Southwest intensified during and after World War I, and U.S. employers continued to encourage Mexicans to come to the United States. Conditions in Mexico, particularly in the aftermath of revolutions and economic instability, prompted a second wave of thousands to migrate to the United States. Between 1920 and 1929, 498,945 Mexicans were admitted to the United States—more than any other national group during that decade.[17]

By 1930, there were an estimated 1.5 million Mexican migrants in the United States,[18] and most settled in the four border states: Texas, California, Arizona, and New Mexico. Texas had the highest population, at 683,681.[19] San Antonio, Texas, was from 1900 to 1950 considered the *capital migratoria de los mexicanos* (migratory capitol of Mexican migrants).[20] Mexican migrants and their families shared the indignities and mistreatment that other immigrants suffered in the communities dominated by Anglo-Americans.[21] In "The Tarnished Golden Door," the Commission described persistent patterns of discrimination against Mexicans and other immigrants and refugees. According to the 1980 Commission's report, "The image of the golden door . . . is a tarnished one." The report stated that "during times of economic stress, American treatment of immigrants has often been cruel. The anti-Catholic, anti-Chinese, anti-Mexican, and other anti-alien eras in American immigration history are replete with examples of such treatment."[22]

In the mid-nineteenth century, nativist anti-immigrant groups protested immigration to the United States of Asians, Southern and Eastern Europeans, and Mexicans. In response, Congress passed explicitly racist laws to prohibit immigration of Chinese laborers, and targeted non-English-speaking immigrants by imposing complex literacy requirements. In 1921 and again in 1924, Congress enacted the national origins quota laws, which imposed an annual ceiling on all immigration, with restrictions on migrants coming from Southern and Eastern Europe.[23]

Targeting Mexican Migrants

Nativists, despite being descended from immigrants themselves, maintained their opposition to Mexican immigration. However, under pressure from U.S. employers and religious groups, Congress exempted from the national origins quota laws natives of the Western Hemisphere.[24] During the Great Depression, calls for the "repatriation" of Mexicans mounted in an era of scarce employment opportunities.

Support among employers and community leaders dissolved as more Mexican workers joined labor unions to resist discrimination and poor working conditions.[25] "With scarcely an exception, every strike in which Mexicans and Mexican-Americans participated in the borderlands in the 'thirties was broken by the use of violence and was followed by deportations."[26]

During the 1930s, the federal government, joined by many state and local officials, forced hundreds of thousands of Mexicans and their U.S. citizen children to Mexico. The Commission estimated in "The Tarnished Golden Door" that during the 1930s, more than 500,000 Mexican migrants were forced to return to Mexico.[27] Other more recent estimates place the number of "repatriated" Mexicans and their families at one million or more.[28]

Congress passed the Immigration Act of 1929, which for the first time criminalized unauthorized entry into the United States. By 1940, the U.S. government had criminally prosecuted tens of thousands of Mexicans for unlawful entry.[29]

Relatively few immigrants were admitted to the United States between 1930 and 1950.[30] However, during World War II, U.S. employers encouraged Mexican workers to return. In 1942, the United States and Mexico negotiated the admission of temporary workers under the "Bracero (seasonal worker) program."[31] The program lasted until 1964.

After the war, Congress began work to modernize immigration laws, and in 1952 passed the Immigration and Nationality Act (INA). The statute consolidated prior laws regarding immigration and citizenship. The INA established categories for employment-based and family-based immigrant visas, while preserving the national origins quotas. It provided for grounds for exclusion and for deportation, and for hearings before "special inquiry officers" (later called immigration judges) to determine questions of exclusion and deportation. The statute defined discretionary applications for waivers or relief from deportation that migrants and long-term immigrants could request from the Immigration and Naturalization Service (INS) or immigration judges, and guaranteed the right to counsel, although "at no expense to the Government."[32]

The Bracero program failed to meet postwar demands for labor in the United States, and thousands of unauthorized Mexican migrants crossed the border. As the unauthorized population grew, the federal government intensified its enforcement. In 1954, more than one million Mexican migrants were apprehended in a campaign called "Operation Wetback."[33]

More than 30,000 Mexicans were formally deported. The rest of the apprehended migrants waived their rights to deportation hearings and were returned immediately to Mexico.[34] The operation resulted in the most Mexicans expelled from the United States since the "repatriations" of the 1930s.

The 1960s: A Turning Point in Immigration History

The 1960s represented a significant turning point in U.S. immigration history and for Mexican migrants. In 1965, Congress repealed the discriminatory national origins quota laws of the early twentieth century.[35] The Immigration Act of 1965 reflected, in part, a more open acceptance of immigrants, and established a system for allocating visas on a per-country basis, with emphasis on reuniting families.[36] In a nod to Mexico, Central America, and South America, the statute imposed a per-country quota only on the Eastern Hemisphere. However, with growing opposition to Mexican immigration, Congress established for the first time a ceiling on total immigrant visas for natives in the Western Hemisphere.

European immigration to the United States steadily declined during the twentieth century. In the 1960s immigration surged to levels not seen since 1910, and included immigrants from areas previously restricted.[37] In 1968, immigrant admissions to the United States from all countries increased to 454,448, the highest number of new immigrants since the 1924 quota laws.[38] Of those, the United States admitted 43,500 Mexicans for legal residence.

At approximately 685,000, Mexican immigrants represented the largest nationality group of legal residents in the United States in 1968. In the next fifty years, immigration to the United States from Mexico, from other Latin American countries, and from Asia would reach levels previously held by Europeans prior to 1910 (see Figure 1).

In 1968, the INS had 12,000 employees engaged in all aspects of the agency's service and enforcement functions. They processed petitions for immigration and citizenship benefits, inspected incoming migrants at U.S. ports of entry, arrested and detained unauthorized migrants, and issued legal rulings in deportation/exclusion proceedings.

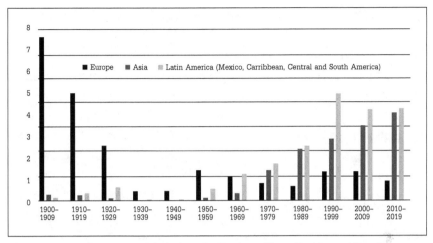

Figure 1. Legal Immigrant Admissions by Region of Last Residence (decade totals in millions), 1900–2019. *Source:* Immigration and Naturalization Service and Department of Homeland Security, Yearbooks of Immigration Statistics (1966–2019).

The INS employed approximately 1,500 Border Patrol agents in 1968, and most were assigned to the United States-Mexico border. After Operation Wetback, the number of INS apprehensions had dropped significantly.[39] However, by the mid-1960s, the federal government had renewed enforcement efforts in response to mounting public pressure against Mexican migrants following a decline in the U.S. economy.[40] In 1968, the INS had expanded its operations along highways and communities north of the border to stop migrants moving north in their search of employment.[41]

The Border Patrol apprehended approximately 212,000 migrants in 1968, a 40 percent increase over the previous year. Of the migrants arrested, 72 percent were from Mexico. Most Mexicans apprehended by the Border Patrol at or near the United States-Mexico border waived their rights to a hearing and were "returned" to Mexico within hours. In 1968, nearly 180,000 Mexicans were "returned," and about 9,600 individuals were detained and removed with a formal order of deportation issued by an immigration judge.[42]

The 1970s: Evolving Immigration Changes

In the 1970s, Mexican immigration to the United States continued to climb in numbers. Between 1970 and 1979, 621,218 Mexicans were admitted to United States, the largest single group of immigrants and close to 15 percent of the total immigrant population admitted during that time period.[43] Most Mexican immigrants were beneficiaries of family-based visas. However, in 1976, Congress abandoned its commitment to natives of the Western Hemisphere and amended the INA to impose worldwide the per-country limit of 20,000 immigrant visas.[44] While the per-country visa quota did not affect the admission of Mexican "immediate relatives" (spouses, parents, or children) of U.S. citizens, the new limits resulted in a years-long backlog of visa applications. The waiting period expanded from seven to fifteen years for admission of other eligible Mexican relatives of U.S. citizens and residents.[45]

The number of unauthorized migrants grew substantially through the 1970s. By 1980, an estimated five million unauthorized migrants were residing in the United States. Mexican workers came in search of jobs, and Mexicans joined their U.S. families as they waited for visas. The INS maintained

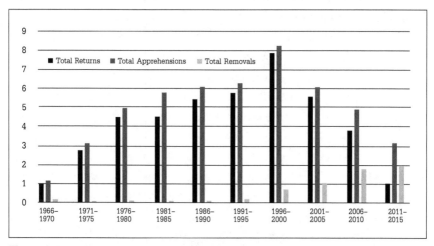

Figure 2. Migrant Apprehensions, Returns, and Removals (five-year totals in millions), 1966–2015. *Source:* Immigration and Naturalization Service, Department of Homeland Security, Yearbooks of Immigration Statistics (1966–2015).

the Border Patrol presence on the United States-Mexico border. In 1970, the number of individuals apprehended by the INS exceeded 345,000; by 1979, the total was in excess of one million individuals. Most apprehensions and immediate "returns" involved Mexicans. The government steadily increased its resources to formally deport unauthorized migrants, and most were from Mexico (see Figure 2).

THE COMMISSION CONVENES AGAIN

The U.S. Commission on Civil Rights began its examination of immigration and civil rights in 1977, after receiving "allegations and complaints of civil rights violations in the enforcement of immigration laws" from migrants, U.S. citizens, and long-term immigrants.[46] The Commission interviewed hundreds of individuals representing a broad range of social and business groups, immigrant organizations, the INS, the State Department, and other government officials. One hundred fifty individuals spoke at open hearings in Texas, New York, and California. In November 1978 the Commission held a hearing on civil rights and immigration in Washington, DC, and heard testimony from thirty-two witnesses.[47]

The report "The Tarnished Golden Door" began with a review of the history of U.S. immigration history and, in particular, its effects on Mexican immigrants and their families. The Commission found that the per-country limits violated the central purpose of the INA to reunify families, and determined that the limits discriminated against Mexicans. The Commission recommended that Congress provide for an allocation of visas within the worldwide quota on a first come, first served basis.[48]

As the Commission conducted its investigations, Congress was deliberating changes in immigration law, including implementation of a compulsory national identity card and sanctions against employers of unauthorized migrants. The Commission considered the effect of unauthorized migrants on U.S. labor, and determined that while unauthorized migrants had an undetermined adverse effect on domestic workers, employer sanctions and a national ID would have more significant negative consequences. The Commission recommended that the Department of Labor more vigorously enforce labor laws and that the United States explore bilateral and multilateral agreements with the countries of origin of unauthorized migrants to better regulate the flow of migrants.[49]

"The Tarnished Golden Door" examined what were often seen as "the conflicting missions of the INS—service and enforcement."[50] The INS was charged with the dual responsibility of providing immigration and citizenship services to the public and providing for apprehending and expelling deportable noncitizens. The Commission report was sharply critical of the structure and the negative effect the INS enforcement duties had on its service functions.[51]

The Commission commended the INS for its efforts to diversify its workforce (28 percent minority, and 35 percent women, in 1978). However, most female and minority employees were assigned to low-level positions with lower pay. Non-Hispanic white employees held the vast majority of high-paying jobs, comprising 92 percent of upper management and supervisory positions in the agency.[52]

The Commission's report found that INS service functions were lacking. Applicants for immigration benefits experienced long delays and were unable to track information on the status of their applications. INS adjudications were viewed as arbitrary and inconsistent. The Commission recommended that the INS institute more efficient and computerized filing systems, improve access to information, and issue guidelines to improve the quality and consistency in decision making. The Commission also recommended that Congress pass legislation to separate the service and enforcement functions of the INS, and appropriate more resources to improve INS services to the public.[53]

VIOLATIONS OF CONSTITUTIONAL PROTECTIONS

A major concern for the Commission was the violation of constitutional protections by INS officers. The report "The Tarnished Golden Door" described INS enforcement operations in which officers conducted sweeping stops and interrogations based solely on ethnic appearance, resulting in illegal arrests and detentions of unauthorized migrants, legal residents, and U.S. citizens. The Commission found that local police improperly enforced immigration laws, leading to violations of constitutional protections

afforded migrants, legal residents, and U.S. citizens. The Commission recommended that INS cease policies and procedures that violated the Constitution and immigration laws, and that Congress pass legislation to clarify
that only the INS enforce immigration laws.[54]

The Commission found that Border Patrol efforts to expedite deportations undermined migrants' crucial rights to impartial hearings before
immigration judges. Most migrants who were apprehended by the INS
did not have hearings before an immigration judge but were processed for
immediate "voluntary departures." The Commission recommended that
INS direct its officials to cease forcing noncitizens to waive their rights to
a hearing.

The Commission called on Congress to adopt legislation to separate
the immigration courts from the INS and form an independent judicial
agency.[55] The Commission also recommended that the INS provide migrants with notice of the availability of free legal services, and that Congress pass legislation guaranteeing the right to counsel at "all crucial stages
of the deportation process."[56]

INS misconduct, which had resulted in the violation of the civil rights
of migrants and U.S. citizens, comprised a large part of the final chapter of
the Commission's "The Tarnished Golden Door" report. The Commission
found that the government had improved its "complaint-process procedures through the reorganization of its internal investigations unit and
the implementation of a new Operations Instructions," but concluded
that a significant backlog of complaints existed. The Commission determined that the public was unaware of the complaint process, and that
complainants received no notice of the status or result of an investigation.
Guidelines for assignments of investigators, particularly minority officers,
were insufficient.[57]

The 1980s: Unauthorized Migration Continues

During the 1980s, Congress and the federal government continued to wres-
tle with a number of issues concerning immigration, including many that

had been the subject of the Commission hearing. The U.S. government made significant changes to address unauthorized migration, to improve law enforcement, and to modernize the legal system for identifying and processing refugees. However, by the end of the decade, unauthorized migration had climbed to the same levels reached in the early 1980s.

LEGAL REFORMS AND REFUGEES

In 1980, Congress enacted the Refugee Act, and brought the United States into compliance with its obligations under international law for the protection of refugees. The statute broadened the definition of refugees, and instituted comprehensive procedures for the admission of refugees and asylum seekers.[58]

In 1983, the Department of Justice followed a recommendation of the U.S. Commission on Civil Rights to separate the immigration courts from the INS. The Justice Department created the Executive Office for Immigration Reform (EOIR) to house the immigration courts, and the Board of Immigration Appeals.

In 1986, Congress enacted the Immigrant Reform and Control Act (IRCA).[59] The IRCA implemented civil and criminal sanctions against employers who hired unauthorized migrants, a provision the Commission had opposed. The IRCA authorized substantial funding for enforcement, particularly for border enforcement. The IRCA also established a legalization program for unauthorized migrants.

A NEW ROUTE TO RESIDENCY

The IRCA's legalization program provided a path to legal residence for two groups: former agricultural workers, and unauthorized migrants who arrived in the United States prior to January 1, 1982.[60] Approximately three million migrants gained legal status, and the majority were from Mexico. However, IRCA legalization provided no benefit for those unauthorized migrants who had entered the United States after 1982, or who had not worked in agriculture.[61] The IRCA also failed to include immigration benefits for the family members of eligible migrants.[62] The number of family visa applications soared as newly legalized immigrants sought to reunite with families. A substantial visa backlog developed in the years after the IRCA. Between 1980 and 1989, the United States admitted more than one million Mexican immigrants.

In the 1980s, civil wars in Central America and harsh conditions in Haiti and Cuba prompted thousands to seek refuge in the United States. The Refugee Act of 1980 established uniform and non-country-specific standards for determining refugee and asylum status, and the law was soon tested by the influx of migrants from Central America and the Caribbean. Advocates for refugees reported that the INS routinely denied asylum claims brought by many migrants from El Salvador and Guatemala, who fled countries considered friendly with the United States.[63] The INS imposed punitive measures, detention, and high bail bonds and expedited deportation, to discourage migrants from seeking asylum.[64] It even instituted a program to interdict Haitian refugees caught at sea to prevent them from landing on U.S. soil.[65]

After the IRCA was passed and the legalization program ended, the population of unauthorized migrants in the United States dropped from five million to about two million. Total apprehensions from 1980 to 1984 were 5.3 million. Then, between 1985 and 1989, apprehensions of unauthorized migrants increased substantially, reaching a total of 6.2 million migrants.

Immigration Patterns in the 1990s

Between 1990 and 1999, 2.7 million Mexicans immigrated to the United States. During this period, there was also an increase in immigration from all parts of the world, most notably from Asia, and a steady rise in immigration from Central Americans. In the 1990s, Congress enacted some legislation that benefited migrants. The Immigration Act of 1990 increased the cap on immigrant visas, although the per-country limits remained in place.[66] Congress established a lottery for an additional 55,000 "diversity" immigrant visas assigned to nationals from countries that were undersubscribed within the worldwide quota. The lottery system did not benefit nationals from high-admission countries, such as Mexico. The statute provided for temporary protected status (TPS) to benefit nationals from countries plagued by disasters or civil wars.

In 1994, Congress passed the Violence Against Women Act (VAWA), comprehensive legislation to deal with the serious problem of domestic violence in the United States.[67] The law included a process for abused spouses and children of U.S. citizens and legal residents seeking to obtain immigrant visas and/or relief from deportation.

The primary focus for Congress and the federal government during the 1990s, however, was on three issues: crime, drug trafficking, and unauthorized migration at the United States-Mexico border. Although studies confirmed that migrants are less likely than U.S. citizens to commit crimes, Congress targeted immigrants in crime-related legislation.[68] In the Anti-Drug Abuse Act of 1988, Congress added a new ground of deportability for immigrants who had been convicted of an "aggravated felony," defined initially as a murder, drug trafficking, or weapons trafficking offense.[69] In 1990 and again in 1994, Congress expanded the definition of "aggravated felony" to include hundreds of other offenses.[70] Congress also limited the availability of relief from deportation to any immigrant with an aggravated felony conviction and a jail term longer than five years.

MILITARIZATION OF THE BORDER

As part of a "war on drugs" that had been declared by several U.S. presidents since Richard Nixon, the Border Patrol received expanded authority in drug interdiction cases in the 1990s.[71] Militarization of the United States-Mexico border progressed rapidly as Congress earmarked funding for border and drug enforcement and authorized hiring more Border Patrol agents.[72] By 1992 the Border Patrol had approximately five thousand agents and a budget of $325 million.

The Border Patrol added stations and checkpoints, built detention centers, and received more equipment, including night-vision goggles, surveillance systems, and helicopters for each sector.[73] In 1991, the government built a steel wall seven miles long along the United States-Mexico border, and in 1993 expanded the length to fourteen miles. New Border Patrol initiatives, "Operation Hold the Line" and "Operation Rio Grande," placed more agents along established migration corridors. The INS sharply increased formal deportation proceedings against deportable migrants, and Congress authorized more funding to expand immigration courts.

The INS further launched a coordinated and expansive use of criminal and administrative sanctions.[74] Criminal prosecution rates for the offense of unlawful entry into the United States had dropped after the 1930s. By the 1990s, U.S. Attorneys had been directed to increase criminal prosecutions in immigration-related cases. INS apprehension rates increased substantially. More than one million individuals were apprehended by the Border Patrol from 1990 to 1995. Between 1992 and 1998, the number of immigration-related criminal prosecutions doubled.[75] By 1998, 93 percent of cases referred by the INS to the Department of Justice for criminal prosecution were accepted. Between 1992 and 1998, the median sentence to incarceration rose from two months to twelve months.

In 1998, more than 170,000 individuals were formally deported.[76] An additional 1,570,000 were apprehended and returned "voluntarily" to Mexico. Another consequence of the government's heavy enforcement soon developed. Reports showed an increase in the death rate of migrants at or near the border. The Border Patrol increased its presence on traditional migratory routes, pushing migrants into more dangerous territory and harsher climates. Between 1993 and 1997, more than one thousand migrants were reported to have died at or near the United States–Mexico border.[77]

ADVISORY COMMITTEES ADDRESS ABUSES

In "The Tarnished Golden Door," the U.S. Commission on Civil Rights had called for "a responsive complaint investigation system" to deal with a rise in INS and local police abuse of migrants and U.S. citizens.[78] However, reports of violence and abuse continued to surface, and in 1990, Congress requested that the Commission study the problems of violence on the border. Four advisory committees to the U.S. Commission on Civil Rights from the four border states of California, Arizona, New Mexico, and Texas convened, and conducted a series of hearings between 1992 and 1993.[79]

The advisory committees voiced concern with the growing militarization of their states' borders with Mexico, and an increase in violence against migrants and residents. Border Patrol personnel ranks had increased by 50 percent, and the authority of Border Patrol officers to conduct drug interdiction had expanded.

Most INS and Border Patrol operations (90 percent) targeted the United States-Mexico border. The committees questioned the ability of the INS to adequately screen, train, and supervise the Border Patrol. Witnesses expressed concern that the dramatic expansion in policing, technology, and resources reflected a new perception of migrants—not as laborers in search of jobs, but as an invading force. "The logical extension of viewing immigration as an 'invasion' is that the national boundary must be defended at gunpoint," one advisory committee report stated.[80]

The advisory committees representing the four states heard considerable testimony from individuals, citizens' groups, and advocacy organizations about incidents of violence and abuse against migrants, immigrants, and U.S. citizens who resided in the targeted communities. The American Friends Service Committee, a Quaker organization, submitted a report of complaints in March 1990 that listed 380 cases of civil rights violations in five areas between 1988 and 1989. The report included a chapter describing the objects the Border Patrol allegedly used to inflict injury, including "flashlights, nightsticks, vehicles, rings, pistols, handcuffs, and windshield scrapers."[81]

The American Friends Service Committee issued a second report in 1992, with data on 1,274 cases of alleged Border Patrol abuse between 1989 and 1991. While the four state advisory committees could not confirm unverified complaints, their report stated that "the sheer statistical numbers and severity of abuse complaints are a cause of deep concern."[82]

The advisory committees to the Commission also recommended litigation involving INS abuse brought in El Paso, Texas. The INS maintained that its officers had unrestricted authority to stop, question, and arrest individuals at and near the border. That notion was challenged in 1982 in *Mendoza v. INS*, a case heard before Judge Lucius D. Bunton.[83] The plaintiffs charged that Border Patrol officers patrolled El Paso bars near the United States-Mexico border and subjected bar patrons and employees to illegal searches and seizures. Judge Bunton issued an injunction and noted that if he were to permit the INS to continue its activities, Border Patrol would "stop and interrogate more than half of the legitimate population of the border town of El Paso."[84]

Ten years later, in 1992, Judge Bunton presided in another El Paso case, *Murillo, et al. v. Musegades,* a class action lawsuit claiming violations of the Fourth and Fifth Amendment rights of El Paso residents.[85] The plaintiffs were students, staff, and faculty members at Bowie High School in El Paso. They alleged that Border Patrol agents systematically stopped and questioned individuals based on their Mexican "appearance." Some plaintiffs said they were verbally or physically assaulted when they resisted INS actions. Judge Bunton issued an injunction, and stated in his order that "the government's interest in enforcing immigration laws does not outweigh the protection of the rights of U.S. citizens and permanent residents to be free from unreasonable searches and seizures."[86]

In March 1997, the Arizona, California, New Mexico, and Texas advisory committees to the Commission issued their report. The committees found that the increase of federal law enforcement officers in the Southwest was a threat to the protection of civil rights in border communities, and "a cause of deep concern," due to the large number and severity of abuse complaints.[87] The report also concluded that procedures for redress of misconduct, the deficiencies of which were exposed in the Commission's "The Tarnished Golden Door" report, remained "inadequate, inaccessible, and lack the confidence of the communities most directly affected."[88]

THE FULL COMMISSION'S REPORT ON VIOLENCE AT THE BORDER

In 2002, the Commission on Civil Rights was briefed by the California and Arizona advisory committees. The Commission heard additional testimony concerning the rise in violence on the United States-Mexico border. The Commission was told about Border Patrol operations in the 1990s—called "Operation Hold the Line" in El Paso, Texas, "Operation Gatekeeper" in San Diego, California, "Operation Safeguard" in Tucson, Arizona, and "Operation Rio Grande" in South Texas—that contributed to an increase in migrant deaths. Witnesses testified that since 1994, more than two thousand migrants had died. In 2002 alone, three hundred migrants died while crossing the border, and 130 died from exposure in the deserts of Arizona, the witnesses testified.[89]

The Commission also considered the rise in vigilante violence.[90] Reports of migrants injured or killed by U.S. landowners and militia groups increased in the 1990s. The American Friends Service Committee testified that two migrants were shot and killed by men in camouflage, and added that they suspected some vigilantes were members of white supremacist organizations. The Commission recommended that the INS reexamine operations that increase mortality rates, and that the Department of Justice investigate border vigilantism.[91]

A Harsher Role in Federal Immigration Enforcement

The militarization of the border, and the increased dangers in crossing under harsher conditions, did not stop migrants from coming to the United States. In a thriving U.S. economy, the population of unauthorized migrants increased. By 1992, an estimated 3.4 million unauthorized migrants resided in the United States. In 1997, the INS estimated that 300,000 migrants were entering the United States each year, and the unauthorized population reached in excess of five million, the level it had been in 1986, when the

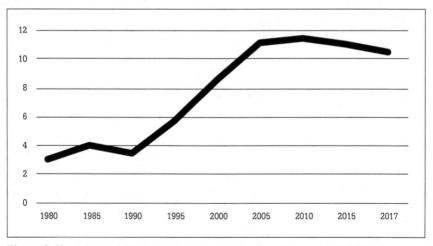

Figure 3. Unauthorized Migrants in United States (in millions), 1980–2017. *Source:* Jeffrey Passel, (1980–89) Pew Research Center; Hispanic Trends (1990–2017), May 3, 2017, online at pewresearch.org.

IRCA was enacted. The majority of unauthorized migrants were from Mexico. They entered without inspection at the United States-Mexico border, or came with short-term visas, and then overstayed the authorized entry (see Figure 3).

In 1996 Congress considered even harsher measures to address crime and unauthorized migration, and enacted two broad-based changes to immigration law: the Anti-Terrorism and Effective Death Penalty Act (AEDPA),[92] and the Illegal Immigration Reform and Immigrant Responsibility Act (IIRIRA).[93] Together, the AEDPA and IIRIRA increased funding for enforcement against unauthorized migrants and immigrants convicted of crimes. The statutes streamlined removals and appeals, mandated detention, and repealed or limited long-standing forms of discretionary relief from removal.

The IIRIRA went into effect after the advisory committees to the Commission issued their report, which recommended that the federal government change course and ease up on enforcement on the border. Then, following the events of the terrorist attack on New York City on September 11, 2001, or 9/11, the government dismantled and overhauled the INS and other federal agencies dealing with customs and security.

Congress continued to direct enormous sums to support border enforcement. By 2012, federal spending for immigration enforcement had reached $18 billion, and became the highest priority for federal law enforcement.[94]

NEW LAWS AND HARSHER PROVISIONS

The 1996 IIRIRA and AEDPA legislation dramatically expanded the federal government's ability to arrest, detain, and expeditiously remove many more unauthorized migrants and immigrants. Congress amended the definition of "aggravated felony" to include hundreds of new deportable offenses, and to retroactively include convictions that predated the IIRIRA.[95] The legislation diminished forms of relief from removal, and rights to appeal removal orders to federal courts.

The IIRIRA gave low-level immigration officers the authority, once reserved to immigration judges, to reinstate an order or deportation/removal against migrants previously deported/removed, and to issue expedited removal orders against newly arrived migrants. Congress added new grounds of inadmissibility based on unlawful presence, restricting the ability of unauthorized migrant relatives of U.S. citizens and legal residents to immigrate to the United States.

In 2000, Congress considered measures to ameliorate the more punitive portions of the 1996 legislation and a plan for legalization of the millions of unauthorized migrants residing in the United States. Congress passed the Victims of Trafficking and Violence Protection Act to provide immigration benefits, known as "T" and "U" visas, for victims of crime and severe forms of trafficking.[96]

In early September 2001, the George W. Bush administration planned discussions with the government of Mexico about legislation to benefit unauthorized migrants. The talks were interrupted by what became known as 9/11, and efforts to adopt comprehensive immigration reform dissolved.[97]

After 9/11, attention to immigration law and policy converged with a focus on terrorism and national security.[98] The U.S. Patriot Act authorized increases in numbers of Border Patrol agents.[99] In 2002, the Homeland Security Act reorganized federal agencies and dismantled the INS.[100] The Enhanced Border Security and Visa Entry Reform Act added security measures for visa issuance and mandated data collection and sharing.[101]

During the George W. Bush administration, twenty-two federal agencies overseeing security, customs, and immigration combined to form the Department of Homeland Security (DHS). For the first time, the enforcement and service functions of the former INS were separated. The Department of Homeland Security comprised three subagencies. Citizenship and Immigration Services (CIS) assumed the service portion. The Immigration and Customs Enforcement (ICE) and Customs and Border Protection (CBP) subagencies combined interior and border enforcement functions.

IMMIGRATION, TERRORISM, AND NATIONAL SECURITY

In the past fifty years, U.S. immigration law and policy has changed dramatically, and the role of immigration enforcement officers—once limited to the tasks of locating, arresting, and processing unauthorized migrants— evolved into a far more complex mission. The IRCA, the "war on drugs," and anticrime legislation expanded enforcement responsibilities in areas of employer sanctions, drug interdiction, and criminal apprehension. After 9/11, the Department of Homeland Security assumed a role in antiterrorism and national security.

By September 2000, the Border Patrol had nine thousand officers, more than 90 percent assigned to the United States–Mexico border, and the agency's budget was $1 billion. Other resources for the border included remote video surveillance systems and construction of seventy-six miles of fencing. Under the newly organized Department of Homeland Security, the Border Patrol became part of the CBP (Customs and Border Protection), and its mission was expanded to include national security concerns, the prevention of terrorism, and seizure of terrorism-related weapons. CBP maintained a strong presence on the Southwest border.[102]

Post 9/11 legislation substantially increased funding for new officers, equipment, and technology directed to the border. CBP justified the buildup as an effort to secure the border from terrorists and other dangerous people.[103] By 2011, there were in excess of 21,000 Border Patrol agents in CBP. Despite the new focus on international terrorism, most Border Patrol agents were stationed at the United States–Mexico border (see Figure 4).

The Border Patrol continued its enforcement of criminal and civil immigration laws. In 2011, half of all federal criminal prosecutions in the United States were immigration related, with most for entry without inspection, and illegal reentry after deportation. The Border Patrol referred more cases to U.S. Attorneys for criminal prosecution than did the FBI.[104] CBP also organized and expanded its staff at the United States–Mexico ports of entry. The inspection process changed as the agency modernized data collection and increased cooperation with other government agencies. "Today, noncitizens are screened at more intervals, against more databases, which contain more detailed data, than ever before," the Migration Policy Institute reported in 2013.[105]

Post-9/11 funding to CBP equipped the United States–Mexico border with additional fencing, lighting, sensors, and patrol planes. Between 2007 and

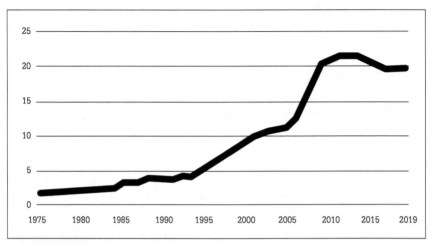

Figure 4. Total U.S. Border Patrol Staff, 1975–2019 (in thousands). *Source:* TRAC Immigration and the Department of Homeland Security; U.S. Border Patrol Staffing by Fiscal Year, online at cpb.gov.

2015, the federal government spent $2.4 billion on fencing the United States–Mexico border, increasing the barriers from 119 miles in length to 654 miles.[106]

THE RISE OF ICE

Congress tied national security concerns with immigration enforcement, and earmarked added funds for ICE and its operations in the interior of the United States. The federal government expanded its efforts to locate and remove convicted immigrants under the Criminal Alien Program (CAP). In 2002, the National Fugitive Operations Program (NFOP) was formed to locate fugitive migrants, and by 2008, funding to NFOP alone climbed to $230 million.[107] In 2012, ICE had a budget that exceeded $6 billion.[108]

ICE increased its alliances with state and local police to locate and hold unauthorized migrants and convicted immigrants. IIRIRA section 287(g) authorized the federal government to increase immigration enforcement through contracts with state and local police, and the program grew quickly. By 2008 there were sixty-one agreements between the Department of Homeland Security and local authorities.[109]

In 2008, ICE organized a separate cooperative program, Secure Communities, which was not burdened by the training and contract requirements mandated by section 287(g). Under Secure Communities, ICE sought to identify migrant detainees in state and local jails, and requested that local officials submit detainee fingerprints to immigration databases. ICE issued detainers for the transfer of targeted inmates to ICE custody.[110] In 2010, local authorities referred more than 3.4 million individuals to ICE, which issued more than 100,000 detainers.[111]

IMMIGRATION AND DETENTION

The IIRIRA required that the Department of Homeland Security detain most individuals who were removable based on crimes. The U.S. Patriot Act mandated detention for individuals considered a national security threat. The federal agency also tightened detention policies relating to those who remained eligible for release.

Congress passed several appropriations bills to fund immigration detention, and, in fact, based funding on a specific number of required beds.[112] In 2012, Congress set the minimum level of detention beds at 34,000.[113] The federal government used a network of approximately five hundred facilities for detention, including DHS's own "service processing centers," federal prisons, local and county jails, and, more recently, contract facilities from a growing industry of private for-profit prisons.[114]

In 2013, the Department of Homeland Security's detention costs exceeded $2 billion.[115] For-profit prisons, including the two largest, GEO Group Inc. and CoreCivic (formerly known as Corrections Corporation of America or CCA), were awarded in excess of $100 million.[116] Texas led the country in the number of individuals detained for the DHS, with more than twenty facilities in the state dedicated to DHS detention. Most were located at or near the United States–Mexico border, in the cities of El Paso, Del Rio, Laredo, Pearsall, Dilley, Karnes City, and Port Isabel.

The Department of Homeland Security also began detaining migrants and refugees who were not subject to IIRIRA's mandatory detention. In 2005, DHS announced an end to its policy of "catch and release" pending removal proceedings. In 2006, DHS opened the T. Don Hutto facility in Taylor, Texas, and dedicated the site exclusively to detention of unauthorized migrant mothers and young children.

The federal agency attracted widespread public condemnation for its decision to detain families.[117] In 2007, the American Civil Liberties Union (ACLU) filed a lawsuit challenging the Hutto facility's failure to comply with health and educational standards for the care of children, and in 2009, Hutto was dismantled as a detention center for children, although it remained a center for detained women. The for-profit CoreCivic company operated the facility.

IMMIGRATION COURTS

Congress allocated significant funding to expand federal immigration courts to, as of 2018, sixty-one courts throughout the United States.[118] The Department of Justice, which oversees the Executive Office for Immigration Review and its system of immigration courts, prioritized the setting and completion of removal cases involving individuals in detention. Many immigration courts operated within detention centers.

In Texas, for instance, in 2018 there were four detention centers with permanent assignments of immigration judges to hear detainee removal cases: Southwest Detention Complex in Pearsall, Texas (four judges); Port Isabel Service Processing Center (five judges); Houston Service Processing Center (three judges); and El Paso Service Processing Center (four judges). Other immigration courts in the state, including the court in San Antonio, Texas, regularly conducted removal hearings from remote detention centers via televideo conferencing.

The federal government expedited hearings—commonly called "rocket dockets"—for removal cases that the government determined deserved emergency consideration.[119] In 2014, following the influx of mothers and their children fleeing violence in Central America, the Department of Justice prioritized the setting of all removal cases relating to the Central American mothers.[120]

Despite the expansion of immigration courts and expeditious processing of hearings, there were more than 500,000 backlogged cases pending at EOIR in 2018. The workload per immigration judge also increased, particularly in the immigration courts located near the Southwest border.[121]

EVEN AS MIGRATION SLOWS, ARRESTS AND DEPORTATIONS RISE

Post IIRIRA, the rate of apprehensions by the Border Patrol exceeded more than one million each year. In 1996, Border Patrol agents apprehended 1.5 million migrants. By 2000, the number of individuals arrested by the Border Patrol exceeded 1.6 million, the most apprehended in a single year since 1986.[122] Between 2001 and 2005, more than six million individuals were arrested, and 5.5 million were from Mexico.

The number of individuals removed from the United States also climbed considerably after IIRIRA. Between 1996 and 2000, 730,506 individuals received formal removal orders, including more than 577,000 from Mexico. U.S. authorities returned 7.8 million individuals to their countries without a hearing, and most were Mexicans. From 2001 to 2005, one million individuals received removal orders, more than 700,000 to Mexico. During the same period, 5.5 million were returned without hearings, with the majority returned to Mexico.

In 1995, the INS detained 85,730 individuals, and the daily detainee population was 7,475.[123] Following the passage of the IIRIRA and the suspension of the DHS's "catch and release" policy, immigration detention rates increased sharply. In 2012, the Department of Homeland Security detained 464,190 individuals, with the majority from Mexico. The average length of stay was subject to debate. DHS reported that ICE detention was, on average, twenty-nine days,[124] but advocates charged that the average detention stay was triple that amount.[125]

After 2006, apprehension rates, including the arrests of Mexicans, began to decline. Heavy law enforcement at the border was one factor, but there were other reasons that appear to have discouraged migrants from crossing the border. During the Great Recession of 2008, demand for labor decreased. The serious drug violence centered in northern Mexico discouraged migrants from traveling to the border, and promising economic conditions in Mexico encouraged many to stay home.[126]

Between 2006 and 2010, total apprehensions declined to 4.8 million. Of those, 4.1 million involved Mexicans. From 2011 to 2015, only 3.1 million were apprehended; two million were from Mexico. However, apprehensions of Central Americans increased as nationals from El Salvador, Honduras, and Guatemala fled drug- and gang-related violence. In 2015, 160,615 migrants from El Salvador, Guatemala, and Honduras were apprehended; in 2016 the number rose to 224,854.[127]

Enforcement, ICE, and Punishment

The Obama administration received considerable criticism for its harsh enforcement against unauthorized migrants and long-term immigrants convicted of crimes. While the Department of Homeland Security maintained that its enforcement efforts targeted criminals and national security threats, the majority of individuals apprehended and removed had never committed a crime.

Community advocates and police officials argued that ICE operations swept up unauthorized migrants, leading to separation of families and disruption in local communities. Between 2003 and 2008, 73 percent of individuals apprehended under ICE's fugitive program, NFOP, had no criminal record, and more than 55 percent of those ICE located through Secure Communities, and placed in removal proceedings, had no criminal record or had a record for minor/traffic crimes.[128] While apprehension rates declined after

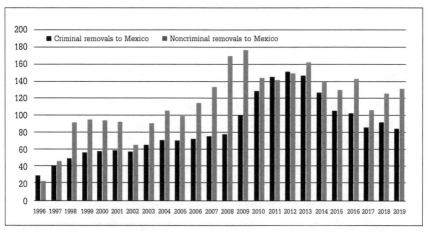

Figure 5. Criminal and Noncriminal Removals of Immigrants to Mexico, 1996–2019 (in thousands). *Source:* Immigration and Naturalization Service and Department of Homeland Security, Yearbooks of Immigration Statistics (1998–2019).

2006, the rates of removals increased. Between 2006 and 2010, more than 1.7 million migrants (1.2 million Mexicans) were removed from the United States, and most were not criminals (see Figure 5).[129]

A SHIFT IN PRIORITIES

In the face of mounting criticism, the Obama administration shifted its enforcement priorities to focus more on apprehension of individuals with convictions.[130] In 2014, the administration discontinued the Secure Communities program and replaced it with the Priority Enforcement Program (PEP).[131] ICE was to limit its issuance of detainers to migrants and immigrants who had been convicted or who posed a national security threat.

The Obama administration also vowed to change its detention policies and to expand alternatives to detention.[132] Detention rates declined somewhat, to 352,882 in 2016. However, as the administration expanded enforcement at the border—particularly against Central American migrants from Guatemala, El Salvador, and Honduras—DHS reauthorized detention for families. It opened two "family residential facilities" in Texas, one in Karnes City and the other in Dilley, with a combined capacity of more than three thousand mothers and children.

The decline in apprehensions continued. In 2016, apprehensions of

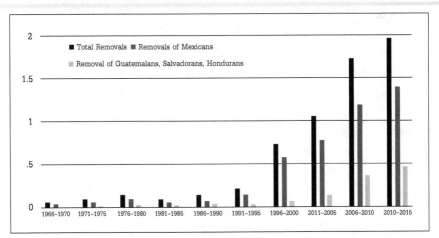

Figure 6. Removals of Mexicans, El Salvadorans, Guatemalans, and Hondurans (five-year totals, in millions), 1966–2015. *Source:* Department of Homeland Security, 2016; Yearbooks of Immigration Statistics (1966–2016).

Mexicans dropped to 265,747.[133] So, too, did the rates of returns.[134] However, the number of individuals who received formal removal orders climbed, and the administration increased its use of administrative removal orders, expedited removal, and reinstatement of removal—summary orders issued without an appearance before an immigration judge.[135]

From 2011 to 2015, there were 1.9 million removals, 1.4 million of them to Mexico. In 2013 alone, the total number of individuals removed reached 433,034, with the vast majority, 308,828, from Mexico, and 104,466 from Central America (see Figure 6).

In 2016, the number of removals was lower—340,056, with 245,306 from Mexico and 75,747 from Central America. Notwithstanding, individuals removed who had no criminal record continued to outpace the numbers with criminal records. More than 60 percent of those removed were listed as noncriminal.[136]

REORGANIZATION AND THE EMERGENCE OF CIS

The U.S. Commission on Civil Rights in its 1980 "The Tarnished Golden Door" report raised many concerns regarding the services the INS provided to the public. Over the years, as the INS reorganized its district offices and expanded regional centers, it addressed some concerns. To free district offices from their considerable workload, the INS transferred tasks to regional offices. The agency reduced delays by routing and processing many applications for benefits to regional offices.

The INS also developed regional centers with special expertise. Petitions for crime victims (U and T visas) and for battered spouses and children (VAWA petitions) were adjudicated by officers at the regional office in Vermont who received training on issues related to domestic violence and abuse. The INS established specialized asylum offices, where officers trained in asylum law and on the specific conditions in countries of origin handled requests for asylum. New technology permitted tracking of files, and the provision of online information about immigration and citizenship services. These and other measures improved productivity, as well as the consistency and uniformity of agency decisions.

A significant recommendation by the Commission, that the INS separate its service and enforcement functions, was accomplished when the federal government abolished the INS and developed the Department of Homeland Security (DHS). Citizenship and Immigration Services (CIS) was established as a separate subagency within DHS. Citizenship and Immigration Services (CIS) met regularly with local immigration attorneys and conducted outreach to other community-based organizations. The CIS website provided all benefit applications online, including detailed eligibility information and instructions. Under INS, a single legal team dealt with both service and enforcement components of the agency. CIS developed its own team of attorneys, which specialized in immigration benefits and provided advice to CIS adjudicators.

Notwithstanding, many concerns remain. CIS receives substantially less funding than the enforcement arms of DHS, CBP, and ICE. CIS must rely on fees paid by the public for operations. Over the years, fees have climbed to very high rates, making some applications, including naturalization, out of reach to low-income applicants.[137]

The number of applications filed with CIS has climbed considerably, but the agency does not have sufficient staff numbers to expeditiously process and adjudicate cases. Applicants for benefits complain about the long waiting periods, and report that they receive little information about their pending cases.

The Commission on Civil Rights had recommended attention to workforce diversity, and INS and its successor agency, DHS, have recruited more representatives of minority groups, as well as women. However, most are in low- and mid-level positions. During the Obama administration, the DHS continued efforts to increase the number of minority and women employees, and assigned more women and minorities to upper-level positions. Examples include the CIS Director Eduardo Aguirre, and Mario Ortiz, a former aide to Senator Lloyd Bentsen, D-Texas, who was appointed the District Director of the Central Region of CIS (the Central Region encompasses the states of Texas, Oklahoma, Colorado, and New Mexico).

Diversity in upper level positions within the DHS remains a concern. The Obama administration issued a number of executive orders to promote diversity in all federal agencies. In October 2016, the administration issued an executive order specifically addressed to national security agencies, including the DHS, after the administration found that the U.S. national security agencies were less diverse than the rest of the federal government.[138]

DACA AND "DREAMERS"

Advocates for immigrants continued lobbying for comprehensive immigration reform, but Congress failed to reach agreement on any significant immigration legislation. The Obama administration relied on its own executive power to provide some relief to migrants facing removal. In 2011, the administration directed ICE to exercise prosecutorial discretion in setting its enforcement priorities to reduce the number of removals of migrants with no criminal record and with close ties to U.S. citizens and legal residents.[139] Between 2011 and 2013, DHS established new guidelines and temporarily closed more than 29,000 removal cases.

Then in June 2012, the Obama administration implemented, through an executive order, the Deferred Action for Childhood Arrivals (DACA).[140] The program enabled close to 800,000 young unauthorized migrants, who had entered the United States as children, to apply for temporary permits and employment authorization. These young people became known among supporters and advocates as "Dreamers." In 2014, the administration announced an extension of DACA to expand the number of young migrants. A new program, DAPA (Deferred Action for Parents of Americans), to provide protections to the unauthorized parents of U.S. citizens and legal residents, was introduced.[141] However, after several states sued and obtained an injunction, the program for parents was never implemented.[142]

Immigration Under President Trump

Possibilities for change in law and policy that would benefit migrants and their families dimmed considerably after Donald Trump was elected president in November 2016. A new and virulent form of nativism dominated his 2016 presidential election campaign, harking back to a similar era in the early twentieth century.[143] As he announced his candidacy for president,

Donald Trump capitalized on fears from a marginalized segment of "white" Americans and attacked Mexican migrants, calling them criminals and rapists.[144] Throughout his campaign, Trump vowed to limit the number of refugees and immigrants admitted to the United States, to round up and deport unauthorized migrants, and to build a wall along the entire United States-Mexico border.[145]

Donald Trump's immigration related campaign promises dominated the start of the administration in 2017.[146] In his first week, Trump issued a controversial executive order to ban refugees from Syria, and to ban the entry of all nationals from seven Muslim-majority countries.[147] In September 2017, the Trump administration set the limit for refugee admissions to the United States at 45,000, the lowest since 1980.[148]

A ZERO-TOLERANCE AGENDA

On January 25, 2017, President Trump issued additional executive orders to dismantle Obama-era policies and to forge ahead with a policy of "zero tolerance" toward unauthorized migrants at the border and in the interior.[149] The order, "Border Security and Immigration Enforcement Improvement," directed the DHS to create funding plans for a border wall, to hire five thousand more Border Patrol agents, to prioritize detention, and to construct new detention facilities. The order also called for more 287(g) programs with state and local officials, and for an increase in federal criminal prosecutions of immigration offenses, including illegal entry.[150]

The Trump administration's companion executive order, "Enhancing Public Safety in the Interior of the United States," set a priority for enforcement against unauthorized migrants who were convicted of, charged with, or had committed crimes. The order essentially expanded removal against any individual who entered the United States illegally.[151] The order authorized the hiring of ten thousand ICE officers, reinstated the controversial Secure Communities program (terminating Obama's more limited PEP program), and directed state and local authorities to cooperate with DHS or face withholding of federal funding.[152]

During 2017, numbers of removals and returns at the border remained consistent with those of prior administrations.[153] However, following the

Trump directives, there was a sharp increase in the numbers of apprehensions and removals by ICE. In 2017, there was a reported 42 percent increase in the number of individuals arrested by ICE.[154] Cooperation with state and local officials led to 112,493 detainers, 81 percent more than the detainers ICE issued in 2016.[155] Removals at the border declined by 17 percent in 2017, while removals attributed to ICE enforcement in the interior increased by 25 percent.[156]

ICE maintained the agency focused on removing criminals, but in 2017, apprehensions of migrants with no criminal charges or convictions more than doubled.[157] Many of the individuals ICE reported as "criminals" had no convictions. Of those with convictions, the crimes were most often minor and nonviolent, such as traffic and misdemeanor immigration offenses.[158] By mid-2017, the Trump administration had located an additional 33,000 bed spaces for detention.[159] The first new contract for a detention facility was awarded to the GEO Group to construct an immigration detention facility in Conroe, Texas, with a capacity for one thousand detainees.[160] In 2017, the average daily population in immigration detention rose by 25 percent.[161] DHS expanded its detention policies to include many unauthorized migrants who, under earlier administrations, were routinely released pending removal proceedings.

At the Laredo Detention Center in Laredo, Texas, a facility for women, advocates discovered Mexicans among newly arrived Central American refugees. Many of the incarcerated migrants from Mexico had no criminal records, and indeed had viable claims to relief from removal due to lengthy and substantial ties to the United States, including children who were U.S. citizens.

PRESIDENT TRUMP AND THE DIVISION OF FAMILIES

In October 2017, President Trump rescinded the DACA program, effective March 2018, ostensibly so Congress could enact legislation to aid the approximately 800,000 "Dreamers."[162] The president also declined to extend temporary protected status (TPS) to another 300,000 migrants—190,000 El Salvadorans, 59,000 Haitian, 2,500 Nicaraguans, and 86,000 Hondurans.[163] For decades, TPS provided safety and economic security to Central Americans and Haitians displaced by earthquakes and hurricanes.[164]

The actions taken by the Trump administration meant that more than one million migrants from Mexico, Central America, and the Caribbean who had temporary permits to live and work in the United States were suddenly vulnerable to deportation. The president resisted Congressional proposals to provide legalization for "Dreamers" and other unauthorized migrants. Donald Trump and his team throughout 2018 continued their demands to fund more border enforcement and to reduce immigrant visas, including an end to diversity visas and a limit on family-based visas, referred to by the administration as "chain migration."[165]

While initially the Trump administration expressed some sympathy for "Dreamers," the administration rejected all legislative compromises that did not include substantial increases to the Department of Homeland Security for enforcement and detention, complete funding for a wall along all 1,954 miles of the United States-Mexico border, and the elimination of diversity and some family-based immigrant visas.[166] President Trump's efforts to end DACA and TPS protections prompted litigation in a number of federal courts in the United States, and the Trump administration vowed to protest any ruling reinstating the programs.

A WAR ON REFUGEES

In early 2018, the flow of migrants seeking refuge from drug and gang violence in Central America increased.[167] The Trump administration launched new efforts to discourage the migrants' journey, including calls for deployment of the National Guard to the border and demands that Mexico handle the migrants.[168] In May 2018, the administration announced plans to prosecute all migrants who entered the United States illegally. It was a particularly cruel option, given that migrant mothers and their young children were separated while mothers were prosecuted and sentenced to jail terms.[169]

The Trump administration continued policies of "zero tolerance" toward migrants and refugees, and began more dramatic and unprecedented measures to end migration to the United States-Mexico border. In 2019, President Trump shut down the federal government for two months in an effort to force Congress to fund the border wall. When Congress refused,

Trump redirected federal funds from other agencies to the Department of Homeland Security for construction of the wall.[170]

By 2019, officials loyal to President Trump had assumed leadership positions in the Department of Homeland Security, and the president pushed the agency to block all migrants from seeking asylum at the United States-Mexico border.[171] With little regard for the safety and well-being of detainees, including children, the DHS pursued a policy to detain all migrants apprehended at the border. Detention conditions rapidly deteriorated at Border Patrol stations, built decades before to temporarily process single men. Migrant families were housed in filthy cages, with no beds or showers and little food. During the summer 2019, members of the House of Representatives and a team of lawyers visited the Border Patrol station at Clint, Texas, and reported on migrants, including children, housed in cramped cells, suffering from "outbreaks of scabies, shingles and chickenpox," and overwhelmed by "the stench of children's dirty clothing."[172]

The Department of Homeland Security, determined to slow, or altogether stop, migrants from filing asylum claims at the United States-Mexico border, began in 2018 to process asylum applications by appointment only for migrants who lawfully sought asylum at the border ports of entry. In the interim, the migrants had to remain in Mexico pending appointments, and many were forced for weeks to camp with their children on or under international bridges.[173] In January 2019, the Department of Homeland Security issued the Migrant Protection Protocol (MPP) order, which forced all asylum-seeking migrants arriving in the United States from Mexico to remain in Mexico pending processing of asylum applications before immigration judges in removal proceedings.[174] The Mexican government authorized temporary permission for the migrants to reside in Mexico pending asylum proceedings. The Department of Homeland Security constructed immigration courts housed in tents at key ports along the United States-Mexico border.[175] Despite DHS assurances that Mexico would provide protections to migrants, advocates reported that migrants faced extremely dangerous conditions in border cities, where they were subject to kidnapping, violent attacks, and abuse at the hands of gangs and others affiliated with area drug cartels.[176]

Along with the procedural hurdles, the Trump administration imposed new legal standards for gaining asylum in the United States. Many asylum applicants, including Central Americans, had won asylum in the United States under a statutory category of persecuted "members of a particular social group."[177] In two decisions, one in 2018 authored by Attorney General Jeff Sessions[178] and another in 2019 by Attorney General William Barr,[179] the Department of Justice overturned earlier precedent decisions that defined social group categories to include survivors of severe domestic violence and family members of persecuted individuals. In July 2019, the Trump administration imposed a new rule drawn from a statutory provision that bars asylum to an applicant who has traveled through a "safe third country."[180] With no evidence that El Salvador, Guatemala, Honduras, or Mexico provided safe alternatives for asylum seekers, the rule barred Central Americans from qualifying for asylum in the United States absent evidence that they applied for and were denied asylum in a transited country.[181]

Many migrants, frustrated by and frantic about obstacles to applying for asylum imposed by the Trump administration and the frightening conditions in Mexico, tried to cross the border into the United States. Border Patrol agents reported increased numbers of sick and exhausted migrants at the border and, in some cases, the bodies of migrants who failed to make the crossing alive.[182] During one month in June 2019, Border Patrol agents found seven bodies, including a woman and her three young children who died of heat exhaustion and dehydration near McAllen, Texas.[183]

Reforming Our Immigration Laws and Practices: Congressional Action

In the early twentieth century, Texas was the first destination for Mexican migrants as they traveled north to build the railroads, ranches, and mines of the Southwest. The ebb and flow of migration of Mexicans and Central Americans, most seeking jobs, safety, and reunification with family, have been met with ever greater restrictions. Ultimately, Texas and other Southwest states that border Mexico have become militarized zones dedicated to large-scale federal immigration enforcement, based principally on unfounded charges that migrants and immigrants are a threat to the safety and security of the United States.

In the past twenty-five years, the federal government has deported and removed more individuals, most from Mexico and Central America, than at any other time in its history. More than eleven million unauthorized migrants reside in the United States. One and a half million live in Texas. Most are from Mexico and Central America, have resided in the United States more than ten years, and live in fear that they will be rounded up and banished from their families and communities.

Each year Congress pours billions of taxpayer dollars into funding immigration enforcement and the detention centers that blanket the Southwest. At the same time, Congress has stripped from immigration law measures that would provide relief from removal, and has refused to pass reforms beneficial to migrants and refugees. Without changes in law and direction, a comprehensive package of immigration reform, hundreds of thousands of migrants, their families, and other border residents will continue suffering incalculable losses and hardships.

In 2018, fifty years had passed since the U.S. Commission on Civil Rights met in San Antonio, Texas, to consider challenges facing Mexican Americans in the southwestern United States, especially those living along the United States–Mexico border. The U.S. Commission on Civil Rights now should initiate a comprehensive investigation into the conditions that migrants, immigrants, and other border residents face in the southwestern United States, affecting the lives of Mexican Americans already living in these states. As part of its investigation, the following recommendations for reform should be considered.

ENFORCEMENT AND MILITARIZATION ON THE UNITED STATES–MEXICO BORDER

In 1995, an estimated 5.7 million unauthorized migrants resided in the United States. By 2000, the number had reached 8.6 million, and in 2007, it climbed to approximately 12.2 million individuals.[184] Following a decline in 2009, the population of unauthorized migrants reached a peak of 12.2 million in 2007 and dropped to 10.5 in 2017.[185] The U.S. government has failed in its mission, "if one measures the effectiveness of border enforcement by the size

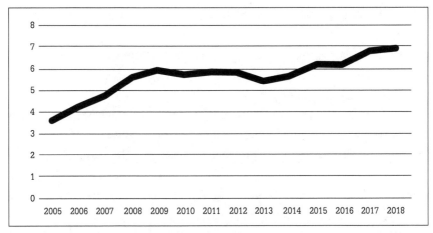

Figure 7. ICE Annual Budget (in billions of dollars), 2005–2018. *Source:* J. Rachel Reyes, "Immigration Detention: Trends and Scholarship," Center for Immigration Statistics, citing records obtained from Department of Homeland Security and Immigration and Customs Enforcement.

of the undocumented population."[186] The annual budget for ICE enforcement has almost doubled since 2005; however, despite billions of taxpayers' dollars spent of enforcement efforts, unauthorized migrants continued to cross the border, and most migrants already in the United States have chosen to stay and not risk capture on a fortified border (see Figure 7).

Costs to the taxpayer are not the only expense. The advisory committees to the U.S. Commission on Civil Rights reported in 1997, and the Commission found in 2003, that increased enforcement and changes in Border Patrol tactics force traveling migrants into more dangerous areas. Between 1994 and 2009, from 3,381 to 5,607 migrants died on the border from heat exposure, exhaustion, and dehydration.[187] Migrants are increasingly dependent on smugglers, who are part of dangerous trafficking rings and sometimes abandon their charges in the heat of the desert.[188]

Unauthorized migrants have established strong ties to the United States. Experts state that a majority of them (66+ percent) have resided in the United States longer than ten years.[189] Migrants who have settled in the United States and are then removed suffer severe hardships. They are separated from their families and communities, and they may be barred from returning to the United States for years or for life.

Harsh immigration enforcement disrupts migrant families and entire communities. In studies organized between 1998 and 2009, Jacqueline Hagan, Brianna Castro, and Nestor Rodriguez interviewed migrants, their families, and community leaders in several locations, including in Texas.[190]

Their research, published in the *North Carolina Law Review*, found that migrants and their families were constantly in fear and withdrew from community events, school activities, and government-funded services.[191] Many reported that they had been stopped by immigration officials for verification of their citizenship. A majority knew of someone who had been arrested by local officials and then deported. Increased enforcement had "dramatic economic, social, and psychological effects on immigrants, their families, and the communities where they live and work."[192]

The damage caused by heavy enforcement is not isolated to a few communities. An estimated 11.1 million unauthorized migrants and their families reside in the United States.[193] The number of Mexicans represented in the population has dropped slightly, but in 2016, Mexicans accounted for about 50 percent of the total.[194] It is Central Americans who are growing faster than any other national group. Between 2007 and 2015, the unauthorized population of Central Americans grew by 26 percent.[195]

California leads with the highest population—2.35 million, of which 71 percent are from Mexico. Texas is reported to have the second highest number of unauthorized migrants living in the United States—approximately 1.65 million, with 71 percent from Mexico. The combined populations of unauthorized migrants in the four border states of California, Arizona, New Mexico, and Texas is 4.4 million. This number represents approximately 40 percent of the total population of unauthorized migrants in the United States (see Figure 8).[196]

The effect of immigration enforcement is most severe on the children of migrants. An estimated four million U.S. citizen children live with an unauthorized migrant parent.[197] In their interviews with migrants who had been deported, Hagan, Castro, and Rodriguez found that 73 percent were parents of young children and 90 percent of the children were U.S. citizens. They report that the deported migrants and their children suffered from the financial and emotional effects of separation.[198]

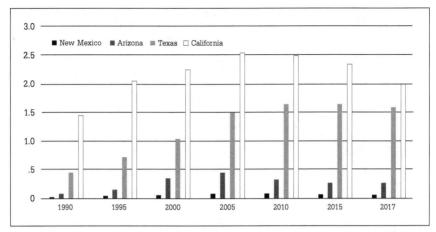

Figure 8. Unauthorized Immigrant Population in Southwestern States, 1990–2017 (in millions). *Source:* Jeffrey Passel, "Unauthorized Migration: Numbers and Characteristics," Pew Research Center; Pew Research, "Unauthorized immigrant population trends for states, birth countries and regions," June 12, 2019, online at pewresearch.org.

In 2010, the Urban Institute examined the impact on children in a study of eighty-five families following the arrest, detention, and removal of a parent.[199] The report found that family income dropped, housing conditions declined, and children experienced significant behavioral problems even during a short-term separation from a detained parent. "In the short term, six months or less after a raid or other arrest, about two-thirds of children experienced changes in eating and sleeping habits. More than half of the children in our study cried more often and were more afraid, and more than a third were more anxious, withdrawn, clingy, angry, or aggressive," they wrote. "A majority of children experienced four or more of these behavior changes."[200]

RECOMMENDATIONS ON BORDER ENFORCEMENT

- Congress should conduct hearings on the state of federal enforcement on the United States-Mexico border.
- Congress should suspend additional funding for immigration enforcement pending passage of comprehensive immigration reform.

- The federal government should suspend removal proceedings against unauthorized migrants and long-term immigrants who would benefit from comprehensive immigration reform.
- U.S. officials should consider initiating long-term bilateral talks with source countries of unauthorized migration, principally Mexico and countries in Central America, to implement solutions to the regions' economic instability and violent conditions.

DETENTION OF IMMIGRANTS

In 1996, under the IIRIRA, Congress mandated detention for a broad range of immigrants who were arrested pending removal proceedings, and the federal government has expanded immigration detention as it has rescinded prior policies for release of those unauthorized migrants not covered by mandatory detention rules. The result is a dramatic increase in detention facilities and a new industry of for-profit prisons.

Advocates have expressed alarm, particularly over the deteriorating conditions of confinement and the inability of detainees to locate attorneys or defend themselves in removal proceedings. A number of investigations have been conducted, including one launched by the U.S. Civil Rights Commission in 2015. Among the recommendations proposed by the Commission was a call on Congress to reduce funding for immigration detention (see Figure 9).[201]

Immigration advocates have charged that substandard health services in immigration detention facilities have contributed to injuries and deaths of many detainees. There are reports that between 2003 and 2015, at least 150 individuals died while in immigration detention.[202] The causes of deaths include cancer, heart conditions, suicide, and other injuries/conditions.[203] Advocates and families of the deceased contend that ICE and contracted officials have undercounted the number of deaths and covered up details of cases to avoid liability and scrutiny by the media.[204] The nonprofit, nonpartisan group Texas Appleseed investigated immigration detention in Texas, where it found that health care services varied in the facilities and that detainees with mental health conditions received little or substandard care.[205]

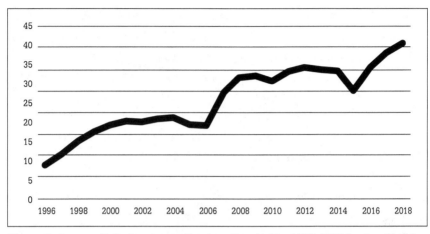

Figure 9. Average Daily Immigrant Detainee Population, 1996–2018 (in thousands). *Source:* J. Rachel Reyes, "Immigration Detention: Recent Trends and Scholarship," Center for Immigration Statistics.

Women comprise 10 percent of the population in immigration detention, and investigations conducted on women's facilities have found that detainees receive little, if any, specialized care, and are often the victims of abuse. In 2009, Human Rights Watch reported that, based on its investigation, "ICE policies unduly deprive women of basic health services. And even services that are provided are often unconscionably delayed or otherwise seriously substandard."[206] Reports surfaced that women were sexually abused by detention staff at Hutto, Willacy County, and Port Isabel. Some officers were terminated and even prosecuted.[207] In 2011, the ACLU sought data on sexual abuse, and obtained two hundred written allegations of abuse. The majority of allegations, fifty-six, came from Texas facilities.

The Obama administration vowed to improve conditions of detention, and in 2008 and 2011 ordered ICE to comply with national detention standards.[208] Yet ICE continues its expansion of immigration detention and a reliance on the same jails and for-profit prisons.[209] In its 2015 report, the Civil Rights Commission found that ICE facilities were not in compliance with detention standards for medical care.[210] Facilities, including some in Texas, ignored serious medical conditions and delayed transfer of detainees to hospitals.[211] The Commission also found that the Department of Homeland Security failed to properly train its staff regarding sexual abuse, or to provide detainees with procedures to report sexual abuse.[212] The Commission recommended that DHS comply with all appropriate detention standards, and that it ensure compliance in its contract facilities.[213]

U.S. laws guarantee that individuals in immigration cases have a right to counsel, although "at no expense to the Government."[214] Without federally funded legal services, individuals in removal proceedings must rely on representation by private attorneys or the few nonprofit legal assistance programs found generally in large urban centers or law schools. The Commission found that immigration detention impedes access to counsel.[215] ICE detention facilities are located in remote areas, far from the urban population centers where detainees and their families could more easily access immigration lawyers and nonprofit legal organizations. The South Texas Detention Complex in Pearsall, Texas, the Family Residential Centers in Dilley and Karnes City, Texas, and the Laredo Detention Center in Laredo, Texas, are all one hour or more driving distance from San Antonio, Texas.

Furthermore, immigration detention facilities have limited space allocated for visitation. Consequently, lawyers often wait hours to see their detainee clients. The Southwest Detention Complex in Pearsall, Texas, is operated by the GEO. The for-profit company's facility was opened in 2005, and has a capacity to detain 1,900 individuals. The space allocated for attorney/client consultation consists of only four rooms.

The Laredo Detention Center offers only two rooms dedicated for attorneys to meet with clients. Lawyers who provide legal representation to detainees from these facilities report that they may wait from two to five hours before they can gain access to a client.[216] Many private immigration attorneys decline to accept detained clients due to the costs and time constraints involved in traveling to remote facilities and waiting hours to speak to a client.[217]

The Civil Rights Commission also found other obstacles to obtaining counsel at immigration detention facilities. Detainees must use pay phones, access to translators is restricted, and lawyers cannot bring cell phones or computers into facilities. In a study on access to individuals in removal proceedings, published in the *University of Pennsylvania Law Review*, researchers analyzed 1.2 million removal cases from 2007 to 2012. They found that 86 percent of those individuals who were detained did not have an attorney, compared to 34 percent of individuals who were not detained.[218] Mexicans and Central Americans have the highest rates of detention and, according to the study, are the least likely of all national groups facing removal proceedings to obtain legal counsel.[219] The study also confirmed that obtaining legal counsel is critical to success for an individual in a removal case. "Their cases are more likely to be terminated, they are more likely to seek relief. And they are more likely to obtain the relief they seek."[220]

The Commission concluded that "Congress should pass, and the President should sign, legislation extending the right to counsel in immigration detention proceedings for all indigent detainees."[221]

RECOMMENDATIONS ON DETENTION

- Congress should suspend funding for immigration detention pending implementation of uniform standards of care.
- Congress should suspend funding to for-profit prisons and pass legislation prohibiting immigration detention in for-profit prisons.
- Congress should repeal mandatory detention and reinstate the rights of all immigration detainees to release from detention under bond.
- Congress should amend the Immigration and Nationality Act to guarantee the right to free legal services to indigent immigration detainees.

FAMILY DETENTION AND REFUGEES SEEKING ASYLUM

IIRIRA empowers low-level immigration officers to order the removal of newly arrived migrants without providing a hearing before an immigration judge. Expedited removal orders are a serious impediment to seeking asylum, even though the statute provides the right to overcome an order if a migrant demonstrates a "credible fear" of returning to his or her country. Many migrants are unaware of their rights under U.S. immigration law and the intricacies of asylum law, and are arrested and detained in locations far from legal advocates.

The federal government has also expanded detention to include women and their children, first during the George W. Bush administration and then again during the Barack Obama administration, when an influx of refugees fleeing severe violence in Central America sought refuge in the United States. In 2014, ICE determined that the refugees were a risk to national security and should be detained without bond. ICE reinstituted "family residential facilities," at Karnes City, Texas, and Dilley, Texas. The vast majority of the detained mothers and children were survivors of severe violence and persecution in Central America. Both facilities are in remote rural areas of South Texas, far from immigration lawyers, nonprofit legal organizations, social workers, and psychologists.

Most of the detained families were subject to expedited removal proceedings. Immigration lawyers, law firms, and law school clinics joined in an effort to provide the refugees with emergency legal assistance needed to protect the detainees' rights to asylum and to be released from detention.[222] A number of legal challenges charging that the family detention violated laws for the protection of refugees and children were filed in state and federal courts.[223] Litigation was successful in forcing ICE to release most mothers and children within a month of apprehension.[224]

The Commission visited facilities that house mothers and children as part of its investigation into immigration detention. The Commission recommended that "DHS act immediately to release families from detention" and, further, that Congress cease funding family detention.[225]

Meanwhile, the Trump administration has seriously undermined the rights of asylum seekers. Central American asylum seekers who enter illegally, including mothers with children, have been prosecuted for illegal entry. Even after the administration claimed it would stop separating children from their parents, it stalled reunification of the families, continued expansion of family detention facilities, and sought to indefinitely detain asylum seekers and their children.[226] In 2018-2019, the administration took extraordinary steps to turn away Central American asylum seekers at the United States-Mexico border. The administration required that all asylum seekers remain in Mexico under dangerous conditions for the duration of processing asylum claims. The Trump administration has undermined

Central American asylum claims by changing legal standards for gaining asylum and mandating that migrants first seek asylum in Mexico and other Central American countries.

RECOMMENDATIONS ON ASYLUM SEEKERS

- Congress should suspend funding for family detention of those seeking asylum.
- The federal government should immediately release asylum seekers and their children from detention and end all practices that discourage refugees from seeking asylum.
- The federal government should immediately cease returning asylum seekers to Mexico and should permit expeditious and fair processing of asylum claims made at the border.
- The federal government should immediately cease denying asylum applications of Central Americans based on "safe third country" transit through Central America and Mexico.
- Congress should repeal expedited removal and reinstate the right to removal proceedings before an immigration judge.
- Congress should pass legislation that guarantees the rights of asylum seekers to petition for asylum free from detention and prosecution for illegal entry.
- Congress should pass legislation that guarantees the right to free legal services for indigent refugees and applicants for asylum.

LEGALIZATION AND APPLICATIONS FOR RELIEF FROM REMOVAL

The federal government has built a capacity to arrest, detain, and remove hundreds of thousands of unauthorized migrants. This includes a generation of young migrants, or "Dreamers," who were brought to the United States by their parents, and Central Americans, who have until recently been protected from removal by permits under temporary protected status permits.

The IIRIRA, passed by Congress in 1996, exposed thousands of long-term immigrants with criminal convictions to removal without regard to their length of residence or family ties. The IIRIRA increased the chances that most unauthorized migrants and long-term immigrants who are placed in removal proceedings would ultimately be removed. While immigration judges once "wielded broad discretionary authority to prevent deportation," the IIRIRA "limited the authority of judges to alleviate the harsh consequences of deportation."[227] To date, Congress has failed to pass any comprehensive immigration reform that would restore applications for relief from removal. Congress as of 2018 also refused to provide any form of legalization to protect unauthorized migrants from removal.[228]

The IIRIRA repealed a provision known as 212(c) relief, a benefit that, since 1917, provided relief to most immigrants charged with deportation based on a criminal conviction. Congress replaced the section with a new application, cancellation of removal, but made relief unavailable to any immigrant convicted of an aggravated felony. Because the IIRIRA also expanded the list of aggravated felonies, the restrictions on relief left hundreds of thousands of immigrants with no opportunity to convince immigration judges that removal would result in permanent banishment and incalculable hardship to U.S. family, friends, and community.

Post-IIRIRA long-term immigrants facing certain removal took their cases to federal courts. They challenged provisions in the IIRIRA that limited their appeal rights and maintained that Congress's repeal of section 212(c) relief could not be applied retroactively. In 2001, the U.S. Supreme Court held in *INS v. St. Cyr* that the IIRIRA did not bar rights to appeal to federal court.[229] The Court also restored 212(c) relief, but only to individuals convicted of offenses prior to the new legislation.

In the years that followed, advocates for immigrants continued to challenge the IIRIRA and the federal government's unrelenting efforts to detain and remove long-term immigrants charged with crimes. In many appeals to the Supreme Court, immigrants have successfully argued that the government unlawfully detained immigrants,[230] applied excessively broad interpretations for "aggravated felonies,"[231] and otherwise overstepped boundaries under the Constitution.[232]

Since 1940, immigration laws have also provided some form of discretionary relief to unauthorized migrants who could establish long residence in the United States. The 1962 statute required that an unauthorized migrant seeking "suspension of deportation" prove a minimum of seven years of presence and good moral character in the United States, and provide evidence of "extreme hardship" to the applicant and/or to immediate U.S. citizens or legal resident family members.[233] The IIRIRA dismantled "suspension of deportation" and replaced it with "cancellation of removal" for unauthorized migrants.[234]

The requirements for canceling removal—and a grant of legal status—are far more restrictive than the prior "suspension of deportation." The law requires a longer period of presence, ten rather than seven years. The IIRIRA increased the level of hardship, from "extreme" to "exceptional and extremely unusual."

The IIRIRA also changed the statute in a way that impacts those unauthorized migrants who will personally suffer hardships if removed, but who have no U.S. citizen or legal resident family. The terms of the 1962 statute allowed an immigration judge to grant "suspension of deportation" in cases where the unauthorized migrant demonstrated extreme hardship to him- or herself.[235] The IIRIRA deleted that language from the terms of the statute. Cancellation of removal is available strictly to those unauthorized migrants who have a close U.S. citizen or legal resident relative and who can demonstrate that their relatives will suffer from the heightened level of hardship.

The changes Congress made to the old "suspension of deportation" statute increase the chances that most unauthorized migrants placed in removal proceedings will be removed. This includes the "Dreamers." It is this group of talented young migrants who benefited from the DACA program in 2012,[236] and who lobby for immigration reform that will benefit them and their families.

Proposals for comprehensive immigration reform made by "Dreamers" and others include some form of legalization, the means by which unauthorized migrants can emerge from the shadows, apply for permanent resident status, and eventually apply for naturalization. Congress passed legislation in 1986, under the IRCA, which provides a model for a present-day legalization. First, the IRCA amended a section in the INA, known as "registry," which had allowed unauthorized migrants with continued residence since

1948 to apply for permanent status with the INS. The IRCA updated the "registry" residence requirement to 1972. The IRCA also instituted two forms of legalization for unauthorized migrants with residence since 1982, and for special agricultural workers. The "registry" statute remains in effect, although it benefits only those few individuals who have resided in the United States since 1972. The legalization application periods for residents (since 1982) and for special agricultural workers ended by 1988.

RECOMMENDATIONS ON RELIEF FROM REMOVAL

- Congress should pass legislation to redefine "aggravated felony" as limited to felony drug trafficking, weapons trafficking, and murder.
- Congress should pass legislation to restore pre-1996 relief from removal.
- Congress should pass legislation to restore the full rights of judicial review of removal proceedings.
- Congress should amend the statute to update the residence requirement for "registry."
- Congress should pass legalization legislation with a path to naturalization for unauthorized migrants who meet a specified length of presence in the United States and for unauthorized migrants who are parents of a U.S. citizen or legal resident child.

IMMIGRANT VISAS AND "UNLAWFUL PRESENCE" BARRIERS

Mexican admissions for legal residence, most from family-based visas, continue to outpace other national groups. Between 2000 and 2010, 1.7 million Mexican immigrants were admitted to the United States, and by 2015, the population of Mexican immigrants residing in the United States rose to 12 million. Immigrant admissions from Central America are increasing at a rate even higher than that for admissions of Mexican immigrants. Between 2007 and 2015, immigrant admissions from El Salvador, Guatemala, and Honduras grew by 24 percent.[237]

Notwithstanding, the legal process for obtaining immigrant visas discriminates against nationals, such as Mexicans, from countries with high rates of migration. Applicants wait years, even decades, for visas to become available for family-based visas.[238] The Trump administration in 2018 proposed reducing or eliminating family-based visas, posing a threat to family unification for Mexicans and Central Americans with relatives in the United States. About 20 percent of Mexican and Central American immigrants are admitted to the United States based on family-based visas.[239] The administration also proposed to eliminate diversity visas, which provide an avenue for 55,000 immigrants each year from countries with low rates of immigration.[240]

Even when visas become available, applicants with a history of unlawful presence in the United States face legal barriers that prevent them from reuniting with family for an additional ten years. The "unlawful presence" rules in the U.S. immigration laws target Mexican and Central American migrants.

RECOMMENDATIONS ON IMMIGRANT VISAS

- Congress should reject proposals to eliminate family-based and diversity immigrant visas.
- Congress should increase immigrant visas to reduce the backlog in family-based visas and amend the INA to permit issuance of family-based visas on a first come, first served basis.
- Congress should repeal the "unlawful presence" grounds for inadmissibility.

ADDRESSING GOVERNMENT MISCONDUCT

In "The Tarnished Golden Door," the U.S. Commission on Civil Rights found that enforcement of U.S. immigration laws resulted in the denial of civil rights of migrants and U.S. citizens. The Commission also found that the federal government's response to public complaints of official misconduct was deficient. In March 1997, when the Arizona, California, New Mexico, and Texas advisory committees to the Commission issued their report, the Committees found "a cause of deep concern" due to the large number and severity of abuse complaints, and concluded that procedures for redress of misconduct remained "inadequate, inaccessible, and lack the confidence of the communities most directly affected."

Federal immigration enforcement has increased dramatically, far beyond those conditions and circumstances considered by the Commission and its advisory committees. Researchers attribute increased violence toward migrants to the militarization of the border and "its accompanying security discourse."[241] Most migrants pose no threat. They come to the United States in search of jobs, for safety, or to reunite with family.[242]

Immigration lawyers, nonprofit organizations, and civil/human rights advocates maintain that migrants, U.S. citizens, and residents in border communities continue to suffer abuse by Border Patrol officers, ICE officials, detention guards, and local or state officers. The American Friends Service Committee, Amnesty International, Human Rights Watch, and the ACLU have reported cases of abuse on the border, in immigrant communities, and in detention centers. Border community organizations, such as the Southern Border Communities Coalition[243] and No More Deaths,[244] monitor abuse. In 1990, the Lawyers' Committee for Civil Rights opened the Immigrant and Refugee Rights Project in San Antonio, Texas, and for sixteen years, the committee investigated and/or litigated hundreds of cases involving INS/DHS abuse.[245]

These organizations and advocates have alleged that Border Patrol and ICE officers conduct searches and arrests based on ethnic appearance, and violate rights under the Fourth Amendment. In communities where there are high concentrations of migrants, particularly near the border and in poor border *colonias* (unincorporated neighborhoods), officers frequently stop and detain individuals at homes, on streets, and at bus stops.[246] In patrols by joint federal and state/local officers in immigrant communities, U.S. citizens and legal residents have been detained.

These organizations allege that Border Patrol officers coerce migrants and refugees to forego hearings before immigration judges, and accept immediate voluntary departure. Border Patrol officers have been accused of preparing arrest reports with false information. Frequently, arrest reports prepared by Border Patrol officers pertaining to Central American women who requested asylum will contain boilerplate language denying any fear of return to Central America. These groups report that Border Patrol and ICE agents have engaged in excessive force and, in some cases, sexual abuse of women. From 10 percent to 20 percent of individuals detained by the Border Patrol report they have been physically abused by agents. This is a significant number, considering the Border Patrol apprehends more than 400,000 individuals each year.[247]

Researchers report that injuries and deaths perpetrated by armed Border Patrol agents have increased in the past twenty-five years. In 2010, Sergio Hernández Guereca, a fifteen-year-old Mexican boy in Cd. Juarez, Mexico, was shot and killed by a Border Patrol agent standing on the United States side of the border. In 2012, José Antonio Elena Rodríguez was killed in Nogales, Mexico, by a Border Patrol officer firing his weapon from Nogales, Arizona.[248] Between 2008 and 2013, six Mexicans have died after U.S. Border Patrol officers shot across the border.[249]

Reports state that migrants have been subject to prolonged and indefinite detention even after their removal proceedings and criminal cases are completed. In one case, a detainee from El Salvador was "forgotten" by the agency after an immigration judge ordered his release. He remained detained in a detention facility in San Antonio, Texas, for 140 days.[250] Advocates allege that U.S. citizens have had their birth certificates and other documents taken by CBP inspectors at the border and by Border Patrol Officers. U.S. citizens have been detained and even removed, some with summary expedited removal orders. Many individuals who acquired U.S. citizenship through their parents have been detained and removed from the United States even when their files contain evidence of U.S. citizenship.[251]

Local and state officers have illegally stopped and detained individuals, these groups report. Migrants are targeted at traffic stops and held for the Department of Homeland Security. Local and state officers subject migrants to prolonged, indefinite detention awaiting arrival of DHS officers. Texas state officers have engaged in border policing and used military weapons and tactics that have resulted in injuries and death, according to the research of these groups.

In 2005, Governor Rick Perry declared a border emergency, and deployed state officers from the Texas Department of Public Safety to the Texas-Mexico border. The Texas Department of Public Safety (DPS) acquired military-style weapons, a helicopter, and several armored gunboats, with a plan to engage in drug interdiction. On October 25, 2012, a DPS officer flying in the helicopter shot at a pickup truck that carried unarmed migrants and no drugs. Two migrants were killed.[252] State and federal immigration officials have largely ignored vigilantes, particularly in Texas and Arizona, who have stopped, detained, and even injured migrants.[253]

Complaints of law enforcement abuse persist, yet the Department of Homeland Security has done little to improve its response.[254] A 2014 report by the American Immigration Council found that of the 809 complaints of physical, sexual and/or verbal abuse lodged against DHS from 2009 to 2012, 97 percent resulted in no action taken, and 40 percent were unresolved.[255] An ACLU report concerning 142 complaints filed against the Border Patrol from 2011 to 2014 found that only one resulted in action against an officer.

The Public Executive Research Forum (PERF), a police research and policy organization, conducted a study of Border Patrol operations following the deaths of the two teenage Mexicans, and found that Border Patrol actions contributed to deaths of unarmed individuals.[256] In March 2016, the Homeland Security Advisory Council submitted a report to the Department of Homeland Security on issues relating to DHS officer corruption and abuse. Among its findings, the council reported that U.S. Customs and Border Patrol had failed to develop an effective process for receiving complaints, and that the disciplinary process was too long to be effective.[257]

RECOMMENDATIONS FOR ADDRESSING GOVERNMENT MISCONDUCT

- Congress should conduct hearings on violence and denial of civil rights perpetrated by DHS, local and/or state police, and vigilante groups against migrants, immigrants, and residents at the United States–Mexico border.
- Congress should pass legislation to designate a federal office to receive and remedy abuse by federal immigration officers.
- Congress should pass legislation to limit the authority of state and local authorities to engage in immigration enforcement.

Notes

1. U.S. Commission on Civil Rights (USCCR), *Hearing before the United States Commission on Civil Rights: San Antonio, TX, December 9–14, 1968* (Washington, DC: GPO, 1969), testimony of Dr. Héctor García, 11–13. Also available at https://catalog.hathitrust.org/Record/001874430.
2. U.S. Commission on Civil Rights (USSCR), "The Tarnished Golden Door: Civil Rights Issues in Immigration," 1980.
3. USCCR, "The Tarnished Golden Door," iii.
4. U.S. Commission on Civil Rights (USCCR), "The State of Civil Rights at Immigration Detention Facilities," 2015, 2.
5. Arizona, California, New Mexico, and Texas Advisory Committees to the U.S. Commission on Civil Rights, "Federal Immigration Law Enforcement in the Southwest: Civil Rights Impacts on Border Communities," 1997, (hereinafter, Advisory Committees report).
6. Advisory Committees report, 80.
7. U.S. Commission on Civil Rights, "Migrant Civil Rights Issues Along the Southwest Border (2003)," (hereinafter "Migrant Civil Rights").
8. U.S. Commission on Civil Rights, "The State of Civil Rights at Immigration Detention Facilities," 2015, (hereinafter, "State of Immigration Detention").
9. "State of Immigration Detention," 171.
10. USCCR, *Hearing*, 24–36.
11. USCCR, *Hearing*, Jack B. Forbes testimony, 26–28.
12. USCCR, *Hearing*, Jack B. Forbes testimony, 25.
13. Carey McWilliams, *North From Mexico* (Greenwood Press, 1968), 61. "From El Paso to Brownville, the Rio Grande does not separate people: it draws them together." See also USCCR, *Hearing*, 461–62, Testimony, Laredo resident and VISTA Volunteer, "Chaca" Ramirez. He lamented the loss of jobs to Mexican "commuters" but recognized the ties between U.S. residents and their migrant "brothers" who are exploited by the same U.S. employers.
14. David Spener, *Clandestine Crossings: Migrants and Coyotes on the Texas-Mexico Border* (Ithaca, NY: Cornell University Press, 2009), 26; see also Neil Foley, *Mexicans in the Making of America* (Cambridge, MA: Harvard University Press, 2014), 3. For more than 150 years, the Mexican migration to the United States has been "virtually unstoppable."
15. Lawrence Cardoso, *Mexican Emigration to the United States: 1897–1931* (Tucson: University of Arizona Press 1980), 9–20, 24–27. See also Kelly Lytle Hernández, *Migra! A History of the U.S. Border Patrol* (Berkeley: University of California Press, 2010), 22–26; Foley, *Mexicans in the Making of America*, 43.
16. Cardoso, *Mexican Emigration*, 18.
17. 2015 Yearbook of Immigration Statistics, Table 2. In contrast, during 1910–1919, 185,334 Mexicans immigrated to the United States, far fewer than immigrants admitted during the same time period from countries in Europe: 1.2 million Italians, 1.1 million Russians, and 371,878 British.
18. Cardoso, *Mexican Emigration*; Kelly Lytle Hernández, *City of Inmates: Conquest, Rebellion, and the Rise of Human Caging in Los Angeles, 1771–1965* (Chapel Hill: University of North Carolina Press, 2017), 132.
19. McWilliams, *North from Mexico*, 163.
20. Jorge Durand and Patricia Arias, *La Vida en el Norte* (Guadalajara, Mexico: University of Guadalajara, 2005), 119.

21. Cardoso, *Mexican Emigration*, 21-23. "To be sure, the white community's consensus at this time labeled the Mexican as an inferior being." But workers who could only earn $0.12 per day in Mexico were willing to migrate even if conditions were harsh. U.S. employers who had economic needs for Mexican labor sent recruiters to Mexico, and opened hiring offices at the border.

22. USCCR, "The Tarnished Golden Door," 1.

23. Quota Act of 1921, 42 Stat. 50; National Origins Quota Act of 1924, 43 Stat. 153; see Foley, *Mexicans in the Making of America*, 49.

24. Cardoso, *Mexican Emigration*, 120. Employers of Mexican workers in the Southwest, joined by the Catholic and Protestant churches, lobbied to exclude Mexicans workers from quota laws. To be sure, employers were interested in their own economic stakes and expressed their openly racist views toward the workers. John Nance Garner from Texas testified that Mexicans could never become U.S. citizens because they were inferior to Anglos, and assured Congress the worker was like a "homing pigeon" and would return to Mexico. Cardoso, *Mexican Emigration*, 125. S. Parker Friselle, from California, stated that he and other growers did not intend to "build the civilization of California or any other western district upon a Mexican foundation. We take him because there is nothing else available to us." Cardoso, *Mexican Emigration*, 125-26. See also McWilliams, *North From Mexico*, 190, quoting a lobbyist who testified in Congress that Mexican laborers prefer "the sunshine against an adobe wall with a few tortillas and in the oft time he drifts across the border."

25. McWilliams, *North From Mexico*, 193-94. Mexican workers were very effective labor organizers, and they led strikes in California, Arizona, Texas, Colorado, Idaho, and Washington. See also Hernández, *City of Inmates*, 119.

26. McWilliams, *North From Mexico*, 194.

27. USCCR, "The Tarnished Golden Door," 10.

28. Francisco E. Balderrama and Raymond Rodríguez, *Decade of Betrayal: Mexican Repatriation in the 1930s* (Albuquerque: University of New Mexico Press, 2006), 151. In 2012, the Los Angeles Board of Supervisors officially apologized for the city's part in the "repatriations" and estimated that close to two million Mexicans and their U.S. citizen children were forced to relocate to Mexico during the 1930s.

29. Hernández, *City of Inmates*, 137-38. The 1929 criminalization of unauthorized border crossings was a compromise between nativists who sought to ban Mexicans and Western employers who wanted to preserve their labor force. To incarcerate the Mexican prisoners, the United States built three prisons, La Tuna at El Paso, Prison Camp #10 at Tucson, and Terminal Island in Los Angeles. *City of Inmates*, 139-44.

30. 2015 Yearbook of Immigration Statistics, Table 2. The United States admitted approximately 1,550,000 during the two decades, compared to the admission of more than 10,600,000 immigrants in the two decades between 1910 and 1929.

31. Balderrama and Rodríguez, *Decade of Betrayal*, 287. In 1942, 4,203 workers were admitted; by 1944 there were 67,860. Some of the Braceros were reported to have been deported during the "repatriations" of the 1930s.

32. PL 82-414, 66 Stat. 163. The Immigration and Nationality Act (INS) is codified at Title 8 of the United States Code (8 U.S.C.).

33. USCCR, "The Tarnished Golden Door," 11.

34. 2015 Yearbook of Immigration Statistics, 103, where it is reported that in 1954, 1,074,277 individuals were "returned."

35. USCCR, "The Tarnished Golden Door," 11.

36. PL 89-236, 79 Stat. 911.

37. 1968 Statistical Yearbook of the Immigration and Naturalization Service. Between 1960 and 1969, 3,213,749 immigrants were admitted to the United States. More than 440,000 were from Mexico, the most Mexicans to be admitted since the 1920s.

38. 1968 Statistical Yearbook of the Immigration and Naturalization Service, 3.

39. 1968 Statistical Yearbook of the Immigration and Naturalization Service. In 1960, for instance, the total number of individuals apprehended by the INS was slightly over 70,000.

40. USCCR, "The Tarnished Golden Door," 11-12.

41. 1968 Statistical Yearbook of the Immigration and Naturalization Service. The 1968 report found that 58 percent of arrests were on the border compared to 68 percent in 1966 and 81 percent in 1965.

42. 1968 Statistical Yearbook of the Immigration and Naturalization Service.

43. 1978 Statistical Yearbook of the Immigration and Naturalization Service, 2.

44. PL 94-571, 90 Stat. 2703.

45. PL 94-571, 90 Stat. 2703. The 20,000 per-country quota limits visas issued under family- and employment-based preferences. For Mexicans, family visas were backlogged in the family preference categories for adult children and siblings of U.S. citizens and the spouses and children of legal residents.

46. USCCR, "The Tarnished Golden Door," 2.

47. USCCR, "The Tarnished Golden Door," 2-3.

48. USCCR, "The Tarnished Golden Door," 13-19. The Commission also considered issues relating to the U.S. State Department and its role in issuing visas. USCCR, "The Tarnished Golden Door," 45-54. The findings and recommendations of the Commission are beyond the scope of this chapter and not discussed.

49. USCCR, "The Tarnished Golden Door," 57-75.

50. USCCR, "The Tarnished Golden Door," 23.

51. USCCR, "The Tarnished Golden Door," 40-43.

52. USCCR, "The Tarnished Golden Door," 23-31.

53. USCCR, "The Tarnished Golden Door," 31-40.

54. USCCR, "The Tarnished Golden Door," 79-95.

55. USCCR, "The Tarnished Golden Door," 96-101, 104-12.

56. USCCR, "The Tarnished Golden Door," 101-4.

57. USCCR, "The Tarnished Golden Door," 117-29.

58. PL 96-212, 94 stat. 102 (March 17, 1980).

59. PL 99-603, 100 Sta. 3359 (November 6, 1986).

60. The IRCA also amended a section of the INA, called "registry." The statute had permitted an unauthorized migrant who had been in the United States since 1948 to seek legal status. The IRCA changed the entry date to January 1, 1972, providing many unauthorized migrants another path to residency.

61. For instance, unauthorized migrants who worked on ranches did not qualify as "special agricultural workers" for purposes of IRCA legalization.

62. Congress did authorize a temporary benefit, called Family Unity, but only for the family members of legalized immigrants who entered the United States prior to May 1988. §301 of IMMACT90, PL 101-649, 104 Stat. 4978 (November 29, 1980).

63. *American Baptist Church v. Meese*, 712 F.Supp. 765 (N.D. Cal. 1989). Between 1980 and 1989, 49,786 El Salvadorans and Guatemalans were deported from the United States, 22% of the total number of individuals deported. See 1982 and 1990 Statistical Yearbooks of the Immigration and Naturalization Service.

64. *Haitian Refugee Ctr. v. Civiletti*, 503 F. Supp. 442 (S.D. Fla. 1980), modified sub nom. *Haitian Refugee Ctr. v. Smith*, 676 F. 2d 1023 (5th Cir. 1982)

65. *Sale v. Haitian Ctrs. Council*, 509 U.S. 155 (1993).

66. PL 101-649, 104 Stat. 4978 (November 29, 1990).

67. PL 103-322, 108 Stat. 1902.

68. Ruben G. Rumbaut and Walter A. Ewing, "The Myth of Immigrant Criminality and the Paradox of Assimilation: Incarceration Rates Among Native and Foreign-Born Men," Immigration Policy Center 2007, 1-2. Study of the incarceration rates of men, aged eighteen to thirty-five years, shows that native-born men are five times more likely to be jailed than the foreign-born.

69. PL 100-690, 102 Stat. 4181 (November 8, 1988).

70. Immigration Act of 1990, PL 101-649, 104 stat. 4978; Immigration and Nationality Technical Corrections Act of 1994, PL 103-416, 108 Stat. 4305. The statutes broadened the definition of "aggravated felony" to include such offenses as theft, burglary, and "crimes of violence."

71. Debra W. Meyers, "U.S. Border Enforcement: From Horseback to High Tech," Migration Policy Institute, November 2005, 4.

72. Meyers, "From Horseback to High Tech," 4. Border enforcement received 57 percent of funding, and employer sanctions only 27 percent.

73. Meyers, "From Horseback to High Tech," 3.

74. Alan Bersin, "Reinventing Immigration Law Enforcement in the Southern District of California," Federal Sentencing Reporter, March/April 1996.

75. Transactional Records Access Clearinghouse (TRAC) Special Advisory (July 26, 1999).

76. Transactional Records Access Clearinghouse (1999).

77. Karl Eschnach, Jacqueline Hagan, Nestor Rodriguez, Rubén Hernández-León, and Stanley Bailey, "Death at the Border," *International Migration Review* 33, no. 2 (1999): 430.

78. Advisory Committee Report, 1.

79. Advisory Committee Report, 3-5. In April 1990 hearings were held by the House Committee on Foreign Affairs on "Allegations of Violence Along the U.S.-Mexico Border." Newspapers reported on violence at the border. The *Washington Post* published an article stating that "U.S. Border Patrol agents shot six Mexicans in the last year, killing four of them," and that none of the agents had been prosecuted. In November 1990, the presidents of Mexico and the United States met and discussed border violence.

80. Advisory Committee Report, at 10, quoting from Kitty Calavita, "The Immigration Policy Debate: Critical Analysis and Future Options," paper published in Wayne A. Cornelius and Jorge A. Bustamante, *Mexican Migration in the United States* (San Diego: Center for U.S.-Mexican Studies, University of California, San Diego, 1989), 166.

81. 1997 Report, 33.

82. 1997 Report, 80.

83. 559 F. Supp. 842 (W.D. TX. 1982)

84. 559 F. Supp. at 850-51.

85. 809 F. Supp. 487 (W.D. Tex. 1992).

86. 809 F. Supp. 487, 497.

87. Advisory Committees Report, 80.
88. Advisory Committees Report, 80.
89. "Migrants Civil Rights Issues."
90. "Migrant Civil Rights Issues."
91. "Migrant Civil Rights Issues."
92. PL 104-132, 110 Stat. 1214 (April 24, 1996).
93. PL 104-208, 110 Stat. 3009 (September 30, 1996).
94. Doris Meissner, Donald M. Kerwin, Muzaffar Chishti, and Claire Bergeron, "Immigration Enforcement in the United States: The Rise of the Formidable Machinery," Migration Policy Institute, January 2013, at 9.
95. The statute increased the number of offences included in the definition of "aggravated felony" by decreasing the sentencing requirements. For instance, pre IIRIRA, a theft offense required a five-year sentence to qualify as an "aggravated felony." IIRIRA reduced the threshold sentence to one year.
96. PL 106-386, 114 Stat. 1464 (October 28, 2000).
97. Barbara Hines, "An Overview of U.S. Immigration Law and Policy Since 9/11," *Texas Hispanic Journal of Law and Public Policy* 12 (2006): 12.
98. Kevin R. Johnson and Bernard Trujillo, "Immigration Reform, National Security After September 11, and the Future of North American Integration," *Minnesota Law Review* 91 (2000): 1369, 1370; Barbara Hines, "An Overview of U.S. Immigration Law," *Texas Hispanic Journal of Law and Public Policy*, 12 (2006): 10, 13.
99. PL 107-56, 115 Stat. 272 (October 26, 2001).
100. PL 107-296, 116 Stat. 2135 (November 25, 2002).
101. PL 107-173, 116 Stat. 543 (May 14, 2002).
102. Meyers, "From Horseback to High Tech," 9.
103. Johnson and Trujillo, "Immigration Reform," 1369, 1370; Jeremy Slack et al., "The Geography of Border Militarization: Violence, Death and Health in Mexico and the United States," *Journal of Latin American Geography* 15 (2016): 1, 10.
104. Meissner et al., "Immigration Enforcement in the United States," 7, 10.
105. Meissner et al., "Immigration Enforcement in the United States," 10.
106. John J. Hudak, Elaine C. Kamarack, and Christine Stenglein, "Hitting the Wall: On Immigration, Campaign Promises Clash with Policy Realities," Brookings Center for Effective Public Management, June 22, 2017.
107. Meissner et al., "Immigration Enforcement in the United States," 102.
108. Meissner et al., "Immigration Enforcement in the United States," 102.
109. Meissner et al., "Immigration Enforcement in the United States," 104.
110. Meissner et al., "Immigration Enforcement in the United States," 107.
111. Meissner et al., "Immigration Enforcement in the United States," 110.
112. The Intelligence Reform and Terrorism Prevention Act of 2004, PL 108-458, 118 Stat. 3638 (December 14, 2004), appropriated funds for a minimum of eight thousand beds.
113. Meissner et al., "Immigration Enforcement in the United States," 19. The lock-up quota of 34,000 beds has been criticized as an authorization to ramp up enforcement and as protection for the private for-profit prison industry; Michelle Chen, "The Deportation System's 'Lock-up Quota' Is Just as Bad as It Sounds," *The Nation*, July 11, 2016.
114. Meissner et al., "Immigration Enforcement in the United States," 125.
115. Meissner et al., "Immigration Enforcement in the United States," 131.

116. Livia Luan, "Profiting from Enforcement: The Role of Private Prisons in U.S. Immigrant Detention," Migrant Policy Institute, May 8, 2018.

117. "Halfway Home: Children in Immigration Custody," Report, The Women's Refugee Commission, 2007. The report condemned the detention of children, and describes the scene at Hutto: "Young children wore prison jumpsuits and played behind concertina wire on the days when they were allowed outside at all."

118. EOIR, U.S. Department of Justice, https://www.justice.gov/eoir .

119. Ingrid V. Eagly and Steven Shafer, "A National Study of Access to Counsel in Immigration Court," *University of Pennsylvania Law Review* 164 (2015): 35-36.

120. "Immigration, Central American Deportation Cases Dominate U.S. Immigration Courts," TRAC Reports (August 2015).

121. Meissner et al., "Immigration Enforcement in the United States," 13. Between 2000 and 2003, the workload was four hundred cases per judge; from 2008-2009, the workload rose to six hundred per judge; "Justice for Immigration's Hidden Population (2010)," Texas Appleseed Report, 14.

122. Meyers, "From Horseback to High Tech," 4.

123. Meissner et al., "Immigration Enforcement in the United States," 126.

124. "Justice for Immigration's Hidden Population (2010)," Texas Appleseed Report, 9.

125. "Justice for Immigration's Hidden Population (2010)," Texas Appleseed Report. In its investigation of immigration detention, Texas Appleseed found detainees who had been in detention for four months and some for as long as a year.

126. Meissner et al., "Immigration Enforcement in the United States," 12. By the mid-2000s, changes in Mexico, including "lower fertility rates, fewer younger workers entering the labor force, steady economic growth, and the rise of the middle class," contributed to reducing the rate of border crossings.

127. 2016 Yearbook of Immigration Statistics.

128. Meissner et al., "Immigration Enforcement in the United States," 114-15.

129. 2007, 2016 Yearbooks of Immigration Statistics.

130. Meissner et al., "Immigration Enforcement in the United States," 104-5. The administration changed its policies regarding 287(g) programs in response to charges of racial profiling by many local authorities; U.S. Department of Homeland Security Advisory Council, "Immigration Task Force on Secure Communities, September 2011, 7. Recommendations made to DHS to focus on enforcement against individuals with serious criminal convictions, rather than persons with no criminal record, young individuals brought to the United States as children, and military veterans.

131. American Immigration Council, "Immigration Detainers Under the Priority Enforcement Program," January 25, 2017.

132. Meissner et al., "Immigration Enforcement in the United States," 128-30. The administration sought to increase alternatives to detention, reduce contracts with for-profit prisons, permit release of asylum seekers who demonstrated a credible fear of return to their countries, and improve conditions in immigration detention facilities.

133. 2016 Yearbook of Immigration Statistics.

134. Meissner et al., "Immigration Enforcement in the United States," 125; As the rates of apprehensions of Mexicans have declined, so has the number of "voluntary returns." 2016 Immigration Annual Report: Immigration Enforcement Action, 11.

135. 2016 Immigration Annual Report: Immigration Enforcement Actions, 8, Table 6. In 2010, 40 percent of removal orders were issued by immigration judges, and 60 percent were administrative orders issued by DHS officers. By 2016, the number of administrative orders increased to 83 percent of the total.

136. 2016 Yearbook of Immigration Statistics.

137. As of 2018, the filing fee required for a naturalization application was a total of $725. U.S. Citizenship and Immigration Services, http://www.uscis.gov.

138. Executive Order, "Promoting Diversity and Inclusion in the National Security Workforce," October 5, 2016.

139. Department of Homeland Security, "Exercising Prosecutorial Discretion Consistent with Civil Enforcement Priorities of the Agency for the Apprehension, Detention and Removal of Aliens," June 17, 2011.

140. Department of Homeland Security, "Exercising Prosecutorial Discretion with Respect to Individuals Who Came to the United States as Children," June 15, 2012.

141. Department of Homeland Security, "Deferred Action for Parents of Americans and Lawful Permanent Residents," November 20, 2014; The U.S. Commission on Civil Rights commended President Obama on his DACA and DAPA executive orders. "State of Immigration Detention," 6.

142. See *Texas v. U.S.*, 787 F. 3d 733 (5th Cir. 2015).

143. Vivian Yee, "In Trump's Immigration Remark, Echoes of a Century-Old Racial Ranking," *The New York Times*, January 13, 2018, https://www.nytimes.com/2018/01/13/us/trump-immigration-history.html; Steve Phillips, "Trump Wants to Make America White Again," *The New York Times*, February 15, 2018, https://www.nytimes.com/2018/02/15/opinion/trump-wants-to-make-america-white-again.html.

144. Michael D. Shear and Julie Hirschfeld, "Stoking Fears, Trump Defied Bureaucracy to Advance Immigration Agenda," *The New York Times*, December 23, 2017.

145. Ariel Dorfman, "A Lesson on Immigration From Pablo Neruda," *The New York Times*, February 21, 2018. The United States was not alone in facing anti-immigrant campaigns. In the 2017 presidential campaign in Chile, politicians blamed immigrants for crimes and demanded that a wall be built on the borders with Peru and Bolivia. The article recounts a similar time in 1939 when right-wing Chileans protested the admission of refugees, and Pablo Neruda and other humanitarians succeeded in rescuing two thousand refugees of the Spanish Civil War.

146. See Adam Serwer, "Jeff Sessions's Unqualified Praise for a 1924 Immigration Law," *The Atlantic*, January 10, 2017. Sessions was reported to have criticized the 1965 Immigration Act and called for a return to the 1924 quota laws.

147. "Timeline of the Muslim Ban," American Civil Liberties Union of Washington, 2017–2018, https://www.aclu-wa.org/pages/timeline-muslim-ban; Hudak et al., "Hitting the Wall," 2. The order was hastily issued without any review within government channels, and it was poorly drafted. It trapped legal permanent residents who were traveling to the United States from the targeted countries. It caused confusion, and massive protests, at airports in the United States and around the world. Within days, the order was blocked by several federal courts. Trump issued two revised orders, and ultimately he prevailed on appeal to the Supreme Court.

148. Paul Steven Zoltan, "Immigration Law," *The Texas Bar Journal*, January 2018, 36.

149. The Brennan Center for Justice, "Criminal Justice One Year Into the Trump Administration," 2017, 2. The Trump administration continues to link crime and drugs to a need for greater border enforcement, in spite of research to the contrary.

150. "Summary of Executive Order, 'Border Security and Immigration Enforcement Improvement,'" American Immigration Council, February 27, 2017; Hudak et al., "Hitting the Wall," 4, 9. The Trump administration's insistence on building a wall and hiring thousands of enforcement officers has been challenged as unnecessary and exorbitantly expensive. Estimates to build a wall range from $25 to 70 billion, costs that do not include the yearly maintenance expenses. Hiring massive numbers of enforcement officers also entails challenges and enormous expenses. Hiring just 3,500 Border Patrol officers is estimated to cost more than $6 billion over a ten-year period.

151. Nick Miroff and Maria Sacchetti, "Trump Takes 'Shackles' Off ICE, Which Is Slapping Them on Immigrants Who Thought They Were Safe," *The New York Times*, February 11, 2017. "The Trump administration has given street-level ICE officers and field directors greater latitude to determine whom they arrest and under what circumstances, breaking with the more selective enforcement approach of President Barack Obama's second term."

152. "Summary of Executive Order, 'Enhancing Public Safety in the Interior of the United States,'" American Immigration Council, May 19, 2017.

153. 2017 Yearbook of Immigration Statistics, Table 39.

154. 2017 ICE Enforcement and Removal Operations Report (2018).

155. Brennan Center for Justice, "Criminal Justice," 7. There was also, however, an increase in the number of detainers that cities refused to honor, and some cities have sued to challenge the administration's threats to cut off federal funds.

156. 2017 ICE Enforcement and Removal Operations Report (2018).

157. 2017 ICE Enforcement and Removal Operations Report (2018).

158. 2017 ICE Enforcement and Removal Operations Report (2018); Brennan Center for Justice, "Criminal Justice," 6.

159. David Nakamara, "U.S. Devising Nationwide System for Mass Deportations of Illegal Immigrants," *The Washington Post*, April 12, 2017.

160. Meredith Hoffman, Associated Press, "First New Immigration Detention Center to Build in Conroe," *Houston Chronicle*, April 13, 2017; Ben Protess, Manny Fernandez, and Kitty Bennett, "Some Contractors Housing Migrant Children Are Familiar to Trump's Inner Circle," *The New York Times*, July 18, 2018. The prison industry, which stands to earn billions in profits, has strong ties to the Trump administration: https://www.nytimes.com/2018/07/18/us/migrant-children-family-detention-doctors.html.

161. Brennan Center for Justice, "Criminal Justice," 7.

162. Alicia Parlapiano and Karen Yourish, "A Typical 'Dreamer' Lives in Los Angeles, Is From Mexico and Came to the U.S. at 6 Years Old," *The New York Times*, January 23, 2018. Most DACA recipients, more than 222,000, live in California; 124,300 live in Texas. The majority are Latino, with 79% from Mexico. The median age when DACA beneficiaries entered the United States is six years, and the most common age is three.

163. Miriam Jordan, "Trump Administration Ends Temporary Protection for Haitians," *The New York Times*, November 20, 2017; Miriam Jordan, "Trump Administration Says that Nearly 200,000 Salvadorans Must Leave," *The New York Times*, January 8, 2018; Miriam Jordan, "Trump Administration Ends Protected Status for Thousands of Hondurans," *The New York Times*, May 4, 2018.

164. D'Vera Cohn, Jeffrey S. Passel, and Ana Gonzalez-Barrera, "Rise in U.S. Immigrants From El Salvador, Guatemala and Honduras Outpaces Growth From Elsewhere," Pew Research Center, December 7, 2017, 13.

165. Steve Phillips, "Trump Wants to Make America White Again," *The New York Times*, February 15, 2018, https://www.nytimes.com/2018/02/15/opinion/trump-wants-to-make-america-white-again.html. However, efforts to roll back racial and ethnic diversity in the United States are unlikely to succeed. When the Immigration Act of 1965 eliminated the visa quotas of the 1920s, 12 percent of the U.S. population was non-white. In the decades that followed, the non-white population of the United States has risen to 39 percent.

166. Editorial Board, "Trump Dangles Hope for Dreamers," *New York Times*, January 25, 2018.

167. 2018 Border Patrol Report on Southwest Border Apprehensions by Sector (2019). By the end of the 2018 fiscal year, the Border Patrol had apprehended more than 450,000 individuals at the border, the most in twelve years.

168. Julie Hirschfeld Davis, "President Wants National Guard to Block Border," *The New York Times*, April 4, 2018; Kirk Semple, "A U.S. Plan to Handle People Seeking Asylum: Force Mexico to Do It," *The New York Times*, May 18, 2018.

169. Miriam Jordan and Ron Nixon, "Trump Administration Threatens Jail and Separating Children From Parents for Those Who Illegally Cross Southwest Border," *The New York Times*, May 7, 2018. The Attorney General also sent to the border an additional thirty-five prosecutors and eighteen immigration judges to handle the increased caseload.

170. Alice Hunt Friend, "The Pentagon Is Moving Money to Pay for Trump's Border Wall," *The Washington Post*, September 6, 2019. The Secretary of Defense announced the transfer of $3.6 billion from military construction projects to fund the wall.

171. Jason Zengerie, "How America Got to 'Zero Tolerance' on Immigration: The Inside Story," *The New York Times*, July 16, 2019.

172. Simon Romero, Zolan Kanno-Youngs, Manny Fernandez, Daniel Borunda, Aaron Montes, and Caitlin Dickerson, "Hungry, Scared and Sick: Inside the Migrant Detention Center in Clint, Tex.," *The New York Times*, July 9, 2019.

173. Molly Hennessey-Fiske, "Caught in Limbo, Central American Asylum-Seekers Are Left Waiting on a Bridge Over the Rio Grande," *The Los Angeles Times*, June 7, 2018.

174. "Policy Guidance for Implementation of the Migrant Protection Protocols," Department of Homeland Security, January 25, 2019.

175. Alicia Caldwell, "Trump's Return-to-Mexico Policy Overwhelms Immigration Courts," *Wall Street Journal*, September 5, 2019; Nick Miroff, "Along Texas Border Administration Sets Up Tent Courts for Virtual Asylum Hearings," *The Washington Post*, September 18, 2019. As many as 42,000 individuals have been forced to wait in Mexico for processing of asylum claims at the border, and some are living in "the most fearsome places for migrants along the length of the border."

176. "Human Rights Fiasco: The Trump Administration's Dangerous Asylum Returns Continue," Human Rights First Report, December 2019. By December 2019, there were "636 public reports of rape, kidnapping, torture, and other violent attacks against asylum seekers and migrants returned to Mexico under MPP."

177. INA §101(a)(42)(A), 8 U.S.C. §1101(a)(42)(A).

178. *Matter of A-B-*, 27 I&N Dec. 316 (A.G. 2018).

179. *Matter of L-E-A*, 27 I&N Dec. 581 (A.G. 2019).

180. INA §208(a)(2)(A), 8 U.S.C. §1158(a)(2)(A). The statute bars asylum to an applicant who had "access to a full and fair procedure" for asylum or temporary protection in a safe third country.

181. Michael D. Shear and Zolen Kanno-Youngs, "Most Migrants at Border With Mexico Would Be Denied Asylum Protections Under New Trump Rule," *The New York Times*, July 19, 2019.

182. Caitlyn Dickerson, "Desperate Migrants on the Border: 'I Should Just Swim Across,'" *The New York Times*, September 29, 2019; Abigail Hauslohner, "Border Patrol's September on the Rio Grande," *The Washington Post*, September 24, 2019.

183. Andrew Hay, "Seven Migrant Deaths Reported in 'Extreme Heat' at U.S. Border," *Reuters*, June 24, 2019.

184. Jeffrey Passel and D'Vera Cohn, "A Mexican Share Declined, U.S. Unauthorized Population Fell in 2015 Below Recession Level," Pew Research Center, April 25, 2017.

185. Passel and Cohn, "As Mexican Share Declined"; Mark Hugo Lopez, Jeffrey S. Passel, and D'Vera Cohn, "Key Facts about the Changing U.S. Unauthorized Immigrant Population," *Pew Fact-Tank*, April 13, 2021, at PewResearch.org.

186. Kevin Johnson and Bernard Trujillo, "Immigration Reform, National Security After September 11, and the Future of North American Integration," *Minnesota Law Review*, 91 (2007): 1371-72.

187. Maria Jimenez, "Humanitarian Crisis: Migrant Deaths at the U.S.-Mexico Border," ACLU of San Diego and Mexico's National Commission on Human Rights, October 1, 2009, 12; American Public Health Association, "Border Crossing Deaths: A Public Health Crisis Along the US-Mexico Border," November 10, 2009; Jeremy Slack et al., "The Geography of Border Militarization: Violence, Death and Health in Mexico and the United States," *Journal of Latin American Geography*, University of Texas Press, March 2016, 16. Since 2000, there have been 2,100 migrant remains recovered in southern Arizona, and 6 percent were children younger than age eighteen. The figures do not include the migrants who disappeared and whose remains have not been found.

188. Slack et al., "The Geography of Border Militarization," 16.

189. Passel and Cohn, "As Mexican Share Declined."

190. Jacqueline Hagan, Brianna Castro, and Nestor Rodriguez, "The Effects of U.S. Deportation Policies on Immigrant Families and Communities: Cross-Border Perspectives," *North Carolina Law Review* 8, no. 12 (2012):1799.

191. Hagan et al., "Effects of U.S. Deportation Policies, "1813-16.

192. Hagan et al., "Effects of U.S. Deportation Policies," 1822.

193. Pew Research, "U.S. Unauthorized Immigration Population Estimates," November 3, 2016.

194. Passel and Cohn, "As Mexican Share Declined."

195. Passel and Cohn, "As Mexican Share Declined.".

196. Passel and Cohn, "As Mexican Share Declined." Other states that have large unauthorized migrant populations are Florida (850,000), Illinois (450,000), New Jersey (500,000), and New York (775,000).

197. Pew Hispanic Center, "A Portrait of Unauthorized Immigrants in the United States, 2009." See also U.S. Department of Homeland Security, 2009, "Removals Involving Illegal Alien Parents of United States Citizen Children," OIG-09-15 2009. In 2009, the DHS estimated that in ten years it had removed 100,000 parents of U.S. citizen children. Recent decisions to end TPS protections affect the approximately 53,500 U.S. citizen children with a Honduran parent. Miriam Jordan, "Trump Administration Ends Protected Status for Thousands of Hondurans," *The New York Times*, May 4, 2018.

198. Hagan et al., "Effects of U.S. Deportation Policies," 1819-20.

199. The Urban Institute, "Facing Our Future: Children in the Aftermath of Immigration Enforcement," 2010.

200. The Urban Institute, "Facing Our Future," ix.

201. "State of Immigration Detention," 129.

202. Megan Granski, Allen Keller, and Homer Venters, "Death Rates Among Detained Immigrants in the United States," Center for Health and Human Rights, New York University, 2015, 1.

203. Texas Appleseed, 11. Texas Appleseed reported that in its investigation of Texas facilities, approximately 34 percent of detainees suffered from some chronic condition, and at least 15 percent had a mental disorder.

204. Nina Bernstein, "Hurdles Shown in Detention Reform," *The New York Times*, August 20, 2009; Brianna M. Mooty, "Solving the Medical Crises for Immigration Detainees: Is the Proposed Detainee Basic Medical Care Act of 2008 the Answer?," *Law and Inequality: A Journal of Theory and Practice*, University of Minnesota Law School, Vol. 28, 2010. Between 2003 and 2008 ICE reported eighty-seven deaths, but failed to include deaths that occurred after release from detention.

205. Texas Appleseed, 1-11.

206. Human Rights Watch, "Detained and Dismissed."

207. Women's Refugee Commission, "Halfway Home."

208. Granski et al., "Death Rates."

209. ACLU, Detention Watch Network, National Immigrant Justice Center, "Fatal Neglect: How ICE Ignores Death in Detention," 2012. An ACLU investigation of eight deaths in immigration custody between 2010 and 2012 found that problems persist, even after promised reforms.

210. "State of Immigration Detention," 124.

211. "State of Immigration Detention," 124.

212. "State of Immigration Detention," 124.

213. "State of Immigration Detention," 126; American Medical Association, "AMA Adopts New Policies to Improve Health of Immigrants and Refugees," June 12, 2017, http://www.ama-assn.org/ama-adopts-new-policies-improve-health-immigrants-and-refugees. On June 12, 2017, the American Medical Association, in response to inconsistent access to medical care in immigration detention, called on ICE to revise its standards.

214. See INA §292, 8 U.S.C. §1362. However, following a federal court directive in *Franco-Gonzalez v. Holder*, 767 F. Supp. 2d 1034 (CD Cal. 2010), the EOIR began appointing counsel in removal cases involving individuals suffering from mental disabilities.

215. "State of Immigration Detention," 126-27; Ingrid Eagly and Steven Shafer, "A National Study of Access to Counsel in Immigration Court," *University of Pennsylvania Law Review* 164, no. 1 (2015): 30-31.

216. Christopher Maynard, attorney with the firm Jones Day, which provides *pro bono* legal services to migrants detained in Laredo, Texas, and David Armendariz, attorney with the firm DeMott & Assoc., San Antonio, Texas, interviewed by the author, February 2, 2018.

217. Anne Monahan, attorney in San Antonio, Texas, and Christopher Maynard, interviewed by the author; Ingrid Eagly and Steven Shafer, "A National Study," 35.

218. Eagly and Shafer, "A National Study," 35, 36.

219. Eagly and Shafer, "A National Study," 45-46. Mexican detainees had a 78 percent chance to be detained, and only a 21 percent chance to obtain counsel.

220. Eagly and Shafer, "A National Study," 9.

221. "State of Immigration Detention," 126.

222. Immigration lawyers from throughout the United States traveled to Artesia, New Mexico, to provide *pro bono* assistance to Central American women. After 2014, when ICE opened new facilities in Texas, a coalition of lawyers and law students, including representatives from major law firms and law schools, the American Immigration Lawyers Association, the National Lawyers Guild Immigration Project, and RAICES, traveled to the border and provided valuable

legal assistance to families in detention.

223. In 1996, the INS and immigration lawyers representing detained children reached an agreement in the case *Flores v. Meese*, CV 85-4544-RJK (CD Ca.), and the INS agreed to release children or hold them in the least restrictive manner. The case was reopened, and in July 2015, a U.S. district judge ordered the Department of Homeland Security to comply with the *Flores v. Meese* terms of settlement with regard to all children in detention, including children with parents. Litigation was also brought against the Texas Department of Family and Protective Services for its grant of child care licenses to the Dilley and Karnes City facilities.

224. Pam Cody, "Use of Ankle Monitors for Immigrants on the Rise," *Brownsville (Texas) Herald*, March 28, 2017. The ankle monitors, which women are required to wear twenty-four hours a day, are distributed by a company contracted by GEO, a private for-profit prison company.

225. "State of Immigration Detention," 126, 129. On June 12, 2017, the American Medical Association joined social workers, psychologists, and other health professionals in calling for an end to "family immigration detention, separation of children from their parents in detention, and any plans to expand these detention centers."

226. Miriam Jordan, Katie Benner, Ron Nixon, and Caitlin Dickerson, "As Migrant Families Are Reunited, Some Children Don't Recognize Their Mothers," *The New York Times*, July 10, 2018. The Trump administration has continued its focus on mass detention, including of children, in spite of criticism from its own staff; Miriam Jordan, "Whistle Blowers Say Detaining Migrant Families 'Poses High Risk of Harm," *The New York Times*, July 18, 2018.

227. Meissner et al., "Immigration Enforcement in the United States," 113, quoting from *Padilla v. Kentucky*, 130 S.Ct. 1473, 1478 (2010).

228. Meissner et al., "Immigration Enforcement in the United States," 1. When considering immigration reform, Congress's response has been "enforcement first."

229. 533 U.S. 289 (2001).

230. *Zadvydas v. Davis*, 533 U.S. 678 (2001) (rejects indefinite detention under IIRIRA mandatory detention).

231. *Leocal v. Ashcroft*, 543 U.S. 1 (2004) (rejects government position that DWI is an aggravated felony crime of violence); *Lopez v. Gonzales*, 549 U.S. 47 (2006) (rejects government position that all state drug felonies are aggravated felony drug trafficking offenses); *Carachuri-Rosendo v. Holder*, 560 U.S. 563 (2010) (rejects government argument that aggravated drug offenses extend to second simple drug possession); *Moncrieffe v. Holder*, 133 S.Ct. 1678 (2013) (rejects government argument that conviction for possession of small amount of marijuana was aggravated felony); *Sessions v. Dimaya*, 138 S.Ct. 1204 (2018) (declared the "crime of violence" section of aggravated felony as unconstitutionally vague).

232. *Padilla v. Kentucky*, 559 U.S. 356 (2010) (guaranteed right to immigration advice by criminal defense attorney); *Vartelas v. Holder*, 132 S.Ct. 1479 (2012) (rejects government position that legal resident's brief departure following pre-IIRIRA offense supports deportability); *Pereira v. Sessions*, 138 S.Ct. 2105 (2018) (a defective notice to appear for removal proceedings does not cut off right to apply for relief).

233. Immigration and Nationality Act (INA), §244(a) (1962).

234. Immigration and Nationality Act (INA), §240A(b)(1) (1996).

235. See *Matter of OJO*, 21 I&N Dec. 381 (BIA 1996).

236. In 2012 President Obama issued an executive order, Deferred Action for Childhood Arrivals (DACA), which permitted young undocumented migrants between the ages of sixteen and thirty-one to apply for permission to stay in the United States and obtain employment

authorization. Approximately 800,000 young migrants applied for, and were granted, DACA status. President Trump rescinded the DACA executive order effective March 2018.

237. D'Vera Cohn, Jeffrey S. Passel, and Ana Gonzalez-Barrera, "Rise in U.S. Immigrants from El Salvador, Guatemala and Honduras Outpaces Growth from Elsewhere," Pew Research Center, December 7, 2017.

238. U.S. Department of State, "Visa Bulletin," January 2018. A U.S. citizen who petitions to bring from Mexico to the United States an adult son or daughter must wait twenty-two years for the visa to become available; twenty-three years for a married son or daughter; and twenty-one years for a sibling. In contrast, in January 2018 the time a U.S. citizen was scheduled to wait to bring relatives from countries not oversubscribed was considerably less: seven years for an adult child, thirteen years for a married child, and fourteen years for a sibling.

239. Thomas Kaplan and Sheryl Gay Stolberg, "House Immigration Bill, Pitched as Compromise, Tilts to a Harder Line," *The New York Times*, June 14, 2018. The Trump administration recommends reduction or elimination in the family-based visa categories, and introduction of a merit-based system. Family-based visas are issued to adult children and siblings of U.S. citizens, and spouses and children of legal residents. (The family-based visa category does not include "immediate relative visas" issued to spouses and children of U.S. citizens, which account for about 48 percent of the total visas issued, and are not part of Trump's plans to eliminate.) In 2016, more than 34,000 family based-visas were issued to Mexican relatives of U.S. citizens and legal residents. Only 6,078 Mexicans received employment-based visas. For the three Central American countries of El Salvador, Guatemala, and Honduras, there were more than 11,000 family-based visas issued; only 4,700 employment-based visas were issued.

240. Vivian Yee, "In Trump's Immigration Remarks, Echoes of a Century-Old Racial Ranking," *The New York Times*, January 13, 2018. In 2016, there were 49,805 diversity visas issued. Approximately 40 percent were received by nationals from the continent of Africa; 31 percent went to natives of Asia; and 24 percent went to Europeans. Trump was widely criticized when he was reported to have claimed that too many U.S. visas are issued to natives of "shit-hole" countries in Africa, and not enough visas to Norwegians.

241. Slack et al., "The Geography of Border Militarization," 21–22.

242. Slack et al., "The Geography of Border Militarization," 12.

243. Southern Border Communities Coalition, "Border Patrol Abuses" (undated). The coalition, formed in 2011, is a coalition of sixty border organizations from California, Arizona, New Mexico, and Texas, and tracks abuse by the Border Patrol. The organization alleges that since 2010, more than seventy individuals have suffered from abuse or died while in Border Patrol Custody. See Southern Border Communities Coalition, http://www.southernborder.org.

244. No More Deaths, "A Culture of Cruelty: Abuse and Impunity in Short-Term U.S. Border Patrol Custody," 2011. No More Deaths was formed in Arizona to prevent deaths of migrants traveling in desert climates. The organization provides food and water on migration trails. In 2012 the organization published a report, "A Culture of Cruelty," documenting allegations of Border Patrol abuse. See No More Deaths, http://www.nomoredeaths.org.

245. The Lawyers Committee for Civil Rights served as lead counsel in the case *Murillo, et al. v. Musegades*, a case involving abuse by the Border Patrol reviewed by the commission's advisory committees.

246. David Armendariz, interviewed by the author, February 2, 2018. Mr. Armendariz, of San Antonio, stated that in the previous six years, he often had removal cases in which he would file motions to dismiss based on misconduct against his clients by Border Patrol and ICE officers.

247. Slack et al., "The Geography of Border Militarization," 19; Francisco Cantú, *The Line Becomes a River* (New York: Riverhead Books-Penguin Group) 2018. The book is a memoir in which Cantú, a former Border Patrol agent, recounts incidents he witnessed of verbal, physical, and sexual abuse of migrants perpetrated by other agents.

248. John Carlos Frey, "Over the Line," *Washington Monthly* (May/June 2013).

249. Frey, "Over the Line."

250. *Arevalo v. U.S.,* CA No. 8-0066-FB (W.D. Tex., January 24, 2008).

251. Lee J. Terán, "Mexican Children of U.S. Citizens: 'Viges Prin' and other Tales of Challenges to Asserting Acquired U.S. Citizenship," *The Scholar* 14 (2012): 583.

252. Melissa del Bosque, "Death on Seven-Mile Road," *Texas Observer*, March 2, 2015.

253. Gabriela Gallegos, "Border Matters: Redefining the National Interest in U.S.-Mexico Immigration and Trade Policy," *California Law Review* 92 (2014): 1756; Hines, "An Overview of U.S. Immigration Law and Policy," 25.

254. Slack et al., "The Geography of Border Militarization," 19-21.

255. Daniel E. Martinez, Guillermo Cantor, and Walter Ewing, "No Action Taken: Lack of CBP Accountability in Responding to Complaints of Abuse," American Immigration Council, May 4, 2014.

256. Slack et al., "The Geography of Border Militarization," 21.

257. Homeland Security Advisory Council, "Final Report of the CBP Integrity Advisory Panel," March 15, 2016, 4-6; General Accounting Office, Report, "Additional Actions Needed to Strengthen CBP Efforts to Mitigate Risk of Employee Corruption and Misconduct," December 4, 2012. The GAO report found that between 2005 and 2012, 2,170 CBP officers were arrested for offenses such as driving while intoxicated and domestic violence. In total, 144 were arrested for corruption, such as smuggling or drugs, and 125 had been convicted.

JOSÉ ROBERTO JUÁREZ, JR.

Mexican American Voting Rights in Texas

When Congress established the U.S. Civil Rights Commission (the Commission) in 1957, the first charge Congress gave to the Commission was "to investigate sworn allegations that citizens are being deprived of their right to vote by reason of their race, color, religion, or national origin."[1] Yet at the Commission's 1968 hearing in San Antonio on discrimination and economic challenges faced by Mexican Americans, the focus was not on voting rights.

This oversight is remarkable, for voting discrimination has confronted Mexican Americans in Texas since statehood in 1845. Early laws prohibited native *Tejanos* from using their Spanish language, organizing political rallies, or serving as election judges.[2] From the early 1900s until the mid-1900s, Texas used poll taxes, direct primaries, and Anglo-only primaries to exclude Mexican American voters. The Texas Rangers were regularly used by Anglo political bosses to forcibly exclude Mexican Americans from attaining political power. Anglo-led structural barriers also discriminated against Mexican Americans during this period. They included multimember districts, racial gerrymandering, and malapportionment of districts.[3]

After extensive testimony regarding language discrimination in the electoral process, the Voting Rights Act was amended in 1975 to provide protection for language minorities, including Mexican Americans.[4] Under the preclearance requirement in Section 5, the State of Texas and its political subdivisions could not "enact or seek to administer any voting qualification or prerequisite to voting, or standard, practice, or procedure with respect to voting" that was different from what was in force or effect on November 1, 1972, unless the change was approved in a declaratory judgment filed by the U.S. District Court for the District of Columbia, or was not objected to by the U.S. Attorney General. Voting changes could not be made that were determined to have either a discriminatory purpose or a discriminatory effect.[5]

From 1975 until 2013, the U.S. Department of Justice repeatedly objected to proposed changes in election procedures submitted by the State of Texas and its political subdivisions. Numerous lawsuits were also filed against Texas and its political subdivisions under the Voting Rights Act, and many of those lawsuits led to court decisions declaring proof and patterns of illegal discrimination against Mexican Americans.

Despite those proven violations, an apparently less concerned U.S. Supreme Court in 2013 struck down the Section 5 coverage formula that required Texas and its political subdivisions to submit voting changes to the U.S. Department of Justice for preclearance, or to obtain approval from the U.S. District Court for the District of Columbia.[6]

Section 2 of the Voting Rights Act was unaffected. Section 2 states: "No voting qualification or prerequisite to voting or standard, practice, or procedure shall be imposed or applied by any state or political subdivision in a manner which results in a denial or abridgement of the right of any citizen of the United States to vote on account of race or color, or in contravention of the guarantees set forth in section 10303(f)(2) of this title [protecting language minorities]."[7] Federal courts continue to find intentional discrimination by Texas against Mexican Americans in Section 2 cases, even though the Fifth Circuit Court of Appeals has increasingly reversed those lower court findings by adopting legal standards that are inconsistent with long-standing discrimination case law.

Mexican American Voter Participation: 1968–2018

THE 1968 HEARINGS

While the 1968 hearings did not focus on voting rights, issues of voting rights appeared occasionally in the testimony of witnesses at the hearing.[8] Acting Staff Director Howard Glickstein asked one witness, Texas farm worker Luis Chávez, whether he had voted in the last elections in Edcouch, Texas.[9] Arnulfo Guerra of Roma, Texas, testified that chronically high poverty rates in Starr County, Texas, caused many voters there to vote for those who provided government food benefits.[10] In response to questions from Commissioner Héctor García, witness Alva Archer, a Texas district attorney from Monahans, Texas, acknowledged that no Mexican Americans served as county commissioners in Reeves County, Texas, and no Mexican Americans served as city commissioners in Pecos, Texas, even though more than 40 percent of the population was Mexican American.[11]

Only one Mexican American in California served as an assemblyman, and no state senators were Mexican Americans.[12] Anglos in the portion of eastern New Mexico known as "Little Texas" failed to support Mexican American candidates.[13] A Commission staff report stated that residency requirements for voting disenfranchised Mexican American migrant workers.[14]

A report prepared in 1968 for the Commission also noted that language laws had inhibited Mexican American participation in voting since the turn of the century.[15] The report noted:

> Although more than 85 percent of the Mexican American population is native born, political participation is relatively low, and Mexican Americans have few elected representatives in Congress and, except for New Mexico, only a handful in the State legislatures, with none at all in California. Mexican American organizations totally lack the funds and resources necessary to mount effective voter registration drives, and neither political party has shown much inclination to provide them.[16]

While representation of Mexican Americans in elected office in Texas has improved since 1968, Latinos continue to be underrepresented in many electoral posts, especially due to new obstacles to electoral participation by Mexican Americans imposed by the State of Texas in recent years. The U.S. Supreme Court's 2013 decision in *Shelby County v. Holder*, eliminating the requirement that Texas and its political subdivisions submit voting changes to the U.S. Department of Justice or to the U.S. District Court for the District of Columbia, has emboldened Texas to adopt practices that continue to limit the potential electoral power of Mexican Americans.

POPULATION CHANGES SINCE 1968

Since 1968, the racial and ethnic composition of the Texas population has shifted dramatically. The proportion of Latinos and Asian Americans has increased, although the total population of Asians remains relatively small. The proportion of African Americans has been relatively stable. The proportion of non-Hispanic white Texans has decreased significantly.[17]

By 2018, Texas was considered a "majority-minority" state, since the majority of the population comprises people traditionally considered "minorities" in the United States (see Figure 1).

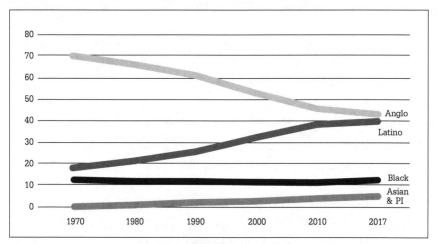

Figure 1. Percentage of Texas Population by Race, 1970–2017. *Source:* U.S. Census Bureau, decennial census counts for 1970–2010, population estimates, July 1, 2017.

However, the picture is altered when one views the persons eligible to vote. Latinos are much younger than other racial and ethnic groups and some are not citizens.

Even so, the rapid growth of the Latino population since 1968 has been accompanied by an increase in the number of eligible Latino voters. The citizen voting-age population (CVAP) of Latinos has increased from 1,876,000 in 1980 to 4,781,000 in 2016 (see Figure 2).

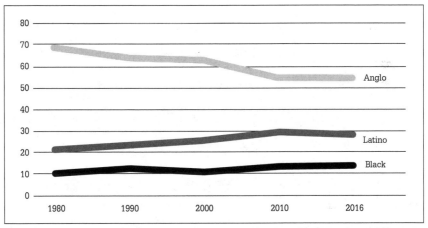

Figure 2. Percentage of Citizen Voting-Age Population (CVAP) by Race/Ethnic Group, 1980–2016.

REGISTERED VOTERS BY ETHNICITY

The number of Latinos registered to vote has also increased from 1980 to 2016. However, registration rates for Latinos lag well behind those for every other group except Asians. After 1996, just over half of eligible Latinos registered to vote in Texas. The proportion registered of eligible Latinos has never exceeded 60 percent (achieved in 2000). By contrast, registration rates for Anglos and, in recent years, African Americans regularly exceeded 70 percent (see Figure 3).

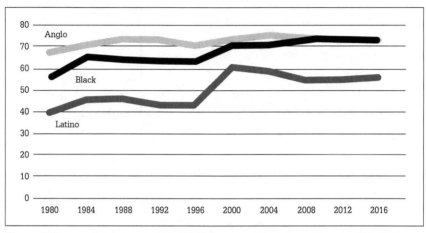

Figure 3. Percent Registered of Eligible Voters by Ethnicity in Texas, 1980–2016. *Sources:* U.S. Census Bureau, *Reported Voting and Registration by Race and Spanish Origin for States* series, Tables 5, 4, 4a, and 4b, for 1980, 1990, 2000, and 2016, respectively. Data on eligible voters sometimes extrapolated from percentages provided in the census reports.

VOTER TURNOUT BY ETHNICITY

The difference between the registration rate for Latinos and the registration rate for the group with the highest registration rate has always exceeded 12 percentage points. The average difference in registration rates since 1980 has been 22 points.

In the last ten years, the average difference has been 19 points. Not only are proportionately fewer Latinos registered to vote, but Latino turnout rates for registered voters have lagged behind that of other ethnic groups in Texas (see Figure 4). The difference between the turnout rate for Latinos and the turnout rate for the group with the highest turnout rate always exceeds 9 percentage points. The average difference in turnout rates since 1980 has been 14 percentage points (see Figure 5). While the difference in the 2016 election narrowed to 10 percent, this was not the result of any significant increase in Latino participation; instead, participation decreased among African Americans (see Figure 5).

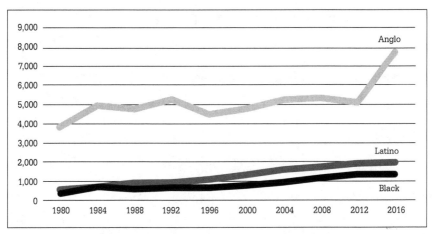

Figure 4. Estimated Number (in thousands) of Texas Voters by Ethnicity, 1980–2016. *Sources:* U.S. Census Bureau, *Reported Voting and Registration by Race and Spanish Origin for States* series for presidential election years 1980 to 2016.

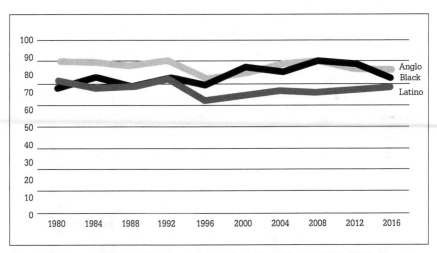

Figure 5. Percent Voting of Registered, by Ethnicity, in Texas, 1980–2016. *Sources:* U.S. Census Bureau, *Reported Voting and Registration by Race and Spanish Origin for States* series for presidential election years 1980 to 2016.

Mexican Americans in Public Office: 1973–2018

There are limited data available regarding Latino officeholders prior to 1973.[18] No Latinos were elected to statewide offices before 1973. Those Latinos holding local offices were almost entirely elected in parts of South Texas and West Texas where Latinos comprised the majority of the voting population.

CONGRESSIONAL REPRESENTATION IN TEXAS

Ted Cruz, a Cuban American born in Canada, in 2013 was elected the first Latino U.S. Senator from Texas. No Mexican American has represented Texas in the U.S. Senate. Congressman Henry B. González, a Democrat, was the first Mexican American elected to the U.S. House of Representatives, in 1961.[19] U.S. Rep. Eligio "Kika" de la Garza (D-TX) was the second; he first served in 1965.[20] Representing heavily Latino districts, Congressmen González and de la Garza were the only Latinos in the Texas delegation until the Voting Rights Act took effect in Texas and was applied to 1980 Congressional redistricting.

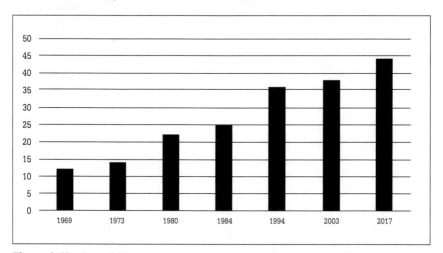

Figure 6. Number of Texas Latinos in U.S. House, 1969–2017. *Sources:* Data for 1973 to 1984 from García, *The Voting Rights Act*; 1994–2003 from Texas Politics Project, *Latino Elected Officials in Texas*; 2017 from NALEO, *National Directory of Latino Elected Officials* (2017).

The number of Mexican Americans elected to Congress increased because of initial and subsequent redistricting, as well as steady increases in the Latino population in Texas. However, the effect of gerrymandered districts, later approved by the U.S. Supreme Court, resulted in a decrease in Latino representation (see Figure 6).

LATINO REPRESENTATION IN STATE OFFICES

There are nine nonjudicial officials elected statewide in Texas.[21] No Latino has ever served as governor, lieutenant governor, Texas comptroller of public accounts,[22] or Texas agriculture commissioner.[23] Dan Morales served as Texas attorney general from 1991 to 1999. George P. Bush has served as Texas land commissioner.[24] Three Latinos have been elected to the three-member Texas Railroad Commission:[25] Lena Guerrero (1991-1992), Tony Garza (1999-2002), and Victor Carrillo (2003-2011).[26]

Judges on Texas's two highest courts of appeal, the Texas Supreme Court and the Texas Court of Criminal Appeals, are elected statewide. Four Latinos have been elected to the nine-member Texas Supreme Court: Raúl A. González (1984-1998), Alberto R. Gonzales (1998-2000), David M. Medina (2004-2012), and Eva Guzmán (2009-2018).[27]

The combined years of service by Latino justices on the Texas Supreme Court totaled 20.9 years as of 2018. This is 8 percent of the 261.2 years of service of that court since 1986.[28] Only one Latino has been elected to the nine-member Texas Court of Criminal Appeals: Elsa Alcalá. She was elected in 2011.[29]

LATINOS IN THE STATE LEGISLATURE

Prior to 1973, Latinos were able to win elections to the Texas Legislature only in those districts where Latinos comprised the majority of the population—in South Texas and in West Texas. With the abolition of multimember districts after the Supreme Court's decision in *White v. Regester*, along with the extension of Voting Rights Act protections to Texas, and the growth in the Latino population, the number of Texas legislators has steadily increased (see Figure 7).

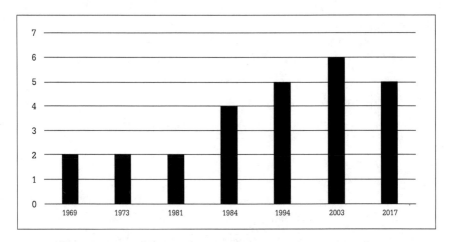

Figure 7. Number of Latino State Legislators in Texas, 1969–2017. *Sources:* Data for 1969 from Texas Politics Project, *Race and Ethnicity in the Texas Legislature*; for 1973–1984 from García, *The Voting Rights Act*; for 1994–2003 from Texas Politics Project, *Latino Elected Officials in Texas*; for 2017 from NALEO, *National Directory of Latino Elected Officials* (2017).

LATINO LOCAL OFFICIALS

Large Latino populations in southern and western counties of Texas led to the election of more Mexican American local officials in those areas. With the protections of the Voting Rights Act, and the dramatic increase in the Latino population throughout the state, the number of Latino city, county, and school district officials increased substantially (see Figure 8).

Barriers to Registration and Voting

Flagrant violations of the voting rights of its Mexican American citizens have led to dozens of lawsuits and court rulings in recent decades. African Americans are a significant proportion of the population of Texas, and many voting-rights cases in Texas were brought on behalf of both Latinos and African Americans. Other voting-rights cases were brought solely on behalf of African Americans—largely in East Texas, where, until recently, the Latino population was small. Some of these cases benefit Latino voters or will benefit them in the future.[30]

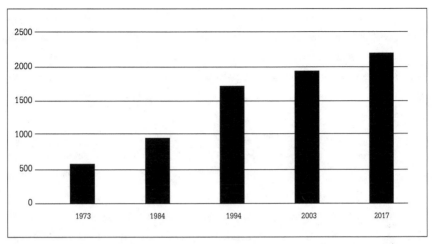

Figure 8. Latino Locally Elected Officials in Texas, 1973–2017. *Sources:* Data for 1973 and 1984 from García, *The Voting Rights Act*; for 1994 and 2003, Texas Politics Project, *Latino Elected Officials in Texas;* for 2017 from NALEO, *National Directory of Latino Elected Officials* (2017).

The adoption of the Twenty-Fourth Amendment to the U.S Constitution and the enactment of the Voting Rights Act in 1965 resulted in the elimination of some of the mechanisms used in the past to disenfranchise Latino and African American voters in Texas, such as the poll tax. The 1975 amendments to the Voting Rights Act, which required Texas to provide election materials in Spanish, represented a significant milestone in the path toward equality for Latino voters, even though many Texas jurisdictions still do not comply with these requirements.

Perhaps the most important achievement of the Voting Rights Act has been its use to dismantle at-large election systems throughout Texas. Racially polarized voting has persisted in Texas. As a result, Latino candidates, and the candidates preferred by Latino voters, were often unable to win elections in an at-large system where Latinos did not comprise a majority of the population. Voting-rights litigation has resulted in the widespread change from at-large systems to single-member district or hybrid (single-member districts with a few at-large seats) systems.

The representative of a single-member district is elected solely by the voters in that district; districts with a majority of Latino voters thus serve to better ensure that candidates preferred by Latino voters have a fairer chance of being elected. Some smaller jurisdictions have adopted cumulative voting, in which candidates are elected at-large, but voters cast votes based on the number of open offices. Under cumulative voting, Latino voters can cast all of their votes for their preferred candidate, thus providing for representation in an at-large system.

Even with single-member districts, however, discrimination can occur. District lines can be drawn so that Latino voters are splintered among multiple districts, rendering them unable to elect representatives of their choice. While the Supreme Court has required that districts be drawn so that the population of the jurisdiction is divided evenly among the districts, this "one person, one vote" requirement has been consistently ignored by Texas jurisdictions.[31] As a result, even in counties where Latinos were a majority of the population, the candidates preferred by Latino voters did not comprise a majority of the governing body.

Jim Wells County, for example, adopted a districting plan in 1975 for the election of its four county commissioners that provided only one district with a Mexican American population of at least 65 percent. After a federal court banned the use of this plan because it had not been precleared under Section 5 of the Voting Rights Act, the county eventually adopted a plan that provided for three districts with a Mexican American population of at least 65 percent.[32]

Violations of Voting Rights by the State of Texas

In the past, the federal Fifth Circuit Court of Appeals has recognized the persistent resistance of the State of Texas to fully guaranteeing the voting rights of Texas Latinos.

> For example, the record shows that as late as 1975, Texas attempted to suppress minority voting through purging the voter rolls, after its former poll tax and re-registration requirements were ruled unconstitutional . . . It is notable as well that "[i]n every redistricting cycle since 1970, Texas

has been found to have violated the [Voting Rights Act] with racially gerrymandered districts." . . . Furthermore, record evidence establishes that the Department of Justice objected to at least one of Texas's statewide redistricting plans for each period between 1980 and the present, while Texas was covered by Section 5 of the Voting Rights Act. Texas "is the only state with this consistent record of objections to such statewide plans." Finally, the same Legislature that passed SB 14 [Voter ID law] also passed two laws found to be passed with discriminatory purpose. (2013).[33]

MEXICAN AMERICAN VOTING RIGHTS PRIOR TO 1975

Immediately after the U.S. Commission on Civil Rights 1968 hearings in San Antonio, Latinos in Texas began to challenge violations of their voting rights. In a lawsuit brought by three Latinos, the Fifth Circuit Court of Appeals in 1971 affirmed a lower federal court's finding that Texas statutes banning assistance to illiterate voters violated the U.S. Constitution.[34] Two years later, the U.S. Supreme Court held that multimember districts in Bexar County for the election of members of the Texas House of Representatives invidiously excluded Mexican Americans from effective participation in political life.[35]

A three-judge court's finding in 1974—that multimember districts in Tarrant, McLennan, Travis, Lubbock, El Paso, and Nueces counties unconstitutionally diluted the votes of Mexican Americans—was subsequently vacated after the Texas Legislature adopted redistricting plans providing for single-member districts in these six counties.[36] A settlement was later reached after the Department of Justice objected to the state legislature's single-member district plans in Nueces and Jefferson counties.[37] The U.S. Supreme Court rejected Texas's congressional redistricting plans in 1973, finding the districts were not as equal as mathematically possible, as required under the Constitution.[38]

AFTER 1975 EXTENSION OF SECTION 5

With the extension to Texas of Section 5 of the Voting Rights Act, subsequent challenges to violations of the rights of Latino voters were generally brought under both the U.S. Constitution and under the Voting Rights Act. The courts found multiple violations of the voting rights of Latinos after Texas reapportioned its districts following the 1980 Census.

The Texas Supreme Court ruled that the 1980 reapportionment plan for the Texas House of Representatives violated the Texas State Constitution's analog to the Fourteenth Amendment's one person, one vote requirement, because Nueces, Denton, and Brazoria counties were divided, even though their populations entitled them to at least one district.[39]

A three-judge court of the U.S. District Court for the Northern District of Texas held that Texas's 1980 plan for reapportionment of the Texas Senate violated the one-person, one-vote requirement of the Fourteenth Amendment after the plan failed to secure Section 5 preclearance from the Department of Justice.[40] A consent decree resolving the Voting Rights Act claims brought by Latino interveners was subsequently approved by the three-judge court.[41] The U.S. Supreme Court affirmed another lower court's order requiring changes to the 1980 Congressional redistricting plan for two South Texas districts after the Department of Justice objected to the plan.[42]

The 1990 reapportionment plan for the Texas House of Representatives was challenged in multiple lawsuits in state and federal courts—all resulting in judgments against the State of Texas. A state court enjoined the state's original reapportionment plan in a lawsuit brought by Latino voters, because it relied on 1990 U.S. Census data that undercounted minorities; an agreed judgment for a new Texas House plan was subsequently entered.[43] However, the Texas Supreme Court reversed the decision, ruling that a state district court cannot order a reapportionment plan without the participation of the Texas Legislature.[44] The Texas Legislature then adopted the plan agreed to in the lawsuit.[45]

Shortly after the Texas state district court issued its injunction, the U.S. Department of Justice objected to the Texas House plan, finding it diluted

Latino voting strength in El Paso, Bexar, and Dallas counties. The agency also expressed concerns about voting rights in districts in other Texas counties, including the state's Río Grande Valley, which stretches to the Texas-Mexico border.

A three-judge federal court found merit in Department of Justice objections under the Voting Rights Act, and ordered the adoption of an interim plan that addressed the dilution of Latino voting rights.[46] A three-judge federal court subsequently ordered adoption of an agreed settlement in a lawsuit alleging the districts were unconstitutionally racially gerrymandered.[47] This court-ordered settlement, with some changes, was ultimately adopted by the Texas Legislature in 1997.[48]

Many of the lawsuits challenging the Texas House plan also challenged the Texas Senate reapportionment plan. As with the Texas House plan, the Texas Senate plan was enjoined by the same state district court, stating that it used 1990 Census data that undercounted minorities. After the Texas Supreme Court issued a stay in this first state court lawsuit pending an appeal, a second state court lawsuit was filed by the plaintiffs in the first lawsuit to enter an agreed judgment providing for a new plan approved by a majority of Texas state senators and the Texas Attorney General.[49]

The Department of Justice granted preclearance approval of this agreed plan. However, the Texas Supreme Court voided the agreement because the district court failed to hold an adversary hearing. The same three-judge federal court that ordered interim plans for the Texas House also ordered an interim plan for the Texas Senate, finding that the original Texas Senate plan diluted Latino voting strength in Harris, Dallas, and Bexar counties, as well as in other districts in South Texas and West Texas.[50] After the Supreme Court held that a state district court cannot order a reapportionment plan without the participation of the Texas Legislature, the Texas Legislature adopted the agreed plan ordered by the state district court in the 1991 *Quiroz v. Richards* case.[51]

Relying, in part, on support from minority legislators and minority rights advocacy organizations for this plan, the plan was subsequently approved by the U.S. District Court for the District of Columbia.[52] However, another federal court suit alleged the Senate plan was unconstitutionally racially gerrymandered.[53] An agreed settlement was entered in this lawsuit in 1995, and the agreed plan was subsequently enacted by the Texas Legislature in 1997.[54]

The federal courts also struck down the state's redistricting plan for seats in the U.S. House of Representatives. Here, however, the federal courts began a trend in which these courts have since failed to protect the voting rights of Latino and African American voters. The 1990 congressional plan provided for three additional seats for Texas, reflecting the increase in the population of Texas—an increase attributable to growth in South Texas, and in Dallas and Harris counties.

The Texas Legislature responded by providing for new majority African American districts in Dallas and Harris counties, as well as a new majority Latino district in Harris County. A three-judge federal court held these congressional districts were unconstitutionally racially gerrymandered, and the U.S. Supreme Court affirmed.[55] On remand, the three-judge court ordered an "interim" plan. This plan was used, however, until the 2000 reapportionment, because state officials refused to hold a special session to adopt a new congressional plan.[56]

REDISTRICTING VIOLATIONS AFTER 2000

The Department of Justice objected to the Texas Legislative redistricting board's original reapportionment plan for the Texas House of Representatives following the 2000 U.S. Census. A federal three-judge court subsequently ordered a remedy providing for additional majority-Latino Texas House districts.[57]

After the state legislature failed to adopt a new congressional redistricting plan, a federal three-judge court ordered a new redistricting plan that preserved Latino-majority districts.[58] The U.S. Supreme Court subsequently found that Texas violated Section 2 of the Voting Rights Act, when the state in 2003 reduced the percentage of Latino voters in U.S. Congressional District 23.[59] A federal court later extended the period for early voting for the election in this district after the state scheduled the run-off election on December 12, 2006—a religious feast day (the Day of the Virgin of Guadalupe) celebrated by many Roman Catholic Latinos.[60]

There was no challenge to the redistricting plan for the Texas Senate. However, a federal court found that the reapportionment plan for the Texas Board of Education violated the one-person, one-vote mandate of the U.S. Constitution, and adopted the plaintiffs' proposed plan.[61]

REDISTRICTING AFTER 2010

The U.S. District Court for the District of Columbia denied Section 5 pre-clearance to the reapportionment plans adopted by the State of Texas after the 2010 Census for the Texas House, the Texas Senate, and the U.S. Congress.[62] This judgment was vacated for further consideration, however, after the U.S. Supreme Court in *Shelby County v. Holder* struck down the provisions that required Texas to obtain Section 5 preclearance for voting changes.[63] Even without the protections of Section 5, a federal court found Texas intentionally discriminated in its reapportionment plan for the Texas House in Bell, Dallas, Nueces, and Tarrant counties.[64]

The U.S. District Court for the District of Columbia found that Texas had failed to meet its burden of showing that the reapportionment plan for the Texas Senate was adopted without discriminatory intent, and found discriminatory purpose with respect to Senate District 10.[65] This order was vacated by the U.S. Supreme Court in the wake of *Shelby County*. A federal court later found that the state's Texas Senate plan violated the one-person, one-vote requirement.[66]

A federal court in Texas ordered an interim redistricting plan for Congressional districts in 2011, pending the decision of the U.S. District Court for the District of Columbia in *Texas v. United States*. This court expressly noted its ruling was not final on the merits of any claims by the plaintiffs.[67] The Texas Legislature adopted the court's interim plan in 2013, after the District of Columbia court found that Texas's original congressional redistricting plan was motivated, at least in part, by discriminatory intent.[68] This finding was vacated by the U.S. Supreme Court after *Shelby County v. Holder*.

A three-judge court subsequently found that the 2013 plan violated Section 2, in terms of both intent and effect, against Latino voters, and found an equal protection violation for two districts.[69] The three-judge court confirmed its finding of intentional discrimination against Mexican American voters, in violation of Section 2 and the Fourteenth Amendment, as well as for its discriminatory effect, with respect to the state legislature's adoption of the court-ordered interim plan in 2013.[70]

The U.S. Supreme Court in 2018 not only rejected the lower court's findings of intentional discrimination against Latinos, it found an impermissible racial gerrymander when the plan moved Latinos into a district to create a Latino-majority district.[71] This decision came to exemplify the Supreme Court's failure to protect Mexican American voting rights under Section 2 of the Voting Rights Act, after eviscerating the protections of Section 5 in *Shelby County v. Holder*.

VOTER IDENTIFICATION IN TEXAS

In-person voter impersonation in Texas is very rare. In the ten years prior to the adoption of Senate Bill 14 (SB 14)—when the Texas legislation required for the first time that voters provide limited, specific forms of photographic identification—20 million votes were cast in Texas. Only two cases of in-person voter impersonation were prosecuted to conviction.[72] Nonetheless, the Texas Legislature in 2011 enacted SB 14, the strictest voter identification law in the United States. Under SB 14, only four types of identification were acceptable: (1) a Texas Department of Public Safety-issued driver's license, personal ID card with photo, or license to carry a handgun; (2) a U.S. military ID card with photo; (3) a U.S. citizenship certificate with photo; (4) a U.S. passport. Latino and African American voters are much less likely to possess one of these photo identification cards, which often can prove expensive to obtain, or involve costly travel to a faraway Department of Public Safety office. A federal court found that SB 14 violated the First and Fourteenth Amendments to the U.S. Constitution, had a discriminatory effect on Latino and African American voters, purposefully discriminated against these voters, and imposed a poll tax in violation of the Twenty-Fourth and Fourteenth Amendments.[73]

The *en banc* (all judges involved in the decision) Fifth Circuit affirmed the lower court's finding of discriminatory effects on Latino and African American voters, but remanded the case to the lower court for a reweighing of the evidence regarding its discriminatory purpose.[74] In addition, the Fifth Circuit ordered the lower court to fashion an interim remedy.

On remand, the lower court again found that Texas enacted its voter identification law with a discriminatory purpose, in violation of Section 2 of the Voting Rights Act.[75] The lower court entered an agreed interim order that allowed voters without such identification to vote upon completing a Declaration of Reasonable Impediment.

The Texas Legislature responded by enacting Senate Bill 5 (SB 5), which added a U.S. passport card to the list of acceptable photo identifications, and increased the amount of time a qualifying ID can be expired from sixty days to four years. Voters over seventy years of age have no limit on the amount of time their ID can be expired. SB 5 authorized mobile units to issue Election ID Certificates for voters who cannot obtain other forms of permissible identification, but provided no funding for such units or means to notify jurisdictions when such units might be available in a specific locale. Disability and illness were added as permissible reasons to vote without a qualifying ID.

The Declaration of Reasonable Impediment (DRI) procedure established as part of the agreed interim remedy was codified in SB 5 but required that the DRI include a threat of criminal penalties for perjury, and increased the penalty for perjury on a DRI to a felony. The statutory DRI process also excluded the "other" category as a reason for voting without one of the required photo IDs.

SB 5 did not include any programs to educate voters; nor did it include funding for such education programs. The federal court found that SB 5 did not remedy the violations found with respect to SB 14 and violated Section 2 of the Voting Rights Act, as well as the Fourteenth and Fifteenth Amendments to the U.S. Constitution. The court enjoined enforcement of SB 14 and SB 5.[76]

The Fifth Circuit Court of Appeals reversed the district court's injunction against SB 5, finding that the district court abused its discretion.[77] Despite the findings of illegal discrimination by all members of the Fifth Circuit, two judges on that court have since permitted the State of Texas to enforce this discriminatory practice that addresses a nonexistent problem. Once again, the Fifth Circuit failed to protect the rights of Latino voters in Texas.

Violations of Voting Rights by Political Subdivisions

Political subdivisions of the State of Texas—such as cities, counties, school districts, water districts, and utility districts—have repeatedly violated the voting rights of Latinos. The State of Texas unsuccessfully challenged the U.S. Attorney General's initial determination that the state was covered by the 1975 amendment protecting language minorities.[78] Texas political subdivisions vigorously challenged the application of Section 5's preclearance requirement to them. San Antonio lost its challenge,[79] as did Frío County.[80]

The city of Pecos was required to preclear voting changes.[81] In 1978, in *United States v. Commissioners of Sheffield, Alabama*, the U.S. Supreme Court held that municipalities and school districts in states subject to Section 5 must preclear their elections changes under Section 5.[82] This ruling was applied to multiple Texas school districts in *Hereford Independent School District v. Bell*.[83] Despite the clear findings in these cases, many Texas political subdivisions refused to seek Section 5 preclearance of voting changes, forcing the federal courts to enjoin the application of voting changes that were not precleared.

FINDINGS OF ILLEGAL DISCRIMINATION BY TEXAS POLITICAL SUBDIVISIONS

The federal courts have found illegal discrimination against Texas Latinos in at least twenty-two cases involving Texas political subdivisions (see Appendix 2). The earliest such case appears to have been *Mata v. White*, decided the year after the 1975 amendments extending the Voting Rights Act to Texas.[84]

While many of these cases involve smaller jurisdictions, the courts have found illegal discrimination by large cities, such as the City of Dallas,[85] and large urban school districts, such as the 67,000-student North East Independent School District in San Antonio.[86] Such illegal discrimination is not limited to the distant or recent past. In 2017, a federal court found illegal discrimination by the city of Pasadena, a Houston suburb.[87] In 2014, the Irving Independent School District, in the Dallas-Fort Worth Metroplex, was found to have violated Section 2 of the Voting Rights Act.[88]

VOTING RIGHTS SETTLEMENTS

Most voting rights cases do not go to trial. As with many other kinds of litigation, these cases are more frequently settled. At least 191 voting rights cases brought against Texas political subdivisions have been settled with an agreement favorable to Latino voters.

IN TEXAS CITIES

For example, settlements have resulted in the adoption of single-member district systems by most of Texas's largest cities. A lawsuit was filed challenging the City of Dallas's at-large election system in 1971. Eight of the eleven members of the city council were elected at-large but were required to live in one of eight "residential districts." The three remaining members were also elected at-large but were not required to reside in any district.

After a federal court found that this system unconstitutionally diluted the votes of African American voters, the City adopted an 8-3 system, in which eight members of the city council were elected from single-member districts, and three, including the mayor, were elected at-large.

Because Mexican Americans at this time represented less than 10 percent of the population of the City of Dallas, Mexican Americans were not a majority of the population of any of the single-member districts.[89] With the dramatic growth of the Latino population in Dallas in subsequent years, a federal court ruled in 1990 that the 8-3 election system violated the rights of Latino and African American voters under Section 2 of the Voting Rights Act. The City of Dallas was forced to adopt a 14-1 plan, with fourteen single-member districts and the mayor elected at large, in 1991.[90]

In 1975, the city of San Antonio sought to annex areas adjacent to the city. A federal court required preclearance of the proposed annexations under Section 5 of the Voting Rights Act.[91] Preclearance was granted after the city agreed to adopt a 10-1 election system, in which ten members of the city council were elected from single-member districts and the mayor was elected at large. This agreement was ratified by San Antonio voters in a January 15, 1977, referendum.[92]

Initial challenges to the at-large election system of the City of Houston by Latino and African American voters were unsuccessful. The U.S. Attorney General objected, however, when the City of Houston submitted proposed annexations for preclearance, because these annexations diluted minority voting strength, given the use of an at-large election system. Voters then approved a referendum providing for nine single-member districts and five at-large seats. The Attorney General approved the districting plan and withdrew his objections to the annexation.[93]

With the notable exception of Plano, where Latinos comprise only 14 percent of the population, the ten largest cities in Texas now use single-member districts to elect their city council members.[94] This is a revolutionary change attributable largely to the successful enforcement of the Voting Rights Act. The positive experience of Texas cities with single-member districts led to the voluntary adoption, without voting rights litigation, of single-member districts in the state capital of Austin in 2012.[95]

Smaller Texas cities have also adopted single-member district election systems as a result of settlements in voting rights lawsuits. (For a complete listing, see Appendix 2.) Small Texas towns have sometimes adopted cumulative voting, which can ensure Latino voters have an opportunity to elect candidates of their choice when the town is too small to be divided into districts.[96] Cumulative voting is one of several methods of achieving proportional representation.[97]

IN TEXAS SCHOOL DISTRICTS

Settlements have also resulted in the adoption of single-member district, hybrid (single-member districts with some at-large positions), or cumulative voting election systems (in which voters are given as many votes to cast as positions to fill, and may cumulate their votes on as many or few candidates as they wish) in several school districts across Texas. All of the largest urban districts use single-member district or hybrid election systems.[98] There is greater variety among the large suburban districts in the state's largest metropolitan areas.

While suburban districts in San Antonio utilize single-member districts, some suburban districts in Houston and Dallas continue to use at-large, by-place election systems. These include four of the ten largest school districts in the state: Cypress-Fairbanks Independent School District (ISD) in Houston, Katy ISD (Houston), Aldine ISD (Houston), and Arlington ISD (Dallas).[99] One of these four—Aldine ISD—elects a board with a majority of African American and Latino members using the at-large election system.[100]

Numerous smaller school districts have also adopted single-member district election systems or hybrid systems in settlement of voting rights lawsuits alleging violations of the rights of Latino voters. Smaller school districts have sometimes adopted cumulative voting in settlement of such lawsuits. The plaintiffs in one small school district agreed to modify an earlier agreement providing for single-member districts by moving to cumulative voting after the single-member districts did not result in the election of Latinos.[101]

IN OTHER TEXAS POLITICAL SUBDIVISIONS

While cities, counties, and school districts comprise the bulk of the defendants in voting- rights cases in Texas, numerous other types of political subdivisions have also adopted single-member district, hybrid, or cumulative-voting systems to settle voting-rights litigation. These include community college systems,[102] hospital districts,[103] river authorities,[104] and water districts.[105]

With the 1975 amendments to the Voting Rights Act, Texas and its political subdivisions became subject to the preclearance requirement of Section 5 of the law. Before enforcing any voting change, all of these jurisdictions were required to obtain preclearance from the U.S. Attorney General of the Department of Justice to ensure that the change did not have a discriminatory effect or purpose. Alternatively, the jurisdiction could file suit in the U.S. District Court for the District of Columbia to obtain approval of the voting change.

Absent approval from the U.S. Attorney General or the District of Columbia federal court, the voting change could not go into effect. One of the more important features of Section 5 was that it applied broadly to any change affecting voting. This requirement applied from 1975 until 2013, when in *Shelby County v. Holder* the U.S. Supreme Court struck down the formula in Section 4 of the Voting Rights Act that subjected Texas and other jurisdictions to the Section 5 requirement.

SECTION 5 OBJECTIONS IN TEXAS

From 1982 until 2013, Texas received the second largest number of Section 5 objections from the Department of Justice.[106] (Mississippi led with 124 objections; Texas followed with 116.) These objections prevented discriminatory voting practices in seventy-three of Texas's 254 counties. About 72 percent of the state's non-white voting-age population resides in these counties.[107] The large number of objections is, in part, explained by the size of Texas. It has many more jurisdictions than other states subject to Section 5. However, the number of objections is also explained by the persistent attempts by state and local officials to deprive Latinos of their right to vote in Texas.

The scope of Section 5's coverage is very broad. Of the 116 Section 5 objections issued against Texas and its political subdivisions since 1982, more than half involved redistricting plans.[108] Other objections involved methods of election, such as single-member districts, at-large elections, majority-vote requirements, and numbered-place elections. Others involved voting procedures, including polling-place locations, the form of ballots and absentee ballots used, election dates, general voter-registration requirements, and bilingual election procedures.[109]

Section 5's deterrent effect extends beyond the formal objections issued by the Department of Justice. Texas had far more Section 5 withdrawals than any other state.[110] The Department of Justice regularly asks for additional information regarding the impact of a proposed change. From 1982 to 2005, Texas and its political subdivisions withdrew at least fifty-four proposed changes after the Justice Department signaled they would not be precleared under Section 5.[111]

Jurisdictions subject to Section 5 of the Voting Rights Act could also sue in the U.S. District Court for the District of Columbia, seeking a judgment that a proposed voting change does not violate the Voting Rights Act. Preclearance has been denied in fourteen such lawsuits. Three of these fourteen suits sought preclearance of statewide redistricting plans or a state statute.

SECTION 5 ENFORCEMENT ACTIONS

Texas was subject to Section 5 preclearance from 1975 to 2013. While many jurisdictions incorporated the Section 5 preclearance process into their procedures, the Department of Justice and private litigants regularly had to file suits to enjoin voting changes because Section 5 preclearance had not been obtained. From 1975 to 2004, the Department of Justice participated in thirty such lawsuits in Texas—twice as many as in any other state.[112] From 1975 to 2013, at least fifty-four enforcement actions were brought against Texas. Four of these suits required the State of Texas to seek preclearance.

Section 5 enforcement actions do more than force a jurisdiction to comply with the Voting Rights Act and seek Section 5 preclearance. Such lawsuits have often provided leverage for the plaintiffs in these cases to force the jurisdiction to withdraw a proposed discriminatory voting change, or to adopt a nondiscriminatory voting change. For example, Medina County, Texas, agreed to a revised apportionment plan after a federal court barred enforcement of the county's original apportionment plan for county commissioner and justice of the peace precincts.[113] After enjoining the state's redistricting plan for the Texas Senate, another federal court adopted the plaintiffs' proposed interim redistricting plan.[114]

SHELBY COUNTY V. HOLDER

In *Shelby Counter v. Holder*, the U.S. Supreme Court struck down the formula set out in Section 4 of the Voting Rights Act that required Texas to obtain preclearance of any voting changes under Section 5.[115] As a result, one of the more important and effective protections for Mexican American voters in Texas was eliminated. The effect of *Shelby County* was felt almost immediately. The U.S. District Court for the District of Columbia denied preclearance to Texas's voter identification law. That denial was subsequently vacated after the U.S. Supreme Court's decision in *Shelby County*.[116]

Minutes after the decision in *Shelby County* was announced, then-Texas Attorney General Greg Abbott tweeted, "Texas#VoterID law should go into effect immediately."[117] Although Texas federal courts have twice found that this law intentionally discriminated against Mexican American voters, the Fifth Circuit Court of Appeals approved the state's adoption of the photo identification requirement, with only minor modifications. Without *Shelby County*, more than 600,000 Texas voters lacking photo IDs would have been able to cast ballots.

The U.S. District Court for the District of Columbia also denied preclearance of redistricting plans for the Texas House, Texas Senate, and U.S. Congressional districts. After *Shelby County* was announced, this decision was vacated; extensive litigation in multiple federal courts in Texas ensued.[118] Although the most discriminatory features of the original redistricting plans were eliminated in these lawsuits, the lawsuits were expensive—not just for the plaintiffs, but also for the State of Texas. The expense of this litigation would have decreased, had the original ruling that the plans were not precleared been allowed to stand.

The U.S. District Court for the District of Columbia preliminarily prohibited implementation of the Beaumont Independent School District's reapportionment plan, as well as other voting changes ordered by a state court of appeals. Following the decision in *Shelby County*, the lawsuit was dismissed.[119]

Prior to *Shelby County*, a Texas three-judge federal court barred changes to Galveston County's reapportionment plan, which had not been precleared under Section 5 and which reduced the number of justice-of-the-peace precincts, thereby reducing the opportunity for Latino and African American voters to elect candidates of their choice. The Department of Justice subsequently objected to the plan, and the court permanently banned the plan.[120]

Two months after *Shelby County*, Galveston County adopted a plan reducing the number of justices of the peace districts, thereby eliminating all but one of the districts that provided an electoral opportunity for Latinos and African Americans. The lawsuit alleges these changes violate Section 2 and the Fourteenth and Fifteenth Amendments.

A trial was held in 2014; however, as of late 2018, no decision had been reported. Even if the court ultimately decides in favor of the plaintiffs in this case, the effect of *Shelby County* is apparent: the reduction in justice of the peace precincts continued for years, while the reduction would never have gone into effect had Section 5 protection been available.

EFFORTS TO REVIVE SECTION 5

Shelby County has diminished the protections the Voting Rights Act previously afforded to Texas Latinos. Proposals have been advanced for a revised coverage formula that would resurrect Section 5. For example, the Voting Rights Advancement Act of 2019, sponsored by 229 members of Congress, would reinstate Section 5 coverage for any state with ten or more voting rights violations in the previous twenty-five calendar years, as long as at least one of these violations was committed by the state itself.

A political subdivision would be subject to Section 5's preclearance requirement if there were three or more voting-rights violations during the previous twenty-five years. Coverage would exist for ten years.[121] The act was approved by the U.S. House of Representatives in December 2019, but was not approved by the U.S. Senate. Advocates should continue to pursue such proposals so that they can be adopted when protection of voting rights—historically an issue supported by both major political parties—once again is politically possible.

Section 2 of the Voting Rights Act remains in effect, and is available to strike down discriminatory voting practices. But Section 5 is a more cost-effective means. Section 2 litigation requires private parties to spend judicial and their own resources, is time-consuming, and leaves Latino voters with no remedy until the case is finally successfully resolved. Section 5, in contrast, is cost-effective.

From 1982 to 2013, 116 objections and 366 voting changes were modified or withdrawn following formal "More Information Requests" from the Department of Justice. Without Section 5, each of these would have required a lawsuit to block the discriminatory change.[122] The requirement of Section 5 preclearance deterred many jurisdictions from proposing discriminatory changes.

Spanish Language Protections of the Voting Rights Act

All Texas political subdivisions are required to provide language assistance to Spanish-speaking voters in statewide elections. In addition, eighty-eight counties are separately covered for Spanish because of high rates of limited English proficiency (LEP) and illiteracy among language minority citizens.[123]

These protections are important in ensuring all Latino voters are able to participate fully in our democracy. Of the 10,405,000 Latinos in Texas in 2014, 76 percent spoke a language other than English at home—presumably Spanish.[124]

Many of these Spanish speakers also speak English. However, significant numbers have limited proficiency in English: 23.7 percent of Spanish speakers in Texas speak English "not well" or "not at all."[125] While many Latinos with limited English proficiency (LEP) are immigrants (and therefore ineligible to vote), there are also as many as 535,000 native-born U.S. citizens who are of limited English proficiency.[126] In the 2000 Census, it was estimated that there were 818,185 Latino voting-age citizens in Texas who are not yet fully proficient in English; among them, 473,099 were native-born Texans.[127]

The language protections of the Voting Rights Act have made a critical difference in the ability of limited-English Latinos to participate in our democracy. Unfortunately, many Texas jurisdictions have failed to carry out the Voting Rights Act's mandate in Section 203. In a 2005 study, the Mexican American Legal Defense and Educational Fund (MALDEF) requested translated voting materials from the 101 counties that were then covered by Section 203.

Of the sixty-seven that responded, forty-seven (70 percent) did not provide voter registration forms, a ballot, a provisional ballot, and written voting instructions in Spanish. Of the twenty counties that responded with some compliance, only one could show that it fully complied with Section 203. Many of the Spanish-language materials provided had incomplete and/or inaccurate translations.[128]

The Department of Justice's enforcement of Section 203's mandate has been sporadic. The federal agency objected under Section 5 to three Texas counties' efforts to decrease spending on Spanish-language translations in 2009 and obtained a consent decree in a lawsuit against Fort Bend County, Texas. Consent decrees were also obtained against nine counties from 2005 to 2007. Five language-related objections were issued under Section 5 in 1994 and 1995.

Texas Election Observers

Section 3(a) of the Voting Rights Act authorizes a federal court to require the Department of Justice to send election observers to states to protect voters' rights. Prior to *Shelby County*, the Department of Justice also had the authority to send election observers to jurisdictions covered under Sections 4(b) and 8 of the Voting Rights Act.

These election observers served "to help deter wrongdoing, defuse tension, promote compliance with the law, and bolster public confidence in the electoral process."[129] Election observers were sent under Section 4(b) to Texas on eighteen different occasions—the fourth highest total of the states previously identified under the coverage formula in Section 4.[130] From 1975 to 2014, the agency sent 1,400 federal election observers to seventy Texas jurisdictions.[131]

Even after *Shelby County*, the Department of Justice can send election observers to a jurisdiction. After a federal court found that a city of Pasadena redistricting plan intentionally discriminated against Latino voters, the federal agency sent observers to the city for the May 2017 city election.[132]

Recommendations

The Voting Rights Act has played a critical role in protecting the voting rights of Mexican Americans, African Americans, and Asian Americans in Texas. As a result, Texas has undergone fundamental changes in its political structures. The number of Latino officeholders in Texas has climbed since 1968, at both the state and local levels. Institutional changes, such as the adoption of single-member districts, have been made in the wake of the law's passage.

Nonetheless, Latinos in Texas continue to face discrimination in voting in a state that has willfully flouted federally mandated voter rights protections regardless of the cost of defending illegal Texas actions. Such discrimination is not a historical relic; it is, unfortunately, a continuing problem. We therefore make the following recommendations:

- Congress should enact a new coverage formula for Section 4 of the Voting Rights Act, so that Texas and its political subdivisions are once again required to preclear voting changes under Section 5 of the law. Proposals for such a formula, which would include Texas, already are pending in Congress.[133]

- Congress should consider codifying the intent standard set out in *Village of Arlington Heights* so that courts such as the Fifth Circuit Court of Appeals no longer evade findings of discrimination by the lower courts by manipulating the standards of proof. Such manipulation occurred repeatedly in the voter ID case. Congress should also make clear that appellate courts cannot overrule a lower court's finding of intentional discrimination unless the finding is clearly erroneous.

- The federal courts should refuse to allow jurisdictions to escape scrutiny by adopting interim remedies used by the courts in emergency situations where an election is to be held in the near future. In the 2010 Congressional redistricting case, and in the voter ID case, the Fifth Circuit allowed Texas to implement statutes that fell far short of fully protecting Latino voters because the lower federal courts had adopted an interim remedy. In the absence of U.S. Supreme Court action, Congress should amend the Voting Rights Act.

- The U.S. Department of Justice should enforce the language protections of the Voting Rights Act. The agency did so briefly in the 2000s, but these efforts focused on small jurisdictions. The MALDEF survey shows that jurisdictions are regularly flouting the language requirements of the Voting Rights Act, and they are aware that they are likely to suffer no consequences for their illegal actions.

Notes

Ernest Herrera, staff attorney at the Southwest Regional Office in San Antonio of the Mexican American Legal Defense and Educational Fund (MALDEF), assisted with the chapter. He holds a juris doctorate from the University of New Mexico School of Law. The author also wishes to thank Dr. Robert Brischetto and Richard Avena for their invaluable assistance in the preparation of the tables and editing of the text. Any errors are solely the author's.

1. U.S. Commission on Civil Rights (USCCR), *Hearing before the United States Commission on Civil Rights: San Antonio, TX, December 9–14, 1968* (Washington, DC: GPO, 1969), 2. Also available at https://catalog.hathitrust.org/Record/001874430.
2. Nina Perales, Luis Figueroa, and Griselda G. Rivas, "Voting Rights in Texas: 1982–2006," *Report of Law and Social Justice,* 17, no. 2 (2008): 713, 720; citing David Montejano, *Anglos and Mexicans in the Making of Texas, 1836–1986* (Austin: University of Texas Press, 1987).
3. Perales et al., "Voting Rights in Texas," 720-22.
4. Voting Rights Act Amendments of 1975 §§ 101, 202, 203 & 206, 89 Stat. 400-402. Texas became subject to Voting Rights Act (VRA) Section 5 preclearance requirements under the 1975 amendments because (1) at least 5 percent of Texas's voting-age population spoke a single language other than English; (2) less than 50 percent of eligible citizens turned out to vote or registered to vote in the 1972 presidential election; and (3) Texas provided voting materials solely in English in places where more than 5 percent of the population spoke a single language other than English.
5. 52 U.S.C. § 10304.
6. *Shelby County v. Holder*, 570 U.S. 2 (2013).
7. 52 U.S.C. § 10301.
8. USCCR, *Hearing, supra* note 1, 2. The commission stated the hearing was "concerned with the issues of education, employment, economic security, and the administration of justice as they affect Mexican Americans, not only in Texas but in Arizona, California, Colorado, and New Mexico."
9. USCCR, *Hearing*, 66.
10. USCCR, *Hearing*, 448.
11. USCCR, *Hearing*, 701.
12. USCCR, *Hearing*, 752.
13. USCCR, *Hearing*, 758.
14. USCCR, *Hearing*, 972 (Exhibit No. 27: Staff Report on Farm Workers).
15. USCCR, *Hearing*, report by Helen Rowan: The Mexican American, 9.
16. USCCR, *Hearing*, report by Helen Rowan, 13.
17. U.S. Census Bureau, Population Estimates, July 1, 2017. Data for Native Americans are not included, because the population of Native Americans has remained small throughout this period. American Indians were estimated to be 1 percent of the population in 2017. https://www.census.gov/quickfacts/TX.
18. John A. García, *The Voting Rights Act and Hispanic Political Representation in the Southwest* (Oxford, England: Oxford University Press, 1986), 59, 53-54.
19. U.S. House of Representatives: History, Art and Archives, "Henry B. González," undated, http://history.house.gov/People/Detail/13906?ret=True.
20. U.S. House of Representatives: History, Art and Archives, "Eligio 'Kika' de la Garza," undated, http://history.house.gov/People/Detail/12083.

21. Texas Secretary of State, "Statewide Elected Officials," undated, https://www.sos.state.tx.us/elections/voter/elected.shtml.

22. Texas Comptroller of Public Accounts, https://comptroller.texas.gov.

23. Texas Department of Agriculture, https://texasagriculture.gov

24. Texas General Land Office, *The Commissioner*, https://www.glo.texas.gov/index.html. His mother was Hispanic.

25. The Texas Politics Project, "Texas Politics—Number of Latino Elected Officials in Texas," University of Texas, Austin, undated, https://texaspolitics.utexas.edu/archive/html/vce/features/0503_04/latinos.html.

26. Texas Railroad Commission, "Railroad Commissioners Past through Present," undated, http://www.rrc.state.tx.us/about-us/commissioners/commissioner-list.

27. *López v. Abbott*, No. 2:16-cv-00303 (S.D. Tex. July 16, 2017), Appendix E, Expert Witness Report of José Roberto Juárez, Jr. Xavier Rodríguez was appointed to the Texas Supreme Court in 2001, but lost his election in 2002. U.S. Courts, "Court Staff: U.S. District Judge Xavier Rodriguez of Texas," https://www.txwd.uscourts.gov/court-staff/u-s-district-judge-xavier-rodriguez; Office of the Texas Secretary of State, "Race Summary Report: 2002 Republican Primary Election," http://elections.sos.state.tx.us/elchist89_state.htm.

28. *López v. Abbott, supra* note 27, 52.

29. Texas Courts, "Judge Elsa Alcala, About the Court Judges," undated, http://www.txcourts.gov/cca/about-the-court/judges/judge-elsa-alcala. Fortunato (Pete) Benavides was appointed to the Texas Court of Criminal Appeals in 1991, but lost his election in 1992. Office of the (Texas) Secretary of State, "Race Summary Report: 1992 General Election," http://elections.sos.state.tx.us/elchist5_state.htm.

30. *Taxpayers for Better Representation v. Everman Independent School District*, No. 4:92-cv-00841-Y (N.D. Tex. January 31, 1994) (entering Final Order of Agreed Judgment providing for 5-2 election system); *The Texas Tribune*, "Everman ISD," undated. While this lawsuit was brought by African Americans, 56 percent of the students in this district are Latino: Everman Independent School District, Board, undated. There is now a Latina on the Board of Trustees. https://www.eisd.org/domain/616. See also other examples of cases brought by African Americans, but likely to benefit Latinos: *Alexander v. Texas City Independent School District, No. G-91-226* (S.D. Tex. October 9, 1992) (implementing 6-1 election system in district where Latinos in 2009 were 35 percent of the population); *Hoskins v. Hannah*, No. 3:93-cv-00012 (S.D. Tex. August 19, 1992) (entering consent judgment in Section 5 suit challenging Galveston County constable and justice of the peace precincts); and, *Sam v. City of LaMarque, No. 3:90-cv-00177* (S.D. Tex. April 6, 1992) (entering agreed judgment providing for 4-1 election system in city where Latinos are 22 percent of the population). Non-Hispanic white voters can also benefit from voting rights lawsuits brought on behalf of minority voters. See *Curtis v. Smith*, 121 F.Supp. 2d 1054 (E.D. Tex. 2000) (requiring preclearance of Polk County Registrar's en masse challenge of registered voters. even though "a relatively small fraction" of challenged voters were minority voters).

31. *Reynolds v. Sims,* 377 U.S. 533 (1964).

32. *Arriola v. Harville,* 781 F.2d 506 (5th Cir. 1986) (summarizing litigation history).

33. [3]*Veasey v. Abbott,* 830 F.3d 216, 239-40 (5th Cir. 2016) (*en banc*) (citations omitted), cert. denied, 137 S. Ct. 612 (2017).

34. *Garza v. Smith,* 450 F.2d 790 (5th Cir. 1971).

35. *White v. Regester,* 412 U.S. 755 (1973). A multimember district is represented by two or more legislators elected at large by the voters of the district; *Whitcomb v. Chavis,* 403 U.S. 124, 128 (1971).

36. *Graves v. Barnes*, 378 F.Supp. 640 (W.D. Tex. 1974) (three-judge court), *vacated on other grounds sub nom., White v. Regester,* 422 U.S. 935 (1975) (per curiam).

37. *Graves v. Barnes*, 408 F.Supp. 1050 (W.D. Tex. 1976).

38. *White v. Weiser*, 412 U.S. 783 (1973).

39. *Clements v. Valles*, 620 S.W.2d. 112 (Tex. 1981) (finding a violation of Article III, § 26 of the Texas Constitution).

40. *Terrazas v. Clements*, 537 F.Supp. 514, 524 (N.D. Tex. 1982) (three-judge court).

41. *Terrazas v. Clements*, 581 F.Supp. 1319 (N.D. Tex. 1983) (three-judge court).

42. *Seamon v. Upham*, 536 F.Supp. 931 (E.D. Tex. 1982) (three-judge court) (affirmed in part, and reversed in part), 456 U.S. 37 (1982) (affirming changes to South Texas districts and rejecting changes to Dallas County districts).

43. *Mena v. Richards*, Civil Action No. C-454-91-F (332nd Judicial District Court, Hidalgo County, Texas, 1991).

44. *Terrazas v. Ramírez*, 829 S.W.2d 712 (Tex. 1992).

45. See *Richards v. Mena*, 907 S.W.2d 566 (Tex. App.—Corpus Christi 1995) (summarizing proceedings in lawsuit).

46. *Terrazas v. Slagle*, 789 F.Supp. 828 (W.D. Tex. 1991) (three-judge court).

47. *Thomas v. Bush*, Civil Action No. 1:95-cv-00186-SS (W.D. Tex. September 15, 1995).

48. Texas Legislative Council, "Texas Redistricting 1990s Cycle," undated, http://www.tlc.state.tx.us./redist/history/1990s.html.

49. *Quiroz v. Richards*, Civil Action No. C-4395-91-F (332nd Judicial District Court, Hidalgo County, Texas 1991).

50. *Terrazas v. Slagle*, 789 F.Supp. 828 (W.D. Tex. 1991) (three-judge court).

51. *Richards v. Mena*, 907 S.W.2d 566 (Tex. App.—Corpus Christi 1995) (summarizing proceedings).

52. *Texas v. United States*, 802 F.Supp. 481 (D.D.C. 1992) (three-judge court).

53. *Thomas v. Bush*, 1:95-cv-00186-SS (W.D. Tex. September 15, 1995)

54. Texas Legislative Council, "Texas Redistricting 1990s."

55. *Vera v. Richards,* 861 F.Supp. 1304 (W.D. Tex. 1994) (three-judge court), *affirmed sub nom. Bush v. Vera,* 517 U.S. 952 (1996).

56. *Vera v. Bush*, 933 F.Supp. 1341 (W.D. Tex. 1996) (three-judge court).

57. *Balderas v. Texas*, 2001 WL 34104833 (E.D. Tex. 2001) (three-judge court).

58. *Balderas v. Texas*, 2001 WL 36503750 (E.D. Tex. 2001) (three-judge court).

59. *League of United Latin American Citizens v. Perry*, 548 U.S. 399 (2006).

60. *League of United Latin American Citizens v. Texas*, No. 5:06-cv-01046-XR (W.D. Tex. December 5, 2006).

61. *Miller v. Cuéllar*, No. 3:01-cv-01072-G-L (N.D. Tex. October 5, 2001).

62. *Texas v. United States*, 887 F.Supp.2d 133 (D.D.C. 2012) (three-judge court).

63. *Texas v. United States*, 570 U.S. 928 (2013) (vacating for further consideration in light of *Shelby County v. Holder*). *Shelby County v. Holder* is discussed in greater detail in the following.

64. *Pérez v. Abbott,* 267 F.Supp.3d 750 (W.D. Tex. 2017), *appeal dismissed for want of jurisdiction,* 138 S.Ct. 739 (2018).

65. *Texas v. United States*, 887 F.Supp.2d 133, 166 (D.D.C. 2012) (three-judge court).

66. *Davis v. Perry*, 991 F.Supp.2d 809 (W.D. Tex. 2014) (three-judge court), *reversed on other grounds sub nom., Davis v. Abbott,* 781 F.3d 207 (5th Cir. 2015) (reversing award of attorney's fees).

67. *Pérez v. Perry*, 835 F.Supp.2d 209, 211 (W.D. Tex. 2011) (three-judge court).

68. *Texas v. United States*, 887 F.Supp.2d 133, 161 (D.D.C. 2012) (three-judge court).

69. *Pérez v. Abbott*, 253 F.Supp.3d 864 (W.D. Tex. 2017) (three-judge court).

70. *Pérez v. Abbott*, 274 F.Supp.3d 624 (W.D. Tex. 2017) (three-judge court).

71. *Abbott v. Pérez*, 138 S.Ct. 2305 (2018).

72. *Veasey v. Abbott*, 71 F.Supp. 3d 627, 639–640 (S.D. Tex. 2014) (summarizing evidence at trial regarding rarity of in-person voter impersonation in Texas).

73. *Veasey v. Abbott*, 695–707.

74. *Veasey v. Abbott*, 830 F.3d 216 (5th Cir. 2016) (*en banc*).

75. 249 F.Supp.3d 868 (S.D. Tex. 2017).

76. *Veasey v. Abbott*, 265 F.Supp.3d 684 (S.D. Tex. 2017).

77. *Veasey v. Abbott*, 888 F.3d 792 (5th Cir. 2018).

78. *Briscoe v. Bell*, 432 U.S. 404 (1977).

79. *Martínez v. Becker*, No. SA-75-CA-315 (W.D. Tex. 1975) (requiring preclearance of the City of San Antonio's proposed annexations).

80. *Silva v. Fitch*, No. SA-76-CA-126 (W.D. Tex. October 5, 1975) (enjoining implementation of a reapportionment plan for Frío County commissioners despite objection by Department of Justice).

81. *Perea v. Pigman*, No. P-77-CA-23 (W.D. Tex. 1977).

82. *United States v. Commissioners of Sheffield, Alabama*, 435 U.S. 110 (1978).

83. *Hereford Independent School District v. Bell*, 454 F.Supp. 143 (N.D. Tex. 1978) (three-judge court) (requiring Texas municipalities and school districts to preclear voting changes under Section 5 of the VRA).

84. *Mata v. White*, Civil Action No. DR-76-CA-24 (W.D. Tex. 1976) (holding that Uvalde County's apportionment plan for county commissioners violates the one-person, one-vote requirement).

85. *Williams v. City of Dallas*, 734 F.Supp. 1317 (N.D. Tex. 1990) (holding that the election system providing for eight single-member districts and three at-large seats, adopted in 1975 following a suit finding that the previous at-large election system violated the rights of African Americans, violates the rights of Latino and African American voters under Section 2).

86. *LULAC v. North East Independent School District*, 903 F.Supp. 1071 (W.D. Tex. 1995) (holding the at-large election system violates the rights of Latino and African American voters under Section 2.

87. *Patiño v. City of Pasadena*, 230 F.Supp. 667 (S.D. Tex. 2017) (holding that the City of Pasadena acted with discriminatory intent in violation of the Equal Protection Clause of the 14th Amendment and of Section 2 of the VRA when it changed its election system from eight single-member districts to six single-member districts and two at-large seats).

88. *Benavidez v. Irving Independent School District*, 2014 WL 4055366 (N.D. Tex. August 15, 2014) (holding that the 5-2 system [five single-member districts and two at-large seats] violates Section 2 of the Voting Rights Act).

89. *Lipscomb v. Wise*, 399 F.Supp. 782 (N.D. Tex. 1975).

90. *Williams v. City of Dallas*, 734 F.Supp. 1317 (N.D. Tex. 1990); Robert Brischetto, David R. Richards, Chandler Davidson, and Bernard Grofman, "Chapter 8: Texas," in Chandler Davidson and Bernard Grofman (Eds.), *Quiet Revolution in the South; The Impact of the Voting Rights Act, 1965–1990.* (Princeton, NJ: Princeton University Press, 1994).

91. *Martínez v. Becker*, No. SA-75-CA-315 (W.D. Tex. 1975).

92. Charles L. Cotrell and R. Michael Stevens, "The 1975 Voting Rights Act and San Antonio, Texas: Towards a Federal Guarantee of a Republican Form of Local Government," *Publius: The Journal of Federalism,* January 1, 1978; Robert Brischetto, Charles L. Cotrell, and R. Michael Stevens, "Conflict and Change in the Political Culture of San Antonio in the 1970s," in David R. Johnson,

John A. Booth, and Richard J. Harris (eds.), *The Politics of San Antonio: Community Progress & Power* (Lincoln: University of Nebraska Press, 1983), 75–94; Robert Brischetto et al., "Texas," 124.

93. *Leroy v. City of Houston*, 831 F.2d 576, 578–79 (5th Cir. 1987) (summarizing litigation history in appeal of attorney's fees).

94. Texas State Library, "Population Estimates of Texas Cities, 2010–2017, Arranged in Descending Order," https://www.tsl.texas.gov/ref/abouttx/popcity6.html; City of Plano, "Mayor and City Council," https://www.plano.gov/1345/Mayor-City-Council; Texas Statistical Atlas, "Race and Ethnicity in Plano, Texas," https://statisticalatlas.com/place.

95. City of Austin, "Ten-One City of Austin City Council Districts," undated, http://www.austin texas.gov/department/10-one-city-council-districts.

96. Robert Brischetto, "The Rise of Cumulative Voting," *The Texas Observer*, July 28, 1995, 6–10, 18.

97. Robert Brischetto and Richard L. Engstrom, "Cumulative Voting and Latino Representation: Exit Surveys in Fifteen Texas Communities," *Social Science Quarterly*, December 1997: 973–91.

98. Austin Independent School District, Board Member Elections (Austin elects seven members of the board of trustees from single-member districts, and two at-large), https://pol.tasb.org/Policy/Download/1146?filename=BBB(LOCAL).pdf. A list of the largest school districts in Texas can be found at U.S. Department of Education, "Niche: Largest N School Districts in Texas," undated, https://www.niche.com/k12/search/largest-school-districts/s/texas.

99. Cypress-Fairbanks Independent School District (ISD), Board Elections. Cypress-Fairbanks ISD elects seven members by place, htttps://pol.tasb.org/Policy/Download/587?filename=BBB (LOCAL).pdf; Katy Independent School District, Board Elections. Katy ISD elects seven m embers by place, https://pol.tasb.org/Policy/Download/594?filename=BBB(LOCAL); Aldine ISD: Board Elections. Aldine ISD elects seven members by position, https://pol.tasb.org/Policy/Download/583?filename=BBB(LOCAL).pdf; Arlington ISD, Board Elections. Arlington ISD elects seven members by place, https://pol.tasb.org/Policy/Download/1098?filename=BBB (LOCAL).pdf; Fort Bend ISD, Board Elections. Fort Bend ISD elects three members each from two districts, and one member at-large. https://pol.tasb.org/Policy/Download/483?file name=BBB(LOCAL).pdf.

100. Carter Truett, "Demographic Study: Harris Academy-Aldine ISD 2007–2008," Report, Prairie View A&M University, undated, 3. As of 2007–2008, a majority of the population of Aldine ISD was African American, while 21 percent was Latino. http://www.pvamu.edu/education. Aldine (Texas) Independent School District, "District Celebrates School Board Recognition Month," *Inside Aldine,* January 2017. Three African Americans and two Latinos serve on the Aldine ISD board.

101. *LULAC v. Eden Independent School District*, No. 6-93-CV-16 (January 25, 2007) (granting joint motion for relief).

102. *Hubbard v. Lone Star College System*, No. 4:13-CV-01635 (S.D. Tex. October 11, 2013) (entering consent decree providing for nine single-member districts to replace the prior at-large election system).

103. *Tobías v. Garza County Hospital District*, No. 5-00-CV0293-C (N.D. Tex. March 6, 2001) (entering consent decree providing for 4-1 election system).

104. *LULAC v. San Antonio River Authority*, No. 5:95-cv-cv-00106 (W.D. Tex. 1995) (entering settlement providing for system of fifteen single-member districts to replace an appointive system). The San Antonio River Authority currently has a twelve-member board; six are elected from Bexar County, and two are elected from three other counties (Wilson, Karnes, and Goliad). "San Antonio River Authority," https://www.sara-tx.org/about.

105. *Agüero v. Lubbock County Water Control & Improvement District Number 1*, No. CA-89-77W (N.D. Tex. filed March 31, 1989) (implementing a 4-1 election system).

106. The National Commission on the Voting Rights Act, "Protecting Minority Voters: The Voting Rights Act at Work, 1982-2005," February 2006. From 1982 to 2013, the U.S. Department of Justice objected to 116 voting changes in Texas, and 124 voting changes in Mississippi. https://lawyers committee.org/publication/protecting-minority-voters-the-voting-rights-act-at-work-1982 -2005.

107. Perales et al., "Voting Rights in Texas," 729-30. This study includes data through 2008. Since 2008, only one new jurisdiction has been the subject of a Section 5 objection: Runnels County. Runnels County in 2017 had a population of 10,226, of whom 34 percent were Latino and 2.6 percent were African American; The County Information Program, Texas Association of Counties, "Runnels County Profile," undated, http://www.txcip.org/tac/census/profile. php?FIPS=48399

108. Perales et al., "Voting Rights in Texas." A previous study categorized the Section 5 objections issued against Texas and its political subdivision from 1982 to 2006. Perales et al., *supra* note 2, 731-43. The present study updates these figures by adding the ten objections filed against Texas and its political subdivisions from 2008 to 2013.

109. Perales et al., "Voting Rights in Texas." The percentages add up to more than 100 percent because some objections involved more than one category of voting change.

110. Perales et al., "Voting Rights in Texas," 730 (reporting that Texas had 366 voting changes withdrawn or altered following a request by DOJ for more information); "Protecting Minority Voters," 139. See Map 7, stating that from 1982 to 2004, Texas had fifty-four withdrawals, the most of any state.

111. "Protecting Minority Voters," 139, Map 7.

112. "Protecting Minority Voters," 139, Map 11.

113. *Vásquez-López v. Medina County*, No. 5:11-cv-00945-OLG (W.D. Tex. filed November 10, 2011).

114. *Davis v. Perry*, 991 F.Supp. 2d 809 (W.D. Tex. 2014).

115. *Shelby County v. Holder*, 570 U.S. 2 (2013).

116. *Texas v. Holder*, 888 F.Supp. 2d 113, 143-44 (D.D.C. 2012) (denying preclearance because it is likely to lead to retrogression), vacated in light of *Shelby County*, 570 U.S. 928 (2013) (mem.).

117. Jessica Huseman, "Texas Voter ID Law Led to Fears and Failures in 2016 Election," Pro Publica, May 2, 2017.

118. *Texas v. United States*, 887 F.Supp. 2d 133 (D.D.C. 2012) (denying Section 5 preclearance), vacated for further consideration in light of *Shelby County*, 570 U.S. 928 (2013).

119. *Beaumont Independent School District v. United States*, No. 13-401 (RC) (D.D.C. April 23, 2013) (granting preliminary injunction).

120. *Petteway v. Galveston County, Texas*, No. 3:11-cv-00511 (S.D. Tex. March 2012).

121. Voting Rights Advancement Act of 2019, H.R. 4, 116th Congress, 1st Session.

122. Perales et al., "Voting Rights in Texas," 730.

123. U.S. Department of Justice, 81 Fed. Reg. 87534-35. The coverage formula is set out at Section 4(f)(4) of the Voting Rights Act.

124. Pew Research Center, "Hispanic Trends: Demographic Profile of Hispanics in Texas," 2014.

125. U.S. Census Bureau 2013 American Community Survey, "Language Use in the United States," 2011.

126. Migration Policy Institute, "Total and Limited English Proficient (LEP) Adults, Ages 18 and Older, by U.S. Citizenship Status," 2013, http://www.migrationpolicy.org/sites/default/files/ datahub/MPIDataHub_State-level-LEP-FB-Adults-by-USCitz-Status_2013.xlsx

127. Perales et al., "Voting Rights in Texas," 751–52.
128. Perales et al., "Voting Rights in Texas," 757.
129. U.S. Department of Justice, "Fact Sheet on Justice Department's Enforcement Efforts Following Shelby County Decision," undated, https://www.justice.gov/crt/file/876246.
130. U.S. Department of Justice, "About Federal Observers and Election Monitoring," undated, https://www.justice.gov/crt/about-federal-observers-and-election-monitoring.
131. *Veasey v. Perry*, Expert witness report of George Korbel, No. 2:13-cv-00193, 6.
132. Mihir Zaveri and Keri Blakinger, "Department of Justice will Monitor Pasadena Elections after Voting Rights Ruling," *Houston Chronicle*, May 2, 2017.
133. Voting Rights Advancement Act of 2019; Perales et al., "Voting Rights in Texas"; Lloyd B. Potter and Nazrul Hoque, "Texas Population Projections, 2010 to 2050," Office of the State Demographer, 2014, 4.

HENRY FLORES

Voter Discrimination in Texas

Mexican Americans have suffered discrimination from their fellow Texans since Texas became a U.S. state in 1845. The U.S. Voting Rights Acts of 1965 and succeeding antidiscrimination laws did not end their plight. For decades Texas has avoided the implementation of those federal laws. The state has spent millions of taxpayer dollars unsuccessfully appealing dozens of federal court rulings against Texas state and local governments judged overtly hostile to protecting the voting rights of Mexican Americans.

Fifty years after the U.S. Commission on Civil Rights met in San Antonio to discuss discrimination against Mexican Americans, Texas was appealing yet another federal court ruling declaring the state's onerous voter identification laws a blatant attempt to discriminate against poor and minority voters.

The Role of the U.S. Supreme Court

Two U.S. Supreme Court opinions lay out the requirements that must be met to prove that a jurisdiction has acted with discriminatory intent. In the two cases—*Village of Arlington Heights v. Metropolitan Housing Development Corp*, 429 U.S. (1977) and *Thornburg v. Gingles*, 478 U.S. 30 (1986)—the Supreme Court identified eleven conditions or variables requiring evidence to prove whether discrimination has occurred. The U.S. Senate Committee on the Judiciary had issued a report listing its own factors to consider in discrimination cases. These became known as the Senate Factors becoming the basis for standards to be met in proving discriminatory intent. Utilizing the variables identified by the Supreme Court in both opinions as a template for judging how Texas has met the standards for racial intent allows for a crisp and concise evaluative process to determine how Texas has met the standards set forth by the Voting Rights Act.

The *Arlington Heights* Case

In the first opinion, *The Village of Arlington Heights v. Metropolitan Housing Development Corp*, 429 U.S. (1977), the Supreme Court explained to the plaintiffs how to prove discriminatory intent. To show a history of discrimination, the plaintiffs in the Arlington Heights case were told to present evidence that a "series of official actions" were taken with "invidious purposes." This included that "the specific sequence of events leading up to the challenged decision also may shed some light on the decision maker's purpose."[1] According to the Court's ruling:

> Departures from the normal procedural sequence also might afford evidence that improper purposes are playing a role. Substantive departures (from normal legislative or bureaucratic processes) too may be relevant, particularly if the factors usually considered important by the decision maker strongly favor a decision contrary to the one reached.[2]

The Court continued:

> The legislative or administrative history may be highly relevant, especially where there are contemporary statements by members of the decision-making body, minutes of its meetings, or reports. In some extraordinary instances, the members might be called to the stand at trial to testify concerning the purpose of the official action, although even then such testimony frequently will be barred by privilege.[3]

Plaintiffs were told to provide (1) evidence of official actions taken with invidious intent found in historical records; (2) evidence that decisional processes were compromised to insure that discriminatory effects would result; and (3) evidence from legislative and administrative records leading to contemporary discriminatory effects.

The *Thornburg* Ruling

In *Thornburg v. Gingles,* 478 US 34 (1986), the Supreme Court incorporated some of the conditions for proving discriminatory intent from the Arlington Heights case. The Supreme Court also created nine categories of conditions gleaned from the so-called Senate Factors made part of the U.S. Senate Judiciary's Committee report on the 1981 Amendments to the Voting Rights Act.

In *Thornburg,* the Court pointed out that not all conditions, or even a majority of conditions, must be proven to show discriminatory intent. The confusion over how many would be enough led to legal infighting during the trial and various interpretations during the deliberative stage by judges.[4]

The Texas Voting Rights Report Card

The collection of the conditions decided by the Court rulings to prove discriminatory intent creates the foundation for a Texas civil rights report card on how the state of Texas has performed in fulfilling the requirements of the Voting Rights Acts of 1965, along with other related amendments and laws.

TEST 1: A HISTORY OF OFFICIAL DISCRIMINATION

According to the Thornburg case, proving "invidious discrimination" involves "the extent of any history of official discrimination in the state or political subdivision that touched the right of the members of the minority group to register, to vote, or otherwise to participate in the democratic process."[5]

What the public record shows in voting rights, education, employment, and health-related matters is that Texas has discriminated against Latinos since the two cultures were introduced to one another in the early part of the nineteenth century. Today, Mexican Americans in Texas continue to suffer worse education and health outcomes, and lower paying jobs, than non-Hispanic whites. The historical record indicates a continuing lack of effort on the part of Texas to help remove barriers to Mexican American voting.

Table 1 outlines the history of various election barriers the State of Texas, through legislation, has imposed to suppress the votes of Latinos and African Americans. Prior to the 1965 Voting Rights Act, Texas used various discriminatory measures to suppress the votes of Mexican Americans, including the poll tax implemented in 1902. This law was part of what became known as Jim Crow laws, which proliferated throughout the southern states after the right to vote was extended to all by the passage of the Thirteenth, Fourteenth, and Fifteenth Amendments to the U.S. Constitution.

The poll tax was intended to inhibit the political participation of African Americans and poor Texans. As a result, it also directly affected the political participation of low-income Latinos.[6] Although the poll tax was prohibited in federal elections by the passage of the Twenty-Fourth Amendment, Texas

Table 1. Texas State Election Barriers (1854–present).

Year(s)	Barrier to voting	Legal outcome
1854	The state considers proposed legislation to deny voting to Mexican Americans.	The effort fails at the state level, but is adopted by some local governments.
1902	Poll taxes are enacted to discourage voting by impoverished minority groups.	The law is struck down by the U.S. Supreme Court in *Harper v. VA Board of Elections* (1966).
1920s	Texas explicitly bans African Americans from participating in state primaries.	The law is struck down by the U.S. Supreme Court in *Nixon v. Herndon* (1927).
1920s	The Texas Democratic Party bans African Americans from participating in party primaries.	The policy is struck down by the U.S. Supreme Court in *Nixon v. Condon* (1932).
1920s	The Texas Democratic Party declares itself a private entity to exclude African Americans from membership and voting in party primaries.	The policy is struck down in *Smith v. Allright* (1944).
1920s	The state adopts at-large elections.	The law is struck down by the U.S. Supreme Court in *White v. Regester* (1973).
1990, 2003, 2012	Gerrymandering leads to changes in congressional district boundaries to favor non-Hispanic white voters.	Changes are struck down by the U.S. Fifth Circuit Court in *Terrazas v. Slagle* (1992); *LULAC v. Perry* (2006); and *Perez v. Perry* (2012).
2012	Texas adopts one of the strictest voter ID laws in the country.	In process of appeals in 2018 before the Fifth Circuit Court in *Veasey v. Abbott*.

continued to use the poll tax in state elections until state-level poll taxes were found unconstitutional by the U.S. Supreme Court in *Harper v. Virginia Board of Elections*, 383 U.S. 663 (1966).

Another mechanism employed by Texas to suppress the votes of racial minorities was the so-called "white primary." A Texas law explicitly banning African Americans from participating in primary elections was found unconstitutional by the U.S. Supreme Court in *Nixon v. Herndon*, 273 U.S. 536 (1927). Texas tried to bypass the decision by declaring that the state would no longer set rules on who could participate in party primaries, leaving the decision up to the state's major political parties. The Texas Democratic Party obliged by passing a rule that African Americans could not participate in their primaries. That rule was struck down by the Supreme Court in *Nixon v. Condon*, 286 U.S. 73 (1932). The Texas Democratic Party then declared itself a private entity in an attempt to continue the exclusion of African

Americans from its primaries, but this was also found unconstitutional by the Supreme Court in *Smith v. Allright*, 321 U.S. 649 (1944).

The adoption of at-large elections for state legislative offices in Texas was found to contribute to diluting minority votes in *White v. Regester*, 412 U.S. 755 (1973). The at-large election scheme, coupled with the racially polarized nature of the electorate and the growth of non-Hispanic white voting blocs, had made it almost impossible for minority populations of Bexar and Dallas Counties to elect candidates of their choice to the state legislature.[7] Racially polarized voting worked against Latinos, particularly in unusually large districts, such as those that existed under the at-large election structure of Texas.[8] Under the at-large structure, minority candidates would enjoy overwhelming support from minority voters, but not enough support from non-Hispanic whites to win elections. Under these circumstances, the U.S. Supreme Court ruled that the at-large scheme diluted minority voting strength in violation of the Fourteenth Amendment.

Racial gerrymandering dilutes the political participation of Mexican Americans and African Americans. The Texas Legislature has racially gerrymandered the single-member districts of the Congressional delegation, state assembly chambers, and the State Board of Education. In every round of redistricting since 1975 following the reapportionment of Congress, and after each decennial census, Texas has been ordered to redraw Congressional, state House, state Senate, or state board of education districts due to the manner in which specific districts have been drawn. I served as an expert witness in *Terrazas v. Slagle*, 821 F. Supp. 1154 (1992), *League of United Latin American Citizens v. Perry*, 548 U.S. 399 (2006), and *Perry v. Pérez*, 565 U.S. 388 (2012) redistricting lawsuits. In every instance, the finding was that the state had manipulated population data to dilute the Latino and African American vote.

In the most recent case, *Perry v. Pérez,* a three-judge U.S. District Court panel found direct evidence that the state acted with racial intent to dilute the Latino vote. That intention was spelled out in an email between state legislative offices during the redistricting deliberations of the 2010 Texas Legislative Session. Gerardo Interiano was a staff attorney to Texas Representative and House Speaker Joe Straus (R-San Antonio). Eric Opiela, a

Republican political counsel to the state Senate Redistricting Committee, initiated the email exchange that triggered overtly discriminatory racial gerrymandering. In the email, the two lawyers discussed creation of a metric to manipulate Latino voter registration and voter numbers in various precincts. They labeled the metric OHRVS, for "Optimal Hispanic Republican Voting Strength."

Texas's Infamous Voter ID Law

More recently, the Texas Legislature passed Senate Bill 14, one of the stricter voter identification (ID) laws in the country, during the 2011 state legislative session. These laws require voters to present photo identification cards before being allowed to vote in an election. The identification cards initially approved by the Texas Legislature proved too expensive to obtain for low-income Texans, including Latino, African American, and older and younger citizens. The Federal District Court for the District of Columbia ruled the law discriminatory during the Voting Rights Act Section 5 hearing in July 2012 in *Texas v. Holder*, Civil Action No. 12-cv-128 (DST, RMC, RLW). the U.S

Nevertheless, Texas was able to implement the voter ID law without any modifications after the Supreme Court struck down the pre-clearance triggering provisions in *Shelby County v. Holder*, 570 U.S. 529 (2013). The voter ID law was again challenged, and in *Veasey, et al. v. Abbott, et al.*, No. 14-41127 (5th Cir. 2016). District Court for the Southern District of Texas and the U.S. Court of Appeals for the Fifth Circuit ruled against the state, concluding that the voter ID law had a discriminatory effect on minority voters. The Southern District court noted that the voter ID law was enacted with racial intent. The Texas voter ID law allowed the state of Texas to begin a voter roll purging process that eliminated "approximately 363,000" voters from the "voting rolls in the first election cycle after *Shelby County*."[9] The Brennan Center for Justice at the New York University School of Law in 2018 reported that "between 2014 and 2016, states removed almost 16 million voters from the rolls" nationwide.[10] The center's researchers wrote that many of the purges were based on the use of "error-ridden practices, that voters were purged secretly and without notice, and that there were limited protections against purges." The report concluded, in part, that "little about purge practices has improved and that a number of things have, in fact, gotten worse."[11]

Persistent Voting Rights Violations

Texas has also led the country in formal objections to the U.S. Department of Justice over state voting laws. Objection letters filed under Section 5 of the Voting Rights Act totaled 1,076 from all states from 1975 through 2013. The 198 objections against Texas during that time period represented the most of any state. By comparison, New York attracted thirteen objections, and New Mexico attracted one.

Table 2 documents the number of objections by each state fully or partially covered by the Voting Rights Act.

Table 3 describes the nature of the 198 objections against Texas and its political subdivisions (counties, cities, school districts, and other special districts). Sixty-seven were for redistricting violations. Eighty objections protested changes in election systems in local and state jurisdictions, including objections to the numbered or place systems, reapportionment restructurings, and majority vote systems. The fifty-one violations listed under the "other" category included violations such as annexations,

Table 2. Voting Rights Act Violations Objections by State.

State	Number of objections	Percent	State	Number of objections	Percent
Texas	198	18.4	Arizona	22	2
Georgia	178	16.5	New York	13	1.2
Mississippi	173	16.1	California	6	.6
Louisiana	148	13.8	Florida	5	.5
South Carolina	121	11.2	North Dakota	4	.4
Alabama	107	10	Alaska	1	<.1
North Carolina	65	6	Michigan	1	<.1
Virginia	33	3.1	New Mexico	1	<.1

Source: U.S. Department of Justice, www.justice.gov.

Table 3. Texas Voting Rights Act Section 5 Objections by Type, 1975–2013.

Redistricting	Method of election	Other
67	80	51

Source: U.S. Department of Justice, www.justice.gov.

elimination of offices, moving polling places to discourage voting, and elimination of elected offices.

Texas's Congressional, state Senate, and state House plans have been objected to in every redistricting year since 1975, demonstrating the state's reputation for persistence in violating the Voting Rights Act with the intent to discriminate against Mexican Americans and African Americans. Additionally, the National Commission on Voting Rights reported that between 1995 and 2014, 172 Section 2 cases were litigated. Of those, ninety-six were tried in Texas.[12]

VOTER DISCRIMINATION BEFORE 1965

While the federal government keeps extensive data on voting violations in Texas against Mexican Americans and African Americans since the inception of the Voting Rights Act of 1965, no comprehensive data have been collected on voter discrimination by Texas or any subjurisdictions prior to 1965. The early history of voting discrimination by local jurisdictions can be gleaned from various histories of Mexican Americans in well-researched books such as Minority Vote Dilution and Race and Class in Texas Politics by Chandler Davidson, V. O. Key's seminal Southern Politics in State and Nation, Anglos and Mexicans in the Making of Texas: 1836–1986 by David Montejano and J. Gilberto Quezada, and Quezada's Border Boss: Manuel B. Bravo and Zapata County.[13]

Davidson's *Minority Vote Dilution* documents minority voter suppression efforts, including the use of at-large election systems, gerrymandering, private slating organizations, runoff requirements, anti-single-shot devices, and decreasing the size of the governmental body after minorities have been elected to offices in Texas from 1837 through 1989. Davidson's work presents empirical evidence in each of these categories for jurisdictions ranging from school districts to the State Legislature.[14]

The forced manipulation of Mexican voters throughout South Texas has been chronicled in the works of Montejano and Quezada, who describe how Mexican Americans were ordered to comply with various "political bosses" that controlled many counties throughout South Texas. These bosses were generally locally elected officials, mostly county judges, who rallied enough support to ensure their reelections and the elections of others who would support their agendas. These practices persisted in parts of South Texas into the 1960s. Some of these political bosses were Mexican Americans, while others were Anglos.[15] Quezada's books describe one instance of Anglo ranchers lobbying to partition one of the counties to escape the electoral effects of a Mexican American political boss.

Political bosses threatened Mexican American voters with the loss of their jobs or homes should they show up to cast ballots. The clearest example of how the Mexican American vote was manipulated in a South Texas town can be found in John Staples Shockley's *Chicano Revolt in a Texas Town*.[16] The book describes how voters in Crystal City were intimidated into staying home on election day. Mexican Americans were told that if they wanted to keep their jobs they would have to vote for Anglo school board and city council officials.

The Crystal City case is not unique. I found evidence of economic coercion of Latino voters as recently as 1991 in Rocksprings, Texas, while conducting research for *Rodriguez and Reyes v. Rocksprings Independent School District* (DR-89-CA-29). Anglo ranchers told a Latino businessman that his business, providing fencing for ranches, would "dry up" if he persisted in mounting an election campaign for one of the county commissioners' positions. The threats became so serious that the Mexican American businessman closed his business and relocated to Big Springs, Texas, in another county.

The manipulation of Mexican American voters by local Anglo political bosses was documented initially by the famous Texas political scientist V. O. Key in his seminal work, *Southern Politics in State and Nation*.[17] The history of suppressing the Latino vote began with the in-person manipulation of large numbers of Mexican American farm and ranch hands subject to coercion by political bosses. The practice has evolved into the more sophisticated use of technology, which obscure discriminatory intent, to gerrymander the state's Congressional, state legislature, and school districts in recent times. Technology requires no interactions with minority voters to create statistical matrices for use in racial gerrymandering and other discriminatory practices.

TEST 2: A HISTORY OF RACIALLY POLARIZED ELECTIONS

One of the conditions for proving discriminatory intent in violations of the Voting Rights Act is to present evidence of racially polarized elections, or, as written in Thornburg, "the extent to which voting in the elections of the state or political subdivision is racially polarized."[18]

Research presented in the 2012 Congressional redistricting case, *Perez v. Perry,* heard before the U.S. Supreme Court, provided evidence of a well-documented pattern of racially polarized voting throughout the recent history of Texas. Research presented to the Court in earlier 1991 and 2003 Congressional redistricting cases also described a clear pattern of racially polarized voting in the state. Since this type of research was conducted in voting rights cases, there is no evidence that this pattern of racially polarized voting has ended. More than thirty years of analyses indicate that racially polarized elections in Texas are the norm, not anomalies.

TEST 3: ELECTORAL MECHANISMS THAT ENHANCE OPPORTUNITY TO DISCRIMINATE

In Thornburg, another condition established for proving discriminatory intent in Voting Rights Act cases was to show a history of "electoral mechanisms" designed to discriminate against Mexican Americans. The Supreme Court wrote that this condition would be based on "the extent to which the state or political subdivision has used unusually large election districts, majority vote requirements, anti-single shot provisions, or other voting practices or procedures that may enhance the opportunity for discrimination against the minority group."[19]

Pure at-large voting systems in Texas and other states allowed the majority non-Latino white voting population to outvote Latinos in communities where there were substantial numbers of Mexican American voters. Historically higher election turnout by non-Latino white voters guaranteed, in the pure at-large configuration, that Latinos would not have an opportunity to elect a candidate of choice.

Under the pure at-large system with no majority requirement, the candidates for all the seats run against each other. The top several vote-getters are the winners. For example, if there are five seats to be filled, and fifteen candidates running, each voter can choose up to five candidates. This system would allow minority-group voters to decide to limit their choices to a particular candidate on the ballot, known as the "single-shot or bullet vote," withholding their remaining votes. This puts more weight on their vote for the preferred candidate, since it deprives the other candidates of votes.[20] If the voter is required to cast as many votes as allowed, and has not marked all the choices to which he or she is entitled, then the "single-shot" vote would be thrown out because of an anti-single-shot proscription.

The "place system" similarly discriminates against Mexican Americans. Under the place system, sometimes called the full-slate system, multiple places have candidates running for each place, rather than competing against all other candidates. This can prevent Latino voters in jurisdictions where they represent a substantial minority of voters from "bullet voting" or concentrating their votes on their candidate(s) of choice.[21]

The majority rule holds only for primary elections in Texas. If a candidate does not win at least 50 percent plus one more vote cast in the primary, he or she must compete again in a runoff with the second-place finisher. Generally, when Latino candidates finish their primary election in either first or second place without winning the requisite majority of votes, they must run again in a runoff election held thirty days later. Latino candidates are forced to spend additional funds on the new campaign, and they face the possibility that the second- or first-place winner still will gain the support of the voters who had voted for the other candidates. A Latino voter who wins the plurality of the votes in the primary might lose the runoff. If there is more than one Anglo candidate in the primary, Anglo voters who voted for the second-, third-, or fourth-place finishers might redirect their support in the runoff to the Anglo candidate to defeat the Latino candidate who initially won more primary votes. This possibility is more likely to become a reality in those jurisdictions where the electorate is racially polarized.

TEST 4: EXAMINE THE EFFECTS OF DISCRIMINATION

In Thornburg, the Supreme Court listed the effects of historical discrimination in "public areas" as among the conditions necessary to prove discriminatory intent in Voting Rights Act cases. The Court described this condition as "the extent to which members of the minority group in the state or political subdivision bear the effects of discrimination in such areas as education, employment, and health, which hinder their ability to participate effectively in the political process."

The federal courts have declared the country's educational system the cornerstone of our democracy, because the system is designed to introduce all who live in the United States to common languages, customs, traditions, lifestyles, and how our government is structured and functions. How our government is structured includes an emphasis on the responsibilities of voting and earning taxable wages.

The judicial historical record is replete with cases in state and federal courts that have found the Texas educational system lacking in the quality of education that has been delivered, particularly for poor, ethnic, and racial minority groups. Those cases have ranged from *San Antonio v. Rodriguez* (411 U.S.1), argued before the U.S. Supreme Court in 1973, to several *Edgewood v. Kirby* state supreme court cases filed from 1984 through 2018.

The *San Antonio* case was filed on behalf of the San Antonio Independent School District, and the *Edgewood* case was filed on behalf of the Edgewood Independent School District. Both districts serve predominantly Mexican American student populations in largely low-income San Antonio neighborhoods. Because school districts rely on local property taxes to fund their campuses and programs, the reliance amounts to discrimination against a school district with a lower property tax base than a district in a higher income neighborhood with a higher property tax base.

The long-term consequences of discrimination in education have been confirmed by historically negative outcomes for students in "poor" districts versus "rich" districts. Districts like San Antonio and Edgewood suffer lower test scores, higher dropout rates in elementary and secondary grades, and lower college attendance rates. This, in turn, has resulted in lower household incomes and higher unemployment and poverty rates for Latinos and

African Americans in the state. The economic disparities have, in turn, led to disproportionately higher rates of poverty-related diseases, lower life expectancies, higher percentages of individuals lacking health insurance coverage, and higher levels of teen pregnancies among minority populations in Texas.

The tables and figures that follow illustrate socioeconomic indicators that characterize the disparities among white non-Hispanic, Mexican American, and African Americans Texans in education, economic security, public health, and safety.

Discrimination in Education

Figure 1 depicts high school dropout levels in grades nine through twelve at Texas public schools, reported by the Texas Education Agency, from 2005 through 2013.

The chart depicts a very gradual decline in dropout rates for both non-Hispanic whites and African American from 2006 to 2013, and a gradual increase in the dropout rate for Latinos. Mexican American children are dropping out at a rate three times higher than that of African American and Anglo children. As of 2013, a Mexican American child had only a 39 percent chance of finishing high school in Texas.

Latinos have never been able to fully recover from the historical discrimination they have suffered at the hands of the Texas educational system. At first, Mexican Americans were banned from public schools. In a later era, Latinos were only allowed to go to public schools through the third grade. The intent was that this level of education was all that was required to perform menial labor tasks in local economies throughout the state. During this era, Texas school districts created "Mexican Schools," where Latino children were taught separately from Anglo children. Today, many Mexican American children attend chronically underfinanced public schools. This legacy of discrimination explains why Mexican Americans trail both Anglos and African Americans in public education outcomes.[22]

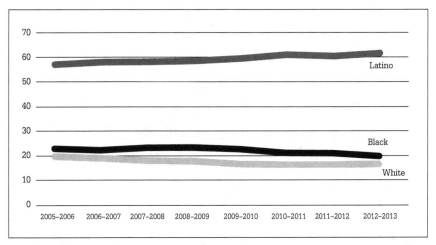

Figure 1. Dropout Rates for Texas Public Schools by Race, 2005–2013. *Source:* Texas Education Agency, *Secondary School Completion and Dropout Rates in Texas Public Schools, 2012–13,* Doc. GE1470107 (Austin, TX: 2014).

The legacy is also reflected in Latino participation rates in the Texas economy. Many Latinos earn lower wages and suffer higher poverty rates. In the San Antonio and Edgewood school districts, neighborhood poverty rates in 2018 ranged upward to 40 percent—more than twice San Antonio's overall 18.5 percent poverty rate.[23]

One significant link to lower wages is lower college graduation rates among Latinos. While one in three non-Hispanic whites earned bachelor or graduate degrees by 2010, fewer than one in nine Latinos had earned college degrees, according to the U.S. Census Bureau.[24] College degrees are critical to obtaining employment at the managerial levels of government agencies and the private sector, and are the gateways to higher income levels.[25] The chronic disparities in average median incomes between Latinos and Anglos in Texas are partially explained by the difference in educational opportunities for Mexican Americans versus non-Hispanic white residents of Texas.

Between 2000 and 2011, of the 282,821 master's degrees awarded by Texas public institutions, 52 percent were awarded to non-Latino whites. Another 14 percent were awarded to Latinos, and 8 percent were awarded to African Americans.[26]

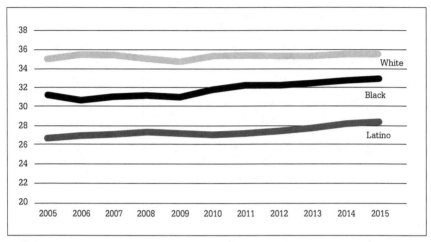

Figure 2. Median Age of Texans by Race, 2005–2015. *Source:* U.S. Bureau of Census, American Community Survey: B01002.

Having an uneducated electorate and work force is not desirable for any state, especially Texas, with its rapidly changing demographics. In this book's chapter by Sáenz, Figure 2 depicts the U.S. Census Bureau's tracking of the rapid growth in the Mexican American population in Texas, from 16 percent of the state's population in 1960, to 40 percent in 2018. The combined Latino and African American populations transformed Texas into a majority-minority state shortly after the 2010 Census.

Adding another layer of complexity to the demographic makeup of Texas is that the Latino population is a much younger one than either the Anglo or African American populations. Figure 2 demonstrates that in the ten-year period between 2005 and 2015 the median age for Latinos was seven to eight years lower than the median age of non-Hispanic white populations, and four and a half lower years lower than the median age of African Americans.

Their higher median age is a principal reason non-Hispanic whites are expected to become the numerical minority before 2050 in Texas, according to Rogelio Sáenz, Dean of the College of Public Policy at the University of Texas at San Antonio. In a report for the *San Antonio-Express News* in July 2018, Sáenz wrote, "Latinos, in particular, will be an increasingly important segment of the future of the country [not simply in Texas] and all of its institutions, including the economy, the healthcare system, universities, the military, places of worship, and the mass media."[27]

The effect of a poorly educated Latino workforce that will become the majority of the Texas labor force will eventually reach a "tipping point" for the state's economy.[28] As the aging non-Hispanic white workforce declines in numbers over time, the younger Mexican American workforce will grow, creating a leadership vacuum in public and private sectors. Too few Latinos will have access to advanced education credentials to fill the vacuum.

Public Health Disparities

Another indicator of the legacy of discrimination suffered by Latinos can be found in public health data. Figure 3 shows the percentage of individuals by race or ethnicity lacking health coverage in Texas from 2003 through 2012. In 2012, 58 percent of Latinos lacked health care coverage, versus 20 percent of non-Hispanic white residents.

Mexican Americans lag far behind both non-Hispanic whites and African Americans in access to health insurance. More Latinos must rely

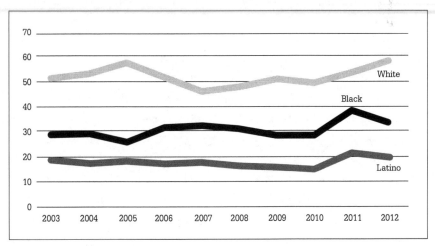

Figure 3. Percent of Texas Adults Lacking Health Coverage by Race, 2003–2012. *Source:* 2014 Health Status of Texas Report: Texas Behavioral Risk Factor Surveillance System.

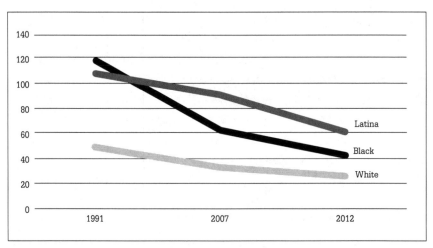

Figure 4. Texas Teen Pregnancy Rate (per 1,000, ages fifteen to nineteen years), 1991–2012. *Source:* National Center for Health Statistics, Division of Vital Statistics, Table 7: Birth Rates for Teenagers Age 15–19 by Race, Hispanic Origin of Mother (NCHS, 2014).

on public health services, because they cannot afford private services normally covered by insurance companies. Even when relying on state support, particularly since Texas has systematically defunded the state's share of Medicaid funding, the majority of lower income Latinos must pay a higher proportion of their incomes for health care services.

One indicator of public health that provides evidence of a legacy of discrimination is the extent of teen pregnancies. The teen pregnancy rate for Mexican Americans has been twice that of non-Hispanic white females for more than twenty years, as evidenced in Figure 4. Mexican American teen pregnancy rates for live births in 1991 stood at 108.5 per 1,000 teens between the ages of fifteen and nineteen, while that of Anglos was 49.7 per 1,000 during the same year. By 2012, the pregnancy rates for all Anglos, African Americans, and Mexican Americans had declined, but Mexican Americans lagged behind. While Mexican Americans had a lower teen pregnancy rate than African Americans in 1991, Latino teen pregnancy rates were higher by 2007 and in ensuing years.

Poverty, Income Inequality, and Unemployment

Latinos in Texas have historically suffered some of the highest poverty rates in the nation, and poverty is directly related to educational attainment and general health levels. Poverty is also associated with lower employment levels and higher teen pregnancy rates. As of a U.S. Census Bureau American Community Survey in 2013, the three poorest metropolitan areas in the United States are in Texas: McAllen-Edinburg-Mission, Brownsville-Harlingen, and Laredo. These metropolitan areas exist in the Rio Grande Valley and along the Texas–Mexico border, where Mexican Americans comprise as much as 95 percent or more of the population.

Figure 5 illustrates that the poverty rate exceeds 30 percent in all three communities. In fact, Texas has four of the ten poorest metropolitan areas in the United States. The poverty rate exceeds 28 percent in the state's College Station-Bryan metro area. No other state has more than two metro areas in the top ten.

Poverty in Texas is also closely associated with race, as demonstrated in Figure 6. While fewer than one in ten non-Hispanic whites live below the

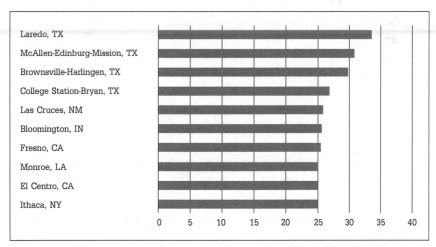

Figure 5. Top Ten Metro Areas in United States by Percent in Poverty, 2016. *Source:* Integrated Public Use Microdata Samples: American Community Survey 2016 Sample.

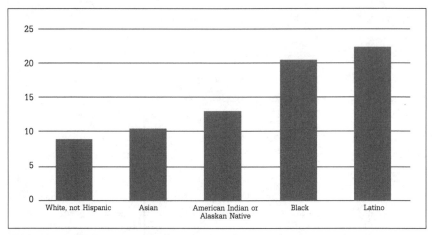

Figure 6. Percent of Persons in Poverty in Texas by Race, 2016. *Source:* Integrated Public Use Microdata Samples: American Community Survey 2016 Sample.

federal poverty line, as many as one in four African Americans and Latinos live below the federally defined poverty level.[29]

Income and Employment

Figure 7 depicts the disparities in median family incomes among Latinos, Anglos, and African Americans since 2005. While the median income level of each group increased from 2005 to 2015, the gaps remain wide between minority and nonminority Texans.

Figure 8 depicts unemployment rates for Anglos, African Americans, and Latinos from 2009 through 2015. African American unemployment rates have been consistently higher. Mexican American unemployment rates hover halfway between the rates for non-Hispanic white residents and African Americans. Apparent similarities in fluctuations indicate that when one group's unemployment rate falls, so do the rates of the other two groups. Like the state's persistent income gaps, the gaps in unemployment between minority and non-minority Texas populations are not closing.

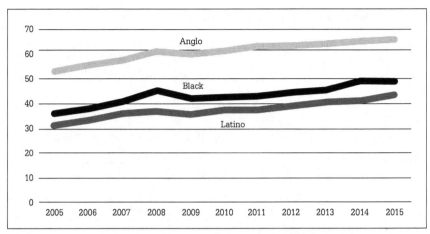

Figure 7. Median Annual Family Income by Race, 2005–2015 (in thousands). *Source:* U.S. Bureau of Census, American Community Survey: B19013.

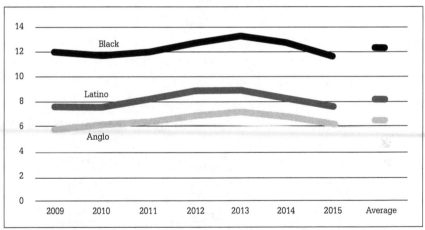

Figure 8. Percent Unemployed in Texas by Race, 2009–2015. *Source:* U.S. Bureau of Census, American Community Survey: S2301.

Higher unemployment rates for Latinos and African Americans are structural because they are the direct result of a poorly funded educational system with discriminatory intent that does not provide the essential certifications required to effectively participate in the state's labor force.

Effects on Voting and Registration

All of the economic, educational, and health data contribute to what the Supreme Court described in Thornburg as the "public area" of discrimination that can have an effect on general political participation. Figure 9 depicts the percentage of each minority and nonminority group's eligible voting population: those eighteen years old and older who were registered to vote between 2008 and 2016.

African Americans and non-Hispanic whites had registered to vote at much higher levels during the past three presidential election cycles than Latinos. While almost three in four eligible Anglos and African Americans are registered to vote in Texas, slightly more than one-half of all eligible Latinos are registered voters.

The lower registration rates of Mexican Americans partially explain why they have lower voting rates than their fellow Anglo and African American Texans. Figure 10 shows that an average of six in ten eligible non-Hispanic white and African American voters cast ballots in the past three presidential election cycles. Fewer than four in ten eligible Latinos voted during those years.

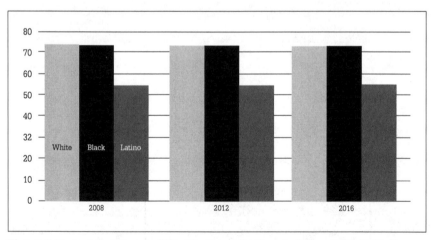

Figure 9. Percent Registered of Eligible Voters by Race in Texas, 2008–2016. *Source:* U.S. Bureau of Census, *Current Population Reports: Voting and Registration in the Election of 2008, 2012, 2016,* compilation of 2007, 2011, 2015.

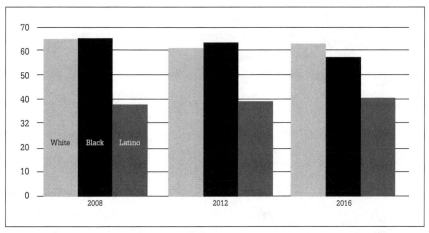

Figure 10. Voter Turnout by Race in Texas, 2008–2016. *Source:* U.S. Bureau of Census, *Current Population Reports: Voting and Registration in the Election of 2008, 2012, 2016,* compilation of 2007, 2011, 2015.

TEST 5: RACIAL APPEALS IN POLITICAL CAMPAIGNS

Another condition described in Thornburg as a condition to meet in order to prove discriminatory intent in Voting Rights Act cases is evidence of explicit appeals to race during political campaigns. The Supreme Court described the issue as "whether political campaigns have been characterized by overt or subtle racial appeals," in *Thornburg v. Gingles,* 478 U.S. 30 (37).

Racial appeals during elections in Texas are not unusual. They are symptomatic of a history of tense relations between non-Hispanic white Texans and Texans who are Mexican American by heritage. For example, during the 1845 Texas Constitutional Convention, a Harris County (Houston) delegate argued against giving "Mexicans" the right to vote. His spurious argument was that if Mexican Americans were allowed to vote in their home state, more than 50,000 people from the country of Mexico would cross the border to vote and elect a government of their own.[30]

Even though the amendment was defeated at the state level, the counties of Bexar (San Antonio), Nueces (Corpus Christi), and Webb (Laredo) refused Mexican Americans the right to vote. A *Corpus Christi Ranchero* newspaper editorial protested that "American men, in an American country should have a fair showing in shaping the destinies of the country."[31] And the *Fort Brown Flag* newspaper in Brownsville, located at the predominantly Hispanic southernmost tip of Texas, declared: "We are opposed to allowing an ignorant crowd of Mexicans (*sic*) to determine the political questions in this country where a man is supposed to vote knowingly and thoughtfully."[32]

In more recent times, overt racial appeals have evolved into less obvious forms. For instance, instead of referring to Mexican Americans as "Mexicans," terms such as "immigrant populations" or "Spanish speakers" have been substituted. References to words and phrases like poverty and public education are also substitute terms, as described in Ian Haney López's book *Dog Whistle Politics: How Coded Racial Appeals Have Reinvented Racism and Wrecked the Middle Class*.[33] López describes how terms such as "welfare queens" and "food stamp recipients" became substitutes for more overt racial labeling of African Americans. The use of overtly racist language has gone underground, he writes, while overt words and uses are practiced in privacy.

TEST 6: DO MINORITY-GROUP CANDIDATES WIN?

The Supreme Court in Thornburg decided that the number of elections won by minority groups could become a condition upon which to argue discriminatory intent in Voting Rights Act cases. The Court described the condition, simply, as "the extent to which members of the minority group have been elected to public office in the jurisdiction."

A stark example of how Mexican Americans in Texas have not been able to elect candidates of choice over the years to state offices can be found in the dearth of Latinos elected to state executive branch offices.

Texas Executive Branch

The Texas state executive branch consists of seven offices. Six have one elected officer per office. The Texas Railroad Commission has three elected commissioners. The other offices are governor, lieutenant governor, attorney general, agriculture commissioner, general land commissioner, and comptroller of public accounts.

Adding the nine executive branch officers to eighteen judges of the state's two supreme courts (the Texas Supreme Court and Texas Court of Criminal Appeals) equals twenty-seven different statewide elected officials who are elected at-large in partisan elections under a primary/general election system. Because the primaries are partisan in nature, and conducted under a majority-rule, runoff configuration, almost all candidates, including court candidates, must rely on generous contributions from individual donors and interest groups to conduct Texas-wide election campaigns in a state that is more than 268,580 square miles in size.

Evidence of the difficulty Latinos have in winning statewide offices can be found in the history of the absence of Latinos in most statewide elected offices. Table 4 documents the number of Latinos who have held executive-level offices. Only six Mexican Americans have served at the executive level and only two of those managed to win a statewide election. The other four were appointed, and lost in reelection attempts. The two Mexican Americans who won statewide elections were Dan Morales, who was Texas attorney general from 1991 through 1999, and Tony Garza, who won a position on the Texas Railroad Commission in 1998, serving one term. Garza was subsequently appointed U.S. ambassador to Mexico by President George W. Bush.

Almost all executive branch offices run for office concurrently, during the same general and midterm election years as the presidential elections. The exceptions are the three railroad commissioners, who run for six-year, overlapping terms. As a result, there is a railroad commissioner position on the general election ballot every two years. The chair of the railroad commission is a rotating position, with the chair generally being the commissioner who will next face reelection. Several members have served as chair for more than one term.

There are no term limits for any of the executive branch offices, although some politicians use state offices as stepping-stones to higher offices. For example, after winning a state land commissioner's race, Texan Rick Perry later became agriculture commissioner, lieutenant governor, and then governor. In 2017, following an earlier, unsuccessful bid to become the Republican candidate for president, Perry moved to Washington, DC, to

Table 4. Texas State Executive Branch Officials by Race, 1845–2017.

Office	Number of elected officials	Non-Hispanic white	Mexican American	African American	Appointed	Elected	Other	Not known
Governor	49	49	0	0	3	43	3	0
Lt. governor	47	47	0	0	6	41	0	0
Attorney general	50	49	1	0	14	33	0	3
Agriculture commissioner	11	11	0	0	2	9	0	0
Land commissioner	28	27	1	0	5	21	0	2
Comptroller	28	25	0	0	5	21	0	2
Railroad Commission (RRC)	50	45	4	1	20	30		
Totals	260	253	6	1	55	198	3	7
		(97.3%)	(2.3%)	(.03%)	(21.1%)	(76.2%)	(1.1%)	(2.7%)

Sources: *The Handbook of Texas Online* (http://handbook/online); Texas Comptroller of Public Accounts (http://www.windows.state.tx.us); Texas Agriculture Commissioner, *A Century of Texas Agriculture Commissioners*; Texas General Land Office, untitled list of Land Commissioners; Texas General Land Office, *Three Centuries on the Land: The Archives of the Texas General Land Office*, revised May 2012; The Texas Railroad Commission, *Commissioners*, retrieved January 2017; Texas Railroad Commission, *Who Regulates Railroads in Texas? Don't Let Our Name Throw You Off Track*, 2010. (All data on individuals who have held executive branch-level offices in Texas since 1845 have been generated from the archives of each office. While most offices have been in place since Texas became a state in 1845, the Texas Railroad Commission and the Office of the Texas Agricultural Commissioner are twentieth-century creations.)

become U.S. Secretary of Energy. Texan Greg Abbott was the state's attorney general before becoming governor in 2015.

The one office that is not perceived as a stepping-stone to the governor's office, or other executive branch position, is the Texas Railroad Commission. This might stem from the agency's unique function, requiring individuals with specialized training and knowledge.[34]

The railroad commission regulates the state's oil and gas industries, gas utilities, pipeline safety, safety of liquefied gas, and surface coal and uranium mining. Although the agency kept the name, the commission no longer regulates the railroad industry. Many individuals elected to the railroad commission have training as either geologists or engineers, with experience working in these industries as well.

The only other executive branch office requiring a specific education is the attorney general's office. Candidates must be lawyers and members of the Texas State Bar. Unlike the vice president of the United States, the lieutenant governor of Texas is not the governor's assistant or governor "in waiting." The lieutenant governor presides as the president of the Texas Senate, providing this officer the unique responsibilities of overseeing the senate's legislative agenda while controlling the senate's internal rulemaking. In fact, the lieutenant governor is often referred to as the most important officer of the state government.[35]

As shown in Table 4 (presented earlier), during the period of 1845 to 2017 only seven members of racial or ethnic minority groups were elected to any of the executive branch offices since their creation. Most recently, 97 percent of all elected or appointed executive branch officials are non-Hispanic white, 2 percent are Mexican American, and 0.3 percent are African American. To declare that members of protected populations have not fared well under the at-large election system in Texas is an understatement.

While there seems to be no evidence of a formal slating process at work, there appears to be an informal vetting process signaling to various candidates which office they should run for because of the "stepping stone effect."[36] Such vetting tends to make the primaries less competitive, unless a candidate is perceived as independent-minded. In this instance, some candidates will eschew the process and file for office, regardless of the wishes of the various political leaders and/or political parties.

Texas Judicial Branch

For the most part, the only state-level offices where Mexican Americans have been successful in winning elections are in single-member districts or at-large districts with substantial Latino majorities. An excellent example of this can be found in the election of intermediate appellate court judges. For instance, three Latina jurists who have attempted to win Supreme Court or Courts of Criminal Appeals elections were recruited to contest seats at the high courts because they had been successful at winning election to their respective appellate courts in Nueces County (Corpus Christi).[37]

Table 5 shows the location and ethnic composition of elected officials to all fourteen intermediate appellate courts in Texas. Latinos have won

Table 5. Justices of Texas's Fourteen Intermediate Appellate Courts by Race, 2018.

Court of Appeal	Number of justices	Location in Texas	Anglo	Black	Latino
First	9	Houston	9		
Second	7	Fort Worth	7		
Third	6	Austin	6		
Fourth	7	San Antonio	3		4
Fifth	12	Dallas	10	2	
Sixth	3	Texarkana	3		
Seventh	4	Amarillo	4		
Eighth	3	El Paso	1		2
Ninth	4	Beaumont	4		
Tenth	3	Waco	3		
Eleventh	3	Eastland	3		
Twelfth	3	Tyler	3		
Thirteenth	6	Corpus Christi			6
Fourteenth	9	Houston	9		
Total	79		65	2	12
Percent	100		82	3	15

Source: www.txcourts.gov.

election to the bench in only three: the Fourth District (Bexar County–San Antonio), Eighth District (El Paso County), and Thirteenth District (Nueces County). These three districts are also the only ones having majority Hispanic voting-age populations (HVAPs).[38] The Fourth District has seven judges, and four are Mexican Americans. The Eighth District has three judges; two are Latino. All six judges in the Thirteenth are Mexican Americans. The remaining eleven intermediate appellate courts had no Latino judges as of 2018.[39]

Texas Final Grade

Elections in the state of Texas are so racially polarized that discrimination is the norm, not an aberration, in any election. Racially polarized elections are the by-products of a long history of racial discrimination in most social arenas, particularly in the realm of education. Latino candidates of choice have little to no electoral success in statewide elections due to the polarized nature of the elections and the lack of an adequate non-Hispanic white crossover vote. The lack of Latino candidates' success in statewide elections is directly linked to the state's discriminatory at-large election system.

The totality of circumstances of a history of official discrimination, manipulation of the Latino electorate, legacy of discrimination in public services, and the state's at-large election schemes makes it almost impossible for Mexican Americans to elect a candidate of choice in statewide executive office and judicial elections in the state of Texas.

On the Texas voting rights report card, Texas earns an "F" for failure. The state and its elected officials have illegally avoided implementing federal voter protection laws. The state has manipulated election data sets for racial and partisan reasons and has gerrymandered voting districts for Congressional and state legislative offices in every redistricting cycle.

Texas discriminates against Mexican Americans and other minority populations in public service delivery as well. This is particularly true for public elementary and secondary systems with predominantly Mexican

American student populations that remain chronically underfunded, despite decades of court battles demanding equal funding.

The history of widespread discrimination against Mexican Americans in Texas portends a bleak future for Latino voter rights. The Texas legislature has consistently failed to take positive steps to rid the state's electoral system of blatantly discriminatory voting rules such as racial gerrymandering, error-plagued voter purging practices, and unfair at-large election systems.

These systems also effectively prevent Mexican Americans from winning elections to statewide offices, stifling their voices by essentially barricading their way to positions of political influence. Rather than abide by federal law designed to protect all voters' rights, the state wastes millions of taxpayer dollars unsuccessfully defending illegal voting practices in state and federal courts. Without meaningful reforms, and without diverse new voices in elected positions to lead the way, the future will be bleak for all Texans in a state that continues to squash voting rights, and economic and leadership opportunities, for the state's youngest and most rapidly growing ethnic population.

Recommendations

- Since Texas historically has refused to abide by federal antidiscrimination and voter rights laws already in place, the U.S. Congress should be persuaded to implement harsher penalties for violating these laws for states like Texas guilty of multiple attempts to skirt the law.
- Congress should implement rules removing the overly strict requirements for proving discriminatory intent.
- In Texas, there is clearly a need for a Texas Voting Rights Act that protects the rights of all voters, with severe penalties to local, county, and state jurisdictions for violations.
- Include in state legislature orientations classes on racial/ethnic sensitivity and the contributions and history of all racial and ethnic minority groups. These orientations should be required for members of the State

Senate, State House of Representatives, lieutenant governor, governor, and executive branch directors.

- Create a voter registration process that is proactive, ensuring more eligible voters are registered and understand the registration and voting process. A broad voter education process would ensure all voters are more knowledgeable about candidates and propositions placed on ballots.
- Lawmakers should eliminate overly long ballots to avoid "decision fatigue" from being faced with deciding on too many issues listed in one election cycle. Instead, spread the number of issues to two cycles instead of one.

Notes

1. *Reitman v. Mulkey,* 387 U.S. 369, 387 U.S. 373–376 (1967); *Grosjean v. American Press Co.,* 297 U.S. 233 (1936); 297 U.S. 250 cited in the original opinion.
2. *Village of Arlington Heights v. Metropolitan Housing Development Corp,* 429 U.S. (1977); 429 U.S. 268.
3. *Tenney v. Brandhove,* 341 U.S. 367 (1951); *United States v. Nixon,* 418 U.S. 683, 418 U.S. 705 (1974).
4. *Thornburg v. Gingles,* 478 US 34 (1986).
5. *Thornburg v. Gingles,* 34.
6. David Montejano, *Anglos and Mexicans in the Making of Texas, 1836–1986* (Austin: University of Texas Press, 1989); Chandler Davidson, *Race and Class in Texas Politics* (Princeton, NJ: Princeton University Press, 1990).
7. Ian Haney López, *Dog Whistle Politics: How Coded Racial Appeals Have Reinvented Racism & Wrecked the Middle Class* (New York: Oxford University Press, 2014). "Racially polarized" voting occurs when voters of one race or ethnic background vote extraordinarily differently from voters of another racial or ethnic group. In Texas, Latino and Anglo voters tend to vote against each other's favored candidate or issue. This voting pattern has held since data of this sort were initially gathered in the 1970s.
8. The three-judge panel of the Western District of Texas ruled that the 2011 round of redistricting was performed with racial intent. CA No. 11-CA-360-OLG-JES-XR, December 2, 2011: Notice of Appeal, *Shannon Perez et al. v. State of Texas et al.,* 5:11-cv-00360-OLG-JES-XR Document 1568 W.D. Tex. San Antonio Division, September 9, 2017.
9. Jonathan Brater, Kevin Morris, Myrna Pérez and Christopher Deluzio, *Purges: A Growing Threat to the Right to Vote* (New York: The Brennan Center for Justice, New York University School of Law, 2018).
10. Brater et al., *Purges: A Growing Threat.*
11. Brater et al., *Purges: A Growing Threat.*
12. National Commission on Voting Rights, *Protecting Minority Voters—2014—Our Work Is Not Done* (Washington, DC: Lawyers' Committee for Civil Rights Under Law, 2014).

13. Montejano, *Anglos and Mexicans*; Chandler Davidson, *Minority Vote Dilution* (Washington, DC: Howard University Press, 1989); J. Gilberto Quezada, *Border Boss: Manuel B. Bravo and Zapata County* (College Station: Texas A&M University Press, 1999); John Staples Shockley, *Chicano Revolt in a Texas Town* (Notre Dame, IN: University of Notre Dame Press, 1974); V. O. Key, *Southern Politics in State and Nation* (New York: Alfred A. Knopf, 1949); Chandler Davidson, *Race and Class in Texas Politics* (Princeton, NJ: Princeton University Press, 1990).

14. Davidson, *Minority Vote Dilution*, 6.

15. Montejano, *Anglos and Mexicans*; Quezada, *Border Boss*.

16. Shockley, *Chicano Revolt*.

17. Key, *Southern Politics*.

18. *Thornburg v. Gingles*, 34.

19. *Thornburg v. Gingles*, 34.

20. Davidson, *Minority Vote Dilution*, 7.

21. Davidson, *Minority Vote Dilution*.

22. Gilbert G. Gonzalez, *Chicano Education in the Era of Segregation* (Denton: University of North Texas Press, 2013).

23. Joshua Fechter, "Report: Poverty in San Antonio Disproportionately Hits Hispanic, Black Residents," *San Antonio Express News*, July 30, 2019.

24. U.S. Census Bureau, 2010.

25. Patrick J. Kelly, *As America Becomes More Diverse: The Impact of State Higher Education Inequality* (Boulder, CO: National Center for Higher Education Systems, 2005).

26. Somer L. Franklin, John R. Slate, and Sheila A. Joyner, "Ethnic Disparities in Master's Degree Attainment at Texas Public Institutions: A Multiyear Statewide Investigation," *In Progress*, 2013, available at inprogressjournal.net; J. R. Allum, N. E. Bell, and R. S. Sowell, *Graduate Enrollment and Degrees: 2001–2011* (Washington, DC: Council of Graduate Schools, 2012).

27. Rogelio Sáenz, "Declining White Population Is Spawning Fears, Bias," *San Antonio Express-News*, July 22, 2018, F1–F6.

28. Malcolm Gladwell, *The Tipping Point: How Little Things Can Make a Big Difference* (New York: Little, Brown, 2002).

29. U.S. Census Bureau, *Historical Poverty Thresholds*. The official federal poverty level for a family of four as of 2017 was $24,858.

30. Montejano, *Anglos and Mexicans*, 38–39.

31. Montejano, *Anglos and Mexicans*, 39.

32. Montejano, *Anglos and Mexicans*, 39.

33. López, *Dog Whistle Politics*.

34. Lyle C. Brown et al., *Practicing Texas Politics, 2017–2018*, 17th ed. (Boston, MA: Cengage Learning, 2017).

35. Brown et al., *Practicing Texas Politics*.

36. Brown et al., *Practicing Texas Politics*.

37. Linda Reyna Yañez and Gina M. Benavides, Texas 13th District Intermediate Appellate Court Justices, interviewed by author.

38. Author's calculations of Hispanic voting-age population (HVAP). The 4th District has a 55.4 percent HVAP, the 8th District has a 72.8 percent HVAP, and the 13th District has a 66.6 percent HVAP. Texas Legislative Council, District Viewer, 2017, https://gis1.tlc.texas.gov.

39. Texas Judicial Branch, "About Texas Courts," online at txcourts.gov.

KEVIN MORRIS AND MYRNA PÉREZ

Barriers to the Ballot Box in Texas

I n January 2019, David Whitley, the acting secretary of state of Texas, drew national attention with claims that more than ninety-five thousand noncitizens had registered to vote in Texas, and that nearly sixty thousand of these individuals had cast a ballot in at least one election.[1] Within days, Whitley had to walk back his claim, but in that short period his actions had already provided yet another example of racial and ethnic hostility corrupting our electoral process.

Within days of Whitley's announcement, it became clear that the process that the secretary of state's office had been using was flawed. Counties immediately began announcing that the lists provided by the states included naturalized citizens.[2] Individuals who had not been citizens when they last visited the Department of Motor Vehicles had subsequently become naturalized and then registered to vote as full American citizens. Four days after the initial announcement, officials in five of the largest counties in Texas confirmed that the secretary of state's office had called them to inform them that many of the flagged individuals had been flagged inaccurately and had already provided proof of citizenship.[3]

Naturalized citizens who had been wrongfully flagged and civil rights organizations sued to stop the voter list review from going forward, and the state eventually agreed to not remove these voters.[4] By focusing on only noncitizens who were registered instead of all voters with invalid registrations, Whitley and the secretary of state office explicitly questioned the right of Latinos to participate in their elections.

Before the walk back and the lawsuits, Texas Attorney General Ken Paxton tweeted a "VOTER FRAUD ALERT" about illegal votes depriving Americans of their voice.[5] Two days later, President Donald Trump also used his Twitter account to argue that these voters identified by Whitley were "just the tip of the iceberg."[6]

Although this episode was particularly egregious, it is not out of line with the trajectory of the battle for civil rights in the Lone Star State and throughout the nation.[7] Individual incidents throw the larger trends into sharper relief. As we move into the next decade, questions about who should get a say in the future of their communities are continually being raised. Texans from all walks of life should be pushing back against rhetoric and policy that cheapen democracy.

Voting Rights and Texas: A Fraught—and Fought—History

The barriers to voting in Texas are nothing new. Texas has a long history of making it difficult for racial minorities—particularly Latinos—to cast their ballots. This history, however, is not limited to discrimination against Latinos. At various times in the state's history, Texas has moved to make it harder for various minority groups to participate in the democratic process. Nevertheless, given both the size of the Latino population in Texas and the unique challenges that face a minority group that is less likely to speak English, the situation facing Latino Texans is especially complicated.

Although the Fifteenth Amendment in 1870 granted Black men the right to vote, the protections afforded to Black voters were quickly eroded post Reconstruction. As Jim Crow reared its head in the late nineteenth and early twentieth centuries, poll taxes and literacy tests proliferated throughout the Southern states, limiting minorities' access to the ballot box. One of the most damaging of these tactics was the so-called white primary. Although states could not bar racial minorities from voting in general elections, the Democratic party—a private organization—could and did bar any nonwhite voters from participating in nomination contests. Because of the Democratic Party's virtual stranglehold on statewide politics (just one Republican presidential candidate won the state between 1872 and 1948), the white primary effectively shut nonwhites out from the contests with the most significance.[8]

The white primary, in concert with other suppressive tactics, was devastatingly effective. According to the Texas Politics Project at the University of Texas, 87 percent of Texas's eligible voters cast a ballot in 1896.[9] By 1916, turnout had shrunk to 34 percent—barely half the national average.[10] Importantly, the white primary was not limited to Texas's hands-off approach to the regulation of private organizations. In 1923 the state formally adopted a law barring African Americans from primary elections. When the law was struck down in 1926 by the U.S. Supreme Court in *Nixon v. Herndon*, the state responded by changing the law to allow executive committees to bar voters from their primaries.[11] When this too was struck down by the Supreme Court in *Nixon v. Condon*, the Democratic Party of Texas's annual convention passed a resolution that excluded Black voters.[12] Not until *Smith v. Allwright* was decided by the Supreme Court in 1944 were white primaries finally deemed illegal, regardless of the state's involvement in their origination.[13]

Texas's problematic stances toward voting rights did not end with the overturning of the white primary, the Twenty-Fourth Amendment of 1964 (banning poll taxes), or the Voting Rights Act (VRA) of 1965. Texas was not originally covered by the VRA's preclearance condition found in Section 5 of that act. In 1975, however, when Congress included new protections for language minorities, the entire state became covered by Section 5. This was due largely to the prevalence of Spanish-dominant communities throughout the state.[14]

Although Texas's relationship with equitable voting rights has improved somewhat since the passage of the Fifteenth Amendment, it has hardly done so enthusiastically. Voter protections in Texas have instead hinged on congressional action and Supreme Court decisions for Latino voting rights. Voter purges, electoral resource allocation, restrictions on early voting, and aggressive prosecution of fraud that continue to this day show that the fight for Latino voting rights in Texas is not a history lesson; it is an ongoing struggle that will likely continue into the decades ahead.

Increases in Purges in Section 5 States

In 2013, the Supreme Court dealt the 1965 Voting Rights Act a crippling blow. Prior to the decision in *Shelby County v. Holder*, states and counties with a demonstrated history of racially discriminatory voting policies were required to pre-approve any changes with the federal Department of Justice or with a federal court.[15] Texas was one of these covered jurisdictions. *Shelby County v. Holder*, however, invalidated the formula that determined which jurisdictions were covered by this preclearance condition, effectively killing the preclearance condition entirely. As the chapter in this volume by Henry Flores relates, Texas Governor Greg Abbott aggressively moved to implement a strict voter ID law in the wake of the Supreme Court's decision. The *Shelby County* decision also had major ramifications for voter list maintenance in jurisdictions throughout the country that were formerly covered under Section 5 of the VRA.

Reports from the Brennan Center for Justice published in 2018 and 2019 demonstrate that prior to the *Shelby County* decision, jurisdictions covered under Section 5 purged their voters at roughly the same rate as those not covered. After 2013, however, purge rates in these formerly covered jurisdictions increased substantially, while purge rates in parts of the country that were not covered by the preclearance condition did not go up (see Figure 1).

The Brennan Center analyses are based on the biennial Election Administration and Voting Survey (EAVS) administered by the U.S. Election Assistance Commission. Because Texas did not report its purge data to EAVS in 2012, it is excluded from the chart in Figure 1. The Brennan Center report, however, presents evidence that fourteen of the twenty most populous counties in Texas increased their purge rates from 2010—the midterm cycle

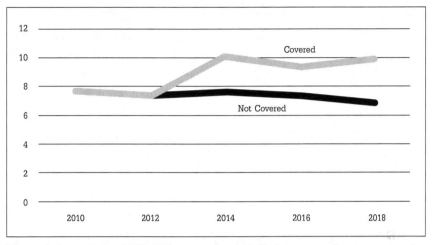

Figure 1. Purge Rates, 2008–2018: comparing jurisdictions covered vs. not covered by Sec. 5 in regard to percent of voters purged over two-year period. *Source:* Election Administration and Voting Survey. *Notes:* Shows data for counties reporting in each period. Texas not included due to missing data.

immediately before the *Shelby County* decision—to 2014, the midterm cycle in which Section 5 of the VRA was invalidated.[16] In 2018, Texas's purge rate returned to roughly the same level as in 2010—but only after hundreds of thousands of voters were removed from the rolls in the year following the removal of the preclearance condition. And, as the botched attempted purge in 2019 makes clear, targeted purges can be hugely problematic for impacted communities, even if the number of voters affected is not high enough to significantly distort statewide purge rates.

Voter Purges Since *Shelby County*

In this post-*Shelby County* environment, more attention is being paid to voter purges than ever before. In 2018, the Supreme Court decided in *Husted v. A. Philip Randolph Institute* that Ohio could purge voters who had not voted for six years and failed to return a postcard, even if the state received no affirmative information indicating that a voter had moved, died, or was otherwise ineligible to vote.[17] At the same time, millions of voters have been purged in recent years in states like Georgia.[18] Because these purges are often based at least in part on how long a registered voter goes without voting, communities with low turnout are especially at risk. As the chapter by Henry Flores in this volume, and work by scholars such as Bernard Fraga, make clear, eligible Latinos are less likely than any other racial or ethnic group to cast a ballot.[19]

Texas itself is no stranger to problematic purges. In 2012, the *Houston Chronicle* reported that thousands of voters across the state were matched with deceased individuals all around the country.[20] State officials had apparently used the Social Security Death Master List to come up with what they called "weak matches"—matches based solely on name and dates of birth. These weak matches unsurprisingly turned up large numbers of false positives, leading to the purge of thousands of voters. The *Houston Chronicle* noted that voters from minority districts in Texas were overrepresented on the list of individuals who had been flagged as deceased in the Social Security database. State officials need not have explicitly targeted voters of color for the purge to have had a racially discriminatory outcome: 16 percent of Latinos and 13 percent of African Americans have one of the ten most common American surnames, while that is true for just 4 percent of white Americans.[21] Because repeated surnames are so much more common among racial minorities, any matching process that uses last names as a primary criterion is likely to return far more false positives for minorities, potentially threatening their ability to cast a ballot.

Election Day Experiences

Over the past few decades, the United States, and Texas in particular, have seen the Latino population increase rapidly. The United States is becoming increasingly non-white, and Texas is one of the states leading that change. Even under the best of circumstances, increased racial diversity can pose problems for the fair administration of elections. In the case of Texas and other states in the Southwest and with growing Latino populations, the complications are further exacerbated by the fact that some of these citizens are not fluent in English and therefore find themselves at a disadvantage inside the voting booth. The update to the Voting Rights Act in 1975 sought to address these problems, requiring jurisdictions with large linguistic minority groups to provide election materials in other languages.[22] Because the coverage formula used to determine which jurisdictions are required to provide language assistance is updated only every five years, the federal protections are not flexible enough to deal with rapidly changing communities. Voters in a jurisdiction that is just below the coverage threshold in an update year are at risk of receiving inadequate resources for three federal elections.

These inadequate resources translate into real problems for voters of color, and Latinos in particular, on election day. This is demonstrated using survey data that asks voters how long they waited in line to cast their ballot. The Cooperative Congressional Election Survey (CCES) is administered after each federal election.[23] In addition to their wait times, the CCES asks voters a host of other information about their sociodemographic characteristics and their experience on election day. A number of papers in recent years have demonstrated that racial minorities wait in longer lines all around the country.[24] Unfortunately, the CCES is not weighted to be representative for individual states. Nevertheless, it can help us to understand the experience of racial minorities on election day, and how those experiences are changing over time.

Although Black voters waited in much longer lines across the nation in the early part of the past decade, the wait times for Latinos were just as elevated as those for Black voters in the past few elections—and were substantially above the wait times for white voters (see Figure 2).[25]

Not only did Latinos face longer wait times on average than white voters, they were also far more likely to face the longest lines. In 2014, the bipartisan Presidential Commission on Election Administration said that no voter should wait for more than thirty minutes to cast a ballot.[26] Between 2014 and 2018, however, the CCES indicates that Latinos were 79 percent more likely to wait thirty minutes than white voters. This gap cannot be explained by other sociodemographic characteristics. Figure 3A demonstrates that racial minorities—and Latinos in particular—have been more likely than white voters to report waiting more than thirty minutes since

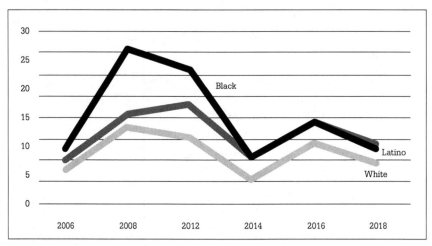

Figure 2. In-Person Reported Wait Times (in minutes). *Source:* Cooperative Congressional Election Survey.

2014. Figure 3B presents the coefficients from national regression models after controlling for available characteristics.[27] Even after controlling for county population density, county share of non-Hispanic white, county share over sixty-four years old, voter education, voter age, voter party, voter marital status, family income, state, and year, Latinos were 24 percent more likely to wait at least thirty minutes to vote than white voters (see Figures 3A and 3B).[28]

To better understand why voters of color might wait in such long lines, the Brennan Center interviewed election administrators from thirty-two counties around the country and seven counties in Texas. These interviews demonstrated that many election administrators may be unprepared to grapple with demographic changes in the coming years. Despite knowing that they would be serving more voters for whom English is not a primary language, these overburdened election administrators explained that they continue to rely on the same poll workers year after year— poll workers who reflect the historic, not contemporaneous or future, demographics of their jurisdictions. Officials in Fort Bend County, for instance, explained that they narrowly avoided being required to provide Vietnamese materials under the language provision of the Voting Rights Act ten years ago. Despite the large Vietnamese population, the county has not begun providing

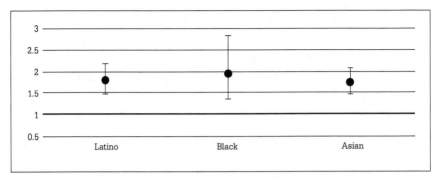

Figure 3a. Latinos and Other Racial Minorities Wait Longer Than White Voters, 2014–2018. Probability relative to whites of waiting thirty minutes or more in line to vote. *Notes:* Relative gap for each racial group measured against white voters. Ninety-five percent confidence bands shown. Robust standard errors clustered by state.

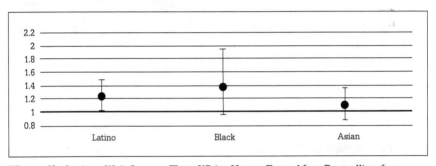

Figure 3b. Latinos Wait Longer Than White Voters Even After Controlling for Other Factors, 2014–2018. Probability relative to whites of waiting thirty minutes or more in line to vote. *Notes:* Relative gap for each racial group measured against white voters. Ninety-five percent confidence bands shown. Robust standard errors clustered by state. Model includes controls for county population density, county share non-Hispanic white, county share over sixty-four years old, voter education, voter age, voter party, voter marital status, family income, state, and year.

resources in Vietnamese.[29] Moreover, many election administrators detailed the difficulties they had finding bilingual poll workers. Considering that counties where the white share of the population has declined the most had the fewest resources per voter in 2018,[30] this is especially troubling.

More troubling still is the fact that the racial/ethnic wait gap in Texas will expand even further in the coming years if the state continues to implement and extend its current voting policies. As related in the chapter in this volume by Henry Flores, the Texas legislature enacted a strict voter ID law the very same day that the Supreme Court invalidated the preclearance formula in 2013. Today, the worst effects of the law are being held at bay: Voters in Texas who do not have the requisite identification can sign a "reasonable difficulty" form that acknowledges that obtaining an identification card is a material difficulty for them.[31] The governing powers in Texas would like to see this exception removed. Unsurprisingly, its removal would have a racially disparate impact: Black and Latino voters are more likely to lack the necessary identification than white voters.[32] Not only would the removal of the reasonable difficulty provision disproportionately disenfranchise Latinos in Texas; it could also lead to confusion in the polling places where these voters try to cast a ballot, leading to longer lines even for voters of color who do have the requisite identification.

Underlying demographic trends and the legal infrastructure in Texas indicate that Latino voters are at risk of facing major problems at their polling places in the coming years. And just as Latino voters have started using the convenience of other electoral reforms like early voting at comparable rates to white voters, they face additional bureaucratic barriers to voting.

Mobile Voting Sites/Early Voting

In years past, Texas has allowed for the use of mobile early voting sites. These sites enabled county election administrators to provide early voting locations for multiple communities throughout their counties. Such mobile early voting sites were particularly helpful for large and lower income counties; rather than provide early voting locations for a small number of neighborhoods for each day of the early voting period, they could offer early voting—albeit with fewer days—to a far larger set of communities.

In 2019, however, the Texas legislature enacted a ban on the temporary early voting sites. Republican supporters of the bill said that the use of mobile early voting sites allowed for the selective harvesting of the votes of certain communities. Although they were not explicit, these legislators were understood to be using coded language to refer to communities of color and areas with younger voters. Texas Democrats pushed back, calling the legislation an attempt to make it harder for marginalized groups to

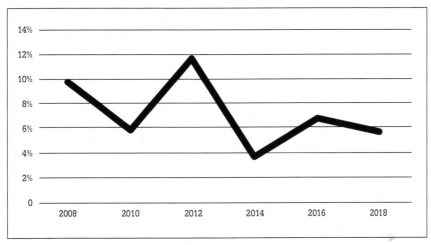

Figure 4. Early Vote Gap Deficit for Latino Voters in Texas. *Source:* L2 Texas Voter File. *Note:* "Early vote gap" calculated by subtracting the proportion of Latino voters who voted early from the proportion of white participants who did so.

participate.[33] Under the new law, any early voting location must remain open for the entirety of the early voting period.

Dana DeBeauvoir, the Travis County clerk, explained that the curtailing of mobile early voting will disproportionately impact Spanish speakers, who live in areas where these sites had been deployed with the most success. In the 2018 midterm election, Travis County had sixty-one mobile early voting centers; as of November 2019, the county was still struggling to decide what it would do as it prepared for massive turnout in the 2020 presidential election.[34]

An analysis of voting patterns in Texas makes clear that the new restrictions on early voting come on the heels of major elections in which the share of Latino voters who cast their ballots early rose dramatically. We leveraged Texas's registered voter file to understand who voted on election day, and who voted early. Figure 4 demonstrates the gap between the early voting rates of white and Latino voters. In 2008, for instance, 65 percent of white voters who participated voted early, while 55 percent of Latino voters voted early. The gap in that year, therefore, was ten percentage points.

Although white voters were substantially more likely to vote early than Latinos in 2008, that gap has largely narrowed over the past decade. In

2014, the gap was just 3.6 percent, and it was only 6.7 percent in 2016—a far smaller gap than in the preceding midterm and presidential elections, respectively. It should come as no surprise that as Latinos have started to use early voting at rates comparable to white voters, restrictions are being put in place. There is a long and documented history of states changing laws once they no longer disproportionately benefit white residents.[35]

Increasingly Aggressive Prosecution of Fraud

Against the backdrop of structural barriers to participation for Latino Americans in Texas is a troubling trend toward more aggressive prosecution against imagined fraud. This can be easily seen in the story with which this chapter opened: Texas Attorney General Ken Paxton rushed to proclaim that his office would bring charges against all noncitizen voters even before he or his office had a chance to examine the evidence and determine whether there were any likely problems. In addition to these statewide investigations into widespread voter fraud, prosecutors in Texas have made examples out of individuals who unknowingly cast a ballot when they were not allowed to do so. Here, we detail the stories of two women who were aggressively prosecuted for accidentally voting when they were not eligible to do so.

ROSA ORTEGA

Rosa Ortega came to the United States from Mexico as a young child; although two of her brothers are American citizens, she never obtained citizenship. She was, however, a legal permanent resident—and, according to her brother, the entire family thought that she was a citizen.[36] According to her lawyers, she did not understand the legal distinction between legal permanent residency and citizenship, and did not know that she was precluded from voting. According to her brother, Ortega indicated on a voter registration form in 2012 that she was a citizen because the form lacked an option for legal permanent residents. Upon moving to Tarrant County she attempted to re-register. Her registration was denied after she submitted a form indicating that she was not a citizen. Upon having her registration rejected, she submitted a new form on which she indicated that she was a citizen. This aroused suspicions, and she was eventually prosecuted for illegally voting.[37] Ultimately, Ortega was sentenced to eight years in prison and will almost certainly be deported upon her release.[38]

CRYSTAL MASON

Crystal Mason cast a ballot in the 2016 presidential election while she was on federal supervised release after serving time in prison in Texas.[39] She did not know, however, that Texas law prohibits individuals from casting a ballot until their full sentence has been served. In Texas, this includes any period of supervised release, even though individuals who are under federal supervised release have "completed the entire term of their incarceration."[40] According to Mason's attorney, no state agency ever informed her that her eligibility to vote was suspended while she was on supervised release—and yet, despite the state's failure to notify Mason of her curtailed rights, she was held individually responsible for the ineligible provisional ballot she cast. Although her provisional ballot was not ultimately counted, she was sentenced to five more years in prison for voting.[41]

The prosecution of these individuals stands in sharp contrast to how the criminal justice system has treated other Texans. Just five days after Crystal Mason was sentenced to five more years in prison, Ethan Couch was released from prison. Couch killed four people while driving under the influence. After a psychologist told the court that Couch suffered from psychological distress due to growing up in a rich family—or "affluenza"—he was sentenced to ten years of community supervision.[42] After he and his mother fled to Mexico to avoid potential jail time, he was sent to prison, where he spent just two years.[43] He was prosecuted in Tarrant County, the very same county as Crystal Mason. The *Houston Chronicle* Editorial Board blasted these disparate sentences. "Something's wrong with the criminal justice system in Fort Worth," they said flatly.[44] Indeed, that a white man should spend less time in prison for killing four people than two women of color who thought they were allowed to vote is hard to explain.

This aggressive prosecution is meant to, and does, have chilling effects on marginalized voters across the state. Formerly disenfranchised individuals, for instance, are often confused about their eligibility to cast a ballot.[45] It is entirely possible that individuals whose rights have been restored but were formerly disenfranchised due to a felony conviction will be scared away from participation by such high-profile prosecution. This could be true even for individuals who are almost positive that they are eligible. When the cost of being wrong is so high, and the state makes its intention to prosecute clear, some would-be voters will inevitably determine that the risks are too high. Mason herself makes clear the chilling effect of these prosecutions. "I don't think I'll ever vote again," she told the *Fort Worth Star-Telegram.* "That's being honest. I'll never vote again."[46]

Conclusion

As this book demonstrates, Latinos in Texas are all too used to having to fight to secure their civil rights. This has been true in housing, employment, health care, and voting. The gains from the past fifty years should be celebrated—but the work is far from over. Despite a period of increased federal oversight of American elections, minority voting rights are in many ways at greater risk now than they have been since the landmark civil rights cases of the 1960s. As the Latino population in Texas and around the country grows, we expect others to try to thwart efforts to translate those numbers into political power.

Recommendations

There are many policies that Texas can and should adopt to ensure equitable access to the ballot box for Latino American voters. Nevertheless, the following policies are among those that would provide the strongest protections and get the ball rolling:

- **Enact automatic voter registration (AVR).** AVR would ensure that Latinos and others are reregistered to vote if they are accidentally purged. It would allow for automatic updates when voters move, and when they become citizens.

- **Make early voting easier, not harder.** Early voting allows workers with inflexible schedules to participate easily in elections. In particular, early voting in Texas should allow for mobile early voting sites that can serve multiple communities without requiring huge financial and resource investments.
- **Recruit multilingual poll workers.** Election administrators in counties with many dominant languages should ensure that poll workers are able to assist them on election day.

Notes

1. Caitlin Yilek, "Nearly 60,000 Noncitizens May Have Illegally Voted in Texas, Officials Say," *Washington Examiner*, January 25, 2019.
2. Alexa Ura, "In Advisory, Texas Implies Its List of Thousands of Voters Flagged for Citizenship Reviews Could Include Naturalized Citizens," *The Texas Tribune*, February 1, 2019.
3. Alexa Ura, "Texas Quietly Informs Counties That Some of the 95,000 Voters Flagged for Citizenship Review Don't Belong on the List," *The Texas Tribune*, January 29, 2019.
4. Alexa Ura, "Texas Will End Its Botched Voter Citizenship Review and Rescind Its List of Flagged Voters," *The Texas Tribune*, April 26, 2019.
5. Ken Paxton (@KenPaxtonTX), Twitter (January 25, 2019, 3:37 pm), https://twitter.com/kenpaxtontx/status/1088898595653386240?lang=en.
6. Donald J. Trump (@RealDeonald Trump), Twitter (January 27, 2019, 8:22 am), https://twitter.com/realDonaldTrump/status/1089513936435716096.
7. The absurdity of the voter fraud charges made in Texas is illustrated in a study of a database of voter fraud convictions at the Heritage Foundation. See Robert Brischetto, "A Number on Voters," *San Antonio Express-News*, March 10, 2019, F1–F6.
8. Texas Secretary of State, "Presidential Election Results," at Texas Secretary of State website.
9. Texas Politics Project, reference to Jerrold G. Rusk, ed., *A Statistical History of the American Electorate* (Washington, DC: CQ Press, 2001).
10. Texas Politics Project, *A Statistical History*.
11. *Nixon v. Herndon*, 273 U.S. 536 (1927).
12. *Nixon v. Condon*, 286 U.S. 73 (1932).
13. Michael J. Klarman, "The White Primary Rulings: A Case Study in the Consequences of Supreme Court Decisionmaking," *SSRN Electronic Journal*, 2001; *Smith v. Allwright*, 321 U.S. 649 (1944).
14. U.S. Department of Justice, Section 4 of the Voting Rights Act, available online at justice.gov.
15. *Shelby County v. Holder*, 570 U.S. 529 (2013).

16. Because the EAVS data measure all removals between federal elections, the 2014 data includes all voters removed between 2012 and 2014. The 2014 period therefore includes some time before, and some time after, the *Shelby County* decision.
17. *Husted v. A. Philip Randolph Institute*, 138 S. Ct. 1833 (2018).
18. Jonathan Brater et al., "Purges: A Growing Threat to the Right to Vote," *Brennan Center for Justice*, New York University School of Law, 2018.
19. Bernard L. Fraga, *The Turnout Gap: Race, Ethnicity, and Political Inequality in a Diversifying America* (Cambridge, UK: Cambridge University Press, 2018).
20. Lise Olsen, "Texas' Voter Purge Made Repeated Errors," *The Houston Chronicle*, November 2, 2012.
21. Joshua Comenetz, "Frequently Occurring Surnames in the 2010 Census," *U.S. Census Bureau*, October 2016.
22. See Section 203, 42 U.S. Code 1973aa-1a, at Department of Justice website, justice.gov.
23. The CCES also includes pre-election waves in even years, and a smaller survey in odd years.
24. M. Keith Chen et al., "Racial Disparities in Voting Wait Times: Evidence from Smartphone Data," working paper, National Bureau of Economic Research, 2019; Stephen Pettigrew, "The Racial Gap in Wait Times: Why Minority Precincts Are Underserved by Local Election Officials," *Political Science Quarterly* 132, no. 3 (2017): 527-47.
25. We use the CCES's vote-verified postelection weights.
26. The Presidential Commission on Election Administration, "The American Voting Experience: Report and Recommendations of the Presidential Commission on Election Administration," Cal-Tech MIT Voting Project, January 2014.
27. These are logistic regressions, where the dependent variable takes the value 1 if a voter waited thirty or more minutes and 0 otherwise. To aid in with the interpretation of the coefficients, the coefficients have been exponentiated in the figure. Some of the wait gap can be explained by sociodemographic variables, which are included in 3B.
28. These regressions incorporate individual-level information from the CCES, as well as county-level data from the Census Bureau's 2018 five-year American Community Survey.
29. Fort Bend County, Texas, interview by Brennan Center for Justice, November 12, 2019.
30. Hannah Klain et al., "Waiting to Vote: Racial Disparities in Election Day Experiences." *Brennan Center for Justice*, New York University School of Law, 2020.
31. Texas Secretary of State, Texas Election Code, Section 63.001(i).
32. Charles Stewart III, "Voter ID: Who Has Them? Who Shows Them?," 66 *Okla. L. Rev.* 21 (2017).
33. Alexa Ura, "Texas Ended Temporary Voting Locations to Curb Abuse. Now Rural and Young Voters Are Losing Access," *The Texas Tribune*, October 10, 2019.
34. Travis County, Texas, interview by Brennan Center for Justice, November 11, 2019.
35. See, for instance, Jacob S. Rugh and Jessica Trounstine, "The Provision of Local Public Goods in Diverse Communities: Analyzing Municipal Bond Elections," *Journal of Politics* 73, no. 4 (October 2011): 1038-50.
36. Sam Levine, "This Woman Got 8 Years in Prison for Illegal Voting. Texas Is Showing No Mercy," *The Huffington Post*, November 30, 2018.
37. Michael Wines, "Illegal Voting Gets Texas Woman 8 Years in Prison, and Certain Deportation," *The New York Times*, February 10, 2017.
38. Michael Barajas, "The Casualties of Texas' War on Voter Fraud," *Texas Observer*, September 9, 2019.
39. Taylor Barnes, "Texas Mother Crystal Mason Appeals Five-Year Sentence for Illegal Voting," *CNN*, September 11, 2019.

40. Sue Halpern, "How Crystal Mason Became the Face of Voter Suppression in America," *The New Yorker*, December 18, 2019.

41. Halpern, "Crystal Mason."

42. Manny Fernandez, Richard Pérez-Peña, and Azam Ahmed, "Ethan Couch, 'Affluenza' Teenager, Had Last Party Before Fleeing, Officials Say," *The New York Times*, December 29, 2015.

43. Daniel Victor, "Ethan Couch, 'Affluenza Teen' Who Killed 4 While Driving Drunk, Is Freed," *The New York Times*, April 2, 2018.

44. Houston Chronicle Editorial Board, "Blatant Injustice for Mistaken Voters in Fort Worth," *The Houston Chronicle*, April 5, 2018.

45. See, for instance, Ernest Drucker and Ricardo Barreras, "Studies of Voting Behavior and Felony Disenfranchisement Among Individuals in the Criminal Justice System in New York, Connecticut, and Ohio," research report. Sentencing Project, 2005; Christopher Uggen and Jeff Manza, "Lost Voices: The Civic and Political Views of Disfranchised Felons," in *Imprisoning America: The Social Effects of Mass Incarceration*, edited by Mary Pattillo, David Weiman, and Bruce Western (New York: Russell Sage Foundation, 2004), 165-204.

46. Anna M. Tinsley and Deanna Boyd, "Convicted Felon Indicted on Illegal Voting Charge in Tarrant County," *Fort Worth Star-Telegram*, March 1, 2017.

DAVID HINOJOSA, MARÍA "CUCA" ROBLEDO MONTECEL,

AND AURELIO M. MONTEMAYOR

Unmet Promises in Texas Education

For a week in December 1968, more than seventy witnesses presented to the U.S. Commission on Civil Rights (USCCR) an ugly panorama of civil wrongs against Mexican Americans in the southwestern United States. The USCCR, meeting in San Antonio, Texas, dedicated almost one-third of its public hearing days to educational inequities.

Professors, social scientists, community activists, school administrators, teachers, and students described institutional animosity that permeated the state's education agency and public school system. One student testified, "I mean, how would you like for somebody to come up to you and tell you what you speak is a dirty language. You know, what your mother speaks is a dirty language."[1]

Until 1968, in Texas, "Mexican American children were prohibited from speaking their native language anywhere on school grounds. Those who violated the 'No Spanish' rule were severely punished."[2] Students were charged fines and regularly subject to humiliation from teachers and administrators. As United States District Court Judge William Wayne Justice attested, "Both the language and cultural heritage of these children were uniformly treated with intolerance and disrespect."[3]

Mexican American history and culture were absent from textbooks. Administrators often relegated Mexican American students to limited courses of study and segregated them in schools starved for resources and lacking adequately prepared teachers. The combined institutional ills resulted in the miseducation of Mexican American children. Many Spanish-speaking children faced insurmountable challenges in comprehending the all-English instruction and curriculum.

In 1964, the Laredo United Independent School District began experimenting with bilingual classes for elementary grades (albeit for only Spanish-speaking students), with other Texas school districts following suit. However, Texas legislation supporting bilingual education would not arrive until 1973.

Even as bilingual education was finally recommended, it was still the rare exception. It took the court's intervention in 1981 to bring about further reforms in bilingual education; however, poor implementation and ineffective monitoring continue to negatively impact tens of thousands of English language learners in classrooms across the state each year.

The 1981 court decision in *United States v. Texas* stated that Mexican Americans had suffered "pervasive, intentional discrimination throughout most of this century" and that "members of this minority group have been severely disabled in their struggle for equal educational opportunity."[4] These wrongs could not be healed overnight. The psychological wounds inflicted on the schoolchildren of Texas were deep and lasting. Judge Justice ruled:

> The long history of prejudice and deprivation remains a significant obstacle to equal educational opportunity for these children. The deep sense of inferiority, cultural isolation, and acceptance of failure, instilled in a people by generations of subjugation, cannot be eradicated merely by integrating the schools and repealing the "No Spanish" statutes.[5]

One indication of the prejudiced view teachers and administrators had toward Mexican American students was the disproportionately high number who were assigned to vocational courses, instead of academic ones. Most Mexican American students were not perceived to have the intelligence needed for college, and therefore were not counseled about a path to higher education. Schools classified students as "retarded" or "mentally deficient," based solely on inappropriate, culturally biased testing. Overemphasizing the significance of essentially useless test data became a structural limitation placed on the children. Commission testimony highlighted the biases of purportedly objective practices in the Texas education assessment system. In 1968, high dropout rates were the norm. Mexican Americans had a median of 6.2 years of education, compared to 10.7 years for Anglo students and 8.7 years for African American students. Of the state's total population of residents ages twenty to forty-nine years, 42 percent of Hispanic children never completed high school. Large percentages of Mexican American students read below grade level, were retained in elementary school two and three times, and were located in districts with the largest numbers of dropouts.[6]

The illiteracy rate among those fourteen years old and older was 11 percent for the general population; for Latinos, it was 38 percent. The dropout rate from the top seven grades was 23 percent for the combined population; for Latinos, it was 34 percent.[7]

Testimony at the USCCR hearing confirmed clear inequities in school funding across Texas and in Bexar County. (San Antonio is the county seat.) Majority Mexican American districts often had (and still have) lower taxable property per student than majority Anglo districts. Because Texas relies substantially on local property taxes to fund local education, districts that primarily enrolled Mexican American students had much smaller budgets and inherently fewer resources, despite taxing their residents at higher rates.

The financial inequities resulted in low teacher salaries, lack of teaching materials and resources, and substandard school buildings. These inequities continued for decades until a decision in 1989 by the Texas Supreme Court, *Edgewood v. Kirby*, declared the state's inequitable funding of schools unconstitutional. This opened a period of more equitable funding, though future rulings by the Texas Supreme Court watered down the strong equity ruling.

At the time of the 1968 USCCR hearing, history textbooks reflected strong biases toward an Anglo interpretation of events, often presenting negative stereotypes of Mexican Americans. Even after fifty years of supposed progress, the Texas Board of Education found itself embroiled in controversy over Mexican American studies courses and social studies curriculum.

Schools especially miseducated migrant students, who moved with their families every year to harvest crops in northern states. Testimony showed that in 1966 and 1967, 60 percent of Mexican American students dropped out before graduating from high school, but the dropout rate for migrant children was "substantially worse." One-fifth of all migrant children never enrolled in any school.[8]

Students who had recently immigrated did not receive as much attention at the 1968 hearing as citizen migrant students. However, some testimony—even from the Mexican American community—reflected prejudice against immigrant students and families. A key U.S. Supreme Court decision in 1982, *Plyler v. Doe*, held that any child of a family that lived within the bounds of a school district must be educated, regardless of the legal status of the child or the parents. In 2001, Texas became the first state in the country to pass a law allowing undocumented immigrant students to pay in-state tuition at state colleges.

More recently, a strong pro-immigrant movement, spearheaded by a young generation of "Dreamers," has advocated for immigration reform. During the Obama administration, the federal Deferred Action for Immigrant Arrivals (DACA) program was created, allowing qualified undocumented applicants an opportunity to obtain a work permit and to stay in the United States without fear of immediate deportation.

The Chicano Movement

The year 1968 was marked by racial unrest and protests across the United States. The civil rights movement had expanded from the South and toward the cities in the North. The Black Power Movement became a national phenomenon. African American athletes raised clenched fists as a salute to human rights solidarity at the 1968 Olympics. Students staged sit-ins at segregated lunch counters in the South.

It was also a time when the Chicano Movement spread across the Southwest, from California to Texas. In San Antonio, student protests and walkouts challenged segregated and inferior schools. The 1968 USCCR hearings revealed an array of ills afflicting the Chicano community, from limitations in employment and housing, to abuse by law enforcement officers. But the spotlight was on educational inequalities, which fueled the marches and protests from Los Angeles to South Texas. A year later, in Crystal City, the students presented a litany of demands that seemed to reflect the testimony at the USCCR hearings in San Antonio.

More than five decades later, the struggle for equality continues in an unequal Texas. Though graduation rates and college completion have improved for Latino students, barriers remain. Youth are still suffering in the juvenile justice system, and attrition rates are still a serious concern.

A large gap continues to exist between Anglo students and students of color, from academic achievement through advanced degree completion. The exclusion of Mexican American children from the courses and effective instruction that would prepare them for college is still a pervasive problem. Texas prisons have much greater representation of Mexican Americans than do Texas colleges and universities. For male students of color, the path is often from school to prison rather than from school to college.

In 1970 a project to create an independent Chicano college in the lower Rio Grande Valley of South Texas professed its educational philosophy with an essay that began:

> The Chicano child is being miseducated. There is no extension of what is learned at home into the classroom. What the child was rewarded for at home, he is punished [for] in the classroom. The teacher does not fit his parents' image. There is an attempt to change the child's language, eating habits, and even his physical appearance. The classroom is an extension of the (non-Hispanic) white middle-class home, and the child is made an agent for change of the Chicano household.[9]

Despite several advances made by Mexican Americans and other advocates, much of the same rings true five decades later. The Texas Latino Education Coalition and other activists persist in advocating for educational equity. What is needed is a framework—supported by a foundation of good government and fair funding—for creating an ecosystem of reforms that can build positive change for all students. Communities and schools can work together to strengthen their capacity to be successful with all students.

The Undereducation of Latino Youth: Considerable and Persistent

Educational opportunity remains an unmet promise for many young Mexican Americans. Testimony before the U.S. Commission on Civil Rights in 1968, based on 1960 U.S. Census Bureau data, described a wide gap between Hispanics and Anglos in school completion rates.[10] In 1970, the U.S. Census Bureau data showed that the median school years completed by persons twenty-five years old and older was almost twelve years for Anglos, but only seven years for Mexican Americans, and ten years for African Americans.[11]

The Intercultural Development Research Association's (IDRA) analysis of 1980 trend data from the Census Bureau's Current Population Surveys indicated that undereducation among minority youth was considerable and persistent. In Texas, Hispanics had a higher undereducation rate at 34 percent than Anglos at 15 percent.[12]

IDRA conducted the first comprehensive study of school dropouts in Texas with the release of a landmark study in October 1986.[13] The study, published in seven volumes, found that 86,276 students (33 percent) had not graduated from Texas public schools, costing the state $17 billion in foregone income and lost tax revenues, while increasing costs for job training, welfare, unemployment, and criminal justice.[14] Attrition rates that year were 27 percent for Anglo students, 34 percent for African American students, and 45 percent for Hispanic students. Nearly half of the Hispanic students who dropped out of school did so before leaving the ninth grade, compared to 18 percent of Anglo students.[15]

Time-series data indicated that from 1986 to 2017 Texas public schools had lost a cumulative total of more than 3.7 million students before high school graduation, including more than two million Hispanic students (55 percent of those lost). While overall attrition rates in Texas had declined to about 24 percent, racial and ethnic gaps continued unabated. In 2017, Texas schools were still twice as likely to lose Hispanic students before they graduate, compared to Anglo students.[16]

At the national level, the National Center for Education Statistics (NCES) reported a decline in overall school dropout rates by nearly half from 1990 to 2015 (from 12 percent to less than 6 percent). The rates for Anglos declined to less than 5 percent, while rates for African Americans and Hispanics, although declining, remained higher, at nearly 7 percent for African Americans and greater than 9 percent for Hispanics.[17] The undereducation of American Latino youth over the last fifty years has been considerable and consistent.

Dropping out of high school has serious negative consequences for the individual and society. According to the U.S. Census Bureau Current Population Survey in 2014, the difference in the median annual income between people eighteen to sixty-seven years of age who had a high school credential (including an alternative such as a high school equivalency GED) and those in the same age group without a high school credential was $18,000 per year ($45,000 for credentialed versus $26,000 for non-credentialed persons).[18] This is equal to $690,000 in lost income over a lifetime.

Adults without a high school education have higher odds of being underemployed or unemployed, have worse health regardless of income, and are more likely to be institutionalized. According to the Census Bureau, "The average high school dropout costs the economy approximately $262,000 over his or her lifetime in terms of lower tax contributions, higher reliance on Medicaid and Medicare, higher rates of criminal activity, and higher reliance on welfare."[19]

In its *Theory of Incompatibilities*, IDRA determined that the "lack of compatibility of the characteristics of minority children and the characteristics of a typical instructional program" caused students of color and economically disadvantaged students to fail.[20] IDRA identified more than forty "incompatibilities" in the areas of poverty, culture, language, mobility, and societal perceptions. Through extensive research IDRA found:

> While much has changed over the years, still today, compared to their more affluent peers, poor and minority students are far more likely to be assigned to classrooms with less qualified teachers and fewer opportunities to prepare for and take advanced and dual credit courses. Educational segregation is on the rise.

Rather than blaming students and families and expecting them to adapt, a fundamental belief in the genesis of IDRA was that adults, in schools and in public decision-making positions, are responsible for transforming school practices and policies so that all students have the opportunity to learn. Poor children and families do not cause schools to be poor; rather, poorly performing schools are caused by poor educational practices and poor educational policies.[21]

Latino Representation in Schools and Leadership Positions

According to information presented at the 1968 USCCR hearing, nearly 3.5 million Latinos lived in five southwestern states in 1960. These people constituted nearly 12 percent of the region's population. Texas had approximately 1.4 million Latinos.[22] Fast-forward fifty years, and in 2018 there were 10.4 million Latinos in Texas, representing nearly two of every five (38 percent) persons residing in the state.[23]

At the same time that the Latino population has grown over the years, growth in professional Latino representation in classrooms, central administration, and school boardrooms has not kept pace. Representation has increased at all professional levels, but it still pales in comparison to the overall Latino population in Texas.

State and School Board Representation

The Texas State Board of Education (SBOE) is an influential force. Among other duties, its members are responsible for setting curriculum standards, adopting instructional materials, establishing requirements for graduation, overseeing the Texas Permanent School Fund, providing the final review of rules proposed by the State Board for Educator Certification, and reviewing awards of new charter schools. When the USCCR reconvened in 1978, it noted that the Texas SBOE was made up of eighteen men and five women, including only one African American member and two Mexican American members.[24] Over the next five decades, the SBOE achieved parity with regard to female representation, but still lagged behind in representation of people of color. By 2018, seven men and eight women comprised the fifteen members: four Hispanic, one African American, and eleven non-Hispanic whites.[25]

Local school boards oversee the management of Texas school districts and enact local policies to govern their public schools. Communities choose members through local elections, with the exception of privately operated charter schools, which appoint board members. Overall, school boards are less racially diverse than the demographics of the United States, but they are more diverse than other elected bodies at the state and national level.[26] In 1968, a USCCR survey of 4,700 school board members in the five Southwestern states showed that only 10 percent were Mexican American.[27]

Of the 7,256 school board members in Texas in 1978, nearly 93 percent were white, and more than three out of four were men. Mexican Americans accounted for approximately 6 percent of the school board population, and nearly all were men.[28] Over the past forty years, representation has improved marginally, as shown in Figure 1. This is likely due to demographic changes and several successful lawsuits brought by the Southwest Voter Registration Education Project and others seeking single-member elected districts in school boards. According to figures provided by the Texas Association of School Boards (TASB), there were approximately 7,271 school board members in 1998. Of the 5,673 who reported their race or ethnicity, approximately 82 percent were Anglo, 13 percent were Latino and 6 percent were African American.

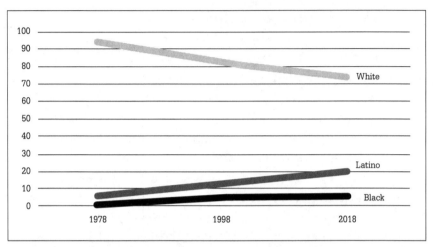

Figure 1. Percent of Local School Board Members in Texas by Race: 1978, 1998, 2018. *Source:* TASB Excel Spreadsheet, 2018 (on file with authors).

School consolidation resulted in fewer school districts and fewer school board members twenty years later. In 2018, there were approximately 7,113 total school board members. Of the 4,662 board members disclosing their race/ethnicity, approximately 74 percent were Anglo, 20 percent were Latino, and 6 percent were African American. In 1998 and 2018, the total number of board members represented by other racial/ethnic groups amounted to less than 1 percent (Figure 1).

By gender, women accounted for 23 percent of all board members in 1998 and 30 percent in 2018. Latina women saw the largest growth. Among those reporting their race, the number of Latina board members grew from 178 in 1998 to 276 in 2018.[29]

SUPERINTENDENT REPRESENTATION

While school boards establish policies for school districts, superintendents implement those policies and manage day-to-day operations. As the top educators in a district, superintendents serve as role models for students in their respective communities, and shape educational programs. In 1978, only twenty-nine of Texas's 1,066 superintendents were Hispanic (less than 3 percent), and two were African American. Only one was a woman.[30]

Twenty years later, the number of Latino superintendents rose to 6 percent of the total superintendents in the state (sixty-six of 1,040). Of the sixty-six Latinos, fifty-seven were men and nine were women. Two decades later, the number of Latino superintendents had doubled, but remained low. In 2018, there were 1,189 superintendents in Texas; 13 percent, or 151, were classified as Latino. Of the Latinos, 74 percent were men, while only 26 percent were women. Nationally, less than 3 percent of schools have Latino superintendents.[31]

While women have seen larger representation as superintendents in the twenty-first century, these female leaders are predominately Anglo (90 percent). Most women (69 percent) serve as superintendents in rural districts with small populations of 500 to 1,499 students.

SCHOOL PRINCIPAL REPRESENTATION

Principals are school leaders who set the tone and culture of their campuses. They play vital roles in student achievement, with national research showing that effective principals who support their teachers can improve student achievement in just one school year.[32]

In 1998, there were 6,418 school principals employed in the state of Texas. Latinos comprised 1,092 (17 percent) of all principals. The distribution of male and female principals during this period was roughly equal. Twenty years later, the percentage of Latino principals had increased to approximately 24 percent. Latinas accounted for 1,365 (of 5,427 women total), and there were 654 Latino men serving as principals that year (of 2,989 total).[33]

Principals are often selected from among teachers already in the schools, so shifts in teacher demographics should ideally be reflected in principal demographics, yet despite an increasing number of Latino teachers, the number of Latinos in school leadership roles lags behind.[34]

EDUCATOR REPRESENTATION

Teachers remain the single most important factor in student success controlled by schools. Studies show that diversity in the teaching profession also matters for all students. This is especially true for students from ethnically diverse backgrounds, who demonstrate greater academic achievement and social-emotional development in classes with teachers of diverse ethnic backgrounds.[35]

Over the last fifty years, the number and percentage of Latino teachers in Texas continue to rise, likely resulting from the population increase. In 1968, Mexican Americans comprised 5 percent of all teachers, compared to 20 percent of all students. In 1998, there were 40,323 Latino teachers in the state of Texas. They represented nearly 16 percent of the 257,400 educators in the workforce. The majority—73 percent—were women.[36]

In 2018, there were 98,252 Latino teachers in Texas, representing 27 percent of the overall educator workforce. This compares to the 52 percent Latino student population. Nationally, the gap between the percentage of Latino teachers and students is larger than for any other racial or ethnic group. More than 21 percent of students are Latinos, while Latino teachers represent fewer than 8 percent of teachers.[37]

Since the late 1980s, the overall number of teachers has dramatically increased. This is especially true for teachers of color, whose numbers have more than doubled from about 325,000 to 666,000 since the 1980s. The number of teachers of diverse ethnic backgrounds increased from 12 percent to 18 percent of the overall teaching workforce. Hispanics also have higher percentages of males entering teaching.[38]

State Funding of Education

Texas continues to struggle to fairly and equitably fund its public schools, despite several decades of advocacy by Mexican American-led organizations, legislators, and legal advocates. While school finance is only one part of a larger ecosystem needed to support equal educational opportunity, it plays a significant role. For example, school finance impacts the number of teachers hired, which can affect class size and student achievement; the quality and extent of professional development offered to teachers and school leaders to help better prepare them to reach and teach all student groups; advanced coursework and co-curricular and extracurricular activities that can lead to greater high school and college graduation rates;

the safety, condition, and technology of school facilities; and availability of full-day prekindergarten with certified staff. There is very little in a school that is not affected by budgets. Yet Texas still largely funds its schools based on ZIP codes rather than on need.

TEXAS SCHOOL FINANCE IN 1968

During the 1968 USCCR hearing, school finance played a prominent role. Experts and advocates testified regarding the school funding advantages favoring property-rich, majority-Anglo communities over property-poor, majority-Mexican American communities. One analysis of nine San Antonio-area school districts by the USCCR's research team showed stark differences between expenditures in property-rich and property-poor districts. Among its findings:

- The majority-Anglo Alamo Heights Independent School District (ISD) had more than ten times the property value per pupil ($23,343 per pupil), compared to the 90 percent Mexican American Edgewood ISD ($2,208 per pupil), the poorest district in the state.
- San Antonio's Alamo Heights ISD spent nearly 40 percent more per pupil ($653) than Edgewood ISD ($465).
- The majority-Mexican American Harlandale ISD, located on the south side of San Antonio, had the second lowest property value in 1968, and taxed its residents seventeen cents higher in property taxes than the majority-Anglo North East ISD (second highest assessed value). Despite Harlandale residents' significant efforts to raise educational funds, North East ISD spent nearly 60 percent more per pupil than its peer district located just across town.
- A strong relationship existed among property values, school expenditures, and the percentage of Mexican American students. The three wealthiest districts, each located north of downtown San Antonio, enrolled between 7 percent and 16 percent Mexican American students. They outspent nearly all other districts analyzed, which enrolled between 24 percent and 89 percent Mexican American students.[39]

Table 1. Select San Antonio-Area School District Expenditures, Assessed Property Value per Pupil, and Tax Rate: 1968, 2016–2017.

District	Percent Hispanic Enrollment		Expenditures per Pupil		Assessed Property Value per Pupil		Real Tax Rate	
	1968	2017	1968	2017	1968	2016	1968	2016
North East ISD	7%	58%	$745	$12,007	$11,414	$453,799	0.71	1.45
Alamo Heights ISD	14%	41%	$653	$12,614	$23,343	$1,139,281	0.78	1.19
Northside ISD	16%	68%	$578	$11,763	$9,429	$365,477	0.86	1.37
East Central ISD	25%	73%	$604	$11,304	$5,939	$256,468	0.68	1.26
Southwest ISD	39%	90%	$543	$12,089	$5,279	$148,934	0.34	1.41
San Antonio ISD	58%	91%	$425	$11,054	$9,783	$242,258	0.72	1.38
South San Antonio ISD	60%	97%	$593	$11,510	$6,807	$140,315	0.91	1.45
Harlandale ISD	62%	98%	$466	$12,603	$4,858	$80,674	0.88	1.52
Edgewood ISD	89%	98%	$465	$11,803	$2,208	$87,600	0.70	1.35

Sources: Texas Education Agency, PEIMS Standard Reports 2016–17 (Student Enrollment). Texas Education Agency 2016–17 Actual Financial data (Total Expenditures, All Funds). Texas Education Agency 2018 Spreadsheet (Total Property Value/Enrollment).

Table 1 presents the property valuations, expenditures, and tax rates for San Antonio-area school districts ranked by percent Mexican Americans enrolled in 1968 and compares them with the same districts in 2017.

An analysis of a USCCR survey of Texas districts in 1968 shows that similar patterns existed across the state. Districts enrolling between 10 percent and 19 percent Mexican American students had property values more than twice the values of districts enrolling between 80 percent and 100 percent Mexican Americans. The districts with low Mexican American student concentrations outspent the districts with high percent Mexican American students by 57 percent. Table 2 compares property values and expenditures in Texas districts by their concentration of Mexican American student enrollment in 1967–1968.

These expenditure advantages allowed the wealthier districts to pay higher salaries and to recruit more teachers with advanced degrees. A survey of Texas districts in 1971–1972 found that districts with low concentrations of Mexican American students (0–25 percent)—even after state aid was added to local revenue share—raised $216 more per pupil and were able to pay teachers 14 percent more and attract more qualified teachers than districts with 75–100 percent Mexican American students. Thirty percent of districts in which Anglo students predominated were able to hire teachers

Table 2. Estimated Market Value, Assessed Value, and Expenditure per Pupil for Texas School Districts of 10 Percent or More Mexican American Pupils, 1967–1968.

Percent Mexican American of District Enrollment	Market Value per Pupil*	Assessed Value per Pupil*	Per Pupil Expenditure, 1967–1968†
10–19.9%	$48,326	$18,413	$464
20–29.9%	$66,943	$16,518	$484
30–49.9%	$56,137	$15,273	$450
50–79.9%	$30,334	$10,674	$383
80–100%	$20,813	$7,224	$296

* Source: Governor's Committee on Public School Education, The Challenge and the Chance, Supplement, December 1968. Reprinted from USCCR 1972c: 21 Table 10.
† Source: USCCR Spring 1969 Survey of School Districts of 10 Percent or More Mexican Americans Enrolled. Reprinted from USCCR 1972c2: 26, Table 14.

with advanced degrees, compared to only 12 percent of districts with a high percentage of Mexican American students.[40]

Francis Knorr and Sally Knack, analysts with the USCCR, noted several effects on educational opportunity related to the unequal funding in the majority Mexican American school districts:

- Almost 90 percent of nondegreed teachers were employed by the four predominantly Mexican American school districts. Disparities in local financial capabilities were also reflected in the quality of facilities.
- These inequalities of opportunity had a strong influence on achievement levels of Mexican American children. Mexican American students on San Antonio's predominantly Hispanic west side tested at achievement grade levels below the grade level they had attained.
- Proportionately, more Mexican American youth, enrolled in schools with student bodies that were almost exclusively Mexican American, were reading two or more years below grade level than those of mixed or predominantly Anglo enrollment.
- College-bound Mexican American students at high Mexican American enrollment school districts were less prepared for college-level work than senior high school students at ethnically balanced or predominantly Anglo schools.
- A disproportionate number of Mexican American students were classified as "mentally retarded" in almost all nine districts, notwithstanding

the questionable validity of biased IQ tests in measuring the innate abilities of Mexican Americans.

• Many Mexican American students were dropping out of school before completing their education. By far the largest number of dropouts occurred in districts with large Mexican American populations.

• In 1967, the San Antonio ISD and Edgewood ISD combined accounted for more than 77 percent of all dropouts, although they accounted for only 7 percent of the collective nine-district enrollment.[41]

RODRÍGUEZ V. SAN ANTONIO ISD

The inequalities built into the Texas school finance system were met with great resistance by Mexican American activists, students, and parents. They staged a student walkout in May 1968 at Edgewood High School in San Antonio to protest the poor quality of education.[42] At the time of the hearing, parents of students attending Edgewood ISD schools had filed a lawsuit, *Rodríguez v. San Antonio ISD*, in federal court, challenging Texas's highly inequitable school finance system. They alleged that the low level of funding for their property-poor school district, compared to other districts in San Antonio and across the state, violated their rights to equal protection under the law and their rights to a fundamental education under the U.S. Constitution.[43]

After a three-judge panel ruled in favor of the *Edgewood* parents in 1971, Texas appealed, and the U.S. Supreme Court reversed the lower court ruling in 1973. The Court held that the parents in the property-poor district did not have a right to equitable funding under the U.S. Constitution, and refused to hold education as a fundamental right. It was a tremendous blow to the community. "The poor people have lost again," lead plaintiff and parent Demetrio Rodríguez told news reporters.[44]

POST-1968 SCHOOL FINANCE IN TEXAS: EDGEWOOD I–IV

Eleven years after the *Rodríguez* decision, Mexican American parents again challenged Texas's inequitable school funding system—this time in state court and under the Texas Constitution. Represented by the Mexican

American Legal Defense and Educational Fund (MALDEF), they joined forces with low-property wealth school districts, including Edgewood ISD. Working with several experts, including IDRA's José Cárdenas, the plaintiffs showed large funding gaps between property-rich and property-poor districts, and argued that the grossly inequitable school funding system denied parents and students their right to an efficient funding system and equal educational opportunities.[45]

Following a trial lasting almost three months in 1987, Travis County District Judge Harley Clark found the Texas finance system unconstitutional. The court found stark disparities among low- and high-property wealth school districts. The court also noted that the heavy concentration of high-need children of color in property-poor districts further exacerbated the problem of unequal opportunity. On appeal by the state, the intermediate court of appeals reversed the district court's ruling on grounds similar to those held by the *Rodríguez* court. The appellate court held that education was not a fundamental right, and that the Texas legislature owed no duty to the plaintiffs to equalize funding across districts.

The plaintiffs appealed the ruling to the Texas Supreme Court. In 1989, that court issued its seminal opinion in favor of the plaintiffs. Citing the important relationship between funding and quality schooling, the court held that all "districts must have substantially equal access to similar revenues per pupil at similar levels of tax effort."[46] The court instructed the Texas legislature to fix the system.

Property-wealthy districts dug in their heels to defend their funding advantages. It took the state six years and three more court cases before finally drafting a school finance plan that met the minimum requirements of the Texas Constitution in *Edgewood IV*. However, each time an increasingly conservative Supreme Court heard a school finance case, it watered down the strong equity standards established in *Edgewood I*.[47] In *Edgewood II*, for example, the court held that the state could allow for "enrichment," creating inequality beyond the cost of a basic, adequate education, as long as the enrichment was not too great.

State Senate Bill 7, approved by the court in *Edgewood IV* in 1995, introduced a provision that would help decrease inequities between property-rich and property-poor districts. Known as "recapture," this equalization feature helped reduce the revenue gap between the wealthy and poor districts by requiring wealthier districts to share their excess tax revenues above certain equalization levels. In turn, these revenues were redistributed to low- and mid-wealth districts to help increase their funding to the equalization levels.

However, the wealthiest districts maintained advantages through "hold-harmless"[48] measures that allowed some high-wealth districts to keep much of their excess revenue. These measures were originally put in place to ease the burden of transitioning into the new funding system. But they lingered long after that transition period. The *Edgewood IV* court acknowledged that the hold-harmless measures contributed greatly to the revenue gap, but it also noted that the Texas legislature intended to phase out those measures after a short period of time.

INADEQUATE AND INEQUITABLE FUNDING IN COURT AGAIN

Ten years later, the Texas Supreme Court heard the next challenge in *Neeley v. West-Orange Cove Consolidated Independent School District*. Representatives of three groups of school districts brought the state's first "adequacy" claim.[49] Under this claim, they argued that the state's overall level of funding was insufficient to provide a basic, quality education to all students. The growth of low-income, Latino, and English language learner students across the state, coupled with rising testing and accountability demands, rested at the center of this controversy.[50]

The low-wealth districts, including twenty-two majority-minority districts led by the Edgewood ISD, were again represented by MALDEF. Along with their adequacy claim, the districts raised equity claims involving funding inequalities between property-rich and property-poor districts for instruction and facilities. They presented evidence showing glaring facility needs across South Texas and along the border. The evidence included stories and photographs of students being educated in thirty-year-old portable buildings and in former housing barracks for migrant workers. They described broken school foundations, mold, and leaky roofs, among other stark deficiencies.

Despite strong testimony from IDRA's Albert Cortez, showing equity gaps exceeding $1,000 between property-rich and property-poor districts, and the accompanying effect on educational opportunity, the Supreme Court again denied relief to the low-wealth districts in 2005. The court now ignored the effect on inequities resulting from the hold-harmless provisions built into Texas Senate Bill 7 back in 1993, which had since been made permanent. Regarding facilities, the court acknowledged the substantial record of evidence, but again revised the legal standard, holding that districts needed to show that they could not provide an adequate education with their existing facilities, regardless of disrepair.

In setting the adequacy standard, the court admonished the trial court for focusing too much on educational inputs, including funding. It stated that educational outputs are better measures for adequacy.[51] The court acknowledged the extensive record showing a struggling system, including an increasingly demanding curriculum, large achievement gaps between special populations, high dropout rates, and high teacher turnover. Nevertheless, the Texas Supreme Court ruled that the system minimally met the standards, despite highlighting scant evidence of "improving" test scores.[52]

The court did uphold the trial court's ruling that districts lacked meaningful discretion in setting their tax rates under a separate claim filed by the West Orange-Cove CISD group. The court noted that districts educating three of every five public school children (59 percent) were forced to tax at the cap of $1.50, and that only 10 percent of districts taxed below $1.40.[53] Evidence demonstrated several districts struggling to maintain accreditation ratings under the heightened testing standards, lack of certified teachers, student demographic changes, and growing teacher attrition.[54] The court held that forcing school districts to tax at or near the statutory cap essentially amounted to a state tax in violation of the state's constitutional prohibition on state *ad valorem* taxes.

THE END OF TEXAS SCHOOL FINANCE LITIGATION (FOR NOW)?

Six years later, the state cut more than $5 billion in funding for schools, while expanding high-stakes testing requirements for graduation from four to fifteen exams. A lawsuit against the state was filed in 2011 by four school district groups, parents, the Texas Charter School Association, and Texans for Real Efficiency and Equity in Education (TREEE).[55] The school district groups included the Edgewood plaintiffs, representing five low-wealth districts and four Latino families of high-need students. They alleged that the school finance system was inequitable and inadequate. They further protested that school districts were forced to tax local residents at or near the allowed limits on property taxes. Unlike the other districts that claimed that the system was inadequate for all school children, the Edgewood group—again represented by MALDEF—alleged that the funding and structural educational opportunities for English language learners and low-income children were inadequate. The group hoped that the tighter focus on the student groups who were struggling the most would help direct the courts' attention to the students with the most glaring needs.[56]

The Texas Taxpayer group (composed of more than 300 low- and mid-wealth districts) argued similar equity and tax claims as the Edgewood group. The Calhoun County ISD plaintiffs consisted of six high-wealth districts that aligned themselves with the other district groups on the adequacy and tax claims. However, they sided with the state in defending their funding advantages, and actively opposed the equity claims of the Edgewood and the Texas Taxpayer groups.

The TREEE intervenors sought to advance their own education agenda. They argued that the system was inefficient because Texas failed to adopt "reforms," such as school privatization and teacher evaluations that used student test scores. The charter school group filed adequacy and equity claims, a facilities funding claim, and a claim seeking to lift the state's cap on the number of charters issued.

Following a trial spanning more than three months between 2012 and 2013, Travis County District Court Judge John K. Dietz ruled the school finance system inequitable and inadequate, and in violation of the meaningful discretion tax clause. In his oral remarks from the bench, Dietz reflected upon the tremendous potential of underserved students. He stated that people typically "let our prejudgments guide our thinking," focusing on the deficits, rather than the potential, of children from low-income families.[57] The court rejected the claims of the intervenors, and upheld only the adequacy claim of the charter school group.

Texas lawmakers went to work in the 2013 legislative session as the trial court prepared its written findings. The state legislature replaced $3.4 billion of the $5.3 billion that it previously eliminated, reduced the number of end-of-course exams for high school students from fifteen to five, and revised the required high school curriculum requirements by setting up "endorsement" tracks (focusing on a chosen field of study) in lieu of the previous, more rigorous "four-by-four" track (mastering four basic academic areas).[58]

Upset with the legislature's intention to further close funding gaps between property-rich and property-poor districts, the wealthy Calhoun County districts asked the court to reopen the trial in spite it having prevailed on two of its claims. The court agreed to reopen the case. In 2014, following a supplemental trial lasting nearly three weeks in January and February, the court again found the system unconstitutional and supported its ruling with 364 single-spaced pages of findings of fact and conclusions of law.[59]

Despite an overwhelming one-sided record on appeal favoring the school district and parent plaintiffs, the Supreme Court of Texas reversed the lower court's decision. The Texas Supreme Court again modified its precedent without any rational justification, making it even more difficult for any party to prevail. It did so by giving the legislature substantial deference in designing the school finance system, and by replacing expert opinion on the record with its own views on educational policy.[60]

For example, to counter the substantial record highlighting the ability of underserved children to succeed if provided sufficient resources and programs, the Texas Supreme Court reached back to the 1960s to reference the much-criticized Coleman Report. This report suggested that more resources might not help improve educational achievement outcomes for underserved children. The state supreme court represented that the report's findings remained valid, despite testimony from the state's own expert witnesses acknowledging the positive effects that high-quality prekindergarten programs, smaller class sizes, and well-resourced bilingual programs can have on student learning.[61]

Perhaps most concerning was the Supreme Court's treatment of the Edgewood group's adequacy claim. The trial record in this case was replete with testimony from parents, teachers, school leaders, and experts on the many challenges facing English language learner students and students from low-income families.[62]

Nevertheless, the Texas Supreme Court again changed the adequacy standard for these underserved children. For subgroups like low-income and English language learners to be successful on their adequacy claims, the Texas Supreme Court stated that "the ruling would have to be truly exceptional."[63] This remarkable feat of applying a higher standard for students facing greater inequities is unparalleled in state court jurisprudence, and it was unsupported by any citation to precedent.

Regarding the equity claim, the Texas Supreme Court ignored unrefuted evidence presented by IDRA's Albert Cortez. His analysis showed that the prior gap of nine cents in tax rates in *Edgewood IV* between high- and low-wealth districts had more than doubled to at least twenty cents in favor of the wealthiest districts.[64] In other words, high-wealth districts could generate the funds needed to provide a basic education at a tax rate that was twenty cents less than the poorest districts.

The Supreme Court of Texas rejected all claims of all parties, despite finding that the system was reflective of "a recondite scheme for which the word byzantine seems generous."[65]

SCHOOL FUNDING IN 2018

As recently as 2018, the unfair advantages built into the system continued to favor high-wealth districts serving few students of color. This is largely due to the decision of Texas, which has no state income tax, to rely substantially on property taxes, and the court's reluctance to hold true to the strong equity standards it pronounced in 1989. After much progress in the 1990s, the state government failed to live up to its promises to the children of low-property-wealth communities. The Supreme Court of Texas also has not decided whether education is a fundamental right under the Texas Constitution. Given the makeup of the court in 2018, the question is not likely to reach that court for at least another generation. As a result, school

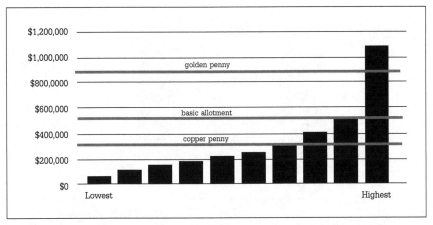

Figure 2. Property Wealth per WADA (Weighted Average Daily Attendance) by Decile of Districts with Equalized Wealth Levels, 2016. *Source:* Intercultural Development Research Association, 2016.

finance and equity advocates have focused greater attention on the Texas legislature.

The state legislature, however, has not been willing to invest in education as the public school population becomes more ethnically diverse and financially poorer. The state's share of paying for education declined from over 50 percent ten years ago to less than 40 percent in 2018, resulting in local property taxpayers bearing an even higher share of the costs. Instead of investing in public education, the state legislature has shifted its focus to supporting failing reforms, including the expansion of ill-performing charter schools. The lack of equitable and adequate funding remains a significant barrier to educational opportunities, especially for underserved Latino-majority and African American-majority public schools.

The wealthiest 10 percent of districts (or deciles) have over ten times the property tax value as the poorest deciles, as shown in Figure 2. In a 2011 analysis, IDRA reported that, on average, the school districts in the lowest decile enrolled approximately 90 percent Latino children, compared to only 50 percent enrolled in the wealthiest decile.[66] IDRA updated the analysis for 2016 (see Figure 2).

Although the state has attempted to equalize funding levels, several exceptions still allow the wealthiest five percent of school districts access

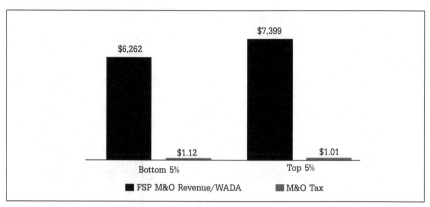

Figure 3. Revenue Advantages for Children in Top 5 Percent versus Bottom 5 Percent of Districts by Property Wealth per WADA, 2016–2017. *Source:* Intercultural Development Research Association, 2017.

to more than $1,100 more per child than the poorest five percent, while taxing ten cents less than the poorer districts, as Figure 3 shows. When that advantage of more than $1,100 is applied to a school or district of one thousand students, the advantage grows to more than $1.1 million. This could translate to expanded prekindergarten programs, more computers or better technology, higher teacher salaries, greater professional development and mentoring opportunities for teachers and school leaders, increased instructional support, more teachers, and reduced class sizes, among other educational opportunities.

Recent research shows that increased funding has contributed to improved student performance and lifetime outcomes, especially for underserved students.[67] Money matters, and how that money is spent, and on which children, also matters. The state legislature created a Texas School Finance Commission to study the topic in 2018. However, to date the commission has largely failed to locate and discuss additional sources of revenue to target the needs of underserved students and to level-up the system for students in property-poor districts. It is not expected to recommend any bold steps to improve funding for public schools, but that has not stopped advocates from informing legislators on the possibilities.

To assist legislators and advocates, IDRA National Director of Policy David Hinojosa developed a research-based School Finance Roadmap to

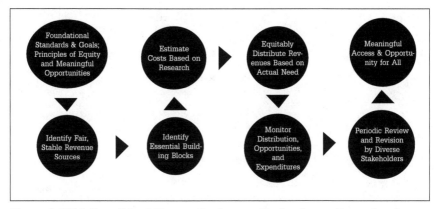

Figure 4. IDRA State School Finance Roadmap to Equity. *Source:* Intercultural Development Research Association, 2018.

Equity and presented it to the commission in 2018. This student-centered framework (shown in Figure 4) enables states to better understand each step policymakers should consider in designing their school finance systems to ensure that all children access the meaningful educational opportunities they need to succeed in school and in life.

As of 2018, the outlook remains bleak for Texas's financial support for the education of its Mexican American students and other underserved students. Texas Governor Greg Abbott's and Lieutenant Governor Dan Patrick's stranglehold on Texas's investment in education continues decades of inadequate and inequitable funding. Until Texas can begin funding schools based on who is in the classroom as opposed to what is above and below the ground in terms of property wealth, the same problems that pervaded Texas's educational system in 1968 will permeate Texas policy.

Bilingual, Bicultural Education in 1968

At the height of the civil rights era in 1968, Latinos faced several institutional challenges in education and assimilation in language, culture, and curriculum. The testimony of many witnesses during the USCCR hearings reflected much of the anger and frustration from the community.

George I. Sánchez, professor of history and philosophy of education and Latin education at the University of Texas at Austin, testified that many teachers and administrators were not prepared to teach diverse populations, and lacked knowledge about their Latino students' culture and language.[68]

State Senator Joe Bernal spoke of the low expectations of Mexican American students. When asked why schools enroll so many Mexican American students in vocational education, he replied:

> We figure that certain people are born innately inferior, and some innately superior, with very little regard as to where you come from a poor area, and that that, in itself, is what is a greater indicator of how you perform in testing. So, when these people test low, the general preconceived idea is that they are not going to go to college. They haven't got the brainpower. They haven't got the facility to understand. They are kind of dumb. So, if they are dumb, we are going to put them in vocational areas where they can work with their hands. You know, these people are very good with their hands, so they tell us.[69]

Manuel Ramírez, an assistant professor of psychology at Rice University in Houston, discussed the challenges confronting Mexican American students when told they cannot reap the economic benefits of the Anglo culture unless they reject their Mexican American culture. The problem, he said, was exacerbated by the stereotypes and portrayals of Mexican Americans in schools and in the media that led to "self-rejection."[70]

Aurelio Montemayor, a former English teacher at San Felipe High School in the Del Rio area of Texas near the Texas-Mexico border, testified that he attempted to find college courses that would help better prepare him to teach Chicano students, but to no avail. The textbook he used for his English literature course was of little use in reaching his students, because the textbook contained nothing about their heritage. He had his students create a textbook of their own that reflected their stories.

James Sutton, a history teacher at Lanier High School in San Antonio and archivist at Our Lady of the Lake University, testified that most Texas history courses were "Anglo-oriented." To teach his students about their heritage, and to better prepare them for college, he taught Texas history reaching further back in time, before the U.S. occupation that would lead to what was then Mexico becoming the state of Texas. He also provided different perspectives from the colonists' viewpoint and the resident Mexicans' viewpoint.[71]

Students spoke of the low expectations of schools, describing the "disconnect" between the curriculum and the communities served. In response to a question about whether he experienced negative portrayals of Mexican Americans in textbooks, Lanier High School student Edgar Lozano stated:

> Yes sir. I mean that is another reason why I felt bad when I was with Anglos, you know. I mean, they kept telling me I'm an outsider, I'm a foreigner. And I said: "Well, I am in the country, you know." So, it is theirs. I am a guest in the country. That is the feeling I always had. And then they, you know, the way they beat us at the Alamo, you know, the way a small handful of men fighting with knives and everything . . . killed off the whole Mexican Army and earned our independence. So that is the crackerjack books that we used to read in elementary and junior high. And then I started reading on my own, a few things I could find. And then I started going to some lectures and looking for some men that I heard had a different point of view, because to me that didn't jibe. I don't care what they told me.

Jack B. Forbes, the research program director at the U.S. Education Department's Far West Laboratory for Educational Research and Development in Berkeley, California, testified that the Anglo-run schools excluded students of color by design. He also noted the strong correlation between alienation and low achievement rates, explaining:

> Now another aspect of this that must be mentioned is that this kind of school quite obviously has not been good for Mexican American children. The same kind of school has not been good for American Indian children; it's not been good for other non-Anglo children. It tends to lead to a great

deal of alienation, a great deal of hostility. It tends to lead also to a great deal of confusion, where the child comes out of that school really not knowing what language he should speak other than English, being in doubt as to whether he should completely accept what Anglo people have been telling him and forget his Mexican identity, or whether he should listen to what his parents and perhaps other people have said and be proud of his Mexican identity.[72]

With little progress in addressing the absence of Mexican American culture and history in the curriculum, momentum was gaining to support bilingual education at the national level. Bilingual education teaches English to children, and gives them a chance to learn core subjects like math and science in their native language. Research clearly shows the benefits to the children's school success in later years, as well as to the community at large. Students in such programs achieve higher academic standards.[73]

In 1968, the U.S. Congress passed the Bilingual Education Act, the first piece of federal legislation supporting the use of a student's home language and culture in learning English.[74] Josue Gonzalez, then the San Antonio ISD's director of the San Antonio Bilingual Education Center, testified at the 1968 USCCR hearing. Using federal Title III funds, the center provided bilingual and English as a second language (ESL) services to 4,000 children in 150 classrooms in nine schools in 1968. Of these, about half the children received bilingual instruction.[75]

Bilingual Education After 1968

Although the Bilingual Education Act did not mandate bilingual education, it opened the door to support bilingual education programs. In 1970, the U.S. Department of Health, Education, and Welfare (HEW) Office for Civil Rights issued a memorandum to school districts that were receiving federal grants and enrolling a student population comprising at least 5 percent English language learners. The memorandum cautioned districts against submerging English language learners in English-only classrooms without any specialized support. It also prohibited schools from tracking students into special education or inferior programs or classrooms based on their lack of English proficiency.[76]

In California, parents of Asian American English language learners sued their school districts, challenging English immersion practices under the equal protection clause of the U.S. Constitution and the Civil Rights Act of 1964. In the case *Lau v. Nichols,* the U.S. Supreme Court held that immersing non-English-speaking students with no support denied them any meaningful opportunity to participate in school.[77]

In response, the HEW issued what became known as the "Lau Memorandum" in 1975, to provide districts guidance in revising their programs and services for English learner students. Although the department did not require any specific language program, it did require school districts to develop and offer a comprehensive plan to ensure the delivery of appropriate language programs that provided for identification, testing, achievement, and program offerings.[78]

At the state level, Texas enacted House Bill 103 in 1969, authorizing—but not requiring—schools to provide bilingual education up to the sixth grade.[79] Following the passage of the Bilingual Education and Training Act in 1973, the state required school districts with twenty or more students in the same grade who spoke the same language to offer bilingual education in kindergarten through third grade beginning in 1974-1975. However, advocates wanted even greater expansion.

The League of United Latin American Citizens (LULAC) and the American GI Forum intervened in the statewide desegregation case, *U.S. v. Texas,* arguing that the state was complicit in the segregation of Mexican Americans in schools. Represented by MALDEF and the Multicultural Education, Training and Advocacy, Inc. (META), they also argued that English language learners were denied equal educational opportunities to learn under section (f) of the Equal Educational Opportunities Act of 1974. The plaintiffs and their experts presented evidence of poorly designed language programs with little state oversight.

In 1981, the federal district court hearing the case agreed, and ordered the Texas legislature to remedy the deficiencies and to expand bilingual education programs to middle and high schools. On appeal, the Fifth Circuit Court of Appeals reversed the ruling on the segregation claim, finding the state did not have an active role or official laws allowing districts to segregate students. It also found that Senate Bill 477, signed into law in 1981 during the appeal, essentially eliminated the need for the additional relief sought by the plaintiffs.[80]

At the time, Senate Bill 477 was among the more comprehensive and progressive language laws enacted by a state. Among its several reforms, it required the provision of bilingual education in elementary schools when there were twenty or more students who spoke the language at the same grade level. It also established criteria for identifying, placing, and exiting English language learners in appropriate language programs; mandated school districts to create school-based committees to evaluate English language learner progress; and directed the Texas Education Agency to monitor districts onsite.

In 2003, the Texas Education Agency replaced its onsite monitoring program with a desk audit that relied heavily on test scores to identify poorly performing schools. An analysis by IDRA showed that the state's monitoring program overlooked several secondary schools where English language learners performed dismally.[81] This occurred because the state often combined the score of higher performing elementary students with lower performing secondary students. Hence, LULAC and GI Forum again sued in 2006.

Following trial, the district court initially declined relief to the plaintiffs. But after the plaintiffs' filed a motion for reconsideration citing error in the court's decision, the district court agreed. Among the state's deficiencies, the court noted that the state's monitors responsible for overseeing interventions were not certified in bilingual or English as a second language (ESL) education. Referring to such a practice as "the blind leading the blind," the court ordered the state to reform its language program monitoring system and its secondary language programs.[82]

On appeal, the conservative Fifth Circuit Court of Appeals reversed the lower court's ruling. The appellate court held that more time was needed to assess the reliability of the newly created monitoring system, and that the plaintiffs should also have sued school districts, since the state did not directly educate anyone. Although the state asked the Fifth Circuit to dismiss the case altogether, the court declined. Acknowledging that the substantial record before it evidenced that English language learner performance is "alarming," it remanded the case to the district court, ordering the plaintiffs to add individual districts as defendants to determine which entity, or both, should be held responsible for the failure.[83]

In 2014 LULAC sued in federal court again, adding the Southwest ISD in San Antonio to their case. The plaintiffs focused on three alleged violations of the Equal Educational Opportunities Act:

- Continuing ineffective state monitoring and intervention of failing district and school programs.
- The state's bare ESL supplemental certification test and procedures that fail to ensure teachers are properly trained and qualified to implement effective language programs.
- The provision of ineffective ESL pullout programs for secondary students.

This case was pending near the end of 2018.[84]

Today, Texas public schools enroll more than one million English language learners, an increase of more than 250,000 students over the past decade alone. English language learners account for nearly one of every five public school students (19 percent), and tens of thousands exit the program each year.[85] About 90 percent of these students in Texas are Spanish speakers. This presents a tremendous asset for Texas—if the state chooses to wisely invest in their education.

Advocates have fought for decades to ensure that English language learners have access to equal educational opportunities, often relying on the courts. Even without litigation, advocates are making some strides. Advocates for bilingual education, including the Texas Association for Bilingual Education, successfully expanded support for dual language programs, which provide dual language services for both English learner and English proficient students. Research shows that when dual language programs are implemented well, the English language learners in those programs outperform general education students.[86] Texas also now has an opportunity for students to earn a performance acknowledgment on their transcripts for outstanding performance in bilingual education and biliteracy.[87]

However, overall support for bilingual education remains challenging. English-only proponents frequently file legislation to undo Texas's strong bilingual education laws. Each year, several dozen districts file for waivers and exceptions to bilingual and ESL teacher certification requirements, citing a shortage of certified teachers. Punitive accountability systems turn some educators and administrators against English language learners and supportive programs.

State funding for bilingual/ESL instruction remains at the same low level established in 1984. This has especially hurt high school English language learners, who are among the lowest performing student groups in the state. IDRA research in 2015 found no secondary schools in Texas that were consistently exceeding academic benchmarks with English learners. The schools with highest English learner achievement levels spent significantly more general funds than other schools on bilingual/ESL programs. Texas is significantly underfunding English language learner education (with supplemental funding of only 10 percent, despite research indicating much higher funding levels are needed).[88]

Mexican American Studies

The fight for the inclusion of Mexican American experiences into the general curriculum remains problematic. The Texas State Board of Education (SBOE) has largely overseen the adoption of curriculum standards, and created its share of controversy on a range of topics. From arguing against the inclusion of Darwinism in science, to shifting the narrative about the role of slavery in the Confederacy, the SBOE has been accused of abusing its authority by injecting its ideological slant into the curriculum. When the board adopted social studies standards in 2010, for example, it refused to consider and include a range of Mexican American figures and experiences. Recent events, however, signal a glimmer of hope, as the Texas State Board of Education authorized the development of a Mexican American Studies course elective.

Following some positive electoral shifts in the board's makeup, advocates for Mexican American studies programs in 2014 approached the SBOE about adopting curriculum standards for an official Mexican American Studies course. In response, the board put out a call for textbooks. Only one textbook was presented to the board, *Mexican American Heritage*, published by a company owned by a former controversial board member, Cynthia Dunbar.

The textbook reportedly included strong anti-Mexican American overtones. Patrick Michels's review in the *Texas Observer* says Mexican Americans are "viewed as lazy compared to European or American workers" and are portrayed as functioning on "*mañana* time," essentially suggesting that Mexican Americans routinely delay taking action until the next day, and the book's author charged that Chicano activists "adopted a revolutionary narrative that opposed Western civilization and wanted to destroy this society."[89]

To the board's credit, it declined to adopt the textbook. Several advocates, including LULAC, MALDEF, the National Association for Chicana and Chicano Studies (NACCS), and the *Tejas Foco* (Texas Focus) Committee pressed forward for the adoption of curriculum standards for a Mexican American Studies high school course. Representatives of the NACCS and other groups cited important research showing such courses led to improved student achievement and graduation rates and increased engagement.[90] In 2018, the SBOE approved state guidelines based on a Mexican American Studies course offered as an elective by the Houston ISD. However, the victory was bittersweet.

David Bradley, a Republican board member seen as politically far-right-leaning, proposed a last-minute name change from "Mexican-American Studies" to "Ethnic Studies: An Overview of Americans of Mexican Descent."[91] Bradley reportedly stated, "I don't subscribe to hyphenated Americanism." A majority of the board, including one Latina Democrat, sided with Bradley on the name change. While some organizations applauded the board's vote, others sharply criticized the name change.

University of Texas at Austin professor and activist Angela Valenzuela publicly stated: "Many of us have expressed just how paternalistic and repulsive this name is—with echoes that go back to McCarthyism and subtractive cultural assimilation to which my parents were subjected in the public schools throughout the 1940s, 1950s, and early- to mid-1960s."[92] Others argued that a specialized curriculum is unnecessary, and that the Mexican American experience and culture should be included in the mainstream curriculum so that all students can learn. Thus, while the potential for reaching more Latino students through curriculum offerings has taken a step forward, challenges remain.

Curriculum and Instruction

Students who speak a language other than English have the right to comprehensible instruction that fosters learning. One key distinction is that many regulations do not specify the methods for achieving high standards. Earlier federal laws specified the development and implementation of exemplary bilingual education programs, development of bilingual skills and multicultural understanding, and development of English and native language skills. However, in many cases, individual schools must determine for themselves how they will implement effective bilingual education programs. And there has always been a shortage of prepared, certified bilingual teachers.

IDRA's research reaffirms what is possible when committed and dedicated individuals use research to develop and provide excellent bilingual education programs for their students. IDRA conducted a national study for the U.S. Department of Education on successful bilingual schools and programs, and identified twenty-five characteristics that contribute to the high academic performance of students served by bilingual education programs.[93]

The characteristics were clustered into five dimensions that are necessary for success: student indicators, student outcomes, leadership, support, and programmatic and instructional practices. Civil rights protections indicate that English language learners should not have to give up their language, their culture, or their diversity as the price for learning English. The inherent value of all students and their characteristics must be recognized, acknowledged, and celebrated. When English language learners walk into a classroom, they should not be limited in their access to an equitable and excellent education. For that to occur, teachers must be prepared to serve them.

Immigrant Education

Immigrants to the United States face nativist and anti-immigrant challenges that were present long before the Civil Rights Commission met in San Antonio in 1968. From anti-Roman Catholic rhetoric, to anti-Chinese movements in the nineteenth century, to former President Donald Trump's "build-a-wall" demands, the proffered "reasons" held in common by those prejudiced campaigns are economic and social.

Laborers seeking low-paying, undesirable jobs are accused of taking away jobs that "belong to white citizens." Some see racial and ethnic visibility and cultural differences as a threat to "American culture, language and values" and to a monocultural, monolingual vision centered on an imagined "white" middle-class, English-speaking way of life. U.S. immigration laws demonstrate a history of discriminatory biases, including Chinese exclusion, literacy tests, national origin quotas, Mexican "repatriation" campaigns, and "Operation Wetback."

The 1968 USCCR hearings focused on education issues of Mexican American students. The litany of exclusionary and discriminatory practices in public schools echoed the broader, painful history of injustices. Forbidding and punishing the use of Spanish reflected the U.S. mainstream phobia of "un-American cultural practices" that deterred "acculturation." Assigning Mexican and Mexican American students to low-level vocational education tracks mirrored the institutional collusion. It was generally believed that immigrant, and particularly undocumented immigrant, students were best at working with their hands, and should only be prepared for the blue-collar market.[94]

While several witnesses testified at the 1968 hearings about the educational needs of English language learners and advocated for bilingual education, little was said about immigrants and their access to public education, given their legal status. Generally, the testimony favored changes in curriculum and instruction that would benefit the children of recent immigrants. The USCCR issued a comprehensive report in 1980, *The Tarnished Golden Door: Civil Rights Issues in Immigration.*[95] But it did not touch on the education of immigrant children. Public schools served undocumented children at will, and many times excluded them because of the legal status of their parents.

School Policies and Assistance

Two years after the San Antonio hearings, the U.S. Department of Health Education and Welfare (which preceded the current U.S. Department of Education) issued a memorandum on May 25, 1970. It stated:

> Title VI compliance review conducted in school districts with large Spanish-surnamed student populations by the Office for Civil Rights have revealed a number of common practices which have the effect of denying equality of educational opportunity to Spanish-surnamed pupils. Similar practices, which have the effect of discrimination on the basis of national origin, exist in other locations with respect to disadvantaged pupils from other national origin-minority groups, for example, Chinese or Portuguese.[96]

Following the *Lau v. Nichols* decision by the U.S. Supreme Court in 1974 requiring local education agencies to provide supplemental language instruction to English learners, the U.S. Department of Education issued mandates for school support that led to the creation and funding of equity assistance centers. These centers originally focused on three distinct issues: national origin, race, and gender equity.

In 1975, IDRA received funding to establish the first generation of equity centers: the Lau Centers (later called the National Origin Desegregation

Centers). These centers were eventually combined into one that served all the issues in focus. IDRA provided critical technical assistance to school districts across the region, including Texas, to assist them in addressing discrimination against immigrant students and the need for more support for English learners. In 1975, the Texas legislature passed a law withholding funds for the education of children of undocumented immigrants. This law also authorized local school districts to deny entry to these children. Represented by MALDEF, immigrant families from Mexico, who were not identified by name because of the legal risk, challenged the law in court.

The resulting U.S. Supreme Court case, *Plyler v. Doe*, focused on the denial of a public education to immigrant families because of their legal status. Consistent with the equal protection clause of the Fourteenth Amendment, the court held that Texas cannot deny undocumented school-age children the free public education that the state provides to children who are citizens of the United States and to legally admitted immigrants.[97] Fourteen years after the USCCR San Antonio hearings, school doors were legally opened to immigrant children.

In Texas, as districts carried out the bilingual education requirements for eligible schools, immigrant children and families were among the beneficiaries of curricula and instruction that used their home or native language. The state developed a process for identifying, testing, and placing children in classes with appropriate instruction. IDRA provided information and conducted training across the state to help school districts implement the new practices and better serve children.

Many immigrant families benefited from the programs that emerged from the "War on Poverty" in the 1960s. Migrant education services in the fields helped some immigrant children continue their education while the families labored in the hot sun. Federally funded Head Start centers across the country availed young children safe places for learning, and invited the children's parents to be part of Head Start governing committees.[98] However, with intensifying enforcement by U.S. Immigration and Customs Enforcement (ICE) in recent years, families became afraid to even attend meetings in their children's schools, concerned that ICE officers might be posted at school entrances.

The Texas DREAM Act

In 2001 Texas became the first state to pass a law authorizing in-state tuition rates for undocumented students.[99] Authored by Texas Representative Rick Noriega and co-authored by several others, HB 1403 (also referred to as the Texas DREAM Act) allows undocumented immigrant students and others who are not citizens or legal permanent residents to pay instate tuition at Texas public colleges and universities.

To be eligible, an immigrant student must have attended high school for three consecutive years prior to graduating; graduated from a Texas public or private high school, or received the equivalent of a high school diploma in Texas; and resided for at least one year in Texas prior to enrolling in higher education.[100] In addition, the person must submit "an affidavit stating that the person will apply to become a permanent resident of the United States as soon as the person becomes eligible to apply."[101] Some immigrant students are also eligible for Texas tuition grants and scholarships.

Unsurprisingly, the Texas DREAM Act has faced repeated opposition in the courts and in the state legislature. In 2009, the Immigration Reform Coalition of Texas (IRCOT)—a politically right-wing, conservative organization—sued the state and the Lone Star College System, arguing that the law and the provision of state tuition grants to immigrant students violated federal law.

MALDEF intervened on behalf of the University Leadership Initiative, an immigrant student advocacy organization at the University of Texas at Austin, to help ensure that the state adequately defended the law. The court in 2011 dismissed the claims challenging the in-state tuition law. Later, following contentious depositions and pretrial discovery work by the defendants and MALDEF, the anti-DREAM Act coalition withdrew its challenge to in-state tuition grants for immigrants.[102]

Legislative advocacy efforts have also stepped up. MALDEF, the ACLU of Texas, and the Texas Association of Business formed the TRUST Coalition in 2007 to counter several legislative attacks filed against immigrant families and their communities.[103] The coalition, Dreamer students, and other advocates have been instrumental in defeating several bills aimed at repealing the Texas DREAM Act.

In 2016, the Texas Republican Party added to its platform a priority aimed at the Texas DREAM Act.[104] The author of a bill filed in the 2017 legislative session, State Representative Jonathon Stickland, stated, "We think that turning off the magnets and the free handouts to illegals is just as important to securing our border, so they have to go hand in hand to really get at the source of this problem."[105] However, the younger "Dreamer" students organized to oppose that legislation. Their concerted efforts helped defeat the Strickland bill and all other similar bills to date.

In 2016 and 2017, school districts across the country issued resolutions and updated their own policies to protect students' rights in light of uncertainty regarding federal immigration enforcement activities. Many of the statements affirmed the districts' missions to ensure all students have a safe and positive learning environment, and they outlined guidance to school personnel on how to respond to requests from ICE agents for information or access to their campus. Some of the resolutions set up timelines for training of school staff, including teachers and campus police.

Migrant Education

The Migrant Education Program was established by the U.S. Department of Education (DOE) in 1966 as part of Title I, Part C, of the Elementary and Secondary Education Act (ESEA) of 1965. Designed to meet the unique educational and social needs of migrant children between the ages of three and twenty-two, the program was designed to ensure equal access to a high-quality education for all migrant children.

The education of children whose families migrated from Texas to other states during growing seasons was given focused attention at the USCCR hearings. Witnesses described the challenges for schools to teach children who left school before the end of the school year with their migrant families and returned after the next school year had begun. These children had the highest rates of in-grade retention and of leaving school permanently. For many of them, completing elementary school was graduation.

José A. Cardenas, Migrant Education Program Director for the U.S Department of Education's Southwest Educational Development Laboratory, testified in 1968:

> Migrant children are consistently underachieving and consistently over-age for their grade as compared to national norms . . . Testimony was given that the dropout rate for Mexican Americans is about 80 percent. I estimate the dropout rate for migrant children to be approximately 90 percent or close to 90 percent . . . One-fifth of all migrant children never enroll in any school, in spite of the state's compulsory attendance laws.[106]

He also testified about the need for a greater number of trained and competent teachers to work with migrant pupils, and the need for effective communication between the school and the migrant home that is both positive and continuous. He added: "Unless we develop some new and better instructional programs for the migrant child that are geared to the special characteristics of the migrant, then you will have very little success in eliminating the educational problem of these children."[107] Commissioner Frankie M. Freeman replied: "Doesn't this seem sort of a sad contrast to somebody who says they are busy getting a man on the moon, and they can't even feed a child or educate a child in this state?"[108]

At the time of the San Antonio hearings, migrant education groups were receiving funding to assist with health and education services for migrant workers and their families. Head Start services provided education to young children in the communities where migrant families resided seasonally. The Colorado Migrant Council was such an entity in the 1970s, and the Texas Migrant Council continues to serve migrants today.

Meanwhile, the numbers of migrant families had dramatically declined. Since the late 1990s, the share of agricultural workers who migrate within the United States fell by about 60 percent. On average over this period, one-third of the drop in the migration rate was due to changes in the demographic makeup of the workforce, while two-thirds was due to government and institutional changes in the market. However, in recent years, demographic changes were responsible for nearly half of the overall

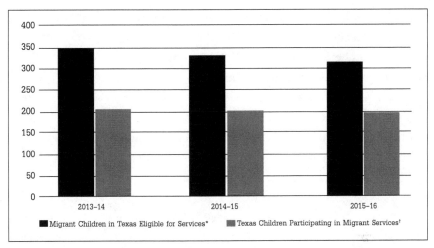

Figure 5. Texas Migrant Program (in thousands). *Within three years of making a qualifying move, resided in a state one or more days, between September 1 and August 31 of a reporting period. †Received MEP-funded instructional or support services at any time. Source: Ed Data Express: Data about elementary and secondary schools in the U.S.

change.[109] Technology changes and mechanization have reduced the need for field workers. The most recent numbers (Figure 5) served in Texas show a decline in total students eligible and served in the past four years.

Migrant education advocacy groups that emerged in the 1970s continue to support improved education and other services for students. Schools receive per-pupil allotments for families identified as migrants, although the criteria to qualify for these funds have become more stringent in recent years. The College Assistance Migrant Program (CAMP) program, in place in Texas and other states, provides support for migrant students to enter and succeed in college.

Mexican Americans and Access to College

In 1968, access to college was largely unattainable for many Mexican Americans. Testimony at the 1968 USCCR hearings showed that preparation, access, and opportunity to complete college were not an option for most Mexican American students. Several witnesses at the commission hearings testified that blatantly low expectations for Mexican American students in schools frequently affected those students' impressions about whether they were "college material." Students attending public schools testified that they felt ill-prepared to go to college.

Richard Teniente, a State Board of Education member, stated: "We have had situations where the ninth-grade counselors have told the youngsters not to prepare for college because there are not enough scholarships available for them to make it through college. We have had the same counselor tell youngsters that it takes money, clothes, and things that you cannot afford, so you better prepare for something else."[110]

In 2000, the Texas Higher Education Coordinating Board introduced an initiative, the "Closing the Gaps by 2015: The Texas Higher Education Plan," designed to reduce achievement disparities to produce an educated workforce that would be needed to avoid economic decline. A 2014 progress report stated that half of Latino students who graduated from Texas public high schools in 2013 went directly to Texas colleges and universities the following fall (46 percent of Latino males; 56 percent of Latino females).[111]

In Texas, two-year persistence rates for Latinos at public universities increased in 2011 from 77 percent to 78 percent. But the two-year persistence rate at public community colleges remained the same, where only about half (51 percent) of Latino students remained enrolled after two years. Of the Latino students who entered a four-year college or university, only 66 percent graduated after six years, the board reported in 2014. More than half of Latino students enrolling in Texas's public colleges and universities required remedial coursework.[112]

In 2013, the Texas Legislature established the Foundation High School Program, which allows for significant local variation in graduation planning, and represents one of the more substantial changes to Texas curricula in recent history. The new policy, known as HB5, lowered graduation requirements for mathematics, science, and social studies. The policy implemented a new graduation requirement for career readiness, called "endorsements," and added a "Distinguished Level of Achievement" designation, which, in reality, aligned with the standards imposed by the previous default graduation program.[113]

The impetus to change the state's graduation requirements came from two different directions. Some proponents, including some school leaders, felt challenged and ill-equipped to meet accountability requirements that measure how many students graduate and how many are college ready. Some business manufacturing interests felt that too many Texas high school graduates were not sufficiently prepared to go directly into their workplaces.

Despite objections by education advocates, community leaders, and many school leaders, these interests succeeded in convincing the majority of Texas policymakers that schools should not be required to provide a high-quality, college-ready education to all students.[114] Many predicted that ultimately, by weakening graduation requirements, fewer high school graduates would be prepared for college.

HIGHER EDUCATION FUNDING

The lack of accessible colleges and strong degree plans in colleges located in areas of the state along or near the Texas-Mexico border was evident at the 1968 USCCR hearings. Commissioner Héctor P. García noted the lack of a public four-year college in San Antonio (157 miles from the border).[115] Over the following decades, the state made little progress in investing in public colleges in areas inhabited by large Mexican American populations near or along the border.

A lawsuit filed by LULAC, the American GI Forum, the Texas Association of Chicanos in Higher Education (TACHE), Latino college student organizations, and fifteen individual Latino students changed this landscape. In 1987, MALDEF filed the suit on behalf of the plaintiffs in state court that described the lack of higher education graduate programs resulting from the state's failure to provide adequate and equitable funding and support to the border region. The plaintiffs alleged that the lack of investment stemmed from a history of discrimination against Mexican Americans, and resulted in depressed educational attainment and economic progress in the region.[116]

In showing the difference in funding and programs between the borderland universities and nonborderland universities, the plaintiffs focused on what the MALDEF attorneys referred to as the three Ds: degrees, distance, and dollars.[117] Among the key findings presented during a seven-week-long jury trial held in 1991 in Brownsville, Texas, were that although about 20 percent of all Texans were living in the border area, only about 10 percent of state funds for public universities was spent on the region.

While the average public college or university student in Texas traveled forty-five miles to the nearest campus offering master's and doctoral programs, the distance was 225 miles for border-area students. Only three of 590 doctoral programs in Texas were available at border-area universities in 1991.

Following the trial in Brownsville, the jury returned a split verdict. The jury found the system of higher education inefficient and discriminatory, but did not find any individual defendant, board of regent members, or then-Governor Ann Richards liable, as individuals, for the discriminatory treatment. The district court entered a judgment in favor of the plaintiffs and threatened to enjoin the entire state public university system if the Texas legislature did not fix the discriminatory funding system during the 1993 legislative session.[118] The state appealed the ruling to the Supreme Court of Texas, but during the appeal, legislators drafted the South Texas Border Initiative in response to the judgment. After being signed into law in 1993, the initiative provided aid to increase undergraduate and graduate course offerings, and funds to expand higher education facilities to the public border area universities and colleges.[119]

Funding for border area higher education institutions has since increased from 10 percent to 18 percent of total state funding for higher education. The plan also included intermediate targets for 2005 and 2010 to ensure progress was on track in keeping with the goals. Some of the targets were modified in 2005 in response to revised population projections, advanced progress toward some of the goals, and contributions made by private institutions of higher education.

THE TEXAS TOP TEN PERCENT LAW

Latino student access to the state's two major universities, widely referred to as its "flagships," the University of Texas at Austin (UT Austin) and Texas A&M University at College Station (TAMU), has been challenging over the years. Since the early 1970s, the federal Office for Civil Rights has investigated the low enrollment of Latino and African American students for discriminatory practices and policies. The lack of access was particularly pronounced in graduate degree programs.

In 1992, UT Austin law school applicant Cheryl Hopwood, an Anglo female, challenged the school's admission practices under the equal protection clause, alleging reverse discrimination. Specifically, she challenged the law school's practice of using a separate committee to review applications from racially or ethnically diverse students, including Latino students.

The case eventually reached the conservative-leaning Fifth Circuit Court of Appeals, which held the practice unconstitutional in its 1995 *Hopwood v. Texas* ruling. The court declined to hold that the limited use of race or ethnicity in considering applications could not be used to remedy societal discrimination or discrimination in K–12 schooling, or to achieve racial diversity.[120] Although the Fifth Circuit did not outright prohibit all affirmative action admissions policies, the Attorney General of Texas holding office at the time, Dan Morales, did. He issued an opinion stating that no Texas universities could use any form of affirmative action for admission purposes, scholarships, or outreach.[121]

African American and Latino student enrollment at the flagship universities decreased in the ensuing years. Advocates and the Texas legislature worked on a race-neutral college admissions plan. In 1997, due in large part to collaboration between rural and urban districts, the legislature passed House Bill 588 in 1997 (also known as the Top Ten Percent Plan).[122]

Essentially, this law allowed automatic admission to all four-year public universities in Texas to students who graduated in the top 10 percent of their Texas high school class and completed certain curriculum requirements. Following the U.S Supreme Court's decision in a University of Michigan case, *Grutter v. Bollinger*, in 2003 UT Austin began studying how to incorporate the limited use of race or ethnic considerations in its admissions policies. In *Grutter*, the court recognized a "compelling interest" in the educational benefits flowing from a diverse student body and upheld the University of Michigan School of Law's limited use of race as one of several factors to achieve the compelling interest.[123]

UT Austin eventually added race as one of several factors considered for freshman enrollment purposes for students not automatically admitted under the Top Ten Percent Plan. Again an Anglo student, Abigail Fisher, sued, challenging the university's consideration of race and ethnic background under its holistic admission plan. In *amicus* (friend of the court) briefs, MALDEF, representing twenty-two Latino national organizations, presented evidence in the *Fisher v. UT Austin* case in 2012, showing that Anglo students were far overrepresented under both the Top Ten Percent Plan admissions policy and the holistic admissions plan, and that Latino students were underrepresented. Fisher had just failed to make the cut.

In IDRA's *amicus* brief submitted in the second appeal to the U.S. Supreme Court, the organization analyzed college entrance test scores to answer Fisher's claim that UT Austin admitted less "qualified" Latino students ahead of her. IDRA demonstrated that Fisher's Scholastic Aptitude Test (SAT) score was thirty-one points lower than the average Latino entering freshman in 2008, and that at least 100 Anglo entering freshman students scored lower than Fisher. After two appeals to the Fifth Circuit Court of Appeals and the U.S. Supreme Court, the courts upheld UT Austin's limited use of race or ethnicity in a holistic fashion to acquire the benefits stemming from a diverse student body.[124]

Although Latino organizations and advocates celebrated the decision, they were also wary of UT Austin's intentions. As the enrollment of Latino Top Ten Percent Plan students at the flagship campus continued to grow, the university continued to pursue approval of a cap on the admission of Top Ten Percent Plan students. UT Austin officials asked for greater discretion over admissions. They wanted to limit Top Ten Percent admissions to 50 percent of the university's total admissions. They eventually persuaded the state legislature to cap automatic admissions under the Top Ten Percent Plan at 75 percent at UT Austin in 2009.[125]

In 2017, state Senator Kel Seliger of Texas filed a bill to eliminate the Top Ten Percent Plan law. IDRA's analysis showed the growth of diversity across geographical, racial, ethnic, and economic lines because of the Top Ten Percent Plan admissions law. The Top Ten Percent Plan helped increase the number of high schools with students who enrolled at UT Austin, from 622 in 1996, to 792 in 2000, to 992 in 2016. Rural schools continued to benefit from the plan, with UT Austin admitting 109 students from eighty-seven rural schools in 2016, up from eighty-five students from sixty-five rural schools in 2010. The plan accounted for 83 percent of admitted rural students at UT Austin in 2016.[126]

The Top Ten Percent Plan is the principal admissions driver for African American, Latino and Asian American students into UT Austin. The plan was responsible for 87 percent of admitted Latino students, 77 percent of African American admitted students, 75 percent of Asian American students, and 69 percent of Anglo students in 2016.[127]

The Future

During the past fifty years, progress in educational opportunities for Mexican Americans in Texas and the Southwest has been bumpy. Bilingual education became the norm in the Southwest, but received too little funding. The academic bar for all Texans was raised and then lowered. The bar was highest under the four-by-four requirement, which required completion of four full-year courses in four basic subjects: English, mathematics, social studies, and science. This approach resulted in 80 percent of Texas high school graduates having transcripts that made them college ready. Since then, the bar has been lowered, producing a confusing array of tracks and endorsements, which involve credit given for completing a series of courses on related topics.

The Common Core movement to implement a common set of curriculum and course standards across states progressed with support from many state governors, and then regressed after being labeled by critics as a government intrusion on local and state decision-making authority. Today, the phrase that "college is not for everyone" is again heard. The numbers and percentages of Mexican American students staying in school, completing high school, and entering college have increased, but high attrition rates are persistent.

In the last thirty-three years, Texas schools have lost a cumulative total of more than 3.8 million students from public school enrollment prior to graduation. At current rates, Texas will not reach universal high school education until the year 2037.[128] The result: more generations lost, even when assuming small but steady progress in graduating students from

Texas high schools; more opportunities lost; more students lost; more productivity lost.

Texas in 2018 had the second largest population of children, at 7.1 million. This is a major issue, because Texas's public education system cannot meet the needs of children who are already attending school. Texas is an incredibly diverse state. In rankings based on fifty states and the District of Columbia, Texas currently ranks third in the percentage of children who are Latino 49.1 percent). However, 33 percent of Latino children live in poverty, and Latino and African American children are three times more likely to live in poverty than children classified as Anglo or Asian Americans.[129]

While more jobs in Texas require a postsecondary education, Texas schools are losing too many students, or not graduating enough students continuing on to college. College is becoming less affordable. For families in the lowest income brackets, the cost of college would require spending 33 percent of their income on community college, 45 percent to 51 percent of their income on a public four-year university, and 99 percent to 120 percent of their income to cover fees at a private four-year university in Texas.[130]

Educate Fir$t, a broad-based group with roots in the San Antonio Hispanic Chamber of Commerce, recently published the report "Why Investing in Education Fuels the Texas Economy."[131] The report recommends full-day prekindergarten education, increased funding for bilingual and English language learner programs, improved teaching methods, and better relationships among families and schools. The group also recommends more financial support for college-bound students, increased funding to universities, and building partnerships among schools and businesses. Educational opportunity can become an engine of shared prosperity for generations of all Americans of all backgrounds and languages.

However, disparities persist. In 2015, the average low-income high school senior score in reading was lower than the average scores for twelfth-grade students in mid- and low-poverty schools.[132] If you are African American or Latino, you are more likely to attend a high-poverty, segregated, underfunded school that is unable to graduate students and unable to prepare students for the future.[133]

EDUCATION MATTERS TO SHARED PROSPERITY

Robust research evidence indicates that the quality of education affects economic opportunity for individuals and outcomes for society across generations. Data from the national Brookings Institution's report on education and potential earnings underscore the connection between education and economic opportunity, and the key role that educational opportunity plays in allowing a fair chance at the American Dream.[134]

There is also strong evidence that education matters to individuals and to society in other critical areas, including health, longevity, and the vitality of civic life. There are many tools for understanding the intersection of opportunity and the many factors, including wealth and education, which contribute to well-being in the United States. These tools include the Common Good Forecaster, an interactive online tool developed by United Way, and the American Human Development Project.

COMMUNITY VOICES MATTER

The quality of education provided in a local school system affects the local community in important ways. To examine the impact of educational quality on the local community, researchers for the nonprofit Rand Corporation found strong evidence of (1) effects on housing values in the school attendance area, with an increase of 1 percent in reading or math scores associated with a 0.5 percent to 1 percent increase in property values; (2) effects on crime rates, with a one-year higher educational level in a community associated with a 13 percent to 27 percent lower incidence of murders, assaults, car thefts, and arson; and (3) effects on tax revenues, with increased earnings and sales, and higher property tax revenues from residences and businesses.[135] There also is ample evidence that educational quality in the community is associated with greater civic participation, including more voter participation, more tolerance and acceptance of free speech, and more involvement in community arts and culture.[136]

Maintaining urgency and clarity in sustainable education reform depends in large measure on the will of the community, and informed engagement at the local community level. Schools, after all, belong to the community, and change is too important to be left to schools alone. Community engagement that is based on active participation by the school and the community produces positive results for students.

IDRA's work in building and informing school-community teams demonstrates success in these partnerships and coalitions.[137] Community buy-in and oversight stemming from shared understanding and data about the why, the how, and the results of school change are critical, but largely untapped, change strategies in school reform efforts. For example, to develop comprehensive action plans to graduate all students, community teams can use data about their local dropout and graduation rates, disaggregated by subgroups, and data on the related school factors of parent involvement, student engagement, curriculum access, and teaching quality.

CHANGE IS POSSIBLE

In recent years, states that have prioritized education and increased funding have made great strides in providing better quality education for students attending low-income schools. New York, Oklahoma, West Virginia, Connecticut, and Wisconsin all have state-funded prekindergarten programs and third-grade course requirement laws. These five states provide high-poverty districts with equal or more funding than higher income districts.[138]

In Texas, student achievement on national tests improved in 2008, due in part to a decade of improved and more equitable funding that had been provided to Texas schools. With dwindling state funding for education in recent years, results from the Nation's Report Card show that Texas has slipped significantly in reading scores. Just 31 percent of Texas students tested at or above National Assessment of Education Progress (NAEP) proficiency level in 2018, while 60 percent tested at or above NAEP's basic level in 2008.

Recommendations

Based on empirical evidence and forty-five years of experience in the field, IDRA's Maria Robledo Montecel spearheaded the development of the Quality Schools Action Framework, which helps schools, communities, families, and business leaders assure that critical features are in place to achieve improved education outcomes for all students. The framework draws from existing theories that suggest that because schools operate as complex, dynamic ecosystems, lasting systems change depends on sustained action within and outside of those systems.

The Quality Schools Action Framework also is intuitive and reflects common sense. For example, research and experience recognize that students are far more likely to succeed when they have the chance to work with highly qualified, committed teachers, using effective, accessible curricula; their parents and communities are engaged in their education; and, students are engaged in their learning. Effective schools depend on good governance to guide their success, and on fair funding to effectively serve all of their students each school day. The framework also can prove useful in making the link between benchmarked standards and sustainable school reform that ties desired outcomes to indicators of quality at the local level. Schools, as public institutions at the nexus of policy and practice, need collective energy, engagement, and leadership if they are to serve all students well. As starting points, IDRA's empirically based Quality Schools Action Framework outlines three indispensable levers of change: engaged citizens, accountable leadership, and enlightened public policy.[139]

Engaged citizens, people who actively express their concern about the quality of education and act as partners in school improvement, are essential to transforming schools. Accountable leaders continuously take stock of school performance and take action to improve it. To leverage change, education policies cannot simply extend the status quo or promote incremental reform. Education policies must reject two-tier (have/have not) solutions, and secure systems that work for all children. At every level, from policy to practice, people need clear, accurate, and timely information to assess what is needed to strengthen schooling, take action, and make sure their actions are on the right track.

In physics, levers apply mechanical force to move or lift heavy objects. Like crowbars, wheelbarrows, and pliers, levers give people a mechanical advantage to accomplish work that might at first seem far beyond their capacity. When it comes to transforming education so that it works for all students, a history of experience and research shows that we must leverage resources beyond school walls. Real, lasting change comes when people are engaged at all levels, from state capitols to boardrooms, from classrooms to community centers and kitchen tables.

At the state level, state boards of education must be driven to promulgate policy to support structures, procedures, and practices that create school success, graduation, and college opportunities for all students. State legislatures must create structures that produce fair funding for local schools so that every student receives an appropriate, equitable, high-quality educational experience that leads to higher graduation rates, no matter the level of community wealth of the school district.

At the local level, boards of education also must create policies that will support student success at every campus, at all levels, wherever students reside within a given school district. School boards must ensure that distribution of the funding needed to implement those policies—be it federal, state, or local—is equitable and appropriate to lead all diverse learners to school success, graduation, college attendance, and completion.

This is not just theory. In the Rio Grande Valley near the southernmost tip of Texas, the Pharr-San Juan-Alamo ISD, under the leadership of Superintendent Daniel King, transformed itself from a district with low achievement levels and low expectations into a district where all students are expected to graduate college ready. This transformation resulted in the district doubling the number of high school graduates, cutting dropout rates in half, and increasing college-going rates. By 2013, half of the school district's students were earning college credits while still in high school.[140]

Latinos generated 29 percent of the country's income growth from 2015 to 2020—more than any other group. The purchasing power of Latinos could reach more than $1.7 trillion by 2020. And Latinos make up 70 percent of the recent growth in the labor market. An additional 11.9 million Latino college degree holders are needed by 2050 to be in line with national average college graduation rates.

No hay peor lucha que la que no se hace, says a Mexican proverb. Indeed, *there is no worse struggle than the struggle that is not waged.* IDRA declares: All children are valuable; none is expendable.

Notes

1. U.S. Commission on Civil Rights (USCCR), *Hearing before the United States Commission on Civil Rights: Hearing Held in San Antonio, Texas, December 9–14, 1968* (Washington, DC: GPO, 1969). Also available at https://catalog.hathitrust.org/Record/001874430.

2. *United States v. State of Texas*, 506 F. Supp. 405, 412 (E.D. Tex. 1981).

3. *US v. Texas*, 506 F. Supp.

4. *US v. Texas*, 506 F. Supp. at 415.

5. *US v. Texas*, 506 F. Supp. at 415.

6. USCCR, *Hearing*.

7. USCCR, *Hearing*.

8. USCCR, *Hearing*.

9. Aurelio Montemayor, "Rationale for a Chicano Learning Center," *HOJAS: A Chicano Journal of Education*, ed. Victor Guerra-Garza (Austin: Juarez-Lincoln Press, 1976).

10. USCCR, *Hearing*.

11. U.S. Bureau of The Census, "Educational Attainment: March 1970," *Current Population Reports*, Series P-20, No. 207, Washington, DC: GPO, 1970.

12. IDRA, *Analysis of US Census Bureau Data* (San Antonio: Intercultural Development Research Association, 1998).

13. María "Cuca" Robledo Montecel, et al., *Texas Dropout Survey Set, Vols. 1–7* (San Antonio: Intercultural Development Research Association, 1986).

14. Robledo Montecel, et al., *Texas Dropout Survey Set*.

15. Robledo Montecel, et al., *Texas Dropout Survey Set*.

16. Roy Johnson, "Texas Public School Attrition Study, 2016–17: High School Attrition Returns to 24 Percent After One Year Bump," *IDRA Newsletter* (San Antonio: Intercultural Development Research Association, 2017).

17. U.S. Department of Education, *Trends in High School Dropout and Completion Rates in the United States: 1972–2012*, by Patrick Stark and Amber M. Noel, Compendium Report, NCES 2015-015 (Washington, DC: National Center for Education Statistics, 2015).

18. U.S. Census Bureau, *2014 Current Population Survey*.

19. U.S. Department of Education, *Trends in High School Dropout and Completion Rates in the United States: 2014*, by Joel McFarland, Jiashan Cui, and Patrick Stark (Washington, DC: National Center for Education Statistics, 2018).

20. José Angel Cárdenas and Blandina Cárdenas, *The Theory of Incompatibilities: A Conceptual Framework for Responding to the Educational Needs of Mexican American Children* (San Antonio: Intercultural Development Research Association, 1977).

21. María "Cuca" Robledo Montecel and Aurelio Montemayor, "Interaction with the Ecosystem: The IDRA Quality Schools Action Framework," and "Beginning with the End in Mind to Establish Equitable, Excellent Education," *IDRA Newsletter* (June-July 2018), available online at idra.org.

22. USCCR, *Hearing*.

23. U.S. Census Bureau, *American Community Survey*, 2018.

24. U.S. Commission on Civil Rights (USCCR), *The Tarnished Golden Door: Civil Rights Issues in Immigration* (Washington, DC: GPO, 1980).

25. "About TEA: State Board of Education Members" (Austin: Texas Education Agency, 2018), available online at tea.texas.gov.

26. F. M. Hess, *School Boards at the Dawn of the Twenty-First Century: Conditions and Challenges of District Governance* (Alexandria, Va.: National School Board Association, 2002).

27. U.S. Commission on Civil Rights, Mexican American Studies Division, *Mexican American Education Study, Report 1: Ethnic Isolation of Mexican Americans in the Public Schools of the Southwest* (Washington, DC: GPO, 1971).

28. USCCR, *The Tarnished Golden Door.*

29. Texas Association of School Boards Excel Spreadsheet, 1998, 2018 School Board Members by Race and Ethnicity. Email from Anisa Pope to author David Hinojosa (September 14, 2018).

30. USCCR, *The Tarnished Golden Door.*

31. Corbett Smith, "Latino Superintendents Lead the Way in Texas' Largest School Districts," *Dallas Morning News* (October 24, 2016); Shelby Webb, "Number of Hispanic Superintendents in Texas Lags Student Population Growth," *Houston Chronicle* (March 28, 2018).

32. Jason Hill, Randolph Ottem, and John DeRoche, *Trends in Public and Private School Principal Demographics and Qualifications: 1987–88 to 2011–12*, Stats in Brief/NCES 2016-189 (Washington, DC: National Center for Education Statistics, 2016), citing Gregory Branch, Eric Hanushek, and Steven Rivkin, "School Leaders Matter: Measuring the Impact of Effective Principals," *Education Next* (2013), 13(1): 62–69.

33. Hill et al., "Trends."

34. Hill et al., "Trends."

35. Desiree Carver-Thomas, *Diversifying the Field: Barriers to Recruiting and Retaining Teachers of Color and How to Overcome Them* (San Antonio: Intercultural Development Research Association, 2017).

36. Carver-Thomas, "Diversifying the Field."

37. Carver-Thomas, "Diversifying the Field."

38. C. Emily Feistritzer, *Profile of Teachers in the US 2011* (Washington, DC: National Center for Education Information, 2011).

39. USCCR, *Hearing.*

40. Robert Brischetto, *Inequalities in the Distribution of Educational Resources: An Empirical Examination of the Southwestern United States* (Ph.D. Diss., University of Texas at Austin, November 1974), 211 and 216.

41. U.S. Commission on Civil Rights, Mexican American Studies Division, *Mexican American Education in Texas: A Function of Wealth: Report IV of The Mexican American Education Study*, by Sally Knack, et al. (Washington, DC: GPO, 1972).

42. David Hinojosa, "*Rodríguez v. San Antonio ISD*: Forty Years Later," in *The Enduring Legacy of Rodríguez*, eds. Kimberly Jenkins Robinson and Charles Ogletree (Cambridge, MA: Harvard Education Press, 2015).

43. José A. Cárdenas, *Texas School Finance Reform: An IDRA Perspective* (San Antonio: Intercultural Development Research Association, 1997).

44. Hinojosa, "*Rodríguez v. San Antonio ISD.*"

45. Cárdenas, *Texas School Finance Reform.*

46. *Edgewood v. Kirby*, 777 S.W.2d 391 (Tex. 1989).

47. Albert Kauffman, "The Texas School Finance Litigation Sage: Great Progress, Then Near Death by a Thousand Cuts," *St. Mary's Law Journal*, 40 (2018): 511–79.

48. These hold-harmless provisions ensured school districts would not receive reduced state funding as a result of policy changes to funding formulas.

49. Albert Cortez, "The Texas Supreme Court Ruling in West Orange-Cove vs. Neeley: A Decision Neither Adequate nor Equitable," *IDRA Newsletter* (February 2006).

50. Hinojosa, "*Rodríguez v. San Antonio ISD.*"

51. *Neeley v. West-Orange Cove Independent School District*, 176 S.W.3d 746 (Tex. 2005), 788.

52. *Neeley*, 176 S.W.3d, at 794.

53. *Neeley*, 176 S.W.3d, at 794.

54. *Neeley*, 176 S.W.3d, at 796.

55. *Texas Taxpayer and Student Fairness Coalition v. Williams*, No. D-1-GN-11-003130 2014 WL 4254969, D. (Tex. 2014).

56. David Hinojosa and Karolina Walters, "How Adequacy Litigation Fails to Fulfill the Promise of Brown," *Michigan Law Review*, 575 (2014): 611.

57. John Dietz, *West Orange-Cove Consolidated Independent School District v. Neeley, Findings of Fact and Conclusions of Law*, 2004 WL 5719215 (Travis County District Court, 2004).

58. Hinojosa, "*Rodríguez v. San Antonio ISD.*"

59. *Texas Taxpayer and Student Fairness Coalition v. Williams*, No. D-1-GN-11-003130 2014 WL 4254969, D. (Tex. 2014).

60. *Morath v. Texas Taxpayer and Student Fairness Coalition*, 490 S.W.3d 826 (2016), 846, 851.

61. David Hinojosa, "In School Finance Decision, the Poor People Have Lost Again," *Texas Tribune* (June 14, 2016).

62. *Texas Taxpayer*, WL 4254969, at 65, 98.

63. *Morath*, 490 S.W.3d 826.

64. *Texas Taxpayer*, WL 4254969 at 202-4.

65. *Texas Taxpayer* (2014); *Morath v. Texas Taxpayer* (2016).

66. "Using the data provided by the state, IDRA initially sorted school districts by the property wealth per WADA (weighted average daily attendance) of individual districts in ascending order of district property wealth per WADA and including all related data for that district provided to MALDEF. Using this sorted data file, IDRA grouped school districts into 10 percent sub-groupings—producing subgroupings of 103 school districts per decile, except for the 10th, which contains 97 school districts." Albert Cortez, "A Report of the Intercultural Development Research Association Related to the Extent of Equity in the Texas School Finance System and Its Impact on Selected Student Related Issues," Prepared for the Mexican American Legal Defense and Educational Fund in Texas Taxpayer & Student Fairness Coalition v. Williams, No. D-1-GN-11-003130, Travis Co. District Court (San Antonio: Intercultural Development Research Association, 2012).

67. C. Kirabo Jackson and Rucker C. Johnson, "The Effects of School Spending on Educational and Academic Outcomes: Evidence from School Finance Reforms," *Quarterly Journal of Economics (Oxford Journals)* 131, 1 (2016): 157-218; Julien Lafortune, Jesse Rothstein, and D. Whitmore Schanzenbach, "School Finance Reform and the Distribution of Student Achievement," *American Economic Journal: Applied Economics*, 10, no. 2 (April 2018): 1-26, doi:10.1257/app.20160567.

68. USCCR, *Hearing*.

69. USCCR, *Hearing*.

70. USCCR, *Hearing*.

71. USCCR, *Hearing*.

72. USCCR, *Hearing*.

73. María "Cuca" Robledo Montecel and Josie Danini Cortez, "Successful Bilingual Education Programs," *IDRA Newsletter* (January 2004).

74. Gloria Stewner-Manzanares, *The Bilingual Education Act: Twenty Years Later. New Focus: Occasional Papers in Bilingual Education*, No. 6 (Washington, DC: Office of Bilingual Education and Minority Languages Affairs, 1988).

75. USCCR, *Hearing.*

76. Angel Noe González, *Bilingual Education: Learning While Learning English* (self-published, 2014).

77. *Lau v. Nichols*, 414 U.S. 563 (1974).

78. José A. Cárdenas, *Multicultural Education: A Generation of Advocacy* (Needham, MA: Simon & Schuster, 1995).

79. E. Midobouche and A. H. Benavides, "Title VII Elementary and Secondary Education Act: Subsequent Amendments," in *Encyclopedia of Bilingual Education*, ed. J.M. Gonzales (Thousand Oaks, CA: Sage, 2008), 840–62.

80. *United States v. Texas*, 680 F.2d 356 ("LULAC I") (5th Cir. 1982).

81. *United States v. Texas*, 572 F. Supp. 2d 726 (E.D. Tex. 2008).

82. *United States v. Texas* ("LULAC II") 601 F. 3d 354 (5th Cir. (2010).

83. *United States v. Texas* ("LULAC II") 2010.

84. *LULAC v. Texas* 6:14-cv-00138-MHS (E.D. Tex. 2014).

85. Research and Analysis Division of PEIMS Reporting Unit, *PEIMS Standard Reports 2016–2017 Student Enrollment* (Austin: Texas Education Agency, 2018) available online at tea.texas.gov.

86. Virginia Collier and Wayne Thomas, "The Astounding Effectiveness of Dual Language Education for All," *NABE Journal of Research and Practice*, 2, 1 (Winter 2004): 1–20.

87. Texas Administrative Code § 74.14(b).

88. IDRA, *New Research on Securing Educational Equity and Excellence for English Language Learners in Texas Secondary Schools, School Finance Fellows Program, 2015 Symposium Proceedings* (San Antonio: Intercultural Development Research Association, 2018).

89. Patrick Michels, "Proposed Mexican-American Studies Textbook: Chicanos Want to 'Destroy This Society,'" *Texas Observer* (May 11, 2016).

90. Angela Valenzuela, "Commentary: How SBOE Could Advance Plan for Mexican-American Studies," *Texas Education Equity* (blog).

91. Michels, "Proposed Mexican-American Studies Textbook."

92. Valenzuela, "Commentary."

93. María "Cuca" Robledo Montecel and Josie Danini Cortez, "Successful Bilingual Education Programs: Development and Dissemination of Criteria to Identify Promising and Exemplary Practices in Bilingual Education at the National Level," *Bilingual Research Journal*, 26, no. 1 (2002): 1–21.

94. Cárdenas, *Multicultural Education.*

95. USCCR, *The Tarnished Golden Door.*

96. U.S. Department of Health, Education and Welfare, "Identification of Discrimination and Denial of Services on the Basis of National Origin," 35 Fed Reg. 11,595 (Memorandum, May 25, 1970).

97. *Plyler v. Doe*, 457 U.S. 202 (1982).

98. U.S. Department of Health and Human Services, *About the Office of Head Start*, available at acf.hhs.gov/ohs.

99. Michael Olivas, "IIRIRA, the Dream Act, and Undocumented College Student Residency," *Immigration and Nationality Law Review*, 25: 323 (2004).

100. Texas Education Code § 54.052(a)(3).

101. Texas Education Code § 54.053(3).

102. Mexican American Legal Defense and Education Fund (MALDEF), "Immigrants' Rights Under a Trump Presidency: FAQs for Students, Educators, and Social Service Providers," Fact Sheet (Los Angeles: MALDEF, 2016).

103. Common Sense Immigration, "About TRUST," online at CommonSenseImmigrationTx.org.

104. Republican Party of Texas, "Report of the Permanent Committee on Platform and Resolutions as Amended and Adopted by the 2016 State Convention of the Republican Party of Texas," 15, available at texasgop.org.

105. LeAnn Wallace, "Texas Lawmakers Consider Repeating DREAM Act to Discourage Illegal Immigration," *Spectrum News* (February 7, 2017).

106. USCCR, *Hearing*, 372.

107. USCCR, *Hearing*, 373.

108. USCCR, *Hearing*, 375.

109. Maoyong Fan and Jeffrey M. Perloff, "Where Did All the Migrant Farmworkers Go?," Policy Brief (Berkeley: UCB Institute for Research on Labor and Employment, July 2016).

110. USCCR, *Hearing*.

111. Josie Danini Cortez, "Barriers Hispanic Students Face Graduating from High School," *IDRA Newsletter* (October 2014).

112. Texas Higher Education Coordinating Board, *Closing the Gaps: 2014 Progress Report* (Austin: Texas Higher Education Coordinating Board, 2014).

113. Hector Bojorquez, *Ready Texas: A Study of the Implementation of HB5 in Texas and Implications for College Readiness* (San Antonio: Intercultural Development Research Association, 2017).

114. Josie Danini Cortez, "A Post Session Assessment of Texas Education Policy Changes Considered, Adopted and Rejected in 2013," *IDRA Newsletter* (2013).

115. USCCR, *Hearing*.

116. Albert Kauffman, "Effective Litigation Strategies to Improve State Education and Social Service Systems," Monograph 17-05, University of Houston Law Center (2005).

117. Kauffman, "Effective Litigation Strategies."

118. Kauffman, "Effective Litigation Strategies."

119. *Richards v. LULAC*, 868 S.W.2d 306 (Tex. 1993).

120. David Hinojosa, "Of Course the Texas Top Ten Percent Is Constitutional, and It's Pretty Good Policy, Too," *Texas Hispanic Journal of Law Policy* (Spring 2016).

121. William Forbath and Gerald Torres, "Symposium: Merit and Diversity After Hopwood," *Stanford Law and Policy Review* (1999): 185–86.

122. Texas Education Code § 51.803 (2015).

123. *Grutter v. Bollinger*, 539 U.S. 306, 337 (2003)

124. Hinojosa, "Of Course the Texas Top Ten Percent."

125. *Fisher v. University of Texas at Austin*, 758 F.3d 633, 655 (5th Cir. 2014)

126. David Hinojosa, "Since When are Good Grades and Diversity a Bad Thing? Seven Recommendations and the Texas Top Ten Percent Plan," *IDRA Newsletter* (February 2017).

127. Hinojosa, "Since When are Good Grades and Diversity a Bad Thing?"

128. Roy Johnson, "High School Attrition Rate Drops by Two Percentage Points From Previous Year," *Texas Public School Attrition Study, 2017–18* (San Antonio: Intercultural Development Research Association, 2018).

129. John D. Gonzalez, *Why Investing in Education Fuels the Texas Economy* (San Antonio: Educate Fir$t, 2017).

130. John D. Gonzalez, *Why Investing in Education.*

131. John D. Gonzalez, *Why Investing in Education.*

132. U.S. Department of Education, *The Condition of Education 2018,* by J. McFarland et al., Report NCES 2018-144 (Washington, DC: National Center for Education Statistics, 2018).

133. "Data Summaries," National Equity Atlas, PolicyLink and USC Program for Environmental and Regional Equity, accessed in 2016 from NationalEquityAtlas.org.

134. Diane Schanzenbach, Lauren Bauer, and Audrey Breitweiser, "Eight Economic Facts on Higher Education" (Washington, DC: The Hamilton Project, Brookings Institution, 2017).

135. S. J. Carroll and E. Scherer, *The Impact of Educational Quality on the Community: A Literature Review* (Santa Monica, CA: The RAND Corporation, 2008).

136. Ann Ishimaru, "Rewriting the Rules of Engagement: Elaborating a Model of District-Community Collaboration," *Harvard Educational Review,* 84 No. 2 (July 2014):188-216.

137. R. G. Rodríguez and B. Scott, "Expanding Blueprints for Action—Children's Outcomes, Access, Treatment, Learning, Resources, Accountability," *IDRA Newsletter,* May 2007; Aurelio Montemayor, "Authentic Consultation—NCLB Outreach Leadership and Dialogues for Parents, Students, and Teachers," *IDRA Newsletter,* June-July 2008.

138. L. Bornfreund, S. Cook, A. Lieberman, and A. Loewenberg, *From Crawling to Walking: Ranking States on Birth—3rd Grade Policies that Support Strong Readers* (Washington, DC: New America Foundation, 2015).

139. María "Cuca" Robledo Montecel and Christie Goodman, eds., *Courage to Connect: A Quality Schools Action Framework* (San Antonio: Intercultural Development Research Association, 2010).

140. Hector Bojorquez, *College Bound and Determined* (San Antonio: Intercultural Development Research Association, 2014).

REBECCA FLORES WITH JUANITA VALDEZ-COX

AND JAMES C. HARRINGTON

The Farmworkers of Texas

When the U.S. Commission on Civil Rights met in San Antonio in 1968 to hear testimony on civil rights challenges faced by Mexican Americans in Texas and other southwestern states, the "unspeakable wretchedness" suffered by farmworkers in Texas was addressed.[1] Even though a farmworker movement had begun in Starr County, Texas, two years before the 1968 hearings, there had been no progress toward better pay and decent living conditions.

The federal minimum wage was raised from $1.40 to $1.60 an hour, but farmworkers were excluded, and Texas at the time had no state minimum wage. Luis Chávez, a farmworker and father of nine from Edcouch, Texas, testified to the civil rights commission that although he was paid one dollar an hour, many of his fellow farmworkers made much less than a dollar per hour. When rain prevented work in the field, there was no pay. If he fell sick, there was no pay. Despite federal child labor laws in place since 1938, Chávez said his eight-year-old and nine-year-old sons worked beside him in the fields when school was not in session.

Written testimony presented at the hearing by Robert Lucey, the Roman Catholic Archbishop of San Antonio, described "the miserable conditions under which the farmworkers of South Texas labor, as well as the unspeakable wretchedness of their lives." The commission's own staff submitted a report describing "allegations of harassment, physical violence and brutality" by growers and by state and local law enforcement officials that followed attempts by farmworkers to organize and publicly voice their desire to improve their "deplorable living and working conditions in South Texas."[2]

The struggles of Mexican American farmworkers in Texas date back to 1836, the year the Republic of Texas was formed following the successful end of the battle to wrest control of land in the Mexican states of Coahuila and Tejas from Mexico. New laws and land grants, essentially land grabs of property that had belonged to Mexicans, meant that once-proud Mexican landowners become poorly paid workers on those same lands. Their meager wages forced them to begin migrating to work on other farms in what became a U.S. state in 1845.

Figure 1. Farmworker children living in one room in a "historical" building in Hidalgo, Texas, 1980s. Alan Pogue.

During the early decades of the twentieth century, groups such as the League of United Latin American Citizens (LULAC), formed in 1929, protested persistent discrimination against Mexican Americans. Lawsuits were filed by these groups, but there was no larger citizens' "movement." Then, in 1966, hundreds of Texas farmworkers led a labor strike, and a protest march through hundreds of miles of Texas. One journalist described the 1966 farmworkers' march as "a handful of unassuming impoverished people normally given to civic passivity [who] have, footstep by footstep, along dusty hot Texas roads, created a feeling of both apprehension and elation among the onlookers of the region."[3]

Another writer described what happened next: "*La Marcha* was symbolic of, and contributed to, the very quickening awakening of the Mexican Americans in Texas. It was symbolic of the end of an era."[4] The strike and march that began in Starr County, Texas, proved the spark that led to a new era of active, organized efforts to create an enduring "Chicano" movement in Texas.

Starr County, Texas: Birthplace of the Texas Farmworker Movement

In Starr County, an impoverished rural county hugging the Texas-Mexico border, the 1960 population was approximately 17,000, of which 90 percent were people of Mexican descent, according to the U.S. Census Bureau. At a time when the U.S. government defined poverty as an income of less than $3,000 for a family of four, the average per-capita income in Starr County was $534. Starr County was ranked the poorest in Texas. In 1966, 70 percent of Starr County families earned less than $3,000 per year, and one-third earned less than $1,000 per year.[5]

In 1966, agribusiness, with annual farm income totaling $11 million (which would equal $83 million in 2017-adjusted dollars), was Starr County's second largest industry (oil was the first). The six major corporate growers were Sun-Tex and La Casita, both owned by California parent companies; Starr Farms; Margo Farms; Elmore & Stahl; and Griffin & Brand. All six were concentrated on 35,000 acres along the Rio Grande,

Figure 2. Workers using short-handled hoes, while crew leader, holding a long-handled hoe, oversees workers. Alan Pogue.

a winding river that forms the natural border between Texas and Mexico. The growers planted crops, irrigated by the Río Grande, requiring intensive hand labor, which was cheap, plentiful, and available. These crops included cantaloupe, watermelon, onions, lettuce, bell peppers, and tomatoes.

Most Starr County residents were United States-born Mexican American citizens who earned their living working in the fields. From March through October each year, many migrated to work in the grape vineyards of California for slightly higher pay. Those too poor to migrate remained to harvest melons from mid-April through mid-June. The public schools would suspend classes during the melon season to allow children to work until the harvesting season ended, at which time classes would reconvene. Wages ranged from forty to eighty-five cents an hour.[6]

Harvesting cantaloupes was backbreaking work during the hottest days of summer in Starr County, when temperatures sometimes reached or exceeded 100 degrees Fahrenheit. Women, men, and children would carry large sacks on their backs, bend over to cut cantaloupes from their stems, and then place the melons in the sacks. They would carry the full sacks on their backs through the fields to loading trucks.

From California to Texas: Early Farmworker Struggles

Texas has had a long anti-worker, anti-labor union history, which continues today. Texas farmworkers had little recourse from the federal government, either, in the early decades of the twentieth century. President Franklin D. Roosevelt's social legislation of the Great Depression, which developed and standardized workers' rights in the United States, specifically excluded agricultural and domestic workers as a group from protections afforded to industrial laborers. Farmworkers originally were excluded from unemployment compensation and social security benefits.

The National Labor Relations Act and the Fair Labor Standards Act excluded agricultural workers from the minimum wage and protections against child labor. "The bill specifically and unequivocally excludes certain industries and certain types of businesses from its scope and effect. It specifically excludes workers in agriculture of all kinds and of all types," U.S. Sen. Hugo Black, D-AL, stated for the Congressional Record in 1937.[7]

The Fair Labor Standards Act first introduced a federal minimum wage in 1938 of twenty-five cents per hour. By 1966, the federal minimum hourly wage was $1.25, but Texas had yet to pass a state minimum wage law.[8] Only those agricultural laborers who worked a minimum of 500 hours per quarter each year for an employer could qualify for the federal minimum wage. That standard excluded most farmworkers from coverage because of the seasonal nature of their work.

Although Texas enacted no worker protection law, the Texas Legislature in 1947 enacted a "right-to-work" law specifically designed to discourage the formation of labor unions. The action followed passage in 1947 of the federal Labor Management Relations Act, also known as the Taft-Hartley Act, over a presidential veto. The law, limiting the power and activities of labor unions, allowed states to adopt right-to-work laws. Texas had already been credited with coining the term right-to-work in an effort underway since 1941 to quell the rise of labor unions. In 1947, the Taft-Hartley Act gave Texas formal permission to adopt its anti-union law. Texas immediately obliged.[9]

FARMWORKERS UNITE IN CALIFORNIA

In 1962, the National Farm Workers Association (NFWA) was founded in Delano, California. César Chávez was elected NFWA's first president, and Dolores Huerta and Gilberto Padilla were elected vice presidents. The NFWA flag, featuring a black eagle on a red background, was designed by Chávez's brother, Richard Chávez, and became the NFWA official emblem. "Viva la Causa" was adopted as the official motto. The NFWA philosophy was expressed as self-sufficiency, service, and nonviolence.

In early 1966, César Chávez called for a nationwide consumer boycott of California table grapes to protest poor wages and working conditions, sending NFWA members to the country's major cities to enlist support for the boycott. NFWA member Eugene Nelson, who would become a major player in the future Texas farmworker strikes, was assigned to Houston, arriving there in early 1966.[10] In August 1966, after four years of organizing

Figure 3. UFW president and co-founder, César E. Chávez, presiding at First Annual UFW Convention in Texas, 1979. Alan Pogue.

grape harvesters in the California fields, and almost a year after the NFWA had joined the Filipino American farmworkers' strike against the California grape industry, the NFWA merged with the Filipino Agricultural Workers Organizing Committee (AWOC). The two groups formed the United Farm Workers Organizing Committee (UFWOC). César Chávez and Dolores Huerta of the NFWA and AWOC Filipino American leader Larry Itliong became the leaders of the new UFWOC.

FARMWORKERS UNITE IN TEXAS

In 1961, Mexican American leaders in Houston established the Political Association of Spanish-Speaking Organizations (PASSO), a partisan organization that grew out of the Viva Kennedy clubs in Texas that supported the presidential campaign of John F. Kennedy in 1960. PASSO promoted the enactment of social and economic measures for the advancement of Mexican Americans. Its leaders were George I. Sánchez, Ed Idar, Albert Peña, and Dr. Héctor García of the American GI Forum. The American GI Forum was founded in 1948 to promote better conditions for Mexican American veterans of World War I and World War II.

When UFWOC member Eugene Nelson opened the Houston boycott office in early 1966, farmworker members of PASSO living in Starr County began communicating with him about organizing farmworkers in the Rio Grande Valley. Responding to the urgency in the workers' calls, Nelson moved to Mission, Texas, in Hidalgo County in early March 1966. Upon Nelson's arrival and after holding a few meetings, which hundreds of farmworkers attended, the farmworkers formed Local 2 of the Independent Workers Association (IWA) as an affiliate of the UFWOC. Seven hundred farmworkers signed authorization cards, asking IWA to represent them.[11]

IWA Local 2 elected officers were Domingo Arredondo, president; Pedro Ríos, first vice president; Baldemar Díaz, second vice president; Rodrigo García, secretary; and Daria Vera, secretary-treasurer. IWA leaders followed the California union's philosophy of nonviolence. Nevertheless, workers would be routinely jailed for actual or nonexistent infractions of various state laws, many of which were later found unconstitutional by federal courts.

The Texas Farmworker Strike of 1966

At a general IWA meeting, four hundred farmworkers voted to go on strike against cantaloupe melon growers at La Casita Farms, Los Puertos Plantation, Starr Produce, and Sun-Tex, beginning June 1, 1966. On that day, more than 80 percent of the labor force did not show up for work, and every packing shed in Starr County shut down.[12] This strike became commonly known by two names: the "La Casita Strike," after one of the major farms, and the Melon Strike (in Spanish, La Huelga del Melón).

Fifty years later, two of the strike leaders, Baldemar Díaz, second vice president of the IWA local, and Librado De la Cruz, recalled the strike in a 2016 interview with *La Voz Newspapers in Texas* for a special Fiftieth Anniversary commemorative edition.[13] Díaz was a labor foreman at La Casita when the strike started and was earning a good wage of three dollars an hour. He said he joined the strike because those in the strike were "my people," and he rejected a Texas Ranger's offer to return to work or go to jail. Díaz was arrested and jailed.

THE STRIKE BEGINS

De la Cruz was arrested seven times during the strike, more than any other striker. He, like other workers, created the fertile planting ground for the growers by painstakingly removing mesquite by the roots. Othal Brand, the owner of Griffin and Brand and, at that time, one of the richer growers in the Lower Rio Grande Valley of Texas, paid De la Cruz forty cents an hour to do the backbreaking work. Workers would go on strike at Brand's Trophy Farms.

Brand and the other wealthy growers, made rich by the work of thousands of poorly paid farm laborers, used their economic power against those workers during the strike. The Texas Rangers, members of the Texas state police force, were on site June 1, 1966, the first day of the strike. Ranger Jerome Priess arrested Eugene Nelson for "inciting a riot" that day. The charge was later changed to disturbing the peace.

Daria Vera, secretary-treasurer of the IWA, and a nineteen-year-old mother at the time of the strike, told *La Voz Newspapers in Texas* that because she believed she had little to lose, she was unafraid.[14] On the second day of the strike, as farmworkers held a rally at San Juan Plaza in Rio Grande City, a jeep drove by and its occupants sprayed the strikers with a caustic pesticide. One of the leaders tried to stop the outsiders, and he suffered chemical burns on his hands.[15]

On June 8, Nelson, one of the strike's principal organizers, stationed himself at the International Bridge at the Texas-Mexico border in Roma, Texas, attempting to persuade laborers from Mexico to support the strike. The Starr County sheriff arrested him, detained him for four hours, questioned him about the strike, and told him the Federal Bureau of Investigation was investigating him. However, no charges were filed against Nelson.[16] Through mid-June, the end of the melon season, law enforcement officers intimidated the striking farmworkers with threats and arrests.

STRIKING WORKERS ENLIST ALLIES IN THE CAUSE

Roman Catholic clergy in the predominantly Catholic communities where the strikes took place became allies of the striking workers. Catholic priests and Protestant pastors held Masses and other religious services, and also picketed and marched alongside the striking workers. Among the participating priests were Fathers Sherrill Smith and William Killian from the San Antonio Archdiocese, Father John McCarthy of Houston (who later became Bishop of Austin, Texas), and Father Henry Casso, executive secretary of the San Antonio Bishop's Committee for the Spanish Speaking.[17] In 1961, Pope John XXIII had issued an encyclical addressing the stark disparities between the wealthy and the poor. The priests' said the Pope's words motivated Catholic pastors and parishioners to support the 1966 farmworkers' strike. Priests, pastors, and Catholic nuns played an important role in the 1966 farmworker strike.

A few years later, because the farmworkers' spirituality was important to the movement, the National Farm Worker Ministry (NFWM) became part of *La Causa*. The NFWM provided volunteer staff to the UFW in California and in Texas for decades. Religious sisters and lay volunteers held staff positions to reach out to faith institutions in the Río Grande Valley. These volunteers were Sisters Carol Ann Messina and Marie-Therese Brown, Sisters of Charity of Nazareth, Kentucky; Maureen Leach, Sisters of St. Francis of Dubuque, Iowa; and Ann Cass, a Catholic layperson.

Other faith groups were also represented in the 1966 strike, including representatives of the National Council of Churches, Texas Council of Churches, and the United Methodist Church. They helped collect food, clothing, and funds for the strikers. Some later marched with the strikers.

Some clergy were arrested. One cleric who drew the particular ire of the Texas Rangers was the Rev. Ed Krueger of the Texas Conference of Churches. He was picketing at a railroad crossing in Mission as trains transported the harvested melons from Starr County eastbound through town. One day, Texas Ranger Capt. A. Y. Allee grabbed Krueger by the shirt, grabbed his head, and held it inches from a moving train, shouting, "You're no priest; you're nothing but a trouble maker."[18]

The Farmworkers March

On the Fourth of July in 1966, about a hundred persons began a peaceful, five-day, fifty-mile march from Rio Grande City to the Shrine of Our Lady of San Juan. Catholic Bishop Humberto Medeiros greeted the workers at the Shrine and celebrated a special Mass for them on July 8.[19] Following the Mass, the workers' union voted to continue their march to Austin, the state capitol, more than 300 miles from Rio Grande City and San Juan. Eugene Nelson and Father Antonio Gonzáles (later joined by Baptist Pastor James Novarro of Houston) agreed to lead the march from San Juan to Austin. Father Lawrence Peguero of Houston loaned his green and white bus, which would carry supplies and pick up exhausted marchers during the march.

Although the original purpose of the marchers was to let the world know about the strike for fair wages and demand union recognition, the march evolved to include a specific demand for an increase in the minimum wage paid to farmworkers. PASSO and political leaders joined the march to seek new state legislation establishing a Texas minimum wage of $1.25 to match the federal minimum wage.

THOSE WHO MARCHED

The number of marchers varied from as few as fifteen on some early days to more than ten thousand as the marchers neared Austin, the state's capital. The closer the march got to Austin, the larger its size. The march lasted 64 days and spanned more than four hundred miles from Rio Grande City to Austin, including detours to towns to gather support. Friends and supporters joined for short stretches along the road. Eight adults and two teenage girls, Herminia and Graciela Treviño, daughters of Benito Treviño, walked the full distance to Austin.

Herminia Treviño, fifty years later, remembered the heat rising through the bottom of her shoes. By mid-day the marchers would be walking on the grass and rocks to avoid the hot asphalt on many roads. She recalled arriving in Falfurrias and being taken to a store where she and other marchers were outfitted with new pairs of shoes.[20]

At thirteen years of age, Herminia was the youngest of the marchers. Her mother had agreed that she could march because she would be with her sister and her father. Herminia remembered that as the marchers passed through Kingsville, cowboys from King Ranch (at 1,289 square miles in size, still the largest ranch in Texas) invited them to a barbecue dinner, complete with white tablecloths at tables shaded by large tents.

The *Texas Observer* published a list of the adult farmworkers who marched the entire route to Austin. They were Jesús Laurel, forty-four, of Los Laureles in Starr County; Reyes Alaníz, sixty-two, of Garceño; Elvira López, fifty-five, who lived near La Casita Farms in Starr County; Gregoria Ramírez Villarreal, forty-one, of La Joya; Cándido Rosa, thirty-four, of Garceño; Julia Ana Ramírez, twenty-four, of La Joya; Valdemar Garza, twenty-nine, of Rio Grande City; and, Roberto Arredondo, twenty-six, of Rio Grande City.[21]

GATHERING SUPPORT ALONG THE WAY

To win public and political support, the march route zigzagged through many towns and villages in South Texas. As the marchers walked from town to town, community members, Catholic and Protestant pastors, and some elected officials came out to support their effort. In Edinburg, Mayor

Al Ramírez left his hospital bed. Traveling by ambulance, the mayor greeted the marchers from a hospital gurney.[22]

The executive board of the Texas AFL-CIO called for a boycott of La Casita products to support the marchers. The Brownsville Meat Cutters local, with one thousand members, led by Franklin García, endorsed the strike and pledged assistance. National AFL-CIO representatives joined the march on the final day in Austin. Members of the Corpus Christi Steelworkers Union, International Brotherhood of Electrical Workers, and Teamsters joined the march. Outside the small town of Bishop, twenty cotton pickers left their cotton sacks on the ground to join the march for a mile.[23]

In many small towns along the march route, the local Catholic priest and nuns greeted the marchers, the parishioners fed them, and marchers slept at parish halls. Hundreds of college students supported the farmworkers. Alex Moreno, then a student (who later became a Texas state representative), when asked fifty years later, spoke about the groups from the cities that joined the efforts. He, along with Ernesto Cortes (who later became an organizer with the Industrial Areas Foundation) and other University of Texas students from Austin, organized farmworker support committees in Austin, San Antonio, Dallas, Houston, Kingsville, and Corpus Christi to gather donated food and clothing for the strikers.[24] Volunteers and local labor unions delivered the supplies. These first efforts became the foundation for a movement that coined the word "Chicano" to define Mexican Americans in Texas. Students involved in the farmworker movement later helped form the Mexican American Youth Organization (MAYO), La Raza Unida political party, and Southwest Voter Registration Education Project (SVREP).

African Americans showed their support. Moses Leroy of the Houston chapter of the NAACP addressed a rally of more than eight hundred people in Corpus Christi.[25] B. T. Bonner of the Southern Christian Leadership Conference organized a group of forty African American supporters to march from Huntsville to Austin to show Mexican Americans "that Negroes are behind them."[26]

A CONFRONTATION WITH THE GOVERNOR

On August 23, as many as thirty to fifty marchers arrived in Floresville, the birthplace of then-Texas Governor John Connally. Although more than three hundred people lined the streets and watched from the courthouse lawn in the "sleepy little town," not one local elected official greeted the marchers. The local Catholic and Methodist churches were the only local establishment to show support for the marchers in Floresville.[27]

On August 30, the marchers arrived in New Braunfels. Fernando Piñón, a college student who would later become a university professor, in a report fifty years later remembered the events of that day:

> [I] was with them when they decided to rest in Landa Park in New Braunfels. It was a casual atmosphere, with the marchers sitting in groups and talking lively as they ate their lunch. This felt more like a church picnic than a political event that had become national news, because most people realized the marchers were fighting, not only for higher wages and social justice, but also to end the unfair labor practices they were subjected to. That casual atmosphere, however, was shattered by a sudden burst of applause. I, like many others, was surprised at the sudden exhilaration. I glanced at where the marchers were looking, and I saw Governor John Connally, Texas Attorney General Waggoner Carr, and Speaker of the Texas House Ben Barnes walking nonchalantly towards the marchers. The applause turned to cheers, as the marchers believed Texas' highest elected officials were there to welcome them and bring them good news.

Father Antonio Gonzales, one of the two religious leaders of the march, with crucifix in hand, walked quickly to greet the Governor as other marchers quickly gathered around him, still in a state of elation. It was then that Governor Connally, without greeting the workers as constituents or as fellow Texans, curtly told the group that he would neither call a special session of the legislature nor meet with the marchers in Austin. He said he would not "lend the dignity of my office" to a Labor Day rally.[28]

Ken Allen, a student at the University of Texas School of Social Work, was working on a master's degree thesis on the farmworkers' strike. He recorded this conversation between Gov. Connally and Eugene Nelson:

> **Connally:** "I do not feel that, as governor of this state, that I should lend the dignity, the prestige of an office, to dramatize any particular march, and so I would not have been with you even if I had not had a previous commitment. I want to make that clear."

(Later in the conversation)

> **Nelson:** "I've come to ask for you to help regarding that you take the leadership and ask for a minimum wage in the state of Texas. Will you do that?"
> **Connally:** "Are you asking me . . . you want me to call a special session?"
> **Nelson:** "Yes, we do."
> **Connally:** "The answer to that is no. I will not."[29]

Lt. Gov. Barnes, to show his support for the governor, said the following Saturday in Dallas: "We did that to show them that a march is not the correct way to get things done."[30] According to Piñón's report:

> Just as the applause and the cheers had exploded spontaneously, so did the jeers. Cries of 'Viva la Raza' (literally, 'long live our people,' in English; but, in general, a call for support for Mexican Americans) echoed throughout the park, and Father Gonzáles pushed the crucifix to the front of Governor Connally's head, as if to exorcise the demons of discrimination and abuse the governor represented. It was in that burst of defiance, coming not from college campuses, but from melon pickers who could hardly read and write, that I became a believer in *La Causa* (the cause).[31]

The teenage girl who marched with the farmworkers, Herminia Treviño, remembers shouting to Connally, "We're not going to see *you*!" Her statement became true. The marching farmworkers were about to step onto a national stage that would be historical in beginning the Chicano political movement in Texas. In one of my conversations with her in 2016, when I asked her how she felt she had changed during the march, she said she had become filled with the "call for justice."[32]

The encounter with Governor Connally had become another turning point for the movement. After the New Braunfels incident, the crowds of supporters became larger. Rey Gaytán, a LULAC (League of United Latin American Citizens) student leader at Southwest Texas State Teachers College (now Texas State University) in San Marcos, remembers that when the marchers reached San Marcos, thousands of people were waiting for them.

THE MARCH ENDS IN AUSTIN

On September 5, 1966, Labor Day, as many as fifteen thousand people arranged themselves into columns of two abreast. The line of marchers, which began at St. Edward's University, where the marchers had spent the night, stretched fifteen blocks—more than a mile.[33] Most of the marchers were Mexican Americans. The marchers included labor union representatives, teachers, college students, housewives, office workers, and state and federal employees.

"The street crowds were fairly good; around the downtown section the spectators were three and four-deep. They were mostly Latin Americans and negroes [sic]; there were, in fact, more members of these minorities downtown this day than one native of the city has even seen there at one time before," the *Texas Observer* reported. A burro, draped with a sign that read "$1.25," was led along the march for the final four miles.[34]

The marchers arrived at the state capitol grounds during the afternoon, sixty-four days and 468 miles after the march had begun. Most reporters agreed the crowd was at least 10,000 strong.[35] In a gesture of solidarity, Andrew Young, executive director of Dr. Martin Luther King's Southern Christian Leadership Conference in Georgia, met with César Chávez, and the two agreed that they "must keep on working," in reference to organizing Southern farmworkers.[36]

A program welcoming the marchers at the south steps of the Capitol included more than a dozen of the state's progressive political Democratic leaders. They included U.S. Senator Ralph Yarborough (D-TX), the only Southern senator to vote yes to all national civil rights bills from the 1950s and 1960s, including the Civil Rights Act of 1964 and the Voting Rights Act of 1965. Among them was Barbara Jordan, then a nominee for the Texas Senate. Later, Jordan would become a state senator and then the first African American woman from the South elected to Congress. She became a powerful voice for civil rights for the national Democratic Party.[37]

After the march, two farmworkers, Benito Treviño and Reyes Alaníz, remained stationed on the steps at the front door of the state capitol each day for months as a constant, visual reminder to the powers-that-be that there was unfinished business. The *Texas Observer* reported that Governor Connally, who usually entered the capitol through the front door, began entering through a side door to avoid the two men.[38]

The Growers Wield Their Political Power

When the workers returned to the Rio Grande Valley of Texas to continue their struggle against the growers in the fall of 1966, the wealthy growers began exerting their political influence over politicians, local and state law enforcement agencies, and even the FBI. Sheriffs, prosecutors, and judges, including 79th District Court Judge C. Woodrow Laughlin, targeted farmworkers. The FBI, under the direction of FBI Director J. Edgar Hoover, began keeping files on Starr County farmworkers.

State and local law enforcement officials "hired" by the growers to stop the ongoing unionizing efforts included Randall Nye, a Starr County prosecutor who also was attorney for Starr Farms. One of the sheriff's deputies, Jim Rochester, was also an employee at La Casita Farms. Five Texas Rangers, led by Captain A. Y. Allee, acted as a private police force for one of the farms in the area. In testimony in a later federal court case, *Allee v. Medrano*, Reynaldo de la Cruz, who had been arrested on November 9, 1966, was told the Rangers were there to break the strike and would not leave until they had done so. Later, a three-judge U.S. District Court found that law enforcement officials illegally "took sides in what was essentially a labor-management controversy."[39]

ARRESTS OF FARMWORKERS ESCALATE

A month after the march ended on Labor Day 1966, the Texas Rangers and Starr County sheriff's officers began arresting the strike organizers, charging them with breach of the peace, abusive language, secondary picketing, impersonating an officer, kneeling while praying at the courthouse, or disturbing the peace. The spurious charges included threatening the lives of the Texas Rangers, trespassing on private property, unlawful assembly, violating mass picketing laws, brandishing a gun, or threatening local police officers. Charges were concocted out of thin air; and bonds for these arrests were set higher than the fines would have been for the "offenses."

On June 1, 1967, Captain Allee and other Rangers severely beat Magdaleno Dímas and Benjamin Rodríguez, and arrested Dímas for allegedly "brandishing" a gun. Because they had no warrant for his arrest, they called the local justice of the peace to issue a warrant at the scene. That same night, they beat up organizers Alex Moreno and Bill Chandler. Dímas's and Rodríguez's beatings were so severe they were hospitalized. Dímas remained hospitalized for four days. Dr. Ramiro Casso of McAllen (himself a long-time activist) treated his injuries. The furor caused by the beatings cast a demoralizing pall over the workers.

GROWERS WIN IN COURT; FARMWORKERS APPEAL

In June 1967, one year after the strike started, Judge C. Woodrow Laughlin of the 79th District Court in Rio Grande City sided with the growers in issuing a temporary injunction that banned all picketing of La Casita Farms. Soon thereafter, the Rangers left the Valley.[40] Eighteen months later, the San Antonio District Court of Appeals affirmed the trial court decision.

Following the temporary injunction, attorneys for the farmworkers filed a lawsuit in the U.S. Southern District Court of Texas at Brownsville, challenging the constitutionality of five Texas statutes: the "mass picketing" law, the "secondary strike" law, an "unlawful assembly" law, the "obstructing the streets" law, and a "breach of the peace" law.[41] Because the case involved the constitutionality of state statutes, a three-judge panel was convened to hear it.

The panel consisted of two U.S. District Judges in the Southern District, Judge Woodrow Seals of Houston and Judge Reynaldo Garza of Brownsville, and Judge John Brown of the U.S. Fifth Circuit Court of Appeals. The three-day hearing ended on June 13, 1968. On June 26, 1972, the trial court issued a decision, declaring all five Texas statutes unconstitutional, and granting injunctive relief against the Texas Rangers, sheriff, deputy sheriffs, and justice of the peace. The decision was appealed to the U.S. Supreme Court.

On May 20, 1974, the Supreme Court justices, in a remarkable decision outlining the facts of the strike, affirmed the lower court's ruling in favor of the farmworkers, noting, however, that since the Texas legislature had already repealed or amended three of the challenged laws, the lower court's ruling on those issues was moot. *Medrano v. Allee* proved that even the vaunted Texas Rangers could be restrained by the law, thus stripping them of the most effective weapon of any oppressive power: the perception that resistance was futile.[42]

Meanwhile, the union organizers became known for more than organizing farmworkers around the issues of wages and working conditions. On September 20, 1967, Hurricane Beulah flooded the Rio Grande Valley communities and farms. The union focused efforts on assisting the farmworkers who lost their jobs for the season, and on assisting those who lost their homes. The strike had ended because of the unrelenting power of the state that was used against a group of oppressed citizens. It ended because the state's laws were set up purposely against its own citizens, and because law enforcement agents enforced these laws with impunity. However, the voices of the farmworkers were not silenced.

Texas Farmworkers Make Their Voices Heard

Following the 1966 strike and march, farmworkers and their unions continued their struggle for better working conditions and higher wages. The United Farm Workers (UFW) hall in Texas moved from Rio Grande City to McAllen. In 1972, a new UFW hall was built on land donated by the United Auto Workers and the Teamsters, and the Catholic Diocese of Brownsville, on the corner of what is now César Chávez Road and U.S. Highway 83, between the Rio Grande Valley towns of San Juan and Alamo.

Antonio Orendain was the union leader until 1975. After another strike in the melon fields, Orendain decided in August 1975 to form the Texas Farm Workers Union. A split occurred; some workers followed Orendain, and others voted to remain with the UFW. When that happened, César Chávez asked Rebecca Flores, Pedro de la Fuente, and José Saldaña to lead the United Farm Workers in the Rio Grande Valley. Eventually, Flores became the sole leader.

In January 1979, after an intensive organizing campaign, the UFW held the first farmworker convention in Texas. César Chávez presided. A thousand delegates from twenty-five organizing committees in Hidalgo, Willacy, Cameron, and Starr counties attended to vote on issues that would direct the work of the UFW in Texas. For the next decade, the UFW succeeded in winning worker protection legislation in Texas, with help from other organized labor groups, including the Democratic Party, Mexican American civil rights groups, and other allies across the state.

FROM LAWSUITS TO LEGISLATION

Passing legislation was not accomplished in the traditional manner. From 1983 to 1987, James Harrington of the ACLU's South Texas Project (and, later, of the Texas Civil Rights Project) filed several winning lawsuits that opened a path to passing legislation protecting farmworkers.[43] The lawsuits, one after another, challenged the exclusion of farm laborers from protective legislation on issues such as workers compensation and unemployment benefits. The lawsuits argued that the exclusions were a violation of the Texas Constitution's equality of rights amendment, especially since farmworkers in Texas were an ethnically identifiable class.[44]

Each piece of legislation stemmed from a lawsuit filed and won in the courts. When ruled successful on appeal, the Texas legislature was compelled to pass legislation to expand legal protections to farmworkers. Eventually, litigation was no longer necessary. Intense lobbying efforts by farmworkers and allies led to later victories, but even then, when the votes were counted, the bills passed the Texas House and Senate by thin majorities.

All this protective farmworker legislation occurred in the 1980s, when Governor Mark White led Texas and Lt. Governor Bill Hobby presided over the Senate. Both were Democrats. The three major laws won for farmworkers through the one-two litigation and legislation approach were:

- **Workers compensation coverage.** Although Texas passed its Workers Compensation Act in 1913, farmworkers were not covered until 1984, seventy years later. The lawsuit that began this campaign was *Puga v. Donna Fruit Company*, filed on behalf of Genoveva Puga, mother of a young man who was killed while working in a citrus orchard when a large bin of citrus fell on him. His body went unnoticed for several hours.
- **Unemployment benefits.** Similarly, while the Texas Unemployment Compensation Act became law in 1936, farmworkers were not covered until 1986, a half-century later. The lawsuit was filed following a 1983 freeze that left thousands of workers unemployed, and without unemployment compensation, because they had been excluded by law.
- **Right to know about use of pesticides in the workplace.** The 1985 Community Right to Know Act had excluded farmworkers from protection. The Texas Agricultural Hazard Communication Law was passed in 1987, covering farmworkers, following a protracted fight, led by the Texas Farm Bureau, against the legislation.

In addition to these changes, protective field sanitation measures were introduced into the agriculture industry. In 1984, access to toilets, potable drinking water, and hand-washing facilities became standard in Texas with a change in health code regulations by the state Health Commissioner. In 1987, the federal Occupational Safety and Health Administration (OSHA) issued this standard for all agricultural workers in the United States.

Other protective laws for farmworkers were adopted in the 1980s. Legislation banning the use of short-handled hoes passed in 1981. This law was followed by another successful bill to outlaw the use of knives by thinning and weeding crews, which passed both the House and the Senate, only to be vetoed at the time by Governor Bill Clements.[45]

The Texas Minimum Wage was established in 1969, in the aftermath of

Figure 4. Texas Senator Lloyd Doggett, who led passage of workers compensation legislation, speaking at 3rd Annual UFW Convention, 1981. From left to right, Rebecca Flores; Jim Hightower, Agriculture Commissioner candidate; Dolores Huerta, vice president and co-founder of the UFW; Lloyd Doggett; and Ann Richards, candidate for treasurer. Farmworker political action committee members/delegates to right and front of podium. Alan Pogue.

the strike and march to Austin in 1966. In 1969, it was set at $1.40 an hour (the federal minimum wage in 1969 was $1.60 an hour). In 1987, the state minimum wage was raised to $3.35 an hour, matching the federal minimum wage. The UFW, and other organized labor groups and allies, lobbied to raise it again, and to permanently match the Texas minimum wage to the federal minimum wage. This effort finally succeeded in 2001, when the federal minimum wage was raised to $5.15 an hour and the state minimum wage matched that amount. Since then, the Texas minimum wage has risen to match federal minimum wage increases. As of 2018, the state and federal minimum wage, set in 2009, stood at $7.25 an hour.

EFFORTS TO MAKE THE "MINIMUM WAGE" REALITY

The minimum wage laws did not guarantee better incomes for farmworkers. Most farmworkers are not hourly employees. They are paid by the

Figure 5. Harvesting green bell peppers. Alan Pogue.

number of units they harvest, a practice commonly called piece rates. The piece rates are intended to guarantee to match at least the minimum wage, allowing workers to earn more than a minimum wage. However, earning more than the minimum wage has rarely been accomplished in the fields of Texas. While the U.S. Department of Labor is the enforcement agency for federal wage complaints, complaints were rarely successful in South Texas. Ongoing strikes in Rio Grande Valley fields helped to raise piece rates, but strikes alone never permanently changed the practice. In the 1980s, Texas Agriculture Commissioner Jim Hightower repeatedly attempted to address the piece rate issue, but he was never successful in changing these agricultural industry practices.

In 1981, at the Texas UFW Convention in Pharr, one thousand farmworker convention delegates were surveyed to determine the actual wages they were earning at the time. The survey showed an average of $1.85 an hour. The Texas minimum wage was $1.40 an hour, and the federal minimum wage was $3.35 an hour. The delegates voted to begin a "March for Wages" to raise the actual daily minimum wage in Río Grande Valley agriculture

Figure 6. Farmworker housing in *colonias* (unincorporated villages) with outdoor toilet. Alan Pogue.

to the federal standard. The seven-day march began simultaneously in Río Grande City and in Brownsville, merging into one march in San Juan. César Chávez led the initial march from Brownsville, alternating march routes each day. Thousands of people supported the march, eventually leading to gradual increases in actual daily minimum wages for Texas farmworkers.[46]

The UFW also played an active role in improving living conditions in unincorporated communities, often populated by farmworkers, in the Río Grande Valley. These unincorporated communities, called *colonias*, are excluded from city and county health and safety codes. Therefore, many *colonias* were left without any public services. The *colonia* land developers offered easy-to-buy contract-for-deed lots, which farmworkers eagerly bought to have land on which to build small homes. There was no access to potable water or a sewage system.

Often, there were no paved roads and no street signs or postal delivery services. The UFW in Texas convinced Hidalgo County commissioners to address the terrible conditions, and to control the growing number of *colonias* being platted and sold. The successes also included bringing potable drinking water, paved streets, sewage and drainage, and trash services to many of the *colonias*. Paved roads were especially important to farmworkers, because they wanted public school buses to be able to pick up their children.

In the 1990s, rules for Model Subdivisions included these successes, but the lots with these conveniences began selling for $30,000, making good housing unaffordable. Model Subdivisions were not considered *colonias*. *Colonias* continued to proliferate; in 2018, Hidalgo County alone had more than 925 *colonias*.

A CHANGE IN FOCUS

During the 1980s, when changes were occurring in agriculture that affected the amount of hand harvesting required, the focus of primarily organizing farmworkers around worker issues also changed. In December 1983, a bitter winter freeze devastated the citrus industry, destroying hundreds of acres of trees. Much of that spoiled acreage was asphalted over and converted to recreational vehicle (RV) parks for tourist trailers. Many farm fields were transformed into nonfarm temporary housing communities. The Río Grande Valley became known as the home of "Texas Snow Birds," the nickname given visitors from cold-weather Northern states during warmer winter months in deep South Texas. In 1989, there was another freeze that further hurt the citrus industry.

In 1993, the North American Free Trade Act (NAFTA) passed. Soon, most of the farming operations with seasonal crops requiring intensive hand labor for cultivation and harvesting moved across the border to Mexico to take advantage of cheaper labor and essentially nonexistent worker protection laws. Today, much of the area's farm acreage is devoted to ma-chine-harvested, low labor-intensive crops such as sugar cane, cotton, and sorghum.

Given the changes in agriculture across South Texas, La Unión del Pueblo Entero (LUPE), a community union concept developed by César Chávez and other national farmworker movement leaders, took the lead in the Río Grande Valley from the UFW in 2000. LUPE continued community organizing efforts in the *colonias*.[47] Juanita Valdez-Cox, a former UFW organizer, became director of LUPE, which continued the *colonia* committee structure for organizing purposes. LUPE focused on the growing crises faced by immigrants during an early twenty-first-century era of harsh anti-immigration policies in the United States, which are still prevalent in 2018.

From 1942 until 1964, the agricultural economy in the southwestern United States relied heavily on the Bracero (temporary worker) program, which authorized thousands of agricultural workers from Mexico to come to the United States to work on farms. Initially, the program was designed to replace the loss of labor when millions of U.S. citizens were drafted to fight abroad during World War II. Valdez-Cox, director of LUPE, wrote in 2018 that her father, Raymundo Valdez, immigrated to the United States as a Bracero in the mid-1940s.[48] His Weslaco, Texas, employer helped him, his wife, and his family become legal residents in 1953.

Thousands of Mexican residents continued to cross the border into Texas after the Bracero program ended in 1964. In the 1960s, farm owners often used immigrants to break strikes by Mexican Americans. In 1965, Congress passed the Immigration and Nationality Act, which established a "family unity" policy that allowed documented immigrants to sponsor family members (their parents, spouses, children). The emphasis was on legal immigration, not deportation. The policy remained basically unchanged through the mid-1980s. The 1986 Simpson–Mazzoli bill that became law imposed stricter identification requirements to ensure that immigrants were authorized to work in the United States. However, enforcement was lax.[49]

Following the terrorist attacks on the United States on September 11, 2001, the United States enacted harsher "border security" measures designed to block the entry of terrorists and violent drug cartels. Immigrant farmworkers were caught up in the political crossfire, and have since faced increased discrimination and deportations, expanding the focus of farmworkers' rights organizations from protecting Mexican American farmworkers to also protecting the rights of non-U.S. citizen immigrants.

The Fiftieth Anniversary

The Texas farmworkers' strike and march of 1966 gave rise to changes in laws that helped labor unions in their organizing efforts in Texas. The Texas Rangers were stopped from interfering with labor union strikes. Students, inspired by the farmworker movement, staged school walkouts to protest inferior education funding. Willie Velasquez in 1974 founded the Southwest Voter Registration Education Project in San Antonio, Texas, to educate Mexican Americans on voting issues in Texas.

Ernie Cortes, who had marched with the farmworkers as a student, began working with the Industrial Areas Foundation (IAF) and organized COPS (Communities Organized for Public Service) in San Antonio in 1974, He subsequently established these faith- and community-based IAF organizations in major cities in Texas. Mexican American voices for change became stronger in education, in labor unions, in communities, and in politics. Arturo Rodríquez, a native of San Antonio, became national president of the United Farm Workers upon the death of César Chávez, serving from 1993 through 2018.[50]

Fiftieth anniversary commemorations were held in 2016 in Río Grande City, Edinburg, San Juan, Corpus Christi, San Antonio, and Austin to remember the events of 1966, and to inspire all to build on that foundation. Hundreds of former farmworkers, allies, students, friends, labor union members, and religious leaders gathered to share memories. The *Texas Observer* covered the Austin celebration, appropriately so, since it was the one English-language Texas periodical that consistently published news about the events of 1966 that had been largely ignored by other media outlets.[51]

The Struggle Continues

In 2016, the *Austin American-Statesman* published the results of the newspaper's four-month investigation into the living conditions of farmworkers in Texas, concluding that the state continues to ignore the needs of the more than 200,000 agricultural workers that the National Center for Farmworker

Figure 7. Hidalgo water tap. Alan Pogue.

Health estimates are working in Texas.[52] Some farmworkers promised temporary housing near the fields where they tend crops were forced to live in shipping containers transformed into shelter with no running water or bathrooms. Some slept in their cars.

The Texas Department of Housing and Community Affairs, responsible for inspecting migrant farmworker housing, had not levied any enforcement actions against operators of migrant farmworker facilities since 2005, the newspaper reported. While other states spend hundreds of thousands of dollars each year to ensure safe, clean living conditions for migrant farmworkers, Texas in 2015 spent less than $2,500 on inspections and licensing. The state housing agency has no funding for migrant housing outreach.[53]

While mechanization has diminished the numbers of farmworkers in Texas, low wages and poor working conditions continue to diminish the quality of life for documented and undocumented farmworkers in the state. The communities in which they work to serve the state's $25 billion agricultural industry still are among the poorest regions in the United States.

Recommendations

- Texas should enforce laws requiring safe, clean living conditions for citizen and noncitizen farmworkers, and safe working conditions in the fields.
- Texas should seek more federal funding for farmworker housing. From 2009 until 2016, California received $105.9 million in U.S. Department of Agriculture grants and loans for farmworker housing. Texas sought and received only $18.9 million.[54]
- Ultimately, Texas should raise the state's minimum wage to a "livable" wage for all workers, as has occurred in other states in recent years. Despite an anti-worker political climate in Congress in 2018 that has not allowed an increase of a $7.25 federal minimum wage unchanged since 2009, other states and municipalities outside Texas have enacted minimum wages totaling as much as $15 an hour in recent years.
- The system of setting piece rates and units of work should be studied as a basis to pass legislation that would establish a just wage. For example, in the 1980s, growers would have onion harvesters fill a five-gallon container for a set piece rate. This container then was changed to a six-gallon and then a seven-gallon container, for the same piece rate.
- Texas should erase its right-to-work laws and policies designed to discourage the formation and power of labor unions, which proved powerful voices for better wages, benefits, and safer working conditions across the United States during the last century. Wages and workers' rights have been suppressed in all states with right-to-work laws.
- Legislation should be passed to end the practice of contracts-for-deeds, a practice that allows an owner/developer to foreclose on a property if the buyer misses one payment.
- The government should establish public hospitals in high-poverty counties that will accept the uninsured and under-insured.

The 1966 farmworker movement in Texas inspired new generations of Mexican Americans to organize in support of better working and living conditions for what will, in a few decades, become the majority ethnic population in Texas.

All Texans can be inspired by what the farmworkers accomplished more than fifty years ago. The Texas Legislature will not act unless it is compelled by millions of new, organized voices and votes.

Notes

1. U.S. Commission on Civil Rights (USCCR), *Hearing before the United States Commission on Civil Rights: San Antonio, TX, December 9–14, 1968* (Washington, DC: GPO, 1969). Also available at https://catalog.hathitrust.org/Record/001874430.

2. USCCR, *Hearing*, Exhibit No. 25, Lucey testimony, 933–941; USCCR, *Hearing*, Exhibit No. 27, Staff Report: Farm Workers, 953–981.

3. James Crutchfield, *It Happened in Texas: Remarkable Events That Shaped History*, 3rd ed., (Lanham, MD: Roman & Littlefield, 2001), 129, citing Greg Olds, "Two Days on the Road," *Texas Observer* (August 5, 1966), 3.

4. David M. Fishlow (ed.), *Sons of Zapata, A Brief Photographic History of the Farmworkers Strike in Texas* (Rio Grande City, TX: United Farm Workers Organizing Committee, AFL-CIO, 1967).

5. Fishlow, *Sons of Zapata*, 5.

6. Fishlow, *Sons of Zapata*, 6

7. Marc Linder "Lost in a Loophole: The Fair Labor Standards Act's Exemptions of Agricultural Workers from Overtime Compensation Protection," *Drake Journal of Agricultural Law*, 10, no. 355, 2005; 81 Congressional Record 7648 (1937).

8. U.S. Department of Labor, Wage and Hour Division (WHD), "History of Federal Minimum Wage Rates under the Fair Labor Standards Act, 1938-2009," https://www.dol.gov/whd/min wage/chart.htm.

9. Gene Lantz, "'Right to Work' is Texas Made," *Dallas AFL-Council*, February 24, 2017; Cole Strangler, "Union-Busting Republicans Lick Their Lips at the Possibility of a Federal Right-to-Work Law," *The Village Voice*, February 21, 2017.

10. History, United Farm Workers of America, AFL-CIO, http://ufw.org/research/history; Susan Ferriss and Ricardo Sandoval, *The Fight in the Fields: César Chávez and the Farmworkers Movement* (New York: Harcourt Brace, 1997); Rebecca Flores (article author), Personnel Recollections and Field Interviews as Organizer, 1975-2005, United Farm Workers Union, AFL-CIO, Texas.

11. Ronnie Dugger, "A Long Struggle with La Casita," *Texas Observer*, June 24, 1966, 3.

12. Fishlow, *Sons of Zapata*, 6.

13. Rebecca Flores and Alfredo Santos (eds.), "Farm Worker Commemoration: 50th Anniversary, 1966 Starr County Melon Strike and March, La Voz *(Texas) Newspapers*, August 27, 2016.

14. Flores and Santos, "Farm Worker Commemoration."

15. Dugger, "A Long Struggle with La Casita," 3.

16. *Allee v. Medrano*, 416 U.S. 802, 806 (1974). The Supreme Court case provides an extensive summary of the facts involved in the 1966 and 1967 strikes.

17. Dugger, "A Long Struggle with La Casita," 4.

18. *Allee v. Medrano.*
19. Fishlow, *Sons of Zapata*, 14–15.
20. Flores and Santos, "Farm Worker Commemoration."
21. Ronnie Dugger, "Eight of the Marchers, They Walked from Valley to Corpus Christi," *Texas Observer*, August 5, 1966, 1–4.
22. Ronnie Dugger, "The Valley Strikers are Walking to Austin," *Texas Observer*, July 11, 1966, 8.
23. Ronnie Dugger, "The March into Corpus Christi," *Texas Observer*, August 5, 1966, 6.
24. Dugger, "The March into Corpus Christi," 5.
25. Dugger, "The March into Corpus Christi."
26. Greg Olds, "Labor Day in Austin, a Bad Day for the Establishment," *Texas Observer*, September 16, 1966, 7.
27. Ronnie Dugger, "Connally Silent as U.S. Labor Approves," *Texas Observer*, September 2, 1966, 3.
28. Fernando Piñon, "Farmers Strike and March is Our Heritage," *Farm Worker Commemoration 50th Anniversary Booklet* (2016); Flores and Santos, "Farm Worker Commemoration."
29. Ronnie Dugger, "The Confrontation," *Texas Observer*, September 16, 1966), 9–10.
30. Olds, "Labor Day in Austin," 6.
31. Piñon, "Farmers Strike and March Is Our Heritage," 8.
32. James C. Harrington, interviewed by the author.
33. On the occasion of the fiftieth anniversary commemorative march, St. Edward's University dedicated a memorial plaque, affixed to a wall in the student union building. Nancy Flores, "Remembering Farmworkers March Fifty Years Later: The Civil Rights Movement Included Many Significant Events, but Here's One That Changed Texas History," *Austin American-Statesman*, September 7, 2016; "United Farm Workers Commemorate 400-Mile March 50th Anniversary, Founder César Chávez," *Spectrum News Austin*, September 12, 2016.
34. Olds, "Labor Day In Austin," 19.
35. Olds, "Labor Day In Austin," 19.
36. Ronnie Dugger, "César Chávez' Plan," *Texas Observer*, September 16, 1966, 12.
37. Ronnie Dugger, "Politicians with the March," *Texas Observer*, September, 16, 1966, 16.
38. Olds, "Labor Day in Austin," 6.
39. *Allee v. Medrano, supra* note 10.
40. Robert Hall, "Farmworkers Strike in South Texas: Pickets Politics and Power: The Farm Worker Strike in Starr County," *Robert Hall Blog*, https://bobsremonstrance.com/farmworkers-strike-in-south-texas. Hall was one of the attorneys involved in the *Allee* case.
41. Vernon's Civ. Stats. Ann. Arts 5154d, 5154f; Tex. Penal Code Arts. 474, 493, 784.
42. *Allee v. Medrano, supra* note 10.
43. James C. Harrington, "From Michigan's Strawberry Fields to South Texas's Rio Grande Valley: The Saga of a Legal Career and the Texas Civil Rights Project," *City University of New York Law Review* 19, no. 2 (September 14, 2016).
44. Harrington, "From Michigan's Strawberry Fields"; Texas Constitution, Article I Sec. 3a.
45. Joshua Barnes, "'Voices of the UFW in Texas': A Documentary on the United Farm Worker Movement in Texas," *Samsonia Way Online Journal*, April 3, 2014.
46. James C. Harrington, "From La Casita to LUPE," *Texas Observer*, December 3, 2004.
47. Harrington, "From La Casita to LUPE."
48. Juanita Valdez-Cox and Vaughn Cox, "The Politics of Immigration in South Texas: 1940s–2018." Unpublished article. Note: Excerpts are from an article prepared for the author.
49. Valdez-Cox and Cox, "The Politics of Immigration."

50. Geoffrey Mohan, "The Longtime Head of the Farmworkers Union Is Stepping Down. His Replacement Is a Woman," *Los Angeles Times*, August 28, 2018.

51. Gus Bova, "Hundreds Gather to Remember the 1966 Texas Farmworkers' March," *Texas Observer*, September 12, 2016.

52. Jeremy Schwartz, "Unlivable: How Texas Fails Farmworkers," *Austin-American Statesman*, March 17, 2016.

53. Schwartz, "Unlivable."

54. Schwartz, "Unlivable."

ALEJANDRO BECERRA AND HENRY CISNEROS

Fair Housing in America and Texas: Mexican American Housing Discrimination and Homeownership Trends

In 1968, the U.S. Commission on Civil Rights held hearings in San Antonio, Texas, on civil rights challenges facing Mexican Americans in the U.S. Southwest. Acting under the authority of the Civil Rights Act of 1957, commissioners invited testimony on education, employment, economic security, and the administration of justice for Mexican Americans in five states: Arizona, California, Colorado, New Mexico, and Texas.

In the same year, President Lyndon B. Johnson, a native Texan, signed Title VIII of the Civil Rights Act of 1968. The law, which came to be known as the Fair Housing Act, was a pivotal piece of legislation that brought to fruition President Johnson's efforts to advance the civil rights of all Americans—a goal pursued by many for generations. The Fair Housing Act followed the enactment of 1964 and 1965 civil rights laws that outlawed racial discrimination in employment, public accommodations, and voting.

Fair Housing for All

When President Johnson signed the Fair Housing Act on April 11, 1968, he stated that the new law filled one of the biggest remaining gaps in the nation's new structure of justice. He declared: "Fair housing for all—all human beings who live in this country—is now a part of the American way of life."[1] Unquestionably, much progress has since been achieved in reducing segregation among America's racial and ethnic communities. The Fair Housing Act mandates protection from discrimination for people when they are renting, buying, or securing financing for any housing. The prohibitions specifically cover discrimination because of race, color, national origin, religion, sex, disability, and the presence of children. The capacity of Mexican Americans and other population groups to benefit specifically from the Fair Housing Act can best be measured by determining how well communities have been integrated across the country. Likewise, properly assessing the full impact of civil rights legislation on housing requires determining the extent to which all Americans, including Latinos, have successfully achieved homeownership or safe and decent rental housing.

President Johnson's national quest was accelerated under the most recent presidential administrations, particularly those of Presidents Bill Clinton and Barack Obama. They made it a priority to reduce or eliminate discriminatory real estate practices that had prevailed over several decades. The most prominent of these unscrupulous real estate practices included racially restrictive covenants, characterized by contractual agreements that prohibited the purchase, lease, or occupation of a piece of property by a particular group of people, usually African Americans.

Redlining involved the ability of banks and other financial institutions to refuse or limit loans, mortgages, insurance, or other services within specific geographic areas, based on their racial or ethnic composition. Over several decades, redlining prevented minority citizens, especially African Americans, from benefiting from federal government subsidies that had been extended to non-Hispanic white neighborhoods. Blockbusting involved profiteering from the buying of homes from non-Hispanic white majority owners below market value, based on the implied threat of future devaluation during minority integration of those previously segregated neighborhoods.

Predatory lending has persisted, relying on unscrupulous lenders luring or tricking borrowers, especially the poor and uninformed, into signing costly and faulty loans. Before the end of the last century, such practices mainly targeted the elderly, minority populations, and the poor. By the early years of the twenty-first century, predatory lending was extended to any gullible borrower, regardless of race, income, or even credit score. This practice contributed to the precipitation of the U.S. housing crisis and the Great Recession that caused the loss of jobs and homes for millions of Americans from 2007 to 2009 and beyond.

Discriminatory Housing Practices before 1968

Prior to the passage of civil rights laws in the 1960s, inequality in housing for people of color was exacerbated when President Franklin D. Roosevelt saved the housing industry, albeit on a discriminatory basis, during the Great Depression, which lasted from 1929 to 1939. During those years, the Roosevelt administration deliberately steered Federal Housing Administration subsidies to "whites-only" neighborhoods, under the spurious pretense that assistance to such neighborhoods would avoid the property devaluation that African American residents would presumably cause by moving to those neighborhoods.

During the 1940s, when the federal government constructed housing for World War II defense plant workers, it did so on a segregated basis. After the war, the Federal Housing Administration (which would serve as a model for President Johnson's later establishment of the U.S. Department of Housing and Urban Development in 1965) and GI Bill housing policies also favored non-Hispanic white suburbs.[2] The precedents had been set for making it extremely difficult to overcome housing inequality and unfairness in housing.

When the Fair Housing Act was adopted in 1968, its basic premise was that the federal government would be fully committed to preventing new discrimination, as well as reversing the damage already inflicted by the government. Today, the federal government has successfully won hundreds of discrimination cases involving overt racial bias and bigotry in renting and selling homes to racial and ethnic minority groups to others covered under the law.[3]

However, what has remained most difficult to achieve is full enforcement of the law's requirement that federally aided local governments take affirmative steps to address and remedy residential segregation. This lack of commitment to proactively deter discrimination in housing has made it more daunting for people of color to live in communities with an abundance of decent, affordable rental housing and homeownership opportunities.

The Long Road Traveled

The civil rights of a nation are nonexistent if they are not self-evident and inalienable for all its citizens. When these rights are fully extended, they lead to economic prosperity, social cohesion, and solid integration into the middle class. Accompanied by public policies that improve education, workforce productivity, and economic strength, civil rights that promote fair and equal housing opportunities help bring more citizens into the mainstream of American life.

Through homeownership, these civil rights provide a direct pathway to economic prosperity for most Americans through the accumulation of assets which constitute most people's primary wealth and security. Over the past fifty years, progress on housing, however, has been slow, particularly for African Americans, whose homeownership rates have barely increased and whose largely segregated living conditions have only slightly improved. The homeownership rate of African Americans dropped from 44 percent in 1975 to 43 percent in 2018.

Although the homeownership rate of African Americans reached a high of 50 percent in 2004, the significant gains African Americans had made until then were essentially erased by the housing crisis and subsequent

Great Recession in 2007 and later years. For Hispanics, including Mexican Americans in Texas and other southwestern states, homeownership has been more readily, yet less than ideally, attainable. Housing finance policies, and outreach and marketing efforts by major financial institutions have consistently failed to fully consider the creditworthiness, aspirations, and market strength of Hispanic homebuyers.

Today, millions of Latino families live in overcrowded, substandard rental housing, often paying as much as 50 percent or more of their monthly income for rent. Rental housing costs and home prices continued to rise in 2018, prodded substantially by unfair competition from institutional investors. Partly because these investors persist in buying existing and new homes strictly for rental purposes, the available housing inventory continued to shrink.

The State of Rental Housing for Hispanics in America

A 2013 study by the nonprofit Equal Rights Center reported that Latino renters experienced discrimination 42 percent of the time. The study documented adverse and discriminatory treatment against prospective Latino renters and homebuyers in Birmingham, Alabama; Atlanta, Georgia; and San Antonio, Texas.[4] The study concluded that discrimination against Latinos in housing has not disappeared since enactment of the Fair Housing Act. It persists, and now reflects more subtle forms of prejudice.

The study finds that Latinos continue to be targeted and to experience some type of adverse treatment when they seek rental housing. The differential treatment experienced by the study's Latino "testers," who posed as potential renters or homebuyers, included numerous patterns of subtle to overt discrimination. Housing agents were less inclined to schedule an appointment with Latino testers than with their matched non-Hispanic white, or Anglo, testers. Agents provided Latino testers with fewer choices in rental properties or homes for sale than they provided to Anglo testers.

In sales tests, agents provided Anglo testers with lender recommendations or other advantageous financing information that was not provided to their matched Latino testers. In rental tests, agents quoted higher fees, costs, or more extensive application requirements to Latino testers. In many cases, agents provided follow-up contact by phone or email to Anglo testers, but not to their matched Latino testers.[5]

In the aftermath of the 2007 housing crisis, caused largely by costly and faulty loans that disproportionately victimized millions of Hispanic and other minority households, the housing discrimination that Latino renters continue to experience has made their recovery and progress even more daunting. Because Hispanic millennials (persons born between 1981 and 1996) comprise as much as one in five of all millennials, the need for an additional supply of affordable rental units for low- and moderate-income Latino households became urgent a decade later, since extremely low vacancy rates continued to push up rental rates.

At the same time, continued budgetary cuts to federal rental assistance have made it essential to increase such funding to close the gap between what low-income households can afford to pay for decent housing and what it costs to provide that housing. According to Harvard University's Joint Center for Housing Studies, investments in permanent affordable housing have the added benefit of preventing displacement in gentrifying neighborhoods. Complemented by amenities such as quality schools and employment centers, improving or constructing affordable rental housing can also help ensure that minority households have access to the economic and social opportunities provided by such neighborhoods.[6]

The need for decent, affordable rental housing for America's fast-growing Latino population is expected to increase substantially, as many continue to live in substandard housing and experience overcrowding. While Latinos made up 20 percent of renter households in 2013, the Joint Center for Housing Studies projected that they will account for more than half of renter household growth through 2023.[7] The Mortgage Bankers Association similarly projects the rapid growth of Latino renter households, reporting that between 2014 and 2024 there will be 2.7 million new Hispanic renter households.[8]

Latino Homeownership in America

As of 2018, the U.S. homeownership rate for Hispanic households was 48 percent, in contrast to the national rate of 64 percent for all households, and the higher non-Hispanic white rate of 72 percent. In 2017, the rate of Latino homeownership in Texas was 57 percent, second highest in the nation, at less than eight percentage points below the national rate, and only five points below the total homeownership rate in Texas.[9]

The national Latino homeownership rate had reached 50 percent at its peak levels in 2006 and 2007. The rate of homeownership of all Americans plummeted during the next decade as a result of the housing crisis that helped trigger the Great Recession. The loss of millions of homes during those years occurred mainly because of the unprecedented large number of unregulated and highly flawed loans that were made to all Americans, regardless of race, income, or even credit scores.[10]

Latinos continue to experience discrimination when seeking to buy a home. The recent study by the Equal Rights Center that documented discrimination as a major housing barrier for Hispanics found that the Latino testers involved in the study did not receive information that could have made buying a home easier. For example, the Latino testers were not provided advantageous financing information, or information about other potential homes in the vicinity.[11]

In spite of such obstacles, the Hispanic homeownership rate today is 16 percent points below the national rate, a five-point decrease from the twenty-one-point gap in 2000. The remarkable recovery of Hispanic homeownership is a testament to the high aspirations of Latinos to own homes, and to improved access to more equitable and fair homeownership opportunities. Equally important, Hispanics have been playing a pivotal role in the growth of the general economy as a result of their expanding population growth, increased purchasing power, and significant employment and entrepreneurial contributions.

Hispanic gains in homeownership are even more exceptional, considering that about half of all Hispanic adults in the United States today are immigrants. Their shorter tenure in this country means that they have had fewer years to earn wages, to establish the financial preconditions for home buying, and to become fully familiar with the complex process of mortgage financing. The variables that continue to hamper the growth of Hispanic homeownership are income, recorded credit history, a younger age profile, and place of residence and work. A low priority given to effectively reaching Hispanic homebuyers and the continuation of discriminatory loan practices also continue to play a role in some regions of the country.

Latino Homeownership Gains in Texas

For Texas Mexican Americans, housing progress has historically depended on their proximity to predominantly Mexican border areas, their length of residency in the state, and finding good jobs in rapidly growing metropolitan areas like Dallas, Fort Worth, Austin, San Antonio, and Houston. Statewide, the rate of Mexican American homeownership is ten points higher than the national homeownership rate of Hispanics in 2017. Texas ranks second only to New Mexico in achieving the highest level of Latino homeownership in the country. Texas also ranks second to New Mexico in having the highest share of Hispanics (39 percent) in the country.[12]

In South Texas and along the United States-Mexico border area, the continued rise in land and home prices has historically exceeded increases in income. The proximity to Mexico long ensured a flow of new immigrants. Thus, the obstacles associated with a person's more recent arrival into the United States—language barriers, residency status, lack of credit, and distrust of financial institutions—remain common in South Texas and more pronounced in rural areas and unincorporated areas known as *colonias*.[13] *Colonia* residents are more likely to own their plot of land and build their home as their finances allow over time. However, they are also more likely to lack standard mortgage financing and to live in substandard housing without adequate water and sewage systems. *Colonia* residents are therefore more vulnerable to environmental health hazards and other bad consequences of poor living conditions.

Nonetheless, for the last half century the rates of Latino homeowner-ship have been high in the following cities and their surroundings: 55 percent in San Antonio; 67 percent in El Paso, Laredo, and parts of San Antonio; 62 percent in Brownsville, Harlingen, San Benito, and Corpus Christi; and as high as 70 percent in McAllen, Edinburg, and Mercedes.[14] Overall, while there is a relatively high rate of Hispanic homeownership in these cities with majority Hispanic populations, lagging economic conditions remain formidable barriers to the attainment of greater Latino homeownership growth and economic prosperity.

The major metropolitan cities of Dallas, Fort Worth, Austin, and Houston have long attracted newcomers, including immigrants from Mexico and Central America, in search of better jobs and living conditions. In particular, Latinos have been flocking to these areas in search of jobs in technology, health, services, and construction sectors. Since 2000, the Latino homeownership rate in these cities has more closely aligned with the national Hispanic homeownership rate of more than 46 percent: 46 percent in Austin, 48 percent in Dallas, and 50 percent in Houston.[15]

Several nonprofit housing organizations have led efforts to increase homeownership in Texas through initiatives that include rehabilitation of existing homes, "sweat equity projects" that reduce construction costs, and utilizing multiple sources of funding from local, state, and federal government agencies. One program in Dallas, Texas, has specifically targeted Latino construction workers in helping them become owners of the homes they themselves helped build.[16]

Latino Homeownership Gains in the United States

As a result of the considerable growth in homeownership, Hispanics continue to play a key role in driving U.S. homeownership gains in recent years. In spite of the housing crisis and a persistent shortage of affordable housing, this trend has largely continued since the start of the twenty-first century. Even with declines in the total number of Hispanic homeowners during the Great Recession—from the last quarter of 2007 to the last quarter of 2010—there was a net gain of three million homes purchased by Hispanics from 2001 thru 2017.[17] Hispanics purchased homes even more rapidly during the first quarter of 2018, with a net first-quarter gain of 258,000 Latino homeowners. The Hispanic rate of homeownership increased from 46.6 percent in the fourth quarter of 2017 to 48.4 percent in the first quarter of 2018.[18]

These numbers support projections by researchers at Harvard University, the Urban Institute, and the National Association of Hispanic Real Estate Professionals, which report that Hispanics will account for more than half of all new homeowners from 2018 through 2028. Importantly, these Latino homeownership gains have not all occurred in isolated or rare instances; these gains have been mostly consistent since 2000.

Prior to 2000, the rate of Hispanic homeownership had dropped substantially from a high of 44 percent in 1975, when the Census Bureau began tabulating these figures, to 39 percent in 1991. From the end of the George H. Bush Administration, when Latino homeownership was at 40 percent, the Hispanic homeownership rate increased to 46 percent by the end of the Clinton Administration.

Similarly, in the aftermath of the housing crisis, during the tenure of U.S. Housing and Urban Development (HUD) Secretary Julián Castro (a native of San Antonio, Texas), the Latino homeownership rate reached 46 percent in 2017. As of the first quarter of 2018, the Census Bureau reports that nearly half of Latinos households (48 percent) had achieved homeownership (see Figure 1).[19]

Since 2000, the continued rise in the number of Hispanic homeowners has been crucial to U.S. homeownership growth. The number of Latino homeowners increased from 4,242,000 in 2000 to 7,424,000 in 2017—a total increase of 3,230,000 Hispanic homeowners. In contrast, the number of non-Hispanic white homeowners increased by only 525,000 homeowners, from 56,868,00 in 2000 to 57,393,000 in 2017, accounting for just 8 percent of net U.S. homeownership growth during those years.[20]

Homeownership gains by Latinos are not isolated events; they follow a consistent pattern. Education, jobs, income, and entrepreneurial gains lead

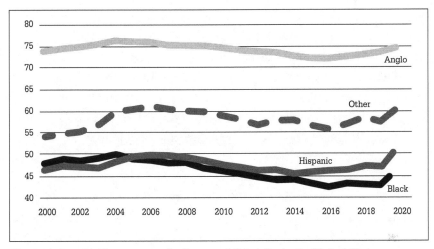

Figure 1. Percent Homeowners by Race and Ethnicity in the United States: 2000–2020. *Note:* "Other" includes Asian and other racial groups. *Source:* Current Population Surveys, U.S. Census Bureau.

directly to homeownership gains. The attainment of homeownership accelerates the accumulation of real estate assets, which enables homeowners to start a business, provide a college education for their children, and "leave something behind" to help future generations become homeowners.

Even with the tremendous growth of Hispanic homeowners in the housing market, the disparities remain large among racial/ethnic groups, as shown in Figure 1. While three in four Anglos (73 percent) owned homes, half of Hispanics (48 percent) and 43 percent African Americans were homeowners in 2019. Other racial groups—comprised mostly of Asian Americans—were in between. This is not surprising since the same persistent patterns of inequality by race are found in regard to economic resources in an earlier chapter of this book by Rogelio Sáenz.

Hispanic Demographic Trends

At 58.9 million, Hispanics currently account for more of the country's population growth than any other demographic. Hispanics are projected to lead U.S. household growth, adding six million additional Hispanic households by 2024. Importantly, 30 percent of Hispanics are millennials, an age cohort that is just entering prime home-buying years. Since 2000, Hispanics have also accounted for more than six of every ten new workers (62 percent) added to the U.S. economy. As of the end of April 2018, the labor force participation of Hispanics (66 percent) exceeded the overall national rate (63 percent). In April 2018 alone, there was an increase of 360,000 employed Hispanics, further demonstrating the key role they play in the nation's employment growth.

Hispanics comprised the only major population group from 2014 to 2017 to show a reduction in poverty, as well as substantive income gains. As further evidence of the economic strength of Hispanics, the gross domestic product (GDP) produced by Latinos in the United States in 2015 was estimated to be $2.1 trillion, the seventh largest GDP worldwide—larger than the GDP of Brazil, Canada, Italy, or India.[21]

A History of Housing Discrimination

Near the end of the first decade of the twenty-first century, millions of Latinos lost their homes due to rampant discriminatory and predatory lending practices. Low-income Latinos were targeted, along with other low-income and elderly populations, and were lured into costly and faulty mortgage loans, which often included nontransparent higher interest rates and excessive fees. Long before then, ample documentation already existed that showed how Latinos have individually and systematically experienced housing discrimination.

As early as 1979, HUD had conducted a study in Dallas that showed that dark-skinned Mexican Americans had a 96 percent chance of experiencing at least one instance of discrimination. The study found they were more than twice as likely to experience discrimination than African Americans or lighter skinned Mexican Americans. They were also less likely to receive favorable lease terms and conditions.[22]

In 1982, HUD funded a study in Denver that used non-Hispanic white and Latino auditors to test incidences of housing discrimination in the sales market. The study reported that non-Hispanic whites and Hispanics received significantly different information from real estate agents. When asking about homes available in a given community, 60 percent of Hispanic auditors were told there was nothing available, while only 31 percent of non-Hispanic white auditors were so informed.[23]

Non-Hispanic auditors were offered much more information than Hispanic auditors in their searches for homes. In 1986, a HUD study in Phoenix reported that in 13 percent of the cases reviewed, Latinos were charged higher rents than Anglos, and Anglos were offered more rental inducements. In 1989, HUD sponsored a much larger national fair housing study conducted by the Urban Institute. The survey was conducted in forty metropolitan areas, and reported a 56 percent discrimination rate for Hispanic homebuyers and a 50 percent discrimination rate for Hispanic renters.[24]

Other studies were conducted in Fresno County, California, in 1995, and in San Antonio, Texas, in 1997. The studies found a 77 percent rate of discrimination against Hispanic renters seeking housing in predominantly non-Hispanic white neighborhoods in Fresno County, and a 52 percent of rate of discrimination against Hispanics seeking housing in Anglo neighborhoods in San Antonio.[25]

In 2006, HUD conducted an analysis of first mortgages in the conventional market and found evidence of discrimination. HUD reported that Hispanics were given lower estimates of how much they could afford to pay for a house, less information on the various mortgage products available, and less positive coaching. HUD specifically found that "even when controlling for differentials in available household, loan, and property characteristics," Hispanics (particularly non-white Hispanics) were given significantly higher interest rates than comparable non-Hispanic white households.[26]

Until that time, an easy opportunity to earn higher levels of profits had often led some lenders or brokers to exploit vulnerable Latino home buyers by charging them higher interest rates and excessive fees. For example, some subprime lenders had during the years leading to the housing crisis chosen not to evaluate a borrower's credit at all, but rather to categorize the borrower as a higher risk borrower in order to charge higher fees.

Some subprime brokers and bank officers did not inform Latino borrowers that providing income and job verification would considerably
lower the cost of their loans. The net result of these predatory and often
discriminatory mortgage loan practices was that large numbers of minority
borrowers, including Mexican Americans, wound up paying unnecessarily
more for these costly and highly flawed loans, which placed them at greater
risk of losing their homes. The HUD study concluded that a better understanding of how credit markets can adversely affect particular consumers
was essential to designing policies that promote equal access to owner-occupied housing.[27]

The Courts Step In

Until 2015, the Fair Housing Act requirement to address residential segregation was given low priority. As a result of such neglect, many communities
became adept at accessing federal funds and diverting these funds away
from serious efforts to integrate America's communities. In 2015, however,
the U.S. Supreme Court ruled in a five-to-four decision that those making
discriminatory claims under the Fair Housing Act in court do not have to
prove that the decisions affecting them were made with intentional bias.

The case *Texas Department of Housing v. Inclusive Communities* broadens
the interpretation of the Fair Housing Act to allow for "disparate impact"
claims. At issue in this case were state tax subsidies granted to build low-income housing developments. The Dallas-based nonprofit Inclusive Communities Project sought to place low-income Texans in affordable housing
within the city's more affluent non-Hispanic white suburbs. The organization reported that the program's subsidy plan supported new affordable
housing in already low-income and racially segregated neighborhoods.[28]

In 2015, the office of HUD Secretary Julián Castro prepared regulations
to enforce a long-dormant but important provision directing local communities to act affirmatively to reduce or eliminate segregation. Had these Affirmatively Furthering Fair Housing (AFFH) regulations been implemented
by President Donald Trump's administration, they would have begun to

counteract the negative effects of local government regulations, including land use restrictions that have long enabled predominantly affluent, non-Hispanic white communities to create their own residential enclaves.

Regulations that have sought to control residential density, establish minimum lot sizes, and enforce zoning limitations have continued to perpetuate segregation by class, race, and ethnicity across the country. Rather than taking advantage of the forward momentum brought about by the 2015 U.S. Supreme Court ruling that the Fair Housing Act prohibited policies that negatively affect protected minority groups (even without an explicit statutory intent to do so), the Trump Administration postponed until 2020 the fulfillment of this requirement.[29]

The requirement established by the Supreme Court ruling, which upheld the application of "disparate impact" under the Fair Housing Act, is that local jurisdictions complete assessments that demonstrate active steps to undo racial segregation and promote fair housing in their communities.

The National Fair Housing Alliance, the state of New York, and two nonprofit Texas groups, Texas Appleseed and the Texas Low Income Housing Information Service in 2018 filed a lawsuit against HUD and its new secretary, Ben Carson, to compel the agency to implement the Supreme Court's ruling in the Fair Housing Act case.[30]

In joining the lawsuit, New York Governor Andrew Cuomo, who served as HUD secretary from 1997 to 2001 under President Clinton, said that the Trump Administration's delay in enforcing the AFFH rule demonstrated an abdication of its responsibility.

Governor Cuomo also asserted that New York could not allow the federal government to undo decades of progress in housing rights. According to Governor Cuomo's office, by delaying the implementation of the Obama's Administration AFFH rule, HUD was effectively quitting "its obligation to provide civil rights oversight for as much as $5.5 billion per year in the funding that is distributed over forty jurisdictions in New York and almost 1,000 jurisdictions across the country."[31]

The Outlook for Latinos and Fair Housing

The ability of Hispanic citizens to exercise their civil rights in every aspect of American life is critical to the economic growth and prosperity of the country. The history of discrimination in housing is replete with findings that support segregation. A 2016 study in Orange County, California, for example, reported that non-Hispanic white respondents felt that an increase in the Hispanic population posed a cultural threat to the "American way of life." Even though Asian Americans had experienced similar population growth, non-Hispanic whites who were interviewed were more positive about Asian Americans, deeming them to be more competent and desirable neighbors, greater contributors economically, and culturally superior. They said they felt generally more comfortable interacting with Asian Americans.[32]

Such views only serve to perpetuate heavily segregated communities, thereby further limiting the possibilities and opportunities of Latinos to improve their living conditions, achieve upward mobility, and gain equal integration into American mainstream life. The net result of segregation in America's communities has meant that a racial hierarchy persists, even if not deliberately planned, with many Latinos at the bottom ranks, subsisting within ethnic enclaves that lack quality amenities, including proximity to good schools and jobs.

Consequently, many Latino households are now only able to find affordable housing within well-established areas or in neighborhoods with older and often substandard housing in the inner cities or close to freeways and other less attractive areas. The concentration of Latinos in such communities across the country has helped lead to increasingly segregated communities.

The positive side is that in such enclaves, Latinos often develop a common bond and community cohesiveness and become over time an invaluable source of social and economic support for each other and for newcomers. George J. Borjas, a public policy professor at Harvard University, who analyzed 1980-2000 Census Bureau data for a National Bureau of Economic Research report, found a statistically significant positive relationship between the probability of homeownership and the relative size of an ethnic enclave in a metropolitan area. His study, "Homeownership in the Immigration Population," found that the growth of ethnic enclaves in major American cities has played an important part in increasing immigrant demand for owner-occupied housing in many metropolitan areas.[33]

Borjas's findings help explain why more Hispanic immigrants move to areas with growing Hispanic populations in search of better jobs, improved housing opportunities, and amenities such as ethnic food stores and restaurants. According to Borjas, the housing markets and mortgage finance systems finally become more accessible as institutions recognize and adjust to meet the needs of the growing market. Borjas suggests that the "warm embrace" of such enclaves helps immigrants escape the discrimination that they might otherwise encounter in the labor and housing markets outside the enclave. On the other hand, in high-cost cities such as Los Angeles and Miami, geographic clustering can have adverse economic effects.

According to Borjas, an ethnic enclave can create incentives for immigrants not to acquire the skills that might be useful in the larger national market, reducing income (and home-buying demand) of families living in the enclaves. Studies by HUD also report that such enclaves can reinforce attachments to substandard neighborhoods and might also decrease the residents' motivation for integration and mobility. In some parts of the country, the flight of non-Hispanic white residents from these increasingly isolated ethnic enclaves, or "barrios," further lessens the capacity of Latinos to attain higher levels of education, obtain better jobs, achieve upward economic mobility, and become homeowners.[34]

Another study, "From Homeland to a Home: Immigrants and Homeownership in Urban America," by Demetrios Papademetriou, found that cities like Los Angeles and Miami, which continue to have large ethnic enclaves, also continue to experience higher housing costs.[35] As more Latinos move into these cities to take advantage of job opportunities or proximity to family members and friends, their population growth creates heightened competition in the job market and higher housing costs. This combination of scarce jobs and costlier housing makes it increasingly difficult for Latino low- and moderate-income families to find affordable homes, even in some otherwise inviting ethnic enclaves.

A study by the Congressional Hispanic Caucus Institute similarly found that the growth of the Hispanic population in rapidly growing cities in the South and Midwest has been followed by the presence of larger numbers of bilingual, culturally sensitive housing professionals. These housing professionals often provide prospective Hispanic homebuyers with more information and assistance to buy a home.[36]

Over time, the growth and migration patterns of Latino households have contributed substantially to the housing boom in the suburbs, averting a decline in urban housing markets and have helped stabilize housing markets in many declining small towns and rural areas.[37] Whether Latinos and other major population groups stay within their own communities, either by choice or necessity, or they opt to move into other geographic areas in search of better jobs and housing opportunities, fair and equitable housing opportunities are essential within any geographic location. Communities receiving federal funds must foster full integration, rather than embrace policies that encourage segregation.

The Road Ahead

Housing discrimination and predatory loan practices have not deterred Latinos from attaining steady gains in homeownership. Today, there are three million more Latino homeowners than at the beginning of the twenty-first century. Nonetheless, millions of Latinos live in substandard rental housing, often paying half or more of their monthly income for rent. Consciously or not, redlining remains a reality as long as major lenders shy away from more assertive marketing and outreach efforts to increase mortgage lending to Hispanics.

Today, Latinos still have to contend with other obstacles to achieving the American dream of homeownership. In addition to persistent discrimination in housing, Hispanic and non-Hispanic millennials in 2018 were each saddled with an average \$23,000 in debt, excluding mortgages, according to a September 2018 study by the research arm of the online loan marketing company LendingTree.[38] Millennials in San Antonio, Texas, a city with a 63 percent Hispanic population, topped larger cities like New York and Los Angeles to rank highest in average per-person debt at \$27,122. One of the study's researchers said that while the cost of living is lower in cities like San Antonio, so are the wages, for an age group traditionally considered a strong first-time homebuyer population.

More than 90 percent of U.S. metropolitan areas in 2018 have experienced a decline in segregation in the past three decades. However, while large metropolitan areas like Houston and Atlanta are now home to an increasing number of Latinos, and have undergone rapid demographic changes, cities like Chicago and Detroit continue to have large areas dominated by a single racial group.[39]

Over the past thirty years, suburbs have increasingly become the most racially and ethnically diverse areas in the country. They include communities that can provide safe and decent rental housing, and affordable homeownership opportunities for Latinos. For example, the metropolitan Washington, DC, area experienced a Hispanic population increase of nearly 300 percent from 1990 to 2016.[40] Similarly, Washington, DC, suburbs such as Silver Spring, Maryland, have also experienced significant increases in Hispanic residents. In San Antonio, Texas, where some inner-city neighborhood populations are 95-plus percent Hispanic, the upscale master-planned community of Stone Oak bordering the city's north side has become an increasingly integrated suburb. In 2016 Hispanics comprised one-third of the Stone Oak community of 31,000 people.[41]

In 1968, the year President Johnson signed into law the Fair Housing Act, Luis and Olivia Chávez of Edcouch, Texas, testified about appalling housing conditions during that year's U.S. Commission on Civil Rights hearing in San Antonio. The family of eleven shared a small two-bedroom house. Four boys slept in one small bedroom, and five girls and their parents slept in the other bedroom. Still, Luis Chávez testified, many of his neighbors in their unincorporated neighborhood, a *colonia*, lived in worse conditions.

Luis Chávez told the civil rights commissioners that "maybe eight or nine houses out of a hundred" had the potable water, bathroom facilities, and gas for cooking that were available in the Chávez home.[42]

Decades later, an estimated 30 percent of more than 800,000 Hispanic *colonia* residents lacked access to safe drinking water, according to a 2015 report by the nonprofit Rural Community Assistance Partnership. Some *colonias* still lack sewage systems. While *colonias* exist in five Southwestern states, an estimated 90 percent of residents of the country's *colonias* are in Texas, a state that has never provided enough funds to meet their most basic needs for adequate housing.[43]

While discrimination remains a challenge, so does the disparity in quality of housing. The median home price in the San Antonio suburb of Stone Oak was approaching $300,000 in 2018, while a house 230 miles south of San Antonio in a *colonia* is worth nothing to a prospective home buyer who refuses to forego basic water and sewage service.[44]

Recommendations

As long as active steps are not taken to undo segregation and prevent future housing discrimination, as prescribed by the Fair Housing Act, the integration of America's communities remains an elusive goal. As a result, unequal and unfair housing opportunities will continue to hamper Mexican Americans and others from living and working in thriving communities with decent, affordable housing.

Closing the door to integration and fair homeownership opportunities for the largest ethnic population in the United States will severely weaken the economy and hamper the economic progress and prosperity of all Americans.

The Fair Housing Act specifies that U.S. "executive departments and agencies shall administer their programs and activities relating to housing and urban development . . . in a manner affirmatively to further "fair housing opportunities." Carrying out this mandate ensures that the Fair

Housing Act lives up to its original intent of opening up fair and equitable housing options and neighborhoods to all Americans who until now have been denied access.

To open the doors of America to integration, and extend fair and equal housing opportunities effectively across the country, we recommend the following government actions:

- The U.S. Department of Housing and Urban Development (HUD) should seek to eliminate the recurrence of inequalities in access to affordable rental housing and mortgage credit in high-opportunity neighborhoods with good jobs and schools through its programs and in the private market.
- In 2015 the Obama Administration issued regulations under the Fair Housing Act that require local jurisdictions to complete assessments that demonstrate active steps to undo racial segregation and promote fair housing in their respective communities. HUD suspended these requirements through a series of steps during the Trump administration. HUD should restore these obligations in order to determine how well local jurisdictions are acting affirmatively to reduce or eliminate segregation within their entire communities.
- The federal government should increase the supply of new rental housing, including new rental vouchers, to effectively address the renter cost burden faced by disadvantaged low- and moderate-income households, especially those headed by minorities, persons with disabilities, and women.
- Rental housing assistance should be increased at all levels of government.
- Texas should use the state's authority over the allocation of low-income housing tax credits to expand the supply of affordable rental housing in high-opportunity neighborhoods, particularly for families with children, and require that units be marketed to historically underserved groups.

There is also a role for government to work with private entities in expanding access to affordable housing for Latinos:

- The leadership and executive management of top mortgage lending and real estate institutions—as well as other housing industry entities engaged in the provision of rental and homeownership options and opportunities—should support increased diversity and inclusion. These institutions should take the lead at the state, local, and national level in providing greater education and information about the current state of residential segregation and the lasting effects of racial discrimination and economic disparities.
- Lenders should support and implement the use of alternative credit scoring models to expand access to mortgage lending for creditworthy minority households and others with limited credit histories. Alternative credit scoring models should incorporate additional data and payment history, including data that would help support the credit scoring for practically "credit-invisible" households with "thin" credit files.

Expanding access to affordable rental housing and to viable homeownership opportunities and promoting racial and economic integration are increasingly being recognized not only as vital Fair Housing Act goals, but also as important local, regional, and national economic development strategies. According to the National Association of Realtors, U.S. regions that have the highest economic integration—where neighborhoods with higher income and lower income households were able to live side by side—were economically stronger and recovered better from the Great Recession than regions with segregated neighborhoods.

Accordingly, a national effort led by HUD must fairly and equitably seek to increase the availability of decent, safe, and secure rental housing, as well as homeownership opportunities, to historically underserved groups. HUD must make meaningful investments to improve all neighborhoods, and successfully connect all prospective underserved homebuyers with housing options in areas that have access to high-quality amenities and services.

Notes

1. Charles Lane, "The Ghettoization of Black Americans Hasn't Been Reversed," *The Washington Post*, April 9, 2018.
2. Lane, "The Ghettoization."
3. Lane, "The Ghettoization."
4. Equal Rights Center and National Council of La Raza, "Puertas Cerradas: Housing Barriers for Hispanics" (report, 2013 NCLR Annual Conference, New Orleans, LA, July 20-23, 2013), available online from EqualRightsCenter.org.
5. Equal Rights Center and National Council of La Raza, "Puertas Cerradas."
6. Joint Center for Housing Studies of Harvard University (JCHS), *America's Rental Housing: Evolving Markets and Needs* (Cambridge, MA: President and Fellows of Harvard College, 2013).
7. JCHS, *America's Rental Housing*.
8. Mortgage Bankers Association, "Housing Demand: Demographics and the Numbers Behind the Coming Multi-Million Increase in Households," July 2015, available online from National Council of State Housing Agencies.
9. U.S. Census Bureau, Current Population Survey/Housing Vacancy Survey, April 26, 2018, available online at census.gov.
10. Alejandro Becerra, "The 2011 State of Hispanic Homeownership Report," National Association of Hispanic Real Estate Professionals, March 2012, available online at nahrep.org.
11. Equal Rights Center and National Council of La Raza, "Puertas Cerradas."
12. Alejandro Becerra and Ron Jauregui, *An Assessment of Hispanic Homeownership: Trends and Opportunities* (Washington, DC: Congressional Hispanic Caucus Institute, 2005).
13. Becerra and Jauregui, *An Assessment*.
14. Becerra and Jauregui, *An Assessment*.
15. Becerra and Jauregui, *An Assessment*.
16. Becerra and Jauregui, *An Assessment*.
17. Marisa Calderon et al., "2017 State of Hispanic Homeownership Report," Hispanic Wealth Project, National Association of Hispanic Real Estate Professionals, February 2018.
18. U.S. Census Bureau, Current Population Survey/Housing.
19. U.S. Census Bureau, CPS/HVS 2018.
20. U.S. Census Bureau, Current Population Surveys.
21. Dan Hamilton and David Hayes-Bautista, *U.S. Latino GDP Report: Quantifying the New American Economy,* Latino Donor Collaborative, September 2019, available at LDC website.
22. Raul Yzaguirre et al.. "The Fair Housing Act: A Latino Perspective," *Cityscape* 4, no. 3 (1999): 161-170.
23. Yzaguirre et al., "The Fair Housing Act."
24. Yzaguirre et al., "The Fair Housing Act."
25. Yzaguirre et al., "The Fair Housing Act."
26. Abt Associates, Inc., *Summary of HUD Research Series Examining Barriers to Hispanic Homeownership and Efforts to Address These Barriers* (Washington, DC: U.S. Department of Housing and Urban Development, 2006).
27. Abt Associates, *Barriers to Hispanic Homeownership*.
28. Texas Department of Housing and Community Affairs v. Inclusive Communities Project, 576 U.S. __ (2015).

29. Kriston Capps, "The Trump Administration Just Derailed a Key Obama Rule on Housing Segregation," CityLab Newsletter, January 4, 2018

30. Bill Chappell, "Carson and HUD Are Sued Over Delaying Anti-Segregation Rule, National Public Radio, May 8, 2018.

31. Ben Lane, "New York Suing HUD, Ben Carson to Enforce Obama Fair Housing Rule," Housing Wire website, May 14, 2018.

32. Celia Lacayo, "Latinos Need to Stay in Their Place: Differential Segregation in a Multi-Ethnic Suburb," *MDPI Journals: Societies* 6, no. 3 (April 2016).

33. George J. Borjas, "Homeownership in the Immigrant Population" (NBER Working Paper No. w8945, Harvard University, 2002), available at ssrn.com; Alejandro Becerra, *Hispanic Homeownership: The Key to America's Housing and Economic Renewal* (Washington, DC: Barclay Bryan Press, 2009).

34. Borjas, "Homeownership"; Becerra, *Hispanic Homeownership*.

35. Borjas, "Homeownership"; Becerra, *Hispanic Homeownership*.

36. Becerra and Jauregui, *An Assessment*.

37. Aaron Williams and Armand Emamdjomeh, "America Is More Diverse Than Ever—But Still Segregated," *The Washington Post*, May 6, 2018.

38. Megan Leonhardt, "This Is the U.S. City Where Millennials Carry the Highest Debt," CNBC, September 10, 2018, LendingTree.com.

39. Williams and Emamdjomeh, "America Is More Diverse."

40. Williams and Emamdjomeh, "America Is More Diverse."

41. Scott Beyer, "Mexican Nationals Are Transforming San Antonio," *Forbes*, June 17, 2016.

42. U.S. Commission on Civil Rights, *Hearing before the United States Commission on Civil Rights: San Antonio, TX, December 9–14, 1968* (Washington, DC: GPO, 1969), 50. Also available at https://catalog.hathitrust.org/Record/001874430.

43. María Esquinca and Andera Jaramillo, "Colonias on the Border Struggle with Decades-Old Water Issues," *The Texas Tribune*, August 22, 2017.

44. Zillow.com, "Stone Oak (Housing) Market Overview: 2009-2019."

ERNEST J. GERLACH

Employment and Economic Security Challenges for Mexican Americans in Texas

When the U.S. Commission on Civil Rights (USCCR) convened a major hearing in San Antonio in 1968 to examine the civil rights concerns of Mexican Americans in Texas and the Southwest, it set the stage for additional initiatives over the next fifty years that changed the civil rights landscape and the role of Mexican Americans in the civil rights movement that followed.[1]

A decade later, the Texas Advisory Committee to the USCCR conducted a follow-up study to determine the state of civil rights in Texas, and to evaluate the changes that had taken place since 1968.[2] The committee found that the status of Mexican Americans in Texas, already suffering the terrible effects of discrimination in employment and economic security in 1968, had not shown much improvement in ten years.[3]

Despite a new era of civil rights activism demanding equity for Mexican Americans, Texas's political leadership was determined then, and is still determined today, to ignore the future consequences of failing to address the challenges facing the state's youngest, most rapidly growing minority population. Today, Mexican Americans in Texas continue to suffer lower pay, worse job conditions, and less economic security, with too many still barred from the pathways to prosperity and leadership.

Defining the Challenges

At the 1968 Civil Rights Commission hearing, newly appointed Commissioner Dr. Héctor García said at the outset that the bipartisan, independent arm of government would be "concerned primarily with the issues of education, employment, economic security, and the administration of justice as they affect Mexican Americans in Arizona, California, Colorado, New Mexico, and Texas."[4] The hearing would explore all "major barriers" to education, employment and economic stability.[5] The goal was, he said, to "point the way to remedial action at the local, state and federal levels for the benefit, the tranquility, the security, and progress of all people, so that the government may truly be a government of the people, for the people, but most importantly, by all the people."[6]

In moving forward with this task, we need to be careful in how we evaluate and interpret terms like "equal employment opportunity" and "economic security." Both are critically important for all Americans, and especially for minorities and women. These terms also establish a range of basic parameters through which we can define just how successful we are in achieving equality under law. Equal employment opportunity, for example, covers a broad range of ideas and rights centered on access to jobs and employment. According to the U.S. Equal Employment Opportunity Commission (EEOC), equal employment opportunity ensures equal access to all jobs without regard to race, ethnicity, gender, disability status, religion, pregnancy status, national origin, and age.[7] It applies to both public- and private-sector employment, state and local governmental units, education institutions, and the federal government.[8] Several key laws provide the legal basis for equal employment opportunity. They include Title VII of the Civil Rights Act of 1964,[9] the Americans With Disabilities Act of 1990,[10] the Age Discrimination in Employment Act of 1967,[11] and the Equal Pay Act of 1963.[12]

To measure equal results of equal employment opportunities over the past fifty years in Texas, the approach applied in this chapter is to examine the extent to which racial and ethnic groups are represented in different job categories at different points in time in proportion to their representation in the employment-age population. Admittedly, this approach does not take into account the qualifications of the individual employees, such as education and other personal qualities. That deeper analysis of the changes in racial disparities is applied in the chapter by Mora and Dávila, which uses a multivariate approach, analyzing individual census records to separate out the effects of education and other characteristics.

The Commission Hearing: 1968

Witnesses at the 1968 Commission hearing cited the 1960 U.S. Census Bureau reports to describe a population of nearly 3.5 million Spanish-surnamed persons living in the five southwestern states, making up nearly 12 percent of the region's population.[13] Of the 1.4 million who lived in Texas, comprising about 15 percent of the state's population, most lived in counties adjacent to the Texas–Mexico border.[14] In all five states, nearly 80 percent lived in urban areas.[15] Mexican Americans represented largely a young population, when compared to the other population groups. In Texas, the median age of the state's Spanish-surnamed population, based on the 1960 Census, was eighteen years, compared to twenty-seven years for non-Hispanic whites, or Anglos, and twenty-four years for African Americans.[16]

The average educational attainment level of the Spanish-surname population was only 6.2 years, compared to 10.7 years for Anglos, and 8.7 years for African Americans.[17] In Texas, 79 percent of the Spanish-surnamed population did not complete the twelfth grade.[18] Texas ranked forty-second among the fifty states in the percentage of all young people who graduated from high school.[19] Contributing to that dismal ranking were high noncompletion rates among Mexican Americans and African Americans.[20] The median personal income for Mexican Americans was only $1,536, or 57 percent of the non-Hispanic white median.[21]

With respect to employment, Mexican Americans in Texas and the other states in the Southwest during the 1960s were largely relegated to low-wage industrial and agricultural jobs.[22] The Texas Council on Migrant Labor in 1965 estimated that there were 167,000 migrant farmworkers in the state, and 95 percent were Mexican American.[23] Mexican Americans were well represented in the public sector, but they were usually concentrated in lower paying positions. At the time of the 1960 Census, 8 percent of the male Mexican American population fourteen years of age and older in Texas was unemployed, compared to only 3 percent of the non-Hispanic whites.[24]

Federal enforcement of equal employment opportunity rules was often lax. To counter this, some federal officials sought to reach out to public- and private-sector employers, encouraging them to comply with equal employment provisions in hiring, but not always successfully. "We have found during the past year and a half (1967–1968) that large numbers of banks are anxious to improve their hiring of minorities, but they often did not know how to recruit them," Assistant U.S. Treasury Secretary Robert A. Wallace testified.[25]

Ten Years Later: 1978

In 1978, the Texas Advisory Committee to the U.S. Commission on Civil Rights conducted a survey of employment in public and private sector businesses, and local governments in the state as part of a follow-up to the 1968 hearing. Among their findings were the following:

- Minority workers in Texas were still relegated to low-paying positions.
- Education decisions at all levels were almost exclusively in the hands of Anglo males.
- Anglo males held 90 to 100 percent of elected positions at all levels.
- Minority groups were underrepresented in law enforcement and judiciary positions.
- The pervasiveness of this pattern from 1968 to 1978 meant that acceptable progress had not been made in providing equal opportunity for all Texans.[26]

With regard to overall employment patterns in local and state government in Texas, the Texas Advisory Committee concluded that Anglo men were overrepresented in state government and higher paying jobs; the same was true for municipal-level government jobs.[27] Those results were the same in San Antonio and Bexar County (San Antonio is the county seat).[28] Moreover, women continued to be underrepresented in the federal-sector workforce, and they were earning less than their male counterparts.[29]

Mexican Americans in the U.S. Workforce Today

In July 2015, the U.S. Equal Employment Opportunity Commission (EEOC) issued a report entitled "American Experiences Versus American Expectations," describing significant changes that had occurred in America's workforce from 1966 to 2013.[30] The report's focus was on the participation of minority and nonminority workers reported in surveys that were required of private employers with one hundred or more workers and all federal employers.

Figure 1 shows the percent of Hispanics by job category in the U.S. private-sector workforce from 1966 to 2013.[31] It is a graphic presentation of the rapid growth of Hispanics in the U.S. labor force.

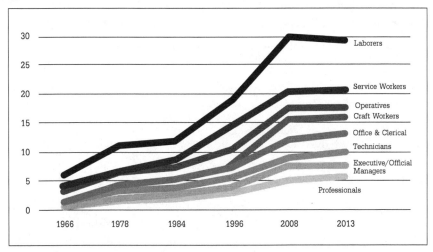

Figure 1. Percent Hispanic by Job Category, 1966–2013 U.S. Workforce. *Source:* Equal Employment Opportunity Commission, American Experience Versus American Expectations, July 2015.

The EEO-1 survey data show that Hispanics in the "laborers" category experienced the largest increase of any race/ethnic group—from 6 percent in 1966 to 29 percent of the total workforce in 2013. The smallest overall change for Hispanics during that same time frame was in the "professional" category, where their proportion increased from less than 1 percent in 1966 to 6 percent in 2013.[32] These changes reflect the tremendous growth of Hispanics relative to other racial/ethnic groups in the population. They also reflect a pattern of being concentrated in lower paying and less skilled jobs.

In 2019, Hispanics made up about 17 percent of the total workforce in the United States. The majority of Hispanics in the U.S. workforce were Mexican Americans (61 percent). In a report released by the Bureau of Labor Statistics (BLS), the overall unemployment rate for the United States was 3.9 percent in October of 2019. The Hispanic unemployment rate was 4.7 percent, slightly higher than the 3.7 percent non-Hispanic white unemployment rate. The unemployment rate for African Americans was almost twice that of whites, at 6.5 percent.[33] However, Hispanics were participating in the labor force in greater proportion to their numbers in the working-age population. The employment/population ratio—the percent of working-age population in the labor force—for Hispanics in the United States was 63 percent; for non-Hispanic whites, it was 61 percent; and for African Americans it was 58 percent. Among adult men (age twenty years and over), eight in ten Hispanic males were participating in the labor force, more than any other racial/ethnic group, albeit in low-paying positions.[34]

Texas Population Changes: 1960–2018

The rapid growth of Hispanics in the Texas workforce can be understood by their just as dramatic increase in the population over the past fifty years. As shown in Figure 1 of the chapter by Sáenz in this book, they contributed to more than half of the growth of the total population in the state, increasing from 1.8 million (16 percent of the population) to 11.4 million (40 percent of the population). Hispanics were also a younger population that was to contribute an even greater share than any other racial/ethnic groups to the workforce. In 2018, their median age was twenty-eight years, compared to forty-two years for the Anglo population.

The Texas Private Workforce

Participation in selected occupations varies by race and ethnicity in the state's private sector. As in the country as a whole, Mexican Americans in Texas and throughout the Southwest tended to cluster in the lower paying, less skilled jobs. That was still true in 2018, when the U.S. EEOC reports indicated that these patterns continue to exist (see Figure 2).[35]

The Hispanic proportion of the 2018 private workforce in Texas was 32 percent, lower than the Hispanic proportion in the population of working age (39 percent). This may, in part, reflect the lower participation rate of

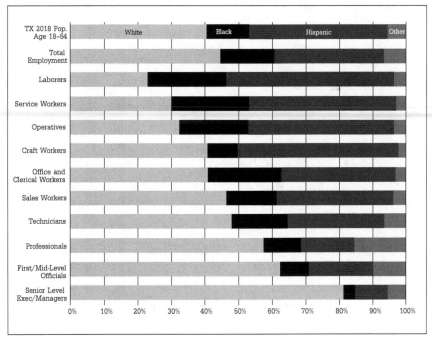

Figure 2. Texas Private Employment by Job Category and Race/Ethnicity: 2018. *Source:* Equal Employment Opportunity Commission, Employer Information Report (EEO-1), 2018. *Other includes Asian Americans, American Indians, Hawaiians, and "two or more races."

Hispanic women in employment (as shown in a previous chapter of this book by Sáenz, Figure 14). Racial disparities by occupational level are also apparent. Hispanics are found in higher concentrations in the unskilled and skilled craft occupations and in lower proportions in the professional, executive, and managerial jobs.

Underlying these patterns are several obstacles confronting minorities and women in Texas, and elsewhere, as they seek parity in the workforce. Certainly, there are differences in occupational status due to educational qualifications. There are also obstacles centered mainly on conscious or unconscious biases, stereotypes, and perceptions on the part of employers as they relate to Mexican Americans, African Americans, and other minorities in the workforce.

The Federal Workforce

The federal sector is especially important because it has often been seen as a gateway for minorities and women to enable them to move ahead in their careers. Opportunities for employment and advancement, especially during and after World War II, were also greater for minorities and women in the federal sector, or at least they seemed to be. Unfortunately, this was not always the reality.

For example, at the 1968 USCCR hearing, employment patterns at Kelly Air Force Base in San Antonio were questioned. The concentrations of Mexican Americans, African Americans, and other minorities in certain job categories, occupations, and grade levels were also discussed at length during the hearing. Similar disparities were found at the U.S. Postal Service and at other federal agencies in Texas as well.[36] The "Ten Years Later" report from the Texas Advisory Committee found "severe examples of unequal pay and opportunity for Mexican Americans and African Americans" in the federal workforce in Texas.[37] For example, while the median annual salary for federal agencies with twenty-five or more employees in Texas in 1977 was $17,000, for Hispanics it was $14,000. The Texas Advisory

Committee also reported that large disparities in median income levels occurred in every federal agency except one: the U.S. Postal Service.[38] The report added:

> Virtually all of the major federal agencies in Texas show extreme levels of underrepresentation and underutilization of minority and female employees. This pattern is most pronounced for minority females, who are virtually absent in the higher-grade levels and have median incomes that are about one-half of Anglo males.[39]

In Texas, the federal government employed 114,166 civilian employees (excluding U.S. Postal Service and military/noncivilian employees). Nearly 26 percent, or about 24,558, were classified as Hispanics. In FY 2015, according to the Office of Personnel Management (OPM), New Mexico and Texas had the highest percentages of Hispanics in the permanent federal civilian workforce, closely followed by Arizona, California, and Florida. Colorado ranked sixth.

Noting the persistent low representation of Hispanics in the federal workforce, the OPM and the U.S. Equal Employment Opportunity Commission agreed to a recommendation made by the Hispanic Council on Federal Employment to require federal agencies with at least one thousand full-time-equivalent employees to conduct a barrier analysis on Hispanic employment. They also committed to continue working on Hispanic recruitment, hiring, retention, and advancement, consistent with the merit system.[40]

Although the Hispanic population in Texas has grown substantially since 2000, Hispanic employment rates in the federal workforce nationally and in Texas have increased only marginally. For example, in Texas, the federal government employed 197,800 workers in 2016. Of that number, 114,166 were civilian employees. Only 26 percent were identified as Hispanic. African Americans made up about 8 percent of the total.

State Government Workforce

The underemployment of Mexican Americans in state and local government jobs in Texas was a topic at the 1968 USCCR hearing in San Antonio, and in the Texas Advisory Committee report in 1978. Testimony at the 1968 hearing indicated that Mexican Americans were underrepresented in state government. Those who were employed were largely confined to lower skilled occupations and lower paying jobs.

In 1977, state government workers in Texas totaled 86,573. Of these, about 74 percent were non-Hispanic whites, about 14 percent were Mexican Americans, and about 12 percent were African Americans. Non-Hispanic whites also were paid higher state government salaries. While about 22 percent of Mexican American males and 56 of percent of Mexican American females earned less than $8,000 annually, only about 10 percent of

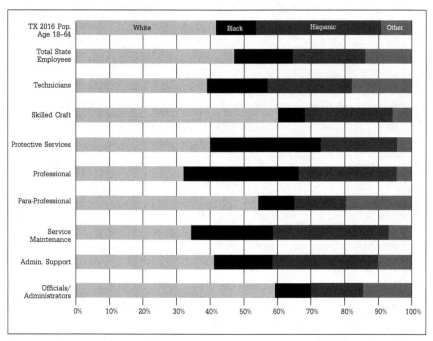

Figure 3. Texas State Government, Employees by Race/Ethnicity/Occupation, 2016. *Source:* Minority Hiring Practices Report, Fiscal Years 2015–2016. Texas Workforce Commission. Austin, Texas, 2017, Table A. *Other includes Asian Americans, American Indians, Hawaiians, and "two or more races."

non-Hispanic white state male employees and 37 percent of all non-Hispanic white female employees were paid less than $8,000 a year.[41]

In 2016, the state of Texas employed 383,921 employees in various job categories, pay systems, and agencies—three times the size of the 1977 state government workforce. Of this total, 186,828, or 49 percent, were Anglos; 68,098, or 18 percent, were African Americans; and, 83,723, or 22 percent, were Hispanics (see Figure 3).[42]

In 2016 Hispanics were found to be underrepresented among state employees (22 percent), almost half of what would be expected from their proportion in the working-age population (38 percent). They were more poorly represented in the state government workforce than they were in the private sector. Hispanics were most underrepresented among state officials/administrators (15 percent) and among professionals (16 percent).

Local Government Employees in Texas

Local government in Texas includes county and municipal government. In its 1978 report, the Texas Advisory Committee noted that a significant number of Texas counties had few, if any, incorporated cities. As a result, county government often served as the primary public deliverer of services. Also, in many parts of the state, especially in the more rural areas, county governments were also major employers.[43] This was true in 1968 and 1977, and remains true today. Even in those counties with major urban areas and municipalities, county government is an important player in providing a wide array of services to local citizens.

In its 1977 report, the Texas Advisory Committee utilized a federal EEOC survey of county government employment. Males comprised about 51 percent and females made up about 49 percent of the employees. Of the county employees, 70 percent were Anglos, 19 percent were Mexican Americans, and 11 percent were African Americans.[44]

The overall county employment distribution at that time was roughly equivalent to the composition of the state's population: 68 percent Anglo, 18 percent Hispanic, and 12 percent African American. The Advisory

Committee pointed out, however, that while the data "appears to show that minority-group members and women have equality of opportunity in county government employment . . . the data masks the fact that women and minorities were disproportionately found in jobs with lower salaries and minimum authority."[45]

In 2013 the EEOC analyzed employment patterns in local governments in Texas. The EEOC surveyed 412 units of governments in the state, focusing on municipal and county governments. These units yielded an overall sample of 60,867 employees classified by job category, and by race/ethnicity. Of this total, 57 percent were non-Hispanic white, 23 percent were Hispanic, and 15 percent were African American. Asian Americans and other race/ ethnicity categories totaled less than 5 percent of the total.[46]

The Texas population in 2013, based on the 2010 U.S. Census, was 45 percent non-Hispanic white, 38 percent Hispanic, and 12 percent African American. While Anglos continued to make up most of the local government workforce in Texas, Mexican Americans tended to be underrepresented in every job category. While African Americans exceeded their overall representation in each of the categories, the exception was the higher paying official/administrators category, where they made up only about 6 percent of those in that category in the sample group. This finding generally reflects previous findings confirming that minorities in local governments in Texas tend to be employed in lower paying positions.[47]

San Antonio: A Case Study on Equal Employment

During the 1968 hearing the city of San Antonio received special attention, not only because it was the site for the U.S. Civil Rights Commission hearing, but also because it was the tenth largest city in the country, and the third largest city in Texas. In addition, it was already a unique city with a strong Mexican cultural tradition, and it was considered to be a triracial city. San Antonio's population in 1968 (588,000) was about 51 percent Anglo, 41 percent Mexican American, and 8 percent African American. Over the years Mexican Americans were a growing segment of the city's population.

In 1900, for example, they made up about 26 percent of the population in San Antonio. By 1940, their share of the population increased to around 40 percent, according to a prehearing report by USCCR staff members.[48]

During the the decade following World War II, the percent Hispanic of the San Antonio population did not increase at all. This was due to the fact that the city began in 1940 to rapidly expand its incorporated area to neighborhoods that were largely inhabited by non-Hispanic white families. The study also noted that the Mexican American population in San Antonio at the time of the hearing was largely confined to

> an area bounded by the original city limits . . . The heaviest concentration of Mexican Americans is in an area of very low income in the west central part of the city extending in a wide band west from the San Antonio River nearly to the city limits and including most of the Edgewood residential area of the city. Culebra Avenue and Kelly Air Force Base serve roughly as perimeters on the north and south, respectively. There is also an intense degree of residential segregation. In 1960, nearly one-third of all the Mexican Americans lived in nine census tracts 90 percent or more Mexican Americans; . . . one-half of the Mexican Americans population lived in 18 census tracts that were 75 percent or more Mexican American.[49]

In 1978, the Texas Advisory Committee to the U.S. Commission on Civil Rights conducted a study of San Antonio's public and private employment sectors as part of a larger study to determine what progress, if any, had been made since the 1968 hearing. The advisory committee reported that while Mexican Americans and African Americans accounted for a large portion of the population in San Antonio in 1978, minorities were still largely concentrated in certain parts of the city. The pattern had changed little since 1968. Most of the new jobs, meanwhile, since 1968 had been developed outside the central city.[50]

MUNICIPAL GOVERNMENT EMPLOYMENT IN SAN ANTONIO

During the 1968 USCCR hearing in San Antonio, Walter McAllister, then the city's mayor, was among the witnesses to testify in support of expanding equal employment opportunities at a time of severe disparities. In its 1978

report, the Texas Advisory Committee to the commission, citing employment statistics from the city's EEO-4 report submitted to the U.S. Equal Employment Opportunity Commission, described a city government workforce
of 5,469 workers in 1973. Of that total, 52 percent were Mexican Americans,
40 percent were Anglos, and 8 percent were African Americans. However, 67
percent of Anglos held top administrative jobs in city government, compared
to 28 percent of Mexican Americans and 4 percent of African Americans.

By comparison, Mexican Americans held 83 percent of all low-paying city government service maintenance jobs.[51] "While the number and
proportion of minorities has increased since 1968, they continue to be
concentrated mainly in the lower paying, less skilled jobs," the advisory
committee reported.

In May 2014, the *San Antonio Express-News* reported a decline in diversity
in city government employment, stating that while San Antonio is "overwhelmingly minority, Anglos hold a majority of the senior positions at City
Hall, and the percentage of Hispanics in those jobs has dropped in the past
five years, San Antonio's payroll records indicate."[52]

While Hispanics filled 42 percent of the top City Hall workforce positions in 2008, that had dropped to 37 percent by 2013. Anglo employees
comprised 32 percent of a city government workforce of nearly 9,700 people
in 2013, but they accounted for slightly more than half of the best-paid positions. Men outnumbered women in those top positions by a ratio of seven
to three, the newspaper reported. The city government's total workforce
was more than 60 percent Hispanic in 2013, in a city that was 63 percent
Hispanic in 2012.

In 2017, the City of San Antonio employed 10,819 workers. Minorities
comprised about 70 percent of the city's total workforce, while Anglos made
up 30 percent (see Figure 4). This figure reflected an overall increase in the
city's minority workforce since 2013. Mexican Americans made up 61 percent of the workforce employed by the city, while African Americans made
up about 6 percent.[53] The overall composition of the city's workforce in 2017
represented well the demographic profile of the city's population.[54] Clearly,
considerable progress had been made toward greater equity in four decades.

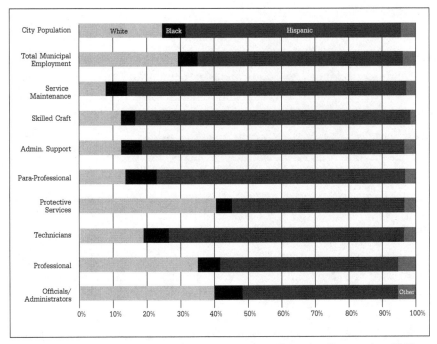

Figure 4. San Antonio Municipal Employees by Race/Ethnicity/Occupation: 2017. *Source:* City of San Antonio, EEO-4 Report, September 2017.*Other includes Asian Americans, American Indians, Hawaiians, and "two or more races."

Still, on the higher occupation levels, there was room for improvement. Although Anglos made up about 30 percent of the city's workforce in 2017, they occupied 40 percent of the city's "officials and administrators," nearly 36 percent of the city's professional staff, and more than 41 percent of its "protective service" personnel. While minorities made up a little more than 70 percent of the city's workforce, they comprised about 60 percent of its officials and administrators, slightly over 64 percent of the city's professional staff, and almost half of its protective service personnel. Minorities matched or exceeded their proportion in the city's workforce in technical, paraprofessional, administrative support, skilled craft, and service/maintenance job categories. Women also made some progress, occupying nearly 48 percent of all "officials and administrators" positions and more than half the city's professional jobs in 2017.[55]

SAN ANTONIO PUBLIC UTILITIES

In 1973 the San Antonio Water Board employed 670 persons. Of that total, 40 percent were Anglos, 8 percent were African Americans, and 52 percent were Mexican Americans. Only about 15 percent of the employees were women. Anglos were mainly concentrated in managerial and technical job categories. Almost half of all the minorities employed with the Water Board were working as laborers. The other major utility company, City Public Service, employed 2,803 persons in 1973. Of this total, 63 percent were Anglos, 2 percent were African American, and 36 percent were Mexican American. Anglos in 1978 still held more than 50 percent of higher paying jobs at both utilities.[56]

Since the 1968 hearing, city utility systems have changed, as they have across the country. In 1992, the San Antonio Water System (SAWS) was created to replace what had been several agencies: the city water board, city wastewater department, and the Alamo Water Conservation and Reuse District. In 2011, SAWS also took over another water provider, Bexar Met, to become the primary public provider of water services to residents and

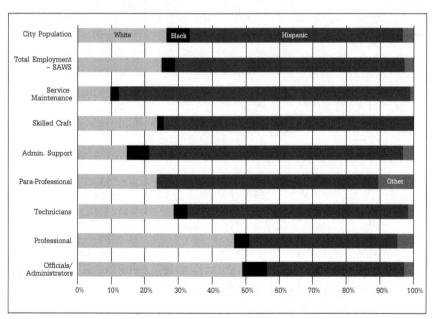

Figure 5. San Antonio Water System Employees by Race/Ethnicity/Occupation: 2017. *Source:* City of San Antonio, EEO-4 Report, September 2017. *Other includes Asian Americans, American Indians, Hawaiians, and "two or more races."

businesses in San Antonio, Bexar County, and surrounding areas. City Public Services (CPS) has also expanded its facilities and service area. Today CPS is the primary energy distributor for more than one million residential and commercial customers in Bexar County, and portions of neighboring Atascosa, Bandera, Comal, Guadalupe, Kendall, Medina, and Wilson counties. CPS employed 3,743 workers in 2018.

The progress made more recently in minority hiring in San Antonio can be seen in the city's water system. In 2017, SAWS employed 1,722 workers, more than three out of four of them minority-group members. The SAWS workforce was 69 percent Mexican American, 24 percent non-Hispanic white, and 4 percent African American and 2 percent other population groups. Although non-Hispanic whites made up less than one-fourth of the total workforce at SAWS in 2017, they occupied nearly 48 percent of all highest salary official/administrator positions. Minorities comprised about half of these positions (see Figure 5).[57]

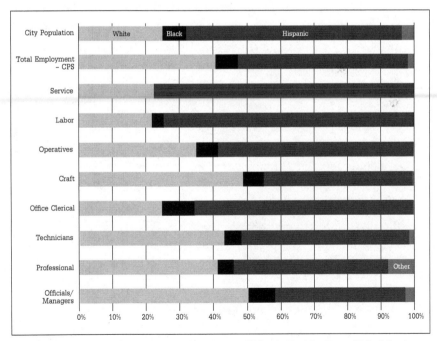

Figure 6. San Antonio City Public Service Board Employees by Race/Ethnicity/ Occupation: 2018. Source: City Public Service Board, Human Resources Department, May 2018. *Other includes Asian Americans, American Indians, Hawaiians, and "two or more races."

The progress in minority hiring could also be seen in City Public Service employment, although not near as great as SAWS. In 2018, San Antonio's City Public Services employed some 3,163 workers. Of this total, 51 percent were Hispanics, 41 percent were non-Hispanic whites, and about 7 percent were African Americans. Slightly more than half of the official/manager jobs at CPS were filled by non-Hispanic whites in 2018.[58] At the same time minorities made up well over half of the workforce at CPS in the service, labor, operative, craft, office/clerical, technician and professional occupational categories (see Figure 6). Much like the pattern found in the analysis of the SAWS workforce, Anglos were twice as likely to occupy positions of officials and managers as one would expect from their proportion of the working-age population.

BEXAR COUNTY GOVERNMENT EMPLOYMENT

In 1973, around 1,200 persons were employed by Bexar County. At that time, the county government's workforce was almost evenly divided between Anglos and minorities. By 1978, minority employment had increased to 58 percent of county government employees. However, Anglos accounted for 83 percent of the higher paying official/administrator positions.[59]

Four decades later, Bexar County government employment had been transformed to accomodate growth in the minority populaltion. In 2017, the county employed around 3,300 personnel. Minorities comprised about 78 percent of the county government's workforce, but 68 percent of the working-age population. Of the total county workforce in 2017, minority groups were even over-represented: 65 percent were Hispanic, and 7 percent were African American. Minorities also comprised 52 percent of the higher paying officials/administrators' jobs, somewhat less than their representation in the working-age population (see Figure 7).[60]

Overall, minorities and women are employed in substantial numbers by Bexar County government. While women made up slightly over 45 percent of the county's work force, nearly half (47 percent) were employed in administrative support positions. Furthermore, they made up nearly 49 percent of the higher salary officials/administration jobs, about 64 percent of the professional staff, and almost 30 percent of technical personnel in

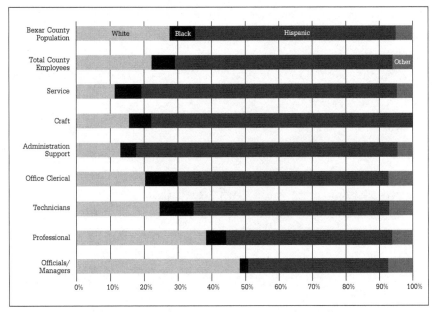

Figure 7. Bexar County Employees by Race/Ethnicity/Occupation: May 2017. *Source:* Bexar County Human Resource Department, EEO Utilization Report, Bexar County Government, May 15, 2017. *Other includes Asian Americans, American Indians, Hawaiians, and "two or more races."

county government. When compared to 1978 employment statistics, Bexar County government appears to have done a good job in employing minorities and women.

STATE EMPLOYMENT IN SAN ANTONIO

In 1968, of the 4,100 state government workers in San Antonio, 41 percent were identified as minorities. In 1978, minorities comprised about 51 percent of the state government workforce in San Antonio. The Texas State Advisory Committee in 1978 reported that while San Antonio's population was more than 50 percent Hispanic, several major state agencies had a much smaller representation of Hispanics in San Antonio, including the Texas Alcoholic Beverage Commission (10 percent), the Department of Public Safety (15 percent), and the Department of Highways and Transportation (26 percent).[61]

Since 1978, the employment of minorities and women in Texas state government has improved. The Texas Workforce Commission reported that

African Americans in state agencies were better represented in fiscal years 2015 and 2016. With respect to Mexican Americans, the Texas Workforce Board reported that they were well represented relative to their availability. However, they did not meet federal benchmarks in higher paying officials/administrators categories.[62]

FEDERAL EMPLOYMENT IN SAN ANTONIO

In 1977, the Texas Advisory Committee to the U.S. Civil Rights Commission reported that the federal government employed more than 34,111 workers in the San Antonio metropolitan area. Minorities made up about half of the federal workforce in San Antonio and women made up 28 percent of the total. These figures represented only a slight increase from the employment data that were presented at the 1968 hearing. At that time, it was reported that minorities comprised nearly 45 percent of the federal workforce in San Antonio.[63]

As of May 2017, there were about 29,000 federal government workers employed in more than 30 agencies in the San Antonio area. Of that number, 14,705—slightly over half—were identified as minority workers. Nearly 42 percent were women. Some of the larger federal agencies having civilian personnel in San Antonio were the U.S. Air Force (12,181), the U.S. Army (7,965), the Department of Defense (1,626), Homeland Security (1,013), Veterans Affairs (4,111), and the Department of Justice (555).[64]

Based on these statistics, Hispanics and other minorities working for the federal government in San Antonio, after almost fifty years, had made progress, but still had not reached parity with their overall population proportion in the city. Hispanics were especially underrepresented in higher paying federal government grade level positions.[65]

Economic Security Challenges for Mexican Americans in Texas

Economic security is multidimensional and multigenerational in terms of its effects and reach. It includes an individual's or family's income status, level of education, ability to access services, securing the kind of housing he or she desires, and more. It also includes the kind of job he or she wants. Measures of economic security are often associated with living standards and one's level of material well-being. Where a family lives is also directly and indirectly influenced by income. It is also, unfortunately, often influenced by one's race or ethnic background.

At the USCCR hearing in San Antonio in 1968, and in a follow-up report by a Texas Advisory Committee to the Commission in 1978, Mexican Americans were described as underemployed, underrepresented, and underutilized in employment and political representation. Despite some progress, minorities and women in Texas are still seeking equity and a standard of living that is compatible with the goals of all Texans and Americans.

DEFINING THE CHALLENGE

Economic security is predicated, in large measure, on having a stable income and other resources that are essential for supporting a particular standard of living in the present and for the foreseeable future. It also encompasses a basic-needs infrastructure that includes access to health services, education, housing, social protection, and employment security.

The Insight Center for Community Economic Development in 2013 described the underpinnings of economic security for working people in America.

> We are an aspirational, goal-oriented nation always striving to reach a next milestone: the better job, the higher wage, a dependable car, or manageable debt. Too often, however, families trying to get ahead just tread water. Single moms work three jobs, multiple generations live together under one roof, and freelancers with companies like TaskRabbit and Uber jump from job to job. They enjoy little breathing room to look ahead and can be squeezed out of opportunities to tap their full talent.[66]

The *New York Times* in 2011 defined the term "economic security" as "the amount of income necessary to cover basic expenses without resorting to public subsidies." The newspaper reported that nearly 45 percent of residents in the United States live without economic security. This means that they are not able to earn enough income to cover basic household expenses, plan for important life events, or save for emergencies."[67]

The *San Antonio Express-News* reported in 2017 that for Mexican Americans living in the terrible poverty of the Rio Grande Valley near the Texas-Mexico border, economic insecurity can be generational. In this region, residents are still paying the price of exclusionary policies and discrimination in the 1940s, 1950s, and 1960s. Today, their children do not have adequate access to quality education and health care services.[68]

If an individual or family unit has limited access to health care, quality education, and a job that pays a living wage, an individual or family will most likely have a poor quality of life, and their well-being will be compromised. Access, in short, shapes opportunities. The lack of economic security especially affects Mexican Americans in Texas. When access is limited by policies and actions that encourage discrimination and a lack of opportunity, governments must develop policies and strategies to address the underlying causes leading to these conditions.

LOW-STATUS JOBS

At the 1968 USCCR hearing in Texas, Mexican Americans were described as a population employed in "occupations of low economic status."[69] Since the hearing in 1968, Mexican Americans, African Americans, and other minorities moved into the workforce in greater numbers. Large numbers also moved into the public sector, seeking jobs at the federal, state, and local governmental levels. Despite this greater engagement in both the public and private sectors of the economy, Mexican Americans continued to be concentrated in lower paying, less prestigious occupations.

In Texas, Mexican Americans suffer lower pay and higher unemployment rates than their non-Hispanic white peers. They also tend to be more likely to be underemployed. In fact, many Mexican Americans hold down more than one job. Median weekly earnings for Mexican American workers are typically less than that of non-Hispanic white workers. The poverty rate for Mexican American households was 25 percent, compared to a 9 percent poverty rate for Anglo households.[70] The median household income for Mexican American families in 2014 was $41,200, compared to $65,800 for non-Hispanic white families. In general, the economic security status of many Mexican American families in Texas is, at best, tenuous.

ECONOMIC SEGREGATION

Economic segregation refers to the degree to which people of different social classes and income groups live among people of their own social, income, or economic level. The majority of families and individuals in Texas and the United States live in what we would call middle-income or mixed-income neighborhoods. However, over the past several decades, economic segregation in Texas communities has increased significantly. More people are living in census tracts, neighborhoods, and communities made up of households with individuals similar to themselves in terms of income, education, and/or occupation, according to the Pew Research Center Residential Income Segregation Index.[71]

This isolation has an effect on housing quality, access to jobs, and other factors that have a bearing on one's quality of life. If you are poor, you are more likely to live in a certain part of the community with other poor people. If you are middle class, or in a higher income bracket, you can afford to live in a better area with others in your income class. This is where economic segregation begins to take shape. Closely linked to this process of exclusion and inclusion is segregation based on race, national origin, and ethnicity. The existence of these economically segregated areas also contributes to a growing class divide in the United States. In many instances, this class divide is reinforced by race/ethnicity disparities in income, education, and employment.

In San Antonio, economic segregation is blatant, according to Christine Drennon, associate professor of sociology, an expert on urban geography and community development at Trinity University. Many San Antonio neighborhoods in San Antonio have either "entrenched poverty or entrenched wealth," she wrote in 2017. Economic segregation has existed for decades, exacerbated by restrictive covenants discouraging integration in higher income neighborhoods and unrestricted development in poorer neighborhoods.[72]

The most economically segregated areas in Texas are the unincorporated communities, called *colonias*, hugging the Texas–Mexico border.

These predominantly Mexican American communities consistently suffer the worst poverty rates in Texas and in the United States. A *Texas Tribune* report in 2017 stated that many lacked basic infrastructure such as potable water, sewage systems, electricity, and paved roads. Poverty rates exceed 40 percent.[73] The 2.5 million deeply impoverished farmworkers in the United States, including Texas farmworkers, as of 2012, were also economically segregated.[74] Most of these farmworkers are Mexican Americans.

LACK OF ACCESS TO HEALTH CARE

Access to health care is a key factor in determining a person's well-being and quality of life. It is also an important component in evaluating one's economic security. Equally important is the idea of equity in providing health services to all members of the community. The Robert Wood Johnson Foundation defines health equity as the condition underscoring the idea that "everyone has a fair and just opportunity to be healthier."[75] This is to be accomplished by removing obstacles or conditions to health "such as poverty, discrimination, and their consequences, including powerlessness and lack of access to good jobs with fair pay, quality education and housing, safe environments and health care."[76] Unfortunately, health equity and access to health care for all are yet to be achieved in Texas.

One indicator of access to health care is the ability of citizens to obtain medical and health care as needed. This is not the case in Texas. Several areas within the state have been designated as medically underserved areas (MUAs) and health professional shortage areas (HPSAs). The federal government reported that 85 percent of all Texas counties are MUAs and 95 percent of all Texas border communities are MUAs in whole or in part.[77]

The poor, in general, and minority groups in particular often suffer more from preventable diseases such as diabetes, hypertension, and heart disease. Passage of the Affordable Care Act would have extended the Medicaid program to poor people in Texas, but Texas was one of the states where leaders have chosen to not expand Medicaid and thus forego millions in federal funding each year, denying health care coverage to poor people.[78]

INCOME INEQUALITY

Income inequality has increased steadily in the United States and Texas over the past several decades, as those at the top have seen incomes rise while those at the bottom have experienced stagnant or declining income. In 2011, for example, the top 20 percent of all working families received about 10 times the total income received by the bottom 20 percent of working families. In other words, the richest 20 percent of all working families in the United States took home nearly half (48 percent) of all income, while those in the bottom 20 percent received less than 5 percent of the total income.[79]

In 2013, 42 percent of all working families in the United States had at least one minority parent, but 59 percent of all low-income working families had one or more minority parents. The high proportion of minorities who are in the low-income bracket is especially significant because of projected changes in the racial/ethnic composition of families in the United States.

The Center for Public Policy Priorities, a nonpartisan, nonprofit policy institute in Texas, released a report in 2017 describing the household income and poverty rate characteristics for Texas, based on the most recent American Community Survey results from the U.S. Census Bureau. Several key findings were released as well. The report found that the overall poverty rate for Texas in 2016 was 16 percent, higher than the national poverty rate of 13 percent. The poverty rate was 22 percent for Hispanics, 20 percent for African Americans, 9 percent for non-Hispanic whites, and 11 percent for Asian Americans. Child poverty disproportionately affects African American and Hispanic children in Texas. The poverty rates for Hispanic (31 percent) and African American (29 percent) children are roughly three times higher than the poverty rates for non-Hispanic whites (10 percent) and Asian American (10 percent) children.[80]

Policy Recommendations

While progress has been made over the past fifty years since the 1968 USCCR hearing in San Antonio, Mexican Americans, African Americans, other minorities, and women still face disparities with respect to equal employment opportunity and economic security in Texas, the Southwest, and the United States.

FEDERAL GOVERNMENT

- The U.S. Equal Employment Opportunity Commission (EEOC) and the Office of Personnel Management (OPM) should develop plans to enhance their Work Group activity to identify barriers to the training and advancement of Hispanics in the federal workforce.
- The Hispanic Work Group should develop a mentoring and leadership program for Hispanics from mid-level to advanced positions, including the Senior Executive Service (SES) in the federal government. In addition, a mentoring and training program should be aimed at providing opportunities for minority and female employees to move from the Wage Board (WB) grades to the General Schedule (GS) pay scale, especially for professional and managerial positions.
- Both the EEOC and the OPM should identify efforts to enforce Title VII of the 1964 Civil Rights Act (prohibiting discrimination in employment) at all levels in public and private employment.
- The U.S. Department of Labor should enhance reporting and antidiscrimination efforts under the Office of Federal Contract Compliance (OFCCP) for all federal contractors.
- The U.S. Department of Agriculture should join with the appropriate state agencies to examine the health, safety, and economic issues of the *colonias* that stretch along the Mexican border, from Brownsville to El Paso.

STATE GOVERNMENT

- The Texas Legislature and the Governor should create a joint task force (Senate and House of Representatives) to monitor the work of the Texas WorkForce Commission. The task force should be directed to develop a plan to identify barriers to the employment and advancement of

Hispanics, women, and other minorities in state and local governments in Texas. All current policies of recruitment and advancement should be evaluated. Mentoring, training, and recruitment programs for minorities and women should be developed and implemented.

- The Texas Legislature together with the Governor's Office should direct the joint task force to examine the barriers to economic security and proper health care for the state population with identification by race, ethnicity, and gender.

- The joint task force should examine economic insecurity and conditions of chronic and other health issues. Special attention should be paid to geographic areas such as south-central, west, and east Texas.

- The Texas Legislature and Governor's Office should immediately reverse its current policy and expand Medicaid coverage to all Texas residents, including the undocumented.

Notes

1. U.S. Commission on Civil Rights (USCCR), *Hearing before the United States Commission on Civil Rights: San Antonio, TX, December 9–14, 1968* (Washington, DC: GPO, 1969). Also available at https://catalog.hathitrust.org/Record/001874430.
2. Texas State Advisory Committee, U.S. Commission on Civil Rights, Texas, "The State of Civil Rights: Ten Years Later—1968-1978: A Report," 1980.
3. Texas State Advisory Committee, "The State of Civil Rights," 1.
4. USCCR, *Hearing*, 12.
5. USCCR, *Hearing*.
6. USCCR, *Hearing*, 13-14.
7. Equal Employment Opportunity Commission (EEOC), "EEOC Glossary for Small Businesses," available at EEOC website.
8. EEOC, "EEOC Glossary."
9. EEOC, "Title VII of the Civil Rights Act of 1964," EEOC website.
10. EEOC, "Americans With Disabilities Act of 1990," EEOC website.
11. EEOC, "Age Discrimination in Employment Act of 1967," EEOC website.
12. EEOC, "Equal Pay Act of 1967," EEOC website.
13. USCCR, "Testimony of Domingo N. Reyes," *Hearing before the United States Commission on Civil Rights*, 21, 22.
14. USCCR, *Hearing*, "Testimony of Domingo N. Reyes," 21, 22.
15. USCCR, *Hearing*, "Testimony of Domingo N. Reyes," 21, 22.
16. USCCR, *Hearing*, "Testimony of Domingo N. Reyes," 22.
17. USCCR, *Hearing*, "Testimony of Domingo N. Reyes," 22.

18. USCCR, *Hearing*, "Testimony of Domingo N. Reyes," 21, 22. This was more than twice the Anglo rate of 33 percent, and higher than the 60 percent rate for African Americans.

19. The Governor's Committee on Public School Education, "The Challenge and the Chance. Report of the Governor's Committee on Public Education," (Austin: USCCR, 1968), 780.

20. The Governor's Committee, "The Challenge and the Chance."

21. USCCR, *Hearing*, 792. The median for African Americans was even less, at $1,150, or 42 percent of the Anglo median.

22. USCCR, *Hearing*, "Testimony of Domingo N. Reyes," Reyes noted that in 1960, about 30 percent of the male Spanish-surnamed and African American population was classified as laborers, compared to 6 percent for Anglo males, while 24 percent of Spanish-surnamed employed males and 13 percent of African American employed males were working in technical, management, and craft-related occupations—compared to 45 percent for Anglo males in 1960.

23. USCCR, *Hearing*, 477. Summary of testimony presented in submission of exhibit, "Summary—Staff Background Paper on Economic Activities and Economic Development in 18 Counties of South Texas," provided by Moses Lukaczer, 477.

24. USCCR, *Hearing*, 477.

25. USCCR, *Hearing*, "Statement of Robert A. Wallace," 1068.

26. Texas State Advisory Committee, "The State of Civil Rights," 4.

27. Texas State Advisory Committee, "The State of Civil Rights," 16.

28. Texas State Advisory Committee, "The State of Civil Rights," 63.

29. Texas State Advisory Committee, "The State of Civil Rights," 65.

30. U.S. Equal Employment Opportunity Commission (EEOC), "American Experiences Versus American Expectations (1966-2013)," report, July 2015.

31. EEOC, "American Experiences," 4.

32. EEOC, "American Experiences," 4

33. U.S. Bureau of Labor Statistics (BLS), "Labor Force Characteristics by Race and Ethnicity, 2019," Report 1082, October 2019, 1.

34. BLS, "Labor Force Characteristics," Texas State Auditor's Office—Summary Report on Full Time Equivalent State Employees—Fiscal Year 2019/U.S. Census, 2018 ASEP Datasets—Annual Survey of Public Employment & Payroll.

35. Equal Employment Opportunity Commission, "Employer Information Reports: EEO-1 Single and Establishment Reports," 2018, EEOC website.

36. USCCR, *Hearing*.

37. Texas State Advisory Committee, "The State of Civil Rights."

38. Texas State Advisory Committee, "The State of Civil Rights," The median for males was $21,000, as opposed to around $12,000 for females. There were also differences in terms of racial/ethnic groups. For example, the median income for Mexican American employees was $14,000. For males, it was $16,000; for females, it was $11,000.

39. Texas State Advisory Committee, "The State of Civil Rights,"

40. Office of Personnel Management, "Annual Report: FY 2015."

41. Texas State Advisory Committee, "The State of Civil Rights," 10-11.

42. Texas Workforce Commission, "Equal Employment and Minority Hiring Practices Report, Fiscal Years 2015-2016: New Hires and Workforce Composition for State Agencies and Institutions of Higher Education," 2017.

43. Texas State Advisory Committee, "The State of Civil Rights," 14-16.

44. Texas State Advisory Committee, "The State of Civil Rights," 11.

45. Texas State Advisory Committee, "The State of Civil Rights," 13-14.

46. EEOC, "EEO Statistical File for Texas: 2013."

47. EEOC, "EEO Statistical File for Texas: 2013."

48. USCCR, *Hearing*, "Staff Report," 1968, 809.

49. USCCR, *Hearing*, "Staff Report," 1968, 809–810.

50. Texas State Advisory Committee, "The State of Civil Rights," 52.

51. Texas State Advisory Committee, "The State of Civil Rights,"

52. Nolan Hicks, "Diversity Declines in City Hall's Top Jobs," *San Antonio Express-News*, May 31, 2014. The newspaper studied workforce conditions to produce its findings.

53. City of San Antonio website.

54. Percentages of total city population by racial/ethnic group are used to compare with employment in the city, since age-specific data were not available at that level of geography.

55. City of San Antonio website.

56. Texas State Advisory Committee, "The State of Civil Rights."

57. San Antonio Water System, "Who We Are," online at SAWS website, https://www.saws.org/about-saws/who-we-are-sidebar-2/

58. City Public Services of San Antonio, Company Profile, 2018.

59. Texas State Advisory Committee, "The State of Civil Rights."

60. Bexar County, "Federal Equal Employment Opportunity (EEO) Utilization Report, Organization Information—Bexar County," May 15, 2017.

61. Texas State Advisory Committee, "The State of Civil Rights." With regard to African Americans, the committee concluded that they were underrepresented to a much greater degree in many state agencies having staff in San Antonio in 1978. The committee also pointed out that ten agencies having offices in San Antonio employed no African American personnel. These included the Attorney General's Office, Parks and Wildlife, and the Railroad Commission. Several other agencies had only a small number of African American employees at that time. These included the State Comptroller's Office (1 percent), the Department of Public Safety (1.3 percent), and the Department of Highways and Transportation (2.3 percent).

62. Texas Workforce Commission, "Equal Employment Opportunity and Minority Hiring Practices Report: Fiscal Years 2015-2016," 9–11.

63. Texas State Advisory Committee, "The State of Civil Rights," 61.

64. Office of Personnel Management, www.opm.gov.

65. Office of Personnel Management.

66. Annette Case, "Economic Security Initiatives," Insight Center for Community Economic Development, Oakland, California, 2013, 1.

67. Motoko Rich, "Economic Insecurity," *The New York Times*, November 22, 2011.

68. Aaron Nelson, "Valley Children's Plight, *San Antonio Express-News*, November 30, 2017, A3, A4.

69. USCCR, *Hearing*.

70. Joint Economic Committee, "Economic State of the Latino Community: Korbel Research, Selected Socio-Economic Data for the State of Texas," 2017.

71. Pew Research Center, "The Rise in Residential Segregation by Income," April 2, 2012.

72. Christine Drennon, "Explaining Economic Segregation: Is San Antonio Really the Most Economically Segregated City in the U.S.?," *San Antonio Express-News*, Opinion Section, December 24, 2017, F1, F6.

73. María Esquinea and Andrea Jaramillo, "Colonias on the Border Struggle with Decades-Old Water Issues," *The Texas Tribune*, August 22, 2017; Jordana Barton, Emily Ryder Perimeter, and Elizabeth Sobel, "Las Colonias in the 21st Century: Progress Along the Texas Border," Federal Reserve Bank of Dallas, April 2015.

74. U.S. Department of Labor, "National Agricultural Worker Survey," July 14, 2014.

75. P. Braveman et al., "What Is Health Equity? A Definition and Discussion Guide," Robert Wood Johnson Foundation, May 2017.

76. P. Braveman et al., "What Is Health Equity?"

77. Vincent R. Nathan, "Health Equity and Minority Health in Bexar County and the City of San Antonio," San Antonio Metropolitan Health District, April 25, 2017.

78. Rachel Garfield, Anthony Damico, and Kendal Orgera, "The Coverage Gap: Uninsured Poor Adults in States that Do Not Expand Medicaid," The Henry J. Kaiser Family Foundation, 2018, available at kff.org.

79. The Working Poor Families Project, Policy Brief, "Low Income Working Families: The Growing Economic Gap," Annie E. Casey, Ford, Joyce, and Kresge Foundations, 2012.

80. Center for Public Policy Priorities, "New Texas Household Income, Poverty Rate Census Numbers, 2017," available at EveryTexan.org.

MARIE T. MORA AND ALBERTO DÁVILA

Achieving Economic Security for Texas Mexican Americans

As the previous chapters in this volume have demonstrated, while Mexican Americans in Texas have made considerable progress with respect to certain economic, social, and political outcomes since the U.S. Commission on Civil Rights (USCCR) presided over a six-day hearing in the U.S. Southwest half a century ago in San Antonio, Texas, this group continues to lag behind non-Hispanic whites in many regards. Given the fact that Mexican Americans now account for a significantly larger share of the state's (and country's) population than in the past—particularly among the youth—and given population projections, their socioeconomic and political outcomes have greater implications for the future prosperity of Texas and the nation overall than in the past.

In light of these issues, in this chapter we compare key economic security outcomes over time between native-born Mexican Americans and non-Hispanic whites in Texas, including employment, earnings, poverty rates, and the likelihood of being in the top 10 percent of the income distribution.[1] Part of our discussion considers the role that education disparities among Mexican Americans have played with respect to disparities in economic security metrics. We focus on native-born adults because in most cases they would have acquired their education in U.S. schools, are fluent in the English language, and would have been exposed to U.S. institutions (e.g., schools, banks, workplaces, civic arenas, etc.) throughout their lives.[2] As such, unlike the case of foreign-born adults who migrate after completing their schooling, homeland disparities in civil rights, equity, and access to resources among native-born children and young adults can have lifelong consequences.

Education

Education plays a key and critical role in determining economic security outcomes given its impact on employment opportunities (hence labor-market earnings, retirement security, Social Security benefits, and others), the likelihood of residing below the poverty line, wealth and asset accumulation, and other outcomes. As Rogelio Sáenz points out in an earlier chapter in this volume, the relatively low education levels among Hispanics, including among native-born Hispanics, have limited this group's future socioeconomic outcomes. In our 2018 Economic Policy Institute (EPI) report, we showed that while on average Hispanics have increased their education levels during the past couple of decades, Hispanics have been unable to close the education gap with non-Hispanic whites.[3] Moreover, even when comparing Hispanic and non-Hispanic white workers with the same schooling levels, we showed in our EPI report that significant and persistent earnings gaps have remained over time.[4]

In the remainder of this chapter, given that Mexican Americans were the focus of the USCCR hearing in 1968, and given that Mexican Americans represent nearly nine out of ten Hispanics currently living in Texas, our analysis and discussion of economic security focus on native-born members of this Hispanic group. To visualize changes in their education disparities with native-born non-Hispanic whites in Texas during the past half century, Figure 1 presents the average years of schooling among adults of prime working ages (i.e., ages twenty-five to sixty-four) between 1970 and 2016 in the state.

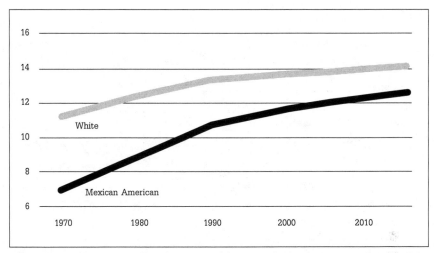

Figure 1. Average Years of Schooling among Native-Born Mexican Americans and Non-Hispanic Whites Twenty-Five to Sixty-Four Years of Age in Texas, 1970–2016.

Native-born Mexican Americans in Texas have made considerable gains in acquiring schooling over time. In 1970, those between the ages of twenty-five and sixty-four had an average of 7.0 years of education, which was 1.7 years less than the 8.7 years of education acquired by native-born Mexican Americans in the United States overall (not shown) and 4.3 years less than the 14.3 years of education acquired by native-born non-Hispanic whites, in both Texas and the United States. By 2016, while these groups had higher average schooling levels than in 1970, the average educational attainment among native-born Mexican Americans in Texas had increased by the largest margin (80 percent), to 12.6 years, essentially reaching parity with their Mexican American counterparts at the national level (12.7 years). They also significantly narrowed their education gap with native-born non-Hispanic whites in Texas, although a substantial gap remained (of 1.5 years), as the latter group also acquired more schooling.

We know from a host of studies on labor-market outcomes that bachelor's degrees (and higher) have become particularly important over time with respect to employer demand and wage growth. In this regard, despite more than quintupling the share of college graduates among native-born Mexican American adults in Texas between 1970 and 2016 (from 3.1 percent

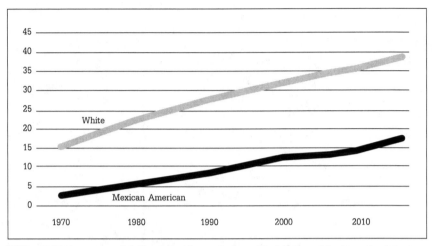

Figure 2. Percentage of College Graduates among Native-Born Mexican Americans and Non-Hispanic Whites Twenty-Five to Sixty-Four Years of Age in Texas, 1970–2016.

to 17.2 percent), this increase does not come close to the magnitude necessary to begin closing the gap with their non-Hispanic white counterparts (see Figure 2). The representation of college graduates among native-born non-Hispanic whites twenty-five to sixty-four years of age (38.7 percent in Texas) was more than twice their representation among native-born Mexican Americans in the state.

Employment, Labor Force Participation, and Unemployment Rates

Having access to jobs is a fundamental component of economic security, not only for today but also in the future, given the implications for asset and wealth accumulation, retirement, access to pensions and Social Security benefits, health care, and others. How have native-born Mexican Americans fared relative to non-Hispanic whites in Texas? We are mindful that the types of jobs people hold matter, but clearly having a job is the starting point in this regard.

Figure 3 presents the employment–population ratios of native-born Mexican Americans and non-Hispanic whites ages twenty-five to sixty-four

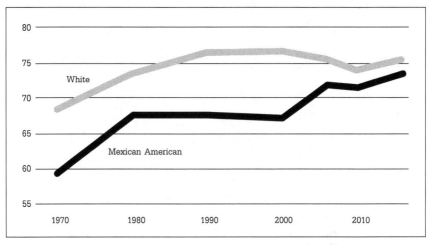

Figure 3. Employment-Population Percentages of Native-Born Mexican Americans and Non-Hispanic Whites Twenty-Five to Sixty-Four Years of Age in Texas, 1970–2016.

between 1970 and 2016 in Texas. This figure shows that since 1970, native-born Mexican Americans made considerable progress in narrowing the employment gaps with non-Hispanic whites in the state, although a gap still remains. In 1970, 59.4 percent of native-born Mexican Americans in Texas in this age range were employed, which was nearly nine percentage points below the comparable ratio of 68.3 percent among non-Hispanic whites in the state. This gap was larger than the national level of 6.2 percentage points (not shown) because, compared to their counterparts in Texas, the employment-population ratio was higher for native-born Mexican Americans (60.8 percent), but lower for non-Hispanic whites in the United States (67.0 percent).

By 2016, the employment-population ratio difference between Mexican Americans and non-Hispanic whites had narrowed considerably, to around two percentage points in Texas (73.4 percent versus 75.3 percent, respectively), with the sharpest gains made in the 1970s and after 2000 before the Great Recession. The narrowing of the Mexican American/non-Hispanic white employment gap in Texas during the past 50 years is a positive indicator of progress for economic security among Mexican Americans in Texas.

Part of the reason for this narrowing of the employment gap was the disproportionate increase in the labor force participation (LFP) rate among native-born Mexican Americans, particularly in Texas. In 1970, Mexican Americans in Texas of prime working ages had an LFP rate 8.3 percentage points below the LFP rate for non-Hispanic whites (61.5 percent versus 69.8 percent, as seen in Figure 4), and 2.5 percentage points below the one for native-born Mexican Americans at the national level (64.0 percent). However, by 2016 the LFP rate of Mexican Americans in Texas (77.2 percent) differed by one percentage point from non-Hispanic whites (78.2 percent), and by 0.7 percentage points from native-born Mexican Americans overall (77.9 percent). Similar to what we observed for the employment-population ratios, the greatest progress native-born Mexican Americans made in Texas, in terms of narrowing the LFP-rate gaps with non-Hispanic whites, occurred in the 1970s and the early part of the 2000s.

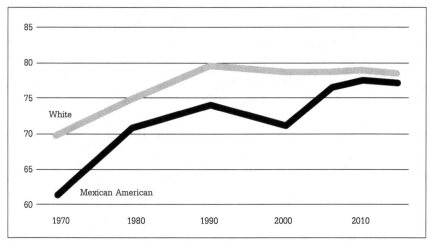

Figure 4. Labor Force Participation Rates of Native-Born Mexican Americans and Non-Hispanic Whites Twenty-Five to Sixty-Four Years of Age in Texas, 1970–2016.

UNEMPLOYMENT RATES

Additional progress, albeit less striking, made by native-born Mexican Americans vis-à-vis non-Hispanic whites in the Texas labor market is

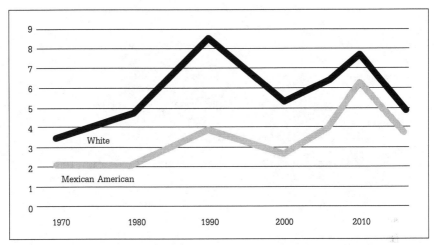

Figure 5. Unemployment Rates of Native-Born Mexican Americans and Non-Hispanic Whites Twenty-Five to Sixty-Four Years of Age in Texas, 1970–2016.

reflected in relative changes in unemployment rates, as seen in Figure 5. Unemployment rates were higher for both groups in Texas in 2016 than in 1970 (which relates to general labor-market and demographic trends outside the scope of this chapter, including the growing labor-force participation of women). It is also worth noting that unemployment rates increased by a smaller margin among native-born Mexican Americans (from 3.5 percent to 4.9 percent) than among non-Hispanic whites (2.1 percent to 3.7 percent) in the state. As such, the increase in the LFP rates among native-born Mexican Americans in Texas since 1970 did not disproportionately push up their unemployment rates. (It is generally expected that as more workers join the labor force, some first join the unemployed ranks as they begin to search for employment). The rising labor-force participation rate of Mexican Americans represents another sign of progress made by this group with respect to achieving economic security.

A CLOSER EXAMINATION OF THE EMPLOYMENT–POPULATION RATIO

Are the higher schooling levels driving the narrowing of the employment gap between native-born Mexican Americans and non-Hispanic whites in Texas over time? Consider the role that education plays in affecting the likelihood of being employed. For this purpose, we break down the

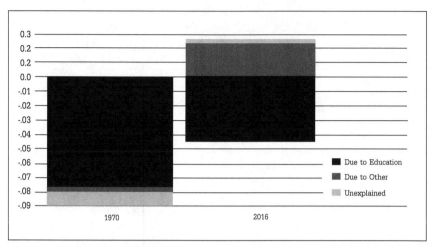

Figure 6. Breakdown of the Employment-Rate Gap between Native-Born Mexican Americans and Non-Hispanic Whites Twenty-Five to Sixty-Four Years of Age in Texas, 1970 and 2016.

Mexican American/non-Hispanic white employment-rate gap in Texas into three components: (1) the portion of the gap explained by differences in education; (2) the portion of the gap explained by differences in other demographic and socioeconomic characteristics, such as age, gender, and family structure (e.g., marital status, having children); and (3) the portion of the gap not explained by education and other observable characteristics.[5] As we move into this discussion, it is important to point out that a negative difference contributes to a wider gap between the groups (i.e., Mexican Americans lag behind whites in this regard), while a positive difference relates to a narrower gap.

Figure 6 presents these breakdowns for 1970 and 2016. Note that the sum of the three portions is the total employment-rate gap between native-born Mexican Americans and non-Hispanic whites.

In 1970, the employment/population ratio of native-born Mexican Americans in Texas was 8.9 percentage points below the one for non-Hispanic whites (59.4 percent versus 68.3 percent); hence, Figure 6 displays the total gap as -8.9 percentage points. Differences in education between the two groups accounted for the vast majority (-7.7 percentage points, shown in the diagonally striped portion) of this difference, while differences in other characteristics essentially played an inconsequential role (0.3 percentage points, shown in the solid black portion). It follows that the remaining unexplained difference in employment rates (shown in vertical stripes) was approximately one percentage point.

Given their average education levels and other demographic and socioeconomic characteristics, we would have expected the employment-population ratio of native-born Mexican Americans in Texas of prime working ages to have been about one percentage point higher if they encountered labor-market conditions similar to those of non-Hispanic whites. This "unexplained" percentage point may reflect employer discrimination against Mexican Americans, as well as differences in unobserved socioeconomic and demographic characteristics between the groups, such as lower schooling quality or lower geographic mobility (hence reduced access to jobs) among native-born Mexican Americans in the state.

Still, examining these breakdowns for 2016 reveals that the relative employment prospects of native-born Mexican Americans improved in Texas. Their employment-rate gap with non-Hispanic whites was 1.9 percentage points (73.4 percent versus 75.3 percent). However, based on education differences, this gap should have been larger, by an estimated 4.5 percentage points. Other demographic and socioeconomic characteristics worked to offset part of this effect (by 2.3 percentage points), resulting in a modest (and positive) unexplained employment-rate gap of 0.3 percentage points. To the extent that discrimination was behind the relatively low employment-population ratios of native-born Mexican Americans in Texas in 1970, this form of discrimination appears to have dissipated, at least in 2016.

Of course, this result should not be interpreted as a sign that discrimination against Mexican Americans has ceased to exist in Texas. We venture several alternative explanations for this result for future research endeavor. First, the quality of education for Mexican Americans might have risen during this time. Second, as Mexican American schooling levels rose, the substitutability between this group and Mexican immigrants fell, leading to more employment opportunities for the former group. The increasing economic development of the Texas-Mexico border region over this time period, and the relatively high concentration of Mexican Americans in that area, also likely helped their employment outcomes.

Moreover, discrimination takes on many forms beyond employment, including through the access to resources necessary to acquire human and financial capital. We cannot with our data explain why native-born Mexican Americans who tend to be products of the American educational system continue to acquire less schooling on average than their non-Hispanic white counterparts, especially at a time when education has become increasingly important with respect to labor-market opportunities and socioeconomic prosperity.

Labor-Market Earnings, Poverty, and Income Distributions

While native-born Mexican Americans in Texas (and the nation overall) have made progress during the past several decades in terms of securing work, employment represents one dimension of economic security. Earnings, benefits, having full-time as opposed to part-time positions, job stability, and many other dimensions exist. To fill in additional details, in this section we analyze three additional outcomes: labor-market earnings, the incidence of impoverishment, and position in the income distribution.

LABOR-MARKET EARNINGS

Figure 7 shows the natural logarithm of real (i.e., inflation-adjusted) annual earnings (in 2016 dollars) for native-born Mexican American and non-Hispanic white workers ages twenty-five to sixty-four in Texas between 1970 and 2016. We use the natural logarithm, given the skewed nature of earnings distributions that often masks important differences when comparing average earnings across groups. Comparing the end of the time frame with the beginning, both of these groups achieved considerable gains in their labor-market earnings when accounting for inflation, with their greatest gains made during the 1980s and 1990s (especially the latter). Despite a dip for both groups in the early part of the 2000s, they resumed growth at a pace greater than the national average since then (details available from

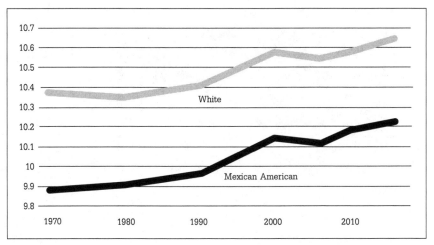

Figure 7. Natural Logarithm of Real Annual Earnings (in 2016 dollars) of Native-Born Mexican Americans and Non-Hispanic Whites Twenty-Five to Sixty-Four Years of Age in Texas, 1970–2016.

the authors). Of the years shown, both groups achieved their highest real earnings in 2016.

Comparing 2016 to 1970, the earnings growth of native-born Mexican Americans in Texas outpaced those of non-Hispanic whites at the national level (not shown). Despite this progress, they continued to earn significantly less than non-Hispanic whites. In 1970, native-born Mexican Americans earned 48.9 percent less ($19,459 versus $31,698, or 9.876 versus 10.364 in natural logs) than non-Hispanic whites in Texas.[6] By 2016, their earnings disparity had narrowed to 41.3 percent ($27,723 versus $41,898, or 10.230 versus 10.643 in natural logs) but remained sizeable at a time when their average educational attainment had been increasing. Moreover, a closer examination of Figure 7 indicates that a substantial amount of this earnings improvement vis-à-vis non-Hispanic whites in Texas occurred in the 1970s, and has been relatively stable since then.

As with employment, we break down the earnings gap between native-born Mexican Americans and non-Hispanic whites in Texas into three parts: (1) the part explained by education, (2) the part explained by other demographic and socioeconomic characteristics, and (3) the unexplained gap.[7] Figure 8 presents these breakdowns for 1970 and 2016. In 1970,

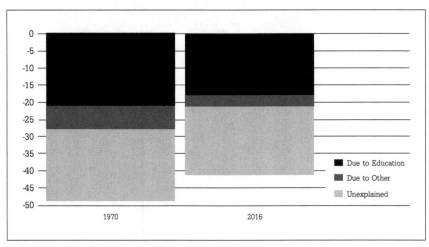

Figure 8. Breakdown of the Earnings Differentials between Native-Born Mexican Americans and Non-Hispanic Whites Twenty-Five to Sixty-Four Years of Age in Texas, 1970 and 2016.

education differences explained nearly half (21.5 percentage points, shown in the diagonally striped area) of the 48.9-percentage-point earnings gap between native-born Mexican Americans and non-Hispanic whites in the state, while other observable demographic and socioeconomic characteristics explained another 6.6 percentage points (in solid black). It follows that a substantial portion of the earnings disparity (20.7 percentage points, shown in the vertically striped area) between these groups was not explained by such characteristics. As with employment, this unexplained gap may reflect labor-market discrimination against Mexican Americans, as well as differences in other unobserved socioeconomic and demographic characteristics between the groups, such as the quality of education.

Unlike what we observed for employment, however, the unexplained earnings gap between native-born Mexican Americans and non-Hispanic whites in Texas differed little between 1970 and 2016, with the latter estimate being 19.9 percent. That is, nearly all of the narrowing of the Mexican American/non-Hispanic white earnings gap observed between 1970 and 2016 can be explained by relative improvements in the schooling levels and changes in other observable characteristics, rather than by a reduction in the unexplained wage gap. While it is important to note that other confounding effects could be explored in this analysis (such as the high concentration of Mexican Americans in low-cost-of-living areas such as the Texas-Mexico border), it follows that even when accounting for differences in education, age, the time spent working, and other characteristics, native-born Mexican Americans made approximately $0.20 less for each dollar earned on average by comparable non-Hispanic whites in Texas in 2016.

In previous work, we identified a "wide and relatively steady" earnings gap between Hispanics and non-Hispanic whites at the national level (see note 3). The results shown in Figure 8 suggest persistent earnings gaps between native-born members of these groups in Texas covering a longer time frame.

THE INCIDENCE OF POVERTY

In addition to labor-market earnings, a commonly used measure of economic insecurity is the incidence of poverty, a measure based on family income as opposed to individual earnings. We now compare the share of adults of prime working ages who were impoverished between native-born Mexican Americans and non-Hispanic whites in Texas in 1970 and 2016, as seen in Figure 9. Similar to the trends discussed in the chapter by Rogelio Sáenz, poverty rates have declined over time for Mexican Americans in Texas (and the nation), especially during the 1970s, but remain considerably higher than those of native-born non-Hispanic whites. In 1970, 30.7 percent of native-born Mexican Americans of prime working ages in Texas resided below the poverty line. This was 1.5 times higher than the national poverty rate (20.1 percent) among members of this group, and 4.5 times higher than the poverty rate among native-born non-Hispanic white adults in Texas (6.8 percent).

Still, poverty rates declined among Mexican Americans in Texas and, to a lesser degree, in the United States in general. The poverty rate for native-born Mexican American adults in Texas fell by more than half, to 13.1 percent by 2016, nearly reaching parity with the national average for members of this ethnic group. This relatively sharp decline, coupled with the increase of poverty among native-born non-Hispanic white adults,

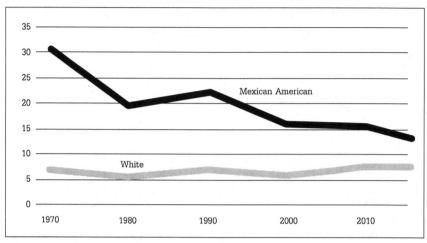

Figure 9. Percentage below Poverty of Native-Born Mexican Americans and Non-Hispanic Whites Twenty-Five to Sixty-Four Years of Age in Texas, 1970–2016.

substantially reduced the poverty-rate gap between these groups over time. Nonetheless, the incidence of poverty among native-born Mexican Americans in Texas remained nearly twice the rate of impoverishment among non-Hispanic whites (7.6 percent in 2016).

Increased educational attainment as well as changes in other socio-economic and demographic characteristics explain a considerable portion of the reduction in their poverty-rate gap with native-born non-Hispanic whites. Figure 10 shows the breakdowns in this gap in 1970 and 2016 attributed to differences in schooling, differences in other characteristics, and an unexplained component.[8] In 1970, education disparities accounted for 9.6 percentage points (the diagonally striped area in Figure 10) of the 23.9-percentage-point difference in poverty rates between native-born Mexican American and non-Hispanic white adults in Texas, and other characteristics (including being employed, age, family structure, etc.) accounted for another 5.1 percentage points (the solid area). This left a sizeable unexplained poverty-rate gap of 9.2 percentage points (the vertically striped area) that year, which may reflect discrimination against Mexican Americans, such as through reduced access to higher wage jobs, lower quality of education, and reduced access to other resources.

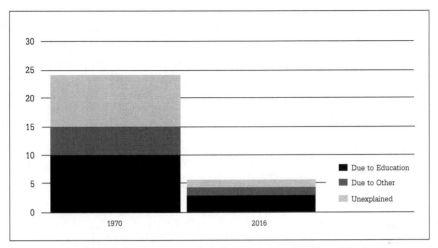

Figure 10. Breakdown of the Poverty-Rate Gap between U.S.-Born Mexican Americans and Non-Hispanic Whites (Ages Twenty-Five to Sixty-Four) in Texas, 1970 and 2016.

By 2016, as Figure 10 shows, poverty rates were 4.1 percentage points higher among native-born Mexican Americans than among non-Hispanic whites due to differences in education (which contributed 2.9 percentage points) and other observable characteristics (1.2 percentage points). The incidence of poverty not explained by differences in observable characteristics had fallen substantially, to 1.4 percentage points (shown in the vertically striped portion), again reflecting the relative progress made by native-born Mexican Americans in moving toward economic security. This analysis suggests that even if Mexican Americans reached parity in education and employment with non-Hispanic whites, they might continue to have a higher incidence of impoverishment, in excess of one percentage point. Again, discrimination, potential differences in the quality of schooling, and other differences to which we have alluded might explain this small gap.

TOP TEN PERCENT OF THE INCOME DISTRIBUTION

We showed earlier in this chapter that native-born Mexican Americans in Texas encountered a substantial and persistent earnings gap compared with non-Hispanic whites over time unexplained by differences in educational attainment and other observable characteristics. At the same

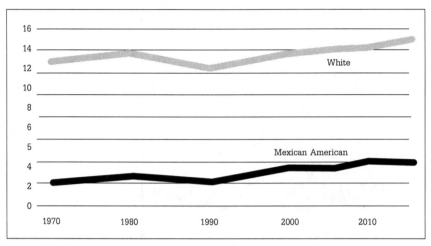

Figure 11. Percentage of Native-Born Mexican Americans and Non-Hispanic Whites Twenty-Five to Sixty-Four Years of Age in Texas in the Top 10 Percent of the Income Distribution, 1970–2016.

time, they made considerable progress in reducing their relatively high rates of impoverishment vis-à-vis non-Hispanic whites. An additional consideration in assessing economic security is whether inroads have been made in the distribution of income; location in income (and wealth) distributions is commonly used to gauge the extent of income inequality.[9] Income—as opposed to labor-market earnings—also serves as a broader measure of economic security because it encompasses additional sources of wealth.

For this purpose, for each year in our time frame of interest, we generate the distribution of income at the national level for adults (regardless of birthplace) twenty-five to sixty-four years of age, based on total personal income, which includes income generated by employment, self-employment/ business activities, interest, dividends, rental property, public assistance, Social Security and Supplemental Security, and other sources. We then estimate the percentage of native-born Mexican American and non-Hispanic white adults in the same age range in Texas in the top ten percent of this income distribution. Figure 11 presents these estimates between 1970 and 2016.

Consistent with other measures of economic security, native-born Mexican Americans of prime working ages in Texas made some progress with respect to increasing their representation in the top decile of the national income distribution over the past half century, but a considerable disparity relative to non-Hispanic whites remains. In 1970, native-born Mexican American adults in Texas accounted for only 2.2 percent of the adults in the top ten percent of the income distribution in the country. This proportion was less than half of the corresponding percentage (4.9 percent) for native-born Mexican Americans in the country overall, and one-sixth of the percentage (13.0 percent) for native-born non-Hispanic whites in Texas. By 2016, 4 percent of native-born Mexican American adults in Texas were positioned in the top income decile, which remained below the national average for this group (4.6 percent) and represented approximately one-fourth of the corresponding share (15 percent) of native-born non-Hispanic whites in the state. That year, as Figure 11 shows, Mexican Americans and non-Hispanic whites in Texas also had a slightly wider gap in this measure in terms of percentage points than in 1970. Eleven percentage points separated these groups in 2016, compared to 10.8 percentage points in 1970.

This information indicates that income inequality along ethnic lines among adults in Texas has been growing. The representation of native-born non-Hispanic whites in Texas in the top ten percent of the income distribution has increased since 1990, reaching its peak (in the time frame analyzed) in 2016. Among native-born Mexican American adults in Texas, this share dipped slightly after 2010.

When decomposing the difference in the percentage of adults in Texas in the highest income decile represented by native-born Mexican Americans versus non-Hispanic whites in 1970 and 2016 (10.8 and 11.0 percentage points, respectively) into explained and unexplained components (see Figure 12), mirroring previous analyses,[10] despite being slightly wider, a smaller proportion of this difference can be explained by education in 2016 than in 1970 (4.7 versus 6.7 percentage points, respectively, shown by the diagonally striped portions). The role of differences in other observable characteristics (the solid portions) rose between 1970 and 2016 with respect to explaining the gaps in the shares of Mexican Americans vis-à-vis non-Hispanic white adults in the top ten percent of the income distribution.

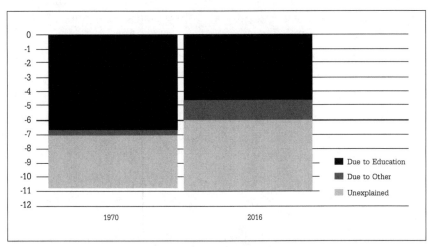

Figure 12. Breakdown of the Top-Income-Decile Gap between Native-Born Mexican Americans and Non-Hispanic Whites Twenty-Five to Sixty-Four Years of Age in Texas, 1970 and 2016.

It follows that higher education levels played a role in explaining the increased placement of native-born Mexican Americans in the top decile of the income distribution between 1970 and 2016 in Texas, but acquiring more education alone did not eliminate this gap with native-born non-Hispanic whites. Indeed, the vertically striped areas in Figure 12 show that in 2016, the representation of native-born Mexican Americans in Texas in the top ten percent of the income distribution was 4.9 percentage points less than the representation of otherwise similar non-Hispanic whites, and this unexplained difference had widened since 1970 (then at 3.7 percentage points). This unexplained (and growing) advantageous positioning of non-Hispanic whites represented nearly half of the entire gap between these groups in 2016. Limited access to resources for entrepreneurial ventures and professional networks that are needed to acquire human capital (such as business and on-the-job experiences) and financial capital might continue to exist for Mexican Americans in Texas.

Discussion and Recommendations

In this chapter, we examine how native-born Mexican Americans fared in Texas over the past half century with respect to a variety of economic security measures. We found that native-born Mexican Americans in the state have been making mixed progress with respect to narrowing disparities in their economic security vis-à-vis non-Hispanic whites. They made progress in terms of the likelihood of being employed and reducing the incidence of poverty, at least partly stemming from their higher levels of schooling attainment. At the same time, even for these socioeconomic outcomes, native-born Mexican Americans in Texas have a long way to go before coming close to eliminating these disparities.

Moreover, our findings suggest that eliminating disparities in education would be a means to *narrow*—but probably not eliminate—economic security disparities between native-born Mexican Americans and non-Hispanic whites in the state. Indeed, our analyses of labor-market earnings in Texas fit with other findings showing large and persistent earnings gaps between Hispanics and non-Hispanic whites at the national level—even for those with the same schooling levels.[11] In addition, the native-born Mexican American/non-Hispanic white gap in the likelihood of being in the top decile of the income distribution widened in Texas between 1970 and 2016, seemingly driven by an increase in the portion of the gap unexplained by differences in education and other observable socioeconomic and demographic characteristics. This finding, reflecting an increase in income inequality along ethnic lines, points to additional policy remedies beyond increasing educational access as means to enhance the relative economic security of Mexican Americans. Such policies could include ensuring access to the same quality of education as non-Hispanic whites in Texas, the enforcement of existing antidiscrimination laws in the labor market and elsewhere, and increased access to other resources such as access to financial capital and professional networks, among others.

In light of changing demographics and the fact that Hispanics have been driving U.S. population growth, the outcomes of such policies have become an increasingly important determinant of economic prosperity in Texas and the nation.[12] And while younger than non-Hispanic whites, the Hispanic population is aging; in fact, Hispanics had one of the largest increases in median age in the nation between 2008 and 2018.[13] Mexican Americans (who comprise the vast majority of the Hispanic population—nearly 60 percent at the national level, and nearly 90 percent in Texas) also have longer life expectancies than non-Hispanic whites.

As such, addressing their economic security disparities in the near term will likely have far-reaching consequences with respect to retirement security, pensions, access to health care, and asset and wealth accumulation, thus affecting long-term national prosperity.[14] While these findings suggest that improving the educational levels of Mexican Americans is fundamental to the continued economic security of this population in Texas and the nation, so too are future investigations into other potential barriers (stemming from labor-market discrimination, relatively weak professional networks, limited access to financial and quality physical capital, and potential regional immobility to areas with relatively more employment opportunities) to inform policy in this regard.

Notes

1. Unless otherwise specified, all of our analyses in this chapter use public-use microdata from the 1970-2000 decennial censuses and the 2006, 2010, and 2016 American Community Surveys, made available through the Integrated Public Use Microdata Series (IPUMS): Steven Ruggles, Sarah Flood, Ronald Goeken, Josiah Grover, Erin Meyer, Jose Pacas, and Matthew Sobek, *Integrated Public Use Microdata Series USA: Version 8.0 [Database]*, Minnesota Population Center (2018), https://usa.ipums.org/usa.
2. We realize that not all native-born adults grew up in the United States or went to U.S. schools. U.S. border communities, for example, provide opportunities for children to come of age in more than one country and to encounter non-U.S. institutions as part of their upbringing. However, it is not possible with our data to identify U.S.-born people who spent considerable time outside of the United States as children.
3. Marie T. Mora and Alberto Dávila, "The Hispanic-White Wage Gap Has Remained Wide and Relatively Steady: Examining Hispanic-White Gaps in Wages, Unemployment, Labor Force Participation, and Education by Gender, Immigrant Status, and Other Subpopulations," *Economic Policy Institute Report* (July 2, 2018).
4. Mora and Dávila, "The Hispanic-White Wage Gap."
5. We partition the gap into these portions based on the "Oaxaca Decomposition" technique; for example, see Ronald Oaxaca, "Male-Female Wage Differentials in Urban Labor Markets,"

International Economic Review 14, pp. 693-709 (1973). Specifically, we estimate two probit regression models for the likelihood of being employed for native-born Mexican Americans and non-Hispanic whites in Texas between the ages of twenty-five and sixty-four. The first regresses education on the employment variable (which equals one for employed individuals, and equals zero otherwise) for native-born Mexican Americans and non-Hispanic whites; based on these estimates, we predict the likelihood of being employed for both groups, given their schooling levels. The second probit regression model (from which we obtain predicted values) includes education and other demographic and socioeconomic characteristics (namely, age, age-squared, gender, limited English fluency [for those who did not speak the English language well], marital status, the number of children at home, and residence outside a metropolitan area) as regressors. The difference between the predicted employment gaps between Mexican Americans and non-Hispanic whites based on results from the first model reflects the portion of the Mexican American/non-Hispanic white employment gap that stems from differences in education. The difference between the predicted employment gaps between Mexican Americans and non-Hispanic whites based on the second model minus the portion explained by education reflects the portion of the employment gap that stems from differences in the other characteristics. The remaining difference in the employment-rate gap between native Mexican Americans and non-Hispanic whites is the unexplained gap. Because the role of education in the labor market changes over time, we conduct this empirical exercise separately for 1970 and 2016.

6. For readers unfamiliar with using values expressed in natural logarithms, percentage differences can be estimated by the difference in the natural log values (in this case, 9.876 - 10.364). They can also be estimated by dividing the difference in the nonlogarithmic amounts by the average of the two: ($19,459-$31,698)/$25,579.

7. For this analysis, we only include adults who reported labor-market earnings. Following the methodology described in note 5, we use ordinary least squares to estimate of regression models with the natural logarithm of earnings as the dependent variable. The control variables in the extended model include education, age, age-squared, gender, limited English fluency, categorical information on the number of weeks people worked, the number of hours they usually worked per week, and residence outside of a metropolitan area.

8. For this analysis, following the methodology described in note 5, we use probit regression to analyze factors related to the likelihood of being impoverished, with a binary dependent variable equal to one for adults living below the poverty line, and equal to zero otherwise. The control variables in the extended model include education, age, age-squared, gender, limited English fluency, employment status, marital status, the number of children living at home, and residence outside of a metropolitan area.

9. For examples, see Thomas Piketty and Emmanuel Saez, "Income Inequality in the United States: 1913-1998," *Quarterly Journal of Economics* (February 2003); and Emmanuel Saez, "Striking It Richer," in David B. Grusky and Jasmine Hill (eds.), *Poverty and Inequality in the 21st Century* (New York: Routledge, 2018), 39-41. For a recent discussion of race and wealth distributions, see William Darity, Jr., Darrick Hamilton, Mark Paul, Alan Aja, Anne Price, Antonio Moore, and Caterina Chiopris, *What We Get Wrong about Closing the Racial Wealth Gap* (Samuel DuBois Cook Center on Social Equity, April 2018).

10. We obtained these estimates following the methodology described in note 5. In particular, we use probit regression to estimate the likelihood of being in the top decile of the income distribution; the control variables in the extended model are the same as in the analysis of

the likelihood of being impoverished: education, age, age-squared, gender, limited English fluency, employment status, marital status, the number of children living at home, and residence outside of a metropolitan area.

11. Mora and Dávila, "The Hispanic-White Wage Gap."

12. Antonio Flores, "How the U.S. Hispanic Population Is Changing," Pew Research Center Fact-Tank (September 18, 2017), https://www.pewresearch.org/fact-tank/2017/09/18/how-the-u-s-hispanic-population-is-changing.

13. Antonio Flores, Mark Hugo Lopez, and Jens Manuel Krogstad, "U.S. Hispanic Population Reached New High in 2018, but Growth Has Slowed," Pew Research Center Fact-Tank (July 8, 2019), https://www.pewresearch.org/fact-tank/2019/07/08/u-s-hispanic-population-reached-new-high-in-2018-but-growth-has-slowed.

14. Jorge Bravo, Nicole Mun Sum Lai, Gretch Donehower, and Ivan Mejia-Guevara, "Aging and Retirement Security: United States of America and Mexico," in William A. Vega, Kyriakos S. Markides, Jacqueline L. Ángel, and Fernando M. Torres-Gil, *Challenges of Latino Aging in the Americas* (2015), 77–89; Rogelio Sáenz, "The Demography of the Elderly in the Americas: The Case of the United States and Mexico," in Vega et al., *Challenges of Latino Aging*, 197–223; and Marie T. Mora, "The Growing Importance of Educational Attainment and Retirement Security of Mexican-Origin Adults in the U.S. and Mexico," in Vega et al., *Challenges of Latino Aging*, 3–10.

JUAN H. FLORES

Chicano Activism: Pathway to Healthy Communities

This chapter assesses the health of the Mexican American community on the fiftieth anniversary of the 1968 U.S. Commission on Civil Rights hearing.[1] Policy recommendations are provided to improve the health and *bienestar* (well-being) of Mexican American families. The six-day hearing in San Antonio provided almost no data on the health status of Mexican Americans in Texas. Nonetheless, health status was a major civil rights concern in the testimony:

> A minimum wage is needed to encourage the development of standards of living necessary for health, efficiency and general well-being of the people and to reduce as rapidly as possible labor disputes arising out of such conditions and inequities.[2]

This presaged the *social determinants of health* framework for assessing both health status conditions and causes for disparities and inequalities in health care. Since the 1990s, public health researchers have increasingly investigated external social factors as contributing reasons for individual,

Table 1. Social Determinants of Health.

Economic stability	Neighborhood & physical environment	Education	Food	Community & social context	Health care system
Employment	Housing	Language	Hunger	Social integration	Health coverage
Income	Transportation	Literacy	Access to healthy options	Discrimination	Provider availability
Medical bills	Safety	Early childhood education		Support system	Quality of care

Health outcomes

Mortality, morbidity, life expectancy, health care expenditures, health status, functional limitations

Source: Beyond Health Care: The Role of Social Determinants in Promoting Health and Health Equity, Henry J. Kaiser Foundation.

family, or community health conditions.[3] Social determinants of health include factors like socioeconomic status, education, employment, housing, and neighborhood and physical environment, as well as access to health care.

Health research has contributed in broadening the policy discussions of health care, beyond simply whether one has an illness and access to medical care. Indeed, social determinants are the circumstances of the family and community environment in which people live and work, as well as the systems put in place to deal with medical issues. These circumstances are in turn shaped by a wider set of forces: economics, social policies, and politics. It is from these everyday realities that we investigate the health status of Mexican Americans.

Texas's social and economic policies and politics were on full display throughout the six-day U.S. Commission on Civil Rights hearing. Testimony chronicled problems of disease, developmental delays in children, substandard housing, toxic pesticides, poor education, and lack of access to medical care.

The study of Mexican American health and trends considers Texas's health data developments, geographic diversity, population growth and dispersion, political environment, and health system change. The approach in this chapter (summarized in Table 1) does the following:

- Uses a version of the World Health Organization definition (circa 1948) of health expressed as the state of physical, mental, spiritual, and social-economic well-being of the individual, not simply the absence of disease or infirmity.
- Adheres to the Mexican American concept of *bienestar*, defined as a perceived quality of life status among individuals, families, and communities affected by social, environmental, and systemic factors. *Bienestar* also embodies social justice concerns given the Latino experience with racism, institutionalized biases, and harmful public policies.
- Defines health equity as everyone having a fair and just opportunity to be as healthy as possible. This requires removing obstacles to health such as poverty, discrimination, and their consequences, including powerlessness and lack of access to good jobs with fair pay, quality education and housing, safe environments, and access to health care.

U.S. Health Care, Chicano Health, and States' Rights

The complexities and politics of health care continue to present major challenges for equitable solutions, particularly among low-income populations and people of color. The United States, where many of the world's most significant scientific and medical advances are developed, has a health care system that continues to bleed health disparities and inequities.[4] With decades of increasing costs now reaching 3.5 trillion dollars annually, the U.S. system has a per-capita expenditure of $10,739, two to three times that of any other modern industrialized nation.[5] However, the health of Americans ranks last or near last in health outcomes dimensions of access, efficiency, and equity.[6] For more than twenty-five years Americans have consistently viewed the U.S. health care system as poor or in crisis.[7]

From the perspective of Mexican American advocates, disparities and inequities in the health care system are the more salient issues, especially in care quality and access. Beginning in the civil rights years of the 1960s and through the early 1990s, "Chicano health" was the call for changes in the health care system affecting Mexican Americans.

In 1972 Chicanos from the southwestern United States met in San Antonio to develop recommendations addressing issues of health services availability, accessibility, acceptability, and accountability to their community health concerns. They noted, "It is unforgivable that in a country as wealthy and technologically advanced as the U.S., Chicanos must continue to suffer ill health without access to services."[8]

Martin Luther King's 1966 statement on health inequities was prophetic: "Of all the forms of inequality, injustice in health care is the most shocking and inhumane."[9] Testimony at the 1968 civil rights hearing in referring to rural communities and farmworkers included:

> The health service they get is not only inadequate in extent but seriously deficient in quality. It is badly organized, underfinanced, rarely related to the needs of the individual or the family. Such health service as there is too often is discriminatory in terms of race and income and heedless of the dignity of the individual.[10]

Health research involving Mexican Americans that began in the 1970s, coupled with Chicano activism, helped identify widespread changes needed. The activism engaged urban and rural Mexican Americans, migrant and seasonal farmworkers from Texas to California, and farmworkers migrating and establishing new growth communities in the Northwest and in Midwestern states.[11] The stated scope of health issues they targeted was comprehensive. These included physical and mental illnesses; behavioral health risks such as nutrition, smoking, substance abuse; and teen pregnancy. The inadequate responses to the identified Chicano health concerns by the major sectors of the health care system were also targeted, including access to quality health care and facilities, dental and mental health professionals, insurance coverage costs, and insufficient medical research.[12]

Chicanos challenged social and health service delivery and research frameworks that use a deficit model explaining poor health. The deficit approach views Mexican Americans' language barrier, lack of knowledge, and culturally based behaviors as the central causes for health problems. Instead, Chicanos advocated for community health development approaches, culturally oriented service delivery policies, and competencies.[13] Latino health data were also advocated for as a crucial need.[14] It was nearly a decade after passage of national legislation in 1976 that federal health agencies began to identify Latinos in their data collection.[15] The lack of available Latino health data persisted in state-level public social and health agencies. For example, the Texas Department of Health only began publishing limited fertility and mortality vital statistics data on the Hispanic population in the late 1980s.

The preceding description situates Latino health activism within a growing, costly, and complex U.S. health care system. It underscores that health care and politics are deeply intertwined. Several contributions are discernable from the documented activism during this period (1970–1990):

- Chicano health was at the forefront in calling for health care systems change. The advocacy expanded into the more inclusive "Latino health" frame, which bridged activism among Mexican American, Puerto Ricans, and Cubans, raising Latino voices for health care system changes to the national level.
- Latino health activism cuts across national and state health legislation and programs that contain opportunities in addressing their health concerns. Examples include programs to expand health insurance coverage (Medicaid); regular access to primary medical and behavioral health services (community health centers); disease prevention services (maternal and child, chronic health illnesses, substance abuse); health professions education and training; and nutrition-based programs, such as Women, Infant, Children (WIC) and the Supplemental Nutrition Assistance Program (SNAP, formerly known as food stamps).
- Social determinants of health are culturally integral to Chicano advocacy and research. Advocates understood that inequities in education, employment, housing, and voter suppression required parallel solutions to truly achieve improvements and maintenance of good health

Federalism and health policy are inextricably linked, creating additional challenges to influence health care issues at the state and local levels.[16] The modernization of health care noted earlier created an explosion of programs targeting health insurance coverage, improvement in the quality of care, preventive medicine, and health professions research. Coinciding with this explosion was the transition to a new federalism that provided more authority and responsibility to the states for the implementation of these programs.

Notably, national and state differences and battles over federalism are more than two hundred years old. However, "new federalism," which began with President Nixon in the late 1960s and was implemented more aggressively by President Reagan in the 1980s, sought to reverse war-on-poverty approaches and reduce the welfare state through devolution of federally run programs to the states. There were expansive business-focused policy deregulations to allow the private corporate sector to work its free-market magic in creating wealth that would trickle down in the form of more jobs and increased wages. The expectation was that there would be less need for social and health welfare programs. These federalism goals continue today and include complimentary use of judicial actions for their support.[17]

Health care devolution examples include Medicaid and state block grants for maternal and child health, women's health, mental health, and substance abuse. After the Affordable Care Act passed in 2010, Texas officials took a states' rights position with administrative and legal efforts to undermine and reverse the law.[18] State elected officials have also refused to expand Medicaid, which can increase health insurance coverage under the Affordable Care Act. The state's policy decisions relative to new federalism's social welfare and health initiatives have been consistently guided by its philosophy that these programs create dependency.[19] State policymakers opted for economic free-market approaches as the purported means to create equal opportunities for "all Texans."

The argument here is not for or against new federalism; it is about Texas's underlying processes in developing corresponding policies, rules, and implementation strategies. Are current inequalities being considered? Are there efforts to create opportunities to significantly reduce what one researcher called "capability deprivation," where poverty is not simply a low income level?[20] This appears germane to Mexican Americans, as one witness explained in the 1968 civil rights hearing:

> Because if people are earning more money, they can give their children a better education, they give them better health, they can have better housing. The economic factor is a terribly important factor in this whole problem.[21]

Today, Mexican American health continues to be situated in a health care system with disparities and equity problems.[22] The prevailing trend is toward less support and increasing restrictions on safety-net programs related to social determinants of health.[23] Given these structural limitations, how is the health of Mexican Americans in Texas affected?

The Epidemiological Paradox

Mexican Americans are frequently characterized as a hardworking and often exploited low-wage labor force that significantly contributes to Texas's economy and population growth.[24] Their resiliency is reflected in better than expected health status based on death rates and life expectancy data, lending credence to the observed phenomenon of the epidemiologic paradox, first identified in Texas among Mexican Americans.[25] Public health researchers increasingly observed that Latinos—natives and immigrants—in the United States are less likely to suffer from chronic disease or die prematurely than Anglos or Blacks. This is despite factors that are typically linked to poor health—high rates of poverty, poor education, and less health care access.

The Hispanic age-adjusted death rates are lower than those for whites, Blacks, and the state's overall rate during the thirty-five-year period illustrated in Figure 1. Death rates for Latinos continued to be lower than for whites and much lower compared to Blacks from 1980 to 2015.

The same patterns can be seen in life expectancy (Figure 2). Latino life expectancy was only two years less than for whites in 1970 and in 1980;

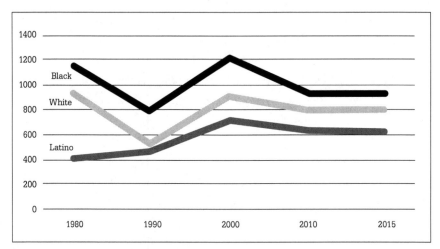

Figure 1. Age-Adjusted Death Rates in Texas by Race, 1980–2015.

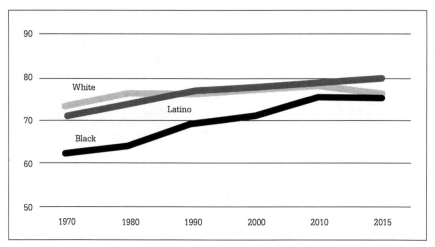

Figure 2. Life Expectancy of Texans by Race, 1990–2015.

Latino life expectancy increased to four years above that of whites by 2015. Black life expectancy is eight to twelve years lower compared to both whites and Latinos throughout most of the forty-five-year period; however, by 2015 their life expectancy gap with whites and Latinos narrowed to one and five years, respectively.

Infant deaths and low birth weight rates are often also cited as indicators of the Mexican American health paradox. Tables 2 and 3 illustrate that Latinos and whites are very close on these two measures. However, Blacks

Table 2. Texas Infant Death Rates (per 1000 live births) under Age One Year by Race and Ethnicity, 1990, 2000, 2010, 2015.

Year	White	Black	Latino	Texas
1990	7	15	7	8
2000	5	11	5	6
2010	6	11	6	6
2015	5	11	5	6

Source: Texas Department of State Health Services.
Note: White includes other and unknown race and ethnicity, but not Latino.

Table 3. Texas Low Birth Weight (<2,500 grams) Infants by Race and Ethnicity: 1990, 2000, 2010, 2013–2015.

Year	White	Black	Latino	Texas
1990	6	13	6	7
2000	7	13	7	8
2010	8	14	8	8
2013–2015	7	13	8	8

Source: Texas Department of State Health Services.
Note: White includes other and unknown race and ethnicity, but not Latino.

have nearly twice the number of infant deaths and percentage of low-birth-weight infants compared to Latinos and whites.

Myron Gutmann's pivotal paper examined the origins of the Mexican American health paradox surrounding infant and neonatal mortality.[26] He found:

- Initial decreases in Mexican American and Black infant mortality began in the post-World War II era with improvements in sanitation and housing conditions.
- Infant mortality was higher for Mexican Americans than for African Americans and whites throughout most of the twentieth century until the late 1950s. The paradox emerged from the data in the 1950s or early 1960s, at which time Mexican American infant and neonatal mortality began to reach rates lower than that for Blacks and nearly equal to that of whites.
- More significant evidence of the epidemiologic paradox surfaced in 1974. Spanish-surname infant deaths were only slightly higher than for whites, and neonatal deaths were slightly lower.

Research on the Latino health paradox has expanded across population targets (e.g., immigrants, children, women, and senior-based research) and health issue focuses (e.g., chronic and mental illnesses, disabilities, maternal health, substance abuse). Evidence supports lower mortality from heart and chronic lung disease, strokes, major types of cancers, and mental illness.[27] Counterevidence includes higher incidence and prevalence of illnesses and/or mortality such as disabilities, cervical and liver cancer, and diabetes. Higher prevalence of select chronic conditions in young children and immigrants was also identified.[28] Studies that compared Mexican immigrants and native Mexican Americans resulted in evidence for an immigrant health paradox despite their much lower social and economic conditions and more stressful living conditions.[29] Access to health care was a frequently identified concern across many of the health paradox studies.

Indeed, Mexican American infant mortality and life expectancy in Texas have improved since 1968. Mexican American life expectancy has equaled or exceeded that of whites for nearly three decades. This paradox has not been defined as better health, nor does it apply to all types of health and mortality outcomes. The paradox has been attributed to family support networks, cultural practices, selective migration issues, genetic heritage, fertility rates, and dietary factors.[30]

To gain a more thorough description of Mexican American health trends in Texas, we must consider Mexican American demographic characteristics and potential health implications, political policy influences, and Mexican American subgroup differences.

Latino Growth, Governing Structures, and the Politics of Health Care

Texas is the second largest state in the country in area and population. It covers 267,000 square miles divided into 254 counties, of which 172 are designated as rural and eighty-two as urban. About 11 percent of the state's 27.7 million population in 2016 lived in rural counties.[31]

Texas had been a Democrat-controlled state for more than a century when the U.S. Civil Rights Commission (USCCR) in 1968 vividly illustrated examples of racism and socioeconomic inequalities affecting Latinos and African Americans. To address these disparities, we must understand the state and local governmental structures that challenged equitable solutions to social, economic, and health-related issues impacting Mexican Americans.

Reacting to their post-Civil War Reconstruction experience, the framers of the 1876 Texas Constitution emphasized states' rights rather than federal supremacy to strongly affirm the doctrine of separation of powers. The Constitution of the State of Texas expressly prohibits officials in any one major arena (executive, legislative, or judicial) from exercising powers identified as belonging to the others unless the authority is expressly specified.[32] The 254 Texas counties since 1931 have constitutional and legislative-based county and municipal-level governmental responsibilities, which include working with state-supported social, education, and health-related agencies.[33]

Before 2004, when state legislation consolidated ten major independent state agencies, having so many independent agencies was troubling for modern government, specifically in the efforts of the state legislature to delegate rulemaking authority to the almost 190 administrative agencies.[34] Prior to 2004 there were sixteen separate state agencies, commissions, and boards across the states, each with multiple geographic delivery boundaries. For example, the Department of Health contained eight administrative regions, the Department of Aging twenty-eight, and the Department of Mental Health and Mental Retardation sixty-three.[35]

Since the county government is an administrative arm of the state government, county-elected officials also greatly influence the availability and quality of Texas health care services. The 254 separate county government bodies have both local and regional responsibilities in health. Because of the traditional Texas attitude that local control is preferable, county judges and other county officials have considerable latitude. County officials can largely determine how state-mandated services will be financed and administered in their county; they have almost total control over which, if any, state and federal optional programs will be implemented. The county judge plays a major role and has authority cutting across all spheres of interests—executive, legislative, judicial, and administrative.

The effects of the political geography and governmental decision structure were evident in the ten-year follow-up report to the 1968 civil rights hearing.[36] The report demonstrated how the fragmented layers of local and state governmental political, policy, and administrative authority over education, social and health public agencies, and judiciary institutions prevented progress in increasing Mexican American and African American employment.

Lacking political clout, Latinos encountered the same local and state governmental obstacles for decades in the development of federally funded nonprofit migrant and community health centers. The centers were established as part of the arsenal of the War on Poverty programs to address health resource shortage areas and uninsured/underinsured populations through "consumer-run" health organizations.[37] Begun in the early 1970s by neighborhood residents and Chicano activists in the Rio Grande Valley, El Paso, and San Antonio, the first Texas community health centers met with considerable opposition. There was pushback from many different authority figures, including city mayors, county judges, health department officials, and medical associations. Criticisms against the centers called into question their legitimacy, saying they were not staffed by real doctors, calling them radical elements and communists, and claiming federal intrusion.

In particular, the Texas Board of Medical Examiners and Texas Medical Societies created significant barriers and opposition to the development of community health centers. Components of the Texas Medical Act were interpreted and utilized to prevent physicians from working on straight salary in a community health clinic. Physicians who worked in such clinics were often ostracized by their peers and harassed by medical society medical review boards. Community and migrant health centers were further hampered because their grant requests required a letter of approval from the local county medical society.[38]

Health care is a human capital investment—like employment, education, and housing—that involves legislative and governmental structures. As demonstrated by the authors of this book, decades of community organizing, legislative advocacy, and legal actions are often required to advance Mexican American equity outcomes.

Texas–Mexico Border Health

The Texas-Mexico border stretches 1,254 miles from the Gulf of Mexico to El Paso. Officially, a sixty-two-mile distance on either side of the border is accepted through the La Paz Agreement between the United States and Mexico. In Texas, this radius encompasses thirty-two counties with fourteen border counties that have eight sister cities with Mexico.[39] The significance of the Texas-Mexico border to the state's economy, as well as to the Upper Rio Grande and South Texas border regions, is well known.

In 2015 there were three million residents living within thirty-two counties that make up the federal definition of the border area (shaded area within sixty-two miles of the border). Nine in ten of the residents were Latino.[40] Since 1980, the border population has grown 114 percent, compared to the state increase of 86 percent. Approximately 80 percent of the border population reside in the four counties of El Paso, Hidalgo, Cameron, and Webb. The Texas-Mexico Border is viewed as a community with historical, cultural, commercial, and health ties that extend across the border.

The border counties have historically been the most neglected region of the state in terms of political representation, basic infrastructure, and human capital investments, particularly education and health resources.[41] Poverty has been a central result of this neglect. Indeed, between 1970 and 2003, poverty rates on the border improved only marginally compared to other regions of the state.[42] While improvements have occurred across border communities, the population is still economically poorer compared to the state average and has lower health status and greater at-risk health concerns.

In 1988, the deplorable health conditions on the South Texas Border caused then Senator Lloyd Bentsen to ask the U.S. General Accounting Office (GAO) to investigate the availability of health care in the whole Texas-Mexico Border area. The GAO report documented extensive poverty, higher fertility rates, and health status results for the nineteen border counties it investigated. Obesity, diabetes type II, gallbladder disease, and viral diseases that included hepatitis A, shigellosis, and mumps were reported as

Table 4. Infant Mortality Rates for Texas and Selected Texas–Mexico Border Counties, 1991.

Morality	Texas	Thirty-two border counties
Infant	8	6
Neonatal	5	4
Fetal	7	5
Perinatal	11	9

Source: UT System Texas–Mexico Border Health Coordination Office, June 1994.

Table 5. Death Rates from Ten Leading Causes for Texas and Selected Border Counties, 1991.

Cause of death	Texas	Thirty-two border counties
Heart disease	226	164
Malignant neoplasms	167	121
Cerebrovascular disease	48	32
Accidents	35	36
Chronic obstructive pulmonary disease	31	24
Pneumonia and influenza	21	17
Diabetes	21	25
Homicide	16	9
Suicide	12	9
HIV/AIDS	12	3

Source: UT System Texas–Mexico Border Health Coordination Office, June 1994.

significantly more prevalent compared to the rest of the state. Further, the health conditions on the border were worsened by higher uninsured rates, health workforces and facilities shortages, and underserved migrant and seasonal farmworker and *colonia* populations.[43]

Three years later, similar health status and limited health resource conditions were reported in a University of Texas System Statistical Report that included the thirty-two border counties.[44] The population totaled 1.7 million. Tables 4 illustrates slightly lower infant, neonatal, perinatal and fetal death rates in 1991. Table 5 shows lower death rates in eight of the ten causes in the border counties, despite high poverty and lower education characteristics.

Lower infant death rates were again reported in a 2003 study by the Center for Health Economics and Policy at the University of Texas (UT) Health Science Center at San Antonio. The study provided detailed data for each of the eleven targeted counties from Val Verde to Cameron in the lower Rio

Grande Valley. Overall, viral disease and diabetes rates were higher across most border counties compared to the state averages. For example, the rates for hepatitis A and salmonellosis were 44 and 20 compared to 13 and 11 percent for the state, respectively, and most counties had a diabetes rate of nearly 8 percent, compared to the state rate of 6 percent. The recurring health conditions of higher uninsured rates, health workforce shortages, and *colonia* impoverished living conditions were also prevalent.[45]

Higher rates of chronic and viral diseases and other public health problems were found in a 2007 health disparities study of thirty-seven South Texas counties.[46] The study population totaled 4.1 million, of which 68 percent were Hispanic. Two-thirds of the study area were state-recognized border counties. Table 6 illustrates the comparative health status results among 23 indicators measured:

- Fifty-seven percent of the indicators were higher in South Texas compared with the rest of Texas.
- Seventy-nine percent of the indicators were higher for South Texas Hispanics compared with non-Hispanic whites in South Texas.
- Ninety-one percent of the indicators were higher in South Texas Hispanics compared with Hispanics in the rest of Texas.

The institute's report also showed that twenty-one of the thirty-eight South Texas counties were designated as health-professional shortage areas, and an estimated 33 percent of the adult population was uninsured, causing significant barriers to addressing the health disparities.

Texas's 1,254 border miles cover more than one-half of the total United States–Mexico border. In 2010, the United States–Mexico Border Health Commission released its most comprehensive health report ever undertaken. The report drew on multiple federal, state, and private research data sources for the four border states. The health measures targeted included environmental health, communicable diseases, oral health, HIV/AIDS, maternal and child health, breast and cervical cancers, injuries, heart disease and stroke, mental health, substance abuse, health insurance coverage, availability of health workforce, teen pregnancy, and access to health care.[47]

Table 6. Select Health Indicators by Ethnicity and Region, 2007.

Health status indicator	South Texas, compared with the rest of Texas	South Texas Hispanics, compared with non-Hispanic Whites in South Texas	South Texas Hispanics, compared with Hispanics in the rest of Texas
Tuberculosis	Higher	Higher	Higher
HIV/AIDS	Lower	Higher	Lower
Syphilis	Lower	Higher	Lower
Chlamydia	Higher	Higher	Higher
Gonorrhea	Lower	Higher	Higher
Breast cancer	Lower	Lower	Higher
Cervical cancer	Higher	Higher	
Colorectal cancer	Lower	Lower	Higher
Prostate cancer	Lower	Lower	Lower
Liver cancer	Higher	Higher	Higher
Stomach cancer	Higher	Higher	
Gallbladder cancer	Higher	Higher	
Leukemia	Higher		
Neural tube defects	Higher	Higher	Higher
Other birth defects	Higher		
Infant mortality	Lower		
Diabetes	Higher		Higher
Heart disease mortality	Lower		Higher
Cerebrovascular disease mortality	Lower		
Obesity (adult)	Higher	Higher	Higher
Childhood lead poisoning		Higher	
Pesticide poisoning	Higher		Higher
Homicide		Higher	Lower
Suicide	Lower	Lower	

Source: South Texas Health Status Review, Institute for Health Promotion Research, UT Health Science Center.

Texas's thirty-two-county border population had grown to 2.1 million, of whom 84 percent were identified as Hispanic. The border's health status measures were compared to the U.S. population. Findings were similar to previous data. Hispanics had lower infant and adult mortality rates, yet greater health risks for cervical cancers, diabetes, serious psychological distress, injuries, tuberculosis, shigellosis, and teen pregnancies were illustrated. Again, severe problems remained with high uninsured rates, shortages in health workforce, and lack of access to care.

The Texas border has experienced health improvement in lower infant deaths, premature births and diseases of early infancy, and in some viral and infectious diseases since the 1968 civil rights hearing. However, there is an array of health status disparities that continue to impact Mexican Americans throughout the border area. The explosion in population growth since 1968, along with improved data collection and research, has broadened our understanding of their social determinant conditions, health status disparities, and inequities in health care access.

Health of *Colonia* Residents

A *colonia* is a residential area or neighborhood that often lacks some of the most basic living necessities, such as potable water, septic or sewer systems, electricity, paved roads, or safe and sanitary housing.[48] Many *colonias* had their beginning in the 1950s because counties lacked home-rule powers and areas outside the city limits were regulation-free zones. As a result, developers purchased tracts of land, platted their tracts, bulldozed roads, and sold the undeveloped lots. Third-world living conditions developed and persisted for decades. There have been steady incremental improvements from poor living conditions because of state legislative actions closing county regulatory gaps and from the hundreds of millions in state, local, and federal dollars in infrastructure investments targeting mostly water, waste management, electricity, roads, and housing development efforts.

One of the earliest recorded studies of *colonias* (1977)—in the Lower Rio Grande Valley counties of Cameron, Hidalgo, and Willacy—identified sixty-five *colonias* with an estimated combined population of 34,000.[49] The study found that the first 15 percent of the Valley's *colonia* developments occurred between 1908 and 1948. Most *colonia* homes in the study were resident-owned, single-family wooden dwellings with an average of four rooms, including a bathroom and a kitchen, which would be considered substandard by any measure. In addition, well over one-half of the homes had no telephone, received no garbage removal service, received no treated water, and had no adequate means of disposing of waste.

Colonia residents were found to differ significantly from other Texas Latino residents. They were younger and less educated; most lacked year-round full-time employment; nearly one-half were farmworkers; and most were low-income wage earners.

The physical location of *colonias* meant they were often isolated from basic resources, including transportation, food markets, social and health services, and legal services. Not surprisingly, viral and communicable diseases were recorded health problems. The study found higher levels of hepatitis, bacillary and amoebic dysentery, and typhoid, which are commonly spread by water-borne fecal contamination.

These living conditions did not abate the resilience of *colonia* residents or their continued desire to own land and their own homes. The *colonia* population was increasing by 48 percent every five years.[50] The most recent (2014) reliable data indicate that there are approximately 2,294 *colonias* in Texas with an estimated combined population of more than 500,000.[51] About 80 percent of the *colonias* are located in the six border counties of El Paso, Maverick, Hidalgo, Webb, Starr, and Cameron.

Since the 1960s, the growth of Texas border *colonias* has invariably increased the challenges in addressing the complexity of infrastructure, economic, social, and health concerns impacting these distinct communities. Basic services—such as clean water and waste disposal—are environmental health concerns. Ample evidence exists that third-world living conditions in *colonias* result in poor health conditions and disparities.[52]

The Texas Office of Border Health produced a report in 2000 on the health status and living conditions of non-*colonia* and *colonia* residents in six of the fourteen contiguous Texas–Mexico border counties.[53] The study's sampling procedure allowed for the survey results to be generalizable to the entire border region and provided a representative sample (ninety-six) of *colonias*. This included counties that happen to be in the Texas Water Development Board's Economically Distressed Areas Program. The counties selected also allowed for comparisons of the different border areas and represented a substantial proportion of the total border population (approximately 20 percent). The *colonias* had a history of poor social determinant conditions, poor infrastructure and public services, and a high potential of disease and exposure to environmental contaminants.

These inferior social determinants and environmental conditions were related to indicators of poor health. *Colonia* residents had higher rates of hepatitis A, greater exposure to pesticides, and higher prevalence of diarrhea in children age five years and younger. They were more likely to purchase medications in Mexico than non-*colonia* residents.

Other studies have also documented the detrimental impact of these *colonia* environmental conditions on the health of their residents and the decline in their health affected by their limited access to care.[54] One health needs assessment study in 2011 was based on 2,000 household surveys in 289 *colonias*, in which 7,744 interviews were conducted with families with and without children.[55] Once again, the results confirmed a young, severely impoverished population of *colonia* residents with a large percentage lacking basic infrastructure and social services. Families with children indicated that their most pressing health needs were access to regular health services for children, diabetes, and vision care. Families with no children indicated care for diabetes, heart disease, and high blood pressure as their most pressing health needs. Among all families, children's health, diabetes, vision care, tuberculosis, and heart disease were the top health care priority needs. High rates of being uninsured and lack of health care access were persistent among all families.

According to the Federal Reserve of Dallas, progress has been made in bringing resources into the *colonias* to improve residents' quality of life.[56] Their 2015 report, "*Las Colonias* in the 21st Century," describes the work of elected officials, government agencies, residents, and community organizers to address infrastructure, housing, education, economic opportunity, and access to health care. The report demonstrated varying levels of progress and obstacles in the counties that have the highest concentration of *colonias*: El Paso, Maverick, Webb, Starr, Hidalgo, and Cameron. As Table 7 illustrates, compared to other Latinos in Texas, *colonias* residents are in counties with populations that are younger, with higher unemployment

Table 7. Demographic Differences between Six Counties with *Colonias* and Texas Demographic.

Indicator	Six-county area, Texas border*	Texas
Median age	27	34
Mexican American	96%	38%
Speak English less than very well	43%	15%
Foreign born	35%	16%
Citizenship rate eighteen years and older	61%	87%
Less than high school diploma	55%	20%
Unemployment	11%	7%
Not in labor force	43%	35%
Median income	$28,928	$50,920
Poverty rate	42%	17%
Public assistance or food stamps	40%	9%

Source: *Las Colonias in the 21st Century*, 2015.
*Six counties are: El Paso, Maverick, Webb, Starr, Hidalgo, and Cameron

and poverty rates, and with a greater percentage foreign-born than in Texas overall.

Continued priority challenges and obstacles were identified in education and employment training opportunities, as well as the need for asset building through affordable home ownership. The work on basic infrastructure was also far from complete: Approximately 900 *colonias* still required improvements, and 337 lacked nearly all the basic services.

The living conditions in *colonias* are contributing causal factors to poor health, as evidenced from social determinants research. However, "there is a paucity of health data specific to *colonia* residents."[57] Nonetheless, their health risks for viral and certain infectious and chronic diseases are higher from current studies and the severity of living conditions, the result of long-standing economic, social. and political inequalities.

Health of Migrant and Seasonal Farmworkers

Since the early 1900s, agricultural labor needs, immigration laws, labor agreements with Mexico, and labor and wage laws have evolved and intersected purportedly to meet the nation's increasing and fluctuating demands for farm labor to harvest our nation's food. Unfortunately, many of the corresponding social policies were discriminatory and inequitable toward farmworkers, resulting in an entrenched cycle of poverty, labor abuses, and poor health.[58] The exploitation of farmworkers, particularly immigrant workers, became an established legacy of American agricultural history.

In 1960 Edward R. Murrow's CBS documentary "Harvest of Shame" brought to the attention of a national television audience the third-world living conditions of migrant farmworkers.[59] At the peak of the civil rights decade, César Chávez emerged in California to form the National Farmworkers Association. The NFWA gave a national voice to migratory and seasonal farmworkers for political and policy changes addressing higher wages, improved housing, and workers' safety and health.

In 1968, Texas farmworkers numbered between 350,000 and 450,000. About 88,700 of these left the state for several months each year along the northern and western stream to harvest many of the nation's crops.[60] More than one-half of them came from the four counties in the Lower Rio Grande Valley. They lived under pervasively poor third-world living conditions.[61] Such work conditions were reflected in a local Rio Grande Valley newspaper report that fourteen Mexican American farm hands were hospitalized,

> felled by deadly parathion sprayed on the cotton field in which they were working. Three were nearly dead when they arrived at the hospital. The examining doctor reported that the workers apparently absorbed through their skin the poison which (the morning dew) contained. He said symptoms of parathion poisoning are, progressively, tightness of the chest, nausea, vomiting, diarrhea, fluid in the lungs, convulsions, and death.[62]

Most descriptions on the health status of migrant and seasonal farmworkers contain major data gaps because of their work mobility, isolation, and inadequate public and private health research.[63] Much of the demographic, social, and health data is national in scope. The most referenced descriptive demographic and socioeconomic data are from the periodic National Agricultural Workers Survey (NAWS) conducted by the U.S. Department of Labor.

Nationally, the number of farmworkers has been steadily declining, in part because of slower immigration from Mexico after 2000. The result has been lost agricultural production, even while the demand for agricultural workers has persisted.[64] There were between three and four million migrant and seasonal farmworkers in the 1960s, decreasing to an estimated two to three million by 2016.

While the number of migratory and seasonal farmworkers has decreased overall in the past five decades, periodic surveys report their general demographic characteristics have not substantively changed. Basically, farmworker demographic characteristics from the NAWS in 1997–1998 indicated:

- One-half were undocumented, while another 30 percent were U.S. citizens, and 20 percent legal permanent residents.
- Most identified Spanish as their primary language, and 30 percent spoke no English at all.
- Approximately 75 percent had been in the United States for at least ten years.
- Nearly two-thirds were male.
- Their median age was thirty-eight.
- One-half were married with children.[65]

The 2015–2016 NAWS survey illustrated some farmworker improvements from 1997–1998.[66] Median education increased from sixth to eighth grade; overall poverty rate dropped from 61 to 33 percent; and farmworkers were not often found sleeping in tents, vehicles, or open fields. Nonetheless, poverty remained inordinately high for a family of six or more (65 percent), and for migrants (52 percent) compared to settled seasonal workers (28 percent). Further, only 15 percent of farmworkers lived in housing provided by their employer, while 57 percent lived in detached, single-family houses. Approximately 33 percent of farmworkers lived in housing defined as crowded, and problems of compliance and enforcement of national or state-level housing standards continue to surface.

Health researchers have identified the poor health status of farmworkers resulting from poor social determinants in their work and living conditions. One researcher reviewed 485 health research articles targeting agricultural workers written between 1966 and 1989, 152 of them specifically related to migrant families. Pesticides and health care delivery and obstacles to care comprise 57 percent of the main topic areas of all the migrant health-focused articles, followed by infectious diseases, dental care, and child health status.[67]

In 2003 researchers compiled updated available published information to identify some of the most salient health issues of farmworkers.[68] The results demonstrated significantly higher rates compared to the general population for occupation-related deaths and disabling injuries, tuberculosis, parasitic and viral infections, pesticide poisoning, dermatitis, musculoskeletal disorders, and dental decay. Also, children were at a much higher risk for a multitude of health problems.

The preceding studies surfaced gaps in data on morbidity and mortality arising from cancers, heart disease, stroke, diabetes, or other possible occupation-related disabilities. Evidence of underreporting was significant among farmworkers because of limited access to health services, job insecurity, illiteracy, and cultural conceptions of health. The available health research suggested the following issues impacting farmworkers:[69]

- More frequent delay of necessary care with acute health conditions.
- Higher prevalence of chronic conditions such as hypertension, anemia, and obesity.
- Difficulties monitoring chronic illnesses like diabetes, hypertension, tuberculosis, and HIV.
- Increased hospitalization rates among migrants.
- High prevalence and risks for mental illnesses.
- Migrant health clinics established under the Public Health Service Act reached only 12 to 15 percent of the migrant population annually.

The 1968 USCCR hearing gave added emphasis to the 65,000 migrant children enrolled in Texas public schools who were not adequately receiving needed medical, dental, nutritional, and psychological support services. More than 20,000 migrant children were identified as coming to school hungry and malnourished, and lacking access to an adequate education.[70] For many of these children, home conditions contributed further to their health risks. USCCR testimony provided evidence of the unsanitary and primitive housing in which migrant families lived.[71]

Access to health care was reported at the time of the hearing to be almost nonexistent for most farmworker families. The average per-capita health care expenditure for the nation's one million migrant workers and their families was $11, as compared to $209 for the U.S. population.[72] More than half of the migrant per-capita health care expenditure came from the Department of Health, Education, and Welfare for the National Migrant Health Program in support of the few primary health clinics established to serve them. In Texas an estimated one-third of the farmworker population had access to a migrant clinic.[73]

By 1990, the Texas farmworker population numbered 500,348, three-fourths of them in the Texas border counties. Thereafter, their numbers began to decline, to an estimated 200,000 in the year 2000, and the population appears to have stabilized at this number, as it continues to be the most cited estimate as recently as 2016. These estimates included only hired farmworkers and not nonhired family members.[74]

Most health research studies involving Texas farmworkers were produced during the period 2000–2010. Their predominant study focus was occupation-related health issues (work injuries and pesticide-related illnesses). A few studies targeted breast and cervical cancer risks and prevention, oral health prevalence, the nexus of children's education and health issues and needs, and health care access barriers. Most of these studies were conducted in the Lower Rio Grande Valley of South Texas.

An estimated 12,000 farmworkers and their families live and work on the U.S. side of the border in the Paso del Norte, a region inside the Chihuahua Desert encompassing much of West Texas and parts of Northern New Mexico. Two studies conducted by researchers from the University of Texas at El Paso exemplify a few of the population-based research efforts to determine the health status of farmworkers beyond simply identifying a health risk, illness, or disease.

One study targeted 150 migrant farmworkers from two Texas border counties (El Paso and Hudspeth) and one New Mexico (Doña Ana) border county. Diagnosed chronic disease and mental health conditions were found to be three to four times greater than the general population. Also, more than one-half of the farmworkers assessed their health as poor or fair, had suffered symptoms of pesticide exposure, and expressed concerns about their working conditions.[75]

The focus of the second study was food insecurity and health status effects, targeting 100 migrant farmworkers from Texas's El Paso County and Doña Ana County in New Mexico.[76] More than 80 percent had experienced some degree of food insecurity, and nearly one-half experienced hunger. Adults who were food insecure with hunger were at higher risks of obesity, hypertension, and metabolic syndrome. Adults had two to four times higher rates of diagnosed diabetes. More than 50 percent reported musculoskeletal related problems (knee, hand, foot, or neck) that lasted at least a week.

Although the third-world work and living conditions have improved with the implementation of federal and state labor-, wage-, housing-, and environment-related laws and regulations, poor working conditions, abuses, and discrimination persist for farmworkers.[77]

Immigrant Population Health

Immigrants have gained a significant demographic presence since the 1960s, increasing from 3 percent (298,791) to 17 percent (4.9 million) of the state's population by 2018. Latino's are two-thirds (3.2 million) of the state's immigrant population.[78] This alone poses significantly more questions regarding their health status and health care access, and the state's health care system.

Undocumented immigrants have experienced heightened challenges over the past decade because of new federal and state anti-immigration policies and enforcement strategies. The resulting stress and anxiety have worsened from the fear of deportation and added barriers relating to social-cultural integration.[79] These negative impacts are further evidence of social determinant indicators resulting in poor health and disadvantageous effects on *bienestar* (well-being).

Overall, the state's immigrant population has grown more diverse while migrating to the state's largest urban cities and border counties of Houston, Dallas, Ft. Worth, Austin, San Antonio, and El Paso. Children in families with at least one immigrant parent comprised 36 percent (2,489,261) of all Texas children.[80]

According to the American Immigration Council, more than a quarter of all adult immigrants in Texas had a college degree in 2018 while over one-third had less than a high school diploma, compared to one in three and 11 percent, respectively, for native Texans. Almost two-thirds spoke English well or very well.[81] Immigrant workers comprised 22 percent (2.9 million) of the state's labor force across a range of occupations. They make up the largest shares of building and grounds maintenance workers (46 percent) and construction and extraction occupations (42 percent).

The demographic profile for the estimated 1.6 million unauthorized immigrants in Texas indicates distinct differences from legal immigrants.[82] The key difference puts the unauthorized at greater risks of poor health because of less education, limited occupational skill sets, and lower incomes. Approximately 53 percent had less than a high school education, while only 12 percent had a bachelor's or higher degree. Sixty-five percent were in the labor force, and they had a low unemployment rate of 4 percent. One-third of their families were in poverty and two-thirds were below 200 percent of the poverty line.

The Latino immigrant population parallels the earlier description of the native-born Mexican American population as a hardworking, resilient, and often exploited low-wage labor force; however, these people experience the added challenges of overcoming immigration policies and related discriminatory actions. It's also clear from their demographic profiles that their ongoing integration is impacted by the social and economic factors that help determine health status, including economic stability, education, social and community context in which they live, and access to health care. These factors provide support that immigration itself should be viewed as a social determinant of health.[83]

One groundbreaking comprehensive national study in 2013 drew from eight major federal data systems to examine health differences between immigrants and U.S. natives across the life span.[84] It included a wide range of health and social indicators encompassing chronic and infectious diseases, mortality, disability, maternal and behavioral health, and neighborhood conditions. Some highlights of the findings were:

- Immigrant life expectancy was 3.4 years longer than for U.S. native Hispanics.
- Life expectancy for Hispanic immigrants was 81.6 years, 2.9 years more than United States-born Hispanics and 4.2 years more than non-Hispanic whites.
- Overall, immigrant infant, child, and adult health was better, with lower disability and mortality rates than for those born in the United States. This pattern was particularly prominent among Hispanic immigrants.
- Immigrant children and adults fare substantially worse than the United States-born in health preventive areas such as obesity, prenatal care, immunization, and regular preventive exams.

On average, immigrants have better health outcomes than native-born Latinos and Anglos, with lower rates of adult and infant mortality, fewer underweight babies, and less likelihood of dying from cardiovascular disease and all cancers combined. The health advantage, while not fully understood, provides preventive health protection. However, there is also a growing body of research evidence that as Latino immigrants become more "acculturated" to some native-born social and behavioral norms, their health advantage declines. This is found in those adopting the American eating habit of consuming more processed foods, and foods high in fats and sugars. Over time, their advantages decline and their health status converges with the native-born. They begin to experience increases in obesity, diabetes, and high blood pressure and decline in health from first to second generations, among both children and adults.[85]

Of greater concern is that while immigrants may be healthier than native-born Latinos and non-Latino whites, they continue to be subjected to systematic marginalization and discrimination, which have accelerated health problems among Latino immigrant families. Health providers across service sectors have increasingly observed and expressed concerns about the negative mental and physical health impacts from punitive national and state immigration policies and actions.

Discrimination and fear of deportation create trauma, which turns into chronic stress, leading to mental and physical health problems. In addition, well over one-half the immigrant families will not have health insurance coverage or a regular source of health care and will often delay seeking any health care. Studies of undocumented Latino immigrant families from Houston to El Paso to North Texas have demonstrated the relationships between immigration policy fears and health problems. Added to this is limited access to health care such as public hospitals, federally funded health clinics, and charity care.[86] The fact that many of these families are mixed-status households has added to both the reluctance to report and confusion about eligibility for both children and adults to access needed social and health services.[87]

Most members of the Latino immigrant population, particularly the undocumented, rely on emergency service providers and hospital systems. Immigration policies that limit health care access have far-reaching negative health implications.[88] Three laws have terminated or reduced unauthorized immigrants' access to public benefits programs such as welfare and Medicaid:

- 1986: Emergency Medical Treatment and Labor Act (EMTALA).
- 1996: Personal Responsibility and Work Opportunity Reconciliation Act (PRWORA).
- 2010: Patient Protection and Affordable Care Act (Obama Care).

These national laws have made it increasingly difficult for Texas's undocumented residents with end-stage renal dialysis (ESRD) needs to receive timely, cost-effective care. Diabetes and high blood pressure are the most common cause for ESRD.[89] It's estimated that more than one thousand undocumented residents needed ESRD in 2014. Many of them acquired medical intervention on an emergency basis, costing 3.7 times more per patient because of the delayed care, emergency room costs, and more frequent hospitalizations. The care was provided by the state's major public hospitals in the largest cities of Houston, Dallas, San Antonio, and El Paso. The total estimated cost for the ESRD care was $10 million from taxpayers.

Another study examined peer-reviewed publications from 1986–2016 and identified key pathways through which state-level immigration policies influence Latino health.[90] They found structural racism affecting access to education, health care, and social determinant resources such as food, wages, and housing.

The health status consequences to Latino immigrant families include foregoing preventive care; greater chronic and communicable disease rates; and mental health-related illnesses. According to a senior health researcher at Human Rights Watch, Megan McLemore, "Every time you make immigration policy more punitive or increase the chances of deportation, you're driving immigrants away from seeking health services."[91] Immigrant health disparities and inequities are worsened by:

- Confusion and conflict between federal, state, and local definitions of statutorily terms "qualified" and "unqualified" immigrants affecting both safety-net health and human service programs, and law enforcement.
- Nonprofit service providers are increasingly put in a position to deny services to immigrants, making service coordination more challenging.
- Notwithstanding existing fears ("silent crisis") or mistrust about accessing "any" services, Latino immigrants are the least informed about available service or about legal/civil rights to access them.

The dominant Mexican immigrant population in 1968 experienced overt discrimination and huge challenges to acquire citizenship, gain a better education, achieve a middle-class income, and improve opportunities for better health. Fifty years later, the Texas immigrant population has increased ten times over and has become more demographically diverse. The Latino immigrant population has also become more diverse, with greater numbers from countries other than Mexico.

Unfortunately, the negative assaults on immigrants are continuing today, arguably with even greater injustices. Punitive immigration policies delay immigrants from reaching social and economic integration and their path to citizenship. From a purely economic perspective, immigrants consistently contribute to state economic growth. They contribute more to the state's tax income than they utilize in public benefits. Punitive immigration policies only worsen health disparities and inequities at a greater cost to society.

The Future Health of Mexican American Communities

The relationship between poor living conditions and poor health presented during the U.S. Commission on Civil Rights hearing in 1968 was grounded in a long history of racially based discriminatory policies at the local and state governmental levels. The results were poor health status and health risks impacting the Mexican American population. Unlike many other advanced industrialized countries, the United States has not achieved universal access to health care as a basic human right. The Mexican American population suffers from the effects of unequal social determinants on people's health, as well as inequities in the health care system (e.g., access to care) necessary to adequately address these.

In 1968, Mexican Americans comprised 16 percent (1.7 million) of the Texas population, most residing in South Texas and the Texas–Mexico border counties. Many families lived under third-world conditions, whether working as farmworkers, living in *colonias*, or going hungry in the neglected barrios of West Side San Antonio. For decades, Texas public policies intentionally under-resourced these regions, racially profiled and politically disempowered them, and thereby perpetuated limited opportunities for social and economic mobility.

Mexican American health issues have become increasingly more salient with better Latino-specific health research and data. With Latinos in Texas increasing in number at a far greater rate than the rest of the population, more attention will likely be paid to mounting Latino health concerns. Latino children and adults are projected to surpass Anglos and Blacks in the incidence and prevalence of chronic diseases and disabilities by 2040 based simply on their greater growth.

Fundamentally, the public policy concerns raised share a common underlying question: If Latino well-being or *bienestar* continues to be disadvantaged by inattention to the social determinants of health, what are the ramifications not only for the future of Latinos but also for local communities, economic regions, and the state?

Demographic Impacts on Health

It's clear that the Latino population has changed dramatically since 1968. Cities such as Houston and Dallas are now more than 40 percent Latino. In addition, in the once predominantly white rural and semirural West and High Plains Texas regions, the Latino populations have increased across rural areas, small towns, and medium-size cities due to immigration and natural increases in these areas.

Latinos are on target to be the largest ethnic group in Texas by 2021. Their youthfulness and high fertility rate compared to the significant aging of the non-Latino white population will soon transform the state's labor force to majority Latino. For nearly two decades, demographers, civic leaders, Latinos, and others have raised state-level public policy concerns regarding the social and economic significance of these demographic changes, and the state's inadequate human capital investments in education, employment training, wage improvements, housing, and health care.[92]

Demographic characteristics are fundamental drivers in the development and allocation of health care resources (facilities, health, manpower) when combined with knowledge and understanding of a population's health epidemiology (types of risks, illnesses, needs) across age and gender groups.[93] However, the health care system has yet to fully realize the organization and allocation of health care resources from a human rights and equity perspective.

In an earlier chapter, Rogelio Sáenz described how the Latino population in Texas, because of immigration and its greater fertility, grew from 16 percent of the state's population in 1960 to 40 percent in 2018. He estimated

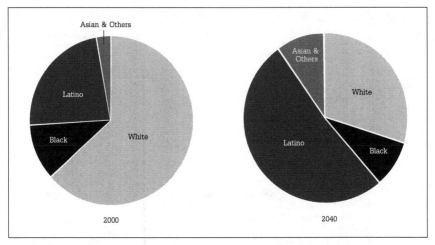

Figure 3. Projected Distribution of Adults with Disease/Disorders by Race, 2000 and 2040.

that by 2021 they would reach twelve million and become the largest racial/ethnic subgroup in the state.

Sáenz analyzed Latino demographic growth in concert with Latino social and economic trends. Large disparities were found between whites, on the one hand, and African Americans and Latinos, on the other. For example, while incomes have increased for all groups, major inequalities persist. Latinos earned 54 cents for every dollar white families earned in 1960; by 2018 Latinos had barely increased to 55 cents for every dollar earned by Anglo families. While the gap in poverty rates has narrowed considerably, Latinos and Blacks in 2018 still had poverty rates 2.6 and 2.5 times higher than whites, respectively. These demographic changes and persistent inequalities will have harmful impacts on Latino families and Texas's economic future if not addressed.[94]

On health status, demographer Steve Murdock and colleagues collected detailed disease prevalence data to make projections of their population impacts over time.[95] They did not consider changes in social and economic conditions or other determinants (e.g., health insurance access). They provide evidence that even if the race and ethnic groups maintained the current rates of chronic health illnesses, Hispanics will

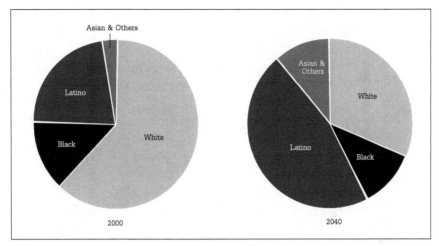

Figure 4. Projected Distribution of Adults with Disabilities by Race, 2000 and 2040.

surpass all other groups in the prevalence of disease, given their demographic growth.

Figure 3 illustrates the projections for disease/disorders among Texas's racial and ethnic populations for year 2000 and 2040. Thirty percent of all adult diseases and disorders in the state in 2000 were found among Hispanics. By 2040, Hispanics will be burdened with more than half of all adult diseases and disorders.

Figure 4 projects that Latinos will more than double their share of the state's disability rate from 2000 to 2040. By then, those with disabilities are more likely to be Latino than white or African American.

Figure 5 is baseline projected changes in the prevalence of diseases and disorders impacting Texas children between 2000 and 2040, also under existing rates. Because they are a younger population, Latinos will account for almost two-thirds of all childhood diseases and disorders by 2040.

In short, the younger age and greater growth of Latinos are generating an increasingly greater need for health care. Demographers are challenging policymakers to address persistent social determinant inequality issues raised in the 1968 civil rights hearing. The issues are intertwined with the state's history of political oppression, some of which still exists in new policy forms.

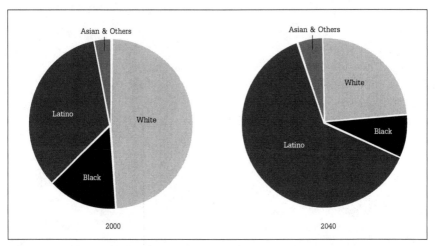

Figure 5. Projected Distribution of Children with Disease/Disorders by Race, 2000 and 2040.

The political and policy inequities illustrated during the U.S. Commission on Civil Rights hearing of 1968, followed by decades of Mexican American political organizing, advocacy, and litigation to remedy them, have been extensively chronicled. While important accomplishments were achieved, fifty years later the state's policymaking still creates an unequal playing field for civic engagement, economic mobility opportunities, and good health. The fact that Mexican Americans are still politically and legally fighting for equal education funding is but one major example.[96]

As indicated, education is a major health determinant. It is one of a group of social determinants (e.g., income, employment) that together account for 40 percent of health outcomes. Health behaviors account for another 30 percent; clinical care accounts for 20 percent; and the physical environment accounts for 10 percent. These factors support a health influence framework that has evolved through years of health disparities research, and increasingly drive efforts to address public policies that have created barriers to good health.[97]

Texas continues to present formidable public policy challenges for Latinos in the twenty-first century that if not addressed are likely to worsen. Health disparities among the state's people of color are estimated to cost billions of dollars to families, employers, insurers, and governments due to excess medical care spending, lost productivity, and lost life years. The disparities and costs weigh most heavily on Latinos.[98] Moving forward, strategies and actions to address social determinants of health must consider the intertwined political, public policy, and health system realities:

- Poor education and poverty created by decades of inequitable public policies do not get solved without political power. As such, social determinants are situated in the political and policymaking process. Texas has spent more than two decades on concerted efforts at voter suppression legislation (e.g., gerrymandering, voter ID laws) to keep Latinos, Blacks, and low-income populations from voting and gaining greater choice in political representation and power. These efforts continue unabated.[99]

- Texas's minimalist approach to policymaking has not significantly changed as it continues to limit human capital investments and to create unequal opportunities for many of its citizens. The "Texas Public Policy Way" is underpinned by the rhetoric of limited government, lower taxes, and individual responsibility, and often blames the individuals (Latinos) for purported failures to succeed.[100] This has resulted in the state performing poorly in a wide range of social determinant policy areas in national ranking reports. A few examples include poverty (thirty-eighth), education (thirty-ninth), income inequality (thirty-seventh), regressive taxation (second worst), teen births (seventh highest), low-income housing (seventh worst), asset-prosperity building (forty-first), food insecurity (eleventh), and family and child well-being (forty-third).

- Health care is a major election touchstone for Texas. The issues include availability, accessibility, quality, and costs.[101] The increasing cost of health insurance with higher deductibles and out-of-pocket expenses is exceeding wage growth and fueling additional concerns.[102] Overall, health care in Texas ranks among the worst in the nation.[103] The primary reasons include largest number of uninsured populations, leaky safety net, poor access to health care, and poor performance in addressing equity issues for low-income and people-of-color populations.[104]

Renewed strategies and comprehensive engagement of the Latino community are needed. Otherwise, state minimalist public policy efforts will continue to have limited impacts. For example, the Texas Office of Minority Health, currently the Office for the Elimination of Health Disparities, was created by the legislature in 1993. The office was intended to address health disparities and inequities. In the 2015 report to the 84th Regular Session of the Legislature, the Texas Health and Human Services (lead agency) reported tremendous strides exemplified by

> providing cultural competency training with an equity lens; evaluating Texas' Children's Health Insurance Program Medicaid Managed Care Organizations' plans for culturally and linguistically appropriateness; and providing system staff, interns from academic institutions and community members the opportunity to develop into transformative leaders. These actions ensure more communities have access to programs and services that strengthen opportunity for all Texans.[105]

Cultural competency is important; however, it exemplifies a minimalist approach to addressing health disparities and inequities, not tremendous strides. After twenty-six years, the office has had minimal state funding support ($250,000 annual average), produced no reports documenting meaningful reductions in disparities, and demonstrated even less organizing and advocacy activities to mitigate health disparity and equity issues across the state. Documented realities include:

- The uninsured: Latinos have been the most uninsured Texans for over four decades. They comprised 61 percent (2,816,816) of the state's uninsured population in 2017. Uninsured Latinos included nearly 1.7 million citizens and more than 1.1 million noncitizen immigrants. The uninsured rate for native Latino children (ages zero to seventeen) was 14 percent, compared to 6 percent among Anglo children. Among adults ages eighteen to sixty-four years old, one in four Latinos were uninsured, compared to 13 percent of Anglo adults. The uninsured rate for noncitizen immigrant children and adults in 2017 was 37 percent and 54

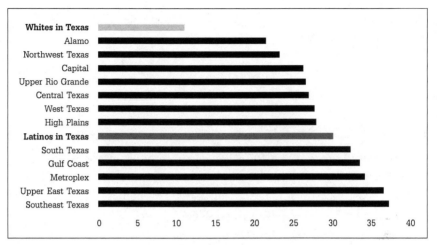

Figure 6. Ranking of Economic Regions by Percent Latinos without Health Insurance, 2012–2016. *Source:* 2012–2016 ACS Five-Year Estimates, prepared by Rogelio Sáenz, dean, College of Public Policy, University of Texas at San Antonio, October 2018.

percent, respectively.[106] Figure 6 illustrates the Latino health uninsured crisis across economic regions. The data include all uninsured for native Texans and nonnative immigrants.

• Chronic disease: The Office of the State Demographer projects that by 2040, nearly eight million adult Texans will have diabetes, costing Texas businesses $32 billion annually. More than 59 percent (4.7 million) of diabetics will be Latino. Latinos have an 87 percent higher risk of diagnosed diabetes than non-Latino whites, with 45 percent of the boys and 52 percent of girls developing diabetes during their lifetimes. The overall cost of diabetes among Latinos, including medical expenses and lost productivity, was $10.7 billion in 2010.[107]

• Growth in regional populations and disparities: A Latino health study covering fifty-three counties in the Texas Panhandle (High Plains and part of West Texas) from 2011 to 2016 was precipitated by ramifications for Latino health care and health outcomes given their population growth, particularly in Latino-majority counties. The results indicated that in Latino-majority counties, all health indicators worsened between 2011 and 2016. The indicators included children in poverty, uninsured adults, low primary-care physician to population ratio, adult obesity, diabetes, and teen birth rate.[108]

Recommendations

Latino civic leadership, legal initiatives, and electoral engagement must build political power and gain greater capacity to influence health policies. The Texas Senate Hispanic Caucus and Mexican American Legislative Caucus, in concert with Latino advocacy organizations and allies, should develop a legislative agenda with a ten-year strategic plan to address health disparities and the development of healthy Latino communities. Goals should include:

- Improve parity in health insurance coverage regardless of health status.
- Expansion of Medicaid coverage to include uninsured adults.
- Fully utilize available federal funding and where allowed provide additional state funding for safety-net programs focusing on issues such as women's health, teen pregnancy, and substance abuse prevention.
- Ensure health professions training that meets the state's population growth and demand for health professionals across community needs.
- Increase the representation of Latinos in health professions.
- Improve opportunities for undocumented immigrants to gain needed access to state and local health and human services programs.
- Establish a statewide expert review panel to critically assess and provide recommendations on major Texas health and services-related plans that require federal review for compliance and funding allocation.
- Improve education on health and nutrition in K-12 public schools.
- Establish a commission to review health disparities and inequities throughout the state with members from Latino and African American health and human services organizations.

A state legislative committee could be formed to evaluate progress on the strategic plan. Every effort should be made to include local governments and advocacy organizations in the legislative agenda.

Notes

1. The term "Mexican American" is used because people of Mexican origin predominate among Latino subgroups in Texas. The term "Chicano" is used purposefully to signify Mexican American empowerment and civil rights health activism. It was activism that first identified the need to focus on social determinant conditions, long before they were given serious health research and health care policy attention. The data presented in charts and tables include Latinos of all national origins.

2. U.S. Commission on Civil Rights (USCCR), *Hearing before the United States Commission on Civil Rights: San Antonio, TX, December 9–14, 1968* (Washington, DC: GPO, 1969), Exhibit No. 45, Archdiocesan Council of Catholic Women Resolution, 954. Also available at https://catalog. hathitrust.org/Record/001874430.

3. Paula Braveman, Susan Egerter, and David R. Williams, "The Social Determinants of Health: Coming of Age," *Annual Review of Public Health* 32 (2011): 381-98; Paula Braveman and Laura Gottlieb, "The Social Determinants of Health: It's Time to Consider the Causes of the Causes," *Public Health Reports* 129, Suppl. 2 (2014): 19-31; "NIH Conference Highlights Importance of Social and Behavioral Influences on Health," from the Consortium of Social Sciences Association website, accessed March 10, 2019.

4. Nancy E. Adler et al., "Addressing Social Determinants of Health and Health Disparities: A Vital Direction for Health and Health Care," *NAM Perspectives* (Washington, DC: National Academy of Medicine, 2016).

5. U.S. Department of Health, Education, and Welfare, Cambridge Research Institute, *Trends Affecting the U.S. HealthCare System: Health Planning Information Series*, by Carol Cerf, DHEW Publication No. HRA76714503 (Washington, DC: GPO, 1976).

6. Kimberly Amadeo, "The Rising Cost of HealthCare by Year and Its Causes," at TheBalance.com, June 25, 2019.

7. Justin McCarthy, "Seven in 10 Maintain Negative View of U.S. Healthcare System," *Gallup News Service*, January 14, 2019.

8. Southwest States Chicano Consumer Conference on Health San Antonio, *Report of the Southwest States Chicano Consumer Conference on Health, San Antonio, Texas, January 26–29, 1972* (Rockville, MD: U.S. Department of Health, Education and Welfare, 1972).

9. Amanda Moore, "Tracking Down Martin Luther King, Jr.'s Words on Health Care," at HuffPost. com, January 18, 2013.

10. USCCR, *Hearing*, 970.

11. Carlos W. Molina and Marilyn Aguirre-Molina, eds., *Latino Health in the US: A Growing Challenge* (Washington, DC: American Public Health Association, 1994); R. B. Valdéz et al., "Improving Access to Health Care in Latino Communities," *Public Health Reports,* 108, no. 5 (Los Angeles: UCLA School of Public Health, 1993): 534-39; Salvador E. Balcorta, *Migrant Health: A Social Justice Movement History* (presentation, National Migrant Health Conference, Denver, CO, May 9-12, 2012).

12. U.S. Government Accountability Office, "Hispanic Access to Health Care: Significant Gaps Exist," no. PEMD-92-6 (Washington, DC: GAO, 1992); Jerry L. Weaver, "Health Care Costs as a Political Issue: Comparative Responses of Chicanos and Anglos," *Social Science Quarterly* 53, no. 4 (1973): 846-54; A. L. Estrada, F. M. Treviño, and L. A. Ray, "Health Care Utilization Barriers Among Mexican Americans: Evidence from HHANES 1982-84," *American Journal of Public*

Health 80 (December 1, 1990): 27-31; R. Burciaga Valdéz et al., "Insuring Latinos Against the Costs of Illness," *JAMA* 269, no. 7 (February 17, 1993): 889-94.

13. W. A. Vega and H. Amaro, "Latino Outlook: Good Health, Uncertain Prognosis," *Annual Review of Public Health* 15 (1994): 39-67; Sally J. Andrade and Charlene Doria-Ortíz, "Nuestro Bienestar: A Mexican-American Community-Based Definition of Health Promotion in the Southwestern United States," *Drugs: Education, Prevention and Policy* 2, no. 2 (January 1, 1995): 129-45; Jane L. Delgado, "Meeting the Health Promotion Needs of Hispanic Communities: Policy and Research," National Coalition of Hispanic Health and Human Services Organizations (COSSMHO), *American Journal of Health Promotion* (March 1, 1995); Carlos W. Molina, Marilyn Aguirre-Molina, and Ruth Enid Zambrana, eds., "Health Issues in the Latino Community" (San Francisco: Jossey-Bass, May 2001).

14. Carmela Alcántara et al., "Disaggregating Latina/o Surveillance Health Data Across the Life Course: Barriers, Facilitators, and Exemplars" (a report to the Robert Wood Johnson Foundation, March 2017).

15. Ruth E. Zambrana and Olivia Carter-Pokras, "Health Data Issues for Hispanics: Implications for Public Health Research," *Journal of Health Care for the Poor and Underserved* 12, no. 1 (2001): 20-34.

16. Carol S. Weissert and Jaclyn Bunch, "Federalism: Cooperation and Conflict Between State and Federal Health Care Responsibility (1960-Present)," in *A Guide to U.S. Health and Health Care Policy*, Thomas R. Oliver, ed., (Washington, DC: CQ Press, 2014), 127-40.

17. Christopher Banks and John Blakeman, eds., *The U.S. Supreme Court and New Federalism: From the Rehnquist Court to the Roberts Court* (Washington, DC: Rowman & Littlefield Publishers, 2012).

18. Benjamin D. Sommers, "Medicaid Expansion in Texas: What's at Stake?," *Issue Brief* (April 2016).

19. Nancy Pindus et al., *Income Support and Social Services for Low-Income People in Texas* (Washington, DC: Urban Institute, 1998); Crystal Kuntz and Margaret Sulvetta, *Health Policy for Low-Income People in Texas* (Washington, DC: Urban Institute, 1997).

20. S. P. Udayakumar, "Globalization as If the Entire Globe Mattered: The Situation of Minority Groups," in *Global Transformation and World Futures—Volume 1* (Encyclopedia of Life Support Systems, 2009).

21. USCCR, *Hearing*, 570.

22. U.S. Department of Health and Human Services, Agency for Healthcare Research and Quality, *2016 National Healthcare Quality and Disparities Report* (Rockville, MD: AHRQ, 2017) .

23. D'Ann Petersen and Laila Assanie, *The Changing Face of Texas: Population Projections and Implications* (Dallas, TX: Federal Reserve Bank of Dallas, October 2015).

24. Pia Orrenius and Madeline Zavodny, *Trends in Poverty and Inequality Among Hispanics* (Working Paper 1109, Federal Reserve Bank of Dallas, June 2011); John Weber, *From South Texas to the Nation: The Exploitation of Mexican Labor in the Twentieth Century* (n.p., University of North Carolina Press, 2015); K. S. Markides and J. Coreil, "The Health of Hispanics in the Southwestern United States: An Epidemiologic Paradox," *Public Health Reports* 101, no. 3 (1986): 253-65.

25. Myron P. Gutmann et al., *Dating the Origins of the Epidemiologic Paradox among Mexican Americans* (paper prepared for the Annual Meeting of the Population Association of America, Washington, DC, March 26-29, 1997, Texas Population Research Center Papers, No. 97, revised April 1998): 98-107.

26. Gutmann et al., *Dating the Origins*, 98-107.

27. Leo S. Morales et al., "Socioeconomic, Cultural, And Behavioral Factors Affecting Hispanic

Health Outcomes," *Journal of Health Care for the Poor and Underserved* 13, no. 4 (November 2002): 477-503; John M. Ruiz, Patrick Steffen, and Timothy B. Smith, "Hispanic Mortality Paradox: A Systematic Review and Meta-Analysis of the Longitudinal Literature," *American Journal of Public Health* 103, no. 3 (March 2013): e52-60; Centers for Disease Control and Prevention, "Vital Signs: Leading Causes of Death, Prevalence of Diseases and Risk Factors, and Use of Health Services Among Hispanics in the United States 2009-2013," *MMWR*, CDC website, May 8, 2015, 469-78.

28. Mark D. Hayward et al., "Does the Hispanic Paradox in U.S. Adult Mortality Extend to Disability?," *Population Research and Policy Review* 33, no. 1 (February 1, 2014): 81-96; Maria Teresa V. Taningco, *Revisiting the Latino Health Paradox* (Los Angeles: Tomas Rivera Policy Institute, 2007); Yolanda C. Padilla, Erin R. Hamilton, and Robert A. Hummer, "Beyond the Epidemiological Paradox: The Health of Mexican American Children at Age 5," *Social Science Quarterly* 90, no. 5 (December 1, 2009): 1072-88.

29. Kathleen A. Cagney, Christopher R. Browning, and Danielle M. Wallace, "The Latino Paradox in Neighborhood Context: The Case of Asthma and Other Respiratory Conditions," *American Journal of Public Health* 97, no. 5 (May 2007): 919-25; Jennifer J. Salinas, Dejun Su, and Soham Al Snih, "Border Health in the Shadow of the Hispanic Paradox: Issues in the Conceptualization of Health Disparities in Older Mexican Americans Living in the Southwest," *Journal of Cross-Cultural Gerontology* 28, no. 3 (September 2013): 251-66; Elizabeth H. Baker, Michael S. Rendall, and Margaret M. Weden, "Epidemiological Paradox or Immigrant Vulnerability? Obesity Among Young Children of Immigrants," *Demography* 52, no. 4 (August 2015): 1295-320; Osea Giuntella, "The Hispanic Health Paradox: New Evidence from Longitudinal Data on Second and Third-Generation Birth Outcomes," *SSM—Population Health,* 2 (2016): 84-89.

30. Merit P. George, "The Mexican American Health Paradox: The Collective Influence of Sociocultural Factors on Hispanic Health Outcomes," *Discussions* 9, no. 2 (2013); John M. Ruíz, Belinda Campos, and James J. Garcia, "Special Issue on Latino Physical Health: Disparities, Paradoxes, and Future Directions," *Journal of Latina/o Psychology* 4, no. 2 (2016): 61-66.

31. M. Ray Perryman, "An Urban-Rural Divide," The Perryman Group website, December 5, 2016.

32. Harold H. Bruff, "Separation of Powers Under the Texas Constitution," *Texas Law Review* 68, no. 7 (June 1990): 1337-67.

33. Texas Association of Counties, "About Texas Counties," available online at County.org.

34. House Research Organization, "Health and Human Services Reorganization: Consolidation, Call Centers, and Councils," *Interim News,* no. 78-5, May 26, 2004.

35. Center for Health Policy Development, *The Texas Health Promotion Initiative: A Strategic Plan Responding to Diversity* report (n.p.: Center for Health Policy Development, 1991).

36. U.S. Commission on Civil Rights, Texas Advisory Committee, *Texas, The State of Civil Rights: Ten Years Later, 1968—1978: A Report* (Washington, DC: GPO, 1980).

37. RCHN Community Health Foundation, *Community Health Centers: Chronicling Their History and Broader Meaning,* at CHCChronicles.org.

38. Gustavo M. Quesada and Peter L. Heller, "Sociocultural Barriers to Medical Care among Mexican Americans in Texas: A Summary Report of Research Conducted by the Southwest Medical Sociology Ad Hoc Committee," *Medical Care* 15, no. 5 (1977): 93-101.

39. Texas Health and Human Services, Office of Border Public Health, "Texas-Mexico Border," at DSHS.texas.gov.

40. U.S. Department of Transportation, Bureau of Transportation Statistics, "Bureau Crossing/ Entry Data," at BTS.gov.

41. Texas Health and Human Services, Office of Border Public Health, "Texas-Mexico Border"; Al Kaufman, "Border Higher Ed Gains Began with a Lawsuit," *San Antonio Express-News*, May 21, 2016; Texas Higher Education Coordinating Board, *Texas-Mexico Border Health Education Needs: A Report to the 77th Legislature* (Austin: Texas Higher Education Coordinating Board, 2000).

42. Amy K. Glasmeier, *An Atlas of Poverty in American: One Nation, Pulling Apart, 1960—2003* (New York: Routledge, 2006).

43. U.S. General Accounting Office, *Health Care Availability in the Texas-Mexico Border Area* (Washington, DC: GAO, 1988).

44. Rumaldo Z. Juarez, *Lower Rio Grande Valley Demographics and Health Statistics, 1994* (Edinburgh: University of Texas System Texas-Mexico Border Health Coordination Office, University of Texas-Pan American, 2004).

45. David C. Warner and Lauren R. Jahnke, *U.S./Mexico Border Health Issues: The Texas Rio Grande Valley* (San Antonio: Regional Center for Health Workforce Studies, Center for Health Economics and Policy, The University of Texas Health Science Center at San Antonio, 2003).

46. University of Texas Health Science Center at San Antonio, *South Texas Health Status Review* (San Antonio: IHPR, 2007).

47. United States-Mexico Border Health Commission, *Border Lives: Health Status in the United States-Mexico Border Region* (Washington, DC: GPO, 2010).

48. Federal Reserve Bank of Dallas, *Texas Colonias: A Thumbnail Sketch of the Conditions, Issues, Challenges and Opportunities* (Dallas: Community Affairs Office of the Federal Reserve Bank of Dallas, 1996).

49. LBJ School of Public Affairs, *Colonias in the Lower Rio Grande Valley of South Texas: A Summary Report, PRP 18*, by Mark Estes, Kingsley E. Haynes, and Jared E. Hazleton (Austin: University of Texas at Austin, 1977).

50. LBJ School of Public Affairs, *Colonias in the Lower Rio Grande Valley*, 16.

51. Jordana Barton, Emily Ryder Perlmutter, and Raquel R. Márques, *Las Colonias in the 21st Century: Progress Along the Texas-Mexico Border* (Dallas: Federal Reserve Bank of Dallas, 2015).

52. Office of Disease Prevention and Health Promotion, "Healthy People 2020, Promote Health for All Through A Healthy Environment," at HealthyPeople.gov, updated March 26, 2020.

53. Ronald J. Dutton et al., "Executive Summary," *Survey of Health and Environmental Conditions in Texas Border Counties and Colonias: A Technical Report* (Austin: Texas Department of Health, 2000).

54. Nelda Mier et al., "Health-Related Quality of Life Among Mexican Americans Living in Colonias at the Texas-Mexico Border," *Social Science & Medicine (1982)* 66, no. 8 (April 2008): 1760-71; Larry Ortiz, Lydia Arizmendi, and Llewellyn J. Cornelius, "Access to Health Care among Latinos of Mexican Descent in *Colonias* in Two Texas Counties," *Journal of Rural Health: Official Journal of the American Rural Health Association and the National Rural Health Care Association* 20, no. 3 (2004): 246-52.

55. A. L. Ramirez et al., "Family-Based Health Needs Along the Texas-Mexico Border," *Journal of Public Health* 33, no. 4 (December 1, 2011): 579-86.

56. Barton et al., *Las Colonias in the 21st Century*.

57. Barton et al., *Las Colonias in the 21st Century*, 23.

58. Mary E. Mendoza, "Mexican Farm Labor and the Agricultural Economy of the United States," *The Hispanic Legacy in American History*, Winter 2019; Robert Holly, "More than Half-Century After 'Harvest of Shame,' Migrant Farmworkers in the U.S. Still Face Deplorable Conditions," Investigate Midwest website, November 7, 2016.

59. Byron Pitts, "Harvest of Shame, 50 Years Later," CBS Evening News website, November 24, 2010.

60. USCCR, *Hearing*, 953-54.

61. USCCR, *Hearing*, 953.

62. USCCR, *Hearing*, 968.

63. A migrant farmworker is someone who travels from place to place to work in agriculture and moves into temporary housing while working, whereas a seasonal farmworker works primarily in agriculture but lives in one community year-round.

64. Stephen G. Bronars, *A Vanishing Breed: How the Decline in U.S. Farm Laborers Over the Last Decade Has Hurt the U.S. Economy and Slowed Production on American Farm* (New York: Partnership for a New American Economy, 2015), available at NewAmericanEconomy.org.

65. U.S. Department of Labor, Office of the Assistant Secretary for Policy, and Office of Program Economics, *Findings from the National Workers Agricultural Survey (NAWS) 1997–98: A Demographic and Employment Profile of United States Farmworkers*, by Kala Mehta et al., Research Report No. 8 (Washington DC: U.S. Department of Labor, 2000).

66. Trish Hernandez and Susan Gabbard, *Findings from the National Workers Agricultural Survey (NAWS) 2015–16: A Demographic and Employment Profile of United States Farmworkers*, Research Report No. 13 (San Mateo, CA: JBS International, 2018).

67. G. S. Rust, "Health Status of Migrant Farmworkers: A Literature Review and Commentary," *American Journal of Public Health* 80, no. 10 (October 1990): 1213-17.

68. Eric Hansen and Martin Donohoe, "Health Issues of Migrant and Seasonal Farmworkers," *Journal of Health Care for the Poor and Underserved* 14, no. 2 (May 2003): 153-64.

69. Don Villarejo, "The Health of U.S. Hired Farm Workers," *Annual Review of Public Health* 24 (2003): 175-93; Thomas A. Arcury and Sara A. Quandt, "Delivery of Health Services to Migrant and Seasonal Farmworkers," *Annual Review of Public Health* 28 (2007): 345-63; *Agricultural Workers and Mental Health* (Buda, TX: National Center for Farmworker Health, 2017), available at ncfh.org.

70. USCCR, *Hearing*, 953-54.

71. USCCR, *Hearing*, 968.

72. USCCR, *Hearing*, 348.

73. USCCR, *Hearing*, 342.

74. Alice C. Larson, *Migrant and Seasonal Farmworker Enumeration Profiles Study: Texas, Larson Assistance Services*, Prepared for Migrant Health Program, Bureau of Primary Health Care (2000); "Agricultural-Worker Population Estimates," Legal Services Corporation website, updated August 8, 2016, at lsc.gov.

75. Jane E. Poss and Rebecca Pierce, "Characteristics of Selected Migrant Farmworkers in West Texas and Southern New Mexico," *California Journal of Health Promotion* 1, no. 2 (2003): 138-47.

76. M. Margaret Weigel et al., "The Household Food Insecurity and Health Outcomes of U.S.-Mexico Border Migrant and Seasonal Farmworkers," *Journal of Immigrant and Minority Health* 9, no. 3 (July 2007): 157-69, doi:10.1007/s10903-006-9026-6.

77. Shedra Amy Snipes, Sharon P. Cooper, and Eva M. Shipp, "'The Only Thing I Wish I Could Change Is That They Treat Us Like People and Not Like Animals': Injury and Discrimination Among Latino Farmworkers," *Journal of Agromedicine* 22, no. 1 (January 2, 2017): 36-46; John Burnett, "In South Texas, Fair Wages Elude Farmworkers, 50 Years After Historic Strike," NPR website, accessed July 22, 2019.

78. For 1960: Office of the State Demographer, "The Foreign-Born Population in Texas: Sources of Growth," 2015; for 2018: https://www.migrationpolicy.org/data/state-profiles/state/demographics/TX

79. Cecilia Ayón, "Economic, Social, and Health Effects of Discrimination on Latino Immigrant Families," Migration Policy Institute, September 2015, available at MigrationPolicy.org.

80. "State Immigration Data Profiles: Demographics for Texas, 2017," Migration Policy Institute, available at MigrationPolicy.org.

81. "Immigrants in Texas" Fact Sheet, August 6, 2020, American Immigration Council, available at AmericanImmigrationCouncil.org.

82. "Profile of Unauthorized Population: Texas, 2012-2016," Migration Policy Institute, available at MigrationPolicy.org.

83. National Academies of Sciences, Engineering, and Medicine, *Immigration as a Social Determinant of Health: Proceedings of a Workshop* (Washington, DC: National Academies Press, 2018).

84. Gopal K. Singh, Alfonso Rodriguez-Lainz, and Michael D. Kogan, "Immigrant Health Inequalities in the United States: Use of Eight Major National Data Systems," *Scientific World Journal*, 2013, https://doi.org/10.1155/2013/512313.

85. Marielena Lara, Cristina Gamboa, M Lya Kahramanian, Leo S Morales, and David E Hayes Bautista, "Acculturation and Latino Health in the United States: A Review of the Literature and Its Sociopolitical Context," *Annual Review of Public Health* 26 (2005): 367-97; John M. Ruiz, et al., "Special Issue on Latino Physical Health," Journal of Latina/o Psychology 4, no. 2 (2016) 61-66.

86. Vivianne R. Aponte-Rivera and Boadie W. Dunlop, "Public Health Consequences of State Immigration Laws," Southern Medical Association website, accessed June 2, 2019; M. L. Berk et al., "Health Care Use among Undocumented Latino Immigrants," *Health Affairs (Project Hope)* 19, no. 4 (August 2000): 51-64.

87. Heide Castañeda and Milena Andrea Melo, "Health Care Access for Latino Mixed-Status Families: Barriers, Strategies, and Implications for Reform," *American Behavioral Scientist* 58, no. 14 (December 1, 2014): 1891-909, doi:10.1177/0002764214550290.

88. Rohit Kuruvilla and Rajeev Raghavan, "Health Care for Undocumented Immigrants in Texas," *Texas Medicine* 110, no. 7 (2014): e1.

89. Kuruvilla and Raghavan, "Health Care."

90. Morgan M. Philbin et al., "State-Level Immigration and Immigrant-Focused Policies as Drivers of Latino Health Disparities in the United States," *Social Science & Medicine (1982)* 199 (2018): 29-38, doi:10.1016/j.socscimed.2017.04.007.

91. "Immigration Is a Public Health Issue, But Not for the Reasons Some Politicians Claim," HuffPost website, accessed June 5, 2019.

92. "Coming to Our Census," *Texas Monthly* website, February 11, 2014.

93. "How Demographics Impact Healthcare Delivery," accessed April 11, 2019, Ensocare website.

94. Ray R. Marshall and Leon F. Bouvier, *Population Change and the Future of Texas* (Washington, DC: Population Reference Bureau, 1986); Steve H. Murdock et al., *The New Texas Challenge: Population Change and the Future of Texas* (College Station: Texas A&M University Press, 2003); Cal Jillson, *Lone Star Tarnished: A Critical Look at Texas Politics and Public Policy* (New York: Routledge, 2015).

95. Steve H. Murdock et al., *Changing Texas: Implications of Addressing or Ignoring the Texas Challenge* (College Station: Texas A&M University Press. 2014).

96. Will Weissert, "Texas Court Finds School Funding Flawed but Constitutional," WOAI radio website, May 13, 2016.

97. "What Is Health?," County Health Rankings & Roadmaps website, accessed May 22, 2019.

98. "Economic Impacts of Health Disparities in Texas—MHM," Methodist Healthcare Ministries of South Texas website, accessed June 3, 2019,

99. "Federal Judge Orders Texas to End 'Flawed' Effort to ID Non-citizen Voters," NPR website, accessed June 3, 2019.

100. Juan H. Flores, "The *Bienestar* (Well-Being) of Texas Hispanic Children" (report, La Fe Policy Research and Education Center, 2016).

101. "Texas Residents' Views on State and National Health Policy Priorities," *The Henry J. Kaiser Family Foundation* (blog), June 14, 2018.

102. "2018 Employer Health Benefits Survey," *The Henry J. Kaiser Family Foundation* (blog), October 3, 2018.

103. Alvaro "Al" Ortiz, "Report: Texas Ranks Last in U.S. in Health Care Access and Affordability," Houston Public Media website, June 12, 2019.

104. David C. Radley, Douglas McCarthy, and Susan L. Hayes, "2018 Scorecard on State Health System Performance" (May 2018), The Commonwealth Fund website.

105. Center for Elimination of Disproportionality and Disparities, "Equitable Practices for Texas Systems" as required by Senate Bill 1 (Regular Session, 2015), Texas Health and Human Services, 4.

106. U.S. Census, *Current Population Survey 2017.*

107. Flores, "The *Bienestar*," 55.

108. Lawrence E. Estaville and Edris J. Montalvo, "Latino Health in the Texas Panhandle: Policy Implications," *Papers in Applied Geography* 3 (August 7, 2017): 1–12.

LUPE S. SALINAS

Mexican American Criminal Injustice in Texas

R acial conflicts pervade American history. The nation began with a Caucasian government that subjugated Native Americans and enslaved Africans. More than half a century later, distinct peoples, specifically Mexican-descent persons, predominantly of Indian and mestizo blood, joined the nation as a conquered people via the treaty that ended the Mexican-American War in 1848.[1] Mexican, African, and Native Americans patiently endured a pitiful lack of fairness in the U.S. legal system.

Having actively observed the past five decades of the Texas criminal enforcement system, I describe it as one of "criminal injustice" that requires corrective action. This chapter provides a fifty-year synopsis of the administration of Texas justice after the 1968 San Antonio hearing conducted by the U.S. Commission on Civil Rights (hereafter "the 1968 hearing").[2] At the 1968 hearing, testimony included a report on investigations by the commission of numerous complaints regarding abuses within the courts and among police officials.[3] The accusations included physical and verbal abuse, harassment by law officers, exclusion from juries, both grand and trial, punitive use of bail, lack of and inadequate representation by counsel, and disproportionately low numbers of Latinos in law enforcement. The 1968 hearing did not address illegal and unethical prosecutorial actions, although the later report included some of these violations.[4]

The 1968 Hearing: Criminal Justice Summary

POLICE BRUTALITY

The complaints about abusive officers in the report included the use of excessive force and harassment among Mexican Americans, in stark contrast with treatment of Anglos.[5] In addition, police presence in minority neighborhoods was less adequate, and the findings indicated widespread law enforcement prejudice that undermined proper police-community relations.[6]

The hearing testimony addressed police interference with Mexican American organizational efforts, citing an effort by the Texas Rangers and ranchers along the Texas-Mexico border to retaliate against farmworker organizing.[7] This incident included use of excessive force by Captain A. Y. Allee, a Texas Ranger known for his violent tactics, against a union activist. Federal litigation declared several Texas statutes unconstitutional and upheld injunctive relief.[8] The hearing found that citizens merely want to be heard and to have appropriate remedial action taken. Instead, victims often encounter obstacles that lead to frustration among civilians and those who suffer serious injury or death while in the custody of or while being confronted by an officer.[9]

The commission concluded in its report that administrative and judicial remedies for illegal police actions inadequately provided prompt and fair review. Worse, police complaints often elicit physical retaliation and threats of charges for false statements, and seldom lead to discipline.[10] Witnesses reported excessive use of force and questionable "investigation" arrests and "stop and frisk" practices in Mexican American neighborhoods. Nonetheless, witnesses complained of inadequate police protection.[11]

JURY REPRESENTATION

The grand jury decides whether criminal charges will be filed against the accused under the lesser probable cause standard, while the trial jury determines the accused guilty or not guilty, utilizing the beyond a reasonable doubt standard of proof. During the 1950s Mexican Americans faced barriers in both grand jury and trial participation, since officials seldom permitted Mexicans to serve. After complaints lasting a half century, the Supreme Court unanimously declared that Mexican Americans constitute an identifiable class distinct from other whites and merited protection from systematic exclusion from grand and trial juries.[12]

The state failed to explain the apparent racial discrimination. The Supreme Court concluded that "differences in race and color have defined easily identifiable groups which have at times required the aid of the courts in securing equal treatment under the laws."[13] It further held that the Spanish-surnamed population constituted an identifiable class that differed sufficiently from the white Anglo citizens, and that its systematic exclusion from jury service violated the Fourteenth Amendment equal protection clause.[14] The 1968 complaints have been generally corrected, but Latinos seek advances in representation and controls over challenges that remove minorities from service.[15]

Texas grand juries that determine whether to charge a person with a state crime also faced complaints.[16] The now-defunct Texas grand jury selection "key man" system allowed district judges to appoint commissioners who selected fifteen to twenty citizens.[17] In 2015, legislators amended the process to allow grand jury selection as done in district court civil cases, permitting a more representative racial, ethnic, and gender group.[18]

DISPARATE BAIL PRACTICES

Bail is designed to permit the release of an accused from custody with the assurance that she will appear for trial. The Eighth Amendment prohibits excessive bail, but cases rarely address this issue since judges enjoy discretion regarding the amount set.[19] The 1968 hearing questioned bail practices and their improper use against disproportionately poor Mexican

Americans. The major concern involved the role poverty plays in inducing innocent persons to plead guilty to gain release.[20]

INADEQUATE COUNSEL REPRESENTATION

Experts consider effective assistance of counsel the most essential constitutional right.[21] The 1968 hearing addressed this critical topic, made famous by Clarence Gideon, a poor man forced to defend himself in a burglary. The court had ruled in 1963 that the Constitution guaranteed poor persons the right to have counsel in state felonies just like a rich person could easily have.[22] Upon his retrial, with the lawyer's aid, Gideon won an acquittal.

In addition, the 1968 hearing addressed concerns of incompetent legal representation. As in bail matters, Latinos encounter barriers in hiring counsel.[23] Besides indigent status, the underrepresentation of bilingual lawyers in private practice obstructed access.[24] The Sixth Amendment grants the accused a right to effective assistance of counsel. Further, confrontation and cross-examination of witnesses require interpreter assistance.[25]

EMPLOYMENT IN LAW ENFORCEMENT

The 1968 hearing addressed the absence of Mexican Americans in administration of justice positions. Public officials and private citizens articulated that respect toward the justice system could be improved by the inclusion of Latino law enforcement and judges who expressed sensitivity to Latino culture.[26] Witnesses provided a critique of the justice system as distrustful and hostile, especially among those Mexican American descendants of Spanish settlers who lost their land via the treaty that ended the war with Mexico in 1848.[27]

Predictably, negative attitudes developed among persons of Mexican descent as a result of mob lynching, fatal attacks by police and Anglo landowners who received assistance from Texas Rangers,[28] jury exclusions,[29] school segregation,[30] denial of voting rights,[31] and exclusions from public accommodations.[32] As confirmed by the various cited sources, Mexican Americans experienced racial discrimination analogous to that inflicted on Blacks by the dominant white leaders of Texas and the South.

Case Studies Since 1968

The Fourteenth Amendment of 1868 forbids "any state" to "deprive any person of life, liberty, or property, without due process of law."[33] Shortly thereafter, Congress enacted the Civil Rights Act of 1871 that provided a damages avenue for anyone deprived of life, liberty, or property without appropriate legal procedures and safeguards.[34] Further, curbside justice or infliction of physical punishment would violate due process of law since the criminal codes, not the police, set forth the appropriate punishment for a wrongdoer.[35]

The cases that follow are examples of injustices that Latinos faced in the past half century.

JOE CAMPOS TORRES—POLICE USE OF DEADLY FORCE, 1977

The police killing of José "Joe" Campos Torres in 1977 is an example of the worst police brutality and the failure of prosecutors and juries to act upon it. Upon his arrest for public intoxication, an offense that carries a mere $200 fine, and after police talked about shooting "wetbacks" swimming across the river, police took Torres to "The Hole," a secret hideaway that later became iconic for police human rights violations. Five police officers beat Torres so savagely that the jail sergeant refused to accept the bloody prisoner.

Instead of providing Torres with medical attention, the officers returned him to The Hole, on the edge of Buffalo Bayou in downtown Houston. An officer removed the handcuffs and reminded Officer Denson that he wanted to see if the "wetback" could swim. The cops marched Torres to the water's edge, and Denson pushed Torres. This act led to a drowning, since Torres, dressed in combat boots and army fatigue pants, also had an extremely high blood-alcohol level of .22.[36]

In the state trial for murder, the jury returned a negligent homicide verdict and granted a probation to the officers.[37] A few months later, after the federal jury conviction for civil rights conspiracy resulting in death, U.S. Judge Ross Sterling inexplicably rationalized that the officers' actions toward Torres stemmed from the police department's faulty management.

In a death case, the accused is punishable up to life in prison. Judge Sterling sentenced the officers to one year and a day in prison.[38]

RICHARD MORALES—USE OF A SHOTGUN TO OBTAIN A CONFESSION, 1975

The murder of Richard Morales by Chief Frank Hayes of the Castroville Police Department recalls memories of the anti-Mexican lynching days of the nineteenth century in Texas.[39] Hayes directed an officer to serve a misdemeanor warrant, and, without a search warrant, to enter Morales's residence to inspect items with serial numbers.[40] Hayes arrived, exited his car, and punched Morales in the stomach, stating, "Let the son of a bitch go; uncuff him and let him run, so I can shoot him."[41]

Hayes and others traveled to a deserted gravel road. Hayes directed that all lights be extinguished, got a double-barreled 12-gauge shotgun, and struck Morales in the stomach with the breech of the shotgun. Hayes then stated that he had killed one Mexican and was "fixing to kill" another one. Hayes directed removal of Morales's handcuffs and told the cops to leave. Hayes questioned Morales further, pushing him with the butt and then the barrel of the shotgun. Morales pushed the barrel of the gun aside and stepped back. The shotgun discharged, killing Morales. After learning the killing details, the Medina County Sheriff called it "the most cold-blooded murder I've ever seen," adding "It looks like an execution."[42]

After the shooting, with the actual civil rights deprivation completed, Hayes then began his obstruction of justice. He told his deputy to inform the sheriff that Morales had escaped. The coverup continued with Hayes and others loading the body into Hayes's personal car. Hayes's wife and daughter continued efforts to conceal the body, traveling hundreds of miles away to bury the body. Police apprehended them as they disposed of bloody garbage bags and shovels, with Mrs. Hayes eventually directing police to Morales's body.[43]

A federal grand jury returned an indictment charging Hayes with depriving Morales of the right to liberty without due process of law.[44] A jury found Hayes guilty, and the judge later sentenced Hayes to life imprisonment.[45] The Fifth Circuit affirmed the conviction, rejecting his double-jeopardy claim.[46]

SANTOS RODRÍGUEZ—THE RUSSIAN ROULETTE TACTIC TO COERCE A CONFESSION, 1977

Although the shooting death of a twelve-year-old boy by a Dallas officer ended in a murder charge, the ultimate disposition angered Latinos. The officer tried to coerce a confession, utilizing the extremely dangerous Russian Roulette tactic.[47] The jury assigned a meager five-year sentence for the murder.

It all began when another officer observed two youngsters, known to him as the Rodríguez brothers, behind a service station. The officer gave their home address. Both Officer Darrell Cain and the other officer arrived and entered the house.[48] Police took Santos and David, both juveniles, placing Santos in the front of the vehicle while David sat in the back with Cain. Cain took out his pistol. David saw the twirl of the cylinder and the bullets in all the chambers. David claims Cain never unloaded the pistol.

Cain shut the cylinder, aimed at Santos's head, and asked Santos to admit they burglarized the station. When he denied it, Cain clicked the gun, stated the pistol had a bullet, and told him to confess. Cain continued threatening, the gun discharged, and Santos died. Cain jumped out, saying, "Oh, my God."[49] Within ten seconds, an investigator took Cain's gun from him, later stating at trial that he did not see Cain replace any bullets.[50] Investigation did not reveal fingerprints from the Rodríguez boys.[51]

At trial, Cain contradicted the state's version, asserting he had unloaded the weapon and merely tried to "make him tell the truth."[52] Cain definitely violated the right of an accused to remain silent and to have a lawyer.[53] As a juvenile suspect, Santos should have received more consideration from the Justice Department since, as a child, he had additional rights and needed more protection than adults.[54]

LUIS ALFONSO TORRES—POLICE USE OF DEADLY FORCE, 2002

Luis Alfonso Torres died on January 20, 2002, shortly after an alleged "fight" with three Baytown officers. The police car video documented that Torres did not throw a punch or attack officers to justify their use of force or violence. No "fight" or struggle ever had a chance to occur. Police, instead, jumped Torres from behind and took him down. Torres never attempted to harm or subdue any officer. In fact, he appeared quite cordial with the officers before the physical encounter. One of the officers applied his knee on or near the neck while Torres was on the ground. To aggravate respiratory matters, an officer then pepper-sprayed Torres, who died at the scene a few minutes later of mechanical asphyxiation, suffocated by an officer's improper and unnecessary force.[55]

The case went before a Harris County grand jury, and the grand jury returned a no bill, concluding they did not have probable cause to indict any of the officers who applied the fatal force. The grand jury would not even justify a negligent homicide charge.[56] Any person would know that the weight and force of a knee on a person's throat is life-threatening. Pepper-spraying a victim's face can only predictably result in the asphyxiation that ended Torres's life within a few minutes. In spite of these facts, the Department of Justice declined prosecution of the officer.

That Torres was a resident alien might cause some to conclude that he had no rights.[57] The civil rights remedies statute provides protection for "any citizen of the United States or other person within the jurisdiction thereof."[58] The criminal law seeks to protect any "inhabitant" of the United States. Unfortunately, many U.S. citizens view both lawfully admitted and unauthorized aliens as lacking civil rights, having been brainwashed by the social and political rhetoric.[59]

CHRIS OCHOA—A CROOKED COP COERCES A GUILTY PLEA TO MURDER, 1991

Chris Ochoa and his friend Richard Danziger ended up in the custodial stranglehold of Austin police detective Héctor Polanco. After the robbery, rape, and murder of a fellow Pizza Hut employee, the two men had gone to the scene of the crime to pay their respects. The nervous employees called the police. Once Polanco had Ochoa and Danziger in his custody, the cop subjected Ochoa to threat of a death penalty prosecution if he did not cooperate by waiving his constitutional right not to "be compelled in any criminal case to be a witness against himself."[60]

Polanco first "worked" on Ochoa, and he then tried the same tactics to get Danziger to cooperate and confess to a crime he did not commit. Polanco utilized a fraudulent and threatening approach against Ochoa to close the Pizza Hut investigation, claiming proof of Ochoa's guilt.[61] Ochoa's denials angered the detective, prompting the detective to yell, pound on the table, and threaten to have inmates rape Ochoa. An officer grabbed Ochoa's arm and showed him where the lethal injection would occur if he did not cooperate, telling him, "white guys always walk, and the Hispanics always get the needle."[62]

Ochoa entered a plea of guilty to murder and agreed to testify against Danziger, who proceeded to trial for sexual assault after he refused to confess. Ochoa perjured himself to avoid retaliation from Detective Polanco. Danziger took the stand, asserted his innocence, and expressed his disbelief as to why Ochoa, his friend, and the police were lying. The jury found Danziger guilty and imposed a life sentence.[63] A year later Danziger was attacked by an inmate, and the severe beating resulted in permanent brain damage, requiring assisted care for life.[64]

Twelve years later, the two wrongly convicted men received their freedom after the Wisconsin Innocence Project responded to Ochoa's pleas for help. The real killer, Achim Josef Marino, already in prison for another crime, came forward. Experiencing a need to repent with his newfound faith in God, Marino repeatedly sent confession letters to Austin police and the Texas governor, claiming responsibility. The state eventually found Marino guilty of capital murder, for which he received an agreed automatic life sentence.[65]

DANIEL VILLEGAS—A CORRUPT COP VIOLATES THE RIGHT TO REMAIN SILENT, 1993

In 1993, two young men died of gunshot wounds in El Paso, Texas.[66] Police picked up seventeen-year-old David Rangel and interrogated him about the recent double murder. Detective Al Márquez badgered Rangel, falsely telling him that "others had already implicated him and that he would get life and be raped in prison if he didn't cooperate."[67] Rangel maintained his innocence, but he mentioned that his sixteen-year-old cousin, Daniel Villegas, bragged during a phone call about shooting the two teenage victims with a shotgun.

Rangel quickly admitted to Detective Márquez that Villegas was just joking, but Márquez demanded that Rangel write out a statement implicating his cousin, ordering Rangel to leave out the term "shotgun" since that detail was "was incorrect." The evidence indicates the two victims had been shot with a .22 caliber pistol, further suggesting that Villegas did not know enough about the crime to "properly brag about it."[68]

His first trial ended with a hung jury favoring guilt. In the first trial, his counsel called a former prosecutor who presented character evidence to the effect that he pursued perjury charges twice against Detective Márquez. In the second trial that ended with a guilty verdict, Villegas's appointed counsel, John Gates, neglected to present an opening statement that could have assisted the jury in understanding the confession's lack of reliability. He then called only one witness. Worse, in his final argument, Gates conceded that Villegas might be guilty by stating that "although Villegas may in fact have been the shooter, he was only trying to scare the boys, not kill them."[69]

Eventually, Villegas got a chance at a third trial. First, Márquez arrested juvenile suspect Villegas and initiated an interrogation without taking him to a judge until after he had already interrogated the juvenile suspect. Texas family law considers a child to be in custody if, among other things, he is detained by a police officer.[70]

Villegas spent the next seventeen years in prison until a ruling in 2012 by El Paso judge Sam Medrano that Villegas had been coerced into a false confession. The court not only recommended Villegas receive a new trial but also took the unusual step of declaring Villegas factually innocent. The Court of Criminal Appeals set aside Villegas's conviction and ordered a new trial. After the third trial and eighteen years in prison, a Texas jury acquitted Daniel Villegas of murder.[71]

SERAFIN OLVERA-CARRERA—DELIBERATE INDIFFERENCE TO SERIOUS MEDICAL NEEDS, 2006

In an effort to detain an undocumented suspect, an immigration agent tackled a fleeing Olvera-Carrera. The force resulted in paralysis. Federal prosecutors filed a criminal civil rights charge against three agents for delaying medical care willfully and with deliberate indifference.[72] When the agents realized that Olvera-Carrera was not moving normally, an officer pepper-sprayed him to determine whether he was faking.[73] His inaction confirmed the severe disabling paralysis.[74] Their deliberate decision not to provide medical care constituted a constitutional deprivation.[75]

In contrast to the convict status in *Estelle v. Gamble,* Olvera-Carrera's serious medical needs arose during a pre-deportation detainee status hearing. Regardless, Olvera-Carrera had a right to protection for his serious medical needs while detained. The Fifth Circuit upheld the prosecution's claim that agents subjected Olvera-Carrera to deliberate indifference to serious medical needs during immigration detention.[76]

Death Penalty Cases

RICARDO ALDAPE-GUERRA, HOUSTON—A "WETBACK" AS A SCAPEGOAT, 1982

Houston, Harris County, Texas, has been touted as the nation's Death Penalty Capital.[77] Yet many Texas convictions have resulted in exonerations or reversals. One example involves the death sentence of Mexican immigrant Ricardo Aldape-Guerra (hereafter "Aldape"). While he was not an angel, no credible physical or eyewitness evidence pointed to him as the murderer of Officer James D. Harris.

One witness, Hilma G. Galván, expressed intense prejudice against Mexican aliens, urging the younger witnesses to blame the "wetback" from Mexico, as she labeled Aldape, for the fatal shooting of officer Harris.[78] Galván made her bias evident by the use of derogatory terms and by providing details inconsistent with Aldape.[79] After the actual killer, Carrasco, died in a shoot-out with police, Galván pointed to Aldape and said loudly enough for witnesses and the officers in the room to hear that since Carrasco had died, they could blame the "wetback" for the shooting.[80]

Galván claimed Mexicans only come to the United States to commit crimes and take jobs from U.S. citizens, repeatedly referring to Mexican Nationals as "mojados" or "wetbacks." The *habeas* judge concluded that Galván's attitude toward undocumented aliens explained the inconsistencies between her statement and her testimony.[81]

Another witness, José Heredia, in his *habeas* testimony and his written statement, identified the passenger Carrasco as the shooter, describing details that made it impossible for Aldape to have committed the crime. After hearing Heredia's version, an officer prepared a statement omitting the exonerating information. Heredia could not read English, and the officer directed him, like others, to "just sign it."[82]

Officers also reacted angrily to some witnesses who provided information that would show Aldape was not the shooter. Patricia Díaz testified that she looked at Aldape after hearing shots and observed empty hands. An officer responded with vulgarity, threatening to take her infant daughter unless she cooperated, circumstantially indicating a plan to fabricate evidence against the survivor.[83]

When Herlinda García, a fourteen-year-old with a baby, testified that she told an officer that Carrasco was the shooter, several officers threatened her with arrest unless she cooperated.[84] An unidentified police officer told her "she just did not know what all could happen to her and her husband."[85] At the time, García's husband was over eighteen years old and on parole. She felt threatened and helpless if she did not say what police wanted.

At the pretrial weekend meeting, when the prosecution focused on Aldape as the killer, García told a prosecutor that Aldape was not the man who shot the officer. The district attorney argued with García, telling her she was confused and could not change her mind, claiming she had already made a statement identifying Aldape as the man who shot both the officer and the civilian.[86]

No realistic evidence connected Aldape to the claim that he fired the gun in the cold-blooded murder. Mere presence at the scene of a crime does not presume guilt, nothing probative directly connected Aldape to murder, and, finally, a trial prosecutor courageously admitted during the *habeas* hearing that the physical evidence "totally pointed towards Carrasco as being the shooter."[87] Most incriminating, investigators found Officer Harris's weapon in Carrasco's waistband when they examined his body at the morgue.[88] In spite of this, the police and prosecution manipulated the evidence and threatened young witnesses into claiming Aldape shot the officer.

After a thorough review, U.S. District Judge Kenneth Hoyt ordered a new trial on the basis of police and prosecutorial misconduct.[89] From the totality of the evidence, it appears the DA's office (use of "DA" hereafter will refer to an assistant prosecutor or to the elected district attorney) and the police concocted a plan to implicate Aldape as the shooter while independent witnesses identified a person with Carrasco's characteristics as the killer. In the process, state officials violated long-standing constitutional directives on the production of exculpatory evidence.[90]

Judge Hoyt concluded that prosecutorial misconduct reached the limits when DAs concealed materially exculpatory evidence and used statements mixing truth and falsehood with deliberate intent to deceive, all with the goal of convicting Aldape. The cumulative effect violated Aldape's due process rights.[91]

Furthermore, many witnesses felt intimidated due to their limited English, education, and youth. Some could not review their English-language statements, reporting that police angrily refused to read the statements to them before they signed.[92]

The *habeas* judge found that prosecutors deliberately manipulated witnesses by putting words into their mouths. They persistently cross-examined them on a false basis and made improper insinuations calculated to mislead the jury and discredit testimony unfavorable to the DA.[93] To seek a new trial, Aldape's counsel investigated the record for prosecutorial misconduct and "incontrovertible evidence of innocence that the jury never heard, and exposed a pattern of official intimidation, misconduct, and abuse."[94] During jury selection, for instance, the DA told the jury that Aldape's "illegal alien" status could justify a death sentence.[95] The problem is that mere immigration status is not a crime, particularly one that indicates a propensity to be a continuing threat to society. Offer of undocumented status serves only to prejudice the jury into consideration of a death sentence on irrelevant grounds.[96]

Judge Hoyt determined that finding Harris's weapon on Carrasco supplied police and prosecutors with ample evidence that Aldape was not the killer.[97] In addition, intentional police actions and prosecutorial speculations during trial effectively undermined material defense testimony. The police planted deceit, the prosecutors developed it, and the judge determined the cumulative effect rendered the trial fundamentally unfair and concluded that a properly conducted trial would likely result in a different verdict.[98]

CARLOS DELUNA, NUECES COUNTY—A DEATH SENTENCE THAT DEFIES THE PROOF, 1983

In 1989, the State of Texas executed Carlos DeLuna for the murder of store clerk Wanda López.[99] Decades later, a thorough review established with abundant certainty that Carlos DeLuna did not commit the murder. Instead, the evidence pointed to his alleged friend or tocayo (namesake), Carlos Hernández, as the actual killer.[100] All this is publicly known due to the intensive postmortem review that Professor Liebman conducted of DeLuna's tragic execution.[101]

The author contends that Liebman's thorough investigation indicates that prosecutorial actions, conducted with professional indifference to the actual proof, known in criminal law as willful blindness (knowledge) of the circumstances, resulted in the wrongful execution of an evidently innocent Carlos DeLuna.[102] Countless motives may have driven the prosecutors (Schiwetz and Botary) to focus on DeLuna as the killer. Their motives for convicting DeLuna may have been purely professional—for example, winning a capital murder case could provide a promotion within the DA's office or the publicity to boost consideration for a judgeship. One cannot discount the motive centering on personal prejudice against Mexicans as an ethnic group.[103]

The lead homicide detective negligently contributed to selection of the wrong suspect by conducting a rapid and extremely sloppy investigation that overlooked possible fingerprints of the killer at the extremely bloody crime scene. Notwithstanding the complex murder crime scene, the detective conducting her first capital murder investigation concluded it within two hours and authorized store personnel to clean the crime scene to reopen for business.[104]

In addition, investigators and prosecutors ignored Kevan Baker's face-to-face[105] eyewitness description of the actual killer as "a 'transient,' someone who looked like he'd 'been on the street and was very hungry.' His clothes were shabby and unclean. He had quite a bit of facial hair: a full moustache and whiskers all over his face, like he 'hadn't shaved in, you know, ten days, a couple weeks.'"[106]

In contrast to Baker's detailed description of the male killer, one that included plentiful facial hair and a person wearing blue jeans, police obtained a positive identification of Carlos DeLuna by the same Kevan Baker. When he was arrested, the clean-shaven DeLuna sat in the back seat of a police car, wearing Black slacks as opposed to blue jeans.[107]

Carlos DeLuna's murder prosecution should not have occurred.[108] Although no direct evidence of anti-Mexican prejudice by the DA surfaced, any professional DA who objectively reviews the evidence will observe inconsistencies that substantially undermine DeLuna's guilt. The DA's evidence substantiating guilt has to be clearly probative of guilt. If not, the proof should lead to an acquittal or at least a life sentence, as opposed to death by lethal injection, as occurred to DeLuna only six years later.

America's overtly racist history, resurrected in recent police brutality incidents involving Blacks and Latinos, cannot be ignored. Whether implicit or unconscious bias enters the picture in deciding what incited a police shooting or the degree of violence by an officer, the continued recent victimization of Latinos and Blacks, respectively the two largest racial minority groups in the United States, presents issues as to the questionable use of physical violence by police against civilians and the role of race in this equation.[109]

Whether the DA is Latino or of another race or ethnicity, one has to realize that Latinos can develop into "equal opportunity offenders" against "their own" people. Court cases have not only noted that same-race or -ethnicity discrimination occurs but also explained this puzzling consequence.[110] If a prosecutor acts with racial or ethnic prejudice or with the awareness that the evidence fails to meet the necessary level of proof, the decision to impose a death sentence constitutes an egregiously wrong and possibly criminal act.[111]

In DeLuna's case, two experienced prosecutors had before them the same evidence discussed in this chapter. They knew the detailed description of the killer that Baker provided. They knew that DeLuna's clean-shaven appearance while wearing dark slacks, confirmed by the Arsuaga couple on the night of the López killing, varied significantly from Baker's eyewitness description of a bearded man in blue jeans.[112]

Even more persuasive, the lack of blood on DeLuna's body, on his clothing, or on the money he allegedly stole establishes quite persuasively that he could not be guilty. Specifically, the absence of blood traces proves he could not have been in the store. Unfortunately, the two prosecutors did not adhere to their duty and obligation "not to convict, but to see that justice is done" by dismissing charges against DeLuna as a suspect or investigating further to seek the truth.[113]

Regrettably, the author was not completely surprised that the horrific DeLuna travesty of justice occurred. In 1975, as a rookie prosecutor, the author attended a Dallas County-sponsored training. A veteran prosecutor lectured on pro-state jury selection tactics, advising prosecutors to remove Blacks, Mexicans, Jews, and Catholics to attain a prosecution-oriented jury.[114] The DeLuna case occurred only eight years after this lecture on jury selection. Thirty years later, in 2005, the Supreme Court reversed a Dallas capital murder case that revealed not only the racist jury prosecutorial practices but also the existence of a DA-sponsored training manual.[115]

In DeLuna, the prosecutorial desire to win explains the indifference to the absence of any blood whatsoever on the alleged killer. They seem to have relied merely on DeLuna's suggestive one-on-one identification as he sat in the police car. While DeLuna's lawyers contributed to his demise, the prosecutors and the police had the supreme responsibility to protect the accused.

The prosecutors knew from the blood absence that DeLuna could not have been present inside the store.[116] The State of Texas participated in the promotion of an execution replete with doubt and objective evidence that could not rise to the level of legal sufficiency of guilt beyond a reasonable doubt.[117]

Furthermore, DeLuna's prosecutors knew these ethical obligations yet they intentionally engaged in unethical conduct to win. Prosecutors have a duty to provide the accused with evidence that might indicate lack of guilt, that can impeach a witness against him, or that provides grounds for mitigation of punishment if he is convicted.[118] Evidence indicates DAs Botary and Schiwitz did not adhere to these protective due process rules.[119]

At trial, Schiwitz asked the dispatcher about the manhunt after the killing, information the DA never gave to DeLuna's lawyers and was curiously "destroyed a few days before the trial began."[120] Neither the defense nor the jury ever heard the repeated police reports describing the suspect as wearing a "grey sweatshirt, red flannel jacket, and blue jeans."[121] Finally, they never heard "Sergeant Mejia worrying out loud on the radio that the clean-shaven man in a white dress shirt and Black slacks" seen by a couple jogging in a different area "was 'another' person, different from the scruffy and mustachioed man Baker saw tangling with Wanda [López]."[122]

DeLuna's claim of innocence by declaring he saw Carlos Hernández kill López angered DA Schiwetz, who retaliated in final argument by urging the jury to convict DeLuna for his "pathetic fabrication of '*this phantom Carlos Hernández.*'"[123] Years later, on the eve of DeLuna's execution, DA Schiwetz repeated that DeLuna "lied throughout the trial, and he's lying now," claiming DeLuna had never been in jail at the same time as a *Carlos* Hernández.[124]

However, years after the execution, Liebman sent an investigator to Nueces County who in only one day "uncovered evidence" that the Texas prosecutors, over the six years between DeLuna's arrest and execution, could not—or would not—reveal: "Carlos Hernández did indeed exist."[125] The Liebman study confirmed DeLuna's assertion under oath that both he and Carlos Hernández were in custody in the Nueces County Jail in 1983, shortly after DeLuna's arrest for murder.[126]

Besides dealing with apparently unethical prosecutors,[127] DeLuna received two court-appointed lawyers who quarreled and failed to focus on his trial.[128] Presiding Judge Blackmon surprisingly first appointed Hector De Peña, a lawyer who had never handled a jury trial.[129] Months later, the judge added James Lawrence, a more experienced attorney, who took the lead from De Peña. To make matters worse, the prosecutors failed in their duty to share exculpatory material that Mr. Lawrence could have presented to the jury.

The DeLuna trial unfortunately had the semblance of an official lynching, considering the disregard of respective duties by prosecutors, police officials, and DeLuna's lawyers concerning the conflicting evidence that pointed to DeLuna's innocence. These evidentiary aberrations primarily include the sole eyewitness's identification that did not fit DeLuna and the total absence of blood anywhere on DeLuna's person or clothing, a fact that in itself raised serious doubts about his presence at the bloody crime scene and, specifically, about the imposition of the death penalty.[130]

RUBEN CANTÚ, BEXAR COUNTY—A POLICE-MANIPULATED ARREST AND PROSECUTION, 1984

Another controversial death penalty prosecution occurred when seventeen-year-old Ruben Cantú faced a capital murder charge for a robbery in which one of two victims died.[131] For several months, the survivor, Juan Moreno, could not—or would not—identify anyone.

However, on his third attempt to view a photo spread, Moreno identified Cantú as one of the robbers. Moreno claimed he felt pressured since Cantú appeared in all three identification efforts.[132] At the trial, the detective testified as to his "impression" that Moreno "knew [Cantú] by sight and by name, but was afraid for his life if he identified [Cantú's] photograph."[133]

On March 3, a different detective visited Moreno and his brother at home. Moreno agreed to visit the police station to view the photos again. After reviewing the same photographs he observed on March 2, shown by another detective, Moreno selected Cantú's photograph as the man who murdered Gomez and who shot him. According to the detective, Moreno had admitted recognizing Cantú's photograph before, but was afraid to tell police.[134] The detective testified that Moreno stated he did not know Cantú's name.

The appellate court agreed with Cantú that showing Moreno several photospreads on different occasions, each containing Cantú's photo, constitutes a suggestive procedure. Police showed Moreno photo spreads on December 16, 1984, and on March 2 and March 3, 1985. Cantú's identical photos appeared on March 2 and 3.[135]

After reviewing the overall facts, including youth and the suggestive photo spreads, the prosecutor offered Cantú a life sentence plea bargain in lieu of the death sentence.[136] Judge Roy Barrera, Jr., rejected the plea bargain to a life sentence, forcing the state to trial.[137] While the prosecution could have proceeded with a non-death-penalty case, the elected DA chose to proceed with a capital murder trial, most likely due to election concerns of being viewed as soft on crime. If the judicial involvement is correct, this is unfortunate since a jurist should ethically avoid assuming prosecutorial duties, particularly if done for electoral publicity.[138]

The state obtained a guilty verdict, and Cantú received a death sentence. Contributing to the jury's death decision was Cantú's involvement in a gang. The gang's code of silence kept those who knew the real identity of the accused from cooperating due to retaliation. Cantú persisted in his innocence to the very end, telling the people of San Antonio in a letter four days after his conviction that he had been framed and that an innocent man was to be executed for a crime he did not commit.[139]

Since Moreno was not a legal or resident alien at the time of the robbery, he feared the police who pressured him to identify Cantú. Years later, Moreno, a teenage undocumented immigrant when the crime occurred, recalls that he told police Cantú was not the shooter, specifically describing the shooter as having curly hair, which Cantú did not have.[140]

Coincidentally, the lead investigator assigned to the Cantú investigation happened to be a close friend of an officer Cantú shot in apparent self-defense in a barroom brawl on March 1, 1985. In the next two days, detectives conducted a concentrated effort to have Cantú identified for the capital murder. The lead investigator later told the *Houston Chronicle*, "It was difficult to get (Moreno) to make the identification ... We weren't able to get him for the police shooting, but we were able to get him for the murder."[141]

Cantú's alleged crime partner, David Garza, a juvenile, agreed to a plea bargain. Years later, Garza signed a sworn affidavit saying he allowed Cantú, his friend, to be falsely accused and executed, stating Cantú was not with him during the murder. Garza's adherence to the gang's code of silence, and the violent consequences for disobedience, coerced the confidentiality.[142] Cantú also swore by this code, even if it led to his death.

VÍCTOR HUGO SALDAÑO—LATINO ETHNICITY AS AN AGGRAVATING FACTOR, 2002

The Texas Court of Criminal Appeals permitted a jury to assess the death penalty against Víctor Hugo Saldaño based on evidence that his ethnic background represented a continuing threat to society.[143] The Texas prosecutors argued that ethnicity constitutes an aggravating factor in determining future threat to society, thus opening the door to a death sentence. The argument was based on expert testimony that the proportion of Latinos in the prison system exceeded their group's population at large.[144]

Texas Appellate Judge Price dissented, denouncing racial prejudice before the jury, adding that the use of race or ethnicity as a basis for finding guilt is constitutionally barred.[145] He further noted the impossible task of determining the "extent an assertion of race or ethnicity as an indicator of criminality or future dangerousness influences the deliberations of a given jury."[146]

The state's Attorney General confessed error before the Fifth Circuit on the impropriety of using race as an indicator of a continuing threat and upheld the lower court's denial of intervention by the district attorney, noting that both officials share an identical interest, that is, "to see that justice is done."[147] In confessing error and waiving Saldaño's procedural default for his failure to object, the Attorney General concluded that justice requires that Saldaño be properly resentenced, a discretionary decision the law grants the Attorney General the power to make.[148]

Bail Bond Practices

It is often stated that "the wheels of justice turn slowly, but grind exceedingly fine." From a victim's perspective, justice should not occur gradually, but factors like politics and financial interests, at times, create egregious outcomes. After almost 200 years of the Anglo, Afro, and Mexican coexistence in Texas, criminal justice for people of color has not progressed well. As a Texas federal district judge spelled out in her decision regarding the cash bail system, race and economics adversely impact people of color.[149]

ODONNELL, HOUSTON—INABILITY TO PAY BAIL COSTS, 2017

When police arrested Maranda ODonnell for driving with an invalid license, she became a victim of misdemeanor bail bond practices. Unless she paid the full predetermined $2,500 bail to Harris County or a percentage to a bail surety, she would remain jailed. The single mother depended on benefits to survive. Although eligible, her financial circumstances prevented her release. So, along with others, ODonnell sued Harris County, alleging the county's policies deprived indigents of due process and equal protection by detaining them primarily based on their poverty.[150]

In Houston, when police jail a misdemeanor arrestee, the prosecutor submits a bail amount utilizing a schedule established by county judges. Hearing officers generally set the amount during the initial hearing held within twenty-four hours of arrest, and county judges review the bail and adjust amounts. Texas law requires officials to conduct an individualized review based on five enumerated factors, which include the defendant's ability to pay, the charge, and community safety.[151]

The Fifth Circuit appeals court found that probable cause hearings seldom occur within twenty-four hours of arrest and last only a few seconds at times, with detainees instructed not to speak and not given a realistic opportunity to submit evidence of ability to post bond. The imposition of secured bail adversely impacts poor arrestees, and the flawed procedural framework demonstrates the lack of individualized assessment when officials set bail. Further, after extensive review of numerous bail hearings, the court concluded that hearing officers realized that imposing a secured bail on indigent arrestees ensured their detention.[152]

Eventually, federal district judge Lee Rosenthal entered an order formally approving the ODonnell settlement in November 2019, authorizing the grant of personal bonds for misdemeanor arrestees with the exception of those charged with violent crimes, such as domestic violence and assault.[153] Commissioner Rodney Ellis, a justice advocate during his legislative days in Austin, praised the outcome of "equal treatment and due process for all—no matter how much money you have or the color of your skin," and he observed that the bail settlement will better protect all communities and help end mass incarceration of people of color.[154]

Hate Crimes and Racist Violence

Police brutality and deception have created serious conflicts for American society. However, a greater problem occurs from inaction by police chiefs and prosecutors to deter lawless cops. Aggravating factors include our national and state leaders who engage in fanning hatred and inciting attacks, leading to hate crimes based on racist violence.

DAVID RITCHESON, HOUSTON—AN ATTACK ON A "WETBACK," 2008

David Henry Tuck and Keith Robert Turner met a sixteen-year-old girl and her eighteen-year-old friend, David Ritcheson, a Mexican American. The girl's mother later drove all four to her home, went to the store, and left them to continue their party.[155] They consumed alcohol and drugs and became intoxicated. Tuck and Ritcheson had an argument, and Tuck called Ritcheson a "wetback," angering Ritcheson. The sixteen-year-old girl's younger sister later stated that Ritcheson tried to kiss her. Tuck responded by knocking Ritcheson unconscious.

The two men continued assaulting Ritcheson, but Tuck, wearing steel-toed boots, specifically kicked him in the head and torso repeatedly while yelling "white power," "wetback," and "beaner."[156] To "whiten" this Latino victim, they poured bleach all over his body and face. They stripped Ritcheson naked and kicked an umbrella pole into his anus.[157] Ritcheson required thirty surgeries and apparently never recovered from his year-long trauma, committing suicide by jumping from a cruise ship.[158]

THE EL PASO MASSACRE—2019

History does not have to repeat itself. The anti-Mexican massacres during the pre-1920 era in South Texas and in Porvenir (West Texas) occurred again in El Paso in 2019.[159] The El Paso suspect, a white man, drove ten hours and seven hundred miles from North Texas, told police investigators that he was targeting "Mexicans," and posted a hate-filled statement on the Internet minutes before the shooting began. He warned Americans of a "Hispanic invasion of Texas" and complained that white people were being replaced by foreigners.[160] Domingo García, the national president of the League of United Latin American Citizens (LULAC), attributed the increased attacks to the hate speech and fear mongering by President Trump.[161]

This killer confessed that his goal included primarily targeting Mexican-descent persons with the AK-47 assault rifle and multiple magazines he possessed.[162] The death toll suggests that the killer accomplished his mission, slaughtering twenty-three and injuring about two dozen, mostly Spanish-surnamed, persons.

According to *The New York Times*, during 2018 the FBI's annual report showed a significant upswing in anti-Latino violence motivated by bias or prejudice, reaching a sixteen-year high in 2018, a time during which the tally of all hate crimes remained fairly level.[163] The statistics reveal 485 hate crimes against Latinos in 2018, fifty-five more than in 2017.

Regarding Mexican American hopes for justice, the principal area of concern involving serious accusations is that an accused Latino will face stereotypes by those who serve on juries. Mexican Americans have to endure several typecasts, such as the alleged reputation of having a proclivity for violence, sexual misconduct, dishonesty, and immorality. Sadly, barriers to neutral and diverse juries continue today since prosecutorial misuse of peremptory challenges justified on absurd or even trivial race-neutral reasons will permit discretionary removals of minorities.[164]

Based on past and all-too-recent jury selection practices and prosecutorial decisions, the chances for a fair outcome for Mexican Americans and other minorities have decreased. Detecting latent prejudices during jury selection is difficult. With the quite common televised reports of Anglo and other English-speaking persons berating Latinos who speak Spanish in public, how might this affect jurors who sit in judgment in a case that requires an interpreter for the person accused of a crime?

A decade ago, our Supreme Court encouraged an end to the race debate, stating that the best way to handle the issue is to quit talking about it.[165] Shortly thereafter, the same court ruled that a person's race should not be a factor in punishment or in deciding guilt.[166] The court held that a juror's statements during deliberations were "egregious and unmistakable in their reliance on racial bias" when the juror encouraged others to join in a racially motivated conviction.[167]

Have Police–Community Relations Improved?

Regrettably, police-community relations continue to suffer, most recently exacerbated by the angry protests that resulted from the police homicide of George Floyd in June 2020.[168] In 2018 the Commission on Civil Rights updated comments as to the use of force by police and provided multiple recommendations: police and community interactions; policing free from bias or discrimination; continuing the efforts of the Department of Justice (DOJ) Office of Community Oriented Policing Services (COPS) and the Community Relations Services office (CRS); and the return of the DOJ's vigorous enforcement of constitutional policing, including the use of consent decrees as necessary where constitutional policing standards are not being upheld.[169]

Police brutality and internal corruption create problems for the justice system, especially from the code of silence considered sacred among some police.[170] This practice unfortunately generated the term "testilying" in court lingo, referring to dishonesty under oath.[171] Aggravating matters, many Texas police agencies have arbitration agreements negotiated by unions to review administrative disciplinary action.[172] Texas police have legislative protections in order to keep fire and police personnel "free from political influence" and have "permanent employment tenure as public servants."[173] One might question why such arbitration procedures exist, considering that courts have always determined due process issues. The arbitration avenue essentially permits a lawless cop to remain on the force even if the police chief knows she has a "rotten apple" on the force that can contaminate others.

Recommendations: To Attain a More Just System

The United States has been a model for integrity in most of its governmental standards, including criminal justice and civil rights. After too many modern-day civil rights violations, however, we know that our system is not fully perfect, notwithstanding the statutory protections.

We have attained a system where rich white people can cheat, lie, and commit bribery to gain entry for their children into universities and receive a mere two-week jail sentence.[174] At the same time, an uninformed Mexican woman who grew up from childhood in Texas, believing she was a citizen, voted twice and received an eight-year prison sentence.[175] Hopefully, our leaders will seek improvements in our prosecution policies so that all Americans, regardless of race, color, religion, economic status, or language characteristics, respectfully benefit from the presumption of innocence.

Consequently, I suggest the following recommendations:

- Bail reform. Bail has historically led to the deprivation of equal rights between the poor and wealthier persons. Other states now have a model plan as set forth in the Houston, Harris County, Texas, *ODonnell* litigation.[176] The next step requires development of procedures by which a judge determines who obtains a personal bond and model standards for determining the likelihood that a detainee appears for court.
- Police training. Latino and other communities need police protection. At the same time, the quality of policing must be improved by racial, ethnic, cultural/linguistic, and mental health sensitivity training, along with extensive background checks. The training should include profiling issues and implicit bias testing to minimize dangers that subtle prejudice can have on safety concerns for both police and the public.
- Police internal disciplinary procedures. Removal of certain law enforcement officers must be facilitated in order to protect not only the public but also law-abiding cops. Texas must repeal or amend statutes that permit the annulment of a police chief's final decision to terminate a dangerous or problem officer. Statutorily supported arbitration agreements that obstruct justice must be legislatively repealed in order "to secure efficient fire and police departments composed of capable personnel," as Texas law provides.
- The independent prosecutor. The justice system must clearly define the need for an independent prosecutor to eliminate the inherent conflicts that arise from reliance on local police witnesses. Conflicts arise since state prosecutors realistically depend on local cops for testimony in alleged crimes committed by the public.

- Modification of statutes of limitations. Deprivations involving official oppression and civil rights violations require a review of specific statutes of limitation where police and prosecutorial misconduct might be involved. The justice system should not reward a corrupt official benefiting from fraud, coercion of confessions, conspiracies to defraud or obstruct justice, and concealment of the truth. The limitations period should be extended where evidence of threats, concealment, or fraud circumstances exists until such time as the victim or the prosecution reasonably discovers the misconduct and reports the violation to a police official.

- Peremptory challenges. Jury representation, to be fair, must address peremptory challenge abuses that prejudice any gender, religious, racial, and ethnic group, as interpreted in existing law. The current *Batson* practice permits a challenge by simply giving a "race-neutral" reason, a vague description that opens the gates to injustice. A more acceptable approach would be to demand more specific reasons from lawyers and consider legislation to reduce the number of challenges to three per party.

- Administrative procedures for compensation. The state legislature should take steps to control and diminish the loss attributable to not being able to work due to abusive police practices. These steps should include procedures that permit reasonable and adequate compensation for direct injury and indirect financial claims that arise from police malpractice, without prejudicing any remedial rights available under federal civil rights law.

- Local police departments' internal complaints. Internal complaint procedures of local police departments should be handled by independent agencies or boards with their own autonomous investigative staff members that exercise the power to recommend appropriate disciplinary action against officers or any state agent found guilty of misconduct. A complainant should have a right to be present at the hearings of such agencies and should be represented by counsel who may question or cross-examine witnesses.

- Indigent legal representation. In order to protect critical rights, legal assistance should be made available to indigent defendants immediately after arrest in all criminal cases that arise in state and county criminal courts.

- Affirmative action goals. Federal, state, and local governments should implement affirmative action recruitment programs for language minorities in order to promote cultural diversity and bilingual linguistic abilities at the law enforcement level as well as at agencies, such as the 911 emergency system, that serve the public's safety needs. The state and local jurisdictions should ensure that bilingual personnel are available at all levels and times when the justice system offices are open to serve the public.

- Ending the Texas death penalty. Capital punishment should be repealed. Neither police, prosecutors, judges, nor eyewitnesses are immune from professional and ethical shortcomings. The described case studies of Aldape, DeLuna, and Cantú serve as examples of errors and, worse, intentional efforts to corrupt justice, indicators that the time to eliminate the death penalty in Texas has arrived.

Policymakers should adopt standards of decency that unite us to other more progressive nations in terminating the death penalty.[177] All is done to prevent innocent persons from suffering an execution like Carlos DeLuna experienced.[178]

Notes

The author thanks the Thurgood Marshall School of Law at Texas Southern University, Houston, Texas, for the 2019 summer research stipend that assisted with the research and writing of this book chapter. He extends gratitude to his recent student assistants, Eleazar Maldonado and Summer Cevallos, who assisted in addressing this difficult and emotional death-penalty topic.

1. Treaty of Guadalupe Hidalgo of Peace, Friendship, Limits and Settlement, U.S.-Mex., Feb. 2, 1848, 9 Stat. 922. A *mestizo* is a person of mixed blood, specifically, a person of mixed European and American Indian ancestry.
2. U.S. Commission on Civil Rights (USCCR), *Hearing before the United States Commission on Civil Rights: San Antonio, TX, December 9–14, 1968* (Washington, DC: GPO, 1969). Also available at https://catalog.hathitrust.org/Record/001874430.
3. USCCR, *Hearing*, iv–v.

4. USCCR, *Hearing*, 60–62. In the section of the report dealing with attitudes toward the courts, the comments centered on uncertainty among Mexican Americans due to the justice system's insensitivity to the group's ethnic background and culture. Prosecutors represent a central aspect of the justice system.

5. Any reference to Mexican Americans includes all Latinos of Hispanic origin.

6. USCCR, *Hearing*, 12–13. In addition, police presence in minority neighborhoods was less adequate, and the commission found that law enforcement prejudice is widespread and a serious issue that undermines proper police–community relations.

7. USCCR, *Hearing*, 16–17.

8. *Medrano v. Allee*, 347 F. Supp. 605 (S.D. Tex. 1972), *Allee v. Medrano*, 416 U.S. 802, 815–16 (1974).

9. USCCR, *Hearing*, 23, 28–29.

10. USCCR, *Hearing*, 22, 25.

11. USCCR, *Hearing*, 10, 12, 13. State failures to protect citizens against violence or other deprivations are found in federal civil and criminal code provisions for prosecution for anyone who willfully subjects any inhabitant of any state or territory to the deprivation of any rights protected by U.S. laws or the Constitution (18 U.S.C. § 242, Deprivation of rights under color of law); the civil action arises under 42 U.S.C. § 1983, the 1871 Civil Rights Act.

12. *Hernández* v. Texas, 347 U.S. 475, 479–80 (1954); see *Cortez v. State*, 44 Tex. Crim. 169, 69 S.W. 536, 537 (1902) (Complaint of grand jury exclusion of Mexican race).

13. *Hernández*, 478.

14. *Hernández*, 477. This included the absence of any single Latin American on jury lists during a twenty-five-year period.

15. *Batson v. Kentucky*, 476 U.S. 79, 94 (1986). Batson allowed the state a chance to demonstrate that "permissible racially neutral" reasons existed to justify the removal from a jury.

16. USCCR, *Hearing*, 39.

17. Until the new law, judges selected the actual grand jury from this group. Patrick Svitek, "Texas Grand Jury Selection to Become More Random," *The Texas Tribune*, August 4, 2015.

18. Tex. Code Crim. Proc. Art. 19.01 (2019).

19. This question is discussed further in the section dealing with the unconstitutional use of bail as it adversely impacts indigent persons. *ODonnell v. Harris Co.*, 251 F. Supp. 3d 1052, 1062 (S.D. Tex. 2017); *ODonnell v. Harris Co.*, 892 F.3d 147, 153 (5th Cir. 2018).

20. USCCR, *Hearing*, 48–50.

21. Walter V. Schaefer, "Federalism and State Criminal Procedure," *Harvard Law Review* 70 (1956): 1, 8.

22. *Gideon v. Wainwright*, 372 U.S. 335 (1963).

23. *Gideon*, 372 U.S. 335. A few years before the 1968 hearing, the Supreme Court granted the poor the right to the appointment of counsel in state felony cases.

24. USCCR, *Hearing*, 54.

25. USCCR, *Hearing*, 71–72. In *Negrón v. New York*, 434 F.2d 386, 389 (2nd Cir. 1970), the Second Circuit ruled that the Sixth Amendment means not only that a non-English-speaking accused has interpreter assistance but also that the quality rises to the level such that the accused will be both physically and mentally present at his trial.

26. USCCR, *Hearing*, 60. Finally, in 1961, President Kennedy appointed Reynaldo Garza of Brownsville, Texas, as the first Mexican American federal district court judge in Texas. Years later, the U.S. Senate confirmed José Antonio "Tony" Canales (1977–1980) as the first Mexican American U.S. Attorney in the Southern District of Texas. In order to serve the public from the main

Houston office to Laredo, Corpus Christi, and the Rio Grande Valley in South Texas, Canales appointed eight Mexican American lawyers, exceeding the two Hispanic prosecutors all other predecessors ever appointed in that region.

27. USCCR, *Hearing*, 62.

28. David McLemore, "The Forgotten Carnage between Hispanics, Rangers," *Dallas Morning News*, November 28, 2004 (Latino retaliation to abuses by whites led to a "frenzy of shootings and lynchings by Texas Rangers and Anglo vigilantes" across the Rio Grande Valley).

29. *Hernández v. Texas*, 347 U.S. 475, 479-80 (1954) (the Court found that a twenty-five-year absence of Latinos from the grand and trial juries constituted racial discrimination where the state failed to explain the lack of Latin American venire).

30. *Brown v. Board of Education*, 347 U.S. 483 (1954); *Méndez v. Westminster School Dist.*, 64 F. Supp. 544 (S.D. Cal. 1946), 161 F.2d 774 (9th Cir. 1947); *Delgado v. Bastrop Indep. Sch. Dist.*, Civil No. 388 (W.D. Tex. June 15, 1948) (Unpublished), reproduced in Lupe Salinas, "Gus Garcia and Thurgood Marshall: Two Legal Giants Fighting for Justice," *Thurgood Marshall Law Review*. 28 (2003): 145, 166-68.

31. *White v. Regester*, 412 U.S. 755, 767-70 (1973) (the Supreme Court found the 1970 Texas redistricting plan diluted the voting rights of Mexican Americans in Bexar County by imposing a multimember district approach).

32. In the *Hernández v. Texas*, 347 U.S. 475, 479-80 (1954), jury discrimination case, the courthouse where the trial occurred had a sign on one of the two restrooms that stated "Colored Men" and "*Hombres Aquí*" ("Men Here").

33. U.S. Const. amend. XIV.

34. The 1871 Act is codified as 42 U.S.C. § 1983.

35. *United States v. Hayes*, 589 F.2d 811 (5th Cir. 1979).

36. For more details related to the homicide of Joe Campos Torres and his posthumous mistreatment by the justice system, see Lupe Salinas, "Lawless Cops, Latino Injustice, and Revictimization by the Justice System," *Michigan State Law Review* (2018): 1095, 1159-64, 1185-90 (hereafter Salinas, "Lawless Cops").

37. Salinas, "Lawless Cops," 1162.

38. 18 U.S.C. § 241.

39. William D. Carrigan and Clive Webb, "The Lynching of Persons of Mexican Origin or Descent in the United States, 1848 to 1928," *Journal of Social History* (2003): 37; George Mason University Press (2003), 411, 425.

40. *United States v. Hayes*, 589 F.2d 811 (5th Cir. 1979).

41. James P. Sterba, "Chicano's Death Stirs a Texas Region," *New York Times*, August 16, 1976.

42. Sterba, "Chicano's Death."

43. *United States v. Hayes*, 589 F.2d 811, 816 (5th Cir. 1979).

44. *United States v. Hayes*, 589 F.2d at 816.

45. *United States v. Hayes*, 589 F.2d at 817.

46. *United States v. Hayes*, 589 F.2d at 817, citing *Abbate v. United States*, 359 U.S. 187 (1959), and *Bartkus v. Illinois*, 359 U.S. 121 (1959). Each government has an enforcement interest of its respective laws. The state trial jury found Hayes guilty of aggravated assault and assessed ten years of confinement.

47. *Cain v. State*, 549 S.W.2d 707, 709 (Tex. Crim. App. 1977). "Russian Roulette" is an extremely dangerous practice of loading a bullet into one chamber of a revolver, spinning the cylinder,

and pulling the trigger while pointing the gun at the head of another, used either as a "game" or as an effort to obtain a confession.

48. The probable cause facts at this point appear nonexistent, but entry into a home without a warrant is even more egregious under Fourth Amendment standards.

49. *Cain v. State*, 549 S.W.2d 707, 710 (Tex. Crim. App. 1977)

50. *Cain v. State*, 549 S.W.2d at 710.

51. *Cain v. State*, 549 S.W.2d at 710-11.

52. *Cain v. State*, 549 S.W.2d at 711.

53. Advising a person in custody of his right to remain silent and to have a lawyer before interrogation occurs had been well established and publicized for the previous seven years at the time Cain killed Santos. *Miranda v. Arizona*, 384 U.S. 436 (1966).

54. *In re Winship*, 397 U.S. 358 (1970); Texas Family Code art. 51.09.

55. Lupe Salinas, Editorial, "Learning from Errors in Torres Case," *Houston Chronicle*, September 13, 2003, A41.

56. Negligent homicide is a state jail felony. Texas Penal Code Art. 19.02

57. Salinas, "Learning from Errors," A41. The civil remedies statute, 42 U.S.C. § 1983, provides protection for "any citizen of the United States *or other person* within the jurisdiction thereof" (emphasis added).

58. 42 U.S.C. § 1983 (2000).

59. U.S. Const. amend. V, XIV. The Fifth Amendment, like the Fourteenth Amendment, identically provides that no *person* may be "deprived of life, liberty, or property, without due process of law" (emphasis added). These due process protections do not specify "citizen," as do other constitutional provisions.

60. U.S. Const. amend. V; *Danziger v. State*, No. 3-90-086-CR (Tex. App.—Austin 1991), discussed in Lupe S. Salinas, *U.S. Latinos and Criminal Injustice* (East Lansing: Michigan State University Press 2015), 214-17.

61. Michael Hall, "Under the Gun," *Texas Monthly* (January 2001).

62. Keith A. Findley and John Pray, "Lessons from the Innocent," *Wisconsin Academy Review* 34 (Fall 2001).

63. *Danziger v. State*, No. 3-90-086-CR (Tex. App.—Austin 1991).

64. Hall, "Under the Gun."

65. CBS News, "Bush Office Sits on Murder Plea," October 17, 2000. Salinas, *U.S. Latinos and Criminal Injustice*, 215-17.

66. Nate Blakeslee, "How to Get a Teenager to Admit to a Murder He Didn't Commit," *Texas Monthly* (January 7, 2014).

67. Blakeslee, "How to Get a Teenager." This rape threat tactic is the same approach utilized by Austin, Texas, detective Héctor Polanco to snare Chris Ochoa, another El Paso native, into confessing to a life sentence.

68. Blakeslee, "How to Get a Teenager."

69. Blakeslee, "How to Get a Teenager."

70. Texas Family Code § 51.095 (d) (2); *Dowthitt v. State*, 931 S.W.2d 244, 256-57 (Tex. Crim. App. 1996) (Texas law interprets one to be "in custody" when a reasonable person, under the circumstances, would believe that his freedom was restricted to the point of a formal arrest).

71. Aaron Martínez, "Daniel Villegas Found Not Guilty in His Third Trial for Capital Murder," *El Paso Times* (October 5, 2018).

72. *United States v. Gonzales*, 436 F.3d 560 (5th Cir. 2006), *cert. denied, Gonzales v. United States*, 547 U.S. 1180 (2006). *Reyna v. United States*, 547 U.S. 1139 (2006); *Gonzales v. United States*, 547 U.S. 1180 (2006) for the denial of certiorari for the other two convicted agents.

73. *United States v. Gonzales*, 436 F.3d at 568, 571.

74. *United States v. Gonzales*, 436 F.3d at 573-74 (concluding that a finding of "actual awareness" fit the facts).

75. *United States v. Gonzales*, 436 F.3d at 573. The Supreme Court concluded that "deliberate indifference to serious medical needs of prisoners constitutes the 'unnecessary and wanton infliction of pain'" forbidden by the Eighth Amendment. *Estelle v. Gamble*, 429 U.S. 97, 104-05 (1976).

76. *United States v. Gonzales*, 436 F.3d 560, 573 (5th Cir. 2006). Under the Fifth Amendment Due Process Clause, pretrial detainees enjoy a constitutional right not to have their serious medical needs met with deliberate indifference.

77. Until 2017, Houston, Harris County, Texas, had the dubious title as the "capital of capital punishment." If the county were a state, only one state would have executed more people since 1976, the year the death penalty was reinstated in the United States: Texas itself. Henry Gass, "How Texas' Harris County Went from 'Capital of Capital Punishment' to Zero Executions," *The Christian Science Monitor*, December 27, 2017.

78. *Guerra v. Collins*, 916 F. Supp. 620, 629-30 (S.D. Tex. 1995) (the habeas corpus decision uses the Guerra name, one of Aldape's two surnames as customary in Mexican culture; the text of the chapter refers to him as Aldape).

79. *Guerra*, 628 (statement of Hilma G. Galván).

80. *Guerra*, 629-30.

81. *Guerra*, 630-31.

82. *Guerra*, 633. After Heredia viewed the lineup, he informed an officer that he recognized Aldape as the driver of the Black car and not the man who shot Officer Harris. The officer did not amend or supplement Heredia's statement.

83. *Guerra*, 624.

84. *Guerra*, 625. This threat apparently arose from indications, based on actions by investigators, that since Carrasco was dead, the police and the prosecution would create a case against Aldape.

85. *Guerra*, 625.

86. *Guerra*, 625, n. 3: "Before I [Garcia] got a chance to move I saw this guy with the blond hair reach into the front of his pants and pull out a pistol and shoot the policeman... He then shot the man in the read (sic) car." [Mr. Armijo]." She added that the shooter wore "brown pants and a brown shirt," consistent with Carrasco and not Aldape. The *habeas* record reveals Carrasco wore a maroon shirt and brown pants and that Guerra wore a light green shirt and blue jeans. Guerra, 623.

87. *Guerra*, 630, n. 7.

88. *Guerra*, 623.

89. *Guerra*, 916 F. Supp. 620 (S.D. Tex. 1995), 90 F.3d 1075 (5th Cir. 1996).

90. *Brady v. Maryland*, 373 U.S. 83 (1963).

91. *Guerra*, 624, relying on *Brady v. Maryland*, 373 U.S. 83, 87 (1963), where the Supreme Court stated that "the suppression upon request by the prosecution of evidence favorable to an accused violates due process" where the evidence is material either to guilt or to punishment, regardless of the prosecutor's good faith or bad faith.

92. *Guerra*, 631, 633.

93. *Guerra*, 635.

94. Scott J. Atlas, "Free Aldape: The Saga of an Extraordinary Death Case," *Litigation* 2 (28): 24.

95. Atlas, "Free Aldape," 24. Evidence existed that one of the neighborhood witnesses openly expressed overt prejudice against "illegal" Mexican aliens and urged other witnesses to blame the "wetback" from Mexico for killing officer Harris. *Guerra*, 629-30.

96. See Benny Agosto, Jr., Lupe Salinas, and Eloisa Morales, "But Your Honor, He's an Illegal!"— Ruled Inadmissible and Prejudicial: Can the Undocumented Worker's Alien Status Be Introduced at Trial?," 17 *Texas Hispanic Journal of Law & Policy* 27, 29 n. 2 (2011), citing Elizabeth L. Earle, "Banishing the Thirteenth Juror: An Approach to the Identification of Prosecutorial Racism," 92 *Columbia Law Review* 1212, 1222 (1992) (the danger that a litigant will appeal to prejudice, that "thirteenth juror," exists).

97. See Alfred Allan Lewis and Herbert Leon MacDonell, *The Evidence Never Lies: The Casebook of a Modern Sherlock Holmes* (New York: Holt, Rinehart and Winston, 1984).

98. *Guerra*, 637. Atlas, "Free Aldape," 32. DA Holmes chose not to re-prosecute Aldape, and after fifteen years, he finally obtained his freedom. He lived the next three months in freedom, dying in a traffic accident. His lawyer rationalized that Aldape at least died a free man, reunited with his family.

99. Cindy Tumiel, "Convicted Killer Executed After Court Rejects Appeals," *Corpus Christi Caller-Times*, December 7, 1989, cited in James S. Liebman et al., "*Los Tocayos Carlos*: Part I: The Death of Wanda López," *Columbia Human Rights Law Review* 43 (2012): 724, 755.

100. Brandon L. Garrett, "The Banality of Wrongful Executions: Review," *Michigan Law Review*, 112 (2014): 979, 980. Garrett states the title, *Los Tocayos Carlos*, means "the Carlos look-alikes," but *tocayos* more correctly refers to "namesakes." These two Carloses shared an extraordinary physical similarity in height, weight, and facial appearance, sufficiently puzzling even family who knew them. See, e.g., James S. Liebman et al., "*Los Tocayos Carlos*: Part II: The Lives of Carlos Hernández," *Columbia Human Rights Law Review* 43 (2012): 816, 898-900 (the individuals who misidentified photographs of the two Carloses included DeLuna's own sister Rose and Freddie Schilling, Hernández's brother-in-law).

101. Liebman et al., "*Los Tocayos Carlos*: Part I," 724; Liebman et al., "*Los Tocayos Carlos*: Part II." 816; James S. Liebman et al., "*Los Tocayos Carlos*: Part III: The Prosecution of Carlos DeLuna," *Columbia Human Rights Law Review* 43 (2012): 908; James S. Liebman et al., "*Los Tocayos Carlos*: Part IV: The Passion of Carlos DeLuna," *Columbia Human Rights Law Review* 43 (2012): 1022; James S. Liebman et al., "*Los Tocayos Carlos*: Part V: The Scars of Dina Ybanez," *Columbia Human Rights Law Review* 43 (2012): 1090.

102. *United States v. Jewell*, 532 F.2d 697, 703 (9th Cir. 1976) (*en banc*). In *United States v. Heredia*, 483 F.3d 913, 917 (9th Cir. 2007), the same federal appeals court ruled that deliberate ignorance, otherwise known as willful blindness, is categorically different from negligence or recklessness.

103. *Peña-Rodríguez v. Colorado*, 137 S. Ct. 855 (2017).

104. Liebman et al., "*Los Tocayos Carlos*: Part I," 784.

105. Liebman et al., "*Los Tocayos Carlos*: Part I," 731.

106. Liebman et al., "*Los Tocayos Carlos*: Part I," 733.

107. Liebman et al., "*Los Tocayos Carlos*: Part I," 736.

108. The author's comments derive from his experience of more than twenty-five years as a prosecutor, both state and federal, and as a state criminal district court judge who presided

over three death penalty cases. He focused on civil rights prosecutions as an Assistant U.S. Attorney.

109. For example, consider the brutality death of George Floyd in Minneapolis, MN, and the questionable use of deadly force against Nicolás Chávez in Houston. Ray Sánchez and Ashley Killough, "4 Houston Police Officers Involved in Fatal Shooting Are Fired," *CNN*, September 11, 2020 (Houston, Texas, Police Chief Art Acevedo fired four officers, including Latinos, who engaged in unreasonable deadly force against an incapacitated man who received a final fatal volley of twenty-one shots). Ethnic-based hate crimes have occurred frequently in the post-1964 civil rights era. In August 2019, a white man went on a shooting spree, seeking to control the invasion of Mexican-descent persons into Texas. The bloody terrorist attack at a Walmart in El Paso resulted in twenty-two dead and twenty-seven injured. Robert Moore, "Alleged El Paso Mass Shooter Arraigned in Texas Court, Pleads Not Guilty to Capital Murder," *Washington Post*, October 10, 2019.

110. In *Alcorta v. State*, 294 S.W.2d 112 (Tex. Crim. App. 1956), reversed by *Alcorta v. Texas*, 355 U.S. 28 (1957) (*per curiam*), both the accused and the prosecutor who perpetrated an unethical prejudicial act were of Mexican descent. Twenty years later, in a separate case involving alleged intraethnic discrimination, Justice Thurgood Marshall responded to Justice Powell's claim that "*all* Mexican Americans, indeed *all* members of *all* minority groups, have an 'inclination to assure fairness' to other members of their group." *Castañeda v. Partida*, 430 U.S. 482, 503 (1977) (emphasis in original).

111. The DA's motive cannot easily be determined, but, reviewed objectively, the death of Carlos DeLuna constitutes a homicide as well as a deprivation of one's right not to be deprived of life without due process of law. U.S. Const. amend XIV provides, in part, that no state shall deprive any person of life, liberty, or property, without due process of law.

112. The Arsuagas saw a clean-shaven man in dark slacks. Liebman et al., "*Los Tocayos Carlos*: Part I," 738. Liebman et al., "*Los Tocayos Carlos*: Part I," 731. George Aguirre also described a man in blue jeans. Liebman et al., "*Los Tocayos Carlos*: Part I," 734.

113. *Guerra*, 624.

114. Salinas, *U.S. Latinos and Criminal Injustice*, 168, no. 133.

115. *Miller-El v. Dretke*, 545 U.S. 231, 264 (2005).

116. Tex. Code Crim. Proc. art. 2.01. The prosecutorial goal of doing justice can be compared to the maxim attributed to the famous English legal commentator William Blackstone: It is "better that ten guilty persons escape than that one innocent suffer," a concept related to the goal found in law that exculpatory evidence should be shared with the defendant.

117. *In re Winship*, 397 U.S. 358 (1970), established that the highest standard, proof beyond a reasonable doubt, is grounded on "a fundamental value determination of our society that it is far worse to convict an innocent man than to let a guilty man go free."

118. For example, see *Brady v. Maryland*, 373 U.S. 83, 87 (1963); *Giglio v. United States*, 405 U.S. 150, 153-54 (1972); *United States v. Bagley*, 473 U.S. 667, 674-75 (1985), cases that set forth these protections.

119. Liebman et al., "*Los Tocayos Carlos*: Part III," 950.

120. Liebman et al., "*Los Tocayos Carlos*: Part III," 950.

121. Liebman et al., "*Los Tocayos Carlos*: Part III," 950.

122. Liebman et al., "*Los Tocayos Carlos*: Part III," 950.

123. Liebman et al., "*Los Tocayos Carlos*: Part III," 1002 (italics in original).

124. Liebman et al., "*Los Tocayos Carlos*: Part III," 1033-34 (emphasis in original).

125. Ed Pilkington, "The Wrong Carlos: How Texas Sent an Innocent Man to His Death," *The Guardian*, May 14, 2012.

126. Liebman et al., "*Los Tocayos Carlos*: Part III," 997. County jail records revealed Hernández and DeLuna were in police custody in April 1983, shortly after his arrest for the murder of Ms. López.

127. In October 1986, Richard Anderson, a capital murder appeals lawyer, informed the Nueces County DA's office that he now represented DeLuna. At this same time, Carlos Hernández sat in jail, facing prosecution by the same DA's office for killing Dahlia Sauceda. Ken Botary, Schiwetz's co-counsel against DeLuna, specifically knew of Hernández because the judge pressed him to produce a 1980 transcript of his conversation with Hernández. It appears that "Schiwetz was aware of Hernández at this point," having mentioned this to De Peña in a casual visit over coffee. Aside from DeLuna and his sister Rose, no one said anything to Anderson about Hernández's existence. Liebman et al., "*Los Tocayos Carlos:* Part III," 1029-30.

128. Liebman et al., "*Los Tocayos Carlos:* Part III," 1016 (the defense lawyers did not call a single witness or present any mitigating evidence during the penalty phase, enough inaction to call for ineffective assistance of counsel).

129. Liebman et al., "*Los Tocayos Carlos:* Part III," 936.

130. Understandably, reputable scholars draw a common thread between lynchings and the death penalty, even referring to mob lynchings as more common than official trials. Carol S. Steiker and Jordan M. Steiker, *Courting Death: The Supreme Court and Capital Punishment* (Cambridge, MA: The Belknap Press of Harvard University, 2016), 23. See also Mónica Muñoz Martínez, *The Injustice Never Leaves You: Anti-Mexican Violence in Texas* (Cambridge, MA: Harvard Univ. Press, 2018) (a depiction of the January 1918 Porvenir, Texas, massacre of Mexican males by white citizens and Texas Rangers). Public lynchings during the 1930s prompted Northerners to urge intervention by federal troops to protect Blacks in the South. Southerners then moved the "lynchings" indoors by resorting to court trials that led to executions. Jeffrey Toobin, "The Legacy of Lynching, on Death Row," *The New Yorker*, August 22, 2016.

131. *Cantú v. State*, 738 S.W.2d 249 (Tex. Crim. App. 1987).

132. Lise Olsen, "Did Texas Execute an Innocent Man?," *Houston Chronicle*, November 20, 2005.

133. *Cantú v. State*, 251.

134. *Cantú v. State*, 251.

135. *Cantú v. State*, 251-52.

136. The factual circumstances indicated that Juan Moreno never pointed to the photo of Ruben Cantú until the third time he saw the photo lineup with Cantú in all of the three photo spreads.

137. Susan D. Reed, Criminal District Attorney, Bexar County, *In the Matter of Juan Moreno*, Investigation Relating to The *State of Texas v. Ruben Cantú*, Cause No. 85-CR-1303, at 9 n. 6 (affidavit of attorney Roland García). Judge Roy Barrera, Jr., has maintained he has no memory of a plea deal effort in the Cantú case. Death Penalty Information Center, "Report Fails to Erase Doubt that Texas Executed an Innocent Man," posted on July 10, 2007, https://deathpenaltyinfo.org/news/report-fails-to-erase-doubt-that-texas-executed-an-innocent-man.

138. Based on the author's judicial experience, he understands the political challenges a judge can face at the next election, especially when the public erroneously blames the judge for a bad decision made by the prosecutor. However, political concerns should not force a judge to cross the ethical line and coerce or direct a prosecutor on how to manage her case.

139. Olsen, "Did Texas Execute an Innocent Man?"

140. Rick Casey, "Story Spurs Review of Executed Man's Case," *Houston Chronicle*, November 23, 2005.

141. Casey, "Story Spurs Review."

142. Casey, "Story Spurs Review."

143. Few cases in modern times overtly reveal the existence of racism like the Texas cases of *Saldaño v. State*, 70 S.W.3d 873 (Tex. Crim. App. 2002) (*en banc*) and *Buck v. Davis*, 137 S.Ct. 759 (2017). Both tolerated consideration of race and ethnicity as punishment factors in Texas courts.

144. *Saldaño v. State*, 70 S.W.3d 873, 892 (Tex. Crim. App. 2002) (*en banc*) (Price, J., dissenting).

145. *Saldaño v. State*, 70 S.W.3d at 893 (Johnson, J., concurring in part), citing U.S. Const. amend. XIV, § 1, and Tex. Const. art. 1, § 3a (1972).

146. *Saldaño v. State*, 70 S.W.3d at 893 (Price, J., dissenting); see *Peña-Rodríguez v. Colorado*, 137 S. Ct. 855 (2017) (during deliberations a white juror introduced prejudicial comments about "Mexicans" and their alleged sexual practices).

147. Tex. Code Crim. Proc. art. 2.01 (Vernon Supp. 2004) ("The primary duty of all prosecuting attorneys [is] not to convict, but to see that justice is done").

148. *Saldaño v. State*, 363 F.3d at 556. Saldaño received a new punishment trial, and the jury assessed a death sentence without any improper reference to race. The Texas Legislature thereafter amended Texas law to bar racially oriented evidence in sentencing. Tex. Code Crim. Proc. art. 37.07, Sec. 3 (a) (2) (Vernon's Supp. 2004).

149. *ODonnell v. Harris Co.*, 251 F. Supp. 3d 1052, 1168 (S.D. Tex. 2017), aff'd in part and vacated in part, *ODonnell v. Harris Co.*, 892 F.3d 147, 152 (5th Cir. 2018).

150. *ODonnell v. Harris Co.*, 251 F. Supp. 3d 1052, 1063-1064. The filing occurred under 42 U.S.C. § 1983, the 1871 Civil Rights Act.

151. *ODonnell v. Harris Co.*, 892 F.3d 147, 153-54 (5th Cir. 2018); Tex. Code Crim. Proc. art. 17.033.

152. *ODonnell v. Harris Co.*, 892 F.3d at 154.

153. Shawn Arrajj, "Settlement in Harris County Bail Bond Lawsuit Receives Final Approval," *Community Impact News*, November 22, 2019.

154. Email from Rodney Ellis, Harris County Commissioner, Precinct One, to Lupe Salinas, Professor, Texas Southern University, Thurgood Marshall School of Law, Houston, Texas, November 22, 2019.

155. *Tuck v. State*, 2008 Tex. App. LEXIS 8525, NO. 01-06-01086-CR (Tex. App. [Houston 1st] October 30, 2008).

156. *Tuck v. State*, at *23-24.

157. *Tuck v. State*, at *3-4. A jury convicted Tuck of aggravated sexual assault and sentenced him to life in prison. *Tuck v. State*, at *1.

158. Bill Murphy, Paige Hewitt, and Jennifer Leahy, "Spring Teen Who Survived Pipe Attack Dies after Leap from Cruise Ship," *Houston Chronicle*, July 1, 2007.

159. Jasmine Aguilera, "'I Cry All the Time,' A Century after 15 Mexican Men and Boys Were Massacred in Texas, Their Descendants Want Recognition," *Time*, September 27, 2019; Mónica Muñoz Martínez, *The Injustice Never Leaves You: Anti-Mexican Violence in Texas* (Cambridge, MA: Harvard University Press, 2018) (a book about the January 1918 Porvenir, Texas, massacre).

160. Robert Moore, "Alleged El Paso Mass Shooter Arraigned in Texas Court, Pleads Not Guilty to Capital Murder," *Washington Post*, October 10, 2019.

161. Adeel Hassan, "Hate-Crime Violence Hits 16-Year High, F.B.I. Reports," *New York Times*, November 12, 2019.

162. Cedar Attanasio, Jake Bleiberg, and Paul J. Weber, "Police: El Paso Shooting Suspect said He Targeted Mexicans" *Associated Press*, August 9, 2019.

163. Hassan, "Hate-Crime Violence." According to the FBI, individuals reported 4,571 hate crimes in 2018.

164. *Batson v. Kentucky*, 476 U.S. 79, 98 (1986). The removal of minorities by prosecutors has been so brazen that the only minority on the Supreme Court, the late Justice Thurgood Marshall, proposed the elimination of the peremptory challenge as a means of securing diversity on the jury.

165. *Schuette v. Coaliton to Defend Affirmative Action*, 134 S.Ct. 1623 (2014).

166. Alex Arriaga, "Texas Death Row Inmate Duane Buck Has Sentence Reduced to Life after Supreme Court Orders Retrial," *Texas Tribune* (October 3, 2017). *Peña-Rodríguez v. Colorado*, 137 S.Ct. 855 (2017). A Caucasian juror in a sex assault charge volunteered his opinion to the jury about how Mexican-descent men have a sex drive that inclines them to force themselves on women); *Buck v. Davis*, 137 S.Ct. 759 (2017). The court voided the death sentence, and the trial court entered an agreed plea to a life sentence.

167. *Peña-Rodríguez v. Colorado*, 137 S.Ct. 855 (2017).

168. Paul Butler, "Filing Charges in George Floyd's Death Was the Easy Part. Now Comes the Hard Part," *Washington Post*, May 31, 2020.

169. U.S. Commission on Civil Rights, "Police Use of Force: An Examination of Modern Policing Practices" (2018), 3-5.

170. Salinas, "Lawless Cops," 1217.

171. Joseph Goldstein, "'Testilying' by Police: A Stubborn Problem." *New York Times*, March 18, 2018; Christopher Slobogin, "Testilying: Police Perjury and What to Do About It," *University of Colorado Law Review* 67 (1996): 1037, 1056.

172. Mark Iris, "Police Discipline in Chicago: Arbitration or Arbitrary," *Journal of Criminal Law & Criminology* 89 (1998): 215.

173. Tex. Local Govt. Code § 143.001 (a); Sec. 143.057 (d) sets forth the procedures for firefighters and police officers to appeal to a hearing examiner; Sec. 143.057 (j) provides that a district court may hear an appeal of a hearing examiner's award only on the grounds that the arbitration panel lacked or exceeded its jurisdiction or that the order was procured by fraud, collusion, or other unlawful means.

174. Kate Taylor, "Amid Modest Sentences, Prosecutors Bring New Charges in Admissions Scandal," *New York Times*, October 22, 2019.

175. Michael Wines, "Illegal Voting Gets Texas Woman 8 Years in Prison, and Certain Deportation," *New York Times*, February 10, 2017.

176. *ODonnell v. Harris Co.*, 251 F. Supp. 3d 1052, 1168 (S.D. Tex. 2017), aff'd in part and vacated in part, *ODonnell v. Harris Co.*, 892 F.3d 147, 152 (5th Cir. 2018).

177. *Trop v. Dulles*, 356 U.S. 86, 101 (1958).

178. David Grann, "Trial by Fire: Did Texas Execute an Innocent Man?," *The New Yorker*, September 7, 2009. He is not alone in Texas. Based upon scientific evidence, many believe Cameron Todd Willingham died an innocent man, caught in the middle of the dirty and deplorable machinations of Texas politics.

Contributors

J. Richard Avena, born in Salt Lake City and raised in El Paso, began his federal career at the Library of Congress Legislative Reference Service as a translator and on occasion wrote speeches for members of Congress. He marched with Dr. Martin Luther King, Jr., in the 1966 James Meredith March Against Fear in Mississippi. He was the only Mexican American on the march. In 1968 he came to San Antonio to help the U.S. Commission on Civil Rights direct the hearings held on civil rights issues facing Mexican Americans in the Southwest. In 1986 he retired as the Southwest Regional Director. He served as the first Mexican American Executive Director of the Texas Civil Liberties Union (ACLU). During 2006-2013 he taught a course on U.S. immigration law and policy at the University of San Carlos in Guatemala. He has a bachelor of arts degree in government from the George Washington University.

Alejandro Becerra, a native of Mexico who moved to Texas at the age of eleven, has served in the Office of Fair Housing and Equal Opportunity at the U.S. Department of Housing and Urban Development, at the U.S. Department of Agriculture, and on the U.S. President's Cabinet Committee on Opportunities for the Spanish Speaking. Former director of research for the National Association of Hispanic Real Estate Professionals (NAHREP), he received the 2011 National HOPE Policy Award for promoting minority home ownership and a Lifetime Achievement in Housing Award from NAHREP. He has served as director of the Peace Corps in Paraguay, South America, and in positions for the Congressional Hispanic Caucus Institute and National Council of La Raza. His books include *Hispanic Homeownership: The Key to America's Housing and Economic Renewal* (2010). He holds a master's degree in economics from the University of Texas, Austin.

Robert Brischetto was a professor at the University of Texas at El Paso, Our Lady of the Lake University, and Trinity University from 1970 to 1982. In 1982 he joined William C. Velasquez at the Southwest Voter Registration Education Project as director of research. There he established the Southwest Voter Research Institute (SVRI) and served as its executive director from 1986 to 1995. In recognition of his work at SVRI, he received the 1992 National Award for Sociological Practice from the Society for Applied Sociology. The director of the Bureau of the Census asked him to establish a Census Information Center at SVRI for minority researchers and organizations to access 1990 Census data. He has served as expert witness in more than forty voting rights cases throughout the southwestern United States. He is also author of more than ten dozen academic and popular publications throughout his career. His master of arts (1970) and doctorate (1975) in sociology are from the University of Texas at Austin.

Henry Cisneros, former U.S. Secretary of Housing and Urban Development (1992-1997), is Chairman of American Triple I, and founder and chair of CityView companies. In 1981, he became the first Mexican American mayor of a major U.S. city, serving four terms as San Antonio mayor. The native of San Antonio is a past president and chief executive officer of the Univision television network, and has served as president of the National League of Cities, deputy chair of the Federal Reserve Bank of Dallas, and vice chair of Habitat for Humanity International. He is the author, co-author, or editor of numerous books, including *Building Equitable Cities: How to Drive Economic Mobility and Regional Growth* (2017). He holds master's degrees from Texas A&M University and Harvard University, and a doctorate in public administration from George Washington University. In addition to numerous national awards for public service, he has been awarded more than twenty honorary doctoral degrees from leading U.S. universities.

Alberto Dávila is Dean of the Harrison College of Business & Computing and a professor of economics at Southeast Missouri State University. His research focuses on the economics of the United States-Mexico border, the economics of immigration, and Hispanic labor markets. In addition to numerous journal articles and book chapters, Dávila has published two books (including the award-winning *Hispanic Entrepreneurs in the 2000s: An Economic Profile and Policy Implications*, with Marie Mora), two co-edited volumes (including *Labor Market Issues along the U.S.–Mexico Border*, with Marie Mora), and numerous book chapters and journal articles. His recent recognitions include the Academic Achievement Award (2018) as well as the Outstanding Service Award (2021) from the American Society of Hispanic Economists, of which he is a former president and founding member. Dávila earned his doctorate in economics from Iowa State University.

Henry Flores, distinguished university research professor emeritus of political science at St. Mary's University in San Antonio, Texas, served as an expert in voting rights litigation, providing reports in more than thirty voting rights cases. He was St. Mary's University graduate school dean and chair of graduate programs in both public administration and political science. He received a lifetime achievement award from St. Mary's University for his contributions and continuing dedication to Latino voting rights issues. He is co-author of Mexican Americans and the Law: ¡el Pueblo Unido Jamás Será Vencido! (2004), and the author of Latinos and the Voting Rights Act: The Search for Racial Purpose (2015) and Racism, Latinos and the Public Policy Process (2019). He holds a master's degree and a doctorate in political science.

Juan H. Flores for more than 40 years has engaged both as an activist and in leadership roles to address Latino health and social policy concerns at the local, state, and national levels. He founded the Chicano Health Policy Development, Inc. (1978–1992), for health professions development, health promotion, and health care access and advocacy. He served as administrator at multiple community health centers in Texas (1993–2005) and directed the La Fe Policy Research and Education Center (La Fe PREC) in San Antonio from 2006 to 2013. La Fe PREC was the statewide policy arm of Centro de Salud Familiar-La Fe in El Paso. The center conducted social and health policy research, leadership training, and advocacy. He has a bachelor's degree in public health from Texas State University and a master's in urban planning from the University of Washington in Seattle, with coursework toward a doctorate in public health at the University of Texas in Houston.

Rebecca Flores was born in South Texas to a family of farmworkers. She was trained as a farmworker organizer by internationally known U.S. labor leader César Chávez, co-founder of the United Farm Workers (UFW), and UFW trainer Fred Ross. Chávez named her Texas Director of the United Farm Workers Union in Texas in 1975. Later, she served three years as Texas Director of the National AFL-CIO. She holds a master's degree in community organizing from the University of Michigan. She acknowledges the assistance in writing this report of James C. Harrington, Juanita Valdez-Cox, and Antonia Castañeda. James C. Harrington, a human rights lawyer, founder and director of the Texas Civil Rights Project, provided legal expertise to the UFW in Texas from 1975 through 2000. Juanita Valdez-Cox is executive director of La Union del Pueblo Entero (LUPE). She was part of a migrant farmworker family and lived in a *colonia* near Donna, Texas. She worked with the United Farm Workers in South Texas from the mid-1970's until the end of 2002. Antonia Castañeda is a historian, writer, and former professor at St. Mary's University.

Ernest J. Gerlach has more than 40 years of experience in rural and economic development, community and regional planning, and public policy research and management. From 1973 to 1986 he was a Civil Rights Analyst for the Southwestern Region of the U.S. Commission on Civil Rights. He has authored or co-authored more than 30 studies focusing in on economic, community, and business development and engaged in several major projects centered on development issues in South Texas. He was a senior fellow at the Center for Urban and Regional Planning Research at the University of Texas San Antonio, a coordinator for the Rural Business Program in the South West Texas Regional Small Business Development Center Network-Institute for Economic Development at UTSA, and the director for the Center for Economic Development at UTSA. He received a bachelor's degree in sociology and a master's degree in urban studies from Trinity University, and a master's degree in public administration from the University of Texas San Antonio.

David Hinojosa is the director of the Educational Opportunities Project at the Lawyers Committee for Civil Rights Under Law and a leading thinker and litigator in educational civil rights. As former regional counsel for the Mexican American Legal Defense and Educational Fund, he led several impact cases and policy work resulting in desegregating schools, improving school finance, preserving the Texas DREAM Act, affirmative action and the Top Ten Percent law, and securing driver's licenses for immigrants. At the Intercultural Development Research Association, he led the organization's policy work and Equity Assistance Center. There, he presented reports to Congress and to federal and state agencies and spearheaded the development of the "Essential Building Blocks of School Finance" and "Equity-Based Framework for Integrated Schooling." He is well published with several book chapters and articles on educational equity. A graduate of Edgewood High School, David holds a juris doctorate from the University of Texas at Austin School of Law.

José Roberto Juárez, Jr., is dean and professor of law at Nova Southeastern University's Shepard Broad College of Law in Florida. He is a former staff attorney at the San Antonio and Los Angeles offices of the Mexican American Legal Defense and Educational Fund (MALDEF), and a former professor of law at St. Mary's University School of Law in San Antonio. He is board chair of the Council of Law and Religion and co-president of the Society of American Law Teachers. He has received numerous honors and awards for his work in voting rights, employment and discrimination, history, and law and religion. He received the MALDEF Excellence in Legal Service Award in 2016, and was named one of the Top 100 Influential Hispanics by *Hispanic Magazine* in 2006. Juárez holds a bachelor's degree in history from Stanford University and a juris doctorate from the University of Texas School of Law.

Aurelio M. Montemayor is an IDRA senior education associate and lead trainer, with a career in education that spans more than four decades. As a young teacher, he testified at the 1968 U.S. Civil Rights Commission hearing in San Antonio, Texas. In 1970, he co-founded the first independent Chicano college, Colegio Jacinto Trevino, in Mercedes, Texas. He developed a U.S. Department of Education Investing in Innovation program that later became known as Education CAFÉ. He has been a board member of the National Association for Bilingual Education, National PTA, and Parents for Public Schools. He earned a master's degree in bilingual education from Antioch College Graduate School of Education in Ohio.

Marie T. Mora is Provost and Executive Vice Chancellor for Academic Affairs and a professor of economics at the University of Missouri-St. Louis. A labor economist, Mora has been invited to share her expertise on Hispanic socio-economic outcomes at institutions and agencies across the country, including by the White House and the Board of Governors of the Federal Reserve System. Along with numerous journal articles and book chapters, she has published two books (including the award-winning *Hispanic Entrepreneurs in the 2000s: An Economic Profile and Policy Implications*, with Alberto Dávila), three co-edited volumes (including *Labor Market Issues along the U.S.–Mexico Border*, with Alberto Dávila), and numerous book chapters and journal articles. Mora is the 2015 recipient of the César Estrada Chávez Award from the American Association for Access, Equity and Diversity, the 2016 recipient of the Outstanding Support of Hispanic Issues in Higher Education Award from the American Association of Hispanics in Higher Education, the 2019 Outstanding Service Award from the American Society of Hispanic Economists, and the 2020 Presidential Award for Excellence in Science, Mathematics, and Engineering Mentoring by the White House Office of Science and Technology Policy. She earned her doctorate in economics from Texas A&M University.

Kevin Morris is a quantitative researcher with the Democracy Program at the Brennan Center for Justice at New York University School of Law, where he analyzes voting rights and elections. His research focuses on the impact of laws and policies on access to the polls, with a particular focus on rights restoration and voter list maintenance. Prior to joining the Brennan Center, Morris worked as an economic researcher focusing on housing at the Federal Reserve Bank of New York and as an economist at the Port Authority of New York and New Jersey. He has a bachelor's degree from Boston College

in economics and a master's degree in urban planning with an emphasis in quantitative methods and evaluation from New York University's Wagner School of Public Service.

Myrna Pérez is Director of the Brennan Center's Voting Rights and Elections Program, and leads the program's research, litigation, and advocacy work nationwide. An expert on voting rights and election administration, she has litigated high-profile voting cases across the country and is the author of several nationally recognized reports and articles. She has testified before Congress and several state legislatures on a variety of voting-rights-related issues. Pérez earned her undergraduate degree in political science from Yale University. She obtained a master's degree in public policy from Harvard University's Kennedy School of Government, where she was the recipient of the Robert F. Kennedy Award for Excellence in Public Service. She graduated from Columbia Law School, where she is now a lecturer in law. Her work has been featured in media outlets across the country, including *The New York Times*, *The Wall Street Journal*, MSNBC, and others.

María "Cuca" Robledo Montecel is president emerita and was president and chief executive officer of Intercultural Development Research Association (IDRA). She is a nationally recognized expert on bilingual education and school dropout prevention and was the principal investigator of the first statewide study of dropouts, the Texas School Dropout Survey Project. She is the author and editor of numerous publications on education and was executive editor of the *IDRA Newsletter* for twenty-six years. She has testified to Congress, to the White House Initiative on Educational Excellence for Hispanic Americans, and to state policymakers. She served as trustee of Our Lady of the Lake University for nine years, and is a founding board member of the Mexican American Solidarity Foundation and the CIVICUS World Alliance for Citizen Participation. She received the 2013 Excellence in Community Service Award from MALDEF. She has a master's degree in educational evaluation from Antioch College and a doctorate in urban education from the University of Wisconsin at Milwaukee.

Rogelio Sáenz is professor in the Department of Demography at the University of Texas at San Antonio. He has written extensively in the areas of demography, Latina/os, race and ethnic relations, inequality, immigration, public policy, and social justice. Sáenz is co-author of the book titled *Latinos in the United States: Diversity and Change* and co-editor of *The International Handbook of the Demography of Race and Ethnicity*. In 2018, he received the César Estrada Chávez Award from the American Association for Access, Equity and Diversity for his work in support of workers' rights and humanitarian issues. In 2020, Sáenz received the prestigious Saber es Poder Academic Excellence Award in Mexican American Studies from the University of Arizona's Department of Mexican American Studies, an honor that recognizes an outstanding scholar whose work has demonstrated long-term commitment for advancing the field. He is a regular contributor of op-ed essays for outlets throughout the country.

Lupe S. Salinas is a professor of law at the Thurgood Marshall School of Law at Texas Southern University in Houston, where he teaches criminal procedure, civil rights litigation, and Latino-based civil rights issues. He retired as judge of the 351st Criminal District Court of Harris County, Texas, where he presided over three capital murder trials that resulted in death sentences. He began his career in 1972 with the Mexican American Legal Defense and Education Fund (MALDEF), served as a state prosecutor and as Assistant U.S. Attorney in Houston, and served as Special Assistant to U.S. Attorney General Benjamin R. Civiletti in Washington, DC, and as Chief of the Civil Rights Division of the Houston U.S. Attorney's Office. In 2010 he received the Ohtli Award from the Mexican government for his efforts to improve the quality of lives of Mexicans and Mexican Americans residing abroad. He is the author of several law journal articles and a book, *U.S. Latinos and Criminal Injustice* (2015).

Lee J. Terán retired in 2017 as a clinical professor of law at St. Mary's University School of Law and director of the Immigration & Human Rights Clinic. She is a 1975 graduate of the University of Colorado School of Law and licensed to practice law in Texas. She testified before the U.S. Commission for Civil Rights in 1978 on immigration concerns in South Texas. She was co-director of the Lawyers Committee for Civil Rights, Immigrant and Refugee Rights Project. She litigated numerous civil rights cases on behalf of immigrants and refugees and is the recipient of the 2009 Excellence in Legal Service Award from MALDEF, the Elmer Fried Teaching Award in 2004 from the American Immigration Lawyers Association, and the Jack Wasserman Litigation Award in 1992, the 1990 Carol King Award from the National Immigration Project, and the Pro Bono and Professional Responsibility Award from the American Bar Association Section on Litigation in 1989.